Nine Contemporary Jewish Plays

From the New Play Commissions in Jewish Theatre
of the National Foundation for Jewish Culture

9 contemporary jewish plays

Edited by Ellen Schiff and Michael Posnick
With a foreword by Theodore Bikel

UNIVERSITY OF TEXAS AUSTIN

Requests for permission to reproduce material from this work should be sent to:
    Permissions
    University of Texas Press
    P.O. Box 7819
    Austin, TX 78713-7819
    www.utexas.edu/utpress/about/bpermission.html

♾ The paper used in this book meets the minimum requirements of ANSI/NISO Z39.48-1992 (R1997) (Permanence of Paper).

Library of Congress Cataloging-in-Publication Data

Nine contemporary Jewish plays / edited by Ellen Schiff and Michael Posnick ; with a foreword by Theodore Bikel. — 1st ed.
    p.   cm.
  "From the new play commissions in Jewish theatre of the National Foundation for Jewish Culture."
  ISBN 0-292-70985-4 (cl. : alk. paper) — ISBN 0-292-71290-1 (pbk. : alk. paper)
  1. American drama—Jewish authors.   2. American drama—20th century.   3. Jews—Drama. I. Schiff, Ellen, 1932–   II. Posnick, Michael, 1942–   III. National Foundation for Jewish Culture (U.S.)
PS628.J47N56   2005
812′.60808924—dc22

                                      2005007621

This book is dedicated to

the memory of Simon and Florence Posnick,
to Eileen and Joshua Max Posnick,

and to

Gary Schiff and Stacy Schiff

Contents

Editors' Acknowledgments

THIS BOOK WOULD NOT exist without the inspiration and enthusiastic support of Richard Siegel, Executive Director, and Lawrence Pitterman, Chief Operations Officer, of the National Foundation for Jewish Culture. We acknowledge with gratitude the Board of the NFJC, especially Karen Ganz-Zahler. Our thanks go to Nancy Schwartzman, Jerome Chanes, and to all the theatre practitioners and scholars who have served over the years as jurors of the New Play Commissions competition. We are deeply and warmly indebted to Kristen Runk of the NFJC for her indispensable efficiency and unflappable dedication. It is a pleasure to thank Len Berkman and Julius Novick for their close reading, creative suggestions, and generous encouragement. At the University of Texas Press, we had the good fortune to work with Tim Staley, Development Officer. The manuscript benefited greatly from the meticulous reading and sound judgment of Sue Carter and the editorial guidance of Leslie Tingle.

Foreword

Theodore Bikel

Chair, Artistic Committee of the
National Foundation for Jewish Culture

THE NEW PLAY COMMISSIONS in Jewish Theatre represent one of many ways the National Foundation for Jewish Culture acknowledges excellence in art of significant Jewish content. The commissions encourage new work, nurture forums for play development, and enable experimentation with style and content.

Because right from the initial application the projects involve collaborations between dramatists and theatres, the commissions strengthen the crucial bridges between them. A playwright cannot know the exact shape, focus, or rhythm of the work until it is brought to life on stage before a live audience. Staged readings or, better yet, full productions give dramatists the opportunity to further define and shape their work. The scripts in this collection are all the result of just this kind of support and development. After having won New Play Commissions, they have been refined and polished, ultimately proving their stageworthiness in full productions. Now they are ready to be staged again and again.

The Jewish theatre scene has changed a good deal since the days I co-founded the Cameri Theater in Tel Aviv. For instance, Hebrew theatre at that time had no Jewish villains; these had to come from outside the Jewish world. Later there was a golden period, especially in America, when Jews and Jewishness came to be seen as the paradigm of the human condition. However, as Jews we are not always comfortable with what we see in the mirror, and in art and literature we began to speak of ourselves openly, often critically. Jewish artists who speak freely about themselves and their surroundings are a recent phenomenon. This too is evident in these plays.

This collection represents pieces of a kaleidoscope of Jewish experiences. And it is surely a kaleidoscope rather than a melting pot, where the ingredients lose their shape and color. In a kaleidoscope, each particle is clearly delineated, but the structure is dynamic. So too with each reading and staging of a play, the ensemble changes, creating new impressions.

These plays are Jewish songs, the songs we sing. May their melodies linger.

Preface

The New Play Commissions and
the New Jewish Theatre

Ellen Schiff

THIS BIG BOOK PURSUES a number of ambitions. First and foremost, it illustrates the success of the National Foundation for Jewish Culture's annual New Play Commissions in Jewish Theatre project. *Nine Contemporary Jewish Plays* testifies to the value of the commissions. As one recipient put it, "Without seed money, there wouldn't be any new plays." Second, in representing the accomplishments of both new and established dramatists, the collection demonstrates the variety of their plays and, of equal significance, the range of theatres that cultivate new work. The book's enterprise does not stop there. This volume forcefully demonstrates what the term "Jewish theatre" has come to mean. The expanded definition often comes as a surprise.

Jewish theatre (sans quotation marks) entered the twenty-first century with all the vigor and aplomb appropriate to a well-established entity. Growing steadily on roots nourished by nineteenth- and early twentieth-century Yiddish theatre, it has acquired, over the last century, an impressive international repertoire. Jewish theatre lacks just one thing: a universally understood definition. It is hard for it to get out of the formidable shadow of its Yiddish antecedents—and there is no reason why it should. Jewish theatre *includes* Yiddish; how could it not? But although the Yiddish stage lives on in, for example, New York, Montreal, and Buenos Aires, it has for decades now no longer been the only show in town. Since the 1960s with the work of such playwrights as Paddy Chayefsky, Herb Gardner, and Neil Simon, we in America especially have witnessed a markedly proliferating efflorescence of drama about Jews written and presented in the vernacular. (A phenomenon already apparent in the 19-teens in the work of Montague Glass and Aaron Hoffman.) Hence, the term "Jewish theatre" has rightly come to denote all drama and production to which Jews, Jewish history, or the Jewish experience are central.

Jewish plays are written and produced in the language of every country where Jews live. They are widely and routinely produced for general audiences in theatres of every size. That very prevalence may contribute to the issue of definition. Plays by and about Jews have become so mainstream and popular (think *Brighton Beach Memoirs* or *Driving Miss Daisy*), their ethnic particularity attracts little special attention. Contemporary Jewish theatrical creativity reflects the profile of Jews in today's liberal, multicultural societies.

Nine Contemporary Jewish Plays addresses another lingering misperception: the notion that all Jewish plays are about family. This is not to deny that family figures prominently in the repertoire. For instance, the plots of Donald Margulies' adaptation of *God of Vengeance* and Jennifer Maisel's *The Last Seder* are rooted in familial problems which clamor for attention with equally compelling issues: moral reckoning and societal prejudices in *God of Vengeance,* the ravages of age and illness and the pain of having to pronounce *Dayenu* for the end of a treasured ritual observance in *The Last Seder,* and unconventional lifestyles in both works.

Complexities of this nature figure in a number of recent Jewish plays. In America the stage has come to reflect the chronology and all the prevailing concerns of Jewish life with striking faithfulness and accuracy. A retrospective glance at the twentieth-century repertoire mirrors the confluence of forces that have molded the Jewish experience and shaped Jewish identity in this country and abroad. Plays about immigration, acculturation, and "making it" in America have been succeeded on stage by works that could only have been imagined since the second half of the century's transformative history.

The Holocaust and the Jewish state have acquired huge and recurring presence in all contemporary Jewish art. The Shoah, a subject until recently treated more commonly in European drama, has become increasingly the subject of American plays, sometimes casting its dreadful shadow on scripts about apparently unrelated matters. As two of the works here indicate, the problems of survival have viral endurance. Jeffrey Sweet's *The Action against Sol Schumann* dramatizes the impossibility of rewriting the past and the painful insufficiencies of trying to make amends, or even explaining their necessity. Sweet's play also includes a subject that, unlike the Shoah itself, is very much a part of contemporary American Jewish life: the experience of children of survivors. Motti Lerner's *Exile in Jerusalem* recounts the plight of a woman who escaped the maelstrom, only to search in vain for an elusive identity in Israel. The Jewish state itself is the focus of drama that transcends the sweet appreciations of early works, like *Milk and Honey,* to treat such thorny issues as the coexistence of Jews and Arabs, the subject of Marilyn Felt's *Asher's Command.*

The plays in this collection represent the ease with which Jewish art crosses borders and languages. A novel in Hebrew (David Grossman's *See Under: Love*) and a Yiddish classic (Sholom Asch's *God of Vengeance*) travel gracefully onto the English-language stage, as does *A Certain Raquel,* based on the Spanish translation of letters written in Yiddish by a Polish woman caught up in the white slave trade in Argentina. The Jewish theatre acknowledges the towering presence of its Yiddish heritage in Elise Thoron's *Green Violin,* which pays homage to Solomon Mikhoels, the great actor of the Soviet State Yiddish Theatre. Ari Roth's *Life in Refusal* conflates issues of Jewish and national identities as a disaffected American Jew, whose job takes her to Russia, is drawn irresistibly to helping refuseniks emigrate.

While these widely varied plays delight on the page, they are meant to be appreciated fully in the venue for which they are written, the theatre. As Michael Posnick explains elsewhere in these pages, all these scripts grew out of the collaboration of their authors with a gamut of the creative people who run theatres and bring drama to life. The range of "greenhouse" theatre companies represented here is noteworthy. They span the country, from San Francisco (A Traveling Jewish Theater, *See: Under Love*) to Madison, New Jersey (The Playwrights Theatre, *The Last Seder).* Some of the houses are illustrious (New Haven's Long Wharf Theatre Company, *God of Vengeance),* Chicago's Victory Gardens Theater *(The Action against Sol Schumann);* others, less well known. Yet the Jewish Ensemble Theatre of West Bloomfield, Michigan, sent *Exile in Jerusalem* on its way to productions at the Williamstown Theatre Festival, and in Vienna, Stuttgart, and Ramat-Gan, while *Asher's Command,* developed at the Rainbow Theatre in Stamford, Connecticut, subsequently appeared in Boston, San Diego, Sanibel, Edinburgh, and London.

Perhaps *Nine Contemporary Jewish Plays'* most ambitious aim is to suggest with its nine-course tasting menu the abundance and rich variety of the new Jewish repertoire. We hope this selection whets the appetite of readers, theatres, and audiences. And serves as a *forshspayz* to feasts just waiting to be served and savored.

Introduction

Background and History of the New Play Commissions in Jewish Theatre

Michael Posnick

The National Foundation for Jewish Culture (NFJC)

The National Foundation for Jewish Culture is the leading supporter and advocate for Jewish cultural creativity and preservation in America. Since 1960, it has nurtured new generations of writers, filmmakers, composers, playwrights, choreographers, and scholars. The NFJC's national and international conferences, partnerships with local communities and institutions, and sponsorships of annual grants and awards in the arts and humanities bring the best of Jewish culture to the Jewish community and the American public.

The New Play Commissions

The New Play Commissions in Jewish Theatre were established by the NFJC in 1994 to support the development of new Jewish theatre. Since its inception, the program has granted nearly a quarter of a million dollars for the development of sixty-six new plays and musicals. These plays have been presented in fifty-seven theatres in twenty-three cities and towns across the United States and in seven foreign countries on four continents. Directly or indirectly, the commissions have contributed to more than seventy-five professional productions, staged readings, and workshops of new Jewish drama.

The commissions are designed to encourage collaboration between a dramatist and a producing company willing to commit to developing the new work through to a staged reading. In the application, playwrights describe the proposed project and the process by which it will move toward completion. They must also include a writing sample and a record of prior playwriting experience. The theatre provides its production history, a budget, and curricula vitae of the creative staff who will be directly involved in developing the work. The competition is, of course, open to all applicants regardless of ethnic or cultural background.

The proposed project may take any theatrical style, from traditional plays to performance art, and may be at any stage of development, from intriguing idea to rough draft to completed script. Commissions have been granted to realistic plays, dance and musical theatre, performance art, puppet and multimedia performance. Funds have been used to support playwrights' research, travel or rehearsal expenses, actors' salaries, and production costs. Typically, between fifty and sixty proposals are submitted annually. A dozen or so are selected for consideration by a panel of jurors composed of theatre professionals, scholars, playwrights, producers, and performers. The jury considers four areas of proficiency: the artistic merit of the proposed project, the playwright's experience, the ability of the theatre to produce the play, and the depth and centrality of Jewish content. In terms of Jewish content, the panel asks if the project has at its core some significant Jewish concern, such as identity, historical experience, or an encounter with traditional texts or practices. The plays in this collection offer a wide range of exemplary responses to the ever vital and challenging question of Jewish content.

Commissioned plays have been produced by a broad spectrum of theatres, ranging from the nationally known, such as the Manhattan Theatre Club in New York, The Ensemble Studio Theatre in Los Angeles, The Kennedy Center in Washington, D.C., and Victory Gardens Theater in Chicago, to a prolific and dedicated group of regional, community, and university theatres, including member theatres of the Association for Jewish Theatre.

Funded playwrights report that, along with financial support, the commissions provide encouragement and inspire confidence, credibility, and critical momentum for their work. One playwright wrote: "I'd never really thought of myself as a Jewish artist before. Now I do." Another wrote that the commission was "helpful as a morale boost—knowing that someone else cares that the play and its characters have a voice in the world."

The editors trust that this collection will illustrate the effectiveness and relevance of the NFJC New Play Commissions. We look forward to volume 2 in this series.

Nine Contemporary Jewish Plays

GOD OF VENGEANCE

by Donald Margulies

God of Vengeance. Williamstown Theatre Festival production, 2002. Pictured (left to right) are Diane Venora, Laura Breckenridge, and Ron Leibman. Photograph by Richard Feldman.

I first encountered *God of Vengeance* over twenty years ago when I was collaborating on a musical about a Jewish prostitute in New York in the early 1900s. In the course of my research, I came upon a brief, intriguing reference in Irving Howe's indispensable *World of Our Fathers* to "Sholem Asch's popular play . . . in which the central character is a procurer trying to keep his daughter from the path of shame." A play about prostitution in which the master of a whorehouse was a Jew? *That* I had to read. I got hold of a translation by Joseph C. Landis in the anthology *Three Great Jewish Plays*.

The play was staggering. Although it was written in Poland in 1906, its themes were remarkably contemporary. It dealt with the sacred and the profane, religion and hypocrisy, sex and love, in bold, modern terms. Even more stunning than its gritty milieu was its depiction of erotic love between two young women. The play was indeed popular in the Yiddish repertoire throughout Europe for more than a decade. Its 1923 success in New York, in Yiddish, prompted an English translation and a move to Broadway. It was then, in that mainstream arena, that the play was shut down for indecency and *God of Vengeance* was relegated to infamy.

Like Zola, Dreiser, and Norris, his contemporaries in the realm of fiction, Asch was a social-realist. Yet, while the breadth of Asch's ambition was impressive, and his sensibility distinctly twentieth century, his dramaturgy remained too firmly rooted in the conventions of nineteenth-century melodrama for the play to truly soar. Its construction diminished the play's stageworthiness and prevented it from becoming little more than a literary curiosity. Still, I was thrilled to make its acquaintance.

Years later, in the mid-nineties, I was approached by Long Wharf Theatre to create a new version of a classic play. I briefly entertained the notion of finding a lesser-known Chekhov, or an Ibsen, but found nothing that cried out for a new adaptation. Gordon Edelstein, then the theatre's associate artistic director, asked if I was familiar with a play by Sholem Asch called *God of Vengeance*. As a matter of fact, I was, but it had been ten years or more since I had read it. So, at Gordon's urging, I read it again and was struck anew by the play's astonishing boldness. And by its clunkiness.

I began to reimagine it. I wanted to make it resonant for today's audiences, and I needed to relate to the material more urgently. While other modern adaptations had been faithful to the original locale, I became excited by the notion of setting my version in the immigrant culture of New York at the very time *God of Vengeance* became a *cause célèbre,* a time when my own grand-parents walked the streets of the Lower East Side. Once I decided to relocate it from czarist Prussia to a New York ghetto in the teeming 1920s, my new take on *God of Vengeance* was galvanized. The play became bigger, more personal.

Originally, the play was structured in three acts: the first, set in the home above the brothel; the second, in the brothel; and the third, upstairs again. I decided to place the action on two floors of a tenement building and on the street so that scenes interlocked or played simultaneously. Intrinsic to Asch's original were motifs that have consistently surfaced in my own plays (parents and children, cultural identity, assimilation, marriage), so the "collaboration" seemed especially apt.

I set out to create a play in the tradition of Elmer Rice and Sidney Kingsley, a big play with a big cast and big, operatic themes. And I wanted my *God of Vengeance* to seem as if it were not only set *in* that time, but *of* that time, as if it were a forgotten American play that had been there all along, waiting to be brought into the light once again.

Notes

Donald Margulies' version of *God of Vengeance* received its world premiere at A Contemporary Theatre (Gordon Edelstein, Artistic Director; Jim Loder, Managing Director; Vito Zingarelli, Producing Director) in Seattle, on April 13, 2000. It was directed by Gordon Edelstein; the set design was by Hugh Landwehr; the lighting design was by Robert Wierzel; the original music and sound design were by John Gromada; the costume design was by Anna Oliver; the dramaturg was Liz Engelman; the dialect coach was Juli Rosenzweig; the fight director was Geoffrey Alm; and the stage manager was Anne Kearson. The cast was as follows:

JACK CHAPMAN: Matthew Boston
SARA: Nike Doukas
RIVKELE: Rachel Miner
MANKE: Naama Potok
HINDL: Johanna Melamed
SHLOYME: Mikael Salazar
REYZL: Betsy Schwartz
BASHA: Tricia Rodley

REB ELI: Larry Block
THE SCRIBE (REB AARON): Sol Frieder
AN ORTHODOX MAN: Andrew Traister
LOWER EAST SIDE KIDS: Ian Nelson-Roehl, Scott Ross
THE PROSPECTIVE IN-LAW: Wauchor Stephens
INDIGENTS: Frank Krasnowsky, Jay A. Hurwitz
POOR WOMEN: Ilene Fins, Hinda Kipnis
PARTYGOERS/MINYAN: Mike Christensen, Matt Purvis, Joe Shapiro,
   Mary Unruh

God of Vengeance was subsequently produced at the Williamstown Theatre Festival (Michael Ritchie, Producer; Jenny C. Gersten, Associate Producer; Deborah Fehr, General Manager) in Williamstown, Massachusetts, on July 21, 2002. It was directed by Gordon Edelstein; the set design was by Neil Patel; the lighting design was by Rui Rita; the original music and sound design were by John Gromada; the costume design was by Candice Donnelly; the production manager was Christopher Akins; and the stage manager was Kelley Kirkpatrick. The cast was as follows:

JACK CHAPMAN: Ron Liebman
SARA: Diane Venora
RIVKELE: Laura Breckenridge
MANKE: Marin Hinkle
HINDL: Jenny Bacon
SHLOYME: Bruce MacVittie
REYZL: Jenn Lee Harris
BASHA: Christy Meyer
REB ELI: Larry Block
THE SCRIBE (REB AARON): Sol Frieder
AN ORTHODOX MAN: Joel Rooks
IRISH KID: Michael Jerrod Moore
SECOND KID: Aaron Paternoster
THE PROSPECTIVE IN-LAW: Mort Broch
FIRST INDIGENT: Daniel Deferrari
SECOND INDIGENT: Lee Rosen
FIRST POOR WOMAN: Rosalind Cramer

SECOND POOR WOMAN: Joyce Lazarus

POOR PEOPLE/PARTYGOERS: Sarah Bellows, Nancy Burnstein, Natalie
Jacobson, Melissa Miller, Noam Rubin, Eric Neher

POOR PEOPLE/MINYAN: Cy Beer, Robert James, Michael Lively,
Constantine Maroulis, Eric Neher, Ben Russo, Benjamin Strands,
Mark Weimer

God of Vengeance was adapted from the play by Sholem Asch, based on a literal translation by Joachim Neugroschel.

The author is grateful to all of the people involved in previous productions for bringing this behemoth to life, particularly Michael Ritchie and the irrepressible Gordon Edelstein.

Characters

JACK CHAPMAN

SARA

RIVKELE

MANKE

HINDL

SHLOYME

REYZL

BASHA

REB ELI

THE SCRIBE (REB AARON)

AN ORTHODOX MAN

IRISH KID

KID TWO

THE PROSPECTIVE IN-LAW

FIRST INDIGENT

SECOND INDIGENT

FIRST POOR WOMAN

SECOND POOR WOMAN

POOR PEOPLE/MINYAN

PARTYGOERS

Place: The Lower East Side of New York
Time: 1923

ACT 1

(The Lower East Side of New York. 1923. The set consists of a two-story cross-section of a tenement building, the suggestion of an alleyway, a sidewalk, and a stoop. The tall buildings of the city loom in the background. The upstairs apartment is living quarters to Jack Chapman, a.k.a. Yankel Tshaptshovitsh, his wife Sara, and their daughter Rivkele. The kitchen and master bedroom are not visible but the living/dining room and Rivkele's girlish bedroom are. The living room, decorated with framed family photos and a variety of tchotchkes, is an incongruous mix of old world quaintness and greenhorn pretension. A fire escape is the urban balcony outside Rivkele's window, with a ladder that leads to the alley.

Downstairs, below the staid residence, is a brothel. Brass beds are partly concealed in cubicles behind exotic curtains. A chaise splashed with colorful fabrics is prominently placed in the main reception area. Washstand, liquor stash, Victrola, lamps, secondhand chairs. The walls are decorated with mismatched ornate mirrors and various pictures of women in seductive poses.

A collage of sounds of the teeming city. Lights up: a spring afternoon. We find Rivkele, seventeen years old, sitting forlornly at her window, like a Jazz-Age Rapunzel, humming a Yiddish song while embroidering a vestment. Manke, a streetwalker in her twenties, walks on and fixes her lipstick while looking in a compact. An Orthodox Man of late middle age nervously shields his face as he walks past, but not without noticing Manke. Manke, standing near the stoop, lights a cigarette. Sara comes on, her baskets full of challahs and flowers.)

SARA: *(To Manke)* Move.

(Manke blows smoke in Sara's face and giggles.)

Very funny.

(Sara goes upstairs, where she puts the flowers in a vase and putters around the living room, sets a buffet table, etc. Rivkele sees Manke from her window. Her face brightens.)

RIVKELE: *(Calls in a whisper)* Manke!

(Manke's face loses its hardness when she sees Rivkele.)

MANKE: Rivkele!

RIVKELE: I prayed you'd be there. I said, please, God, I'm going to look out my window, please let Manke be there. And you were!

MANKE: Shh shh shh.

RIVKELE: Look at my stitching. See? I'm doing as you said.

(Shows her the vestment)

MANKE: Yes! You're such a good pupil.

RIVKELE: I want to see you so much.

MANKE: Me, too. Come down!

RIVKELE: I can't. My father's having a party. And I'm the guest of honor.

(The Orthodox Man returns and nervously makes his move; he clears his throat to get Manke's attention.)

ORTHODOX MAN: Can we go somewhere?

MANKE: Yeah, sure. Right this way.

(She takes a final puff and grinds out the cigarette, then blows a kiss to Rivkele and whispers:)

Later.

(Rivkele waves ruefully. She works on a paper flower chain as Manke leads the man into the downstairs apartment. He warily follows, kissing the mezuzah on his way in.)

ORTHODOX MAN: So this is what it looks like.

MANKE: You were expecting the Waldorf-Astoria?

ORTHODOX MAN: You hear about such a place your whole life . . . your imagination . . .

MANKE: It's just a place. Four walls, beds that sag in the middle. My bed is here.

(She pulls open the drape on her cubicle and steps out of her dress.)

ORTHODOX MAN: No no no. Not so fast. *(A beat)* Could we maybe talk a little
first?

MANKE: Talk?

ORTHODOX MAN: Yeah. You know. Talk.

MANKE: We didn't come here for conversation.

ORTHODOX MAN: I know. But, please. Let's sit a minute.

(He sits down on the chaise. She shrugs, then sits next to him. Silence.)

MANKE: *Nu? (Meaning, Well . . . ?)*

ORTHODOX MAN: I walked down this street so many times. Summer, winter. Went out of my way. Just to see you.

MANKE: Oh, yeah? You'd gawk at me, then go home, screw your wife?

ORTHODOX MAN: No. *(A beat)* I just got up from shiva.

MANKE: Oh. I'm sorry.

ORTHODOX MAN: *(Nods his thanks)* She was sick a long time, my wife, may she rest in peace. A long time.

(Manke nods. Silence. He sighs deeply, inhales her aroma.)

What is that?

MANKE: Rose water. I dab some on my neck.

(She lifts her hair so he can smell her neck. He nearly swoons, gets up, moves away.)

What.

ORTHODOX MAN: I never should've come.

MANKE: Why not?

ORTHODOX MAN: It's a sin! That's why not! What goes on here are sinful things!

(She laughs.)

What's so funny?

MANKE: Sin now, atone later. That's what they all do.

(Her laughter subsides. He's charmed.)

ORTHODOX MAN: What's your name?

MANKE: Manke.

ORTHODOX MAN: Manke?! Is that so? I knew a girl named Manke, once.

MANKE: Yeah, yeah, I've heard that one before.

ORTHODOX MAN: No, I did. In the old country. Back in Vilna.

MANKE: Vilna?! You're from Vilna?

ORTHODOX MAN: Yes.

MANKE: I'm from Vilkia.

ORTHODOX MAN: Vilkia! Small world! My mother was born in Vilkia. Her name was Zide.

MANKE: *(Can't recall, shrugs)* I left a long time ago. I was only seven.

ORTHODOX MAN: A child.

MANKE: Once.

ORTHODOX MAN: You're still a child.

MANKE: No. Not anymore. Not for a long time.

ORTHODOX MAN: Oh, but you are. Look at that punim. How does a girl with a face like an angel end up doing something like this?

MANKE: *(Brusquely gets up)* Look, I don't want to talk anymore. Okay? No more talking. Talking's never a good idea. I wanna dance.

ORTHODOX MAN: Dance?

(She goes to the Victrola, puts on a jaunty Tin Pan Alley tune.)

MANKE: There! Come on, let's dance!

(She pulls him to his feet. He resists.)

ORTHODOX MAN: No, no, I can't . . .

MANKE: What do you mean, you can't?

ORTHODOX MAN: It's not allowed . . .

MANKE: "Not allowed"?! Mister! You'll pay to shtup me but you won't dance with me?

(She snatches his hat, puts it on her head and teasingly dances around him.)

ORTHODOX MAN: Hey! What are you doing?! You mustn't do that! Give it back!

(She gets him to move with her, awkwardly, in a dance-like way. He succumbs to her charms in spite of himself. Manke takes off the man's jacket, revealing his traditional garb underneath, and dons the jacket herself. She performs a seductive, sexually charged dance. Meanwhile, upstairs, Rivkele hears the music and dances freely, almost erotically, around her room. Wrapped in her paper flower chain, her romantic reverie is shattered by her mother's call.)

SARA: *(Putting on an apron)* Rivka!

(Rivkele, breathless, stands guiltily in her doorway.)

What are you doing in there? The whole house is shaking.

RIVKELE: Nothing.

SARA: Well, come. Finish with the decorations.

(Sara continues bustling about. Rivkele drapes paper flowers around the room. Downstairs, Manke's dance with the Orthodox Man has become more sultry. Trembling, he kisses her face. She turns off the music and, her back to him, walks to her cubicle and waits at the curtain. He braces himself and follows her in.)

ORTHODOX MAN: *Oy gevalt. (As in, What am I doing?)*

(As the Orthodox Man sits on the bed and begins to remove his shoes, Manke looks at her watch, then draws the drape. Upstairs, Rivkele and Sara continue their preparations.)

RIVKELE: *(Decorating the mirror)* Look, Mama. Look how pretty it looks.

SARA: Yes, yes, very pretty. Stop dreaming. We want to be finished by the time your father gets home. Here, set these out.

(She gives Rivkele breads, etc., which the girl arranges.)

RIVKELE: Will there be music at this party?

SARA: Music? What kind of music?

RIVKELE: I don't know, a little Sophie Tucker, maybe?

SARA: Sophie Tucker?! Your father wants to impress the men from the synagogue; all he would need is Sophie Tucker. He invited the whole neighborhood, practically, your father. If everyone comes who was invited . . . I hate to think what they'll do to this place. I should've rolled up my rugs.

RIVKELE: Will girls be coming, too?

SARA: Girls? Maybe. Some people might bring their daughters. Nice Jewish girls.

RIVKELE: Will the girls from downstairs be coming?

SARA: *(Stops puttering)* The girls from downstairs? What do you think? *(Resumes puttering)*

(During the above, Basha and Reyzl, two hookers both barely in their twenties, enter with two East Side kids. One of the kids is more confident than the other, who lags behind. They go into the brothel.)

IRISH KID: *(Coaxing his reluctant friend)* Come on! Come on!

BASHA: You boys sure you want to go through with this?

IRISH KID: Sure we're sure.

BASHA: 'Cause you don't have to.

IRISH KID: We're sure, we're sure.

REYZL: *(To Basha)* Look how cute, they could be our kid brothers.

IRISH KID: Hey! We ain't your kid brothers.

REYZL: *(Feigns being impressed)* Oh, well, pardon me!

IRISH KID: We been with plenty of girls.

BASHA: Okay, Casanova, who gets who?

IRISH KID: I'll take you.

BASHA: Yeah? That okay with your friend?

IRISH KID: He don't care.

BASHA: Oh. Okay. *(Starts to lead him inside)*

REYZL: *(To Kid Two):* Well . . . ? You coming, or what?

KID TWO: Yeah. *(Takes a step, then backs away)* Uh, on second thought, there's
   something I gotta do . . . See ya, Francis . . . *(He runs down the street.)*

BASHA: *(Teasing)* "Francis"?

REYZL: *(Overlapping, as Kid Two goes)* Hey! What's the matter, you don't like
   my looks?!

IRISH KID: Ah, don't mind him. He's chicken. Hey, why don't you come, too?

REYZL: What do you mean?

IRISH KID: You know. You, me, and her.

REYZL: That's a new one, huh, Basha?

BASHA: *(To the Irish Kid)* You like Jewish girls?

IRISH KID: I like girls.

REYZL: It's gonna cost you double.

IRISH KID: I don't care. *(Shows his cash. Grins.)* Moron gave me his money.

*(Reyzl and Basha giggle as the threesome enter a cubicle and close the drape. Up-
stairs:)*

RIVKELE: What about dancing, Mama? Will there be dancing?

SARA: I said I didn't know if there was gonna be music.

RIVKELE: Oh, I hope so. I hope there is dancing. There's never any music in
   this house. Or dancing. I love to dance. I wish I had a silk dress and elegant, ladylike shoes to dance in, not these clumsy old schoolgirl shoes.

SARA: You wear schoolgirl shoes, my dear, because you are a girl! I hate to break
   it to you!

RIVKELE: But I'm not! I'm seventeen! Papa makes me wear these silly little
   dresses.

SARA: Don't let your father hear you talk like that. He takes such pride in you!

RIVKELE: Pride?! Like for a puppy, yes. Or a doll. For him to dress up and do with as he pleases.

SARA: Let me tell you something, darling. Your father may be smart about a lot of things, but about women . . . ? *(She shakes her head)* Let me give you a little advice: Take what you can get from him. That's what I do.

RIVKELE: If only I could have some new clothes. Like I see in *Harper's* magazine.

SARA: Well, once you're married, young lady—God willing, come Shevuas—you'll be free to dress . . . however your *husband sees* fit.

RIVKELE: But I'm grown up already.

SARA: You're hardly grown up.

RIVKELE: Look at me, Mama.

SARA: Yeah, yeah, very nice.

RIVKELE: Stop what you're doing and look at me.

(She makes Sara stop and actually look at her.)

I am not a child. Am I.

SARA: *(A realization)* No. No, you're not.

RIVKELE: *(Pinches her shirtwaist)* See? I have breasts. And a waist. Manke says—

SARA: Manke!

RIVKELE: Manke says I have a very nice shape.

SARA: Oh, she does.

RIVKELE: She has all these beautiful clothes she says she'd let me wear.

SARA: Oh, really? I've got news for you: You're not putting on any of Manke's clothes.

RIVKELE: You should see, her closet is filled with—! *(She stops herself.)*

SARA: Manke's closet? What do you know from Manke's closet?

RIVKELE: *(A confession)* I've been down there.

SARA: Is that so?

RIVKELE: She's been teaching me how to embroider. Remember you said it would be good for me to learn?

SARA: I didn't mean for you to go down there!

RIVKELE: Then how, Mama, how was I to learn? She's taught me a lot. Wait, let me show you.

(She goes to her room to get the embroidered vestment.)

SARA: *(Calls)* You know the rules. If your father ever found out!

RIVKELE: *(Returns, holds up the vestment)* See? She's such a good teacher. See how well she draws? She drew the Star of David and the olive leaves. Just like the vestment in synagogue.

SARA: *(Impressed)* Manke did this?

RIVKELE: Yes. Isn't it beautiful?

SARA: Whatever you do, don't tell your father Manke had anything to do with this. He'd have a fit.

RIVKELE: I thought it would please him.

SARA: Please him?! It *wouldn't* please him—that you were getting embroidery lessons downstairs from Manke?! That her dirty hands touched something as sacred as this?!

RIVKELE: Dirty hands? Oh, no, Manke's hands aren't dirty. She's my friend.

SARA: Your "friend." Uy gut. He doesn't want you mixing with the girls downstairs. That's all there is to it.

(Downstairs, the Irish Kid, wearing only his underwear and holding his clothes in a bundle, comes out of the cubicle and hurriedly gets dressed. Basha, wrapped in a sheet, and Reyzl follow.)

BASHA: That was fast.

REYZL: I never even got my turn.

BASHA: What's the matter, "Francis"? Got a train to catch?

(The girls laugh derisively.)

IRISH KID: Screw you.

BASHA: You wish.

(He starts to go.)

REYZL: Hey, where you going? Pay up!

(Jack Chapman, a.k.a. Yankel Tshaptshovitsh, comes down the street with a bounce in his step.)

BASHA: Hey! Mister! Stop him!

REYZL: He didn't pay! He owes us both!

JACK: *(Stops the Irish Kid, roughs him up)* Oh, is that so? Trying to get a free
   ride, huh? Huh?

IRISH KID: (Overlapping) Hey! Leave me alone! Let go of me!

JACK: Nobody gets a free ride. You understand? Nobody!

IRISH KID: Get offa me—kike!

JACK: *(More incensed)* Why you little pisher! Who do you think you are? Huh?!
   Pay up! You hear me? Hand it over! Before I wring your pimply little neck!

IRISH KID: *(Overlapping)* Here! Take it! Here's your stinking money!

(He crumples the money and tosses it to the ground.)

JACK: Good! Now get the hell outta here! Go!

(He pushes the Irish Kid, who runs away. He shouts after him:)

And don't show your little Irish putz around here again! Shaygetz! *(He picks
   up the bills and smoothes them out. To the girls:)* What are *you* looking at?

*(They remain silent. He gives them each a dollar and puts the rest in his billfold.
He changes his mind and gives them more.)*

All right, now go fix yourselves up. Go on.

*(Jack putters downstairs while Reyzl and Basha get dressed, fix their makeup.
Meanwhile, upstairs:)*

RIVKELE: Does Papa really think I don't know what goes on down there? When
   I was old enough to ask questions, you know what he told me? He said it
   was a boardinghouse down there! A boardinghouse!

(Reyzl and Basha reemerge, Jack eggs them on; the girls go.)

JACK: The night is young. Go go go!

SARA: *(To Rivkele)* Never mind, you! Everything that man has done—good or
   bad—he's done for you.

RIVKELE: I know, Mama.

SARA: He's trying so hard to change his ways. Give him a little credit, will you?
   (Hears him coming up the stairs) Shhh. Here he comes. Please, darling? Be
   a good girl. Try to show your gratitude. It costs a lot to be pious.

(Jack bursts ebulliently into the room.)

JACK: Well! Let me tell you: Everybody is talking about this party! And I mean everybody!

SARA: Oh, yeah?

JACK: Sara, the whole neighborhood is talking. I saw Dr. Cohen on the street.

SARA: Dr. Cohen! Is that so!

JACK: Oh, yeah, I'm telling you: Everybody. He was quite grateful for the invitation, Dr. Cohen, wished us all the best.

SARA: Dr. Cohen is coming here?

JACK: Well, no, not exactly. He's a very important man that Dr. Cohen.

SARA: I know!

JACK: You should have seen: He was rushing to the hospital with his little black bag when I saw him. A woman was giving birth, he told me; he couldn't talk, he had to run. I don't envy *his* life, let me tell *you*. Klein, the tailor, I saw him, too.

SARA: And?

JACK: He said he would try.

SARA: Try?! That doesn't help me. I need to know who's coming. What if there's not enough food?

JACK: There's enough, there's enough! Relax! I'm the one who should be nervous. My name is on the line, that's all. Big deal, what's a name? Oh, I even invited a bunch of unfortunate souls off the streets, so the machers will see what a big-hearted mensch I am.

SARA: Jack!

JACK: (Gently corrects her) Yankel, Yankel, remember? No more Jack, I'm Yankel again.

SARA: Forgive me: Yankel. It's still so new, I keep forgetting.

JACK: (To Rivkele, who has been trying to disappear) What, you don't say hello to your father anymore? (To Sara) She doesn't say hello?

(Sara nudges Rivkele.)

RIVKELE: Hello, Papa.

JACK: (Teasing) "Hello, Papa." Come here, I'm not gonna bite you. (Sees the vestment) What's that she's holding?

SARA: (To Rivkele) Show him.

RIVKELE: (Displays it) It's a vestment, Papa. For the Torah.

JACK: For the—? Well, how do you like that?! Isn't that wonderful? Where'd it come from?

SARA: Tell him. *(Rivkele says nothing; to Jack)* She made it.

JACK: *(To Sara)* No! Yes?

SARA: Yes; she did.

JACK: *(To Rivkele)* Bring it closer, let me see.

SARA: *(Quietly prodding)* Go on.

(Rivkele tentatively offers it to Jack. He takes it. He's effusive.)

JACK: Will you look at this! Isn't that gorgeous?!

SARA: Yes; it is.

JACK: Such talent! Who knew my little Rivkele had not only beauty but talent? *(To Sara)* Did you?

SARA: Not me.

JACK: It looks professional. Doesn't it?

SARA: *(Nods, while exchanging looks with Rivkele)* Yes; it does.

JACK: *(To Rivkele)* You did this all by yourself?

SARA: With her own two hands.

JACK: Where'd she learn how to make a beautiful thing like this?!

SARA: *(Shrugs)* Here and there.

JACK: *(To Sara)* You see that? You think you know your own child and then she does something like this? Come, darling, let me give you a kiss.

(Rivkele is reluctant.)

What, you won't let your father kiss you?

SARA: Your father wants to kiss you. Go.

(A beat. Rivkele tentatively goes to him. He pats his lap. Uncomfortably, Rivkele sits on his lap. He kisses her cheek.)

JACK: Well, now! Was that so terrible? *(To Sara)* She's getting so grown up she doesn't like to sit on her papa's lap anymore?

SARA: *(Shrugs, then)* I've got to check on that goose.

RIVKELE: *(Suddenly)* No, Mama! *(She doesn't want to be left alone.)*

SARA: What? It's shpritzing fat all over everything. *(To Jack)* You had to have goose . . .

(Sara goes offstage to the kitchen. Jack bounces Rivkele on his knee while humming a Yiddish song. She gets up.)

JACK: What's the matter? You used to love sitting on my lap.

RIVKELE: I'm too big to sit on your lap.

JACK: Don't be ridiculous. You're still my little girl. Remember we used to ride to Coney Island on Sundays in the summertime, just the two of us, you on my lap? Trolley after trolley, all the way to the end of the line, till we could smell the ocean? And I'd buy you salt water taffy and you'd laugh and chase the waves in your little bathing costume?

RIVKELE: That was a long time ago, Papa.

JACK: How long ago could it be? You're still a child. It seems like yesterday. *(A beat)* Something happened. What happened?

RIVKELE: Things changed.

JACK: What changed?

RIVKELE: I grew up.

JACK: No no. Why did we stop going? You lost interest in taffy and the long trolley ride, what?

RIVKELE: Papa, may I go to my room now?

JACK: *(Incensed)* No! When I tell you to go to your room, then you may go!

(She is silent; he is remorseful.)

Rivkele . . . Come back. I don't mean to yell. You know how much your papa loves you, don't you?

RIVKELE: *(With a sigh)* Yes, Papa.

JACK: To the ends of the earth, that's how far I would go.

RIVKELE: I know, Papa. I know.

JACK: All I want . . . I want you should marry well and have children. I want you should walk down the street with dignity! So when people see you—the so-called respectable people—they look you in the eye; not down at your feet. *(He takes her hand.)* Sweetheart, God is being invited back into this house. You'll see. Things are gonna be different. I promise. I'm gonna be different. Once I get that Torah for you . . . A holy man, a scribe, wrote one by hand, in beautiful script, for a man who died. He's coming here, this scribe; Reb Eli is bringing him. And I'm offering him a helluva lotta money for it, too, believe me. But, hey, I don't care about that; that's not important. What is important is you. Your welfare. Your future. *(Beaming)* Eli's been playing matchmaker. He's got his eye on someone for you. A scholar.

(Uncomfortable, she moves away.)

What's wrong?

(She shakes her head, evades him. Sara returns from the kitchen.)

SARA: Uch! Goose fat all over everything. I should make soap.
JACK: *(To Sara)* I'm embarrassing her. Marriage talk has made her bashful.
SARA: Marriage is God's will. What's to be bashful about? God knows everybody does it.
JACK: *(To Rivkele)* See? What would you like?
RIVKELE: What do you mean?
JACK: I want to buy you something, a little present. *(Takes out his billfold)* What should it be?

(Rivkele doesn't answer.)

Hm?

SARA: *(To Rivkele)* Cat got your tongue? Your father wants to buy you something. *(Sotto)* Take him up on his offer.
JACK: Let's see . . . should it be a doll? A little rag doll? Huh? What.
SARA: She'd like a silk dress and a pair of pretty shoes.
JACK: A silk dress and a pair of shoes? What's wrong with the dresses she has?
SARA: You asked what she wanted.
JACK: *(To Rivkele)* Is that what you'd like?

(She nods.)

Then why didn't you say so? Here, go buy yourself that dress and those shoes. *(He gives her money.)* You don't know how to say thank you?
RIVKELE: Thank you, Papa. May I go to my room now?
JACK: Okay. Now you may go.

(Rivkele exits to her room.)

(Calling) You'll come out for the party, though, won't you.
RIVKELE: Yes, Papa.

(She exits into her room. A pause.)

JACK: What's with her?

SARA: *(Shrugs)* It's the age.

JACK: What more can I do for her than I'm already doing?

SARA: Nothing.

JACK: Sometimes I think she doesn't like me.

SARA: Jack.

JACK: *(Corrects her)* Yankel. It's true, Sara. I feel like she's passing judgment all the time.

SARA: It's the age.

JACK: I feel like everybody has an opinion about me, and it's not very good.

SARA: What, all of a sudden, in the middle of your life, it matters to you what people think?, what God thinks?

JACK: Of course it matters. What, it shouldn't?

SARA: Public opinion never stopped you before.

JACK: I was never in the middle of my life before. I'm gonna be dead one day, you know.

SARA: God forbid.

JACK: No, honestly. I ask myself, Do I give a damn what people will have to say about me when I'm dead? And the answer comes back, Yeah, I do, I do care. It's not too late to change.

SARA: Well, don't expect miracles. That's all I'm saying. God doesn't hand out miracles like the pickle man from his pushcart.

(Feeling affectionate, he comes up behind her.)

JACK: You're funny.

SARA: Ha ha.

JACK: *(Calls her by her Yiddish diminutive)* Soyreleh.

SARA: Uy. "Soyreleh" now.

(He nuzzles his face in her neck.)

What are you doing?

JACK: Can't I have a nibble?

SARA: Nibble.

(Pause. He kisses her neck while she gazes into space.)

When I think of the life I would've had if I'd never met you . . .

JACK: *(A beat; his ardor cooled)* You would have died on the street. *(A beat)* I'm gonna change my clothes.

(He exits. Sara finishes what she's doing, then goes off to the kitchen. During the above, Rivkele, in bed embroidering, hits a snag, struggles with it, then decides to find Manke. The vestment in hand, Rivkele climbs out of her window, down the fire escape, and stealthily enters the brothel.)

RIVKELE: *(Whispers)* Manke?

(A moan draws her to Manke's cubicle, from which we hear creaking bed springs. Rivkele's impulse is to go but she stops herself and stays to eavesdrop, becoming excited by what she hears. Meanwhile, on the street: Shloyme, a flashily dressed, streetwise felon, appears, a ribbon-wrapped bundle tucked under his arm. Two hungry Indigents approach from the opposite direction. They converge at the stoop.)

SHLOYME: *(Unfriendly)* Can I help you?

FIRST INDIGENT: This Jack Chapman's place?

SHLOYME: Yeah, what can I do for you?

FIRST INDIGENT: He told us to come.

SHLOYME: Oh, yeah?

SECOND INDIGENT: We're a little on the early side.

SHLOYME: Early for what? You're never too early around here. There's always some girl.

SECOND INDIGENT: Girl?

SHLOYME: Yeah. You're here for the girls, right?

FIRST INDIGENT: *(Realizing the misunderstanding)* Oh, no, not the girls, the goose.

SHLOYME: The goose?

FIRST INDIGENT: Yeah, he told us he's having a party.

SECOND INDIGENT: A party for his daughter.

SHLOYME: A party, huh? What kind of party?

SECOND INDIGENT: Don't ask me.

FIRST INDIGENT: All I know is he said something about a Torah scroll and a goose.

SHLOYME: A Torah scroll? We talking about the same Jack Chapman?

SECOND INDIGENT: Is this his place or not?

SHLOYME: Yeah, this is it. Be my guests, go right on up.

INDIGENTS: Thanks. So long.

SHLOYME: *(Calling as they go)* And save me a piece of that bird!

(The Indigents go upstairs. Both Sara and Jack are offstage. The Indigents admire the room and the spread and begin to put food in their pockets. Meanwhile, Shloyme enters the downstairs apartment and is surprised and amused to see Rivkele listening at Manke's cubicle.)

Well, well, well . . .

(Rivkele gasps. He approaches.)

If it ain't little Goldilocks. What you doing down here, Goldilocks? Picking up a few pointers? *(Mimics panting; cracks himself up.)*

RIVKELE: *(Embarrassed)* I'm sorry . . .

(She tries to go past; he blocks her.)

SHLOYME: Where you going? *(Admiringly)* Look at you! You filled out awfully nice . . .

RIVKELE: Please . . .

SHLOYME: Don't go on my account. Sit. Stay and chat a while.

(He takes her hand, sits her down beside him on the sofa.)

RIVKELE: Please, I have to go back up. I didn't mean to . . .

SHLOYME: *(Takes out a Baby Ruth, unwraps it suggestively)* Want a bite?

(She shakes her head.)

Don't you like chocolate? Sure, you do. Everybody does.

RIVKELE: No, thank you.

SHLOYME: Oh, well. More for me. *(Takes a big bite)* Mmm . . . is that good!

RIVKELE: Please let me go. If my father . . .

SHLOYME: Hey, I hear he's throwing some kind of party for you, is that right?

(She nods.)

What's this about a Torah scroll? Old Uncle Jack a yeshiva bucha all of a sudden?

RIVKELE: Please, Shloyme.

SHLOYME: Uh! You know my name!

RIVKELE: Didn't my father tell you never to show your face around here again?

SHLOYME: Hey, you know everything, don't you?

RIVKELE: Papa said you took him for a ride.

SHLOYME: *(Amused)* Something like that.

RIVKELE: I won't say anything if you won't.

SHLOYME: *(Charmed)* Listen to you! Hey, you're a live one, ain't you, Goldilocks. Come on. Have a little candy. Go ahead. I want you to have a bite. It's not gonna kill ya.

(She hesitates, then slowly takes a bite, her eyes on him.)

Thatta girl. That wasn't too bad, now was it? Pretty tasty, huh?

RIVKELE: Uh huh.

SHLOYME: See? I wouldn't lie to you. How's Hindl doing?

RIVKELE: Hindl? I don't know.

SHLOYME: She still work down here?

RIVKELE: Uh huh. As far as I know.

SHLOYME: She ever talk about me?

RIVKELE: How am I supposed to know? Now, please, can I go? If my father . . .

(He pushes her to her feet.)

SHLOYME: Go. Get outta here. Get your toochis back upstairs. Go! Shoo!

(She heads back up the fire escape, hastily leaving the vestment behind. He finds it.)

What the hell is this?

(He covers his face with it and stretches out to take a nap. Upstairs, Rivkele rushes from her room into the living room, surprising the Indigents, who are busily pocketing food. She and the men share a tense moment.)

FIRST INDIGENT: Jack Chapman sent us.

SECOND INDIGENT: We was invited.

(Jack, now dressed for the occasion, enters, not realizing what's taking place.)

JACK: Well! *(Calls)* Sara?! Our guests are here! *(To the Indigents)* Welcome, gentlemen, welcome!

FIRST INDIGENT: *(Bows obsequiously, covering his theft)* Mr. Chapman! *(Prompts his friend to do the same)*

SECOND INDIGENT: Mr. Chapman, sir!

JACK: Now, now, none of that. You embarrass me, gentlemen. The name's Tshaptshovitsh, actually; I was Chapman for a while but now I'm using Tshaptshovitsh again, the name I was born with. *(Calls)* Sara, come greet our guests!

(Sara, donning an apron, enters. She tries to hide her disdain for the "guests.")

SARA: Well, hello!

FIRST INDIGENT: Mrs. Chap— *(Looks to Jack)*

JACK: Tshaptshovitsh. Tshaptshovitsh.

FIRST INDIGENT: Mrs. Tshaptshovitsh.

SECOND INDIGENT: Madame Tshap—*(His friend elbows him for using "Madame"; he corrects himself)* Mrs. Tshaptshovitsh!

FIRST INDIGENT: The lovely lady of the house!

JACK: *(To the Indigents)* I see you've already met our Rivkele, the light of our lives.

(He puts his arm around her shoulder; Rivkele averts her eyes.)

FIRST INDIGENT: Ah yes, what a girl!

SECOND INDIGENT: Quite a looker!

(His friend elbows him again. During the following, several more Poor People come down the street and arrive upstairs. They're a rowdy bunch. Ad-lib party talk.)

POOR MAN: Our generous host! Our lovely hostess! *(Tries to kiss Sara's hand, Sara recoils.)*

POOR WOMAN: Mazel tov. May the Torah bring you prosperity and happiness.

(Others concur.)

JACK: Thank you, thank you. But let's not jump the gun; it isn't mine, not yet. Let's hope and pray. Please, friends, enjoy, help yourselves! *(To Sara)* See? See? And you were worried there'd be no guests.

SARA: You call these "guests"? Where are all the well-to-do neighbors you were talking about?

JACK: They'll be here. *(To Rivkele)* Mingle. Schmooze. These people have come to see you.

RIVKELE: No they haven't . . .

JACK: Go on, sweetheart. Go say hello.

RIVKELE: Must I?

JACK: Yes!

SARA: Do as your father says. Go on.

RIVKELE: *(Uncomfortably, to a Poor Man)* Hello, I'm Rivkele. Welcome to our home.

POOR MAN: *(Belches, then)* How do you do?

JACK: *(To the guests)* How about a little entertainment? Yes? Would you like that? *(The guests respond affirmatively; to Rivkele)* Sing something.

RIVKELE: What?

JACK: Sing for our guests. Go on.

POOR PEOPLE: Oh, yes! Sing! Sing! *(Etc.)*

RIVKELE: What am I supposed to sing?

JACK: Anything.

RIVKELE: I can't . . .

JACK: Of course you can. A little song! A little song is gonna kill you? Sing, darling. *(Announcing)* My Rivkele will sing for you!

POOR PEOPLE: Wonderful! *(Applause, etc.)*

RIVKELE: No, Papa, please . . .

JACK: Go on! What's the big deal? They'll hear your sweet little voice.

RIVKELE: I don't want to, Papa, please don't make me sing for these people . . .

JACK: *(Angered, sotto)* Enough of this nonsense! You will do as I say. Now sing!

(The gathering eggs her on with applause and words of encouragement. She seems utterly miserable as Jack positions her in the middle of the room. He shushes the assembly and gestures to Rivkele to begin.)

RIVKELE: *(Sotto; desperately)* Mama, I can't think of anything to sing!

(Sara begins to sing a Yiddish lullaby, gently cuing her daughter. Rivkele sings along, shakily but sweetly. Sara stops singing; Rivkele sings alone. The Orthodox Man emerges from Manke's cubicle and exits as Hindl, a weary hooker in her thirties, enters on sore feet. Not realizing Shloyme is asleep on the chaise, she takes off her shoes, rubs her feet. Upstairs, Rivkele finishes her song and the party ap-

plauds her. Jack makes a show of his appreciation. The guests resume eating. We focus on the Poor Women stuffing their faces. Sara winds through with a tray of food and eavesdrops.)

FIRST POOR WOMAN: What a shame! She's a lovely girl.

SECOND POOR WOMAN: I know. You'd think she was raised in a synagogue, not in a place like this.

FIRST POOR WOMAN: How dreck like those two wound up with such a gem . . .

SECOND POOR WOMAN: God only knows.

JACK: *(Approaches, genially)* So, how's everything?

SECOND POOR WOMAN: *(Without missing a beat)* Ah! We were just saying, what wonderful hosts you are!

JACK: Thank you!

FIRST POOR WOMAN: And that daughter of yours!

JACK: Isn't she something?

FIRST POOR WOMAN: Uh!

SECOND POOR WOMAN: A finer girl you rarely see! You rarely see such a girl!

FIRST POOR WOMAN: Even rabbis don't have such daughters.

JACK: *(Confidentially)* You wanna know the truth? I agree with you!

(They share a laugh. He hands them more food.)

Here, take, don't be shy, eat, eat, take some more. We wouldn't want you to go home hungry.

POOR PEOPLE: Oh, thank you! Mmm! This is some party! (Etc.)

SARA: *(Under her breath, to Rivkele)* This is who he shows off to?

(Jack taps a glass to get the attention of the gathering.)

JACK: Ladies and gentlemen. May I have everybody's attention, please.

(They quiet down.)

Up until today, I thought we were all alone. Outcasts. Shunned by our neighbors. But now I look around and see all you wonderful friends and neighbors sharing in our nakhess and it makes my heart burst in happiness! I am overwhelmed. Thank you for coming, my friends. Thank you! And enjoy! *L'khaim!*

POOR PEOPLE: *L'khaim!*

(Amid scattered applause, Sara sidles up to him and coaxes him to the stairs.)

SARA: What is the matter with you?

JACK: Why?

SARA: You talk to these people as if they care about you. They don't care about you, they care about your bread and wine, that's what they care about. They'll take your food and then spit at you behind your back! Remember: A goy may be treyf but his cash is always kosher.

JACK: I want these people to leave here and tell their friends they were guests of Yankel Tshaptshovitsh and he was a gracious host.

SARA: These people? What do you care what these people think? If we're in the street, they're in the gutter.

(She moves away with a tray of dishes. He lingers on the stairs thinking about what she's said, looks at his watch, seems worried. We fade out and focus on downstairs: Shloyme, still unseen by Hindl, sits up and watches her looking at herself in the mirror. She catches his reflection and is startled.)

SHLOYME: *(Imitating Jack)* Why aren't you out on the street?!

HINDL: *(Sees him)* Shloyme!

(He laughs.)

You almost gave me a heart attack. What the hell you doing here?

SHLOYME: Ain't you glad to see me?

HINDL: You want the truth?

SHLOYME: Is that any way to talk?

HINDL: I thought you left the neighborhood. Went to Washington Heights or someplace.

SHLOYME: Yeah, but now I'm back.

HINDL: You're just like the clap, you know that? Just when you think you've gotten rid of it . . .

SHLOYME: *(Amused)* Hey. Hindleh. Is that how you talk to the man of your dreams?

(He presents her with the gift-wrapped bundle. She considers it for a moment before rejecting it.)

HINDL: *(Rubbing her feet)* Dreams? I don't know about dreams . . . Nightmares is more like it. Uy, my feet are killing me.

(He takes over massaging her feet, which she finds suspect.)

What's this for?

SHLOYME: *(Shrugs)* Can't I rub my girl's feet? I missed you.

HINDL: Yeah, sure. You never did this when we were together.

SHLOYME: I never missed you before.

HINDL: *(Slaps his hand away)* Two months! Two goddamn months! Not a card, not a word, nothing!

SHLOYME: I'm sorry! Uncle Jack was making life miserable for me downtown. Only the fellas uptown weren't too crazy about me, either.

HINDL: You never should've sold him that booze. Schmuck.

SHLOYME: I didn't know it was bad. How was I supposed to know?

HINDL: You should've known. What kind of way is that to do business?

SHLOYME: What do you want from me? These things happen in business. First you're mad at me for leaving, now you're mad at me for coming back? Hey . . .

(He touches her breast; she slaps him.)

Ow!

(Laughter from upstairs)

HINDL: What the hell's going on up there?

SHLOYME: Uncle Jack's having a party. For that precious little girl of his. Boy, I got a good look at her: She's turned into some nice-looking piece. *(Refers to the vestment)* She left her knitting.

HINDL: That ain't knitting; it's embroidery. He's calling himself Yankel now, you know.

SHLOYME: What do you mean?

HINDL: Says he doesn't want to be called Jack Chapman anymore; that was his Yankee name. Now he's Yankel Tshaptshovitsh.

SHLOYME: What, he's getting religious, "Reb Yankel"?

(They laugh. Pause. He gives her the bundle again. She sits and opens it. It's a pretty shawl. She revels in it for a moment, then stops herself.)

HINDL: What do you want?

SHLOYME: Why do you always think I want something?

HINDL: Why do you think?

SHLOYME: I came to tell you something.

HINDL: Yeah? Well . . . ? What do you want to tell me?

SHLOYME: *(A beat)* I found a place.

HINDL: What kind of place?

SHLOYME: An apartment. On Rivington Street. Four rooms. Furnished.

HINDL: Four rooms? What do you need all those rooms for?

SHLOYME: What do you think?

HINDL: *(A beat; catching on)* Oh . . .

SHLOYME: I'm gonna open the classiest house on the Lower East Side.

HINDL: Is that so. And how you gonna do that all by yourself?

SHLOYME: I'm not. You're gonna do it with me.

HINDL: So, are you asking me, or what?

SHLOYME: Asking you? I'm telling you.

HINDL: Oh. Excuse me: You're telling me. And you're telling me why?

SHLOYME: So you should know.

HINDL: I see. Well, thanks for telling me.

SHLOYME: Ain't you gonna wish me a mazel tov?

HINDL: Oh, sure. Mazel tov on your new whorehouse. Use it in good health.

SHLOYME: Thanks.

(Pause)

HINDL: You sonofabitch.

SHLOYME: What.

HINDL: You're really not gonna ask me?

SHLOYME: Ask you what?

HINDL: Ask me to *marry* you!

SHLOYME: *Marry* you?! Oh, Jack is gonna love that: Me stealing his girls.

HINDL: He doesn't own me; I'm not their furniture. That Sara looks at me like I'm a—a piece of garbage. So high and mighty she is! Like *she* never had to walk the streets! I'll be the lady of the house. I'll be real good at it, too. You know I would. I've got a good head for business. I'll run a tight house for you, Shloym, you know I would.

SHLOYME: Easy, will ya? Slow down! There *is* no house! There's a vacant four-room apartment! Can't have a house without girls.

HINDL: I'll get us girls.

SHLOYME: You? What, you're a white slave trader and you didn't tell me?

HINDL: What if I get you Manke?

SHLOYME: Manke?! You're gonna get me Manke?

HINDL: If I get you Manke . . . She brings in a lot of business, you know, more than anybody. If I get her for you . . . Marry me. Make an honest woman out of me, Shloym.

SHLOYME: Too late for that.

HINDL: You gotta get me out of here, Shloym. You gotta take me with you.

SHLOYME: Take you where? I'm only talking about Rivington Street!

HINDL: I don't care. I'm dying here, Shloym. *(She kisses him repeatedly. Sultry, suggestive.)* I'll take care of you. You know how well I take care of you, don'tcha? Don't I take good care of my man? Huh? Huh?

SHLOYME: *(Succumbing)* Aw shit . . .

(She leads him into her cubicle. Meanwhile, Sara has rejoined Jack on the landing with a plate of food.)

SARA: You should eat something.

JACK: You were right: No one else is coming. No Reb Eli, no Scribe. We're stuck with the dregs.

SARA: Look: You've got a place to live? Stay there. You've got bread to eat? Eat it. Enjoy. But don't try going where you're not wanted, and don't try being what you're not. Have you forgotten who we are?

JACK: Who are we? Have we robbed anybody? Murdered anybody? I run a business! The need is there, we provide the service. Economics, pure and simple. That's how it works. For this I should be punished? This is America!

(Downstairs, Hindl and Shloyme:)

HINDL: Whataya say? Huh, Shloym? Huh?

SHLOYME: I'm starving; I wonder what they got to eat up there.

(She grabs him by his collar.)

Hey!

HINDL: I want an answer. If I bring you Manke, will you marry me.

SHLOYME: Knock it off! You're cutting off my circulation!

HINDL: Will you?

SHLOYME: Okay! I'll marry you! I'll marry you!

(She releases him and kisses him all over.)

HINDL: Thank you thank you thank you!

SHLOYME: *(Overlapping)* Now can we get something to eat?

HINDL: Sure, let's go stuff our faces.

(Hindl and Shloyme encounter Jack and Sara on the stairs.)

SHLOYME: "Reb" Yankel!

JACK: Uh! You!

SHLOYME: *(Tips his hat)* Sara, you're looking the respectable woman this evening . . .

SARA: Drop dead.

SHLOYME: How long you been holy, "Reb Yankel"? Since lunchtime?

JACK: Get out of here. Now! Go!

HINDL: *(Helping herself to food)* Is that any way to treat your old friends?

SARA: Old friends?! Ha!

JACK: Goniff! The nerve of you showing your face around here!

SHLOYME: We came to pay our respects. To little Rivkele.

JACK: Yeah? Well, nobody invited you.

SHLOYME: You invite bums in off the street but business associates you throw out?

JACK: *(Overlapping ". . . you throw out?")* "Business associates"?! You call what you do business?!

SARA: *(Overlapping ". . . business?!")* Don't even speak to them. Get them out of here!

HINDL: *(Hefts a fork)* Is this real silver?

SARA: *(Snatches the fork)* Out of my house. Vermin!

HINDL: The hell with your house. We're gonna have a house of our own.

SHLOYME: Hindl . . .

JACK: *(Overlapping; skeptical)* Your own house, is that so?

HINDL: That's right. Shloyme's gonna marry me.

SHLOYME: *(To Hindl)* You got a big mouth, you know that?

SARA: *(Overlapping)* Marry you?!

HINDL: Why? *That* prize married *you.* *(To Shloyme)* Tell them!

SHLOYME: She's gonna be my girl now, what do you think about that?

SARA: Oh, really! I wish you luck!

JACK: *(Overlapping; to Shloyme)* I'm not gonna discuss this with you up here. *(Escorting him)* Downstairs, the both of you, now!

SHLOYME: *(Pulling away from him)* Hey! Watch the hands!

JACK: Downstairs! If you have anything to say to me, you say it downstairs. Upstairs, I don't know you and you don't know me.

SHLOYME: I got news for you, Yankel Chapawhozitz or whatever you're calling yourself these days: Upstairs, downstairs, the Devil's the same all over.

JACK: Out of here! Now!

SARA: *(Taking food from Hindl)* Don't you have work to do? You barely earn your keep anymore!

HINDL: Oh, yeah? Let's see *you* go downstairs and peddle *your* ass, see how much you bring in!

SHLOYME: *(To Hindl)* Better yet, tell her to send down little Rivkele.

(He and Hindl laugh.)

JACK: *(Attacking him)* You sonofabitch! How dare you! How dare you even speak her name! You are scum! Scum!

(A fight ensues. The remaining guests disperse. During the commotion, Manke emerges from her cubicle downstairs and listens. Upstairs, Rivkele stands in her doorway, fascinated. Jack roughhouses Shloyme down the stairs to the sidewalk and puts a switchblade to his throat.)

SARA: Oh, my God! Jack!

HINDL: Shloyme!

SARA: *(Overlapping; to Jack)* Stop it!

RIVKELE: Mama?

SARA: *(To Rivkele)* Into your room!

RIVKELE: Mama, what's happening?

SARA: Now!

(Rivkele ducks back into her room.)

JACK: *(To Shloyme)* If I ever hear you speak her name again . . . If I ever see your face again . . .

(Meanwhile, Reb Eli, a matchmaker and all-around go-between, and Reb Aaron, the Scribe, an ancient, mysterious, pious man, come down the street.)

ELI: *(Entering; overlapping)* Oh, my oh my! Gentlemen! Gentlemen! What's all this?

SARA: Jack! Reb Eli.

(Jack stops battling Shloyme.)

JACK: Reb Eli, hello. *(To Shloyme and Hindl, controlling his rage)* Go.

ELI: Shame on you! You should be rejoicing, not fighting.

(Jack's eyes are on Shloyme and Hindl, who is nursing Shloyme's bloody lip.)

JACK: Forgive me. I was evicting some riffraff. They were just leaving.

SHLOYME: *(Fixing his collar)* Come, Hindleh. I can tell when we're not welcome. So long, "Reb" Yankel. *(To Hindl)* Get a load of who he's taking up with. Next thing you know, he'll be running for mayor.

(Hindl laughs. They exit brusquely past Eli and the Scribe.)

JACK: Pardon the intrusion. Please, come upstairs. You open your home to the neighborhood, you're bound to get a few rotten apples. *(A nervous laugh)*

ELI: Yes. Well. *(To the Scribe, making introductions)* Aaron . . . this is Mr. Chapman.

JACK: Tshaptshovitsh. Remember?

ELI: Yes, yes, excuse me. Tshap—?

JACK: Tshaptshovitsh.

ELI: Mr. Tshaptshovitsh.

JACK: Hello, sir. Welcome. Welcome to my home.

(Jack extends his hand, which the Scribe pointedly doesn't shake. Jack withdraws his hand in embarrassment.)

SCRIBE: (To Eli, his eyes on Jack) This is the man who wants to buy the Torah scroll?

ELI: Yes.

SCRIBE: *(Coolly)* Sholem *aleichem.*

JACK: *Aleichem sholem.*

(Sara bows, steps back respectfully as the Scribe comes forward.)

Please, sir. Sit down. Sara?

(Sara sets out a chair for the Scribe.)

Some schnapps? Hm?

(The Scribe shrugs, nods. Jack fills glasses, with Sara's help, gives them to the men.)

ELI: *L'khaim.*
JACK: *L'khaim.*

(Eli and Jack down their drinks but the Scribe does not, unnerving them. Sara steps forward to brightly offer some food but Jack restrains her.)

SCRIBE: *(To Eli, while looking at Jack)* This is the man?
ELI: Yes, Aaron, this is the man. He doesn't have a son, so he wants to serve God by purchasing his own handwritten copy of the Torah. *(To Jack)* Isn't that right?
JACK: Yes.

(Eli prompts him to be more positive.)

Oh, yes! For my daughter's dowry. I thought if I could buy the one you—
ELI: Just answer yes or no. *(Continuing, to the Scribe)* This is very honorable, no? We must celebrate this in any man.
SCRIBE: Tell me: What sort of man is he?
ELI: What sort of man?
JACK: Well, you see Rebbe—
ELI: *(Cutting him off)* What difference does it make? He's a Jew, is he not?
JACK: True. I'm a Jew.
ELI: An ordinary Jew. If you mean, is he a scholar? No. The answer is no.
JACK: No. No scholar.
ELI: But does every Jew have to be a scholar?
JACK: That's right!
ELI: If a Jew wants to do a mitzvah, like this, don't we owe him something? A helping hand at least? Now, come, Aaron, let's drink . . . *(Refills his and Jack's glasses) L'khaim.*
JACK: *L'khaim.*

(Eli and Jack drink; once more, the Scribe does not.)

SCRIBE: Does he know how to conduct himself with a holy book?

ELI: Of course he knows.

JACK: Of course I know.

ELI: What Jew doesn't know what a Torah is?

JACK: Exactly. I was bar mitzvah forty-odd years ago, in Warsaw. A Jew is what I am.

ELI: *(Prepares another round)* L'khaim, l'khaim . . . Let us toast. May God grant us better times.

JACK: Better times. *L'khaim.*

(Jack drinks with Eli. The Scribe does not.)

SCRIBE: A Torah is a magnificent thing.

JACK: Oh, I know.

SCRIBE: Remember that.

JACK: I do, Rebbe, I do.

ELI: Shh. Listen.

SCRIBE: One handwritten scroll enfolds the entire world. Each Torah is like the very Tablets of the Law that were handed down to Moses from Mount Sinai. Every line, every stroke of the pen, is written in purity and holiness. And where a home has a scroll of the Torah, then God is there, too. So, for that reason alone, it must be kept free of contamination. Do you understand what that means?

JACK: *(Terrified by the Scribe's speech)* Yes, Rebbe.

SCRIBE: Do you understand that responsibility?

JACK: Yes, Rebbe, listen, I must tell you something . . .

ELI: *(To Jack)* What are you doing?

JACK: I must tell him everything. I must tell him the truth.

ELI: *(Quietly, to Jack, trying to save the deal)* No no no . . .

JACK: Rebbe, I am a sinful man . . .

ELI: *(Overlapping)* Sh sh sh. *(To Scribe)* Rebbe, the man is a penitent, see? So we have to help him, right? The Talmud says so. Doesn't it?

JACK: I got caught up in business. I forgot about God.

ELI: *(Sotto, to Jack)* Quiet!

JACK: I changed my name. I denied who I was. I tried to hide from God.

ELI: Let me handle this, will you!

JACK: I'm tired of hiding, Rebbe, I don't want to hide anymore.

ELI: What it comes down to is . . .

JACK: I've taken back my name. My Jewish name, the name I was born with.

ELI: What it comes down to is respect. As long as you respect the Torah, and watch your tongue, and be pious and modest, what could go wrong?

SCRIBE: A single word, heaven help us! One single word could disgrace the Torah, and then a huge calamity might descend on not just you but on all Jews, everywhere!

JACK: *(Agitated)* Rebbe . . . Listen . . . I'm not worthy of your presence here, under my roof.

ELI: Don't . . . !

JACK: I have to say this. Rebbe, I am a sinful man.

ELI: *(To himself)* Uy.

JACK: *(Holding Sara by her shoulders)* She is a sinful woman.

SARA: Yankel.

JACK: We don't have the right to even touch a Torah scroll. But there . . . *(Points to Rivkele's room)* In there, Rebbe . . . An angel lives there . . . Let me show you.

(Jack goes into Rivkele's room, surprising her. He takes her by the hand and leads her into the living room.)

This is my Rivkele. The scroll is for her, Rebbe, not for me. *(Takes her hands, lovingly examines them)* These hands, Rebbe, look at these hands. These are the purest hands imaginable. *(To Rivkele)* Go, darling, show the rebbe what you're making for the Torah.

RIVKELE: *(Panicked but trying not to show it)* What?

JACK: The vestment. Show him.

RIVKELE: Um . . .

JACK: Show him.

RIVKELE: Oh, Papa, must I?

JACK: Yes.

RIVKELE: But . . . it's . . . it's not finished.

JACK: So what? Go get it.

RIVKELE: *(Tearfully)* Please, Papa . . . don't make me . . . please don't . . .

SARA: *(Urges gently)* Yankel . . .

JACK: *(To Rivkele)* Uh, okay, dearest. *(To the men)* She's shy. You see what humility?

(He takes her hands and displays them for the Scribe.)

These hands, Rebbe, have embroidered the finest vestment for a Torah I have ever seen. Wait till you see. You will be amazed. My hands won't touch your Torah scroll. *(Points to Sara)* Her hands won't, either. But *these (Rivkele's), these* hands will. She'll take care of it. And honor it. It will stay in her room. And when she marries, she can take it with her wherever she and her husband may go.

ELI: *(To the Scribe)* See? See? Isn't that wonderful?

JACK: "Forget your father," I'll tell her. "Forget your mother. Have pure, decent children of your own." *(Quietly, to Rivkele)* Now, go, sweetheart. Go to your room. *(Kisses her head; smiles, watches as she goes.)* Rebbe, we are the sinful people. *(Meaning Sara and himself)*

SARA: *(Under her breath)* All right, already, Yankel.

JACK: Not her. This is why I went over to the synagogue and went up to this man *(Meaning Eli),* this man who is so wise about other people's lives, and I said to him, "Reb Eli, I need your help. I am a sinful man, but how can I protect my daughter from sin? I may be doomed but how can I save her? How can I make sure she gets the decent husband she deserves?" And he said to me, "Have a Torah put it in your house." He told me you had just copied one, for a man who died. Rebbe, that's all I want, that's all I ask. Please, sir. I must have that scroll.

(Eli confers with the Scribe. Jack and Sara watch expectantly as the old man weighs his verdict.)

SCRIBE: We will need a minyan.

ELI: *(Relieved)* No problem. We'll go to the synagogue, we'll find ten men.

JACK: *(Overlapping)* Thank you, thank you.

ELI: *(Refills glasses)* Now: Good—let's drink. *L'khaim.*

JACK: *L'khaim.*

SCRIBE: *L'khaim.*

ELI: You see, Reb Aaron? Even if a Jew sins, he's still a Jew. A Jewish soul wants the best for his child. *(To Jack)* God loves a penitent, true. But you have to make donations to the scholars.

JACK: Of course.

ELI: If you're not a scholar yourself, then you have to support scholarship. Because *al toyrah oylem oymeyd:* On the Torah rests the whole world. Isn't that right, Reb Aaron? Isn't that the way it is? *(The Scribe nods; to Jack)* Give up your old ways and support scholars.

JACK: Oh, I will, I will.

ELI: Forget the path you've been on and follow a different path.

JACK: I am, I will.

ELI: Do these things and eventually God will forgive you.

JACK: I'm gonna follow a different path, the path that leads to God.

(Eli puts his arm around Jack, walks him away from the Scribe.)

ELI: I've made some progress in lining up that bridegroom for your daughter.

JACK: Oh, yes?

ELI: A scholar. Who's going to college!

JACK: You hear this, Sara? College!

ELI: And now that you have a Torah for a dowry?!

JACK: Oh, thank God!

ELI: Come, let's find a minyan and rejoice in the Holy Book.

JACK: Wait. You're saying I can walk down the street with men such as your-selves?

ELI: Why not?

JACK: *(Moved)* You're not ashamed to be seen with me?

ELI: Look, if God forgives you, then we can certainly forgive you. Isn't that so, Reb Aaron?

SCRIBE: *(Shrugs)* Who can say? Our God is a God of mercy, a God of com-passion—but we mustn't forget: He is also a vindictive God, a God of vengeance. *(Looks at the fading light)* Hm, it's getting late. Come, if we're going to synagogue, we must go now . . .

(The Scribe exits the apartment, starts going down the stairs.)

JACK: What did he mean by that?

ELI: Don't worry about it. *(To Sara)* You think maybe you can prepare a little something for when we come back?

SARA: Consider it done.

JACK: Reb Eli, I am so grateful. How can I ever repay you?

ELI: Let me tell you about our new scholarship fund.

JACK: Could it be in my name?

ELI: Of course it can. If the donation is sizable enough.

(They go down the stairs and down the street. Sara primps in front of a mirror and putters as she calls to Rivkele, who is lying dreamily in bed, alone in her room.)

SARA: Rivkele!

RIVKELE: Yes, Mama?

SARA: The men have gone to get a minyan. They'll be back any minute. Put on your nice blue dress. Hurry.

RIVKELE: Yes, Mama.

(She gets out of bed. Meanwhile, Manke climbs the ladder of the fire escape and soon appears at Rivkele's window. Rivkele is terribly excited to see her but dares not exclaim; Manke slowly moves toward her as Sara continues speaking from the next room. The girls hardly take their eyes off each other.)

MANKE: *(Whispers)* Are you all right?

(Rivkele nods.)

I had to see you.

SARA: I can't believe this day has come.

RIVKELE: *(Whispers, to Manke)* You'd better go. My mother . . .

MANKE: *(Touches Rivkele's lips to silence her)* Shhh . . .

SARA: Your father has talked about this day, sweetheart, for so long. He wants so much for you to have a respectable life. You do know that, don't you, darling?

RIVKELE: Yes, Mama, I know.

SARA: Reb Eli says it's looking very good for this bridegroom! But I should keep my mouth shut. Kinna horee, I should keep my mouth shut. Do you need help in there?

RIVKELE: No! I don't need help. *(Her eyes on Manke)* Tell me about my bridegroom, Mama.

(Manke helps her out of her party dress and into a more austere one.)

SARA: Your bridegroom?! We shouldn't talk about him. It's bad luck.

RIVKELE: Please, Mama, I want to know. What is he like?

SARA: Well . . . he's very special.

RIVKELE: Yes?

SARA: Oh, yes. A treasure.

RIVKELE: A treasure?! Yes!

SARA: A scholar. Very smart. And kind.

RIVKELE: Yes. So kind.

SARA: An honest man. A good provider.

RIVKELE: Where will we live, Mama, my bridegroom and I? Where will we go?

SARA: He'll take you to live in a fine house. Filled with light. With trees all around. And your children—respectable, decent children—will run through the fields, laughing.

RIVKELE: What does he look like, Mama? Is he handsome?

(Manke takes Rivkele's face in her hands and kisses her passionately on the lips. They caress one another.)

SARA: Oh, yes! Very handsome. Beautiful, really.

RIVKELE: Yes. So so beautiful.

SARA: Clear, pale skin—white, almost.

RIVKELE: Yes.

SARA: Shiny black hair. And a smile . . . ! Such a smile!

RIVKELE: What about his eyes, Mama. Tell me about his eyes.

SARA: His eyes are dark. But they sparkle. Like jewels.

RIVKELE: Yes! They do! And his hands, are his hands gentle?

SARA: Yes. But also strong.

RIVKELE: *(Responding to Manke's touch)* Mmm. Will he touch me and caress my hair? Will he, Mama? Will he tell me I'm pretty?

SARA: Yes, yes, always.

RIVKELE: Will he love me, Mama?

SARA: Will he love you?

RIVKELE: Yes. Will he love me, my bridegroom? Will he?

SARA: Oh, yes. Of course he'll love you. Completely. With all his heart.

(We hear sung prayers as holy men in black—ten in all, the minyan, including Jack, Eli, and the Scribe, who holds the Torah, which seems to glow from within— come down the street and begin to go upstairs.)

Oh, my God! They're coming! He's back with the men! Hurry hurry hurry! They're on their way!

(Manke and Rivkele share a parting kiss. Rivkele gets into her dress as Manke descends the fire escape ladder. The men file into the upstairs apartment as the curtain falls.)

ACT 2

(A light spring rain. Later that night. Lights up on the gleaming Torah, now hanging in a cabinet on the wall in Rivkele's room. She is in her nightclothes, dreamily humming while brushing her hair. During the following, she gets ready for bed, turns out her light. Her haunting song continues while Manke comes down the street with a customer walking a few steps behind her. Both are holding umbrellas. She enters the downstairs apartment first; the man follows. He gives her money. They go into her cubicle. Shloyme and Hindl come down the street arguing.)

HINDL: He said hello! What do you want me to do, ignore him? He's just being friendly.

SHLOYME: Friendly?! That ain't "friendly," that's giving you the eye.

HINDL: You're crazy! I know him from the neighborhood. I walk past his hardware store a dozen times a day.

SHLOYME: I saw the way he looked at you, I saw that look.

HINDL: What look?

SHLOYME: "Well hello there, Hindl."

HINDL: That's just Moish. That's how he talks. He's a character.

SHLOYME: Did you do it with him?

HINDL: Uy gut, Shloym, what is the matter with you?

SHLOYME: Did you?

HINDL: What, all of a sudden you're jealous?

SHLOYME: Answer me: Did you screw him.

HINDL: You're nuts, you know that?

(He grabs her by her arm.)

SHLOYME: Did you?! Did you?! You did, didn't you!

HINDL: Let go of me!

SHLOYME: Did he pay? Huh? Did he, you stinking filthy whore? Did he?

HINDL: *(Finally)* No!

(Shloyme tosses her aside; she yelps.)

SHLOYME: And I said I would *marry* you?! What was I thinking?! What the hell was I thinking?!

HINDL: *(Overlapping "What the hell . . .")* He was nice to me! Don't I deserve someone nice now and then?

SHLOYME: *(Overlapping ". . . now and then?")* I said I'd go into business with you?!

HINDL: You'd gone away! How was I supposed to know you were coming back? I thought I was never gonna see you again!

SHLOYME: *(Overlapping "I thought . . .")* I must be outta my mind! We'll go broke! You *give* it away!

HINDL: *(Overlapping ". . . outta my mind!")* You're my man, not him. I don't give a damn about him! He says hello, I'll cross the street—

SHLOYME: You're secondhand goods!

HINDL: Please, Shloym, let's not fight. Come on, baby, don't . . .

(She tries to kiss him; he pushes her away.)

SHLOYME: Get offa me!

HINDL: I promised you Manke. Remember? You said if I got you Manke . . .

SHLOYME: Get offa me, I said!

(He tosses her aside and storms down the street.)

HINDL: Shloyme, no!

(She sobs, her face streaks with mascara. Basha and Reyzl run laughing down the street from the opposite direction, their clothing drenched by the downpour.)

REYZL: Oooh, I love the rain, don't you?

BASHA: Rain makes me homesick.

REYZL: Yeah?

BASHA: Makes me think of the orchard back home . . . The sound of the rain falling on the leaves . . . My mama, may she rest in peace, her borscht on the stove . . . sorrel and beets and dill. *(Inhales)* I can smell it.

REYZL: I remember the goats we had, grazing in the rain. I can smell them, too!

(They laugh.)

BASHA: Oh, and all my old friends, my girlfriends, oh God, I miss them. They'd be out dancing in the fields in a rain like this. And I'd be dancing with them, barefoot and drenched, far from the shtetl, far from our fathers.

REYZL: Would he get mad, your father?

BASHA: Oh God, would he!

REYZL: Mine, too. He used to come after me with a branch!

BASHA: Oh, no!

REYZL: Caught me with a boy once, hit me so hard, it left a scar. See? *(Shows her arm)*

BASHA: *(Winces)* Oooh. My father was a butcher. He had all these sharp knives. He didn't like something I did? He'd put a knife to my throat and threaten to stick it in!

REYZL: Oh God!

BASHA: I don't know if he's alive or dead and I don't care.

REYZL: Basha!

BASHA: He wanted me to marry Notke, the other butcher in town. It was all arranged.

REYZL: What was he like?

BASHA: Notke? Uch, he was awful. These big hairy hands, and he always smelled like beef!

(Reyzl laughs.)

He did! He was disgusting. The thought of spending the rest of my life with him, those rough hairy hands touching me, stinking of blood . . .

REYZL: Ich . . . so what happened?

(They enter the brothel. Hindl, still unseen, shields her tear-streaked face.)

BASHA: I ran away. And came here. To America. My mama didn't want me to be a butcher's wife like her. She gave me every last shekel she saved to pay my way.

REYZL: Ohhh . . .

BASHA: The last time I saw her, my boat was pulling away. She ran to the end of the dock, all the way to the end, till there was nowhere left to run . . . *(A faraway voice)* "Good-bye, Basheleh! Find a better life! God be with you!" *(Silence. Saddened.)* Some "better life."

(Reyzl puts her arm around her.)

Thank God she didn't live to find out what I do.

HINDL: And what's wrong with what we do?

REYZL: *(Surprised to see her)* Hindl.

HINDL: Are we any different from the shopgirls? Or the factory girls, or the secretaries? We're all out to earn a buck. We all gotta survive. You think the middle-class wives are any better off? *They* gotta work hard for their keep, too—by making their fat husbands happy.

REYZL: Hey. What's with your face?

HINDL: *(Self-consciously)* Nothing.

REYZL: You been crying?

HINDL: No . . . *(Fixing her face in the mirror)* Just the rain.

BASHA: *(Still haunted by her mother)* She . . . she comes to me sometimes.

HINDL: Who?

BASHA: My poor dead mamaleh, from deep in her grave.

REYZL: You see her?!

(Basha nods.)

When?

BASHA: At night.

HINDL: What are you talking about?

BASHA: She comes to me, her shroud all torn and tattered, covered in mud . . .

REYZL: Uch! What does she do?

BASHA: She gets into bed with me.

(Reyzl gasps.)

And tears at my hair because of my sins, the terrible things I've done.

HINDL: *(Spooked)* I don't like this; I don't like this at all.

BASHA: She rips hair from my head and scratches my face with her nails.

HINDL: Stop it.

REYZL: Does she speak?

BASHA: She cries. She howls in shame . . .

(Hindl shudders.)

(A haunted, faraway voice) "Basha, how could you!? This is not what I wanted for you! This is not what I wanted!"

HINDL: All right, already! Enough about sins! Enough about ghosts! You're giving me the creeps!

(Meanwhile, Jack, holding a basket of food, comes downstairs.)

JACK: *(Singsong)* Hell-o-o!
REYZL: *(Quietly)* Oh, no!
HINDL: *(To the girls)* What does he want?
JACK: *(Enters cheerfully)* Well! Good evening, girls.
BASHA: Evening.
JACK: Some night, hm? Any business at all?

(Basha and Reyzl shake their heads.)

HINDL: Manke. She's got someone.
JACK: Leave it to Manke. So . . . how are my girls?
REYZL: Don't worry, we're going back out.
BASHA: We just came in to change; we got soaked.
JACK: That's all right, I'm not complaining. You hear me complaining? I didn't come here to yell.
REYZL: No?
JACK: No! I came to tell you girls to call it a night.
BASHA: *(Incredulous)* You did?
JACK: Stay in! Keep dry! God forbid you should get a cold.
REYZL: You mean you're not gonna make us walk the streets in the rain?
JACK: No no no. Better you should stay in and keep your health.
BASHA: Yeah? But you always said, don't come back unless it's with a customer.
JACK: That was the *old* Yankel. This is the *new* Yankel.
HINDL: The new Yankel, huh.
JACK: That's right: The one who's changing his ways.
HINDL: You mean Yankel the mensch, not Yankel the pimp?

(The girls look at one another, expecting the worst.)

JACK: *(With a smile)* You're not gonna get a rise out of me tonight, Hindl. Not tonight. Tonight I begin again. I'm so happy, I could . . . dance around the room!

(He spins Basha, who is aghast.)

BASHA: Mister . . . !

HINDL: What's with you?!

JACK: What's with me? God is with me.

HINDL: Uy vey.

JACK: Make fun all you want. Look what I brought you . . .

(He unveils a splendid basket of food. The girls exclaim but hesitate.)

HINDL: Okay, where's the catch?

JACK: There *is* no catch. My! You're so suspicious, Hindl! Does there always have to be a catch?

HINDL: Generally speaking . . . ?

JACK: Can't I give my girls a little treat now and then? Huh? Look at all this beautiful food going to waste! I want you to have it. Take! Help yourselves!

(The girls warily help themselves.)

There you go! Don't be shy.

BASHA AND REYZL: Oh, thank you, mister . . . thank you. (They savor the bread, etc.)

JACK: *(Overlapping ". . . thank you.")* Uncle. Call me Uncle. No one can say I'm not a good employer. Look at the benefits. There! Now isn't that good?

BASHA AND REYZL: Mmm, yes . . . delicious . . . *(Etc.)*

JACK: Whatever you do, don't tell Sara I gave you. She thinks I'm too generous as it is. *(To Hindl)* Take. It's only gonna go bad.

HINDL: I don't take charity. Not from the likes of you.

JACK: Oh, I see. Well, aren't you superior. You don't want my food? Fine. *(A beat)* Your darling boyfriend around? Excuse me: Your fiancé.

HINDL: What do you care?

JACK: Give him a challah. Tell him it's on me.

HINDL: You gotta be kidding.

JACK: No! I told you: I'm not the same man I was when I woke up this morning. God has been invited back into my house. He's there. He's right upstairs. Big changes are happening around here.

HINDL: Oh, yeah, what kind of changes?

JACK: Big changes. As soon as I get my Rivkele married off . . . I'm closing up shop.

HINDL: You're what?!

BASHA: (Overlapping) What do you mean?

JACK: I'm getting out of the business.

HINDL: What do you mean you're getting out of the business? You're going straight?

JACK: That's right.

HINDL: Ha. What are you gonna do?

JACK: Taxi medallions.

HINDL: Taxi medallions?

BASHA: *(Overlapping)* Taxis?!

JACK: Mark my words: Taxis are gonna be the next big thing in this town. I'm buying a whole fleet's worth.

HINDL: Unbelievable.

BASHA: And what happens to us?!

REYZL: You're kicking us out?

JACK: Nobody's kicking you out.

HINDL: Sure.

REYZL: I *live* here; this is my *home!* The only home I've ever had here!

BASHA: *(Overlapping "The only home . . .")* Where are we supposed to go?

JACK: *(Overlapping; calming them down)* Shh shh shh . . . Don't get hysterical.

HINDL: *(Overlapping)* What does he care? He doesn't give a damn what happens to us.

JACK: Quiet, you! *(To the others)* You think I'd just throw you out on the street? Huh? What sort of man do you think I am?

(Hindl scoffs.)

I'll send you off with a few bucks to get you started. A little something, you'll be fine.

REYZL: And do what? How we gonna live?

BASHA: *(Overlapping "How we gonna . . .")* This is all I've ever done; I don't know how to do anything else!

REYZL: Me, either!

JACK: You're young, you'll find husbands.

BASHA: *(Tearful)* Who's gonna want me?

JACK: *(Soothing)* Basha . . .

BASHA: *(Continuous)* What kind of man'll want to marry a girl like me?

HINDL: Shloyme's marrying me . . .

JACK: You see that?

HINDL: We're opening up a house of our own. You can come work for us.

JACK: Uh! You see that?!

BASHA: *(To Hindl)* Work for *you?* What makes you think I'd want to come work for *you?*

HINDL: Well, the hell with *you!*

REYZL: I'd rather starve to death!

HINDL: The hell with both of you! I offer you a roof over your heads and this is how you talk to me?

BASHA: Screw you!

HINDL: *(Continuous)* We'll see how you feel when winter comes and you're freezing your tootsies off and you got no place to go!

BASHA *(Overlapping ". . . and you got . . ."):* Oh, yeah?

JACK: (Overlapping) Girls, girls! Enough of this! Really, now. You should be ashamed of yourselves. There's a Torah upstairs now. Show a little respect. Now go to sleep and get some rest, all of you. Go!

REYZL: Good night, Uncle.

JACK: Good night. And make sure Manke gets some food. *(He starts to go.)*

BASHA: Yes, Uncle. Good night.

HINDL: Hey. Reb Yankel. You forgot something.

(She balls up Rivkele's vestment and throws it at him. He picks it up.)

JACK: (Realizes) Oh, my God . . . What is this doing here?!

HINDL: I dunno.

JACK: Did you steal it?

HINDL: No!

JACK: *(To Hindl, grabbing her arm)* Did you?! Did you snatch it upstairs from the party?

HINDL: *(Overlapping)* No! Let go of me!

JACK: You stole it when no one was looking!

HINDL: I did not! Stop it! You're hurting me!

BASHA: Leave her alone!

JACK: *(Grabs Basha)* Did you? Did you sneak upstairs?

BASHA: No!

JACK: *(Tosses Basha aside, grabs Reyzl)* Did you?!

REYZL: Uncle! Please!

JACK: Then how did it get here? Huh? Magic? Somebody stole it!

HINDL: Nobody stole it, dear, repentant Uncle.

JACK: What?

HINDL: Somebody left it behind.

JACK: What are you talking about, left it behind?

HINDL: Rivkele! Rivkele left it!

JACK: Rivkele?!

HINDL: Yes, Uncle. Your precious Rivkele. She was down here!

JACK: *(Restrains himself from striking her)* How dare you! How dare you say such a thing!

HINDL: *(Overlapping)* She came down to see Manke!

JACK: What?

HINDL: She and Manke are friends! They're friends! Manke's been teaching her how to embroider! This is *Manke's* work! *She* did it.

JACK: That's not true! Rivkele did it! She told me herself!

HINDL: You stupid, blind man! She comes down here! Your darling daughter!

JACK: Liar!

HINDL: I'm not lying! It's the truth!

JACK: I want you out of here first thing in the morning. You hear me? First thing!

HINDL: With pleasure.

JACK: Now, go! All of you! Go to bed! I want you out of my sight!

(Reyzl and Basha scurry off to their beds. Jack runs upstairs with the vestment. Hindl lingers in the shadows. Jack bursts into Rivkele's room. She wakens, frightened.)

RIVKELE: Papa!

JACK: Look what I found downstairs! Look! Look!

(Sara appears in a robe.)

SARA: *(Overlapping "Look!")* Jack! What's going on?

JACK: *(To Rivkele)* What was this doing there? Huh? Huh?

RIVKELE: *(Crying hysterically)* Papa, please!

JACK: *(Continuous; slapping her with the vestment)* I want an answer! Have you been going downstairs?! Have you? *(Etc.)*

SARA: Jack, leave the girl alone!

RIVKELE: *(Overlapping "Have you . . .")* Papa, don't! Please, Papa! *(Etc.)*

SARA: The Torah! What is the matter with you?!

RIVKELE: Mama?

SARA: Shhh . . .

(Sara comforts Rivkele, tucks her back into bed. She leads Jack into the other room. Rivkele listens.)

JACK: That Hindl, you know what she said? She said Rivkele's been down there!

SARA: What?

JACK: Can you imagine?

SARA: Oh God . . .

JACK: That whore! Such lies! I could kill her!

SARA: I have to tell you something.

JACK: It's jealousy, that's what it is. Jealousy!

SARA: *(Overlapping "Jealousy!")* Listen to me, Yankel. You're not gonna like this.

JACK: Don't tell me that; I hate when you tell me that.

SARA: Sit down.

JACK: I don't want to sit down.

SARA: All right, don't sit down.

JACK: What. Tell me.

SARA: *(Sighs)* This isn't the easiest life we've made for ourselves, you know.

JACK: Yeah, yeah. So?

SARA: All I want is for my family to be happy; I want you to be happy, I want *Rivkele* to be happy. Sometimes that means I have to look the other way.

JACK: What are you talking about?

SARA: It's true. Hindl is telling the truth.

JACK: What?

SARA: Manke's been teaching her how to embroider.

JACK: Oh my God.

SARA: Rivkele wanted to learn, so I mentioned that Manke did nice needle-work and . . .

JACK: *You* did?!

SARA: I'm very sorry, what's done is done!

JACK: What have I been talking about all these years?! Huh? What have I been saying?!

SARA: *(Overlapping "What have I been saying?!")* They're just girls! Like sisters!

JACK: "Sisters"?! What's the matter with you?! Manke is a whore! You want your daughter talking to whores?

SARA: The girl has no friends! She has no friends! Who does she have?

JACK: She has you and me! She has her family!

SARA: She needs more than us. What world are you living in where things are so simple? She's growing up! She's curious about the world! She's lonely! She goes to school and she comes home to her room! Those are the rules you insist she keep. What kind of life is that?

JACK: What do you want, you want your daughter to end up like you?! Huh? Is that what you want?! Like mother, like daughter?

SARA: *(A beat; hurt)* No. God forbid she should end up like me.

JACK: There's already *one* whore in the family, what's another one? Why not?, it's the family business!

(She raises her hand to strike him but he catches it. Pause.)

SARA: You made me a whore.

JACK: I "made" you . . . ?

SARA: I was practically a child. No older than Rivkele.

JACK: How did I "make" you? With promises of food in your stomach, clothes on your back? Your teeth were falling out when I found you; you were skin and bones. "Saved" you is more like it.

SARA: *(Sarcastically)* Thank you, Yankel—is that what you want to hear?— thank you for leading me down the road to prostitution. I can't thank you enough.

JACK: Sara.

SARA: You took my soul—and threw it away!

JACK: We had no choice. Rivkele has a choice.

SARA: We had a choice. You had no faith.

JACK: Faith? The faith was beaten out of me. I had to survive. Things were gonna be different for her. Remember? That was what we wanted. That's what all these years have been about. No mixing between upstairs and downstairs! How many times have you heard me say that? They've gotta be kept separate, like kosher from treyf!

SARA: *(Ironically)* Today was gonna be a new beginning. Remember?

(He falls to his knees repentantly and clutches her. Sara, surprised, holds his head against her.)

(As if to a child) What is this?

JACK: *(Tearfully)* I'm sorry . . .

SARA: Oh, Yankeleh . . .

JACK: I didn't mean what I said.

SARA: *(Stroking his hair, skeptically)* No? Sounded to me like you meant exactly what you said.

JACK: I say things sometimes . . .

SARA: What, you say you're sorry and that makes everything all right?

JACK: What more can I say? *(Sobbing, his face buried in her)* Forgive me. Please. Please, Sara.

SARA: Shhh. All right. *(A beat)* I forgive you. God help me, but I do. *(Pause)* Come. Let's go to bed.

JACK: Sara, what am I going to do?

SARA: You'll talk to her in the morning. *(Helps him to his feet)* Come, tateleh.

JACK: *(Standing)* Yes. You're right. I'll talk to her in the morning.

SARA: That's right. In the morning.

JACK: *(Going, her arm around him)* I'm only looking out for her own good, Sara.

SARA: I know, I know.

JACK: I want her to have a better life.

SARA: Of course you do.

JACK: A respectable life.

SARA: Yes, yes . . .

(They exit to their bedroom. Rumble of thunder. Downstairs, Manke emerges from her cubicle in a camisole; her customer dresses and leaves. She goes to the window and inhales the rain-cleansed air. She climbs out of the window and stands in the rain under Rivkele's window.)

MANKE: *(Whispers, calls)* Rivkele! Rivkele!

(Rivkele hears her, goes to her window. Hindl remains in the shadows, eavesdropping.)

RIVKELE: Oh, Manke! It's you, it's you, thank God it's you!

MANKE: Have they gone to bed?

RIVKELE: I think so.

MANKE: Did he hurt you?

RIVKELE: No, but he scares me so much. It's all my fault. I went down to find you and Shloyme was there—

MANKE: *(Overlapping)* Shhh shhh shhh. It's all right; it doesn't matter. Come down.

RIVKELE: What?!

MANKE: The rain feels wonderful! Come down right now!

RIVKELE: We'll get soaked!

MANKE: So what! Feel how warm the rain is!

RIVKELE: Oh, I would love to . . .

MANKE: Do!

RIVKELE: But what if my father . . . ?

MANKE: The hell with him!

RIVKELE: *(Giggles)* Manke!

MANKE: The night is so sweet. We'll dance to spring! *(Spins herself around a puddle)*

RIVKELE: *(Torn, considering it)* Oh . . . I don't know what to do . . .

MANKE: Rivkele . . . !

RIVKELE: I can't. I mustn't.

MANKE: Stop saying that! Or I'll shout your name and wake up the whole neighborhood!

RIVKELE: Shhh! What if he catches us?

MANKE: What if he does? We have nothing to lose! Our secret is out!

RIVKELE: Yes! You're right. Wait . . .

(She goes to her bed and props up her pillows to make it look like she's sleeping, then returns to the window.)

Oh God . . . I can't believe I'm doing this . . .

(She climbs down the fire escape ladder in her bare feet.)

MANKE: Yay!

RIVKELE: Oooh, it is warm!

MANKE: I told you!

(Manke takes Rivkele's hands and together they gaily swing around. Their laughter subsides. Manke strokes Rivkele's wet hair and face.)

(Gently) Close your eyes. Feel it? Feel how nice that is?

RIVKELE: Mmm.

MANKE: Let the rain wash away your sadness. Doesn't that feel good?

RIVKELE: Oh, yes!

MANKE: And breathe it in.

(They inhale together.)

Do you smell how sweet it is?

RIVKELE: Yes!

MANKE: Who would believe the city night could smell so sweet?

RIVKELE: Oh! My heart.

MANKE: What.

RIVKELE: Feel it. It's pounding.

(Manke puts her hands on Rivkele's chest.)

MANKE: Oooh, yes. Your heart is pumping so fast.

(Silence as she slowly caresses Rivkele's breasts)

Your skin is so cool under my hands . . . like cool white snow . . .

(Rivkele's teeth chatter.)

Oh, my darling, you're shivering. Come, let's go inside . . .

(As Manke helps Rivkele back inside, Hindl hides behind the drape of her cubicle and listens. Manke sits Rivkele down on the sofa, gets a towel and a blanket.)

RIVKELE: I feel so cold all of a sudden . . .

MANKE: *(Wrapping her in a blanket)* Here . . . *(Sits with her)* Cuddle with me. That's right. Snuggle up close. Feel how warm I am?

RIVKELE: Oh, yes.

MANKE: You hold me, and I'll hold you. There.

(They do.)

Better?

RIVKELE: Oh, yes. I love how you hold me. No one ever holds me like this.

MANKE: Me, neither.

RIVKELE: No? But all those men . . .

MANKE: *(A laughable notion)* Those men.

(Rivkele strokes Manke's hand.)

RIVKELE: I love your hands.

MANKE: *(Takes it away; self-conscious)* I hate how they look.

RIVKELE: *(Taking hold of Manke's hands)* Oh, no, they're so long and sleek and warm.

(Manke strokes her own face with Rivkele's hair, inhaling its scent.)

MANKE: Mmm . . . Your hair smells so clean. Like the rain. So fresh, so soft. Let me fix your hair, like a bride. *(She begins to)*

RIVKELE: Oooh, yes!

MANKE: You be the bride. A lovely young bride. And I'll be the bridegroom, your new husband. All right?

RIVKELE: Yes!

MANKE: The night of the wedding: The celebration is over. All the guests have gone home. We're sitting at the table with your mama and papa. And— wait! It's getting late. Your parents go off to bed. We're all alone.

(Rivkele mock-gasps.)

The nervous bride and her bridegroom. And I sit closer to you, as close as can be. And we hug. Like this.

(They hug.)

Oooh, yes! Tight, tight, as tight as can be. And I kiss you. Like this.

(She kisses Rivkele.)

And we blush, both of us. And we go to your bed, now our marriage bed, and we lie there, the two of us, side by side, and no one sees, no one knows, and no one cares, for we're married now, just a bride and her bridegroom, and we fall asleep in each other's arms, like this *(Gets on top of her),* for- ever and ever and ever . . .

(Hindl comes out of her cubicle, feigning surprise at seeing them.)

HINDL: Oops! Pardon me!

(Manke and Rivkele sit up, mortally embarrassed.)

MANKE: Hindl! What are you doing sneaking up on us?

HINDL: I wasn't sneaking, I was coming out to look at the rain.

MANKE: The rain stopped. Go back to bed.

HINDL: Gee, I knew you girls were friendly, but . . .

MANKE: We were only playacting.

HINDL: Oh, sure. Playacting.

MANKE: Mind your own business.

RIVKELE: Please don't tell my father. If he finds out I was down here . . .

HINDL: Boy, he's got some temper, doesn't he! You should've seen him before. I might just go upstairs right now . . .

RIVKELE: Don't! Please!

MANKE: Why don't you leave us alone?

HINDL: All right. I was gonna tell you something I thought you might find interesting but if you don't want to hear it . . .

MANKE: What.

HINDL: *(Singsong)* Good ni-ight!

MANKE: Hindl! What.

HINDL: Okay, you twisted my arm. What if I told you . . . Jack was shutting down the business?

MANKE: He is not.

HINDL: Yes he is. You think I would lie about something like that?

RIVKELE: It's true; I heard him talking about it.

MANKE: When's this supposed to happen?

RIVKELE: Soon. After my wedding.

MANKE: Oh God.

RIVKELE: It's good news, isn't it?

MANKE: No.

RIVKELE: Why?

HINDL: *(Overlapping)* What's so good about it? Think about it, mameleh: If he shuts this place down, where does that leave you and Manke?

RIVKELE: I'll still be upstairs and she'll still be downstairs.

MANKE: No . . .

HINDL: *(Overlapping)* Not if she's booted out and you're someone's little wife.

RIVKELE: Oh God . . .

MANKE: She's right.

RIVKELE: I hadn't thought about that.

HINDL: You're not gonna be able to hop the fire escape and see her anymore.

RIVKELE: Oh, Manke . . . What are we going to do?

MANKE: I don't know.

HINDL: Well, I know what I'm doing.

MANKE: What?

HINDL: Getting the hell out of here. Before he throws me out.

RIVKELE: And going where?

HINDL: Someplace new. Someplace safe. That your father doesn't know from. Or your mother. Where there's no more hitting. No more yelling.

RIVKELE: Where is this place?

HINDL: Not far. A few blocks away. But it might as well be the moon.

MANKE: Okay, Hindl. What's the story?

HINDL: You wanna know the story? Shloyme's gonna marry me. *That's* the story.

RIVKELE: *(Overlapping)* Hindl, that's wonderful!

HINDL: I never thought he'd ask me, but he did.

MANKE: What does Shloyme have to do with this?

HINDL: He found us a place. Of our own. On Rivington Street. Plenty of room for everybody.

RIVKELE: For everybody?

HINDL: Yeah, for you, too, baby.

MANKE: Oh, I see . . .

RIVKELE: What. I don't understand.

MANKE: She means a place like this. No way on earth would I take you to a place like this.

HINDL: You want to be together, don't you?

RIVKELE: Yes!

MANKE: But not like that. I would never do that to you. Never.

HINDL: So how you gonna be together? Huh? He'll do everything he can to keep you apart. You know he will.

RIVKELE: I'd die if I couldn't see you anymore . . .

MANKE: This is no kind of life for someone like you. This is no life for anybody.

RIVKELE: And what kind of life am I looking at now?, living under my father's roof, married off to a man I've never even met?! I want to be with you. I have to be with you. *(She cries.)*

MANKE: I won't let you throw yourself away. You hear me?

RIVKELE: Yes.

MANKE: Not for any man. Not for any reason.

(Manke holds Rivkele tightly.)

HINDL: All right, enough already, girls. Come, if we're gonna go, let's go.

(Hindl gets a suitcase and starts packing.)

RIVKELE: You mean now?!

MANKE: *(Overlapping)* Tonight?!

HINDL: Yeah! I'm outta here tonight. You coming with me, or what?

MANKE: This will change everything. Nothing will be the same after this.

RIVKELE: Let's do it! Let's have an adventure!

MANKE: An adventure?

RIVKELE: Yes! You and me!

HINDL: Thatta girl! Let's get out of here.

RIVKELE: Like this? *(Meaning her attire)* I can't go like this. I have to go back up.

HINDL: No, no, forget about your clothes.

RIVKELE: I just need to pack a few things.

HINDL: Too risky. What if your father hears you?

MANKE: She's right. Forget it.

HINDL: You'll wear *our* clothes.

RIVKELE: *Your* clothes?!

MANKE: Yeah! Let's see, what do I have for you . . . *(She goes through a rack of garments.)* Try this . . .

(Manke gives Rivkele a dress which she puts on with pleasure.)

RIVKELE: Oooh! I love it! It feels so silky.

HINDL: *(Applying lipstick)* I'm not gonna miss this place, that's for sure. Not for one minute.

(She starts applying lipstick to Rivkele's mouth.)

Here, kid . . . Pucker up.

MANKE: *(Stopping her)* No, don't!

RIVKELE: It's okay. I want to see.

(She lets Hindl finish. Hindl takes her to a mirror.)

HINDL: There! How do you like that?! Don't you look pretty.

RIVKELE: *(Looking at herself and Manke in the mirror)* What do you think, Manke? You think I look pretty?

MANKE: *(Rueful)* Yes. Very pretty.

HINDL: Here, try these shoes. Do they fit?

RIVKELE: *(Puts them on)* Yes! Good enough!

HINDL: Good! Now: What you need is a hat!

(Hindl puts a hat on Rivkele's head. Rivkele admires herself in the mirror. Hindl wraps her boa around Rivkele with a flourish.)

Ladies and gentlemen . . . Miss Clara Bow!

(Rivkele and Hindl laugh. Manke does not. Their laughter subsides. Rivkele watches Manke pack in silence.)

RIVKELE: Manke?

MANKE: *(Smiles)* Come. We should go.

(She clicks shut her suitcase and slips her arm through Rivkele's. The three of them begin to exit.)

HINDL: You won't be sorry. Things'll be different with Shloyme and me. I promise: A whole new world. Wait till he sees who I'm bringing home!

(Rivkele lingers to take a final look at her building. Manke takes her hand and they run off together. Lights shift. The dead of night.)
(Upstairs: Jack, in a robe, unable to sleep, enters the living room. Restless, he pours himself some wine, sits, thinks. Downstairs: a shriek. Basha, wraithlike in her nightclothes, comes out of her cubicle in an agitated dream state.)

BASHA: Mama?! Don't hurt me, you're hurting me! . . .

(Reyzl comes out of her cubicle, comforts Basha.)

REYZL: Basha . . . Shhh . . . You're dreaming . . .

BASHA: Please, Mama . . . Stop!

REYZL: Wake up!

BASHA: *(Wakens with a start)* Oh God . . . Reyzl . . . It was my poor dead mama again . . .

REYZL: I know.

BASHA: Howling and weeping and covered with thorny prickles . . . scratching my face, pulling my hair.

REYZL: Shhh . . .

BASHA: *(Haunted voice)* "For this I saved you? For this?" Oh God, I've shamed her so . . .

(She sobs in Reyzl's arms.)

REYZL: Poor Basha. Try to sleep. Come, mamaleh, I'll tuck you back in. Shhh . . .

(She leads Basha back to bed. Upstairs, Jack quietly enters Rivkele's room and approaches the cabinet housing the Torah. It seems to glow from within.)

JACK: *(Whispers, to the scroll)* Hello, God. It's me, Yankel Tshaptshovitsh. Welcome to my home. God, you see everything. You know everything I do. If you want to punish me, punish me. But the innocent girl who sleeps here—this angel—doesn't know the meaning of the word "sin." Have pity on her. Amen. *(Sits, whispers gently to the form lying in bed)* Rivkele? I don't want to wake you. I just want to be near you.

(He pulls up a chair and sits.)

I used to sit by your cradle while you slept, just to listen to you breathe. I couldn't believe the perfect little miracle God gave to two sinners! You are not the work of a vengeful God, my darling.

(A beat)

I had to find my way by myself, on the street. A greenhorn in America, this scrawny orphan. What did I have? I had nobody; I had nothing. Just my wits. But you, my precious, you're gonna have the life in America we only dreamed about. You, and your children, and their children. Yankel's children. You'll live the dream.

(A beat)

(More hurt than anger) So, when I find out you've been going downstairs when I told you never to go downstairs . . . When I find out you're making friends with the wrong sort of people . . . and lying to me! Sweetheart! Is it any wonder I get upset? I'm better now. I had a talk with your

mother. I've calmed down. We'll talk in the morning. Everything will be all right.

(He reaches for "her" and is shocked to find pillows where he thought she lay. He flings off the blanket and shouts in horror:)

Oh my God! NO!!!

(Sara hurries from her room into Rivkele's bedroom.)

SARA: Jack . . . Jack, what is it?
JACK: *(Shouts wildly)* You see your daughter?! Hm? Hm?

(He throws Sara down onto the bed.)

SARA: What do you want from me?!
JACK: You were too easy on her! You said I was too hard, but you . . . !
SARA: How dare you blame me! It was bound to happen! Sin is right down the
    stairs, Jack— *(Mocking)* "Yankel!" Right down the stairs!

(He storms out of the apartment and down the stairs.)

JACK: *(Shouts)* Rivkele?!

(Jack tears into the brothel, pulls Reyzl and Basha out of their beds, manhandles them. They're terrified.)

Where is she? Hm? Where is Rivkele? Is she here? Is she hiding?
REYZL: I don't know!
JACK: *(To Basha)* Do you?
BASHA: No! Let go of me! You're hurting me!

(He releases her, pulls open the drapes exposing the empty cubicles.)

JACK: Up! Everybody up! Manke! Hindl!

(He sees evidence of packing. It dawns on him.)

Oh, my God . . . *(To the others)* Where are they?! Where did they go!
REYZL: We don't know! We were sleeping!
BASHA: We're not their keepers!
JACK: *(Shouts)* Sara? Sara?

(He runs out, encounters Sara on the stairs.)

SARA: Did you find her? Is she there?

JACK: No! She's gone! She went with them!

SARA: With who?

JACK: Manke's gone, and so is Hindl! She ran away! Your precious daughter! She ran away! With those whores!

(He rampages around his living room, tossing furniture around, breaking glassware, etc. Sara and the girls huddle together on the stairs and listen in horror.)

BASHA: *(Frightened)* What's happening?

SARA: God help us! I don't know.

BASHA: It's my mother's revenge!

SARA: Go find Reb Eli. Tell him something terrible has happened. Tell him we need his help. We can't have a wedding without a bride. Hurry!

(Reyzl and Basha don coats and exit. Sara goes back upstairs to find Jack disconsolate and the apartment in shambles. She begins to pick up the pieces.)

Our daughter has run away, but must you destroy our home too?

JACK: *(Quietly)* What difference does it make? It's all shit. *(A mournful wail)* Rivkele!

SARA: Listen to you! So she's run away! What seventeen-year-old girl hasn't done that?!

JACK: What can I do? There's nothing I can do!

SARA: Go out there! Ask around! Ask the scum you know who make their lives in the gutter! Ask them if they've seen your daughter!

JACK: I can't. I can't move my legs. It doesn't matter anymore. Nothing matters. God doesn't want it. He doesn't want it . . .

SARA: God doesn't want it? *You're* the one who doesn't want it!

(She puts on a coat.)

JACK: Where you going?

SARA: To the streets! If you want to sit here eating your kishkes out, fine! I'm going out to look for her!

(Sara hurries downstairs and exits. Lights shift. Minutes pass.)
(Just before dawn. Eli rushes up the street and finds Jack upstairs, sitting amid the wreckage.)

ELI: *(Entering)* Oh my God! Look at you! Look at this place!

JACK: *(Muttering)* Eli, Eli . . . she's gone, Eli. My Rivkele. She's left me.

ELI: Pull yourself together . . .

JACK: She ran away with whores.

ELI: Quiet. Don't speak that way.

JACK: It's true, Eli. The marriage I wanted for her. The future. God doesn't
    want it.

ELI: Shhh!

JACK: *(Overlapping)* He doesn't want it. It isn't meant to be. *(Wails)* Rivkele!
    . . . Rivkele! . . .

ELI: What is the matter with you?! You want the whole world to hear? Things
    like this are best kept private.

JACK: I don't care who hears. My daughter is gone. No more daughter. Riv-
    kele! *(Breaks down sobbing)*

ELI: Enough. You're acting like a crazy man.

JACK: I am crazy. Crazy to believe that my faith would not be mocked. She's
    gone to the Devil, I just know it.

ELI: Stop it. That isn't true.

JACK: Yes. I know what happens out there. She'll feel . . . temptation.

ELI: Yankel!

JACK: She will. And once it starts to grow inside her . . .

ELI: Uy uy uy.

JACK: *(Continuing)* Once it starts, she won't know how to fight it. She'll sur-
    render. Just like the rest of us sinners.

ELI: All right, now stop that right this minute.

JACK: If only she had died before her time . . .

ELI: What kind of nonsense is that now?!

JACK: If she had died, at least I would have known that I buried a pure child.
    But now . . . ?

(Eli takes Jack by the hand into Rivkele's room, stands before the scroll.)

ELI: Come. Let us pray!

JACK: What's the point? He doesn't hear me. He hasn't heard me all along.

ELI: Don't say that! Pray to Him! Pray for His forgiveness!

JACK: *(To the scroll)* Show me! What kind of God are you?!

ELI: Yankel!

JACK: Perform a miracle! Go on! Send down a fire to consume me!

ELI: Enough!

JACK: *(Continuing)* Open up the ground and let it swallow me up!

ELI: Enough with that!

JACK: Please please please, God, please protect my child. Send her back to me as pure, as innocent as she was. Otherwise I say that You are no God at all!

ELI: *(Aghast)* You mustn't speak this way!

JACK: *(Continuing)* You are vindictive! No better than a man!

ELI: That is blasphemy! Beg His forgiveness! Pray with me! Now!

(Eli leads Jack in prayer. Lights shift. Minutes pass. Sara hurries down the street with Shloyme.)

SHLOYME: *(On the move)* This better be good, dragging me out of my poker game . . .

SARA: What do you care, you were losing. Come, I'll give you some schnapps . . .

(She enters the brothel, pours drinks.)

SHLOYME: *(Hesitates)* Uh-uh, no thanks, I don't want to run into your husband.

SARA: Don't worry about him . . . He's fast asleep.

SHLOYME: *(Enters)* I liked him better before he found God.

SARA: *(Hands him a drink)* You and me both. *L'khaim.*

(They drink.)

Got a cigarette?

(He gives her one, holds her hand as he lights it for her.)

SHLOYME: You know? You must've been some looker.

SARA: Yeah? Well, you're right.

SHLOYME: Even now. You're not bad.

SARA: Gee, that's some compliment coming from you — seeing what sophisticated taste in women you have. I mean, really, Shloyme: Hindl?

SHLOYME: Oh, come on, Hindl's not so bad.

SARA: No?! She's bounced around every flophouse on the Lower East Side, that girl! She's all used up! You—you're young, you're smart, you're not bad-looking . . .

SHLOYME: Gee, thanks.

SARA: You could get any girl you want! A girl from a good family, even. Have a little self-respect! Don't sell yourself short!

SHLOYME: How come you're so interested in me all of a sudden?

SARA: *(Her hand inching up his inner thigh)* I just hate to see all that potential go to waste.

SHLOYME: What'd you want to talk about anyway?

SARA: Business.

SHLOYME: Yeah? So talk.

SARA: I want you to do something for me.

SHLOYME: Yeah? And what you ever do for me?

SARA: *(Seductively)* What would you like me to do? Huh? I'll do an-y-thing you want.

(He removes her hand and backs away. She takes cash out of her purse.)

SHLOYME: What's all that?

SARA: Investment for the future. Three or four hundred—I'm not sure, I haven't counted it lately.

SHLOYME: What're you doing walking around with all that money?

SARA: You can have it—it's yours.

SHLOYME: What do you mean, it's mine? How's it mine?

SARA: Just tell me where my daughter is.

SHLOYME: Your daughter?! How'm I supposed to know? Ain't she tucked away upstairs in her bed?

(During the above, Hindl runs up the street and enters the brothel.)

HINDL: I did it, Shloym! I got you the girls! Just like I said. Manke and Rivkele, too!

SHLOYME: *(Comprehending)* Oh . . .

SARA: *(Overlapping; to Hindl)* Where is she?! Huh?! Where'd you take her?!

HINDL: Damned if I tell you!

SARA: Bitch! *(To Shloyme)* Is opening a house with a broken-down whore the best you can dream about? Is it?

HINDL: *(Overlapping "Is it?")* Screw you!

SARA: You can do anything. This is America. This'll help you get started.

HINDL: That Rivkele's a gold mine. That face, that little body of hers? The men are gonna be all over her—they're gonna be lining up!

(Sara thrusts the money at him.)

SARA: Take it. Where is she? What's the address?

HINDL: Don't, Shloym. The girl's worth a lot more than a wad of cash.

(Sara takes off her earrings.)

SARA: Take these, too. Hock 'em. That's a couple hundred right here.

(Shloyme is considering it.)

HINDL: *(To Shloyme)* Don't. We're so close! We're in business, baby. We're all set. We're getting married! Let's do it today!

SARA: *(Overlapping)* You don't need her.

HINDL: Yes, you do. You love me! I know you do!

SARA: Here's your ticket, right here . . . right in my hand . . .

HINDL: Don't listen to her, Shloym . . . We're better than her.

(Shloyme and Hindl look at one another.)

SHLOYME: (While looking at Hindl) Two-eleven Rivington Street.

(He takes the jewelry. Hindl cries out.)

(To Sara) Come, I'll walk you.

SARA: Thanks.

(Sara walks past Hindl, who stands crumpled in the doorway.)

SHLOYME: *(To Hindl)* Hey. Let's face it: It's for the best.

(Hindl slaps his face. Shloyme and Sara exit down the street. Hindl, depressed, goes into her cubicle and draws the drape. Upstairs, Eli paces while Jack sits despondently.)

ELI: All is not lost. We can still save this match. When I talked to the boy's father, I dropped a few hints that the bride's family, well, that maybe she doesn't come from the best of families and he didn't bat an eye. He still wants to meet you. I said I would bring him around first thing this morning.

JACK: This morning?! But how can he come?! There is no match! I have no daughter!

ELI: He doesn't have to meet the girl. He wants to meet you. We can buy some time. Now, please, get dressed and let's clean up this mess; we can't have it looking like this.

(Jack dresses while Eli picks up. Lights shift. Minutes pass.)
(Morning. Sara comes down the street with her arm around Rivkele, who is wrapped in a large shawl.)

SARA: Thank God I found you. You had yourself a misadventure, that's all. What child doesn't get into mischief every now and then?

RIVKELE: Where's Manke?

SARA: Forget about Manke. I don't think you'll be seeing Manke anymore. Now: When your father asks questions, don't say any more than you have to. Remember: The fewer words the better.

RIVKELE: Mama . . .

(At the steps, Sara fixes Rivkele's appearance.)

SARA: Now, let's see . . . if only I had a comb. I'd fix your hair in braids.

RIVKELE: Leave it! I don't want my hair in braids.

SARA: *(Taken slightly aback)* All right. We'll leave it.

RIVKELE: Please don't make me go up there.

SARA: He's not gonna hurt you. I promise. I won't let him.

RIVKELE: You always let him.

SARA: *(Taken further aback)* Rivkele!

RIVKELE: It's all right, Mama, I know: We all take what we can get.

SARA: Hate me all you like . . .

RIVKELE: I don't hate you.

SARA: Hate your father. But don't—I beg you—don't destroy your future out of spite. This marriage . . .

RIVKELE: Mama . . .

SARA: It's a real opportunity! A way out! We can still make it happen! No one has to know *any*thing! Come, sweetheart, whatever you do, don't make him mad.

(They go upstairs. Eli sees them approach from the top of the stairs.)

ELI: Thank God! They're here!

JACK: *(Still dazed)* What?

ELI: Your wife and child. See? God did help you. He punishes but He also
heals. *(To Rivkele)* Hello, dear. Thank God you're home safely. You had us
all so worried there for a time. *(To Jack)* Now: Before anything else should
go wrong, let me quick find the father of the bridegroom and finish the
deal. Pay the dowry right away, whatever it is, today. And no hemming or
hawing about the wedding, either.

JACK: *(To Rivkele, but not looking at her)* I just want to know one thing. And I
want the truth.

ELI: Leave it alone, Yankel. Just thank God for her return and leave it alone.

SARA: He's right, Yankel.

JACK: Just the truth. That's all I ask.

ELI: God will help and, in time, everything will work itself out. *Tshuvah, tefi-
lah, tzedaka:* Penitence, prayer, and charity. *(To Sara)* You might want to
tidy up a little bit more.

SARA: Yes; I will.

ELI: And cheer up, everybody. Smile. You wouldn't want anyone to think something was wrong. I'll be back.

*(Eli goes down the stairs, exits. Jack, Sara, and Rivkele stand in silence, the girl's
face still obscured by her shawl. Jack approaches her. She flinches.)*

JACK: I only want to see your face. Let's see . . .

(He gently reveals her face; she averts her eyes.)

There you are, my darling. *(To Sara, hopefully)* See?

(Sara nods.)

It's still the same girl. Isn't it?

SARA: Yes, it is.

JACK: *(To Rivkele)* Come. Sit with me.

(Rivkele doesn't move.)

Don't be shy.

RIVKELE: I'm not shy.

JACK: Sit with me, I said.

RIVKELE: No, Papa.

JACK: No?

SARA: Your father wants you to sit with him.

RIVKELE: And I told him I don't want to. *(Looking at Jack defiantly)* No, thank you. I'll stand.

JACK: *(To Sara)* What kind of talk is this? She runs away from home and she comes back with a mouth?

RIVKELE: Not a mouth. Just a tongue.

JACK: Well! Well!

SARA: Yankel, don't. We're all tired.

RIVKELE: Not me. I'm wide awake.

JACK: *(To Rivkele)* I have one question. Only one. But I want the truth. You understand?

RIVKELE: Papa . . .

JACK: Do you?

RIVKELE: I understand.

JACK: *(Pauses; gently)* Tell me you're the same girl who left here last night. The same, pure girl. That's all I want to hear. You can tell me, darling.

RIVKELE: I don't know!

JACK: You don't *know?!* What do you mean, you don't know?!

RIVKELE: What is "pure"? I don't know what it means!

JACK: That's ridiculous! Look me in the eye and tell me. Tell me the truth.

(Rivkele looks at him but doesn't say anything. Silence. He unravels her shawl, unveiling her garish dress.)

Oh my God!

(Jack puts his fingers around her neck. Rivkele is not afraid.)

SARA: Don't!

JACK: *(To Rivkele)* If I had done this, long ago . . .

SARA: Jack!

JACK: *(Continuous, ignoring Sara)* If I had twisted your neck off before you grew up . . .

SARA: Oh my God, Jack . . .

JACK: If I had cut off your breath . . . Maybe we all would've been better off.

SARA: Stop it!

JACK: *(Tearfully)* Look at you!

RIVKELE: Go ahead. Do it now. I don't care.

SARA: Rivkele! *(Pulls her away from Jack)*

RIVKELE: *(Continuous, to Jack)* Cut off my breath, just as you've been suffocating me all my life!

(Sara gasps.)

JACK: What are you talking about, suffocating.

SARA: Leave it alone, leave it alone, Jack . . .

RIVKELE: *(Overlapping)* You kept me locked in my room!

JACK: Locked in your room?!

RIVKELE: You made me your prisoner!

JACK: Darling! I was protecting you!

RIVKELE: From what?

JACK: From evil! From sin! It's a sinful world out there! You're just a child!

RIVKELE: No! Not just a child! Not anymore!

JACK: *(A beat)* What do you know?

RIVKELE: Everything! I know everything!

(Meanwhile, Eli and the Prospective In-law, the father of the would-be bridegroom, come hurriedly down the street and mount the stairs.)

ELI: *(Animatedly, while walking)* Yes, yes, he's very eager to meet you. And his daughter! Such a fine girl and a pretty one! A scholarly son-in-law he's after and he'll support them the rest of their lives.

PROSPECTIVE IN-LAW: Ah, good, very good.

(They enter the apartment. Eli feels the chill in the air.)

ELI: Well! Here we are! Aren't we lucky! The entire Tshaptshovitsh family . . . The mother of the bride . . .

PROSPECTIVE IN-LAW: How do you do?

SARA: How do you do.

ELI: The father of the bride . . .

PROSPECTIVE IN-LAW: *(To Jack)* Sir . . .

ELI: And the lovely Rivkele.

JACK: *(Bitterly)* Yes sir, a finer, chaste maiden you will never see.

ELI: Yes, well. *(To the Prospective In-law)* Isn't she something? Can you imagine a better match for your boy?

(The Prospective In-law nods.)

JACK: *(Takes Rivkele's hand brusquely)* Such a fine, chaste girl I have, no?

RIVKELE: Papa . . .

JACK: *(Maniacally)* And what fine, chaste children she will have! *(To Sara)* Right? Oh, what a future! What a bright future! The *years* we dreamed of this . . . Her mother will lead her to the wedding canopy . . . in the whore-house!

(Screams, shouts, cries—a cacophony.)

PROSPECTIVE IN-LAW: What? What did he say?

ELI: *(Overlapping)* Oh, no, have you gone crazy?

JACK: Down to the whorehouse! Go! Get out of here, all of you!

RIVKELE: Papa!

(Jack pushes Rivkele toward the stairs.)

JACK: You're all whores! *(To Sara, evicting her)* You, too!

SARA: Jack! No!

JACK: Go! Everyone! Downstairs!

PROSPECTIVE IN-LAW: *(Overlapping)* What's going on here?

ELI: He's mad!

JACK: *(To Eli)* You can go, too! Go on! Go! Good-bye!

ELI: You fool! You crazy fool!

JACK: Wait! Before you go . . .

(He rushes into Rivkele's room, takes the scroll.)

ELI: Don't throw it all away! Think about what you're doing!

(Jack wields the Torah over his head, as if he is about to throw it at Eli.)

Remember God, Yankel! Remember God!

(Jack instead thrusts the Torah into Eli's arms.)

JACK: *(To Eli)* Take it with you! I don't need it anymore!

(Eli and the Prospective In-law leave with the scroll. Manke runs on and sees Riv-kele, who breaks away from Sara and goes to her. Sara watches as the girls exit together, Manke holding Rivkele. Sara, shattered, resignedly trudges back upstairs to join Jack in the ruins of their home. Downstairs, Hindl robotically applies lip-stick before setting out for another day of walking the streets. Lights fade.)

A CERTAIN RAQUEL
A Play in One Act and Fourteen Scenes

by Nora Glickman

A Certain Raquel. Teatrotaller performance in Puebla, Mexico, 1999. Pictured are María Burgos Ojeda and Alexander Santiago Jirau. Photograph by Melissa Castillo-Garsow.

When Raquel Liberman's granddaughter provided me with an old box containing her grandmother's letters and documents, she had no idea of their contents. The letters were written in Yiddish and the documents were in Polish. Her uncle had kept them hidden under his bed in his apartment. Having been taught not to ask questions about her family's past, the granddaughter was naturally curious. Then, in a TV documentary which featured a notorious Argentinian prostitute of the 1920s, she recognized the image of her grandmother, the same image as a portrait on her family's mantelpiece. She was both ashamed of her newly discovered family history and curious to obtain further information about her grandmother, Raquel. Subsequent translations of the letters revealed a poignant and complex story that clarified family secrets and vindicated Raquel.

My interest in the white slave trade began when I was conducting research for my doctoral dissertation. I examined the impressionistic writings of Albert Londres and the Yiddish stories and plays of Sholom Asch, Sholem Aleichem, and I. B. Singer, and the fiction of Latin American Jewish authors like Moacyr Scliar, Mario Szichman, and Germán Rozenmacher, which amplified this fascinating yet disconcerting topic.

Subsequent study of the historical and literary documentation of prostitution in Argentina and Brazil resulted in several articles and two books, as well as a cotranslation (with Rosalía Rosembuj) of Leib Malach's play *Ibergus*. My chief interest was in understanding the reasons why Raquel Liberman, the woman who denounced the traffickers, was seen at various times as a martyr, a victim, and a manipulator.

A Certain Raquel contains an adaptation of one scene from Leib Malach's play, *Ibergus*, which illustrates essential elements in the lives of the *polacas* —Jewish prostitutes from Eastern Europe, not just Poland: their pride in practicing their religion and in celebrating Jewish holidays, their love of tango and Yiddish music, and most notably, their preservation of the Yiddish language by becoming patrons of the Yiddish theatre. In the theatres they clashed openly with the mainstream Eastern European community, who fought fiercely against the traffickers.

The title of my play, *A Certain Raquel,* refers to the casual response made by a Polish embassy official in Argentina in 1934 to Raquel's request for a travel visa. After inspecting her lifestyle, he was supposed to determine whether or not "a certain Raquel Liberman," a woman of questionable reputation, had sufficiently reformed. Although her travel permit was granted, Raquel never took the trip to Poland. She remained in Buenos Aires, where, within a few months, she died of thyroid cancer.

By the end of her life, Raquel had succeeded in making a name for herself in the Argentine press. Her courageous testimony led to the breakup of the Zwi Migdal traffickers' organization by the Argentine authorities. She accused the traffickers of deceiving Jewish women with false promises of marriage and wealth and then forcing them into prostitution. Raquel's deposition coincided with a new period of legal reform in the Argentine government, breaking a long tradition of bribery and corruption.

In my play, I dwell on Raquel's claim that she was brought to Argentina and forced into prostitution. In truth, she entered the profession voluntarily. Raquel did not disclose to the authorities that she had entered the country legally as a married woman with two children and later decided, on her own, to practice prostitution. She lied in order to safeguard the future of her small children.

The biographical elements which serve as a framework to my play provided the tools for a dramatic collage. By juxtaposing the voices of the past with those of the present, with Raquel summoning her dead grandmother, I could bring together two women separated by generations but determined to fill the void of the past in order to better understand the present.

I consider myself a Latino writer, concerned with issues of identity, assimilation, and integration that pertain to North America and the Hispanic world. The experience of bringing this play to both a Latino and an American audience was particularly appealing to me. Teatrotaller of Cornell University produced the first Spanish version of the play in 1999. After performances in Ithaca, the group staged the play at Columbia University in New York and at various university theatre festivals in Mexico City, Puebla, and Liege, Belgium. I am grateful to Teatrotaller.

My thanks to Raquel's grandchildren for having supplied me with their grandmother's letters; to Rosalía Rosembuj for her translation of Raquel's letters from Yiddish; to Myrtha Schalom, Carlos Serrano, and Humberto Costantini for their inspiring works; to the National Foundation for Jewish Culture for the development of this play; to Ollantay Center for the Arts; and to Roger Hendrix-Simon's Drama Center, where the first workshops of the play took place.

Characters

RAQUEL LIBERMAN (thirty-five)

RAQUEL CELMAN, Raquel's Granddaughter (twenty-five)

YAACOV FERBER, Raquel's Husband (thirty-nine)

BRONIA KOYMAN, A Madam (forty-five)

DOMÍNGUEZ, A Client

SIMÓN BRUTKIEVICH, Head of the Zwi Migdal

MAURICIO KIRSTEIN, Trafficker

JOSÉ KORN, Trafficker

MAX KAUFMAN, Raquel's Friend

CUSTOMER

SOCIETY LADY

JULIO ALSOGARAY, Police Inspector

AUCTIONEER

AUDIENCE

Actors in Malach's play *Ibergus:* Starr (plays the role of Doctor Silva); Actress (plays the role of Reizl).

Three male and three female characters could play all the roles in the cast.

Setting and Music

Place: Buenos Aires, Argentina.

Time: 1900–1935, and the present time.

Music: Jewish music, Klezmer style—"Tayere Malke," "Macheteineste Guetrarier," "A Brievele Der Mamen," "Yiddish Red Zich Azoi Sheyn," "Shloff Mein Kind," "Far Mir Bist Du Sheyn." Argentine—"Milongas" and "Tangos" by Carlos Gardel (from the thirties—"Esclavas Blancas," "Milonguita," "Mi Buenos Aires Querido"). Charleston and shimmie music.

Scenes

SCENE 1:   PROLOGUE

SCENE 2:   THE VOYAGE

SCENE 3:   THE STREETS OF BUENOS AIRES

SCENE 4:   "LA CASA"

SCENE I: PROLOGUE

(Lights on Inspector Alsogaray, standing backstage. There are many chairs facing him. Raquel sits in front of him, her back to the audience. She gets up and takes a few steps forward.)

RAQUEL: *(Pointing)* That woman at the back belongs to the Ezrat Nashim, the Society for the Protection of Women. She offered to be my witness.

ALSOGARAY: Do you know her credentials? Some of these "charity ladies" pass themselves off as your "saviors" when in fact they are working with the traffickers. They even promise to return the girls to Poland, but instead they send them to worse dumps in the provinces.

RAQUEL: The Ezrat Nashim organization is well informed about my case, sir. Its members wait for the boats in Montevideo and try to warn the girls before they reach Buenos Aires.

ALSOGARAY: The real danger comes from Poland and France. This campaign of mine has become my religion, and you are the witness I need to expose the traffickers. I've been collecting evidence against them for months. Are you prepared to provide us with a written record of your deposition?

RAQUEL: Yes, sir.

ALSOGARAY: We need to have the names of the *caften,* and details of their business as evidence against the Zwi Migdal. When you managed to escape them, you opened your establishment in their own territory. That took guts. On October 29, 1928, just a couple of months later, you renewed your health certificate, and returned to prostitution at the *casa* on Valentín Gómez Street, the same one you had managed to leave. What made you go back? If they did not touch you, Raquel Liberman, it was because you were too hard to get rid of. But in this country of immigrants, people of good conscience like yourself must purge this evil from its roots, once and for all.

RAQUEL: *(Hesitant)* Will you protect me if I testify?

ALSOGARAY: Absolutely. I can assure you that your information is invaluable to us. With your testimony we can move ahead with the largest crackdown ever. *(Pause)* Let us begin . . .

RAQUEL: Back in Poland, where I lived, life had become unbearable. Misery, persecution, pogroms. A respectable looking man promised my parents he would take me to Buenos Aires, where I would marry a rich man. I was innocent then, a virgin. He brought me to Argentina, where he sold me to a trafficker and his madam, who kept me prisoner and threatened to kill me if I disobeyed. It took me years to find out who everyone was, and what was their business: Kirstein, Madanes, Brutkievich . . . Korn . . .

(Lights down, and up on Raquel and her Granddaughter, who approaches slowly from backstage. She is holding a box and stops behind Raquel. Both women face the audience.)

GRANDDAUGHTER: Why did you lie to the police, Grandma? Why did you tell them you were a virgin when you arrived here and that you had been kidnapped? Why couldn't you tell them the truth?

RAQUEL: To bring disgrace on my children? It would have ruined their lives and that would have been unbearable.

GRANDDAUGHTER: Grandma, talk to me! Until last night all I had of you was this picture my father kept on the mantelpiece. You look so beautiful, so serene, holding a white rose on your lap, your eyes filled with dreams. But last night, when I saw your picture on the TV screen I couldn't believe it. And the more I looked, the more convinced I became that it was you, Grandma. The same eyes, the same look. The reporter was talking about the Argentinean traffickers' society; they flashed their mug shot, and suddenly they showed one of "a certain Raquel Liberman": Was that, by chance, your maiden name? Tell me, Grandma, was it you?

RAQUEL: Yes, it was me. Mother made my black dress and embroidered it with lace to cover my shoulders. We had no money for food, but the photo had to look dignified *(Softly)* . . . You look shocked.

GRANDDAUGHTER: Of course I am. How could I have imagined you, Grandma, mixed up with white slave traders?

RAQUEL: My poor darling! So now, all of a sudden you want to . . .

GRANDDAUGHTER: I need to know who I am, Grandma. So much was hidden from me. I was so excited last night when the program was over that I went straight to Uncle Mauricio's apartment to see if he had hidden anything of yours. All the years that your son has been in a mental home I kept the keys to his place, but never dared search among his papers. But this time I couldn't resist. *(Opens the box and looks at the letters)* What language is this?

RAQUEL: Yiddish, of course! These are the letters your grandfather Yaacov and I wrote to each other while I stayed behind in Warsaw, with a baby in my arms and another on the way. *(Pause)* Then I thought those were the hardest years of my life. Now I believe they were the happiest.

GRANDDAUGHTER: Uncle Mauricio knew how to hide the letters well . . .

RAQUEL: My children couldn't live with so much shame. *(Lights down)*

SCENE 2: THE VOYAGE

(Jewish music is heard in the background. Actors wearing long coats in the Judeo-Polish fashion enter the stage from all directions. They walk slowly in a "grid," carrying suitcases with scraps of fabric in earth-colored ribbons—sepia, gray, brown—suggesting poverty in the Polish shtetl. They empty their suitcases until the floor is totally covered with their scraps. They also take out of the suitcases the clothes that will be used by the bride and groom. They act out a Chasidic wedding ceremony: They set up and hold the bridal canopy [the chuppah*] under which the groom breaks the ceremonial glass. They all toast the bride and groom ("Mazel Tov" and "L'chaim"). Lights go down slowly. The actors leave the stage one by one. Raquel is now wearing a long skirt, a wide-brimmed hat, and a shawl. She carries a wicker basket. Yaacov is wearing a black hat, a long black coat, and carries a suitcase. The music changes. Lights go up again on Raquel and Yaacov, facing each other at the back of the stage. They walk slowly toward the middle of the stage.)*

RAQUEL: Just a few lines every day, Yaacov. If you repeat yourself, so much the better. It will be like having you at my side.

YAACOV: And you do the same Rochel, my love. Letter after letter. And pictures! Pictures of our dear little son; that way I'll see how he's growing. Your image, I'll carry with me whether my eyes are open or closed.

RAQUEL: But I want to see how you change, if you gain weight or get thin, if you cut your beard . . .

YAACOV: You'll see, my *ketzeleh,* every penny I save in Argentina will bring you more quickly to my side.

RAQUEL: Please, Yaacov, remember the Jewish holidays . . . fast on Yom Kippur.

YAACOV: If I eat the rest of the year, then I promise to fast on Yom Kippur.

RAQUEL: Have faith . . .

YAACOV: But don't expect miracles.

RAQUEL: Learn the language fast.

YAACOV: And you take care of your health.

RAQUEL: Send money! *(Lights fade.)*

(Sounds of gulls. Raquel carries a letter in her hand, to indicate the beginning of her correspondence with Yaacov. They walk slowly across the stage, pausing when the text is longer.)

YAACOV: "Dear wife, the boat landed in Spain, where more passengers came on board. Max Kaufman was one of them. Imagine my surprise! He had come all the way from Warsaw by land and boarded here, in Barcelona."

RAQUEL: ". . . I hope you didn't get seasick . . ."

YAACOV: "It didn't last long . . . When it's your turn to travel, don't be afraid, dear wife. Now we're going straight on, to Argentina, the 'Land of Silver'."

RAQUEL: "Do you think there's any silver waiting for us there, Yaacov? My only consolation is caring for our son and seeing how my stomach grows again with your second child."

YAACOV: "Did you receive the money I sent you in dollars? Was there enough?"

RAQUEL: "I received it, but there's never enough. Try to get some more for the tickets. My sister and her husband can't wait for me to get out of here. But the only one who can help is you, my Yaacov, and no other. Now tell me, how can you be content when your own flesh and blood is struggling in loneliness and misery?"

YAACOV: "Dear wife, You'll soon be leaving Poland for good. I can't find a job here, because I don't know the language. But I'll manage the best I can. My sister Helke is doing even more for me than a mother would for her son. Nine years she spent preparing a wardrobe for me: silk shirts, patent-leather shoes, and a gray suit for the holidays. I put my *kapelush* hat in a trunk, so I don't look so much like a foreigner anymore. The only things missing in my life are you and my dear son at my side."

RAQUEL: "God keep Helke in good health for many years. Tell her that I'm a strong woman. I could lighten her burden. From the depths of my heart I thank her. Please beg her on your knees to rescue your family from this *gehenom*, this living hell!"

YAACOV: "With God's help, we'll soon share the life we deserve."

RAQUEL: "I was hoping, my Yaacov, that in a little while I'd be traveling toward you; that my tear-filled eyes would shine again, seeing you hold your child to your chest and kiss him. But what have I got instead? A sister and a brother-in-law who shout at me and my son. They can't wait for us to leave Warsaw. Oh! Is there no place for us in this world?"

(A stagehand dressed in white quietly wheels a hospital bed to a corner of the stage and helps Yaacov put on a white gown.)

YAACOV: "Dearest Rochel, my eyes burn with pain when I think that I wasn't at your side for the *bris* of Moshe Vélvele, our second son. My recent illness has left me somewhat weak. The doctors can't find the cause. But a healer told me it was because of the evil eye. And I think he was right because, thank God, I'm recovering. As they say, it's darkest just before dawn."

RAQUEL: "Your letter of January 25th brought a new fountain of bitter tears from my eyes. My heart trembles thinking that maybe you're writing me of your recovery only to make me feel better, but that in truth you're actually sicker. Why else haven't you hurried the papers to us? Forgive me, my dear husband, but these thoughts torment me."

YAACOV *(Walking slowly toward his bed. He lies down.)* "Next week, I hope, I'll be able to travel to Buenos Aires and get the passports, tickets, and money for you and the children. I'm sending you a check for thirty-five dollars that I borrowed from my sister. I'm happy you've made peace with our relatives in Warsaw, and now that they know you're leaving soon, they'll treat you with more respect. You'll see, 'all's well that ends well.' Don't worry, my dear wife. We'll be together very soon."

(Lights down indicate Raquel's arrival in Buenos Aires. When lights rise again, a few months have gone by. Raquel removes her hat and puts up her hair in a bun. She rushes to see Yaacov at the hospital. They embrace.)

RAQUEL: Has the doctor been to see you yet? Are you feeling any better, my *lieber?*

YAACOV: About the same.

RAQUEL: They say one becomes accustomed to *tsures*. What a joke! Your illness is my greatest pain . . . Pain within and without! When will it end, my Yaacov?

YAACOV: Why won't they let me go with you to Tapalqué so you can look after me?

RAQUEL: If I had money, I'd take you to the mountains. We've had such a short time together with our two boys!

YAACOV: It was heaven on earth.

RAQUEL: But now we're far away from our dusty village . . . *(Smiling)* where the dogs sleep in the middle of the road . . .

YAACOV: And where people only worry when it's their cow's turn to be mounted by the only bull in town . . . *(They both laugh.)*

RAQUEL: *(Shows him a crumpled note)* Recognize this?

YAACOV: *(Examines it)* Sure I do. I marked this *peso* note before I sent it to Warsaw.

RAQUEL: You told me not to throw it away because here, in Buenos Aires, they pay a *peso* for every twelve hundred Polish *zlatys.* Well, you were wrong my dear; I only get five hundred *zlatys* for a *peso,* and that doesn't go far at all. Max, who traveled with you . . . he's been changing the money for me.

YAACOV: Yes, Max and his brother Aaron! They too struggle to make a living. *(Pause)* Rochel, does my sister Helke treat you all right?

RAQUEL: *(Showing him her coat)* She's given me these clothes. She says that if I want to find work I should dress like a *criolla* . . .

YAACOV: I wrote Helke last week. Did you get my letter?

RAQUEL: Oh, my Yaacov; you should have seen! The hospital put your letter in an official looking envelope, so you can imagine what we felt when it arrived! Helke started yelling: "Gottenyu, put an end to our anguish already!" But when we recognized your handwriting and we knew you were alive, we all sighed with relief.

YAACOV: Even if I'm worthless, God should make me healthy for your sake and for our children.

RAQUEL: You've always been a good husband and a good Jew.

YAACOV: Rochel, there's no cure for my illness.

RAQUEL: Have faith, Yaacov dear . . . please don't give up. Next time I come I'll bring you photos of the children . . .

MAX: *(Interrupting) Sholem aleichem,* dear friends. *(They embrace.)*

RAQUEL: It's so good you're here, Max, to comfort Yaacov. Stay with him awhile, *bríderl.*

YAACOV: I thought we were coming to the Land of Silver, Max. But this Argentina hasn't been good to me.

MAX: What did we know, Yaacov . . . North America, South America? We only wanted out.

YAACOV: What will become of my Rochel and the boys when I die, Max?

RAQUEL: Don't say that, Yaacov!

MAX: You'll soon get better, just be patient.

YAACOV: Promise me you'll look after Rochel, Max.

MAX: *(Puts on his hat and takes Yaacov's hand)* Of course I will. Rochel is like a sister to me.

YAACOV: You're a good friend, Max. And when the time comes, you'll say *kaddish* for my soul, right?

RAQUEL: *(Raising her hands)* Gottenyu! He's asking for prayers! Enough now!

YAACOV: *(Closes his eyes and prays to himself until he falls asleep)* Shma Yisroel, Adenoy Eloheinu, Adenoy echad.

RAQUEL: God can't punish us this way!

(Max and Raquel remain by Yaacov's side. Lights go down on Yaacov. Stagehand removes the bed.)

SCENE 3: THE STREETS OF BUENOS AIRES

(Tango music [Gardel's "Mi Buenos Aires Querido"] and street sounds. Actors dressed as Buenos Aires dwellers, Gardel style: White scarves, slanted hats enter the stage from all directions. They walk in a grid [or imitating tango steps]. Raquel remains center stage, trying to sell the merchandise she carries in her basket. Bronia watches Raquel with great interest, before she approaches her. Everyone leaves the stage, except for the two women. Music stops slowly.)

RAQUEL: *(Pronounces Spanish like a foreigner, replacing the "R" with the "G")* "Comgra señog, compga bagato" [Buy, sir, it's cheap].

BRONIA: *Antshuldik mir, señorita,* excuse me . . . I'm sure I've seen you before, if not at the boat, then in Warsaw. You look so lost . . .

RAQUEL: Ah, to hear *mameloshn* again! I thought I'd have to remain as dumb as a wall until I learned to speak Spanish!

BRONIA: If you want to speak Yiddish, there're plenty of Jews here. Let me introduce myself. My name is Bronia Koyman. I've been here for three years.

RAQUEL: And I'm Raquel . . .

BRONIA: *(Curiously)* And your husband? Isn't he coming to meet you?

RAQUEL: My husband . . . He died a month ago. I had to leave my two little boys in Tapalqué.

BRONIA: So you came to test your luck in the city. You're a brave woman! Do you have a place to stay already? Buenos Aires is a rough city! What kind of work can you do, Raquel?

RAQUEL: I'm a seamstress . . .

BRONIA: Perhaps I can do something for you.

RAQUEL: I'd be so grateful!

BRONIA: *(She produces a photograph from her bag.)* I have a big house and I could offer you a room until you're settled . . . This is the house.

RAQUEL: Lovely flowers . . . And a wrought iron fence! Like a real Spanish house . . .

BRONIA: It's Spanish and Jewish . . .

RAQUEL: Do you think I'll be able to make a living here? That's my greatest worry: to be able to send money to my children.

BRONIA: You will, you'll see you will . . .

(Bronia puts her arm on Raquel's shoulder and guides her toward her house. They walk around the stage until they approach it. Raquel is curious about everything around her. Milonga music is heard inside.)

RAQUEL: What an elegant house! Geraniums in bloom . . .

BRONIA: They're always in bloom . . . The synagogue is two streets away. We'll go together on Yom Kippur.

(A girl dressed in a provocative gown crosses the stage. She wears curlers and chews gum. She gives Raquel a sly smile. The bell rings and the girl lets Domínguez in.)

BRONIA: *(Approaching him)* Señor Domínguez, *buenos días!*

DOMÍNGUEZ: *(He notices Raquel.)* Anyone new for me? Anyone worth waiting for? Young, clean, beautiful?

BRONIA: *(Whispering)* That one's not for sale. She's looking for real work.

DOMÍNGUEZ: A total *greene* . . . that's what I need!

BRONIA: Be patient. I'm keeping her for you. *(Lights fade.)*

SCENE 4: "LA CASA"

(Semi-dark stage. Following the rhythm of a Milonga, the "clients" drop scraps of bright cloth and red ribbons filling up the stage. Then they line up to see the women. Raquel crosses the stage carrying an old sewing machine and pays no attention to what's going on. They all exit, except for Raquel. Bronia enters and watches her. Lights on the two women.)

RAQUEL: *(Produces a letter from her pocket and begins to read it. Sobs.)* The woman who's taking care of my children writes that if she doesn't get the money I owe her, she'll have to send them here, to Buenos Aires *(Pause)* Bronia! Bronia! I can't make it.

BRONIA: *(Tenderly)* I know what it's like, Raquel. I am a mother too. But I keep my boy far away from me.

RAQUEL: *(Insistent)* Maybe I can bring my babies over for a few days. Just for a few days until . . .

BRONIA: You want to bring them here? Ridiculous! You don't want them begging in the streets: There are too many children in the streets already.

RAQUEL: What can I do?

BRONIA: You know Domínguez, Raquel, he likes you . . .

RAQUEL: What are you saying? I couldn't!

BRONIA: He's a rich man, Raquel . . . Take advantage . . .

RAQUEL: I can't!

BRONIA: Your children, Raquel . . . *(Exits)*

(Tango music. Semi-darkness in the brothel. Enter several "clients" and women. With stylized movements the men drop brightly colored ribbons as they surround Raquel and the women. The women stand next to chairs, each chair becoming her "room." They make suggestive overtures facing the public, leaning against the back of the chairs, their legs spread apart. The men freeze in their poses like robots. Domínguez is the first to force Raquel. The other clients follow him. Raquel continues to resist.)

BRONIA: *(Entering)* You lost your voice from so much crying. No more scenes, please. I don't want to hear my clients complain. *(Pause)* Raquel, I can be useful to you.

RAQUEL: The shame . . . the horror! Don't let my children ever find out . . .

BRONIA: No one has to know.

RAQUEL: Swear you'll never say a word to anyone about them.

BRONIA: Not a word. Here's your only chance, Raquel. Most other girls come to this life lured by false promises of marriage. Even I was deceived. When my child was born, I had to send him far away from me. I will never see him again and that's my punishment. Everyone thinks I am a big *macher!* *Imbeciles!* The law, you know, doesn't allow men to manage *casitas* in this country. So Cyssinger . . . my "boss," married me so I would manage this one for him. *(Pause)* I've done well in this profession, Raquel. And you will, too. You'll make enough to save your children!

RAQUEL: I want to go back . . . go back . . .

BRONIA: Go back where? To Poland? What's there in Poland? Pogroms! Misery!

RAQUEL: What a fool I was! I really thought that I'd be a seamstress . . .

(The men walk toward the back of the stage and remain in a line. The women, barely dressed, express weariness.)

BRONIA: What could you trade without money, without a language? You're a *polaca* here, Raquel. And a *polaca* in Buenos Aires gets a good price. French women, they say, are the aristocracy. The *polacas* are worth a little less, and still less goes to the *criollas*. All they get is a lousy *peso* for their services. But you, Raquel, you're different from the rest. You'll get better terms from me. With the cut I give you, in a few years you'll have more than enough to pay for your freedom.

RAQUEL: What if I catch some horrible disease? Gottenyu!

BRONIA: Just keep a record of your services. Check yourself at a clinic. Make sure you don't catch any disease, and you'll see how you master the job . . . how you learn the language *(Exits)*.

(Lights fade as they center on Raquel. Everyone exits.)

RAQUEL: *(Pretends she's writing)* "Dear Max, I don't know how I'll get this note to you. I don't know if it will reach you. You're the only one who can help me get away from here. Please Max, ask for Raquel of the *'casa de los geránios'* on Sarmiento Street. Pretend you're a customer. Come right away."

(Raquel faces the public. Granddaughter enters and remains on side of stage.)

GRANDDAUGHTER: That woman really knew how to con you . . . Why didn't you run right away, Grandma? Why did you give up?

RAQUEL: Bronia made a deal with me: I could visit my sons for short periods, on condition that I came back to work for her.

GRANDAUGHTER: Couldn't you have stayed in Tapalqué instead of coming back here?

RAQUEL: Then we would have all starved to death. Over the years I came to accept my fate. In Buenos Aires I got used to the routine: weekly line-ups at the clinic to renew my good health certificate, turning the mattress upside down, spraying the sheets with cheap cologne. I tried to be a machine, but my poor bones resisted. Stench and sweat and fluid stuck to my skin, spread down into my loins. *(Transported)* Only when my body seemed to float toward oblivion, I'd wake up to reality, under the weight of a stranger's body. *(Lights fade. They exit.)*

SCENE 5: THE ZWI MIGDAL

(Brutkievich is sitting at Bronia's desk, checking on her bookkeeping; Kirstein is holding a drink in his hand. They behave like frequent clients to the brothel.)

BRUTKIEVICH: So Bronia just brought the new merchandise and put her straight to work! She kept her all to herself!

KIRSTEIN: This way the girl's all hers and we get no commission . . . Bronia has been working for the Zwi Migdal long enough. She thinks she knows the ropes.

BRUTKIEVICH: But she doesn't! She can't set the rules. Better watch her, Kirstein, before she becomes too comfortable wearing my shoes! All that's hers, remember, belongs to us.

(Kirstein rests one foot on a chair. Brutkievich remains on his seat, facing the public.)

BRONIA: *(Enters, surprised and annoyed) Gut Morgen,* my friends! Make yourselves comfortable!

BRUTKIEVICH: Good work, Bronialeh . . . good work . . . You've had her a while now, and not a word to us! We hear she has some natural gifts . . . but your sharp eyes must have noticed them right away, isn't that so, my friend?

BRONIA: I was struck by her quality, her self-possession, her class.

BRUTKIEVICH: Watch it, Bronia, she may turn out to be one of the ungrateful types who spread ugly rumors . . .

KIRSTEIN: What can they do, alone in the streets? Claim that they are mere cannon fodder that roll from one brothel to another, amidst flowers and champagne?

BRUTKIEVICH: Nice words, Kirstein . . . fit for a tango! But just remember, Bronia, what your job is here: to keep the girls in line . . . make sure that they don't drink too much, don't take snow, don't get sick, don't have affairs with each other . . .

KIRSTEIN: What did they have back there in the shtetl? If they never leave this place it's because they don't know how to save five cents. *(Pause)* And you, sister, you treat them like queens. Congratulations. You're also a practical woman, Bronia; so let's deal.

BRONIA: No. Raquel's independent. She works on commission. She pays for the use of room and board, and that's it.

BRUTKIEVICH: Don't tell me you're losing your skills as a teacher!

BRONIA: No one ever runs away from my *casita!*

KIRSTEIN: How could they run away? Where would they go? When they first come here the fools can't even wash their own armpits! *(Looking for the girls)* Where's Clarita? Is she over there? *(Exits)*

BRUTKIEVICH: Bronia, you're putting the organization at risk, bringing in a girl this way. If Liberman sings, tell me, who pays the judges and the police in the final round to shut her trap? I do! *(In a patronizing manner)* The last time we met, you said you wanted to increase your production.

BRONIA: I'm always looking for quality. I've taught enough chicks to behave like ladies.

BRUTKIEVICH: We're getting a very special cargo in the next ship coming to Buenos Aires. I'll let you know when we have an auction. *(They exit. Lights center stage. Charleston music.)*

SCENE 6: THE PLOT

(Bronia enters Raquel's room carrying two boxes. Raquel opens the smaller of the two.)

BRONIA: Here's chocolate. Remember, Raquel, what the chocolate is for. If your mouth has blisters, or your lips, make sure you eat chocolate in front of the clients. The brown color covers the blisters.

RAQUEL: What's in this other box? *(Opens the box and takes out an elegant gown)*

BRONIA: Now, what do you think of this? Black is the most elegant color for an evening dress . . . You'll wear it tonight to go to the theatre! Leib Malach, the playwright, would be proud to see such a beautiful woman among his audience.

RAQUEL: *(Changes into the new gown)* Thank you, Bronia, you really know how to choose the best clothes for me.

BRONIA: *(Helps her dress)* Those Jews Malach criticizes in his play chased him out of this country . . . Who would believe it! The Jewish theatre has become a battleground in Buenos Aires . . . *(Pause)* Ah, Raquel, with this dress you'll cause a sensation tonight! Here, wear this ermine fur round your neck . . . *(Enters Max carrying a bundle of trinkets)* Ah! Here's your faithful friend Max . . .

MAX: *(Admiringly)* You look just like a princess, Raquel! Catherine the Great!

BRONIA: What would they say in the shtetl if they saw her now! *(They laugh.)* It's good to see you laughing, for a change! . . . Come here more often, Max! Raquel will teach you how to enjoy life. *(Exits)*

MAX: I spent the whole night traveling. *(Shakes his head)* I knock at every door . . . and sell little or nothing.

RAQUEL: *(Puts an envelope in his jacket pocket)* Here, my friend, take another thousand. Hide it well. You'll have to warn your brother about our plan. He remembers me from Poland, doesn't he? I was very young then, a child.

MAX: Of course Aaron remembers you! You were little Rochel, then.

RAQUEL: *(Hugs him)* Ay, my dear friend! It's so hard to show how I feel! *(Pause)* You know the antique shop on Avenida Callao? The old lady took a liking to me and promised to sell me the store for a low price when I get out of here.

MAX: Yes, the shop on Callao, so close to the Migdal . . . They'll chase you away! Or worse, they'll take revenge. I'm afraid for you, Raquel. You know what became of your friend Sara when she ran away from them? Her body was found floating in the river . . . and no one was blamed.

RAQUEL: That shop is the only place I could afford. It's my only chance.

MAX: *(Comforted)* So I will see my little Raquel selling antiques, like the Argentine *doñas?* Will you treat your customers well? Is your Spanish good enough?

RAQUEL: *(Rolling the r's with a heavy guttural accent)* Of course it is. *¿Un guegalo para su esposa, estimado señog? ¿Algo muy oguiginal?*

MAX: *(Pretending to be a customer)* Busco un guegalo paga mi anivegsagio.

RAQUEL: *¿Paga su anivegsagio? Un bgoche de cameo con bogde de filigrana, señog. ¿Le gusta?*

MAX: *Sí. Me gusta. ¿Es mucho dinego?*

RAQUEL: *¡El mejog pgecio! Mi español* is just fine, *amigo* Max. Behind the counter I'll find the words to persuade the most demanding of *clientes.* I only want to smell clean, use my brains, and be free again. *(Raquel guides Max out of her room and remains alone. Lights fade.)*

SCENE 7: THE PLAY

(Bronia and Raquel, elegantly dressed and bejeweled, walk arm in arm towards the stage. They sit down among the audience. Light on left stage, on Starr's dressing room, as he is getting ready for the performance of Ibergus.*)*

BRONIA: The name of Starr, our best Yiddish actor, used to be printed in the papers, in bold letters. He had admirers all over. But now they're ashamed of him . . . And d'you know why? Because he performs for everyone: for the decent folks, the pimps, and the prostitutes too. He never misses a wedding or a ceremony. Starr is an actor above all; acting is his daily bread. But the "pure" Jews don't want to understand. Don't they sell their merchandise to the "impure" without blinking an eye? Of course they do!

(Loud noise is heard from the street. A Lady from a Jewish organization storms into Starr's room.)

LADY: A scandal! A real scandal! Are you Mr. Starr, the actor?

STARR: I'm Starr. *¿Qué pasa?* What's all the commotion?

LADY: Señor Starr . . . As president of the Lady's Guild, I beg you to understand . . . My people won't let you act tonight.

STARR: What are you saying, *señora?* Who are your people?

LADY: They are people with morals . . . pure morals!

STARR: May their guts rot!

LADY: If you insist, I'm afraid blood will flow here tonight. You know how it is, Señor Starr. You're either with us or with that scum. You'll be paid anyway if you don't perform.

STARR: *(Pushes her out)* Enough already, *doña!* Get out of here

LADY: *(Running out and screaming, as she exists)* Help! This man is attacking me! Help!

STARR: May the devil take you!

(Lights fade. Starr finishes putting on his makeup, exits his room, and returns to center stage, now as Doctor Silva, accompanied by an actress who plays the role of Reizl, from Leib Malach's play Ibergus. *They wear masks over their faces as they perform their melodrama with exaggerated gestures.)*

SILVA: Dearest Reizl, remember you're not a casual woman, nor an occasional lover. You're my true love. Let me open my heart to you: It would be my greatest joy if you'd agree to be my wife.

REIZL: Oh, dear Doctor Silva, I'm still plagued by shadows and fears! My happiness has turned into bitter poison.

SILVA: But I've seen your transformation with my own eyes! And when you give birth to your child, it will be my child too!

REIZL: No, I can't be your wife, Doctor Silva. To have a husband, a woman's heart should be all in one piece. But my heart is shattered. I may be everyone's woman . . . but I wouldn't know how to be one man's wife . . . I can't stay here any longer!

SILVA: Where will you go, tell me?

REIZL: I'll go where every hour is a lifetime; where my blood may end up infected, my body mutilated. I don't care what happens after I die. All I know is that if I dare cross the threshold to the honest life you offer me, the anguish that overcomes me will suffocate me. *(Bitter laughter)* I always wanted to reach the other side, and now it's too late. What evil tricks fate plays on us!

(Several actors wearing masks are now seated among the audience and interrupt the scene. Reizl and Doctor Silva remain on the stage.)

AUDIENCE: *Yidn! Yidn!* Stop this performance! Those actors should not be allowed to play!

—They belong with the impure of the Zwi Migdal!

—Quiet! Don't interrupt!

—Get them out of here! *(Hissing from audience)*

—Down with you!

—Get out of here!

STARR: *(Takes off his mask)* Just a few words, honorable audience! I was just playing the role of Doctor Silva. But you all know my real name: I'm Starr, the well-known actor of the Yiddish theatre.

AUDIENCE: Get off the stage!

—Shame on you!

STARR: Shh! Calm down, gentlemen. Please be patient. *(Voices quiet down.)* This is the Yiddish theatre, a sacred place, and for me it's as sacred as our temple! I've been acting for over twenty-five years, first in Warsaw, then here, in Argentina.

AUDIENCE: This is not Warsaw! This is Buenos Aires!

—Who do you think you are!

—Enough already!

—Let him have his say!

—Down with him! Out!

STARR: I play for everyone at the theatre. Do I ask you for your passport or your papers? We are all brothers.

AUDIENCE: Down with the impure!

—To hell with the unclean!

STARR: If you don't like me as your brother . . . *(Violently, he takes off his fake beard and his costume.)* then . . . here, take everything! You don't deserve that I perform for you! *(Exits with the actress)*

AUDIENCE: *Bravo! Bravo!*

—His best performance yet! *(Applause)*

LADY: *(Nervous and pale, goes upstage)* Bruders und shvesters, we don't need them . . . We have our own, decent actors. And our *kinder,* our dear children are here too. We don't want to set a bad example for them, do we? Then . . . let's clean up the theatre!

AN ACTRESS: *(Climbs on stage and rings a little bell)* I beg you, honorable public, be quiet! Let me say a few words on behalf of Leib Malach's play, and of our great Yiddish actors. Starr, as you saw, was playing the part of a Deputy in the Argentine Congress who fights to defend the good name of a Jewish prostitute. He takes her out of the gutter and gives her a home. Don't you see Reizl is one of your Jewish sisters? Destiny has wronged her!

AUDIENCE: You're one of them too!

—How much do they pay you to talk such nonsense?

ACTRESS: Fight against those who reap huge profits from exploitation! Wage war against the henchmen who lead our innocent girls to damnation! *(Muttering in the audience)* They're a plague that spreads over us in this young country! They are the enemy! Not the actors, nor the girls!

VOICES FROM THE AUDIENCE: That's not true!

—She's lying! . . .

—No! no! Give her a chance!

—Get down, you scum!

—No! She's telling the truth!

(Dramatic Jewish music is heard. Actress exits in confusion. Someone points to Raquel and to Bronia.)

—Look up there, in the front row! The traffickers have found their way into
   this theatre! The *coorvehs* have slipped inside without permission!
—There's Raquel!
—And there's Bronia Koyman, the rich Madam!
—What a nerve, by God!

*(The actors in the audience remain frozen in their seats, while Raquel and Bronia
get up and leave, mumbling angrily. Lights follow them as they walk toward the
exit among the public. Bronia picks up a couple of placards from the floor. When
they reach the end of the corridor, they turn around and walk back to the stage,
which has now become Bronia's house.)*

BRONIA: *(Reading)* "White slavers and whores are forbidden entry!" "War to
   the impure ones!" *(She stamps on placards and tears them.)* It's not enough
   we can't be buried in their cemetery, their synagogue . . . now they want
   us out of their theatres, too!
VOICES FROM THE STREET: *Coorvehs,* go back where you belong!
—Scum! Stay out of our theatres!
BRONIA: *(Looks out to the street)* You hear them, Raquel? They followed us all
   the way from the theatre! *(Yelling)* Do you also want to come in? *(Sarcastic)*
   Not now. You pay to get in here, the same price you pay at the theatre, only
   here you get all the action. But not now; not with your wives at your backs,
   eh? You hypocrites! Bastards! *Mamzerim!* That play didn't teach you a
   thing! *(Pause)* Right! Stare all you want. The streets are public property!
RAQUEL: They treat us like they treated Reizl in the play.
BRONIA: But we won't let them. The theatre belongs to us too . . . There they
   sing our Yiddish songs, they tell our best stories: Sholem Asch, Sholem
   Aleichem, Mendele, all in *mámeloshn* . . . *(Shouts at the men in the street)*
   So we'll go to see our plays any time we feel like, you hear?
RAQUEL: *(Takes off her ermine stole)* They can't stand to see their wives and
   daughters sitting next to us! Their wives envy us . . . What do they envy?
   Our fine clothes? Our diamonds? The furs are dyed . . . the stones are false
   (Pause) And what are we? We're used merchandise. That's what we are.
BRONIA: Listen, Raquel, if it weren't for us, there'd be no theatre. We are its
   best audience. Don't we see the same play two and three times over? Don't
   their best actors come from our own ranks?

RAQUEL: We must be a real threat to them. *(She looks at the program.)* In his play Malach shows they aren't any better than we are.

BRONIA: And that's saying a lot. *(Pause)* . . . I saw you crying during the play, Raquel.

RAQUEL: *(Shakes her head)* Reizl doesn't fight for her life. A distinguished Argentine doctor wants to marry her, and give his name to her son . . .

BRONIA: And what does the silly girl do? She turns him down and has an abortion!

RAQUEL: Reizl didn't know how to be a mother. She had a premonition of her own death. *(Recites from Malach's play)* "Those sharp-nailed fingers, like daggers digging out my flesh . . . let them tear me, let them eat into my guts, let them empty my entrails!"

BRONIA: Ah! You remember those lines by heart, and you recite them with such passion, Raquel!

RAQUEL: That's when Reizl hears those voices calling her from hell . . .

BRONIA: Was she going crazy? Maybe those voices came to blame her for murdering her unborn baby. But you, you had two children, Raquel, you've sacrificed yourself for their sake . . .

RAQUEL: May they forgive me after I'm dead.

BRONIA: Don't be so melodramatic, Raquel. You won't die. For guilt and tears, we go to the theatre. We have a busy day ahead, and that's real, Raquel. *(Exits carrying Raquel's gown)*

RAQUEL: *(Lights fade. She takes her children's portrait out of her pocket and presses it against her bosom)* I want you to grow up healthy and innocent . . . *(Kisses the portrait)* No, my sweets. I can't die yet. I want my freedom now, more than ever. And I want you by my side. *(Lights down)*

SCENE 8: THE AUCTION

(Lively tango music. Carnival atmosphere. Actors enter the stage wearing long black capes, extravagant feathers, and masks. They bring in chairs that will serve as pedestals for the women, who are overly made up and almost naked. They dance around them. Raquel is one of those women. She is wearing a blond wig and is covered by a translucent gown that reveals her crimson-painted nipples.)

MAX: *(Approaches Raquel, wearing a mask and cape)* Did you bring me the rest of the money? There's a big commotion outside.

RAQUEL: *(Gives Max an envelope, which he hides in his pocket)* Here it is. Hide it well.

(A tango by Gardel is heard, while the men [Max among them] wait for the auction to begin. They gather round the women standing on the chairs. They examine their mouths, hair, thighs, and then place bids with the auctioneer.)

AUCTIONEER: What a great cargo we have for you today, gentlemen. These girls crossed the ocean in a filthy cellar of their ship all the way to Buenos Aires, so that today this place looks like paradise to them!

KIRSTEIN: Good merchandise!

AUCTIONEER: All new, except one. *(Approaches Raquel)* Observe, gentlemen, what a desirable prize you've got here! In the time this woman has been at this house, she learned the secrets of her trade to perfection. She knows exactly how to get to men's hearts . . . and pockets. *Sheyne poolkes, sheyn tooches . . . (He shows off her thighs and buttocks.)* Feel the firmness of her flesh, see the shine of her hair, the freshness of her skin. Now, who'll give the first bid? *(Repeats each bid at a faster pace)*

MAX: Nine hundred!

KIRSTEIN: A thousand!

CLIENT: A thousand one hundred!

CLIENT: And two hundred!

KIRSTEIN: Two thousand!

MAX: Five!

KIRSTEIN: Six thousand!

MAX: *(Very tense)* Six thousand five hundred!

KIRSTEIN: *(Tense and furious)* Seven thousand, damn it!

AUCTIONEER: Seven thousand! Anyone offers eight thousand?

MAX: *(More nervous still)* Eight thousand!

(Kirstein consults with his partners, and they agree to let the unknown trafficker "buy" Raquel.)

AUCTIONEER: Eight thousand! Do I hear eight thousand? Eight thousand! Eight thousand going once . . . twice . . . Sold to the gentleman for eight thousand! Mazel tov!

KIRSTEIN: You've done well for yourself, *chevreman.* Don't forget this is our concession to you from the Migdal. I bet you don't have a prize like this one where you come from. But you have to be strict with this woman. She has a reputation for being independent.

MAX: I'll know how to deal with her.

KIRSTEIN: This woman is worth her weight in gold. But you'll need to use a heavy hand with her . . . *(Pause)* Still, the best auctions are in Warsaw. There you could pick the best merchandise.

(The women step off their pedestals to mingle with the men. Raquel signals Max to hurry.)

MAX: All those policemen over there . . . what are they doing here?

KIRSTEIN: Curious spectators; they come to watch the show. They turn a blind eye when necessary.

(Music goes up. Raquel and Max are about to exit.)

BRONIA: *(Very flustered)* What the hell's going on here, gentlemen? Raquel Liberman was not part of this auction! She belongs to me!

KIRSTEIN: Enough concessions, Bronia. Now it's our turn to pick up the earnings. And if you don't go along with us, you'll lose your *casita* . . . So go have a drink and keep your clients happy. *(They chuckle.)*

BRONIA: Watch your mouth, you scum, or I'll have you thrown out of my establishment! And you, Raquel, have you gone crazy? Go back to your room if you know what's good for you.

RAQUEL: *(Takes Bronia aside)* I know what I'm doing, Bronia. This man paid the Migdal with my money to get me out of here.

BRONIA: You've been betraying me all this time . . .

RAQUEL: What choice did I have? You left me no choice. As for your promise to me . . .

BRONIA: I'm no snitch. You see? I'm better than you. Go; go away before I change my mind. *(Raquel and Max exit. Lights fade.)*

SCENE 9: THE BOUTIQUE

(A few months later, Raquel, at her boutique, prepares some jewelry for display. Street sounds are heard.)

KIRSTEIN: *(Entering)* What a pleasure to see you, Raquel, so well settled! Congratulations!

RAQUEL: *(Coldly)* It's no pleasure for me, Kirstein. Please leave my store.

KIRSTEIN: Oh, the lady doesn't believe I'm good enough for her, does she? Then why does she establish herself right in our territory?

RAQUEL: I can open my shop wherever I please.

KIRSTEIN: *(Grabs some jewels on display and puts them in his pocket)* What I'm taking is just an advance, Raquel, for some debts still pending with us.

RAQUEL: Thief! Leave that alone! I don't owe you anything! Try stealing from me and I'll call the police!

KIRSTEIN: Oh, yes, go ahead, call them! And who'll come to your rescue? The policeman who gets ten times the salary from us, or the guard who's on our payroll to warn us of traitors like yourself? Or maybe the inspector who likes to do it for free every Sunday morning, while his wife goes to Mass with the children? God forbid, dear lady, that I should take advantage of you . . . You're a proprietor now. A businesswoman. I respect that, and I'll pay you . . . *(Pulls out a bill from his wallet)* whatever they're worth. Two hundred *pesos* for the lot.

RAQUEL: That's nothing! You're a rotten thief, Kirstein! This necklace alone costs over a thousand!

KIRSTEIN: That's all it's worth to us . . . So tell the police you've been fully paid for the transaction. *(Raquel attempts to hit him. Kirstein threatens to cut her face with a blade, and holds her tight as he speaks. She does not resist.)* You see how close it can get . . . You want to see how deep it can penetrate? Where shall I engrave the initials of the Zwi Migdal? On your forehead? The "Z" and the "M" on your cheeks? *(He tears her blouse. Raquel falls down.)* . . . Or on your breasts? "Migdal" stands for "fortress" . . . Get it? You're trapped, Raquel. Your debt to us will never be over.

RAQUEL: Hungry dogs! You gnaw at my bones until there is nothing left to chew . . .

KIRSTEIN: *(Opening the palm of his hand)* Then come back and eat from our hand. You'll be sorry if you don't . . . *(Exits. Lights on Raquel, frozen in her place.)*

SCENE 10: THE VISIT

(Brutkievich, president of the Zwi Migdal, wearing cuff links with a gold chain, is piling up bills and coins, which he locks away in a little chest decorated with family photos. His prayer book falls to the ground. He picks it up and gives it a loud kiss. Enter Korn and Kirstein, elegantly dressed in Argentine-fashioned clothes.)

BRUTKIEVICH: *(Extending handshakes) Gut Morgen,* gentlemen. *Nu,* Korn, how was the trip to Poland?

KORN: A great cargo this time, Simón. *(Smiling)* During the train journey from Warsaw to Marseilles I met a young man who seemed very impressed with my silk suit, or maybe with the ruby on my ring. *(Shows it)* He didn't stop nagging me with questions about life in Buenos Aires, until he finally asked what he wanted to know from the beginning: "But you sir, how do you make a living?" I thought a lot, and then I answered: "Not precisely from prayer books, my friend . . . not from prayer books." *(They all cheer Korn's answer.)*

BRUTKIEVICH: Now tell me, *señores,* what brings you here today?

KIRSTEIN: Morris Singer's widow is desperate. He died of a stroke and the Chevre Kadisheh found out he had been an old Zwi Migdal client for years.

BRUTKIEVICH: So now the "clean folk" won't bury him on their holy ground . . .

KORN: And that's why the widow is seeking our services.

BRUTKIEVICH: Oh yes. We can give them to her and show how very charitable and generous we are with our Jews . . . Look at the Italians and the French. Do they close the gates of their churches and cemeteries to people in our line of business?

KIRSTEIN: Never! . . . and their brothels are booming!

BRUTKIEVICH: But with Jews, morals always come first.

KORN: *(Chuckling)* Yes, only the "pure" ones are given the keys to heaven, right, Simón?

BRUTKIEVICH: Right! If I wanted to, I could be a high official in the Jewish community . . . but I'm no hypocrite.

KIRSTEIN: What are all these *frume Yidn* afraid of? More pogroms? Are they afraid they'll be thrown out of the country, deported? They forget that in this country we Jews are pioneers!

KORN: Right, Kirstein. First the Argentines wanted to get rid of the Indians. And afterward they set out to civilize the *gauchos* . . .

BRUTKIEVICH: But we Jews, we're Europeans . . . perhaps not exactly what they had in mind, but still, we bring the new blood of the immigrant. They need us. "To govern is to populate," they preach. So we've come to populate, with pleasure . . . or for the pleasure of populating . . . or for mere pleasure . . . taking care not to overpopulate. *(They chuckle.)*

KIRSTEIN: *(Looking at the family photos on Brutkievich's trunk)* Nice photos! Your son, Simón, he's settled down already?

BRUTKIEVICH: Ah! *Kinder!* They have it too easy here in Argentina. Now Alberto wants to be a poet . . . a poet! *(Resigned)* So he'll have to learn from life the hard way.

KORN: And your daughter . . . she's getting married soon, eh?

BRUTKIEVICH: After Passover, God willing.

KIRSTEIN AND KORN: *(They toast.)* Mazel tov!

BRUTKIEVICH: Thank you, *amigos*. But what would make me most happy would be to teach that "certain Raquel Liberman" a lesson. That little scheme she planned with her landsman after the auction so she could open a shop on Avenida Callao . . .

KIRSTEIN: Right on our grounds . . . But we've already taken care of him.

(Kirstein and Korn step aside with their drinks and continue talking to each other, while Brutkievich goes back to his accounts. Soft light on Raquel as she exits her boutique and walks toward Brutkievich's office.)

RAQUEL: I took the liberty, Mr. Brutkievich, because I didn't know where else to turn. I was told you're the most respectable member of the community. As the head of the Jewish Burial Society, I beg you to help me.

BRUTKIEVICH: Of course, my dear. Tell me what's upsetting you. I'll do all I can.

RAQUEL: The Zwi Migdal is after me. They harass me every day, even after I managed to start my own business. But they are set on destroying me. I beg you, Señor Simón . . . use your influence and tell them to let me live in peace! I don't bother anyone, I just want to be left alone.

BRUTKIEVICH: Calm down, please. You've shown a lot of courage by coming here. I'll talk to those bastards. They operate in underhanded ways, you know. They bribe the authorities and go hunting for lonely, desperate women to take advantage of them. You have every right to live your own life.

RAQUEL: *(Humbly)* Thank you, sir.

BRUTKIEVICH: I'll see what I can do. Those pimps are giving our community a terrible name. They should all be deported to leave room for the folks who want to make a decent living.

RAQUEL: I'll be grateful to you for the rest of my life. Good-bye, Mr. Brutkievich. *(Exits and returns to the space of her boutique)*

BRUTKIEVICH: *(Chuckling, to himself)* If she expects me to shoot myself in the foot and let an organization of hundreds of members and millions of *pesos* crumble, she has a nice surprise coming. After all, Raquel is a romantic creature. With her, roses will succeed where thistles cannot. *(Lights down. He exits.)*

SCENE II: THE PROPOSAL

(Raquel is in her boutique. Live music is heard from the street. Men wearing dark masks enter, posing as customers. They threaten Raquel with their gestures.)

—Great cover, Raquel!

—A boutique!

—Jewelry! Antiques!

—You're an artist at your trade!

RAQUEL: *(Distressed)* Who are you? What do you want of me?

VOICES: You look like the perfect shopkeeper, *señorita.*

—What are you selling today? Any reproductions of the *Naked Maja?* *(He strokes Raquel's cheeks and she pushes him away.)*

—I prefer the real thing!

RAQUEL: This is a respectable place!

VOICES: C'mon, you can't fool us!

—You've never left the Migdal! *(They exit.)*

KORN: *(Entering)* Raquel, my darling, you look upset, what's the matter?

RAQUEL: Ah, José, thank God you're here! The agents of the Zwi Migdal. They want to force me out of here . . . They've spread the word that I never left my old "business."

KORN: Let's call the police.

RAQUEL: It's useless. The police work hand in hand with the pimps.

KORN: Why don't you let me help you, my love? Remember Doctor Silva and Reizl, in Malach's play? . . . Silva wanted to save Reizl and she wouldn't let him. You know, Raquel, that I want the best for you. Let me be your knight-errant. Let me take them on . . .

RAQUEL: You won't have a chance against them either, José. They came last week to ask me questions about the man who visits me in the afternoons. You see, you're marked too.

KORN: *(Melodramatically)* In that case, we'll be stronger . . . marked together, you and I. To move ahead in this land, a woman needs the help of a real man . . . Raquel, let me be that man!

RAQUEL: I'm still hurt from many wounds . . .

KORN: Let me heal them with my kisses, dear Raquel. *(Kisses her)*

RAQUEL: *(Turning to him as if she has just discovered him)* We're landsmen, José. We're both healthy and free . . . You have romantic eyes and strong hands, but I'm so afraid . . . What if your promises aren't true? What if you've been deceiving me all this time . . .

KORN: *(Kisses her again)* Do you want proof of my love for you? Let's marry under the *chuppah,* just as the Jewish law prescribes! Let's both sign the *ketubah,* and let ten witnesses help consecrate our marriage. The Migdal will leave you alone then . . .

RAQUEL: I'm afraid of tempting the evil eye . . . May God hear my prayers this time . . . *(Lights fade.)*

SCENE 12: THE WEDDING

(This scene is played in a grotesque style. A combination of distorted carnival music with Hasidic tunes is heard. The body movements of the actors are exaggerated. They wear masks and capes. They help Korn and Raquel get into their wedding clothes. The couple stands under the wedding canopy. A "rabbi" mumbles a prayer. Korn stamps on a glass wrapped in cloth and breaks it. After the ceremony, everybody celebrates by kissing the married couple. Only now Raquel recognizes some of the guests. She looks at them suspiciously.)

RAQUEL: *(Frightened)* Have you seen them?

KORN: Whom?

RAQUEL: Them! Kirstein and the rest! Them! Who let them in?

KORN: Calm down, Raquel. Anyone who wants to can come to a synagogue.

RAQUEL: Thank God Brutkievich is here! *(Runs to Brutkievich)* Just one word, Mr. Brutkievich . . .

BRUTKIEVICH: *(Removes the mask)* Mazel tov, dear lady! Today's your lucky day!? *(His men surround Raquel.)*

RAQUEL: We need your help! These men, they are pimps! They don't belong in here! Get rid of them, I beg you!

BRUTKIEVICH: This is the house of God and it's open to every believer.

RAQUEL: Not to this scum! And even less on my wedding day! *(Confronts them)* You're not welcome, gentlemen! Please leave!

KIRSTEIN: How could we miss this occasion, my dear. It's not nice of you. We came to congratulate you on your choice of a husband.

RAQUEL: *(Barely containing herself)* Now that you have, leave this temple.

KIRSTEIN: Of course, darling bride. And you, proud groom, are you coming with us now, or will you join us later?

RAQUEL: *(Very upset)* What's going on, José?

KORN: You see, Raquel? This *ketubah* is our marriage contract. I'm your husband now, and as your husband you're bound to me, and will do as I say. And I say: "Wife, be nice to our guests!"

(Dramatic music is heard. Raquel attempts to run away, but she is encircled and overcome by the mobsters. Lights fade.)

SCENE 13: REVENGE

(Tango music is heard. A few days later Raquel is held prisoner at a new brothel. Customers provoke her with lascivious gestures. They exit. Raquel remains alone. Bronia enters.)

BRONIA: I can't believe you let them entrap you again, Raquel! When I came back from my vacation in Río, what did I find? Raquel is not a shopkeeper anymore. She's working for the Migdal again!

RAQUEL: I wanted so much to believe in José . . . But even then I never told him about the children. God must have protected them . . . But this time, Bronia, I swear, if it's the last thing I do . . .

BRONIA: *(Examining the place)* You were better off with me, *meydaleh,* than in this fleabag. You fell into the trap like a bird.

RAQUEL: They'll pay for it . . . even if it costs me my life. Bronia, you'll help me, won't you, when I expose them to the police and demand my freedom . . . I know where I have to go. I won't rest till they are all behind bars: Korn, Kirstein, Brutkievich, the whole lot. I have their number.

BRONIA: This is very risky, you know. Why don't you come with me to Río, instead? I found a nice *casita* in Copacabana, and you could be my partner.

RAQUEL: *(Shakes her head)* Go to Río with you and leave my children behind? Never! I'll report every one of those wretches, even if it's the last thing I do.

BRONIA: Wait at least a few days until I go back to Brazil. *(Pause)* Now is the time for you to act, Raquel, now that the judges are engaged in a new cleansing and morality campaign. But don't fool yourself. This business is here to stay. You too should be thinking about leaving the country with your boys if things get nasty . . . *(Lights down. They both exit.)*

SCENE 14: EPILOGUE

(Same music and gestures as in Scene 1. The actors sit down backstage as witnesses [as they did in Scene 1]. Lights on Alsogaray, and on Raquel, on a witness stand, wearing the same clothes as in Scene 1. She is about to give her deposition to the police.)

ALSOGARAY: You are the witness I needed to put an end to the traffic. Are you ready then, Raquel Liberman, to provide us with a written record of your deposition?

RAQUEL: Yes, sir.

ALSOGARAY: You had freed yourself from them; you had set up your place on Callao Street in their territory. Still we know that on October 29, 1929, you renewed your health certificate and went back to prostitution at Valentín Gómez Street. What made you go back when you had already managed to escape?

RAQUEL: A man named José Salomón Korn showed up at my shop one day and pretended to be my friend. We became close. *(Pause)* . . . If we married in a synagogue, I thought, our union had to be blessed by God . . .

ALSOGARAY: *(Sneering)* The synagogue at Junín Street . . . A fake temple for fake marriages . . . And no civil contract, of course . . .

RAQUEL: What did I know about a civil contract . . .

ALSOGARAY: Well, consider yourself lucky you're not dead. Women like you have drowned "accidentally" in the river. Some have been mutilated and fed to the pigs . . . You may start dictating now . . .

(Lights fade as Raquel gives her testimony. Granddaughter enters carrying a large box with newspapers, clippings, and photos, and walks toward Raquel.)

GRANDDAUGHTER: Why was your name never mentioned at home?

RAQUEL: Your father must have wanted to guard you from the reputation of the Migdal. He must have wanted to make sure you'd be able to fend for yourself without depending on men.

GRANDDAUGHTER: That's why he was always so protective. That's why he forced me to finish my education without caring if my brother studied or not, if he married or not. *(Looking at the photo)* In this photo your children must be about two and four . . . And here they are a bit older, dressed in Sunday clothes. *(Reads from the back of the photo)* "22 August, 1925: Dear Mamita: Here we send you a photo of us, so you don't cry so much. Many greetings from Dóvidl and Móishele. We remember you, always."

RAQUEL: "Yánkele" became "David" and "Móishele" changed his name to "Mauricio." All those years I kept asking myself . . . How do they look today? What are they eating? Do they sleep well? Do they miss me at all?

GRANDDAUGHTER: *(Reads)* Who wrote on the back of this card, Grandma? "I'm sending you a picture of your little darlings, so you can see nothing is wrong . . ."

RAQUEL: The woman who took care of the boys wrote often, to make me feel better.

GRANDDAUGHTER: *(Reads another postcard)* "This is us, wearing plain clothes. We just want to cheer you up." *(Shows her another photo)* But look at them here! Red sashes, white stockings . . . Like little aristocrats in Goya's portraits!

RAQUEL: That's the way I've always pictured them. In a romantic, dreamlike, pose . . . And me, happy next to my children.

GRANDDAUGHTER: And here, Grandma? You look so different here. You're standing all alone in an empty street, looking so sad . . . And here again, you're leaning on a street lamp . . . Why?

RAQUEL: They are a reminder of my ruined years . . . and you, Raquel, you carry my name . . . you wanted to see me the way I really was . . .

(Lights down. Granddaughter moves stage left. A stagehand, dressed in white, rolls in a hospital bed, helps Raquel change into a hospital gown, wraps a white bandage round her neck, and exits.)

RAQUEL: *(Lies down in bed)* Hasn't God tested me enough, now that my children are finally by my side? . . . Is this hospital . . . my final home . . . this bed, my grave? . . . *(Feels her neck)* And this awful swelling, this monstrous lump tightening round my neck . . . Tomorrow they'll cut me open and I still haven't brought order into my life. *(Looks around)* White beds, smell of chloroform, wretched women biting their lips to stifle their pain! Make a list, Raquel! Fast, before they stuff you with pills! Think, while you're still awake! Am I to die alone, then, like a rat? It's a curse from hell . . .

to die at thirty-five, when my real life has just begun . . . What a waste, Gottenyu. . . . This is the Angel of Death *(Closes her eyes. Lights fade.)*

(Lights on Granddaughter, who enters quietly and addresses the audience. Raquel and her Granddaughter don't look at each other till the end.)

GRANDDAUGHTER: My grandmother was a Jewish heroine and I didn't even know it! The newspaper headlines published your deposition! *(Reads)* "The greatest scandal of the decade . . . more than four hundred traffickers arrested, and over one hundred brothels shut down!" Grandma, you must have felt triumphant!

RAQUEL: *(In a weak tone, her eyes closed)* I was feeling tired and scared. All I wanted was to have my children by my side and finally lead a normal life. But it was all in vain.

GRANDDAUGHTER: Your life was not in vain. I carry your name. I carry you within me. You should feel proud, Grandma, if you knew poets composed eulogies to the women who saved thousands from slavery and who knew how to turn defeat into victory. You're a new Joan of Arc! *(Pause)* Even though Papá never spoke to us about you, he kept your portrait on the mantelpiece all that time. And when he turned fifty-seven he wrote this inscription on the back of your portrait: "To the most sublime and re-vered figure on earth: Mother. With love, David."

(Granddaughter approaches Raquel and recites a poem softly, like a lullaby.)

Take the whiteness of the jasmine
Take the crystal of the water
And you'll see a sublime *milonga*
Spring to life.
A *milonga* for a heroine,
A *milonga* for Raquel,
who single-handedly
had the courage
To face the Migdal.

(A Yiddish lullaby is heard. Lights fade as Granddaughter bends over the bed toward Raquel.)

Glossary

BRÍDERL:	*(From Yiddish)* Little brother
BRIS:	*(from Hebrew)* "Brit Milá," circumcision
CAFTAN:	(PL. CAFTEN) Used to describe the traffickers
CHEVREMAN:	*(from Hebrew)* Comrade, fellow
CHUPPAH:	*(from Hebrew)* Matrimonial canopy
COORVEH:	*(from Yiddish)* Prostitute
EZRAT NASHIM:	*(from Yiddish)* Society for the Protection of Women
FRUME:	*(from Yiddish)* Religious
GEHENOM:	*(from Hebrew)* Hell
GOTTENYU:	*(from Yiddish)* Dear God!
GREENE:	*(from Yiddish)* Recent immigrant
KADDISH:	*(from Hebrew)* Sacred prayer for the dead
KAPELUSH:	*(from Polish)* Hat
KETUBAH:	*(from Hebrew)* Marriage contract
KETZELEH:	*(from Yiddish)* "Kitten," a term of affection
KINDER:	*(from Yiddish)* Children
MACHER:	*(from Yiddish)* An influential person in the community
MÁMELOSHN:	*(from Yiddish)* Literally, mother tongue, referring to Yiddish
MAMZERIM:	*(from Hebrew)* Bastards
MAZEL TOV:	*(from Hebrew)* Good luck
MEIN LIEBER:	*(from Yiddish)* My darling
MEYDALEH:	*(from Yiddish)* Little girl
MILONGA:	A popular dance from Argentina
SHTETL:	*(from Yiddish)* A Jewish small town in Eastern Europe
TSURES:	*(from Hebrew)* Trouble
YOM KIPPUR:	*(from Hebrew)* Day of Atonement
ZWI MIGDAL:	Jewish traffickers' organization that brought women from Poland to Argentina to employ them as prostitutes

GREEN VIOLIN

by Elise Thoron

Conceived by Rebecca Bayla Taichman and Elise Thoron
Music by Frank London

For MJ Granite and his Layzer

Green Violin. Dress rehearsal, 25 April 2003. Pictured are Raúl Esparza (left) and Hal Robins. Copyright © 2003 Prince Music Theater, photograph by Mark Garvin.

For over fifteen years, I have been active in Russian-American theatre exchanges in New York, St. Petersburg, and Moscow. My work has ranged from early exchanges of "cultural diplomacy" with the Soviet Union to adapting and directing a production of *The Great Gatsby* for a Russian theatre. Through this challenging period of Soviet/Russian history, I have always admired the courage of those who remain in their country in hopes of making it a better place to live.

When my dear friend and colleague Rebecca Taichman approached me about writing a play inspired by murals Marc Chagall painted for the first Soviet Yiddish theatre (GOSET) in 1920, I was thrilled. The history of the theatre after Chagall's departure from the Soviet Union in 1922 is fascinating. GOSET continued to flourish as Yiddish theatre in the thirties and through the war under the artistic leadership of the brilliant actor Solomon Mikhoels, who was murdered by Stalin in 1948. My research led me back to Moscow, where some people dismissed GOSET as a thing of the past. With persistence I found several devoted scholars, archives, and even a surviving member of GOSET, Maria Kotlyarova, who shared recollections, Yiddish songs, and dance steps with me in her small kitchen.

Green Violin aims to recollect and celebrate the extraordinary work and idealism of a group of Jewish artists who, emerging from the Pale of Settlement, exploded with creativity during a brief moment when the Soviet government supported Yiddish culture. *Green Violin* examines artists' choices under an increasingly repressive political system. Many, like Chagall, who left Russia in the early twenties, flourished as individual artists in the West but suffered from profound nostalgia for their native land. Those who stayed in the Soviet Union created a dynamic culture and sustained an advocacy for their people, but for the most part met a horrible end. Their legacy of heroic activism and hope haunts us to this day.

Green Violin focuses on the relationship between Marc Chagall, quintessential individual artist, and Solomon Mikhoels, an actor devoted to his Yiddish theatre company and increasingly a political advocate for Jews in the Soviet Union. When they met as young men in Moscow in 1920, Mikhoels discovered a unique style of acting through working with Chagall's paintings. He became the embodiment of Chagall's art on stage; in Mikhoels, Chagall saw his work living and breathing in three dimensions with music and song. After this unique collaboration, Chagall left Russia and was not allowed to return. The friends met twice: once in Paris in 1928, when GOSET was on a European tour, and once in New York in 1943, when Mikhoels was sent to the United States by Stalin to raise money for the Soviet Red Army's fight against Nazism. Snapshots of these meetings were springboards for my imagination. My task was to dramatize this passionate friendship, which was torn apart by events and the choices each man made in a shattering world.

History is alive within us when we listen and share stories that reflect on choices we are making today. Theatre gives us the opportunity for collective questioning. Chagall painted four marvelous panels for the GOSET, with each representing one of the theatre's four muses—literature, drama, dance, and music. I was blessed to work with wonderful collaborators: composer Frank London of the Klezmatics, and choreographer David Dorfman, who with Rebecca Bayla Taichman, the director, brought the spirit of Chagall's paintings to the stage through dance and movement.

A friend once looked at the Chagall murals and asked me quite honestly: "What's so great about them?" I replied spontaneously: "They twist sorrow into joy." And that has been a guiding impulse in the creation of *Green Violin*.

Notes

Green Violin used the NFJC commissioning grant for a workshop at New York Theater Workshop on December 16, 2002. The first production was at the Prince Music Theater in Philadelphia in 2003.

The author would like to acknowledge the tremendous help of Dr. Zoya Prizel with Yiddish language and literature, and Professor Benjamin Harshav for his invaluable insights and his book *Marc Chagall and the Jewish Theater.* She also would like to thank Alexander Galin and his wife, Galina, for their work on the Russian adaptation of *Green Violin,* which clarified much in the original.

Characters, Musicians, and Setting

CHARACTERS

CHAGALL, a young artist obsessed with his work. Passionate, a bit awkward. Something of the clown. Lives close to his dreams.

BELLA, Chagall's wife and muse. A poet with a deep love of Yiddish culture. Joins Chagall in his flights of fancy, but always keeps one foot on the ground. Mother to their young daughter, Ida.

The Yiddish Theatre:

MIKHOELS, leading actor, extremely charismatic. Highly intelligent. An idealist who becomes a political spokesman. A philosopher by nature, he plays the fool with a profound sense of irony.

GRANOVSKY, artistic director. Brilliant, punctilious, avant-garde stage director. Artistically ambitious and cosmopolitan. He trained in Berlin and does not speak Yiddish.

EFRAIM, the janitor. Small in size, big in voice. Becomes increasingly devoted to the Communist Party.

EFROS, founding producer. Active in petitioning for funds and overseeing the artistic and logistical well-being of the company. A poet.

ZUSKIN, actor par excellence with a gorgeous voice. He plays Sancho Panza to Mikhoels' Don Quixote. Close friends with Mikhoels off stage as well; their clowning never stops, nor their devotion to each other.

MARIA, actress. Outspoken, fun loving, with a generous heart.

IOSIF, actor. A little slovenly and loose tongued, but very talented.

DANIIL, actor. Very diligent, concerned with his performance.

Additional company members, dancers/singers, etc., are welcome, but not essential.

GREEN VIOLINIST, a virtuoso who takes Chagall soaring into his dreams. Brings his paintings to life. He is also visible to Mikhoels, but others are less aware of his existence.

MUSICIANS

In addition to Green Violinist, a small klezmer band: wind, strings, and percussion.

SETTING

Theatre from nothing. An empty room under construction that becomes the
    Yiddish Theatre and stage for later performances. Like a Chagall paint-
    ing, the staging must be fluid, evoking different times and places, floating
    in our imagination like a dream.

Time and Place: Act 1, Part 1, *Agents,* Moscow, 1920. Act 2, Part 2,
    Travels of Benjamin III, Paris, 1928; Part 3, The Terror, or *King Lear,* New
    York, 1943, Moscow 1941–48.

ACT 1

PART I

Agents

(Moscow, 1920. A cold night. Chagall, in the nude, stands high on a scaffold. The young artist has been working feverishly and has just finished painting a mural on the ceiling. Below, in shadows, is the construction of a new theatre: beams, piles of sawdust, old moldings, cans of paint. Lost in his work, Chagall does not seem to notice how night fades, and, as if with the dawn, he hears Green Violinist playing the violin. Chagall, shivering, stares in amazement at what he has created. The violin laughs. With morning light Bella, Chagall's wife, enters, calling to him from the bottom of the scaffold.)

BELLA: Marc! Marc! *(Looking up)* You're crazy—meshugina—it's morning! They're about to begin rehearsal. Come down! *(Chagall descends.)*

CHAGALL: Bella, Bella, Bella . . .

BELLA: You worked all night again! You're shivering! *(Laughing)* Where are your clothes? *(Wrapping him in her coat)* You're numb.

CHAGALL: With you I am warm as a goat . . .

BELLA: *(Rubbing his hands in hers)* I woke up freezing without you . . . the bed was empty . . .

CHAGALL: I slipped out from under the covers . . . you were sleeping so softly . . . *(Kissing her, passionate)* If you had woken, I never could have left . . .

BELLA: *(Loving)* You fool . . . put on your clothes . . .

CHAGALL: *(Kissing her)* Who needs clothes? You just have to take them off to make love or paint . . .

BELLA: Marc! Get dressed. Before the actors get here! *(He gets dressed.)*

CHAGALL: Bella, Bella . . . *(Looking up at ceiling he has painted. Laughing.)* Can you believe it—our own theatre! Where we belong . . .

BELLA: So that's why I spend nights without you?

CHAGALL: A whole company . . . needs my work! *(Teeth chattering, ecstatic, feverishly pointing up)* Look!

BELLA: *(Glancing)* It's wonderful, Marc.

CHAGALL: You didn't even look.

(She really looks up.)

BELLA: What is it?

CHAGALL: A Yiddish circus—

BELLA: At home there's a Yiddish circus . . . nothing to eat . . . the little one
has nothing . . . you sit up there day and night under the ceiling. Come
down to earth. They're tearing down street signs to make firewood . . .

CHAGALL: Listen, he's playing! *(Sings a snatch of first violin melody, moving
about)* He'll keep us warm!

BELLA: You can't burn a violin . . .

CHAGALL: Bella, Bella, Bella . . . *(Loving her)* I'll paint you a shawl, red mit-
tens, a big fur hat, cabbage soup for the little one, a samovar with two
glowing coals . . . like at home in Vitebsk . . .

*(Offstage we hear Actors entering, taking off coats, warming up. They sing "The
Nothing Song." They appear amid the construction, Mikhoels at their center—set-
ting up chairs, grabbing props as they sing. All drab, cold, scruffy—no one notices
Chagall's work on ceiling.)*

COMPANY: We have nothing! More than nothing!
Nothing for lunch or for supper!
Nothing's a feast for a beggar!
Hole in my stomach what can I do?
Half of what I have, I give to you.

BELLA: *(To Chagall)* Let's go.

CHAGALL: *(Over singing)* . . . stay and watch rehearsal . . . look at these wonderful actors . . . there's one—Shloyme—they call him Mikhoels—

BELLA: I'll go alone if you—

CHAGALL: I have to finish sketches for sets and costumes—

BELLA: *(Upset)* We have no family in Moscow. No friends. Nowhere else I can
turn. Our little potato cried her eyes out yesterday. Use your head—

*(He takes off something from around his neck. Hands it to her. Bella shakes her
head adamantly—"no.")*

CHAGALL: Sell it.

BELLA: I gave that to you . . . for our wedding.

CHAGALL: What is the past compared to a future?

BELLA: Is there a future here?

(Bella takes it without looking up at him and heads for the door. Mikhoels grabs her hand, pulls her back into song.)

COMPANY WITH CHAGALL: We have nothing! Less than nothing!
Nothing will feed all our hunger.
Nothing's a meal with a brother.
Forkful of air—we just don't care,
Half of my nothing is yours to share!

MIKHOELS: *(To Bella)* We'll be your family—meet your younger brother, Zuskola, your second cousin Maria, your uncle Iosif, Reb Daniil . . . and me
Shloyme . . . the dog . . .

BELLA: I have a child. A little girl, she can't eat air. *(Exits)*

ZUSKIN AND MIKHOELS: Give us wind, the sound of a horn,
Give us a hole of a bagel.
Give us a bottle without a top,
And we'll put a song on the table.

COMPANY AND CHAGALL: Nothing's mine—nothing's yours.
Nothing will keep us together.
Nothing will keep us together.
Nothing we have we cannot lose,
Nothing is ours forever!
Nai-da-da-dee-dai-dai -na-da-dee-dai . . . (Etc.)

MIKHOELS: *(Over music)* Marc Zakharovich—you're pale, shivering—maybe
you should go home.

CHAGALL: I—I have work to do—see—see—what I painted last night—

MIKHOELS: *(Looks up)* Ah—a violinist—

CHAGALL: *(In agony of indecision)* Bella needs me at home . . .

MIKHOELS: You can't be both places at once. *(Rubbing his hands, he places them
on Chagall's cheeks.)* Your brains froze during the night. *(Mikhoels, laughing, rubs Chagall's face with his hands.)* Warm?

CHAGALL: Warm. They've allowed a bunch of crazy Jews into Moscow to make
a theatre. First time ever. How can I go home? I'll paint a feast . . . enough
for a wedding . . . Where's the bridegroom?

MIKHOELS: *(Flirting)* Marc Zakharovich—who knew?!

ZUSKIN: Wait! I'll make the match . . . *(Tosses a rag on top of Chagall's head,
who becomes the bride. Introduces Mikhoels as the groom.)* The best actor in
the company . . . my brother on stage . . . with a voice like . . .

MARIA: A donkey . . .

IOSIF: An ass . . .

DANIIL: Eeee-on.

ZUSKIN: *(Aside to Mikhoels, referring to Chagall)* Shloyme, what do you think? Did I do well for you?

MIKHOELS: Such a beautiful bride. So shy! So modest! Oy! Such tiny feet! To have such luck!

CHAGALL: And the bridegroom—what hooves? What teeth! *(Mikhoels brays.)*

ZUSKIN: *(As rabbi)* May you live in harmony for the rest of your days.

(Mikhoels mimes breaking a glass with his hoof. Company begins a mock wedding dance—lifting Chagall and Mikhoels in separate chairs. Above, unnoticed on the scaffolding, the Green Violinist plays. With the sound of the violin burning inside him, Chagall can't stop himself, and leaps down—actors clapping—as he dances! Mikhoels joins him.)

MIKHOELS: My God! A painter who can dance!

(Granovsky, the artistic director, appears at the peak of the dance.)

GRANOVSKY: Silence! *(Room freezes at his command—actors stop mid-air, music on a note—all suspended. Chagall slowly stops dancing and also observes the wild frozen circus. Granovsky surveys the resulting tableau.)* There's chaos in the streets, but in the rehearsal room we must maintain absolute order. In stillness we find form, my friends. *(Silently examining the effect of the dynamic tableau)* I like it. Now, shift position on a five count. *(He counts as actors make short move and freeze again. Chagall tries to follow.)* Again. *(They make another short move.)* Move! Move! *(They move in small increments; tableau shifts.)* Stop. Silence. *(They freeze.)* Enough, my doves, at ease. *(All take comfortable positions, attending his every word.)* We dance, we sing, but we must do so with startling rhythms and abrupt silences. It is not enough to caper about as Jews have done through the ages—we need a new vocabulary—our own unique artistic voice. We perform in Yiddish, but our work must speak beyond language, beyond nationality to the essence of who we are in these revolutionary times. Our identity is forming—and form, my friends, is the crucial word—form is everything—

CHAGALL: Because content is a green cow . . . *(Beat. Laughter. He moos.)*

GRANOVSKY: Precisely.

MIKHOELS: Not a green cow, Comrade Chagall, a red bull, a red bull mooing: "Long live the Bolshevik Revolution!"

(He moos. Company moos.)

GRANOVSKY: It's impossible to rehearse under these conditions.

(Efros, the producer, enters with a piece of paper in his hand.)

EFROS: *(To Granovsky)* Alexsei Mikhailovich, I am sorry to interrupt, but I need you to look over this petition to the Soviet—they're deciding on funding this morning—it's our best chance. I wrote it last night—

GRANOVSKY: *(To Company)* Our producer is up all night! *(To Efros)* Let me see—*(Scanning text)* but . . . this is in verse!

EFROS: I thought it would be more effective—

GRANOVSKY: *(Reading under breath)* "Just think . . . just think . . . just think what we can do . . ."

EFROS: *(Reciting)* "No limits . . . no blueprint . . . all we do is new . . . a Yiddish art theatre . . . the words ring in my mouth . . ."

GRANOVSKY: A producer poet—anything is possible! Get this to them right away and post a copy on the wall of the theatre for all to read.

EFROS: Unfortunately, there's no bread or tea this morning, but we'll come up with something by midday.

ZUSKIN: Not again . . . my stomach is howling . . . *(To stomach à la Granovsky)* Silence!

EFROS: My apologies. The idiots running the Revolutionary Arts Commission can't make up their mind about rations for our theatre.

ZUSKIN: If those idiots running the theatres knew a little about art, not just politics—

MIKHOELS: Leave the art to us . . .

GRANOVSKY: Zuskin, if you worked as hard on your vocal range as Efros does petitioning the Soviet, you'd be our leading singer—

EFROS: The Revolution is only as strong as we are. We prove our use—we'll have food. *(Everyone applauds—half mocking, half real.)*

MIKHOELS: He's right. There's no longer someone else to blame . . . no czars . . . no police . . .

DANIIL: It's us.

MARIA: We are free.

GRANOVSKY: Enough proclamations! To work! *Agents*—first scene. *(Looking around)* Where's our stage manager?

ACTORS: *(Shouting)* Efraim! Efraim! Efraim!

(Efraim scurries in. He is short and always working to bring order to the company's chaos.)

EFRAIM: *(Waving an empty tin)* Someone left this! An empty tin of herring— not only did they not share it—but they left their garbage lying—

GRANOVSKY: I don't care about herring—

EFRAIM: Lying about for others to smell. I answer for the cleanliness of the building.

GRANOVSKY: You are responsible for starting rehearsals!

EFRAIM: I am responsible for everything! Last night, that artist of yours went through our supply of candles for the month.

MIKHOELS: What is he supposed to do, paint in the dark?

EFRAIM: Work during the day.

ZUSKIN: We rehearse during the day—

GRANOVSKY: If only!! *Agents!* First scene!

EFRAIM: *(Barks)* Agents—first scene! Actors with briefcases . . . boarding the train . . .

CHAGALL: Where's the violinist?

MIKHOELS: He's late—running on the roof—trying to catch the train—

CHAGALL: Of course. He's flying over the train—

GRANOVSKY: What violinist? There's no violinist in the scene—

CHAGALL: I see a violinist floating above the train—his boots making tracks in the sky!

MIKHOELS: Brilliant! Zuskin will play the boots—I'll be the tracks . . .

GRANOVSKY: *(Whispering)* Marc, you attend to the ceiling, I decide what's on stage.

MIKHOELS: He's like our fate . . . only he knows what will become of us . . .

CHAGALL: Perhaps . . . but I see him standing next to you . . .

MIKHOELS: But who is he? As an actor I have to have something concrete to play—

GRANOVSKY: We'll discuss it later. This is a rehearsal.

CHAGALL: But I rehearsed here all night in the cold—

EFRAIM: In the nude . . .

GRANOVSKY: How original, Marc.

EFRAIM: I have no fuel to heat the room—much less at night!

GRANOVSKY: I do things in the nude. Smoke. Entertain. Rehearsing is not among them.

EFROS: We could burn this parquet!

GRANOVSKY: That's my stage!

CHAGALL: I don't need any fuel.

MIKHOELS: He froze here all night for us—

CHAGALL: I am my own heat! Like a lantern I burn the whole night through—

GRANOVSKY: Efros, is it you who brought this artist to us?

EFROS: He caused a sensation in Paris—

GRANOVSKY: This is Moscow. We don't have time for this nonsense—

CHAGALL: I'm your set designer—talk to me! Tell me what you want—

GRANOVSKY: I want to rehearse. I want absolute silence, so I can hear the rhythm of the action. Rhythm is everything! You have your paints, but you need a blank canvas. Well, I need silence . . . Si-lence! A script is a knot of noisy little words that I must untangle. On stage—I create form. Articulation. For words to have meaning they must spring from silence. Movement from stillness. Is that clear, Monsieur Chagall—

CHAGALL: Bien sûr. *(Touching his finger to his lips)* Silence. *(Retreats to scaffolding to watch)*

(Meanwhile, Violinist drags his sorry ass into the rehearsal room. Only Chagall notices.)

CHAGALL: *(Loud)* You're late.

EFRAIM: Late? Who's late?

CHAGALL: *(To Violinist)* Where have you been? They almost took you off the program. There's no theatre without a violin!

(Trying to warm up fingers. Violinist plays.)

GRANOVSKY: Silence! *(All is quiet. Granovsky composes himself. Violinist retreats.)* We will start with our exercises—partners— *(Starts metronome, which he keeps on a pedestal)* To a ten count. Go. *(To tock of metronome a series of gymnastic exercises, resembling biomechanics, take place in pairs, based on activities in a train compartment.)* Good. Excellent.

ZUSKIN: With all respect, Alexei Mikhailovich, how will anyone in the audience know who we are?

GRANOVSKY: You're Jews.

COMPANY: *(Gesticulating mock revelation)* Jews?!!! . . . My God! We're Jews . . . Yids! . . .

GRANOVSKY: From the provinces—that much is clear—even without acting—

MENAKHEM MENDEL (MIKHOELS): *(Goofing around as character, very funny Jewish stereotype)* My name is Menakhem Mendel . . . that's Me-na-kehm Men-del—with a *khuh*—you see I've never been on a train before—so today's is my lucky day! I was about to be sent on the vacation of my life —to Siberia—when I happened to meet an insurance agent. What luck! Hires me on the spot—because I can talk—that's all that's required! Can you believe it? He bought me a new suit . . . *(Strutting)* Eh? And gave me a briefcase full of blank politics, I mean—policies and a book of institutions . . . er . . . instructions. So I started to work! True, the collar's a little tight . . . and there's my wife, Sheyne Sheyndl . . . what a beauty . . . so full of complaints—I mean compliments . . . for her husband, always a loving word . . .

CHAGALL: *(Laughing) Du bist ein shlemeil.* [Yiddish: You're a loser.]

MIKHOELS: *(Answering) Yah, yah ein luftmenshe.* [Yiddish: Yes, a luftmensh.]

GRANOVSKY: A *luftmenshe?*

MIKHOELS: *(Turning his pockets inside out.)* A man who floats in the air, because he has nothing in his pockets to hold him down.

CHAGALL: But his name floats around the world: Menakhem Mendel Yakhenoz . . .

EFROS: *(Aside to Chagall)* Alexei Mikhailovich does not speak Yiddish.

CHAGALL: The artistic director of a Yiddish theatre does not speak Yiddish?

EFROS: Privileged background, trained in Berlin—consummate artist—

ZUSKIN: A "schlemiel," Alexei Mikhailovich—in Yiddish means "a loser"—

GRANOVSKY: A "loser" is not what I had in mind for opening the first state-funded Yiddish theatre in Moscow—

CHAGALL: Why not?

GRANOVSKY: Not   dignified—we   need   something   symbolic—like Maeterlink—

MIKHOELS: *(As Menakhem)* Maeterlink shmaeterlink. Let's rehearse! My name is Menakhem. I'm selling life insurance for this crumby little life. Where are my customers?

(Signals actors. Musicians begin with a train rhythm. Mikhoels and the Company begin rehearsing "Traveling on a Train," a musical number from Sholem Aleichem's Agents. *Efros exits to office. Mikhoels, as the leading character, Menakhem Mendel, is looking at his reflection in the window of the train compartment. He is admiring his new suit—adjusting the collar, which is too tight.)*

MENAKHEM MENDEL (MIKHOELS): I'm traveling on a train
Do I know where? *(Big pause)*
ALL: Nooooo.
MENAKHEM MENDEL (MIKHOELS): A traveling Jew, what's to complain?
When you're traveling on a train.
ALL: What's to complain?
MENAKHEM MENDEL (MIKHOELS): "You'll make a good agent,
An agent," they said.
"Put food on your table
And feathers in your bed."
A traveling Jew, what's to complain?
When you're traveling on a train.
ALL: What's to complain?
MENAKHEM MENDEL (MIKHOELS): "Your name alone—God knows—"
ALL: What's to complain?
MENAKHEM MENDEL (MIKHOELS): "Menakhem-Mendel Yakhenhoz!"
Traveling on a train.
ALL: Menakhem-Mendel Yakhenhoz,
Menakhem-Mendel Yakhenhoz,
Men-ak-hem-Men-del Ya-ya-ya-ya-ya-khenhoz.
MENAKHEM MENDEL (MIKHOELS): It's a name. What's to complain?
ALL: What's to complain?
CHAGALL: *(Over song, excited, cornering Granovsky)* Menakhem hangs from the ceiling in a compartment, the violinist floats above—
GRANOVSKY: *(To actors/musicians)* Stop—
CHAGALL: The actors at times must seem very large—at times very small. If Menakhem stands alone in the desert he is very small . . . but if in the palm of his hand he holds a grain of sand . . . he becomes a giant.

MIKHOELS: *(Pointing to the floor)* Zuskola—look, a tiny Menakhem Mendel—

ZUSKIN: *(Also pointing to floor)* Oi! Look, Solomon Mikhailovich, a teeny weeny Moishe Moiseevich—

(They both are on the floor speaking in high-pitched nonsense dialogue for their tiny imaginary characters—trying to sell each other insurance. Others join around in a circle. Mikhoels and Zuskin continue in their high squeaky voices under Chagall and Granovsky.)

CHAGALL: And on their costumes—triangles, rectangles, circles hurtling through space—

GRANOVSKY: Pure abstraction won't work on stage—

CHAGALL: *(Passionate outburst)* Who is talking about "pure abstraction"?! Leave it for the gutter! People who talk about "pure" art are usually rolling in their own filth. Do you know why they forced me to leave the Peoples Art College in Vitebsk—an art school that I founded, with my own revolutionary sweat and enthusiasm. Why? Because I paint pictures that look like something. "Dirty" little images of life—red rabbis and green cows— instead of their "pure" white circles, black squares, and red crosses. They turned the students against me, cleared out my studio with a letter from the local authorities. One morning I come in . . . and my room is pure. Abstract. Empty. *(Laughing)* But I'm in Moscow now with a blank canvas *(winking to Granovsky, whispering)*—a very quiet canvas—shh—just think what we can do. *(Sketching)* Look, we'll have . . . a triangular cloud of smoke . . . from a black rectangular train—and a circular goat—

GRANOVSKY: *(Excited by sketch)* It's good, I like it, Chagall—*(Whispering, confiding)* But we have no money for sets or costumes—Efros is doing all he can to petition the Jewish Section—

CHAGALL: Efraim, can you get me a pile of rags, approximately our actors' sizes?

EFRAIM: Rags are not impossible to come by.

CHAGALL: I will paint—every inch—they will be like paintings. But I'll need canvas for the walls.

EFRAIM: No canvas. Bedsheets, maybe. Before the Revolution there was a brothel next door.

CHAGALL: Bedsheets then. With such a history they will be rich.

EFRAIM: Comrade Chagall, I go.

ZUSKIN: Efraim is short, but adept in the marketplace. He'll find your sheets.

(Efraim exits.)

GRANOVSKY: Sheets? Not now! We're rehearsing! Efraim! Come back here this instant!

EFRAIM: I'm back.

GRANOVSKY: I cannot work in this bedlam!!!

CHAGALL: *My apologies.*

GRANOVSKY: Time is impossibly short.

MIKHOELS: The opportunity is too great to . . .

ZUSKIN: Botch.

MENAKHEM MENDEL (MIKHOELS): Exactly. *(Again in character as Menakhem Mendel)* An opportunity comes only once in life! An apostrophe many times—around each corner an apostrophe—apostrophe, apostrophe, apostrophe—I mean catastrophe—take the Bible—take history . . . a catastrophe on every page. But not if you have insurance—you can sleep soundly every night. Dream of sugarplums! Not pogroms! The answer lies right here—*(Tapping briefcase, a major revelation)* Your life is guaranteed! *(Reading policy)* Look, it says: "for a small monthly fee we insure your life . . ." How about that, eh? *(Reading further)* "Make death pay in the event of a catastrophe!" Fantastic! You don't have to worry! For the first time Jews can live without fear—life guaranteed for a little monthly premium! Or pay upfront. I am going to be selling policies like hotcakes— whoever heard of such a thing?! *(Ecstatic)* I'm a rich man—I'm selling life!

(Green Violinist appears. Mikhoels sees him and starts to dance to the Violinist's melody.)

GRANOVSKY: It's good, Mikhoels. But I've seen it before. I will not tolerate stereotypes!

MIKHOELS: We live with Menakhem two inches under our skin.

GRANOVSKY: No "schtick," I believe you call it.

(Mikhoels retreats. Violinist stops playing.)

ZUSKIN: It was funny, Solomon Mikhailovich—really, I was laughing—ha-ha-ha . . .

MIKHOELS: *(Shaking his head)* No. He's right . . . he's right . . . but there is something in that violinist.

EFROS: *(Bursting in)* Comrades—our opening date has been approved—January 1st, 1921—what a New Year! Funds allocated to renovate the building—Yiddish is being proclaimed an official workers' tongue—Hebrew reeks of religion—Russian the tongue of the czars—Yiddish is pure—a pure vessel of socialist thought—how about that? A pure expression of the revolutionary spirit—they want Yiddish poems, essays, plays, newspapers—our own printing presses . . . *(Catches Granovsky's stony gaze)* Sorry to interrupt—I got carried away with the good news.

CHAGALL: Mazel tov!

MIKHOELS: *L'khaim!*

GRANOVSKY: The more you yammer—

ZUSKIN: "Silence!" *(All quiet)* We're all ears.

IOSIF: Eyes.

DANIIL: Noses.

GRANOVSKY: Thank you, Zuskin.

EFRAIM: *Agents*—first scene! Briefcases, comrades—

(As we hear Agents *begin again, Chagall climbs up the scaffolding to his painting. Rehearsal continues beneath as he works.)*

GRANOVSKY: Mikhoels—*(Signals musicians)* from the second verse—

MENAKHEM MENDEL (MIKHOELS): They gave me an advance,
Trained me for a day,
"Insure for a profit,"
That's what they say.
"Better for the living
If death can pay."

ALL: What's to complain?

GRANOVSKY: Pause. And shift. Good.

MENAKHEM MENDEL (MIKHOELS): "You travel and travel and travel," They said.
"Insure your little Jews
Of the life ahead."

ALL: "You travel and travel and travel," they said.
"Insure your little Jews

Of the life ahead."

"You travel and travel and travel," they said

"Insure your little Jews

Of the life ahead."

MENAKHEM MENDEL (MIKHOELS): I'll keep them all alive . . .

GRANOVSKY: Silence!

(Company freezes, in wild pose. Frustrated, Mikhoels breaks out of the tableau)

MIKHOELS: If you stop us every second—how can we work?!

GRANOVSKY: *(Patient)* Do it again.

MIKHOELS: Nothing again is nothing.

GRANOVSKY: Again.

MIKHOELS: More nothing!

ZUSKIN: Mikhoels, "nothing" will happen, unless you give me the cue.

MIKHOELS: The cue has "nothing" to do with it.

CHAGALL: *(Laughing)* Now that's our Yiddish theatre—

GRANOVSKY: A-A-ARGH!

CHAGALL: God forbid you should play Maeterlink.

GRANOVSKY: That's it! Rehearsal has ended. My throat is on fire. There is sawdust in my lungs. If you gentlemen . . . *(Almost in tears)*

EFRAIM: Comrades.

GRANOVSKY: . . . if you comrades . . . can't concentrate . . . then what is the point? I ask you. I could be working anywhere . . . *(Exiting with a dramatic sweep. Zuskin signals musicians, Mikhoels joins in melodrama. Granovsky does not miss a beat, sings to a series of his precise rhythmic movements as he leaves the stage.)*

I calculate the rhythm

Of silence, and a pause.

Alone, prepare a score,

I do not seek applause.

But I need my actors' focus

Every second on the stage

And not to be provoked

Into a choking fit of rage!

(Exits, leaving a shaky silence in his wake. The Company is crestfallen. What to do? Chagall whistles as he works on the scaffold, Mikhoels looks up. Efros rushes in.)

EFROS: Tea in the foyer. With salt fish.

ZUSKIN: Food! *(Heading off)* Shloyme . . . a fish for you, a fish for me . . .

EFROS: Rehearsal resumes in one hour.

EFRAIM: One hour, rehearsal!!!

(Actors head off. Zuskin turns, waiting for Mikhoels, but Mikhoels motions him to go ahead. Mikhoels lies down on his back, opens his eyes to the sky/ceiling. Green Violinist appears above. Solo violin. Mikhoels starts seeing things. His body starts moving in Chagallian shapes—off kilter—dreamlike—he moves. Chagall watches him, then swings down off scaffolding. A painting is coming to life.)

CHAGALL: Make your hand . . . a square . . . a fist turned inside out . . . like you're carrying a kopeck that everyone wants to take . . .

(Mikhoels, working with Chagall, discovers a form for the character of Menakhem. Holds out the imaginary kopeck to Chagall)

MIKHOELS: Your fee for the idea . . .

CHAGALL: *(Taking the imaginary kopeck from Mikhoels)* Thank you . . . this will buy all the nothing I need . . .

(Mikhoels sings with violin; as he moves, Chagall joins. Violinist carrying the two men away.)

CHAGALL: *(Looking up at Violinist)* Why did he turn out green?

MIKHOELS: *(Looking up)* Still young, I guess. Your painting is better than my acting.

CHAGALL: Your acting's not so bad; just not as good as my painting.

MIKHOELS: Give me your sketches.

CHAGALL: Why?

MIKHOELS: I want to eat them.

CHAGALL: Let all who are hungry come eat. *(Passes handful of sketches to Mikhoels)*

MIKHOELS: *(Examining)* Me as Menakhem. *(Takes pose of sketch)* Leaning to the right. Pushing to the left. One hand open, one hand closed. So much tension . . . strength. Fighting everyday with a world that does not value him. I've been playing him weak, a bit of a fool—but you get that in this sketch with the wrists—*(Adjusting)* they're broken, his great strength cannot get to his hands . . . he cannot make anything in the world. But his potential is tremendous—*(Examining more sketches)* It's all here, Chagall—every character . . .

CHAGALL: But no one looks at my work! I can't even get Granovsky—

MIKHOELS: They will. *(Pause)* You know, Chagall, you should paint the whole company. Show us who we are in your eyes . . .

CHAGALL: All of you?

(Efraim enters under pile of bedsheets.)

MIKHOELS: Even Efraim.

CHAGALL: Of course, Efraim—

EFRAIM: Is this enough, comrade Chagall?

CHAGALL: For a mural—or a brothel?

MIKHOELS: You can call it: "The Creation of the Yiddish Theatre."

CHAGALL: Genesis!

EFRAIM: *(Objecting)* That's Hebrew . . .

MIKHOELS: We'll make it Yiddish.

CHAGALL: On the third day, Efros brings Chagall to meet the great Granovsky. I must be carried across the face of the deep . . .

MIKHOELS: And Mikhoels—moves like a wind over the unformed void—

CHAGALL: Clutching the hooves of a goat . . . and chasing a violin . . . *(Sketching again)*

MIKHOELS: Get to work!

(Mikhoels whistles, Efraim echoes loud and shrill. Other company members gather. Mikhoels hands out sketches and shows how to begin working with them. Chagall retreats to his scaffolding. Grumbling: "Finally someone notices what I'm painting." He is observing company members astutely. Actors are trying a new form for their character based on the sketch. Chagall is sketching Efraim, who also poses holding a tray and a glass. Violinist plays and they all begin to move. Each actor is caught in a colored light for a moment of Chagallian transformation. Fracture dance. Efros and Granovsky enter, talking heatedly. Slowly they become aware of the Company's new movement and are captivated by what they see.)

EFROS: Please, Alexei Mikhailovich—the actors need you . . . adore you . . .

GRANOVSKY: If they behave like cockroaches . . . what more can I do? Where's that petition to the Soviet? Tear it up! *(Grabbing piece of paper with Efros' poem off the wall. Efros stops him from ripping it up.)* It's useless if—*(Notices the actors moving)* What is that? Wonderful . . .

EFROS: *(Reciting a line from his poem)* Just think . . . just think . . . just think what we can do . . .

GRANOVSKY: But it has to be rhythmic . . . my doves. *(Setting time for Company)* "Just think . . . just think . . . just think what we can do . . ." *(Company picks up rhythm, repeating as they work and move with music: "Just think, just think, just think." Granovsky looks at Company moving)* Now this is interesting . . .

EFROS WITH GRANOVSKY: *(Company continues repeating as they work and move in time with music: "Just think, just think, just think." Efros declaims his poem in full voice over music.)*

No limits no blueprint,
All we do is new.
"A Yiddish Art theatre,"
The words ring in my mouth,
Vibrate on my tongue—
No permits! No police!
No pogroms! No more czar!
No accidents! No precedents!
We are who we are!

(Company has begun moving as one fantastic Chagallian entity, Mikhoels as the leader. Granovsky, thrilled by what he sees, joins poem. Chagall looking down from above, sketching like mad: a constructivist dream. Green Violinist next to him with an outrageous solo line.)

We make of the present
What was and is to come.
A future, my friends . . .
Rest when we are done!

(Music builds to a climax, Company revitalized, moving as one. Suddenly, Bella enters with small child in her arms. She is in a state of shock, barely able to talk. Chagall rushes to her. Maria takes little child and starts rocking her, singing her a Yiddish lullaby under her breath. Rest of the company gathers around Bella.)

BELLA: . . . the old man . . . the old man with skinny hands . . . lives in the cellar . . . eats next to nothing . . . what harm could he do? Two soldiers. What harm? An old man: Petya. Tells the orphans fairy stories—Baba Yaga with her house on chicken feet—the only time I saw a smile in their eyes—parents dead and he makes them smile with his skinny hands talking like two puppets. They come looking for him—two soldiers—young men scaring the children—"a dangerous war criminal—a White—an Aristocrat." Find him trembling behind the boiler and they drag him out . . . take him out and shoot him in the woods . . . children watching from the window . . . children who'd seen their parents shot into pits. "There! Let that be a lesson to you!" "Long live the Revolution!"

CHAGALL: *(Trying to comfort)* Bella, Bella, Bella . . . this is a civil war. War breeds more war . . . more death—

BELLA: What people could let this happen?

CHAGALL: Unspeakable cruelties on both sides—

BELLA: What good can come of it?

CHAGALL: Wars end. Life is too strong.

BELLA: You can't clean the eyes that saw—can you?

MIKHOELS: *(Passionate)* No, but we can build a society that does not feed on violence and cruelty—that does not fight wars to enrich a few, at the expense of millions . . . where there is food enough for everyone—

CHAGALL: And hearts can be filled with love—

BELLA: *(Angry)* Where? On these streets? You fools living inside this theatre —how beautiful—you make beautiful—you make—how beautiful not to see—not to see what I saw today—I wish I'd closed my eyes—I wish I'd turned my head—*(Breaking down completely)* I wish . . . I'd stopped them . . .

CHAGALL: *(Holding her)* Bella Bella Bella Bella . . .

MIKHOELS: *(Gathering Company around Bella)* We will be your walls. Our hands will become puppets—like Petya—eh? Our voices the stories that must be told . . .

(Mikhoels signals musicians to begin a Menakhem Mendel solo, "What's to Complain?")

MENAKHEM MENDEL (MIKHOELS): I work as an agent,
I travel the land,
An empty bundle in my hand.
Always a hope for a better life,
Always a word from my loving wife

Oh, Sheyne Sheynele,
What's to complain?
After the sun, there's always rain.
After the rain, there's always sun.
Always a dream when the day is done.

Invest in markets,
Invest in stocks,
I always hear when opportunity knocks:
"Menakhem, you fool,
What have you done?!
You've gone and lost what we should have won!"

Oh, Sheyne Sheynele,
What's to complain?
After the sun, there's always rain.
After the rain, there's always sun.
Always a dream when the day is done.

*(Lights fade on Company singing, repeating chorus of last verse. Darkness.
Night. A quiet empty theatre. Above flickers the small flame of a candle, where
among bedsheets we make out the form of Chagall. Mikhoels lies on the floor below,
staring at the ceiling. Chagall finally notices Mikhoels.)*

CHAGALL: Mikhoels, is that you?

MIKHOELS: I came so you wouldn't drop dead from the cold. I brought Rus-
     sia's main source of warmth . . . *(Mikhoels pulls out a bottle, two glasses.)*
     Come down here.

CHAGALL: Not yet. I've never seen you with a bottle in your hands. *(Pause. To
     Mikhoels.)* Move to the left. No, left. Good.

MIKHOELS: Ach—I'm too ugly to paint—paint Menakhem—paint Zuskin—
     anyone but ole monkey face—

CHAGALL: Shut up. *(Continues working)*

MIKHOELS: Marc Zakharovich, do you know why an orangutan has three balls?

CHAGALL: No, Solomon Mikhailovich. Why?

MIKHOELS: Because . . . because . . . *(Laughing)* I forgot. *(Makes orangutan
     noises. Then quiet, gazing up)* Why don't we put the audience lying on the
     floor? Let them stare at your ceiling and walls. And I could stay here for-

ever . . . with something to drink . . . someone to drink with. Paradise. I'll fall asleep like this . . .

CHAGALL: Sweet dreams . . .

MIKHOELS: *(Sitting bolt upright)* The Party is coming to opening in full force.

CHAGALL: Good for them.

MIKHOELS: Good for us.

CHAGALL: *(Pointing to the upper walls, where a mural of a wedding table runs.)* I painted a wedding feast. A place for everyone. *(Chuckling)* One taste of my herring . . . and they'll have indigestion.

MIKHOELS: I'm serious, Marc Zakharovich. It's important for us. Zuskin nearly quit last week. We all have our past lives. Not one of us was a professional actor—Granovsky took us off the street—he wanted to train his company from nothing. Zuskin was a logger—chopping down trees for Socialism . . . Daniil from a family of bakers; Maria was studying medicine and engaged to the son of a wealthy factory owner; Iosif a teacher who fought for the Bolsheviks. So when our work goes poorly and there is no food, each one of us remembers his former life. Zuskin wanted to go back to the woodlot, but when he heard the Party leaders were coming to our opening he decided to stay.

CHAGALL: I painted him with a bird in his throat. He better sing.

MIKHOELS: *(Pause)* If this doesn't work out, Chagall . . . I can become a lawyer . . . You know, when I first applied to law school—there was no chance—not for a Jew . . . Now the sky's the limit . . .

CHAGALL: *(Pointing to paints)* This is all I can do. When I was little I was taken to see a mural my great-grandfather painted on the walls of the Moghilev synagogue. An image of the Eternal City—Jerusalem. He dared to paint a place he would never see. I thought about it: this is what I wanted to do—make the world closer—like we are all held in the palm of some great hand: seeds that grow wherever we are scattered . . . but we must remember the hand. I'm living in a miserable little village outside Moscow. I work at an orphanage teaching art to shaved-headed monkeys who were starving on the streets a few weeks ago. *They* are giving *me* milk for my little girl. *(Mikhoels goes toward Chagall.)* Hold still. *(Chagall painting Mikhoels. Green Violin plays, Mikhoels listens. Solo violin.)* Now move. *(Mikhoels starts dancing to violin, singing* nign. *To Mikhoels, matter of fact)* You're an actor.

(Bella enters with package of food. Notices Mikhoels—opens it.)

BELLA: You've been painting forty days and forty nights. There's no dry land left at home. Only floods of tears. We're sitting on the roof. Come down, Marc, or we will all drown!

MIKHOELS: Bella, it's a miracle—I brought some vodka. And now there's something to eat! Where did you get so much food?

BELLA: A friend of my parents is emigrating.

MIKHOELS: What a feast!!! Chagall! COME EAT!

BELLA: Sold everything. Just like that—gave me his rations. Said he'd be fine wherever he was going. As long as it wasn't here.

MIKHOELS: Chagall! *(Digging in with Bella)* We even have something to drink!

CHAGALL: Ein moment.

(Bella toasting with Mikhoels: "L'khaim!")

MIKHOELS: Mmm.

CHAGALL: A masterpiece!!

MIKHOELS: No, the masterpiece is here. A meal. A real meal like we used to have . . .

BELLA: What's the song? The one you were teaching me—

(Mikhoels starts traditional Yiddish song. Bella joins, singing with him.)

CHAGALL: Wait! Wait for me! *(Leaping down)* I'm almost finished! Two more little figures: Chagall and Bella, in a corner watching. Watching the birth of the new Yiddish theatre! A theatre . . . in our image, our own likeness . . . and we see that it is good. A theatre that speaks to the whole world . . .

MIKHOELS: *(Picking up from Chagall)* "Be fruitful and multiply . . . fill the waters in the sea, and let the birds increase in the skies . . ."

(Lights fade on the three eating, laughing, singing. Darkness. Lights rise on Chagall, having pulled another of his consecutive all-nighters, standing alone in center of room. Bleary-eyed. Exhausted. Green Violinist beside him also flagging. Solo violin.)

CHAGALL: *(To Violinist)* You're drunk. You're tired. What good are you?

(Violinist plays mournful whine: "Me too . . ." Efraim brings Chagall a glass of milk on a tray. Chagall nurses it hungrily.)

CHAGALL: Thank you, Efraim.

EFRAIM: Half water, but better than nothing.

CHAGALL: When the actors arrive, bring them all in here. I'm done.

(Efraim nods. Heads off. Turns, scurries back.)

EFRAIM: Congratulations, comrade Chagall. *(Raising an imaginary toast:)* L'khaim! (Exits.)

CHAGALL: Look at it first . . . perhaps no will like it.

(Violinist continues to play the painters lament. Lights rise full on the Company facing out, staring at the mural Chagall has painted of them. They are seeing it for the first time on the fourth wall, out over the audience. The audience "sees" the mural only through their reactions to it, and the slight shifting of their bodies into the image they are seeing of themselves. A moment of stillness.)

MIKHOELS: It's us.

MARIA: We're all there.

EFROS: Even Efraim—

EFRAIM: Even Efros—

ZUSKIN: Look, Granovsky has no arms—

GRANOVSKY: And Zuskin's a clown—

DANIIL: And Mikhoels can do splits—

MIKHOELS: And fly through the air—

IOSIF: Who's that peeing on the pig? Is that you Daniil?

BELLA: Where am I?

CHAGALL: Over there, watching in the corner—

BELLA: *(Delighted)* Oh, with you . . .

CHAGALL: And tiny little Ida.

GRANOVSKY: *(Hugging him)* Chagall, it's stunning!

EFROS: Our manifesto!

GRANOVSKY: Now let's make theatre!

CHAGALL: *(Pointing to mural)* But that is . . . that is . . . that is our theatre.

(Swirl of activity as theatre is prepared for opening night.)

EFRAIM: *(Barks)* Opening night. Half hour. Half hour, comrades!

(Chagall is painting costumes, constructing them on the spot. Actors move Agents set into place.)

MIKHOELS: Cha-a-aga-a-llll! If you are going to paint my face, do it! It's almost curtain!

CHAGALL: *(Crossing to where Mikhoels stands before a mirror in already painted Chagall costume)* Ah—Menakhem Mendel's face. I'm coming. I'm coming.

MIKHOELS: *(To Chagall in front of mirror)* I like the cap. But no one will see the tiny goats . . .

CHAGALL: God will. *(Beat)* With opera glasses.

(Chagall approaches Mikhoels with palette, starts painting Mikhoels' face. Around them, opening night frenzy. Blare of musicians tuning instruments. Granovsky rushing about: adjusting props, talking to actors/musicians. A large green goat floats into the space. Where did that come from? Efros and Bella are all dressed up in the auditorium, watching the audience assemble.)

EFROS: Look, the audience is so excited!

BELLA: They can't take their eyes off Marc's murals—

EFROS: *(Proudly)* Jews. Russians. Poles. Foreign press—many nations under one roof—

(Chagall intently painting Mikhoels' face. Zuskin appears with costume and face, also painted by Chagall.)

MIKHOELS: Eh? Eh? Zuska!? Zuskola. Now this is a *shayne punem* [Yiddish: a beautiful face]—

CHAGALL: Stop moving!

ZUSKIN: Eh? Eh? Solomon Mikhailovich. Now this is a *shayne punem*—

GRANOVSKY: Gentlemen, it's time. Places.

EFRAIM: Comrades, places. Opening night.

CHAGALL: *Kleyn* moment. Not done.

(Efros, Bella in the house. Granovsky backstage frantically searching for Mikhoels.)

EFROS: Now is the moment.

BELLA: You've been working so hard.

GRANOVSKY: Mikhoels!

CHAGALL: *(To himself)* I'm not done.

EFROS: I hear you singing to Marc at night as he paints—

GRANOVSKY: Where is Mikhoels?

CHAGALL: A few more minutes . . .

BELLA: *(Radiant)* Solomon Mikhailovich is teaching me to sing. We're starting with all the old Yiddish songs from our childhood—

(Efraim follows Granovsky, who is walking in ever tighter circles, getting more and more wound up. Chagall calmly working on Mikhoels.)

GRANOVSKY: Mikhoels! You pour your lifeblood into the theatre. Mikhoels! He was a law student when I found him! Mikhoels! We're holding the curtain. The audience is restless. The critics. Can't you hear them? They're saying this is another bunch of lazy Jews who can't even start a show on time. This is amateur. Not what I spent two years creating. Start the overture.

(Chagall's fingers remain hanging over the face like a question mark. He holds his thumb up to Mikhoels' right eye. Takes several steps back. Shaking his head.)

CHAGALL: Solomon, oh, Solomon. I could do so much, if only you didn't have your right eye.

GRANOVSKY: *(Bursting into dressing room)* Yo-u . . . you y-y-y y—y-i–i-i-d-d-d! Y-y-ou h-h-h-erring monger's son! LET HIM GO!

CHAGALL: *(Grabbing Mikhoels)* No! I'm not finished! I must tear out your right eye!

MIKHOELS: It's good, Chagall.

GRANOVSKY: *(In a state of tug-of-war with Chagall over Mikhoels)* You are not keeping *my* actor a minute longer while the public waits assembled in *my* theatre—

MIKHOELS: Mazel tov. I better go. *(Slipping out, joyous)* Zu-u-uskaaaa! Wait for meeeeeeee!

(Rushes to make his entrance. Musicians are playing overture. Chagall and Granovsky remain as play begins.)

GRANOVSKY: Marc . . . even though you know nothing about theatre, the actors adore you. And I . . . I am grateful. It's our opening, why not make peace?

CHAGALL: You sat the audience facing the stage!!!

GRANOVSKY: Where else should they face?

CHAGALL: Their backs are to my paintings.

GRANOVSKY: So?

CHAGALL: No one will see them!

GRANOVSKY: I also feel as if everything has finished . . . no more crazy rehearsals . . . no more arguments . . . but people will see the performance . . .

CHAGALL: And maybe someone will turn around . . .

GRANOVSKY: We are audience now. Come, let's have a look—you at your walls, me at the stage . . . *(Beat)* And Mikhoels.

(Chagall and Granovsky head off to watch Mikhoels and Company. On stage: Agents' first performance. Mikhoels with Daniil, Iosif, and Maria in railway carriage, now a small Chagallian structure. Painted costumes and faces. Menakhem Mendel (Mikhoels) is looking at his reflection in the window. Other actors, each a little Menakhem Mendel, all tending to their appearance. Moisei Moiseevich Lamp-Squelcher (Zuskin) in rear, peering in and trying to get into compartment, finally tumbles in with huge briefcase. Performance is now lush, musical, effortless, rhythmic harlequinade. Stylized silences, punctuated with humor.)

MENAKHEM MENDEL (MIKHOELS): *(Composing a letter to his wife)* To my wise, redeemed—er—esteemed and pusillanimous—I mean—magnanimous wife, Sheyne-Sheyndl. Look at me now! *(Pose and movement shift)* This time you've got a winner here! *(Silent grotesque pose)* Life Insurance—what a business! *(Another silent pose)* Your husband has a new suit . . . new suit . . . new suit . . . new suit . . . *(Sings "Traveling on a Train")*

MENAKHEM MENDEL (MIKHOELS): I'm traveling on a train
Do I know where? *(Big pause)*

ALL: Nooooo.

(Zuskin tumbles into compartment. Extreme physicality, as we saw in rehearsal, but with Violinist playing and complete fluidity. All reaching over each other for briefcases as they see a prospective client. Tight collars produce rhythmic coughs.)

MENAKHEM MENDEL (MIKHOELS): A traveling Jew, what's to complain?
When we're traveling on a train.

ALL: What's to complain?

MENAKHEM MENDEL (MIKHOELS): "You'll make a good agent,
An agent," they said.
"Put food on your table

And feathers in your bed."
A traveling Jew, what's to complain?
When we're traveling on a train.
ALL: What's to complain?
MENAKHEM MENDEL (MIKHOELS): "Your name alone—God knows—"
ALL: What's to complain?
MENAKHEM MENDEL (MIKHOELS): "Menakhem-Mendel Yakhenhoz!"
Traveling on a train.
ALL: Menakhem-Mendel Yakhenhoz,
Menakhem-Mendel Yakhenhoz,
Men-ak-hem-Men-del Ya-ya-ya-ya-ya-khenhoz.
MENAKHEM MENDEL (MIKHOELS): It's a name. What's to complain?
ALL: What's to complain?
MENAKHEM MENDEL (MIKHOELS): They gave me an advance,
Trained me for a day,
"Insure them for profit,"
That's what they say.
"Better for the living
If death can pay."
ALL: What's to complain?
MENAKHEM MENDEL (MIKHOELS): "You travel and travel and travel," they
    said.
Insure your little Jews
Of the life ahead."
ALL: "You travel and travel and travel," they said.
"Insure your little Jews
Of the life ahead."
"You travel and travel and travel," they said.
"Insure your little Jews
Of the life ahead."
MENAKHEM MENDEL (MIKHOELS): I'll keep them all alive . . . *(Pause)*
It's a business that will thrive.

(Spoken aside) Look, what a nice man, a nice briefcase. Praise God I may be
able to insure him from death—
(Silence—all freeze. Train jolts them all on top of each other. They straighten out.)

LAMP-SQUELCHER (ZUSKIN): *(Aside about Menakhem)* Now, there's my customer—with a briefcase like that he needs a little insurance.

BAKING FISH (DANIIL): *(Aside)* Mnm-Mnm-Mnm. What a fine fellow . . . with a briefcase bulging with food! Must have a loving wife . . . who will love him even more . . . after he dies . . .

TURTLE DOVE (MARIA): *(Aside)* Finally, a good prospect . . . fine looking man, an expensive briefcase. God willing he's got a lot to insure . . .

(Iosif does the identical moment in silence or made-up tongue. All stare at him.)

LAMP-SQUELCHER (ZUSKIN): *(To Menakhem Mendel)* Ah-hem, pleasure to travel by train, isn't it?

MENAKHEM MENDEL (MIKHOELS): Ah yes, a real pleasure . . . a pleasure . . . Not like before . . . *(All agree.)*

LAMP-SQUELCHER (ZUSKIN): Nooo. *(Aside)* He's going right where I want him. *(To Menakhem Mendel)* A calamity at every corner . . .

(All in agreement—silent gestures. Pause. Still as all look at each other: winning smiles.)

MENAKHEM MENDEL (MIKHOELS): *(Aside)* Following me like a duckling . . .

LAMP-SQUELCHER (ZUSKIN): *(To Menakhem)* Remember when we had to go by horse and buggy—

ALL: *(Sputtering cacophony)* Ach! Horse and buggy . . . horse and buggy . . . no, no, no . . . *(Etc.)*

MENAKHEM MENDEL (MIKHOELS): The only advantage was safety. Trains— *(nodding what they all must infer)* God forbid . . .

LAMP-SQUELCHER (ZUSKIN): An accident!? *(All nodding in silence)*

ALL: *(Huge shift—grotesque movement)* Not to utter such words . . . May you live forever . . . Your wife as well *(Etc.)*

LAMP-SQUELCHER (ZUSKIN): *(All leaning in, whispering)* A catastrophe . . .

ALL: *(Pause—intake of air—whistle on the breath out)*

MENAKHEM MENDEL (MIKHOELS): Good to be insured for . . . say . . . a few thousand . . .

LAMP-SQUELCHER (ZUSKIN): A few thousand!?

ALL: *(Excitedly)* Yes.

MENAKHEM MENDEL (MIKHOELS): *(Whipping out pen and paper)* We can do it right here! *(A flurry of papers and pens from everyone—then silence)* Life's short—eternity forever. *(Violin bemoans this fact.)*

LAMP-SQUELCHER (ZUSKIN): So true. *(Filling in form)* How old are you?

TURTLE DOVE (MARIA): *(Filling in form)* How old am I? How old are you?

BAKING FISH (DANIIL): *(Forms flying)* How old am I? How old are you?

MENAKHEM MENDEL (MIKHOELS): You!

LAMP-SQUELCHER (ZUSKIN): You!

BAKING FISH (DANIIL): You!

TURTLE DOVE (MARIA): You!

IOSIF: You!

BAKING FISH (DANIIL): You!

MENAKHEM MENDEL (MIKHOELS): *(Pause)* I'm an agent. *(Accelerates, rhythmic over music.)*

IOSIF: I'm an agent.

BAKING FISH (DANIIL): I'm an agent.

TURTLE DOVE (MARIA): You?

LAMP-SQUELCHER (ZUSKIN): I'm an agent.

TURTLE DOVE (MARIA): I'm an agent.

MENAKHEM MENDEL (MIKHOELS): I'm an agent.

IOSIF: I'm an agent.

BAKING FISH (DANIIL): I'm an agent.

TURTLE DOVE (MARIA): I'm an agent.

MENAKHEM MENDEL (MIKHOELS): I'm an agent.

ALL: *(Alternating then mounting cacophony)* You? You? You? You? You? I'm an agent. *(Etc.)*

MENAKHEM MENDEL (MIKHOELS): *(Holding up his hand)* My fellow agents, what's to complain? We're selling life! With a good policy Eternal Life waits for each of us! *(Leads song: "We Can Live Forever." Agents ecstatic— all dancing)*

We can live forever

If we all insure each other.

COMPANY: *(Considering the idea, assenting)* A little policy for Life,

A little income for the wife.

MENAKHEM MENDEL (MIKHOELS): Who knows what will endure.

In the end what is secure?

COMPANY: Is it family? Is it wealth?

Can a pension bring good health?

MENAKHEM MENDEL (MIKHOELS): Is it history? Is it art?

Sign a contract. Let us start.

Anyone who has to die,

I will now exemptify.

ALL: *(Flurry of signatures)* Exemptify, exemptify . . .

MENAKHEM MENDEL (MIKHOELS) AND COMPANY: We can live forever,

We can all insure each other.

Buy a policy today,

And we can make forever stay. *(3X tempo accelerates, a round)*

(Applause. Lights fade on Efraim in ecstasy, throwing his hat in the air and catching it. Holding it over his head.)

EFRAIM: We did it! We did it! We did it!

(Darkness. Chagall and Mikhoels enter arm in arm, very drunk, with bottle of vodka. Offstage the sounds of the opening night party—music, cavorting.)

CHAGALL: Solomon Mikhailovich, I have something to say . . . and you must . . . you must listen . . . *(Mikhoels objects.)* No, no you must . . . tonight . . . you . . . you were brilliant. I've always dreamed of hiding in my paintings . . . to see what happens when I'm no longer there. They hang on a wall . . . a house, maybe a museum, if they don't get stuffed in some basement . . . but life continues inside them. Tonight . . . with you on stage . . . I saw my paintings . . . living on without me . . .

MIKHOELS: Marc Zakharovich . . . before you . . . before you . . . there was nothing . . . you gave us everything. Let's go. Everyone is asking for you.

CHAGALL: A toast . . . *(Raising glass)* To . . . to . . . *(Can't think of anything)* . . .

MIKHOELS: *(Raising glass)* To . . . to . . . *(Can't think of anything)* . . .

CHAGALL: The green violin . . . *(They drink.)*

MIKHOELS: I mean a tree is green when it has leaves and a violin is like a living tree—its leaves are notes—

CHAGALL: *(Putting finger to his lips)* Shh! *(Pouring another—which with tradition goes to the parents)* To our parents . . .

MIKHOELS: Our dear ones, here and beyond . . . *(They drink.)* Tomorrow is sold out. And the next day and the next. *(Observing Chagall staggering about the space)* What are you doing?

CHAGALL: Collecting my brushes. What's left for me to do?

MIKHOELS: Take a trip to the Promised Land.

CHAGALL: Where? Paris?

MIKHOELS: No. Our next production— *Travels of Benjamin III.*

CHAGALL: Granovsky didn't mention anything.

MIKHOELS: *(Finding this particularly funny)* He doesn't know yet! I want to play the role of poor Benjamin . . . the fool who's never left his little village . . . and suddenly gets it into his head to fulfill his destiny and travel to the Holy Land. Just think of the sets you could design, Chagall: a red sea . . . green camels . . . orange palm trees . . .

CHAGALL: The lights of Paris . . .

MIKHOELS: Why not!? A city Benjamin will never get to . . .

CHAGALL: You've never seen anything like them . . .

MIKHOELS: The city of his dreams . . .

CHAGALL: Golden, riotous . . .

MIKHOELS: He meets the lost tribe of his ancestors . . . A harem . . .

CHAGALL: Paris is a city of painters . . .

MIKHOELS: It's all in his head. He's a dreamer, stuck in his muddy little village . . . but he takes action. And you and I can make his dreams come true . . . eh? Not a million miles away . . . but here . . . here. Eh, Chagall?

CHAGALL: Do you think anyone even saw my murals?

MIKHOELS: What are you talking about? Of course. They're brilliant— *(Sees Granovsky in doorway, celebrating, visibly drunk. To Granovsky:)* Alexei Mikhailovich is thrilled—

GRANOVSKY: They are magnificent! Mikhoels, they're waiting for you . . . Lunacharsky has already asked three times: where is Mikhoels?

MIKHOELS: Let's go, Marc. Didn't the audience love Marc's paintings?

CHAGALL: They couldn't even see them! They were kept in the dark—

GRANOVSKY: Of course, the light was on the stage.

CHAGALL: There was no light on my paintings!

MIKHOELS: Chagall, Chagall, Chagall . . . come on, let's go . . .

GRANOVSKY: The show was a success—the audience ecstatic—

CHAGALL: Ninety people . . . in a dark smelly little room . . . rubbing the backs of their greasy heads against my murals—

EFROS: *(Sticking head in)* It's a triumph! A triumph!

CHAGALL: I need a bigger audience.

EFROS: They're calling for you, Alexei Mikhailovich—

CHAGALL: I paint for everyone . . .

GRANOVSKY: *(Locked into Chagall)* What? My theater is too parochial for you?

EFROS: They want you to give a speech—

GRANOVSKY: Too narrow for your "general" public?

EFROS: All the newspapers are here!

GRANOVSKY: Too Jewish?

MIKHOELS: *(Defending)* Chagall's work is steeped in the shtetl—

CHAGALL: That's a village. I was born in a village next to Vitebsk.

GRANOVSKY: Enough of your "village" patriotism.

EFROS: Stop this nonsense!!

GRANOVSKY: If your village is so wonderful, why did you leave? I'm trying to raise our work to a new international level! So we will be recognized in Paris . . . Berlin . . .

CHAGALL: You think they won't understand you in Berlin? In Paris, they are going to turn their backs on your stage because your actors dance in peyis to a crazy violin? Your Europeans did not turn away from the Bible—Jerusalem is just another "village," isn't it . . . the same Jews lived there . . . or perhaps you do not consider them your relatives?

GRANOVSKY: I will not insulted by . . . by this, this—

(Granovsky and Chagall face off like two snarling dogs.)

EFROS: All of Moscow stands, glasses raised to toast the birth of their new Yiddish theatre and you are here—fighting—like—like—

CHAGALL: You promised an exhibition of my murals!

EFROS: Dogs!

GRANOVSKY: I run a theatre, not a museum!

CHAGALL: You want to revolutionize the arts? Put some light on my paintings—there's your revolution!

(Chagall and Granovsky face off. Snarling and growling, locked in each other's grip. Dogfight.)

MIKHOELS: We are your paintings! Onstage! You said so yourself—

EFROS: *(Yelling)* Efraim, bring a stick and a bucket of water.

MIKHOELS: What in the world do you want?

EFRAIM: *(Heading off)* Stick and a bucket of water.

CHAGALL: *(Outcry)* I have not been paid!!! But I could care less, if someone had even noticed my work . . .

GRANOVSKY: No one has been paid! Not me. Nor Shloyme. Nor Efraim, nor Efros. The theater has nothing! We live on top of each other like pancakes and beg for food.

CHAGALL: GRRRRRRRRRRRRRR!

EFROS: Stop it! *(Efraim arrives wielding stick. Action freezes, stick raised. Efros now losing it.)* Everyone will be paid! Everyone! We have our—our allocation—Lunacharsky is here—the Party—they're all celebrating your performance, singing your praises. *(To Granovsky and Mikhoels)* And you . . . you insult them by not showing up for a toast. They want Mikhoels to lead the "Internationale" at midnight—in Yiddish. So if you don't get out there and be our rising star and his artistic director, I'm . . . I'm quitting!!! *(Exiting)*

MIKHOELS: *(Whistling to Chagall, calling him off like a dog)* Come on Marc Zakharovich . . . come on . . . let's go for a walk . . . *(Chagall lopes toward Mikhoels. Granovsky straightens. Efraim lowers stick.)* We'll present ourselves to these leaders . . .

CHAGALL: No one has asked to see me. And if they asked me, I'd say that they are bureaucrats that know nothing about art—

EFROS: Quiet! Please . . .

MIKHOELS: I won't go in there without him . . .

GRANOVSKY: Let's go, Mikhoels. I am not facing this crowd by myself . . .

MIKHOELS: . . . our theatre's success is his!

GRANOVSKY: They'll want to see the *actor* . . .

MIKHOELS: Chagall. Please . . .

CHAGALL: *(To Mikhoels)* Go, go . . . Shloyme! An actor must receive applause. You've earned it. *(Mikhoels goes off with Granovsky. To Efros:)* For them I don't exist. I'm not an artist of their "First Category," isn't that correct, Efros?

(Offstage. Sounds of great cheers as Mikhoels and Granovsky enter the room. Murmur of speeches. Chagall strips down to paint, grabbing brushes, is on the verge of making a wild, enraged mess. Green Violinist appears drunken and askew, egging him on. Solo violin.)

BELLA: *(Entering)* Marc? It's almost midnight. Everyone's gathered—there's champagne. Come, let's join them!

CHAGALL: *(Throwing himself into her arms like a hapless child)* They don't love me.

BELLA: What? What's wrong? I do.

CHAGALL: They don't love my paintings. They don't need me. No one needs my paintings in Russia.

BELLA: *(Comforting him)* You're exhausted. You've worked too hard, night after night. Your paintings are needed. People may not understand them yet, but they awaken something . . . a memory of their past . . . a dream they no longer have time for. You'll keep painting . . . *(Stroking Chagall's head in her lap. She sings, "You over the Village," rocking him gently in her arms.)*

Nacht gekumen du bist nisht do.
Fenster tunkl ale gasn leydikh.
Di ki zey shlofn hoikh iber di felder,
Kholemen a shtetl:
Zeygers tick tock
Vign voyen
Toibm fliyn in shtumkayt.
Un aleyn ikh ze dayn shotn,
Vi du flist iber dem shtetl.[1]

Night is come and you are not at home.

Windows dark, and all the streets are empty.

The cows are sleeping, high upon the hilltop,

Dreaming of a village:

Clocks are tocking,

Cradles rocking.

Flocks of doves murmur silence.

All alone I see your shadow,

You are flying over the village.

CHAGALL: But in the darkness I can hear a light,

In your voice I can see a candle,

A breathe of flame and

---

1. Yiddish translation: Zalmen Mlotek.

CHAGALL AND BELLA: We shall be together,
Flickering forever
CHAGALL: waltzing slowly
BELLA: burning holy
BELLA AND CHAGALL: melody of flame.
CHAGALL: Hear it rise so
BELLA AND CHAGALL: Bright,
CHAGALL: into the
BELLA AND CHAGALL: night,
CHAGALL: the burning
BELLA AND CHAGALL: light of our love.
CHAGALL: Where can we go?
BELLA: Wherever you can paint.
CHAGALL: You would come with me? Leave our home?
BELLA: Home is inside. Where we need no documents.
CHAGALL: *(Recovering equilibrium)* Then we'll keep house in my left shoe.

(Zuskin reeling in drunk, trying to find himself)

ZUSKIN: Zuska, Zuskola, where are you? I lost him, damn. Have you seen Zuskin?
CHAGALL: There's a bird stuck in your throat. Open your mouth and sing!
ZUSKIN: *(Crowing)* Oh, here I am! *(Words tumble out.)* Everyone is drunk—even Lunacharsky—the Party—Efros is being promoted. They are embracing Granovsky for his bold pioneering form—Alexei Mikhailovich is making extraordinary speeches—Daniil translating them into Yiddish—and Mikhoels—*(Slight awe)* Mikhoels . . .
MIKHOELS: *(Bounding in)* Here I am!
ZUSKIN: Who'd think this all came from what we did on stage . . . two "schlemiels" . . .
MIKHOELS: Zuska, my little Zuska—I'll tell you a secret—*(Loud whispering in his ear)* Tomorrow we get to do it again—

(They both laugh hysterically. Chagall and Bella watch, already in a different plane.)

ZUSKIN (LANTERN-SQUELCHER): A nice man with a nice briefcase . . . Pray God he needs a little insurance . . .

MIKHOELS (MENAKHEM MENDEL): Oi . . . such a nice man, such a nice briefcase . . . (*Launching into song, hugging, dancing*)

MIKHOELS AND ZUSKIN: We can live forever
If we each insure the other.
A little policy for life
A little income for the wife

(*As Company members enter, they join the song/dance.*)

COMPANY, GRANOVSKY, EFROS, AND EFRAIM: Who knows what will endure.
In the end what is secure?
Is it family? Is it wealth?
Can a pension bring good health?
Is it history? Is it art?
Sign a contract. Let us start.
Anyone who has to die,
We will now exemptify.
Exemptify, exemptify . . .

(*A wild Chagallian tableau vivant by the end of the song. Chagall remains on the periphery watching, as frenzy mounts.*)

We can live forever,
We can all insure each other.
Buy a policy today,
And we can make forever stay. (*3×*)

CHAGALL: (*Amid the second repeat of the chorus*) Silence!

(*The whole stage freezes à la Granovsky, each character in a fantastic pose. Chagall slowly approaches Mikhoels, who softens as Chagall speaks to him.*)

Please keep this for me.

MIKHOELS: What is it?

CHAGALL: (*Pulling an old photograph from his pocket. Green Violinist plays behind: melody of "Steppe Prayer."*) A photograph of the walls my great-
grandfather painted in the Mohilev synagogue—his eternal city. I kept it
with me while I painted the murals. "Blow into me, my bearded grandfather, a few drops of Jewish truth!"

MIKHOELS: (*Bemused as he takes photograph*) Why give it to me?

CHAGALL: This is his home. He does not want to leave.

MIKHOELS: *(His whole face a question, directed at Chagall)* You do?

(Chagall nods.) You're leaving. *(Chagall nods, places both his hands on Mikhoels' cheeks, holding his face.)*

CHAGALL: Warm, eh? Remember?

MIKHOELS: Warm.

CHAGALL: *(Trying to say good-bye)* I have never had a friend . . . who helped me . . . maybe even saved me . . . made me paint, when I was about to give up. With you, I was warm . . . like home . . . with a brother . . .

MIKHOELS: Without you . . . I'll be cold.

CHAGALL: Every night a roomful of people breathe with your every breath. While I walk home alone from the train — through a wasteland — nothing in my hands to feed my wife and child.

MIKHOELS: Half of what I have I give to you.

CHAGALL: Half of nothing is nothing.

(Silence)

MIKHOELS: They'll give you a visa?

CHAGALL: For an exhibit in Paris. I think so.

MIKHOELS: And Bella?

CHAGALL: I'll send for her. What else can I do?

(Silence)

MIKHOELS: You'll come back?

CHAGALL: *(Laughing)* For my paintings. How could I say good-bye?

(Chagall embraces Mikhoels, who takes on the shape of a painting.)
(Green Violinist leads instrumental: "Mural Sleeps." Night colors. Slowly Chagall moves among the Company, passing close to each character. The world loses gravity as Chagall passes. It begins to dream its own dreams. Characters and objects lift and float as in one of his paintings. Chagall kisses Bella like a passionate angel, carries her downstage, out the world of the theatre. Efraim, bright-eyed, comes to life for the New Year's countdown.)

EFRAIM: Comrades, it's almost the New Year!!! Good news! Good news, Comrades! The Party is giving us money for a new stage! More seats! The Party will review the script for our next production. The Party is taking a strong interest in our progress. Let's ring in the New Year! To a great New Year!

(Whole stage comes back to life and "real" time to join Efraim for the countdown. Chagall and Bella are gone.)

ALL: Ten . . . Nine . . . Eight . . . Seven . . . Six . . . *(Switching to Yiddish) Finif . . . Fir . . . Dry . . . Tsvay . . . Ein! (Chaos, ecstasy of congratulations)* Happy New Year! To a joyous year to come . . .

(Lights fade as klezmorim burn up the night and bring in the new dawn. "Green Violin Hora.")

ACT 2
PART I
  Travels of Benjamin III

(Paris. 1928. Théâtre de Boulevard. "Paris Overture." Opening night fracas and excitement. Company warms up on stage, setting final props on the set of Benjamin's village of Tunyadevka, reminiscent of a Chagallian painting. Bella and Chagall enter, elegantly dressed, hurrying to make the curtain.)

BELLA: Marc, we're late.

(He grabs her hand.)

CHAGALL: The light catches your ear. And you are ear-resistible. *(Nibbling her earlobe)*

BELLA: Marc—

CHAGALL: How can I resist your ear?

BELLA: We have to go!

CHAGALL: But I am "ear" . . .

BELLA: They'll hold the show for us—you know they will—we have to be on time!

CHAGALL: Granovsky will have a fit—his Paris opening delayed by five minutes . . .

BELLA: Marc, it's not respectful—

CHAGALL: "Delayed by the late arrival of the well-known French artist and his beautiful poetess wife—"

BELLA: What about the actors? Mikhoels, I'm sure, is dying to see you.

CHAGALL: It seems like he is always with me. How many times have I tried
to repaint the Green Violinist—thinking only of him? And I never get it.
You're right . . . it's time to see the original.

BELLA: Then come along . . .

CHAGALL: Bella, I'm scared . . .

BELLA: Nonsense. *(Seeing Efros from afar, waving)* Efros! Abram Markovich!

(Efros rushes to greet the Chagalls and guide them to their box.)

EFROS: At last! In Paris! Bella! And our famous painter—

CHAGALL: Efros! You are here, there, everywhere!

EFROS: *(Shaking his head)* Six years.

CHAGALL: *(Genuinely moved)* Six years. Look at us—we haven't changed . . .

EFROS: It's a miracle. Paris! A European tour . . .

BELLA: We'll celebrate after! Start the show!

CHAGALL: I'm inviting everyone.

EFROS: Granovsky asked me to tell him the minute you arrived! He can't wait
to see you. *(Exits)*

(A busy Efraim scurries past.)

BELLA: Efraim! Efraimushka! Why don't you say hello!?

CHAGALL: *(Fondly greeting)* Efraim, what are you doing here?

EFRAIM: A tour is only for actors? Who sweeps up? Who gets the tea? Who
speaks for the Party?

CHAGALL: In Paris?

EFRAIM: Of course. Communism is international. It's why I'm here.

CHAGALL: At home the Revolution is still alive?

EFRAIM: *(Proudly)* With Comrade Stalin, Moscow is taking charge. Things are
moving forward. If you came, you'd see.

CHAGALL: I'd come, but they won't give me a visa. Not even to visit my sisters.

EFRAIM: There must be reasons.

CHAGALL: It's an outrage. I'm not a criminal. I'm a world-renowned artist—

EFRAIM: Not in the Soviet Union.

BELLA: We love Russia—you have no idea how we ache—

EFRAIM: *(Politely)* It was your choice to leave.

BELLA: —we ache to see our home. Our family. It's not right—

EFRAIM: No one forced you. You ran away. Didn't even say good-bye. *(Exits)*

(Efros returns with Granovsky.)

GRANOVSKY: Chagall! You look—splendid. Bella. Magnificent. Life in Paris agrees . . . *(Quiet, intense)* Marc, I have to speak with you.

EFROS: Alexsei Mikhailovich, we must begin! We were waiting only for you, my friends . . .

BELLA: *(Squeezing Efros' hand)* Start the show! I can hardly wait.

GRANOVSKY: *(To Chagall, aside)* Chagall . . . speak to Mikhoels.

CHAGALL: What?

GRANOVSKY: *(Urgent)* If Mikhoels returns to Moscow, the company goes with him. If he stays in Paris, everyone will stay. We can't go back. You have no idea what horror is starting to happen. People are being killed.

CHAGALL: Doesn't he understand?

GRANOVSKY: He's an actor. His life is on the stage. Comrade Stalin is methodically eliminating the opposition. You, my dears, should feel happy you left.

CHAGALL: Will you go back?

GRANOVSKY: With a noose around our necks . . . *(Tugs gently on the silk scarf wrapped around his)* Mine is French silk . . . I hope.

EFRAIM: *(Appearing suddenly next to them)* Comrade Granovsky, Comrade Efros conveyed your request that the actors meet with *Monsieur* and *Madame* Chagall after the performance. I warn you, as Party deputy for internal affairs of this theatre, that you will be held entirely responsible for this action . . . The Party is against it . . . *(Pause)* And so am I . . .

CHAGALL: Efraim?

EFRAIM: *(Quiet)* It would be better if you stay away. *(Exits)*

GRANOVSKY: You see how we live? *(Hushed, urgent, to Chagall)* We have offers —a tour to America—films in Berlin. Mikhoels always admired you. Your phenomenal success in the West should convince him. Please . . .

CHAGALL: I'll try . . .

EFROS: Alexei Mikhailovich, let Chagall go so we can begin the show!

GRANOVSKY: Watch the actors, I won't disturb you anymore . . . *(Withdraws)*

EFROS: One minute—*(Ecstatic to Chagalls)* Everything is as it was, but was as it is now! *(Seating them)* Enjoy! Mendele Mokher Sforim's *The Brief Travels of Benjamin the Third.* Mikhoels knows you are here. He sends his regards—he says this performance is for you—his two wanderers. *(Exits)*

(Curtain rises on Mikhoels as "Benjamin" and Zuskin as "Sendrel" in Travels of Benjamin III. *Among the Company is a Russian Peasant with a whip for her oxen.* "Benjamin Sets Off.")

BENJAMIN (MIKHOELS): *(Sung) Sendrel, tsi vaystu vos iz vaiter fun Tunyadevka?* [Sendrel, do you know what's beyond Tunyadevka?] [2]

SENDREL (ZUSKIN): *(Spoken)* Do I know what's beyond our village, Tunyadevka? Ai-ai-ai. A tavern with good vodka!

COMPANY: Ahhhh.

BENJAMIN (MIKHOELS): *(Sung) Nayn, nokh vaiter.* [No, Beyond that!]

SENDREL (ZUSKIN): *(Spoken)* Beyond that? I don't know, Binyomin.

BENJAMIN (MIKHOELS): *(Sung) E-e-e-retz Yisruel. Mit alle haylikher erter.* [The land of Israel with all the holy places]

COMPANY: *E-e-e-retz Yisruel! Mit alle haylikher erter.*

BENJAMIN (MIKHOELS): *(Sung)* Yes. And I will go there. Sendrel, will you come with me?

SENDREL (ZUSKIN): *(Sung)* Benjamin, you're crazy! *(Spoken)* How could the two of us travel? We have no money!

BENJAMIN (MIKHOELS) AND SENDREL (ZUSKIN): *(Simultaneous realization)* Steal from our wives.

CHAGALL: Ah-h-h-h-h.

SENDREL (ZUSKIN): But we have no horses?

BENJAMIN (MIKHOELS): Together we have four feet.

SENDREL (ZUSKIN): *(Sendrel counting)* One two three four—feet!

RUSSIAN PEASANT: I'll give you a lift, you two little yids. *(Peasant cracks whip and exits)*

SENDREL (ZUSKIN): But Benya, I'm afraid to cross the street. Even in Tunyadevka.

BENJAMIN (MIKHOELS): Sendrel, my dearest friend,
We will not part
'Til journey's end.
Our road is long,
Our road is hard.
But I will lead us,
To lands afar.

---

2. Yiddish translation: Zalmen Mlotek.

(Two wanderers set off together, bundles on their shoulders, gazing into the distance.)

We'll climb dark mountains,
We'll find lost tribes.
We'll cross rough seas,
We'll chart the skies.
We'll find the river of Sambotyan.
We'll reach our dream,
We'll find our home.
There are no strangers, only friends.
In Eretz Yisruel our journey ends.

SENDREL (ZUSKIN): *(Spoken over underscoring)* I go with you, my Binyomin.
    So many places I have not been. I'll never fear, if you're with me.

BENJAMIN AND SENDREL: *(Sung)* We'll make our journey
As it's meant to be.
There are no strangers, only friends.
In Eretz Yisruel, in Eretz Yisruel, Our journey ends.

(Lights fade. Applause. Music continues under scene change: wanderers walking toward the Promised Land. In theatre box: Chagall clapping, Bella seated beside him. Granovsky appears beside them, whispering to Chagall.)

GRANOVSKY: When Mikhoels heard the Party didn't want you meeting with
    us, he yelled and said he wouldn't go on stage. He got them to agree to it,
    but they will never forgive us. There's going to be a big scandal . . . Cha-
    gall, only you can save this theatre . . . and Mikhoels . . .

BELLA: *(Turning away from stage)* What's wrong?

CHAGALL: Nothing . . . Let's watch the show . . .

(Moon rises. Benjamin and Sendrel have set down their bundles and are going to sleep. Intoned speech.)

BENJAMIN (MIKHOELS): *A gute nacht.*

SENDREL (ZUSKIN): *Gute nacht, Binyomin. Du schlofst?*

BENJAMIN (MIKHOELS): *Schlof. (Pause) Sendrel. Du schlofst?*

SENDREL (ZUSKIN): *Schlof. A gute nacht.*

BENJAMIN (MIKHOELS): *Gute nacht.*

(In theatre box)

BELLA: *(Whispering to Chagall, nearly in tears)* I feel like I am home. My mother tucking me into bed. The sheets smell of winter.

CHAGALL: *(Kisses her forehead)* Gute nacht . . .

BELLA: *Gute nacht . . .*

(Big lush music, exotic motif: "Dream of the Promised Land." A parade of half-men and beasts: camels, palm trees, and a peppernutter *(dinosaur/creature); no goats. Alexander the Great and royal entourage, waving welcome to our heroes.)*

SENDREL (ZUSKIN): Benjamin, Benjamin—Look how beautiful it is here!!!

BENJAMIN (MIKHOELS): Look!!! We have arrived in the Promised Land!!! Look, Sendrel—they are welcoming us!

Their brother Benjamin from Tunyadevka.

SENDREL (ZUSKIN): A guest like you is nothing to sneeze at, Benjamin.

(In theatre box)

CHAGALL: *(To Bella)* Do you know what they are playing?

BELLA: What?

CHAGALL: It's about their return to Russia.

(Exotic vision and creatures have vanished. Benjamin and Sendrel waking with their heads on their bundles.)

BENJAMIN (MIKHOELS): Wake up!

SENDREL (ZUSKIN): Wake up!

BENJAMIN (MIKHOELS): Bugs.

SENDREL (ZUSKIN): Ai! Bugs.

BENJAMIN (MIKHOELS): It's normal.

SENDREL (ZUSKIN): Normal. *(Pause)* Benya, I had such a dream.

BENJAMIN (MIKHOELS): Sendrel, I had such a dream. I saw you.

SENDREL (ZUSKIN): I saw you.

BENJAMIN (MIKHOELS): Quick. Spit three times.

SENDREL (ZUSKIN) AND BENJAMIN (MIKHOELS): Tfu—tfu—tfu.

BENJAMIN (MIKHOELS): Are we awake?

SENDREL (ZUSKIN): Where are we?

BENJAMIN (MIKHOELS): The desert.

SENDREL (ZUSKIN): Benya, I can't go on. I'm scared. I feel like I am dying.

BENJAMIN (MIKHOELS): Let's pray for strength. *(Gets Sendrel on his feet)*

(They walk forward to edge of stage, looking out to the horizon; silence, then sing "Steppe Prayer." They sing their separate meditations simultaneously.)

SENDREL	BENJAMIN
Zul shoyn kumin di geyulah	Why do you stay so far away?
Mesheekh kumt shoyn bald.	Why do we call and you do not answer?
Rebeynu shel oylem meshiekh Ben David	Our foe is near, we're all alone.
Rebeynu shel oylem meshiekh Ben David	Can you hear us? Our hopeful song.
Oy zolshoyn kumen	And if you hear us why won't you answer?
Zolshoyn kumen di geyulah	We hear your silence. Could we be wrong?
Di geyulah meshiekh	Why do we call and you not answer?
Ben David[3]	Why do you stay so far from us?

(Sound of whipping/beating off stage. Disturbing violin underscores.)

RUSSIAN PEASANT (VOICE): *(To Ox)* Get! Get on! On with you! Get on! Get!

BENJAMIN (MIKHOELS): Aiiiiiii! Did you hear? A wild killer. Run!

SENDREL (ZUSKIN): Benya, I'm dying.

RUSSIAN PEASANT (VOICE): Who's there?

BENJAMIN (MIKHOELS): *(Panic)* Me too. I'm going with you. *(Lies next to Sendrel)*

RUSSIAN PEASANT: Hoo-hoo-hoo! What have we here? The two little Yids from Tunyadevka—lying in the field. Crazy. Probably drunk. *(Sound of laughter. Whipping/beating ox)* Get on! Go on. Go on.

(Benjamin and Sendrel lying on ground as voice fades. Granovsky watching behind Chagall and Bella.)

GRANOVKSY: That's *my* ending. Now the finale for our Comrades at home. Mikhoels made it up.

---

3. Let the redemption come. Messiah will come soon. Master of the universe, Messiah, son of David.

(Music swells. Benjamin and Sendrel in the field.)

SENDREL (ZUSKIN): Benjamin, look where we've ended up! The turnip field. It smells like the pigs and we're still in our village.

BENJAMIN (MIKHOELS): It's true, Sendrel, here we are.

SENDREL (ZUSKIN): Benya! How can it be? Our dream nothing? No Promised Land—no palm trees—no carobs, no dates—*(They sing "The World Is Round.")*

BENJAMIN (MIKHOELS): We are home, my dear friend,
A place we know far too well:
Ravaged skies, cold and gray,
Empty stomach eats the day.
Sunk in mud, lost to pain,
Can we find our dream again?
We are two birds
Who've known the sky
Why are we afraid to fly?
It's up to us to conquer fear.
The Promised Land is here.
We will create the dream that we saw.
We'll live a life, a life of awe:
Awe of our village,
Beauty in all we meet.
We are two men
Come home to stay.
Why, you ask, did we go away?

SENDREL (ZUSKIN): Tell me, why did we leave?

BENJAMIN (MIKHOELS): To learn where we are from.

SENDREL (ZUSKIN): Tell me, why were we lost?

BENJAMIN (MIKHOELS): To find our way home.

SENDREL (ZUSKIN): Tell me, why were we scared?

BENJAMIN (MIKHOELS): To learn we have courage.

SENDREL (ZUSKIN): Tell me, why have we come back home?

BENJAMIN (MIKHOELS) AND SENDREL (ZUSKIN): Now, upon our return,
We will teach what we had to learn:
The world is round, around we roam
To find ourselves home.

(Curtain. Wild applause. Zuskin, Efros, and the whole company of actors/musicians pour out from back stage to greet Chagall and Bella. Still half in costume and makeup, rattling tambourines, cartwheels, and headstands, they tumble toward Chagall and Bella, surround them adoringly. Tearful, joyous reunion. A circus on a dime. All trying to talk at once, a cacophonous happy burble. Lines overlap. Efraim is silent, watching.)

CHAGALL AND BELLA: My paintings! You were fantastic! Magnificent! *(Etc.)*

ACTORS AND MUSICIANS: Bravo Chagall!!! Chagall! Chagall!! Our own Chagall! The celebrated artist! Toast of Paris! *(Etc.)*

CHAGALL: Paris adores you! I *loved* the performance!

BELLA: The actors brought me to tears!

CHAGALL: Where's Mikhoels?

ACTORS AND MUSICIANS: Bravo Chagall!!! Chagall! Chagall!!

ZUSKIN: You should have seen us in Berlin—they went crazy.

EFROS: The public who came! We met the great playwright Asch! We met Asch! Chaim Weizmann.

ZUSKIN: Audiences on their feet for hours!

MARIA: Can you believe we meet in Paris!

DANIIL: Your name on the finest lips—

EFROS: When we first got off the train in Poland—it was Passover, imagine, we hadn't celebrated in years. Religion died with the Revolution!

MARIA: Your paintings in every museum in Europe!

EFROS: We were met by some cousins of Zuska's and taken to a seder!

ZUSKIN: Berlin, Prague, Krakow—

MARIA: Moscow is lonely for you!

IOSIF: A Jew is a Jew no matter where he hangs his hat.

MARIA: Come back!

ZUSKIN: It has been too long . . .

CHAGALL: I'm glad you remember me!

EFROS: A seder! We had forgotten how good it is . . . our own food . . .

(Zuskin looks at Efraim, silently watching.)

ZUSKIN: Forget about it.

MARIA: The food, Marc Zakharovich, I've died and gone to heaven . . .

DANIIL: Granovsky took us to parties . . .

IOSIF: In Berlin . . . mm-mm-mm . . .

DANIIL: We were so hungry.

MARIA: We saw the beautiful portrait of Bella . . .

CHAGALL: Which one?

BELLA: He's painted hundreds!

CHAGALL: Where's Mikhoels?

EFROS: At the seder I was a child again singing: *(Sings) Chad gad yo . . . Chad gad yo . . . (Etc.)*

(Zuskin trying to catch Efros' eye to stop the joyous outpouring)

BELLA: The song at the end of the seder!

EFROS, DANIIL, AND BELLA: *(Singing) Chad gad yo—Chad gad yo—(Etc.)*

ZUSKIN: Shh.

EFROS, DANIIL, AND BELLA: *Chad gad yo—*

ZUSKIN: Enough.

(Efraim stands, quiet, observant.)

EFRAIM: Comrades, you forget yourselves . . . religion is no longer necessary for the new Soviet Jew.

ZUSKIN: No cousins of mine.

EFROS: What are you talking about—your father's nephew—

ZUSKIN: *(Sharp to Efros, looking at Efraim)* No cousins. No seder. *(Starts clapping, singing to cover. Musicians join in.)*

Now is the time when we all meet again,

Too many years, the years have come between us.

Too many sorrows and joys we have to own.

Now is a time when we greet and we toast our old friends!

Too many hours they have spent too much alone.

BELLA: I've been so lonely, so lonely

For our friends and for our home.

My heart is with you,

No matter where we go

How far we roam.

We'll find a country,

A land where we can sing and be with friends.

A time together, forever,

Is where our journey ends.

ZUSKIN AND BELLA: But time will vanish in the air,
Soon this moment won't be there.
Throw your hands up—
And catch a rhythm.
Dance a *freylekhs* if you dare.

(Mikhoels enters unnoticed, comes behind Chagall, covers his eyes with his hands. Granovsky follows. Efraim watches.)

MIKHOELS: Guess who?

CHAGALL: I know by your hands.

(They hug each other. Everyone falls silent.)

MIKHOELS: Marc Zakharovich, it has been too long. Bella . . . Beautiful Bella . . .

BELLA: Solomon Mikhailovich, your voice brought me home!

MIKHOELS: Bella, Bella, Bella, we have so many songs to sing!

CHAGALL: Menakhem Mendel comes to Paris! But your eye—remember I wanted to tear out your eye—

MIKHOELS: I know, I know. I have two eyes, what can I do? We work as best we can without you. I beg the chief here everyday to allow us to express a few emotions on stage—

GRANOVSKY: Any more emotion and I won't be able to eat my supper!

ZUSKIN: I'll eat it for you, Alexei Mikhailovich.

GRANOVSKY: I miss you, Chagall—it's hard for pathos to leak through seven layers of green paint.

MIKHOELS: Remember, Chagall—our song—when there was nothing to eat in Moscow—

MARIA: *(Joyous)* There is still nothing to eat in Moscow!

MIKHOELS: *(Mikhoels starts to move, singing "The Nothing Song.")*
I want nothing! Much more nothing!
Nothing for lunch or for supper!
Nothing's a feast for a beggar!
Hole in my stomach, what can I do?
Half of what I have, I give to you.

(Chagall dances with Mikhoels. All clapping. Granovsky silent as stone. Zuskin has slipped off to where Efraim is standing.)

CHAGALL: Give me nothing! Half of nothing!
Nothing will feed such a hunger.
Nothing's a meal with a brother.
Forkful of air—we just don't care—
Half of my nothing is yours to share.
ZUSKIN: We have done nothing wrong!
EFRAIM: Liaisons with foreigners. Parties. Seders—meetings with prominent
    Zionists. Now the artist Chagall—
ZUSKIN: We rehearse, we perform, and do our diplomatic duties—
EFRAIM: Scandals are being reported in the Moscow papers every day.
ZUSKIN: What will happen to our families—
MIKHOELS: Zuska!!! Your verse!
EFRAIM: Go home and find out!

(Efros crosses to Efraim.)

ZUSKIN AND MIKHOELS: *(Sung)* Give us wind, the sound of a horn
Give us a hole of a bagel.
Give us a bottle without a top,
And we'll put a song on the table.
EFROS: This is not the place. We'll have a company meeting tomorrow.
EFRAIM: Tomorrow is too late. Everyone must pack tonight.
EFROS: What?
EFRAIM: Orders from Moscow. I purchased the tickets home.
MIKHOELS: I gotta hole in my pocket
ZUSKIN: See this hole—my left shoe's sole—
CHAGALL: A hole, plus a hole will make us whole—
ZUSKIN, MIKHOELS, AND CHAGALL: Show us a hole and we'll mock it!
Nothing's mine—nothing's yours.
Nothing will keep us together.
ALL: Nothing will keep us together.
Nothing we have we cannot lose,
Nothing is ours forever!
Nai-da-da-dee-dai-dai-na-da-dee-dai . . . *(Etc.)*

EFROS: Who runs this company?

EFRAIM: I am only responsible for purchasing the tickets home.

EFROS: You do what you are told!

EFRAIM: I do what my conscience tells me!

GRANOVSKY: *(Savage, taking center)* No more nothing, we have something—
Something that keeps us together,
Something that joins us forever,
Something we have, that we must not lose—

(Breaks off—silence)

They are trying to take this theatre away from me. Putting people in the administration to watch me. I don't have the constitution for it. Forgive me.

MIKHOELS: Alexei Mikhailovich, we won't let them—the two of us, Efros, the whole company is with you . . .

EFROS: Together we will triumph over short-minded bureaucrats.

MIKHOELS: When we return—but right now I want to hear from Chagall—

(Chagall is silent.)

GRANOVSKY: When? If! If we go back, we may never be able to leave! Don't you understand!? *(Pause. Desperate.)* There is a whole world to create!

MIKHOELS: And there is Russia. Everyone has a place where they are born.

GRANOVSKY: Chagall, tell him!

EFROS: *(To Company)* What are we to do? *(Pause)* Become exotic imports? Granovsky's naïf little Jews from the East? We are building a significant culture for our people in the Soviet Union—

GRANOVSKY: Not for the people—it's the government that summons you back —to show the world that you belong to them.

EFROS: Maybe . . . but our audiences are waiting for us in Moscow . . . and you.

BELLA: Why won't they give Marc a visa!!! Why? Aren't we all free people? Marc's paintings are Russia. Why can't we even visit our old home?

MIKHOELS: In Soviet eyes . . . you defected. That is forever.

(Chagall is silent.)

GRANOVSKY: *(Desperately clutching Mikhoels)* Stay here with me! With Chagall! We'll create a new theatre the likes of which Paris has never seen.

EFRAIM: Now you have overstepped.

GRANOVSKY: With Chagall we can make extraordinary productions.

EFRAIM: Impossible! Art does not exist in a vacuum.

GRANOVSKY: Who is in my company? Mikhoels?

EFROS: *(Overlapping Granovsky)* Do not divide us!

GRANOVSKY: Zuskin? Maria? Iosif? Daniil? Mikhoels?

EFRAIM: *(Overlapping, waving tickets)* I have the tickets home right here!!! We leave tomorrow!!!

EFROS: No action will be taken until I say so!

ZUSKIN: *(Overlapping)* We'll be cut off from our families—

MIKHOELS: We must go back to Moscow—

GRANOVSKY: Chagall—

(Chagall is silent.)

Chagall!

CHAGALL: *(Quiet)* We each decide our own fate.

GRANOVSKY: Chagall—tell him! There's a lifetime's work ahead. Berlin. New York. Paris. Life here is abundant. Bright. Fragrant. If you need Russian audience—Paris is full of Russians and there are plenty of samovars . . .

MIKHOELS: *(To Chagall)* Marc . . . Moscow is the city . . . where our theatre was born . . .

GRANOVSKY: I drink the air here like the French drink wine . . .

MIKHOELS: We fought to create a theatre—for people who remain in Moscow . . .

EFROS: *(Almost breaking)* Marc, they've given us a brand new theatre—a stage the size we always wanted . . . we'll have our own theatre school . . . a new generation of brilliant young actors . . .

GRANOVSKY: All of which they are trying to destroy, eating away at our theatre like so many rats. You think Russians care about Jews. Ha! About your Yiddish culture! Ha! I am going to Berlin to work in Germany, in a civilized environment.

MIKHOELS: The world is round, Alexei Mikhailovich. Round. We will meet again in Moscow.

GRANOVSKY: *(Furious, pushing Mikhoels away)* Go back to your Tunyadevka! GO! See if I care! See if I suffer one whit! Go! GO!

(Granovsky tosses white silk scarf elegantly around his neck, signals musicians. Sings "Exile" in the manner of an elegant cabaret singer)

I depart from any party
With no feelings of regret.
I hear a distant laughter:
All the friends I could have met.
The past I leave behind me
Like smoke from a cigar.
The future I inhale—
It alone knows who we are.
Ya-da-dai-dai-de-da-da *(Etc.)*

(Granovsky exits. Silence.)

MIKHOELS: *(Achingly to Chagall and Bella)* Please help him. Chagall, Bella . . . look after Granovsky for me.

EFRAIM: Granovsky is from a privileged background, contacts abroad. He is not to be trusted with our revolutionary ideals.

MIKHOELS: *(Furious, lashing out)* Granovsky is to be trusted—loved. He is a great artist. And our leader.

(Silence.)

How can we continue without him?

EFROS: *(At a loss)* They'll impose some artistic leadership.

EFRAIM: *(Quiet)* What about . . . comrade Mikhoels? He runs many of the rehearsals already. Coaches the actors. Even suggests our plays. I keep an accurate record of the movement for each performance in my scripts . . . down to every count.

EFROS: It's true, what he says . . .

MIKHOELS: No.

EFROS: So we'll just abandon all of our work now . . .

ZUSKIN: *(Speaking for the Company)* . . . abandon us?

MIKHOELS: *(Searching)* Chagall, Chagall . . .

CHAGALL: *(Sings)* You're traveling on a train; do you know where?

MIKHOELS: *(Quiet)* No.

(Company quietly echoes: "Nooooooooo," à la Agents.)

EFRAIM: Yes. We do. Home to our theatre.

EFROS: Where Mikhoels will take on artistic leadership.

COMPANY: Yes. Mikhoels. *(Etc.)*

MIKHOELS: *(To Chagall)* You see, Chagall, I'm being given a new role—

CHAGALL: The play is rotten—the stage will collapse under your feet—

MIKHOELS: Well then, it'll happen in front of an audience.

ZUSKIN: And they may even laugh if you time it right, Solomon Mikhailovich.

MIKHOELS: With an audience, I get the better of any play. *(As he speaks the text he raises his right hand in a gesture from* Benjamin III, *palm facing forward:)* "If I forget you, O Jerusalem, let my right hand wither . . . Let my tongue cleave to the roof of my mouth, if I do not remember you . . ." 137th Psalm. My character never speaks those words on stage, it's here. *(Holding up his palm)* The psalm of my hand.

CHAGALL: And who do you think will hear it . . . this hand of yours?

ZUSKIN: *(Making his hand speak like a jester's puppet, high gibberish, barely intelligible version of psalm)* "If I forget thee oh Jerusalem . . ."

MIKHOELS: Would you rather I keep it my pocket? Counting my change?

ZUSKIN: *(Hand continues squawking)* "One franc, two franc, three franc, four . . ."

CHAGALL: Let your talents serve whomever you will!

MIKHOELS: I shall. *(Hand agrees, pats Mikhoels on shoulder; Mikhoels strokes it.)*

EFROS: *(Shaking his head, smiling)* We're speaking to different times now, different ears.

CHAGALL: My paintings have one voice—they answer to no one but me.

MIKHOELS: *(Dead serious)* I want to live in a country where there are no rich and no poor . . . Where all nationalities live together . . . undivided . . . where Yiddish can be spoken as freely as . . . French.

CHAGALL: A beautiful vision . . .

MIKHOELS: Give us the courage to live it.

(Turns to leave. Chagall grabs Mikhoels with great force, as if to never let him go.)

CHAGALL: You'll break my heart, Shloyme.

(Mikhoels loosens Chagall's grasp.)

MIKHOELS: The world is round, Chagall. We'll meet again. *(Sings)*
And time will vanish in the air,
Soon this moment won't be there.
Throw your hands up—

And catch a rhythm.

Dance a *freylekhs* if you dare.

MIKHOELS AND COMPANY: Nothing's mine—nothing's yours.

Nothing will keep us together.

Nothing will keep us together.

Nothing we have we cannot lose,

Nothing is ours forever!

Yai-di-di-dai-dai-yai-dai . . . *(Etc.)*

(Mikhoels exits with whole company singing "The Nothing Song." As they walk upstage, deeper into the mural, Bella runs after them. From the set of Benjamin III, *she grabs a little red house from the village before it disappears. Holding it in her arms, she walks forward and shows it to Chagall.)*

BELLA: *(Strong)* Our house is empty, Chagall. Fill it—weddings on the ceiling. Births. Funerals. Paint, Marc.

("Green Violin Hora" [reprise] explodes—dancers whirl, creating a maelstrom around Chagall. Green Violinist appears next to Chagall, a relentless force turning the world on its head.)

PART 3

  The Terror, or King Lear

(Chagall's New York studio. Chagall is alone with a huge, empty canvas. As Green Violinist plays, actors from the Company appear swirling in his memory; Efraim comes closer than the rest.)

CHAGALL: *(Over music)* What am I to paint? Moscow, 1941 . . .

EFRAIM: Moscow, 1941. Red Square in the snow . . . a parade . . . soldiers heading off to the front . . . the great leader Joseph Stalin stands on the mausoleum . . . saluting his country's chosen sons.

CHAGALL: I am French.

EFRAIM: Moscow, 1941. A world torn by war. Stalin leads the battle against Hitler. You move to New York! Poof! No longer French! You aren't American. Who are you?

CHAGALL: Bella! BELLA!

EFRAIM: I know what you are . . . *(Disappears)*

(Bella stands on threshold holding an unlit candle.)

BELLA: What? What's wrong?

CHAGALL: He was here again. I saw him . . .

BELLA: Who?

CHAGALL: Efraim.

BELLA: You live in your imagination, your dreams—without them who would you be?

CHAGALL: We ran away . . . we escaped . . .

BELLA: *(Outburst)* . . . we arrived in New York the day Hitler invaded Russia! German troops storming down the streets of our village as we see the Statue of Liberty in the harbor! And we are safe. *(She lights the candle next to where Chagall is painting.)* What is left of our families?

CHAGALL: Forgive me . . . Bella . . . I shouldn't have spoken.

BELLA: *(Stands behind Chagall)* In New York I am a ghost, whose life continues elsewhere . . .

CHAGALL: I will paint you . . . a red angel over my shoulder . . .

BELLA: Keep me with you. Paint.

(Green Violinist plays as the world of Moscow, 1941, swirls around Chagall: "The Storm." Scenes, songs, silences, and images from Part 1 reappear, twisted by the storm.)

EFRAIM: Moscow, 1941. On the stage of the State Yiddish Theatre: *Keneg Lear*. Mikhoels' greatest role: the raging king who challenges the heavens, a tyrant in a tempest. *(Rattles a thunder sheet)*

(Mikhoels in King Lear costume in front of mirror, putting on a wig, preparing to go on stage. Behind him, Zuskin makes a gesture from Agents, blowing on window to clean it to see his reflection. Mikhoels echoes. They communicate through mirror.)

MIKHOELS: Zuska, I have a rheum.

ZUSKIN: A large room?

MIKHOELS: A cold of colossal proportions. *(Coughs and sneezes)* I'm going to splatter the whole audience. Who's in the first row?

ZUSKIN: Some big goose from the interior security office and several of his goslings.

MIKHOELS: I'll aim for the second . . .

ZUSKIN: More there too . . . and the third . . .

MIKHOELS: Oh I forgot . . . this is a command performance for one of our internal organs . . . .

ZUSKIN: Sneeze on me . . . I'm a fool, I can wipe it off.

MIKHOELS: Better just give me a handkerchief.

ZUSKIN: I'll show you how King Lear sneezes. *(Does a huge exaggerated sneeze. Mikhoels laughs.)*

(Efros and Efraim enter, mid-conversation.)

EFRAIM: Mikhoels never misses a performance.

EFROS: He's doing too much—he should go home.

EFRAIM: We all make sacrifices.

EFROS: You'll kill him with all these performances. Ten Workers' Clubs in five days?

EFRAIM: We have a plan to fulfill.

EFROS: It's inhuman. *(Stands next to Mikhoels, who holds his hand: "I'm fine.")* He's in Committee meetings all day—speeches—*(Mikhoels' hand: "I'm fine, I'm fine. Not to worry.")* And he goes on as Lear every other night—

EFRAIM: What is a theatre if it does not perform? Are you going to walk out in front of the curtain tonight and tell our audience to go home because we are "sick?" The whole country is making sacrifices, and you, the leader of this theatre, cancel a performance because we are "sick?" Perhaps *you* should go home, Comrade Efros. It's very possible that you are overtaxed by this work. *(Tense silence. Mikhoels holds Efros' hand, then lets go. Efros exits.)*

MIKHOELS: Efraim, bring me hot tea with lemon.

(Efraim exits. Mikhoels and Zuskin look at their reflections in the mirror.)

ZUSKIN: *(Into mirror)* Benya, I'm scared . . . without you . . . what would happen to the theatre?

MIKHOELS: *(Sings from* Benjamin III) "Sendrel, my dearest friend,
We will not part 'til journey's end . . ."

EFRAIM: *(Handing Mikhoels tea)* It's Lear tonight.

MIHKEOLS: Thank you, Efraim. It was a joke. Even Shakespeare has jokes.

EFRAIM: Very funny. *(Exits)*

ZUSKIN: We're allowed to say them on stage.

MIKHOELS: Shakespeare spoke Yiddish! Shakespeare's now our Yiddish bard —
speaking for all those whose texts we can no longer perform. Shakespeare
escapes the censors in any language. Fool, what say you?

ZUSKIN: Only a fool speaks his own words.

MIKHOELS: Dost thou call me a fool, boy?

ZUSKIN (FOOL): I prithee, nuncle, keep a schoolmaster that can teach thy fool
to lie: I would fain learn to lie.

MIKHOELS (LEAR): An you lie, sirrah, we'll have you whipped.

ZUSKIN (FOOL): I marvel what kin thou and thy daughters are: they'll have
me whipped for speaking true, thou'lt have me whipped for lying, and
sometimes I am whipped for holding my peace. I had rather be any kind
o' thing than a fool: and yet I would not be thee, nuncle; thou hast pared
thy wit o' both sides and left nothing i'the middle.

EFRAIM: Places.

ZUSKIN: Efraim! My cap!

MIKHOELS: Where are my shoes?

EFRAIM: You'll be stark raving mad soon. You don't need shoes.

MIKHOELS: What scene?

EFRAIM: Banished by his daughters, the old king wanders the heath. *(Rattles
thunder sheet)* The storm.

*(Led by Green Violinist, again a swirl of images appears before Chagall. Lear
[Mikhoels] and the Fool [Zuskin] stand center, caught in the eye of the storm. A
man is buffeted by wind as a huge umbrella turns inside out. Granovsky, dressed
only in a tallis wrapped around his waist, leans into the storm, a wanderer. He
slowly crosses upstage, through the hurricane.)*

LEAR (MIKHOELS): Blow, winds, and crack your cheeks! Rage! Blow!
You cataracts and hurricanoes, spout
Till you have drench'd our steeples, drown'd the cocks!
You sulphurous and thought-executing fires,
Vaunt-couriers to oak-cleaving thunderbolts,
Singe my white head! And thou, all shaking thunder,
Smite flat the thick rotundity o' the world!
Crack nature's moulds, all germins spill at once
That make ingrateful man!

(During Lear scene, Efraim shows two police [Maria and Daniil] to the theatre office, where Efros sits working at the desk. Efraim leaves them. As Efros sees them approach, he reaches for phone, but they twist his arm behind his back and silence him. They quietly collect papers into a briefcase and exit with Efros. The desk is clean. The violence is smooth, routine.)

FOOL (ZUSKIN): *(Sings) Un ver es farmogt khotch a tropele markh,*
Tra la la . . . meg der regn shoyn gisn
Un shtromen un fleytsn . . . er vil gornit visn . . .
Der regn meg shmaysn batog un banakht.
[He that has just a little bit of wisdom —
Tra-la-la — let the rain pour
And flow and flood that he shouldn't know from it
And the rain should come and hit us day and night.]

EFROS: *(Screams as he is removed)* Mikhoels!

EFRAIM: *(To Mikhoels)* Comrade Efros . . . was collected for questioning.

MIKHOELS: What? *(Mikhoels abruptly exits to office, where he begins phoning. Leaving Zuskin to continue singing "The Fool's Song.")*

ZUSKIN: He that has a little tiny wit,
With hey, ho, the wind and the rain,
Must make content with his fortunes fit,
Though the rain it raineth every day.

(Zuskin is escorted offstage by those who took Efros.)

MIKHOELS: *(In theatre office, dials phone #1)* This is Mikhoels, Solomon Mikhoels — State Theatre — give me Comrade Morozhenko — I can't wait, I have to go on stage — get him. *(Holding #1, dials #2. Efraim standing by, livid — Mikhoels glowering at him.)* Efraim, tea, lemon. *(Efraim exits. Into #2)* This is Mikhoels — give me the prefect — there's been a mistake — yes mistake I said — *(Back on line #1)* Morozhenko, look into your subordinates' work — they've taken my managing director — yes I understand — a minute? — I have but a minute *(Into #2)* Then release him — I'll wait until you find the record. *(Holding #1 and 2, dialing #3)* Mashenka — Mashenka — a minute — *(Into #2)* Mikhoels, Solomon Mikhoels — so glad you liked the role — yes, I have a little problem, not to trouble you — yes, I'll come by after the show — *(Hangs up #2)*

EFRAIM: *(With tea)* You'll miss your cue.

MIKHOELS: Go then, and make more thunder—*(Efraim exits.)* "Thou art a boil, a plague-sore, an embossed carbuncle in my corrupted blood." *(Into phone #1)* Ah excuse me—yes, Comrade Zolen, wonderful. I'll give him a call . . . I should mention I am president of the Jewish Anti-Fascist Committee . . . mention your name . . . thank you. *(Hangs up #1, into #3)* Mashenka—Mashenka, I know the apartment is tidy, but the time has come to clean—your husband Efros keeps a messy desk. *(Quietly)* No tears, Mashenka. I memorized his odes. You know his sonnets. He will be back tonight—in time to walk the dog. *(Hangs up—swigs tea. Takes off wig.)* O let me not be mad, not mad, sweet heaven! *(Exits)*

(Chagall watches as the Green Violinist plays and visions appear and disappear around him. Dogfight—two dogs locked into each other [Daniil and Iosif]—savage. Mikhoels enters, leading Efros, whom he has just freed. Late night, street.)

EFROS: *(Falling into his arms)* Thank you, my friend . . . if such words have meaning . . .

MIKHOELS: Good to be insured for a couple of poems. *(Silence)*

EFROS: Mikhoels, be careful. The hatred in that room. They called me a Zionist traitor.

MIKHOELS: It's a popular phrase these days . . .

EFROS: Zionist?

MIKHOELS: Traitor . . . Zionist . . . to them it's one and the same . . .

EFROS: I said: "I'm not a traitor . . . I work for the Soviet State." Then the one behind me hit me on the back of my neck and said: "You'll be whom we tell you to be." He asked me to repeat: "I am a Zionist traitor."

MIKHOELS: Did you?

EFROS: Yes. He had a gun. Then they hit me harder. There was a phone call . . . some other people came in . . . and it stopped. If it weren't for you, I never would have come out . . .

MIKHOELS: As our friend Granovsky would say: "Silence!"

EFROS: Be careful . . . please, Mikhoels. They know all about us. The man who beat me read my poems.

MIKHOELS: But they need us now . . . They are sending me to America.

(Music: "Green Violin Hora." Chagall watches as Efraim appears, handing Mikhoels a jacket, hat. Mikhoels changes into official Soviet suit.)

EFRAIM: Mikhoels—president of the Soviet Jewish Anti-Fascist Committee— sent to America by Comrade Stalin on a mission to raise money for the glorious Soviet Red Army. A great man—

MIKHOELS: *(Fragments of his speech, recorded, as he changes into suit jacket)* "I speak of things you would rather not hear in America. Of women pulling ploughs, of soap made from human flesh."

"The history of a people is in danger!"

"The Soviet Red Army is the first line of defense for humanity."

(Mikhoels, fully dressed, is lowered by dancers onto a set of crutches. Efraim places stand-up microphone in front of Mikhoels.)

EFRAIM: New York, 1943. Solomon Mikhoels. A speech to the American Jewish Council for War Relief.

(Bright lights. Camera flashes. Mikhoels on crutches, making a speech. Efraim watches from side. Chagall watches. The conclusion of a brilliant oration.)

MIKHOELS: *(Delivered to great hall)* Unity is not a word, it is a necessity. Unity is action, unity is battle. Unity of American and Soviet Jews in the war against fascism and Nazism today gives us victory, and tomorrow peace! *(Ovations, etc.)*

CHAGALL: Mikhoels!

(Chagall's New York studio after speech. Large empty canvas with outline of crucifix flies in behind the long table. Pile of sketches on the table.)

BELLA: Shloyme, come rest your broken bones! You've been standing on one foot for hours.

CHAGALL: We'll drink the night into morning. How can you leave us!? *(Mikhoels nods toward Efraim.)* Efraim too, of course.

BELLA: Solomon Mikhailovich, you must be starved.

MIKHOELS: What are you painting, Chagall? That's what I'm hungry for.

CHAGALL: *(Gesturing to the table)* Your meal. Take whatever you like . . .

MIKHOELS: *(Hungrily looking at sketches, taking them in)* I couldn't afford one —eh Marc Zakharovich—eh? Your prices are too high.

CHAGALL: The whole table is yours. Take it. I work like in a tornado . . . fighting the elements . . . Every morning I expect it all to be destroyed . . . to come into the studio and find blank walls. At night I don't paint—but sit in the dark waiting—Bella stays up with her candles, writing . . .

BELLA: We live in the eye of a storm. All the memories of my childhood are coming to me . . . my Papa, my Mama . . . speaking to me in my native tongue. I started to write it down so as not to lose my mind . . . Last night my mother whispered to me: "A star will fall . . . turn into a snowflake on your tongue and melt in your throat . . ." I got so frightened . . .

MIKHOELS: If you're scared, you must sing.

BELLA: *(Touching her throat)* My throat hurts . . .

MIKHOELS: *(Half sung, with great love)* Bella, Bella, Bella, Bella . . . so many songs we must sing together. *(Pointing to huge blank canvas)* And what is this? *(Chagall hands him a sketch.)*

CHAGALL: I am being criticized for painting crucifixes. But I recognize our people on the cross. My friends.

(Silence)

BELLA: *(Breaking mood)* Solomon Mikhailovich must eat. I will light the candles. To celebrate this last night together.

MIKHOELS: Bellochka, I will only eat if you stop worrying about me and come sit. You don't mind, Marc Zakharovich, if I keep your beautiful Bella in my lap.

CHAGALL: Half of what I have is yours and you choose my better half. *(Kisses Bella on the forehead)* Sit, my angel. Solomon Mikhailovich has been away from home for so long . . .

BELLA: *(Laughing, embarrassed)* But he has a broken leg.

MIKHOELS: They stormed the stage in Chicago.

EFRAIM: It collapsed. *(Chuckles)* Poor American construction.

MIKHOELS: A good speech.

CHAGALL: Ach! To paint the two of you! *(Adjusting Mikhoels and Bella into a pose)* Here . . . gently, gently. *(Steps back, pleased)*

EFRAIM: There's not enough time, is there?

CHAGALL: I don't have a camera, but you do, Efraim?

EFRAIM: At the hotel.

CHAGALL: I'll get you a taxi—you'll be there and back in no time.

EFRAIM: But—

CHAGALL: We must have a photo to remember by!

BELLA: Please, Efraim! Well then, off you go!

(Chagall exits with Efraim. Mikhoels heaves a sigh of relief—big theatrical gesture of wiping his brow. Then complete exhaustion.)

MIKHOELS: Thank God. That pygmy never leaves my side. Not even to brush his teeth. Seven months of traveling, it's exhausting.

BELLA: *(Pouring him a glass of vodka)* Soon you'll be home.

MIKHOELS: *(Knocks it back, holds out his glass for another)* No different. I can't be alone. At night I'm afraid to walk the dog. *(Drinks)* I call Efros to meet me in the street. He smokes his pipe, recites his poems. I walk. The dog pees. *(Another shot of vodka)* On stage I am safe—do you know why?

BELLA: Why?

MIKHOELS: Too many people watching . . . they can't arrest me.

BELLA: At home?

MIKHOELS: We don't sleep well. A noise in the stairwell . . .

BELLA: It's true what they say . . .

MIKHOELS: People are taking vacations in Eastern Siberia. Many never come back. They like the cold weather. It's better now. With the war, Stalin evacuated all of Moscow to the East, and the Germans take care of killing us—*(Sucks in air as if someone punched him in the stomach. Doubles over.)* How could I say such words about my own country? *(Silence. She strokes his head.)* Nowhere, nowhere safe . . .

BELLA: *(Sings "Golus March")*
Mit dem vandershtab in hant
On a heym un on a land;
On a goyel, on a fraynd,
On a morgen, on a haynt,
Nit geduldet nor geyogt,
Vu genekhtikt nit getogt,
Imer vey, vey, vey,
Imer gey, gey, gey.
Imer shpan, shpan, shpan,
Kol zman koyakh iz faran.
[With the wanderer's staff in hand
With no home and with no land

No friend or savior on the way
No tomorrow, no today
Chased, not suffered in our plight
Ne'er a day where spent a night
Always pain will knock, knock, knock
Always walk, walk, walk
Always stride, stride, stride
While your strength can still abide]

CHAGALL: *(Bursting in, very pleased)* The driver is making a little extra to show our friend the sights on the way back—a nice long tour. *(Takes in the mood)* We have all night to drink, but not long to talk. *(Pours glass for each)*

MIKHOELS: *(Wrecked)* To . . . to . . . to . . .

CHAGALL: Friends.

MIKHOELS: *(Pulling himself together)* Friends.

(They drink. Mikhoels pours another.)

BELLA: Hope.

(Drinks. Another. Mikhoels exhausted, releasing, cries.)

CHAGALL: Bellochka, bring us some food. *(She exits. Low voice, serious.)* I have connections in the embassy in Moscow to bring your wife and daughters. I have money now, enough for two. There is a Yiddish theatre here, waiting for a star.

MIKHOELS: I would l-ike that—

CHAGALL: Before Efraim comes back. *(Crossing to phone)* We'll call my friend who can help . . . It's your only chance.

MIKHOELS: My country is at war—in America you forget this—

CHAGALL: That's not true—

MIKHOELS: My country's army has fought back—

CHAGALL: Our country. Russia.

MIKHOELS: Soviet soldiers are dying—liberating our people, camp by camp.

CHAGALL: Why put yourself in danger? People need you alive . . .

MIKHOELS: We are collecting eyewitness reports of the war atrocities. No one knows what has been happening—

CHAGALL: Who will report when you die? *(Silence)*

MIKHOELS: Every afternoon in Moscow, I rehearse a play in Yiddish. Then I gather the acting students to smoke my cigarettes and count their heads to make sure no one disappeared in the night. I lecture them on the pronunciation of the language I love. Every evening, I perform. And on stage, I am free. I feel the audience breathing with my every breath. *(Starts clapping, then puts his hands on Chagall's cheeks)* Warm. Mnh?

CHAGALL: *(Holds Mikhoels' hands on his face)* Shloyme, I cannot let you go.

MIKHOELS: You must.

CHAGALL: *(Holds each hand as he takes it away from his cheek)* Your best trait as an actor. Some nights I only watched your hands. *(Unable to let him go)* What would the world be without these hands? *(Raises a hand to his lips)*

MIKHOELS: *(Disengaging, wiping hand)* "Let me wipe it first. It smells of mortality." As Lear would say. Paint me, Chagall. But be quick. So I don't miss my plane.

CHAGALL: Not enough time.

MIKHOELS: Paint me, Chagall.

(Chagall gets small brush and palette. Chagall grabs his hand and starts painting on his hand.)

Oy, no, no. Not on my hand. *(Exuberant, boisterous Mikhoels again)* Bellochka! We want to eat! It's time! Chagall has started to paint—you never know where it will end!

(Chagall paints Mikhoels' hand. Bella enters, singing as she brings in a steaming bowl of soup. A safe haven.)

MIKHOELS: Bella! Bella! Bella! It smells sooooooooo good.

CHAGALL: Don't move! *(Putting finishing touches on Mikhoels' right hand)*—to give you strength . . . *(Breaks)* or what will I paint when I come back?

(Efraim rushes in with camera, quite agitated. He wears a large mink coat and carries another for Mikhoels.)

EFRAIM: He took me for a ride—all over—he wouldn't stop the car. I didn't know where I was or I would have jumped out. Solomon Mikhailovich, we have to hurry back to the hotel.

(Starts bustling about Mikhoels, trying to drape coat over his shoulders)

MIHKOELS: Go hail us a cab. I move more slowly.

BELLA: What coats, gentlemen!

EFRAIM: Given to us by the workers of the Furriers' Union: one for me, one for Mikhoels, and a third for Comrade Stalin.

MIKHOELS: Stalin's measurements are a state secret. So the size is approximate—they guessed extra large.

EFRAIM: All the furriers fought over who would have the honor of making Stalin's coat—a real row. Then they had a competition . . . and the coats . . . They made one just my size.

MIKHOELS: Fits like a coffin. Now we now have to fight over who presents the gift . . . to the boss.

EFRAIM: Not directly to Comrade Stalin.

MIKHOELS: Never.

(Efraim quickly shakes Chagall's hand and hurries off.)

EFRAIM: We must go!

MIKHOELS: *(Touches his breast pocket)* On our way to the United States, we flew from Teheran to Cairo and stopped at the airport in Palestine. We could not get off of the airplane, but I kissed the air. I wanted to kiss the air and the land of Israel.

EFRAIM: Mikhoels!

(Mikhoels raises his painted hand, an open palm, an echo of the gesture he used for 137th Psalm. Chagall raises hand in same silent gesture. Mikhoels turns, walks with Efraim in their heavy mink coats. Mikhoels on crutches they move slowly deeper and deeper upstage. New York vanishes. The big empty canvas rises, revealing a Chagallian painting behind in the depths of the stage: Granovsky shirtless is wrapped in a tallis *and stretched out on a cross. Reminiscent of Chagall's painting:* White Crucifix. *Granovsky sings "Exile" [reprise] in a quivering voice)*

GRANOVSKY: A song that's lost inside me
Cuts me open like a knife.

CHAGALL: *(Seeing the image upstage)* This is what I paint.

GRANOVSKY: In my mouth the desert's singing
As I choke upon my life.

BELLA: *(Calling out for him)* Chagall, I'm scared . . . My throat. I can't breathe.

GRANOVSKY: You will find me in the morning
Hanging high up in the sky

The desert singing kaddish . . .

CHAGALL: *(Taking her hand)* Bella, stay with me. Be an angel over my shoulder. Sing to me.

(Bella turns away from Chagall, slowly walks away deep into the stage until she vanishes. Green Violinist plays. As Bella leaves Chagall, she sings "You over the Village" [reprise].)

BELLA: *Nacht gekumen du bist nisht do,*
Fenster tunkl ale gasn leydikh.
The cows are sleeping, high upon the hilltop,
Dreaming of a village:
Zeygers tick tock,
Vign voyen.
Flocks of doves murmur silence.
Un aleyn ich ze dayn shotn,
Vi du flist iber dem shtetl.

CHAGALL: *(Reacting to Bella, as she disappears)* No—no—

(Zuskin appears in a pool of light, being beaten. Several blows. He continues to testify to unseen interrogator.)

ZUSKIN: *(Testifying, overlaps with Chagall)* No—no . . . He never meant that. Mikhoels was an actor not a politician. He was no traitor. That evening . . . I wasn't even there . . . *(Blow)* I don't know what happened . . . *(Blow)* I was waiting off stage . . . *(Another blow)* Mikhoels arrived late. "Zuska," he said. "Zuska, I have some important words to say—" and he went on as Benjamin. He was an actor . . . he was just playing his part . . .

(Company stands in line behind Mikhoels, facing upstage.)

MIKHOELS (BENJAMIN): Sendrel, my dearest friend,
We will not part,
'Til journey's end.
Our road is long,
Our road is hard,
But I will lead us
To lands afar.
There are no strangers, only friends,

In Eretz Yisruel our journey ends.

(To audience) Today is a historic day. Today we perform these words with the greatest joy. Today my character Benjamin sets off on his journey knowing that there is a road leading to the Promised Land—today in the great United Nations the countries of the world supported the founding of the state of Israel.

(Applause begins like a wave. Company holds arms above their heads, stylized applause building. Mikhoels stops speaking.)

ZUSKIN: There was applause. Deafening. People stood and stamped their feet —ten, fifteen, twenty minutes. Mikhoels turns pale. I stood there. I didn't know what to do. I never would have said such things on stage . . . I would never . . . *(A blow.)* But Mikhoels is no nationalist . . . he loves this country . . . our homeland . . . you must understand he would never betray the country that made him who he is.

MIKHOELS: *(Turning to Zuskin)* Sendrel, tsi vaystu vos iz vaiter fun Tunyadevka?

ZUSKIN: *(To court)* Mikhoels is a great actor.

MIKHOELS: *(Quietly)* Zuska, that was my act of treason. A few words spoken in joy—but so worth speaking—I would speak them again . . . wouldn't you? *(To Chagall)* Wouldn't you?

(Chagall approaches Mikhoels, clapping. He raises his hands to place on Mikhoels' cheeks, in their familiar gesture. Mikhoels steps away before Chagall touches his face, turns to walk upstage with rest of Company. As they walk upstage there is a single gunshot: Mikhoels and Company twist and crumble slowly to the ground. Chagall raises his hands to his own cheeks, feels his own face. He holds his own cheeks tightly in his hands. Green Violinist starts playing. Very simple, barely a song.)

CHAGALL: I am painting a village,
The village I come from.
I am painting the laughter,
The laughter I know.
I'm painting a wedding,
Two lovers, a *khupa*.
I'm painting a horse,
A bouquet in the snow.

I'm painting a sleigh,
Flying over my village.
I'm painting my wife,
An angel of love.
I'm painting an actor—
The stage now is empty.
I'm painting a psalm
To send up above.
I'm painting a hand
To hold us together.
I'm painting a place,
Where I've never been.
I'm painting a song,
That goes on forever.
I'm painting the notes,
Of a green violin.

(*Chagall's mural* Introduction to Yiddish Theatre *descends. We see the painting for the first time. Mikhoels' offstage voice joins. Chagall stops singing, listens as the voices multiply into whole Company singing behind the mural, which now covers the stage. Chagall opens his arms wide, like wings, to embrace the whole mural. Voices taper off to Mikhoels' solo* nign. *Chagall touches image of Mikhoels. Green Violinist appears in a glow, playing a wild riff; musicians join. Chagall feels the music in his body, begins to move with the music as lights fade. The klezmorim play into the darkness.*)

Musical Numbers

PART 1

Green Violin Solo	Green Violinist
"The Nothing Song"	Chagall, and Company
Agents (rehearsal)	
"Traveling on a Train"	Mikhoels and Company
Efros' Poem/Fracture Dance	Efros and Company
Lullaby	Maria
"What's to Complain?"	Mikhoels and Company
Reveller's song	Mikhoels, Chagall, and Bella
Agents (performance)	
"Traveling on a Train"	Mikhoels and Company
"We Can Live Forever"	Mikhoels and Company
"You over the Village"	Bella and Chagall
"Mural Sleeps"	Green Violinist
"Green Violin Hora"	Green Violinist

PART 2

"Paris Overture"	Green Violinist
Travels of Benjamin III	
"Benjamin Sets Off"	Mikhoels, Zuskin, and Company
"Steppe Prayer"	Zuskin and Mikhoels
"The World Is Round"	Zuskin and Mikhoels
"The Nothing Song"	Chagall, Mikhoels, Bella, Zuskin, and Company

PART 3

"Green Violin Hora"	Green Violinist
King Lear	
"The Storm"	Green Violinist
"The Fool's Song"	Zuskin
"Golus March"	Bella
"Exile"	Granovsky
"Painting a Village"	Chagall and Company
"Green Violin Solo"	"Green Violinist"

Sources

PERFORMANCES

Sholem Aleichem's *Agents* (1906) was adapted by the author. It was translated aloud from Yiddish by Dr. Zoya Prizel. I also consulted the brilliant translation of *Agents* by Benjamin and Barbara Harshav; Benjamin Harshav, *Marc Chagall and the Jewish Theater* (New York: Guggenheim Museum, 1992); and *The Letters of Menakhem Mendl and Sheyne-Sheyndl,* translated by Hillel Halkin, in *The Letters of Menakhem Mendl and Sheyne-Sheyndl and Motl, the Cantor's Son,* by Sholem Aleichem, edited by Hillel Halkin (New Haven: Yale University Press, 2002).

Travels of Benjamin III was adapted by the author from the GOSET 1927 adaptation of Mendel Mokher Sforim's *The Brief Travels of Benjamin the Third,* translated aloud by Dr. Zoya Prizel, published by Benjamin Harshav in *The Yiddish Pen* 28/29 (Nov./Dec. 1996). I also consulted the original narrative, *The Brief Travels of Benjamin the Third,* translated from Yiddish by Hillel Halkin, in S. Y. Abramovitsh, *Tales of Mendele the Book Peddler,* ed. D. Miron and K. Friedan (New York: Schocken Books, 1996).

King Lear excerpts from William Shakespeare, *King Lear,* Act 3, sc. 2.

SPEECHES

The text of Mikhoels' speech at the farewell banquet of the National Committee to welcome the Soviet Jewish Delegation, New York, 1943, can be found in M. Goldenberg, *Zhizn' I Sud'ba Solomona Mikhoelsa* (Baltimore: Vestnik Information Agency, 1995).

SONGS

The Yiddish lyrics in Bella's song in Part 3 can be found in Morris Rosenfeld, "A Goles Marsh," in *Shriftn,* vol. 1 (New York: A. M. Evalenko, 1908), cited in Benjamin Harshav, "The Role of Language in Modern Art: On Texts and Subtexts in Chagall's Paintings," in his *Marc Chagall and the Jewish Theater.*

LIFE IN REFUSAL

by Ari Roth

With special thanks and dedication to
Anna and Yadviga Charny
Jerrold and Leona Schecter
Rabbis Ronne Friedman and Bernard Mehlman
And, as always, to
Kate Schecter and our children, Isabel and Sophie

Life in Refusal. Theater J production, 2000. Pictured are Brook Butterworth (left) and Holly Twyford. Photograph copyright © Stan Barouh, 2000.

*L*ife in Refusal began as a one-act play called *Proverbial Human Suffering*, written in 1988 shortly after I returned from the Soviet Union during the height of Mikhail Gorbachev's twinned initiatives of *glasnost* and *perestroika*. I had traveled to Moscow and Leningrad for three months with my wife and her family, who were writing a sequel to their first family memoir, *An American Family in Moscow.* Published in 1976, with seven coauthors, the book chronicled life under socialism from an American family's perspective. The five children attended Soviet public school for two years while their father, Jerrold Schecter, ran the news bureau for *Time* magazine. The Schecter clan returned to Moscow some seventeen years later to write *Back in the U.S.S.R.* Spouses were invited to tag along, and I was encouraged to write about the Soviet theatre scene.

We didn't expect to be approached by rabbis who, in the weeks leading up to our departure, asked us to bring Nikon cameras and other swank items (like Casio digital wrist watches and Chicago Bear blue shoulder bags) to be given away to Jewish refuseniks who could then sell them on the black market. These were Russian Jews who had lost jobs because of their expressed desire to leave the Soviet Union. In many cases, these were sick Russian Jews. And in the case of one refusenik, we were talking about a sick Russian Jew who was in effect being given a death sentence by Soviet immigration authorities. His name was Benjamin Charny. We wanted nothing to do with him.

And so begins the dramatic conceit by which I made this real-life story a saga for the stage. Drawing on twenty-five pages of transcript from taped interviews, I found it easy to create the character of Ben. His exacting diction is lifted right off the tape and suggests a precise, humble, graceful, and gracious man of good humor and an abiding sense of moral outrage and spiritual perseverance. Around this realistic depiction are more stylized compressions, characters of more extreme behavior. There are also other kinds of Russians here, hectoring and self-interested. They come off as less nuanced, an indication of the distance that Alison, the surrogate for my wife and me, kept from so much of the pain and suffering around her.

The one-act I first wrote ended with Ben still in Moscow, awaiting news of his fate. A year later, I wrote an upbeat epilogue that culminated with Ben's real-life departure from the Soviet Union and his dramatic touchdown in the city of Boston. And then ten years after that, after learning of Ben's death, I wrote an expanded version of his story with an entirely new frame and new scenes in the States. The play now asks about the meaning of such moments in history when people fuse together to undo an injustice. What happens when the cause no longer takes hold of the conscience as it once did? Whither the bond with the Jewish refusenik when he or she is no longer refused?

"All relationships have a shelf-life," wrote one reductive critic in response to this play, which most others found to be moving. But as I think about that dismissal, it occurs to me that the relationship whose usefulness has expired doesn't necessarily get tossed out with the garbage. It occupies space in the soul and the conscience, as memory retrieves moments of shared love, anguish, and worry. And then the context changes. The bond slackens. But the resonance is transformed. The changing resonance is what infiltrates Alison's soul and leads her back to reclaim a piece of her heritage: a song from the old country, an identification formerly eschewed. This memory sends the character back to a soulful place, to a way of feeling and behaving, which hopefully can move us to become a bit more soulful in our own present, awakening state.

Notes

This play received an NFJC commission in 1997 and was staged at the Performance Network of Ann Arbor in 1998. It received its Equity world premiere in March of 2000 at Theater J, in the Aaron and Cecile Goldman Theater at the Washington District of Columbia Jewish Community Center, which has been my artistic home for the past eight years. It is a particular joy to have this play included in this volume in that it finds superb company with authors like Motti Lerner, Jennifer Maisel, Donald Margulies, Jeffrey Sweet, and Corey Fischer, all authors whose work I have had the honor to produce at Theater J. *Life in Refusal* was first professionally produced by Theater J in Washington, D.C., from March 4 to April 2, 2000.

Director: Wendy C. Goldberg
Set Designer: Lou Stancari
Lighting Designer: Martha M. Mountain
Sound Designer: Timothy Thompson
Costume Designer: Susan Chiang
Production Stage Manager: Stephanie Nagel
Dialect Coach: Christine Hirrel
Fight Choreographer: Grady Weatherford

CAST

Alison: Holly Twyford

Ben: Lawrence Redmond

Anna, *Washington Post* Reporter, Old Russian Lady, and Tanya: Brook
Butterworth

Michael, Old Russian Man, and Refusenik with Cane: Daniel Ladmirault

OVIR Official, Waiter/Goon, Refusenik with Beard, and Mourner C: Joe
Cronin

Producer, *Chicago Tribune* Reporter, Anna's Fiancé, and Mourner D.:
Jefferson A. Russell

Adam, Victor, Refusenik with Eye Patch, Alison's Father, and Mourner B:
John Dow

Yadviga, Bag Lady, Patience Smith, and Olya: Caren Anton

Refusenik with Back Brace (Fox), Camera Man, Fellow Goon, Chernobyl
Mayor, and Mourner A: Michael Skinner

Characters

ALISON (thirties)

BEN (fifties)

ANNA (thirties); also *Washington Post* Reporter, Old Russian Lady, and Tanya

MICHAEL (thirty); also Old Russian Man and Refusenik with Cane

OVIR OFFICIAL; also Waiter/Goon, Refusenik with beard, and Mourner C

PRODUCER (thirties, African American); also *Chicago Tribune* Reporter, Anna's
Fiancé, and Mourner D

ADAM (forties to fifties); also Victor, Refusenik with Eye Patch, Alison's Father,
and Mourner B

YADVIGA (fifty); also Bag Lady, Patience Smith, and Olya

REFUSENIK WITH BACK BRACE (Fox); also Camera Man, Fellow Goon, Chernobyl Mayor, and Mourner A

Time: 1998 to 1987 and back.

Place: Washington, Manhattan, Moscow, and Boston.

SCENE 1

(Music: A collision of ancient and modern, or Russian and Jewish. Lights up on Alison, an intense, intelligent ex–New Yorker. She holds an ivory envelope.)

ALISON: *(To audience)* I just got the invitation. I knew it'd be coming. Anna called for my address. She told me then. About her news. So I've had a week to think about it. Whether or not I'll be coming—*alone; with a date* —but I should know, either way, that Ben won't be. And that I missed the funeral. That's how it came out. All in a breath. To which I replied, *I'm-so-happy-for-you-Anna-Oh-my-God-I'm so . . . Sorry.*

(A light on Anna, facing out)

ANNA: Please don't be upset with us.

ALISON: No. *God,* no.

ANNA: We were in such hurry.

ALISON: You're getting *married!*

ANNA: We had to make all arrangements. Fly back the body.

ALISON: It's fine.

ANNA: By the time we *tried* to call, no one could find!

ALISON: How did it happen?

ANNA: They said you were traveling. In Sevastopol. And Belarus?

ALISON: Anna, tell me.

ANNA: So you are working for World Bank now? Exciting!

ALISON: Uh-huh.

ANNA: But this means you have left academia?

ALISON: I it; it *me.*

ANNA: And this is good thing?

ALISON: *(Turning to face Anna)* Tell me about your father.

ANNA: What's to say?

ALISON: Where did it happen? You said they had to fly back the body? I didn't know they had *moved!*

ANNA: So we tell you everything when you are here.

ALISON: But it's crazy, isn't it? I mean, isn't it awful? To fall so completely out of touch?

ANNA: So come. Make connection—*anew.* You will celebrate. But no dancing, of course. In memorial.

ALISON: In memorial . . .

BEN: I have hope.

ANNA: So we see you then?

(A light on Ben, as lights fade on Anna)

BEN: You don't have to come.

ALISON: No, I want to. I want to come. It's just . . .

BEN: You have your own life, Elison.

ALISON: I liked mine better, Ben, when it was with you.

BEN: I liked it also.

ALISON: And I miss it. I miss the time. Is that possible? To miss the Soviet Union?

BEN: Don't.

ALISON: But I want it back. Not the place—the *cold;* the kitchens; what Anna said. It's not the same here. And it won't be in Boston.

BEN: How do you know?

ALISON: Because I know myself at weddings in synagogues; in this country. I'm allergic.

BEN: You have Jewish sense of humor, you know this?

ALISON: I'm not *connected* to anything!

BEN: You always are. And will be.

ALISON: I lost you, didn't I? We lost each other. Here, in the maw.

BEN: I still have hope we can see each other.

ALISON: But where? As what? What was I to you, Ben, because I don't think I ever saw you; I mean, as anything more than just a crutch, for my own limp.

BEN: How 'bout one little tango?

ALISON: *(To audience)* "No dancing," she said. In memorial . . .

(He dances, she watches, moves to him, but light fades; Ben is gone.)

I'd only miss him either way. Besides, I'm scheduled to be on mission come June, doling out vouchers in the Crimea—promises with strings—touring poly-clinics with holes in the floor where there should be toilets. Ben always said, "There's so much work to be done. Only so much one can do. So do." And I'm *doing,* right!? A step up from where I was. Before we met. A darker decade. New York pre–K-Mart. Wherein I would bypass human suffering the way a driver might a pothole. Wherein I would take note of a particular barefoot woman, my age, and console myself as follows:

(Lights up on Bag Lady)

"There are problems in this world so intractable, so bewildering, that there's nothing we can do, so why try?"
BAG LADY: Hey, lady.
ALISON: Quite convenient, actually. I'd put a quarter in her cup. Neither of us would feel any better.
BAG LADY: So why bother? Walk away! Hey, lady! Whatch'ya looking at? What's your problem?

(Alison acknowledges the question. The Bag Lady moves on.)

ALISON: I put a quarter in Ben's cup—I think that was the extent of it—servicing a cliché; worse, a dated one. *"Save Soviet Jews!" "Save two, win a free set of steak knives!"* . . . I met Ben and Yadviga Charny, in the summer of 1987, at the dawn of Mikhail Gorbachev's new reforms. Quite reluctantly, of course.

(Enter Michael)

MICHAEL: So you walk into your 47th Street Photo. You get one of the nice little Chasidic men to give you a Nikon 2000. You tell him it's a gift; a gift for one of his oppressed Soviet brethren. He says, "That's very nice. It'll *still* cost you two-hundred-fifty!"
ALISON: *(To audience)* This is Michael.
MICHAEL: So you buy it—he's a schmuck, but it's wholesale.
ALISON: *(To audience)* We used to live together.
MICHAEL: You go to Russia.
ALISON: *(To audience)* It wasn't pretty.
MICHAEL: You go to a pay phone. You dial. You do *not* give your name.
ALISON: I'm trying to remember why it is we got together.
MICHAEL: You say, "I'm a friend of a friend, Social Action Committee, Temple Holy Blossom, West Orange."
ALISON: I'm still trying.
MICHAEL: No, no, wait . . . You do not say "Temple Holy Blossom."

ALISON: Still trying . . .

MICHAEL: You do not say "West Orange."

ALISON: *(A realization)* I think I know.

MICHAEL: You say, "I'm a friend. I'd like to meet."

ALISON: Investment.

MICHAEL: You meet.

ALISON: He had one, and I . . .

MICHAEL: You leave the Nikon. A man's family will live off this camera for six and one half months, and it has cost you next to nothing, as I am giving you the money, just keep the receipt. So, whaddaya think?

ALISON: I don't think I'm going to do it.

MICHAEL: It's a *moral obligation,* you realize.

ALISON: No, it's a major imposition. Besides, I don't agree with the politics.

MICHAEL: A man's life?

ALISON: I don't believe the country I study to be an Evil Empire. I'm sorry that you do. Now, if you don't mind—

MICHAEL: The man is sick, you realize.

ALISON: So am I, Michael. Of you trying to convert me! It's ridiculous! We're the same religion!

MICHAEL: So then take. *Take!*

ALISON: I'm not taking any more brochures!

MICHAEL: This happens to be a certified check!

ALISON: Keep it.

MICHAEL: Oh, great! And what am I supposed to tell my committee? I've just swindled them out of two hundred and fifty BUCKS?

ALISON: You tell your committee you picked the wrong person. You tell your committee I have an internship setting up interviews with people who represent more than one tiny, myopic perspective on Soviet life!

MICHAEL: Alison, you know what the problem is here?

ALISON: You have a tiny, myopic perspective on Soviet life?

MICHAEL: No. You have a grandmother born in Minsk, and a father born in the Bronx who fled her *k'naidlach* the way she fled the *Cossacks,* and so all you know how to do is *flee,* and as a result, you are an island.

ALISON: Do me a favor: Do not reduce me to half a line in a folk song. I happen to be traveling with some pretty heavy hitters!

(Enter Adam, with pipe)

ADAM: Alison. Get me the Gerasimov piece.

ALISON: Yes, professor.

ADAM: You've read this?

ALISON: Yes, professor.

ADAM: What the hell did I say?

ALISON: You liked him. You said "Gennady Gerasimov is the wave of the future."

ADAM: I did?

ALISON: "The Larry King of Soviet foreign policy."

ADAM: *(To audience)* I like that.

ALISON: *(To Michael)* Advisor to three U.S. presidents.

(Enter Producer with Camera Man)

PRODUCER: Hold it! I want that! Adam, I want that shot of you and your boarding pass.

ALISON: Our producer.

ADAM: *(Striking a pose, with pipe)* How's this?

PRODUCER: Whaddaya think? Al? Have a look.

ALISON: *(She looks through the camera.)* I dunno, a touch stagey, maybe? For a documentary?

PRODUCER: Does the girl have an eye? Does this girl have an eye?

ALISON: As a matter of fact, she has two.

PRODUCER: And a gorgeous two. Kindreds, baby.

MICHAEL: *(Sizing up the situation)* Oh, *I see* what kind of a trip this is.

ALISON: Kindreds?

PRODUCER: "This shtetl shit is old, girl." That's what them baby-browns is saying. "I have been there. I have done that. Let's see the world!"

ALISON: This is not about "seeing the world." This is my field. This trip is *work*.

PRODUCER: I'm with ya there.

(Fade on film crew)

MICHAEL: Loud and clear.

ALISON: Look, Michael, I'm really sorry about your friend.

MICHAEL: He's not *"my"* friend.

ALISON: Well then, the man in this picture—your refusenik—and what kind of a word *is* "refusenik"? Is that like "Beatnik"? Or "Peacenik"? Why the "nik"? Is that supposed to get us "riled up?" Because it doesn't. Doesn't work. "Someone denied a permission." Why not say that? We're all denied *some*thing. And by the way, it's a lousy picture.

MICHAEL: It's a lousy situation. A life and death situation!

ALISON: Well, I'm sorry about it. Now if you'll excuse me, I have to get my dry cleaning.

MICHAEL: And you don't notice a pattern?

ALISON: Of you trying very hard to, as you would put, "*hock*" me?

MICHAEL: Of you rejecting your own needs.

ALISON: Michael, you are about the *last* person in the world to know of my own fucking needs. You tell me what schlepping a camera four thousand miles across an ocean has got to do with my own fucking needs!?

MICHAEL: It will help you make peace with your people.

ALISON: But I don't *want* to make peace with my people! I have had it up to HERE with my people!

MICHAEL: Why? Because we talk funny?

ALISON: You don't talk funny. You think funny. You think tiny, Michael. You think like somebody old. Who sells pickles. And eats herring. And wears *galoshes*. And has too much hair sprouting out of his ears.

MICHAEL: What's wrong with a little hair sprouting?

ALISON: It makes it difficult to hear people! Hear this:

MICHAEL: Didn't you used to like herring?

ALISON: No. I used to *experiment* with herring. That's what you were, Michael —My Experiment With Herring. And borsht. And then you started putting back half-drunken glasses of borsht in the fridge, with great big dollops of sour cream floating up at the top, never bothering to use the Saran Wrap I would expressly lay out.

MICHAEL: *(Overlapping "expressly")* Alison-The-Jew-From-The-Bronx-Who-Aspired-To-A-Life-Of-Saran-Wrap!

ALISON: I am not from the Bronx! My *father* is the one from the Bronx, and he got the hell *out* of the Bronx—

MICHAEL: "To discover a much larger world."

ALISON: That's right.

MICHAEL: "At the expense of his family."

ALISON: I never said that.

MICHAEL: "At the expense of his children." Yes you did.

ALISON: I hate Victim shit! I am trying to enlarge myself. I am helping to make a movie about the world's future!

MICHAEL: That's very large of you.

ALISON: All right, fine. EUROPE'S future. All right, all right, RUSSIA'S future. *OUR* future.

MICHAEL: And in this "future," there will be no such thing as Jewish Suffering?

ALISON: I certainly hope not.

MICHAEL: Meaning *"enough about Jews, maybe?"* Hmmm?

ALISON: As a matter of fact—

MICHAEL: *"Enough with your Jewish Misery?"*

ALISON: Could we not do this?

MICHAEL: *"You people really think you have a monopoly. Well, you don't!"*

ALISON: No, you don't. You don't. YOU—

MICHAEL: Yes, *"WE . . . ?"* (Pause, shift, Alison steps forward.)

ALISON: I did not take Michael's check. I did not buy Ben a camera. I took the number, crumpled it in my pocket—and left for Moscow that September wearing several winter coats.

(Fade. And then special on Ben.)

BEN: I dream I am back at my old job . . .

ALISON: *(Emerging, to audience)* When I arrived, I did what I always did.

BEN: I am working, not waiting.

ALISON: I called the usual family friends.

BEN: My assistants are all young. I am old. Like now.

ALISON: But not Ben.

BEN: I am unable to explain my own algorithms!

ALISON: He was just a name on crumpled paper.

BEN: Chief Assistant approaches and says he will be leaving. "Okay," I say. "Where will you be going?" *"I am leaving Soviet Union."* "Okay!" I say. *"Forever."* "Great!" I say. "Where can I write you?" He tells me *"Big Riddle,"* and disappears . . .

I am now trembling, perspiring, swollen thyroid. I must walk out of institute, but am stopped at gate by militia who tells me I must wait. "Why," I say. *"State Secrets."* "Okay," I say, "Where shall I go?" *"Go to hell, Jew,"* he says.

To be exact, he laughs, as if old Russian joke, which, by the way, it is. I walk down cement block hallway. This is my recurring dream.

(Lights shift, as a well-dressed Soviet Man enters with a bottle of vodka and two glasses. He and Alison sit for lunch.)

SCENE 2

VICTOR: *(A toast)* To your project.

ALISON: To *glasnost*.

VICTOR: So you are making a film!

ALISON: *(To audience)* Victor Klimov was a friend of my father's.

VICTOR: We are hot little commodity in your country now.

ALISON: They met during the Brezhnev years. Victor was working for TASS at the time.

VICTOR: And so you are looking for scientist?

ALISON: To be interviewed, yes.

VICTOR: On camera?

ALISON: If possible.

VICTOR: And you have leads?

ALISON: A few.

VICTOR: May I see?

(Victor takes her notebook. Peruses.)

"Gilbo." Hmmm.

ALISON: Have you heard of any of these . . . ?

VICTOR: No. So.

(He does not give back the notebook; motions to waiter.)

ALISON: *(To audience)* I remember Victor and his second wife, Olya, owning a *dacha* along the Volga. There was a sculpture garden of alabaster women with no arms; clay courts; and, set back in the woods, a very old sauna that involved barrels of water, wet eucalyptus branches, and being naked in front of both sets of families. We'd have to whip each other on the back, or the butt, with these steaming hot leaves, in a very odd ritual, having something to with "friendship" and "blood circulation." I remember it hurting. A lot.

VICTOR: So may I offer supplemental thesis?

ALISON: Please.

VICTOR: We are in very beguiling stage as nation.

ALISON: It would seem.

VICTOR: To be Soviet citizen is to be in love with two Woman. First, is Motherland; the womb from which you emerge, to which you can never return,
but always, in some primal way, desire. Second, is wife. This is woman
who cooks for you; cleans for you; darns the hole in your sock. And she,
of course, is state. Every man in Soviet Union has these two lovers. What
we need now as country—

ALISON: Yes?

VICTOR: Is additional lover. And this is our *glasnost* and *perestroika*. She is the
mistress who brings out so-called Inner Child. Every long-term relationship needs such release, yes? The little fling? The imagined adventure? You
like music?

ALISON: Um . . .

VICTOR: *(Calling to waiter) Affitzante! Nyiem-noga muzike.*

ALISON: *(To audience)* Victor Klimov would launch his own private-coopera-
tive-joint-venture later that same year with a publishing magnate in
France. They would call their glossy *"COMMERCE IN U.S.S.R."*

VICTOR: *(To audience)* Sounds like oxymoron, yes? But it's not! And it won't be!

ALISON: *(To audience)* And he was right.

VICTOR: Architects of the Future! No longer frozen in head-lock of competition; arms-race; Super-Power; these rigid categorizations—We must *overcome* them!

ALISON: I agree with that.

VICTOR: There are new challenges before us.

ALISON: In the field of space research.

VICTOR: Yes?

ALISON: It's a segment I'm producing. Or trying to. What's going on in *Baikanor?* The new *Cosmodrome* facility? Star City?

VICTOR: You know your space!

ALISON: I think there are many ways our countries can work to forge new
innovations.

VICTOR: But instead . . . ?

ALISON: I'm sorry?

VICTOR: But instead . . .

ALISON: Instead?

VICTOR: We are subject to, not such mutual cooperation, but orchestrated campaign of brain drain.

ALISON: Huh.

(Waiter brings more vodka.)

What exactly do you mean by "brain drain?"

WAITER: Brain. *Drain.*

(Waiter walks away.)

Jeez.

(Waiter exits.)

ALISON: What I mean is, we hear the phrase, but no one in the U.S. actually believes that you—

VICTOR: I will tell you what "*we* actually believe," my Alyona, because you are curious Production Manager, not to mention open-mind, well-read, and also quite beautiful.

ALISON: Yes, Victor?

VICTOR: I am Male Chauvinist pig, yes?

ALISON: Yes, Victor.

VICTOR: This I like, by the way. When you scold me. Is uniquely Capitalist predilection. So-called Pain and Pleasure Principle.

ALISON: *(As she gets up)* Good-bye, Victor.

VICTOR: Please. Forgive. But don't leave. You have not obtained from me what you desire.

ALISON: Which is?

VICTOR: What "we actually believe." And why list you are working from is so inflammable.

ALISON: I didn't realize there was anything wrong with . . .

VICTOR: So . . .

(As she sits)

You see, certain small-mind, Special-Interest-type lobbyist are right now coordinating massive public relations campaign to help "free" so-called Scientist. "Why?"

ALISON: Go on . . .

VICTOR: Because U.S. is country founded on principle of immigration. You have opened your gates to so-called huddled masses. Now, perhaps you have too many "Huddled." Too many Haitian. Too many "Wetback." Perhaps you would like New Class of Masses? So quietly, you woo ballet dancer; violin player; National Hockey League Detroit Red Wing; now Soviet Scientist—

ALISON: Excuse me, but I was under the impression your country was *looking* for an exchange of New Ideas—

VICTOR: But not people. We are nation that takes great pride in our people. Also great investment. Is there no reciprocal obligation? A person to his place?

ALISON: Well, yes, I can see how . . .

VICTOR: I have met these scientists who make application. All are gone now. Some to Israel. Most, to U.S. Mostly state of Massachusetts; so-called "Boom State." High-tech; route 1-2-8. Scientists all work for defense contract. S-D-I. Life of one-time-Russian-now-U.S.-citizen is seemingly quite comfortable. He has Buick; Bunga*low.* And yet, no Motherland. He knows he will die in Framingham off Turnpike in strange land. "Yes, but he is free!" Free to do *space* research . . . You see, this Wind From West, she is a tantalizing breeze. The smallest spark of curiosity . . . . Brush-*fire* . . .

ALISON: Well if it means anything, I'm not here to "save" any scientists. I just want to talk to a few.

VICTOR: And I am happy to arrange. You know, all names you have in notebook are Jewish.

ALISON: . . . No. No, I didn't.

VICTOR: "Slepak?" "Goldshtein?" *"Ketz?"* I think this will make it exceptionally difficult to present so-called balanced thesis.

ALISON: I . . . agree.

VICTOR: So, may I offer new list? Come. Up to office! I give you whole Rolodex of names!

ALISON: I think I'm okay starting with what I have.

VICTOR: Oh, I don't know. This is your "research?" This list?

ALISON: May I? Please? Victor? Have my notebook back?

VICTOR: Where do these come from? *Who* do these come from?

ALISON: It's not like I *asked* my contacts that every name of every scientist on my list be . . .

VICTOR: "Jewish?"

ALISON: May I?

VICTOR: Is beautiful Rolodex. Super *Size*. Office Depot.

(She takes back her notebook.)

ALISON: *(To audience)* Following the fall of the Wall, the coup, the invasion of Pizza Hut, Victor changed the name of his magazine to *Moscow Gold* and began raking in the rubles. He bought a Mercedes-Benz dealership with his sons; invested in aluminum; published hard-hitting stories on the paltry flow of supply; the government cartel. Victor thought he smelled a rat. Soon Victor would meet the Mafia.

(The Waiter returns, now a leather-jacketed Mob Goon, accompanied by a Fellow Goon.)

WAITER/GOON: Klimov.

ALISON: *(To audience)* In the winter of 1997, the same month I heard the news about Ben, Victor Klimov was mugged outside his garage.

WAITER/GOON: Come.

ALISON: His fur coat stolen. His Mercedes-Benz stripped . . .

VICTOR: Stop.

(The Goon tapes Victor's wrists.)

ALISON: His mouth and nose sealed shut with duct tape.

VICTOR: *(Muffled)* But a fledgling, new democracy needs a vibrant, open press!

(The Goon tapes Victor's mouth shut.)

ALISON: His body was discovered by dogs in his driveway.

WAITER/GOON: Talk too much, you . . .

ALISON: Some speculated it to be an old-fashioned hit.

WAITER/GOON: Stock portfolio . . . Mink coat . . .

ALISON: Others, a random act of thuggery.

WAITER/GOON: Mercedes-*Benz* 600 S.E.L . . .

FELLOW GOON: You, Yid . . .

(They kick him. And then they kill him.)

ALISON: When I heard the news, I thought of the *dacha* in the deep green forest. Alabaster women with no arms. And the sauna. Being whipped with hot, spiked sticks. Sitting there. Taking it. Why had my father brought us to that *dacha?* Why were we water-skiing on the Volga, and not huddled in some synagogue? *(Lights fade on Victor and then appear on an Old Man.)*

OLD MAN: Pssst!

ALISON: I left the House of Foreign Journalists and made my way to the nearest Metro.

OLD MAN: Pssst! You are Jewish?

ALISON: A deranged looking man in a white beard approached—

OLD MAN: Take. Is list.

ALISON: His breath smelling of borsht and smelt herring and old sour cream.

OLD MAN: You see name? You call name. You like name? You marry name. You bring name back to Israel and live free.

ALISON: Uhm. I don't live in Israel.

OLD MAN: You should.

ALISON: I live on the Upper West Side. Close enough.

OLD MAN: So take.

ALISON: No.

OLD MAN: Take. *Take!*

ALISON: No, no, no, NO! I am not taking any more lists. I am not talking to any more *men!*

OLD MAN: So what are you doing?

ALISON: What am I doing? My job! I am doing my job!

OLD MAN: For *shabbis.* What are you doing for *shabbis?* You need family?

(Hold. Then shift.)

ALISON: *(To audience)* I took the endless wooden escalator into the subway, then rode under the city for the rest of the afternoon. As I came up from the cavern, passing couples heading down, or families with strollers, soldiers in a hurry, I thought of all the things I still could love about this country. A woman selling fresh dill wrapped in newsprint against the side of a building. I bought two bunches of carrots from her, and the same kind of meat pie we used to get when my dad was off covering some crisis and Mom was alone with the kids.

(Lights up on the Old Woman)

OLD WOMAN: You are Jew.

ALISON: It wasn't a question. There was no demand. It was a statement. She could just . . . tell.

OLD WOMAN: *(Pointing at Alison)* Eyes.

(A long moment. Alison reaches into her pocket. Uncrumples the piece of paper with phone number on it. Goes to pay phone. Dials. As lights shift, a phone rings. Ben answers.)

SCENE 3

BEN: *Da?*

ALISON: Hello? Uhm, is there a Mr. Benjamin Ch—

BEN: Would you like to meet me?

ALISON: Uhm, actually . . . *Na-skolka va-puni-mayu v'we u-chauw-ney?*

BEN: So how 'bout lunch?

ALISON: Uhm . . .

BEN: I would offer walking tour of Moscow, but I have blood pressure issue today. Not big deal.

ALISON: Walking tour isn't necessary. I've actually BEEN a tour guide here before.

BEN: Oh, really?

ALISON: Also not a big deal. Please, don't go to any trouble—

BEN: I won't. So, you will come to me.

ALISON: It's just a questionnaire, actually, that we—

BEN: You know our Metro system?

ALISON: I love your Metro system.

BEN: I am very impressed. So, you will come to *Kiyevsky Vagzal.* I meet you on lower platform at back wall.

ALISON: Uhm, I—

BEN: You have seen my picture?

ALISON: Once, I think but—

BEN: Is terrible picture, I know. So, I am funny looking man, like hippo. This is nickname my daughter, Anna, gives me. I will invite her as well? Or so, you would like to call her on your own?

ALISON: Uhm, I think you should know, I'm not from any committee.

BEN: So, I will call and see if she is free. You sound like you are both same age.

ALISON: Really?

BEN: So, good. You tell me your name when we meet. And I am looking forward to seeing you, whoever you are.

ALISON: Yes, and I—

BEN: Bye-bye. One o'clock, yes?

ALISON: Uhm—

BEN: *(As he hangs up)* Yaduchka?

YADVIGA: *(Entering)* Da?

BEN: One o'clock lunch. Let's move!

(Lights shift.)
(Alison moves into light indicating a subway platform.)

SCENE 4

ALISON: *(To audience)* Now the thing about Ben's picture that's so terrible . . . or that *was* . . . The bleakness. Gray; featureless; circles under the eyes. And all quite deliberate—I'm sure the people who printed these things must've gone rummaging through old photos, only to pick the most depressing ones they could find—oh, and the inscription, "FREE BEN CHARNY!" with the proverbial exclamation mark! There was always an exclamation mark in Human Rights in those days. Now they've learned. Eliminate the emphatic. So they send out a jolly set of self-sticking address labels with the colorful logo that we use to pay bills, *then* throw the rest of the pack away, because the brochure's *still* got some gray, featureless, utterly helpless . . . It just gets me upset . . . Because when you see Ben . . . When I *saw* Ben . . . That first time . . .

(Ben enters in blue jeans jacket.)

BEN: *(Waving, warmly)* Shalom!

ALISON: Let's just say, I was in trouble, and I knew it.

BEN: I am Ben.

ALISON: Hi.

BEN: Hi. And *your name* is?

ALISON: Alison. Or Alyona, I guess.

BEN: You have Hebrew name, Elison-or-Alyona?

ALISON: No. I mean, uhm, not that I remember.

BEN: I will check this.

ALISON: No, that's—

BEN: I have book given to me by young rabbi from temple in Palm Springs. You have visited this place?

ALISON: Temple?

BEN: Palm Springs.

ALISON: Oh. No.

BEN: You are nervous about meeting me.

ALISON: No! It's just . . . I need to be back at the hotel in—

BEN: You speak Russian.

ALISON: Yes.

BEN: So we speak English. We are only reading English in our house now.

ALISON: Really?

BEN: So, we go.

ALISON: *(To audience)* And he took my arm.

(He holds her, as they walk. He stops.)

BEN: But slow. "Slow-*ly.*" I must take breaks.

ALISON: *(To audience)* Because of the arteries. In his leg. But I didn't know that at the time. He seemed fine. Lots of people have to take breaks.

(They walk slowly.)

BEN: So, I have received extremely good news just recently.

ALISON: Really?

BEN: About the person I have told you I will call.

ALISON: . . . Anna?

BEN: I have found out she is receiving the permission with her husband and Sima.

ALISON: Permission?

BEN: With husband's entire family. Leaving soon. Before Jewish New Year.

ALISON: That must be wonderful news . . . She, and ALL her—?

BEN: On husband's side, yes. Of everything I have wished, it is for Anna to be free. Then, of course, if there is time . . . but my case is more complicated. She is individual, quite separate from me. All the same, when she is in re- fusal eight years, it is because we are all part of "same big happy family."

ALISON: She must feel terrible.

BEN: Why? This is most exciting day in all her life!

ALISON: That can't be true. I mean, exciting, yes. But also—

BEN: She will not let this impede. She will see; there is opportunity; she will take; she will go. I must stop.

(They stop.)

ALISON: . . . Ben?

(They walk, turn a corner, and then stop again.)

BEN: So. Here is building number 3. When you come next time, you will look for tall clock as reference point. Also, you will need apartment code. So, you may try. 2-7-8-8.

(She presses code number. Door buzzer sounds. They proceed. Lights rise on table, set for lunch. Yadviga welcomes them warmly.)

YADVIGA: *Strast-vitye.*

ALISON: *Strast-vitye. Minya zavoot Alyona.*

YADVIGA: *(Affectionately)* Alyonnnna . . . *Pajalsta* . . .

BEN: Also called "Alison."

(He goes to bookcase.)

YADVIGA: So. You know. No Anna.

ALISON: You must be very . . . happy.

BEN: (With book) So, it seems this name can be either biblical "Elisheva," or perhaps simply "Eli."

YADVIGA: Eli! *Eta ochen krasivaya* . . .

ALISON: Yes, but I think I still prefer Alyona.

BEN: Still, you are familiar with your name.

ALISON: I know my name.

YADVIGA: *Eli.*

ALISON: Al*yon*a. I really much prefer Alyona.

BEN: But why?

ALISON: Why? Because I don't know from Elisheva! I don't much know the Bible. I don't feel the need to announce my—

BEN: Yes?

ALISON: . . . I just . . . like . . . Alyona.

BEN: So do we. Come.

YADVIGA: Eat.

BEN: We like "Alyona" very much.

(They eat.)

ALISON: Thank you.

(More eating)

This is nice. Food, I mean. It's good food.

BEN: Is Jewish food. You like Jewish music?

ALISON: I'll have some more potatoes, please.

BEN: So this is familiar melody, or am I little bit—what is expression—off-key-chain?

ALISON: Key. Off key. No chain.

BEN: "Off key." So. Help me. Please. Sing.

(Sings the melody to "Tumbalalaika")

Hai-dai-dai, dai-dai-dai,
Hai-dai-dai, dai-dai-dai . . .
BEN: Come on! Everybody!
(Yadviga joins.)
Hai-dai-dai, dai-dai-dai,
Dai-dai-dai-
ALISON: I can't. I don't know it. I can't . . . Help you . . . With . . . You know, with the song . . .

BEN: Okay.

ALISON: No, I mean, it's just . . .

BEN: Elison . . .

ALISON: I don't sing. I'm sorry. I . . . just . . . don't. Sing.

BEN: So I show you something else. Please. Come. Read.

(Ben takes Alison over to desk, gives her a postcard, as an OVIR official enters through door.)
(Lights shift to indicate that we are now in an office, although a light remains on Alison holding postcard.)

SCENE 5

OVIR: Hello! I am friendly Visa official! May I help you?

BEN: Yes, I have postcard explaining to me my most recent refusal.

OVIR: Yes! This is part of our new policy package! We are now exceptionally open when giving details as to why people are refused!

BEN: And I think this can be extremely useful in my case. You see, you have given here exact years for which my work is considered secret.

OVIR: Is new provision mentioned by General Secretary that no one be refused on secrecy grounds older than ten years.

BEN: Good. So my job at Institute of Automation ended in 1971.

OVIR: Yes? So?

BEN: So, according to statement, there are no longer grounds on which I may be refused!

OVIR: Statement?

BEN: You just mentioned new provision made by General Secretary.

OVIR: Provision?

BEN: Yes, you have just said—

OVIR: You have tape?

BEN: No.

OVIR: *Beta Mex?*

BEN: No, but—

OVIR: You have witnesses?

BEN: I am here alone.

OVIR: So perhaps you are delusional!

BEN: . . . Okay.

(Beat)

May I ask question concerning logic of these so-called secrets?

OVIR: Certainly. Please. Sit.

BEN: *(He stands.)* I have only worked on peaceful space projects in Soviet Union.

OVIR: We only *have* peaceful space projects in Soviet Union!

BEN: Yes, but for instance Surface-to-Air-Missile? My calculations could not even be applied to such invention. I have worked only on flight to moon. Before such technological advances as micro-chip.

OVIR: I am friendly Visa Official. Not micro-chip specialist.

BEN: Yes, but who is? Who, in making any decision about my work, can tell me anything about it?

OVIR: We consult with the Academy.

BEN: And they are first to admit my work is useless! They strip me of my title; openly state I am ungrateful, lousy scientist! They cannot remember what my theories are!

OVIR: They remember your theories. I believe they teach your theories. You seem to me impatient, Benjamin.

BEN: I am most patient, I can tell you.

OVIR: But I am being exceptionally OPEN with you! I am admitting that, yes, you know more about so-called micro-chip. This is stunning admission!

BEN: I understand.

OVIR: No, You must APPRECIATE, *ta-var-ish*. You must not put your need, your ego, above needs of state.

BEN: I am not "comrade."

OVIR: Then friend. We are not hasty country. We are peace-*love*rs in the midst of brutal technological competition. Your time will come.

BEN: When?

OVIR: You have plans?

BEN: I have people who wait for me.

OVIR: Tell you what. Find job. Pay back debt to State. Then we reconsider your case in, oh, let's say . . . eight years.

BEN: Eight years . . .

ALISON: *(Still watching the scene)* Eight years . . . ?

OVIR: Eight years is not such a very long time.

ALISON: But he can't wait eight years, can you? Can he?

OVIR: I'm sorry?

BEN: I said, I have medical issues, that is all.

OVIR: All are equal in our society.

BEN: I have cancer.

OVIR: Yes, this is often used by publicity seeker.

BEN: I am hardly.

OVIR: Or perhaps you don't really have cancer.

BEN: I wish this was so.

OVIR: Perhaps you are *lying* about cancer.

BEN: So I have records of extensive history of melanoma. Thyro-toxicosis.

OVIR: We give no preference to sick or to—

BEN: Myocardial infarction complicated by heart block, treated with temporary pacemaker—

OVIR: This is extremely unnecessary detail—

BEN: I have hypertension, slight angina, circulation disorder—

OVIR: I am not poly-clinic, Charny.

BEN: Also, two new tumors on my neck, seemingly benign. You may touch them.

OVIR: This is most distasteful exhibition—

BEN: You suggest I am lying. Touch.

OVIR: Charny, you are excused please.

BEN: Don't misunderstand. Soviet doctors save my life. Three times I am at the edge of death and they have performed surgery with only minor complications. But now, all *surgeons* refuse me. Because of the seizure, after last time. And I have doctors in the West who will treat me.

OVIR: Where?

BEN: Massachusetts General Hospital—

OVIR: Ah, BOOM-STATE again! This Massachusetts is a busy little state.

BEN: My brother Leon has made all the necessary arrangements.

OVIR: We know. We know all about this brother Leon. He is quite vocal expatriot.

BEN: Please. I am rational person. Why do you keep me? I mean nothing to no one.

OVIR: Fellow Soviet Citizen: You are Pioneer in the field of space. Famed Reviser of Keppler's Law of Planetary Motion. Shining star in Soviet constellation, not to mention, future architect of laser beam flat-screen-coordinate-technologies! You are not "no one." You are *some*one. Be*lieve* in yourself, Benjamin. Be proud.

BEN: I do not need your instructions in this matter.

OVIR: Then be polite. We know about the Hebrew students, Charny. The cassettes you have made. The audio history lessons.

BEN: What lessons?

OVIR: I am glad to see you have stopped. You are advised to be careful. You will leave someday. Only question . . . is when.

BEN: I do not know how much time I have left.

OVIR: And who does? Who of us in this country really knows? We see you in 1995, Benjamin. Oh, and don't tell so much about such illnesses next time. Is quite discomforting for listener.

(Fade on OVIR. Ben turns to face Alison, still holding the postcard.)

BEN: Keep. Is of no use to me.

ALISON: But you'll still need this, won't you?

BEN: In eight years . . . ? I have made miscalculation.

ALISON: Why?

BEN: What you said before . . . That you do not feel need to "announce—"

ALISON: Yes?

BEN: What? What was this thing? "Who you *are?*" I have not been content to just be . . . who I was told. I have asked for more. I have applied for more. For my family. Now look what I have done to them?

ALISON: But Anna will soon be free. She's leaving.

BEN: Exactly. For what may be a very long time. Perhaps it is better to be quiet. Thank you.

ALISON: For?

BEN: Thank you again, Elison.

(Ben exits.)

ALISON: What for? I'm sorry? He said . . .

YADVIGA: Three week he prepare for this. Three week. Work-work-work. Meeting? Nothing! Now?

ALISON: Yes. It must be very . . .

YADVIGA: Thank you. Thank you very much . . .

ALISON: For what? Yadviga? I don't understand! Thank you for . . . ?

YADVIGA: Coming.

(Fade, as Yadviga exits. Alison stares at the postcard. Lights shift as the scene becomes the Berlin Hotel Restaurant. Adam and the Producer sit and eat.)

SCENE 6

PRODUCER: Alison? Ally, sweetie?

ADAM: You've been staring at that vodka for the past hour.

ALISON: I'm fine. *I'm* . . . fine.

PRODUCER: We want you to know—C'mon, Adam—you've been doing a terrific job. Hasn't she?

ADAM: *(Obliging)* You've been doing a terrific—

ALISON: I haven't "done" anything.

PRODUCER: We're going to Baikanor, aren't we?

ADAM: . . . Middle 'a goddamn Siberia.

ALISON: It's in Kazakhstan.

ADAM: I knew that.

PRODUCER: They're launching a satellite, Adam. We're shooting it. Because of her. Because of you, Ally.

ALISON: Why don't we skip it?

ADAM: We could. I've got wall-to-wall meetings—

PRODUCER: With a bunch of talking heads.

ADAM: Walk outside! The story's right in front of our face! A nation on the brink of becoming young! People here are on fire! They're reading the newspaper, for god's sake! Devouring their own history.

PRODUCER: I got it. We'll call it, "Their Woodstock."

ALISON: Catchy.

ADAM: It's your "friend," isn't it?

ALISON: No.

PRODUCER: Adam already explained . . .

ALISON: He isn't "my" friend.

ADAM: Can't *do* unemployed scientists.

PRODUCER: No credibility.

ALISON: I thought he'd be interesting.

ADAM: Interesting? To who? A very select group of viewers in suburban Long Island, maybe.

ALISON: Meaning?

PRODUCER: Meaning, Allie, if we thought there was a picture we would shoot it, believe me.

ALISON: I believe you.

PRODUCER: She's upset. Adam? She's upset with us.

ALISON: *I'm* not upset! *I'm* not the one who's dying, okay!?

PRODUCER: Okay, he's dying. Good. Good. Do we see that?

ALISON: Excuse me?

PRODUCER: Do we *see* the cancer? It's crass, I know, but do we?

ADAM: No tears.

ALISON: The tumors on his neck are benign, so no.

ADAM: This isn't *Oprah,* for chrissake! This is *NOVA* with a news angle. And a major institute paying for it, namely mine.

PRODUCER: Okay, now Adam *does* have a point. We do need a news angle.

ALISON: This *is* a news angle.

ADAM: But where's the "new" in it?

PRODUCER: Is there a "new" in your news angle?

ALISON: A man is suffering. Needlessly.

ADAM: That isn't new.

PRODUCER: How 'bout this? I need pithy. Is he pithy? Because people here still don't think in terms of sound bytes yet.

ALISON: As a matter of fact, he's rather technical. But he has dreams. He has nightmares.

PRODUCER: Allie, sweetie. This is PBS. We don't have budget for nightmares.

ALISON: Let's just forget it.

PRODUCER: No. I don't want to "forget it."

ADAM: Clearly. He wants to work with you.

PRODUCER: Adam. Now this man is suffering. And that's moving. I mean, it's moving to *me.* Cause I know from suffering. I *come* from it. Does anyone wanna hear about it? *No.* They have *been* there. They have *done* that. Is this different? Can we make it different for others?

ALISON: I have no idea.

ADAM: She has no idea!

PRODUCER: Well, does he emote? I mean, can I get quivers? Eye flutters?

ALISON: I don't know if you can get flutters. I don't know if he quivers. I don't know how he emotes! I don't know HIM. That's what I'm saying. I know a bio. I know some facts.

PRODUCER: Like?

ALISON: Like he has a wife.

PRODUCER: Okay?

ALISON: He has a daughter.

PRODUCER: He has a daughter . . . ?

ALISON: Who is leaving for Vienna at eight o'clock tomorrow morning, and neither father nor child have any idea whether they will *see* each other again!

PRODUCER: *(A big beat . . .)* . . . Adam? . . . Do you see a lightbulb?

ADAM: I believe I'm in meetings all day tomorrow.

PRODUCER: But what I'm seeing is a picture—a final farewell airport picture!

ADAM: I believe we have an interview at the Presidium of the Supreme Soviet of the Communist Party at eight forty-five.

PRODUCER: *(To Alison)* She couldn't push her flight back a day?

ALISON: I don't think so.

ADAM: You know, Alison, it sounds to me like the perfect subject for *print.*

PRODUCER: Now, Adam. Bear with me. What I'm seeing is a FINAL-GOOD-BYE-AIRPORT-PICTURE *in English!*

ADAM: And what I see is rank, parochial sentiment.

PRODUCER: But the camera LIKES rank, parochial sentiment. Now I don't mean to be a *noodge,* but I am prepared to go to the mat for this shot. Adam, I want my picture. I want my picture!

ADAM: Then consider an alternate funding source.

(Beat)

PRODUCER: You know, Ally, the more I think of it—

ALISON: Don't tell me.

PRODUCER: Sounds like the perfect subject for—

ALISON: Print. I get it.

ADAM: Op-Ed.

PRODUCER: *Wall Street Journal.*

ADAM: *Hadassah.*

ALISON: You're uncomfortable with the subject?

ADAM: I'm not uncomfortable.

PRODUCER: We're not uncomfortable—

ALISON: I was. Not hot enough. Not hip enough. Not hard enough. Not huge enough.

ADAM: Alison, I don't recall you being one of our campus-radical-hotheads.

ALISON: I'm not. I wasn't.

ADAM: Then I'm sure you can appreciate the importance of a critical dispassion, especially if you plan on continuing with any serious work in the field.

ALISON: I do, but—

ADAM: Then let the vice president and U. S. Congress tell the world how much "We Americans love Freedom." *We Americans love to be reelected,* is what they mean. And therein lies the fallacy. They're still operating under the assumption that somehow three percent of an electorate represents something more than what it is. In fact, Jews are less. If we look at birthrates. The price of oil. We have been letting Fatty Emotions that play well on a certain Banquet Circuit estrange us from an ever-widening body-politic. And therein lies great danger. The danger of being by-passed. We must place ourselves on the right side of history. Speak Truth to the two most powerful nations in the history of civilization. Point them in scientific, demographically sound, new directions. That's why we're academics, Alison. That's what you've signed up for.

(A beat)

PRODUCER: . . . This isn't going to be in the film, is it?

ALISON: I don't think *I'm* going to be, either.

PRODUCER: Ally—

ALISON: No, I'm clearly not "dispassionate" enough, nor terribly convincing, either.

PRODUCER: You've sold me. You could hold a press conference for the guy.

ALISON: You gentlemen can get someone else to make your wake-up calls.

PRODUCER: But don't you see what's happening?

ADAM: You've grown "attached."

ALISON: I have not grown attached! But so what if I did?

PRODUCER: Well, that'd be sweet. Adam, isn't it sweet?

ALISON: It is not sweet! This is not about sweetness. It's about cruelty. Yes, it's been known to happen; a country can be cruel, gentlemen. As can people. Well-fed, comfortable, people. Our sitting here is cruel. MY siting here is especially—

PRODUCER: Ally—

ALISON: No—two weeks ago, Benjamin Charny was a piece of paper I thought I'd thrown away—a horror story to be dismissed, just like the thousands I'd been dismissing every day. Only this isn't a horror story; it's a Hope Story. Ben Charny isn't some gray, featureless photo. He is a scientist who studies stars! Who is being extinguished. Who needs our help. There. I said it. I want to help! . . . I want to help! And the most pathetic thing is . . . ? I have no idea how.

(Beat. Sits. Adam and the Producer just look at each other. Lights rise on Ben, at his table, writing.)

SCENE 7

BEN: "Good-bye my Anna. May you have sweet life for you and for Yuri, and of course, my Sima. May you be accepted to M.I.T., if this is still goal. Be healthy. Have many children. See the good. Love freedom. Find job. . . . Do not be consumed . . ."

(He stops. Folds letter. Yadviga enters in coat, tying a rain hat. She waits for Ben, strokes his forehead. Then exits. He follows off. Cross-fade back to Alison.)

ALISON: *(To audience)* I think about that homeless woman I used to pass. What happened to her? Or the person I was. It's one thing to sit in a sauna and be beaten with spiked sticks; to allow a pain; deny a feeling. But to watch others be beaten; or denied . . . to teach Lenin and assign "What Is To Be Done?" and then, not do . . . What was to be done about Ben? I went to the Meat Pie Lady—The one who sold me fresh dill wrapped in *Pravda*. Someone had to bundle those bunches. There was work to be done everyday.

(Doorbell rings. Alison enters with a bag of food.)

SCENE 8

BEN: Hul-loh.

ALISON: I brought meat pies.

BEN: Nice to see you.

ALISON: And potatoes. Today, *I'm* cooking.

BEN: Sounds good.

ALISON: Where's Yada?

BEN: Out.

ALISON: Oh?

BEN: At Anna's old apartment. Helping new tenant to move in.

ALISON: She's very strong. I admire her.

BEN: Yes.

ALISON: I told 'em I'm not going to Leningrad.

BEN: Beautiful city.

ALISON: *Or* Baikanor. Let 'em fend for themselves.

BEN: But your job? Reason you came?

ALISON: I wouldn't be back 'til Saturday, and then we'd only have—

BEN: I know. You should go.

ALISON: But I leave in a week—

BEN: I am aware. Please. Leave such vegetables. I need you for matter separate from cooking.

ALISON: But I'd like to make something for—

BEN: I understand. So I have been working on letter for past five days intended for distribution amongst membership of U.S. Academy of Science. Is such group, yes?

ALISON: National Academy . . . Yes, there is.

BEN: Good. So, please. Make correction. Is my own translation, and despite excellent dictionary, I think I may have one or two little bump spots.

ALISON: I . . . You want me to read this now?

BEN: If you have trouble with my typing—

ALISON: No, it's . . . it's . . . uhm, just this is a ten-page letter.

BEN: Is clear so far?

ALISON: I'm still on the title. Letters in America don't usually have titles.

BEN: In Russia they do.

(She reads to herself.)

So, how's my spelling?

ALISON: Uhm, this first sentence . . .

BEN: Read to me.

ALISON: ". . . in September five—"

BEN: "On." Is typo.

ALISON: ". . . on September five—"

BEN: Yes?

ALISON: ". . . From cancer Faina Kogan two days after permission died."

BEN: Yes. Is tragic. And most terrible.

ALISON: I don't think people will understand—

BEN: I am presenting initial example of—

ALISON: No, *I* understand. It's just . . . this goes on, about somebody else, for—

BEN: Three pages. Then we move onto discussion on Myth of Peaceful Space.

ALISON: Ben, you don't have to do that.

BEN: Why? This is not story of one man.

ALISON: But this is a personal letter. You want this to be *your* personal letter, right?

BEN: To scientists—

ALISON: But also, maybe, politicians? Newspapers. I think that's important.

BEN: This will be separate, more expansive letter.

ALISON: No, Ben. You don't understand. No one in America will read a ten-page letter.

BEN: Why not?

ALISON: It's too many pages—

BEN: So I retype, single space.

ALISON: No. Look. You don't want to overwhelm people. Trust me. You're going to have to cut.

BEN: So? We cut!

(He gives her pencil.)

Show me.

ALISON: I . . . This is your life.

BEN: Only small part. I have left out many, many details—

ALISON: I know . . . There's just . . . I . . . wouldn't know where to begin.

BEN: So begin with a sentence.

ALISON: But w . . . where do you mention your cancer in this?

BEN: Is not relevant to scientists. Perhaps, in separate letter to Medical Association—

ALISON: No! I shouldn't do this.

BEN: Why? You are asking good questions.

ALISON: But people get lots of letters! You can't just give names; dates; reasons for refusal . . . You have to present yourself.

BEN: So you help to present me.

ALISON: To present you, I'd have to *know* you, and—

BEN: What would you like to know?

ALISON: I don't mean just "know."

BEN: I have no secrets.

ALISON: I know that, Ben . . . I just—

BEN: Yes?

ALISON: Wouldn't know where to start.

BEN: So, we start with meat pie. I bring two plates.

(He exits. She picks up pencil, begins cutting, rewriting a line. Ben returns. He eats.)

ALISON: You're very different from me.

BEN: I think you are quite wrong.

ALISON: You're much more at . . . peace. I mean, despite—

BEN: My situation?

ALISON: You never . . .

BEN: Have *questions?*

ALISON: You do? What kind?

BEN: Simple. The most simple. Childhood story, actually. Fortunately, this, for sure, is irrelevant to issue of letter.

ALISON: I'd like to hear.

BEN: We have to cut.

ALISON: You said there's a story.

BEN: I said we are similar, in simple ways.

ALISON: Please tell me. About your questions. I want to hear.

BEN: But—

ALISON: I need to.

BEN: . . . So . . . I will tell you about 1943. Is quite interesting really, because I also have memory of meat pie. Actually, closer to potato pie, but all the same, texture is similar; this same taste of bread, wet blood, and tears. It is still middle of war, I am five, and we have just returned from Ural Mountains where my family is sleeping in basement of local library. On this very day of my return, young boy stops me on street and asks typical question of this time: "Who are you? Russian, or Jew?" And on answer "Jew," he hits me. "Socks me right in the kisser" is, I believe, the expression. I run to library, my face is swollen, all wet; and when I tell incident to my father, he has answered me in this way: "Benya," he tells me, "You can hit also." I can hit also. And so it began. For all my later life. I would fight any incident quite physically. I would fight it. And I would win. You know I am champion wrestler in high school?

ALISON: No.

BEN: Also, swimming. Age fifteen.

ALISON: Really?

BEN: Free-style. All the same, at this point, something changed. Less in me than in country. Around middle of fifties, acts of personal anti-Semitism became much less visible; much more clever. You see, when you are fighting against Man, you can see what you must hit. When you are fighting

State, you are fighting endless chain. You cannot win or lose. State only allows or disallows, and always in arbitrary manner. In place of combat, spirit fights with self. And this is real genius of State: Elimination of Archetypal Enemy. All is "internal" now. Anti-Semitism exists only within imagination of each Jew. World watches in amusement as Jew eats self to death. Now again, act of brilliance: Refusenik as resister of Peace Train, putting ego and self-interest above "Good of Man," "Fight for Peace." I love peace, I can tell you. I would just like small piece of this peace for myself.

(Beat)

ALISON: Ben, I want to arrange a press conference for you. So you can present yourself.

BEN: I have letter.

ALISON: You need more. You need attention. You and Yada.

BEN: And who else?

ALISON: Who else? No one.

BEN: But there is whole group of Cancer Patient Refuseniks both here and in Leningrad and in . . .

ALISON: But begin with one, right?

BEN: Also, group with disease other than cancer; for example, heart, kidney, liver.

ALISON: Begin with one sentence, isn't that what you said? And then slowly the letter will change?

BEN: But my case is unexceptional.

ALISON: Ben, you are extremely exceptional.

BEN: But there are so many like me!

ALISON: But you and Yada need publicity! The more groups you invite—

BEN: Yes?

ALISON: The less immediate the press conference.

BEN: But there are thousands of—

ALISON: We can't have thousands in this apartment, Ben! I can't *do* anything about thousands! I can *may*be do something about *one.*

BEN: But is not my place—

ALISON: You have to FIGHT this.

BEN: You are not listening!

ALISON: You said you fought when you were five. You can fight when you're fifty! You don't have other choices.

BEN: But is unseemly to call such attention—

ALISON: Ben. Stop. You can't wait. You have to do this.

(Long pause)

BEN: So, may I make phone call on this matter?

ALISON: However you want.

BEN: So, just to friend or two.

ALISON: This is for you, Ben.

BEN: So just to friend.

ALISON: It's for you . . .

(Beat)

BEN: You know, Alison? You are tough little cookie.

ALISON: So are you, Ben.

BEN: So is my Anna . . .

(They eat quietly . . .)

You mind that I am picking at this with my finger and not fork?

ALISON: No.

BEN: Is quite interesting, really. I have close to this same meat pie when I was five.

(They eat in silence. Lights shift. Alison steps forward.)

SCENE 9

ALISON: *(To audience)* I made about six calls before leaving for Leningrad. Ben made one or two to his friends. Word got out. By the Sunday of the press conference, Ben's apartment was a madhouse. A dozen refuseniks with various illnesses; six world-weary Western correspondents; that's eighteen *sick* people in one room. I can't show them all to you now, but I do have my notes and they read: "One Refusenik with eye-patch; one Refusenik with cane; one with back brace and mild-case-distemper." Oh, and my favorite, "Alexander Solzhenitsyn look-alike."

(We hear coughing and wheezing behind Alison as the various Refuseniks enter and complain in animated fashion.)

On the reporters' side, the simple note, "The men are better dressed."

(Enter Reporters from the Post, Tribune, *and Patience Smith from* Times, *carrying a large handbag.)*

Perhaps this is because the men don't have additional burden of staying up 'til three in the morning with child, as Patience Smith surely must have, for she had now caught said child's cold and was letting everyone know it.

(Patience sneezes loudly. All freeze.)

PATIENCE: . . . Excuse me.

ALISON: I'd never really organized anything before. I would now find out why!

(The din returns. Alison takes her place in the circle.)

CANE: *Nu?*

BACK BRACE: *Sha!*

CANE: Who you telling *"Sha"?*

EYE PATCH: Shhh . . .

BEN: Gentlemen . . .

BACK BRACE: *Shh* . . .

CANE: Who's *shushing* me? Who's *shushing?*

BACK BRACE: I'm *shushing!*

BEARD: YOU shut up!

BEN: Thank you, gentlemen.

BACK BRACE: Charny. Begin.

(Ben unfolds a prepared statement.)

BEN: First, may I say thank you to busy members of press for attending. We believe there are good signs coming now from Kremlin—

POST: Excuse me. Can we just go around the room and get the names?

TRIBUNE: We'll need to leave for a briefing at ten thirty—

POST: But we wanna make sure we get the dates, illness—

TRIBUNE: Reasons for refusal—

BEN: Yes, fine. So, we will—

CANE: KOGAN. K-O-G-A-N. First name, FELIX. First refusal, '75.

ALISON: Uhm, Ben—?

CANE: I have phlebitis, bursitis, acute condition pancreatitis, hemorrhage in left kidney—

TRIBUNE: Reason?

CANE: Secrets.

(Patience sneezes loudly.)

POST: Bless you.

PATIENCE: Please. Continue.

TRIBUNE: Next?

CANE: Also, I have wife recently dead from cancer after—

POST: Name?

TRIBUNE: Her name please?

CANE: Faina. F-A-I-N—

TRIBUNE: Thank you. Next?

ALISON: Ben? Would—

CANE: I would like to explain nature of my so-called secrets—

TRIBUNE: We're just going around the room, Sir.

CANE: CHARGES ARE LUDICROUS! My wife would be *alive* today if not
for such—

(Patience sneezes loudly once again.)

POST: Kleenex, hon? You sound terrible.

PATIENCE: No, I have . . . please. Continue.

EYE PATCH: SHUTROFF. S-H-U-T-R-O-F-F. First name, Sasha.

ALISON: Uhm, excuse me?

EYE PATCH: First refusal, '79. Second refusal, '81. Third refusal, '85. Lost job,
'79. Suffer from glaucoma, thrombosis, angina, mild case tuberculosis—

POST: Reason?

EYE PATCH: Also—

TRIBUNE: State Secrets . . .

EYE PATCH: Complicated by fact that my wife speaks Chinese.

(Patience sneezes again.)

TRIBUNE: You sound terrible!

ALISON: Would you like some tea?

PATIENCE: No, thank you. I'm . . . I'm sorry.

BACK BRACE: FOX. F-O-X. Vladimir. I have son in Los Angeles, aspiring actor
in television industry. I have picture.

POST: Just the illness, Sir.

BACK BRACE: Deterioration of spinal cord.

TRIBUNE: And what do *you* think of Gorby's new reforms?

BACK BRACE: I don't see them.

POST: Hey. That's good! I can *use* that!

TRIBUNE: Anything else?

BACK BRACE: Only that medical treatment here is fine for young children, especially poly-clinic. But for serious illness, such as spinal cord, T.B., or phlebitis, colitis, sinusitis . . .

(Patience sneezes again.)

PATIENCE: Oh, fuck!

POST: You are killing me with those eyes!

TRIBUNE: Would you go home and bundle up!

PATIENCE: Guys, I'm fine.

TRIBUNE: You cannot fool around with a cold!

POST: Not in Moscow!

TRIBUNE: First it starts in your nose—

POST: Then your throat—

TRIBUNE: Before you know it, you've got a FEVER!

ALISON: *(To audience)* "Empathy: American Style."

PATIENCE: Gentlemen. Please. Proceed.

BEARD: So. I begin.

TRIBUNE: I'm afraid we *will* have to be going.

BEARD: Sit. Name is KREITMAN. K-R—

POST: We did mention a briefing—

BEARD: I begin again.

TRIBUNE: It's a rather important—

BEARD: I said, sit.

TRIBUNE: Sit.

(They sit.)

BEARD: Name is Kreitman. I am in Siberia eight years for alleged teaching of Hebrew. Now am released on condition I work as coat check in local swim pavilion.

POST: So you like the reforms?

BEARD: Well, this is complicated question.

TRIBUNE: Thank you very much.

POST: I'm afraid we really do have to be—

TRIBUNE: Patience?

PATIENCE: My husband's covering.

POST: Gentlemen. We'll be sure to press this matter.

TRIBUNE: Thank your wife for us.

BEN: Yes, of course.

ALISON: But where are you going?

POST: We can be very tough on the Soviets.

BEN: Yes. Thank you.

ALISON: Ben? This is for you! *(To Reporters)* Excuse me? What could possibly be more pressing than a person's LIFE?

POST AND TRIBUNE: . . . Intermediate Nuclear Force Treaties, Ma'am.

(A moment. Reporters exit.)

BEARD: I begin again . . .

ALISON: *(To audience)* And so Kreitman began and, in truest Solzhenitsian manner, continued for the next two and a half hours . . .

BEARD: In 1963, my wife had Caesar Operation, followed by acute tonsillectomy . . .

ALISON: *(To audience)* . . . And on he went. It was only the *New York Times* at this point, Ben's big opportunity having long been shot. Patience Smith was working on her third packet of Kleenex, and even *she* was beginning to flag and, more importantly, needed to be getting back to her kid.

PATIENCE: I thank you all, and will do my very best to bring your stories to the American public. I can't promise every story we file gets run, but you *have* been heard most clearly.

CANE: What about Ben?

EYE PATCH: Yes, what about our host?

BACK BRACE: Quick. Ben. Tell.

CANE: Hurry.

BACK BRACE: *(Escorting Patience back)* Sit. Please.

BEN: . . . It has been long morning for you.

PATIENCE: Yes, it has.

(She sits. Takes out a Kleenex.)

BEN: You are catching cold from your child. You should be home.

PATIENCE: Please. Begin. I'm listening.

BEN: So, name is Charny. C-H-A—

PATIENCE: I know, Ben. Your brother has worked very hard on your behalf. Especially in the United States Senate.

BEN: Apparently such letters of support come rather easily in election year.

PATIENCE: Just the same, it's a symbol, an important one. You're not forgotten.

BEN: You know, my daughter is arriving just this evening in the city of Boston.

PATIENCE: Ben. I want you to tell me all about your family, and anything else that comes to mind . . .

BEN: So. okay . . .

ALISON: *(To audience)* And so he began to talk, mostly about facts, and then he began to cry, or maybe I did. I'd long stopped taking notes. I do remember Patience leaving some time before one, though. I'm sure she would've liked to have stayed longer, if she could've, but she couldn't; nor could I.

(Lights fade on press conference area as all leave, except for Ben, who acknowledges Alison's help, and then he too exits.)

SCENE 10

ALISON: *(To audience)* I saw Ben a last time before the end of that trip. We went out for dinner, just the three of us . . .

(Ben and Yadviga return.)

BEN: I have hope.

YADVIGA: He will be fine.

ALISON: Yadviga's a really great woman, and anyone who meets them says *she's* the really strong one.

YADVIGA: So long as we have each other, no matter where we live . . .

ALISON: Or that she was. She still struggles. With the language.

BEN: We have many hopes.

ALISON: I wound up leaving a bunch of silly personal items; vitamins, cold pills, toothpaste; anything I could, really. It wasn't much to hold them. I asked them not to give me anything but, of course, they insisted. They gave me a candlestick.

BEN: I would like to see Israel someday.

ALISON: And a meat pie.

BEN: I am most curious about future of this little country. First, though, I must go to U.S. and tiny boom-state called Massachusetts. It will be all my family, brother, grandchild, daughter, all in bottom floor of big house, I imagine. There will be stimulating work, school, temple. These are things to be treasured. Perhaps I must also come visit New York City. Or perhaps you will come visit me. You will visit me in Massachusetts. Or Tel Aviv. Or in Moscow, if I am still here. If I am still here . . . you will, I pray, be welcome.

ALISON: In the immediate days following my return, I scoured the newspaper: A-section, B-section. Anything for an item on the press conference. But there was nothing. A couple weeks later, after I'd long fallen back into my habit of skipping over things, I stumbled into someone who said they'd read a letter in the *Times* a week earlier by a man named Ben. Had I heard of him? I ran to the library and, sure enough, there it was. A personal statement, Op-Ed; the same letter I'd sent to Anna the day I'd gotten back. I don't know how she got it placed, but the letter looked great in there. "Anna? *Isn't* it wonderful!" I said, stupidly, as only someone infatuated with the wand of Media might.

(As in the beginning, Anna appears.)

ANNA: Not so much has changed with his situation —

ALISON: She said.

ANNA: In fact, he is even more depressed now.

ALISON: Why?

ANNA: Well. He misses us . . .

ALISON: *(To audience)* . . . But he just had his letter published in the *New York Times!* . . . Why isn't he better?

(Fade on Anna. Ben attempts to stand.)

A few weeks after the article, Ben collapsed during a reception at the Australian Embassy.

(He sits back down.)

He sat by himself for several hours, then paid for a cab ride home. A week after that, while delivering a paper at yet another press conference . . .

BEN: Subject of today's meeting will be devoted, uhm . . . Excuse, please. Excuse me?

ALISON: He was forced to stop after just five minutes. Too hot for him to stand. There were just too many people in the room.

BEN: So sorry . . .

(Ben walks off under his own power.)

ALISON: I remember going to rallies in Washington; or in front of the U.N.; the routine of it; increasingly less routine. Then a volunteer thing out in Brighton Beach. The same. I eventually made it out to Temple Holy Blossom one Friday night. Turned out it was Passover weekend, I didn't even know! The rabbi there called it The Holiday of Freedom. That seemed pretty simple. And the simple seemed sufficient. Just about.

(Michael appears.)

MICHAEL: So you *finally* made it.

ALISON: Made it? Oh, you mean, out here?

MICHAEL: The peace. With your people.

ALISON: I'm trying.

MICHAEL: And this is gonna be a regular thing? 'Cause I can sign ya up. Homeless Committee, Ritual Committee. You wanna carpool? We can carpool. Wanna get engaged? We can do that too.

ALISON: The services were nice, Michael. Just . . .

MICHAEL: "Not for you?"

ALISON: Maybe.

MICHAEL: Must be pretty happy about your friend, though.

ALISON: Friend?

MICHAEL: You know. The news! Didn't you hear?

ALISON: And then he told me . . .

MICHAEL: We're all driving up—we could squeeze one more in. Or, no, you'd "prefer to take the train. So you can read." See? I'm learning!

ALISON: No, that's . . . I can squeeze.

MICHAEL: Great! Let's go!

(Sound of an airplane. Michael takes Alison by the arm as a light reveals Ben and Yadviga holding carry-on baggage. A crowd gathers.)

BEN: *(To audience)* On July sixteen, nineteen-hundred and eighty-eight, after so much work on my behalf from my brother, my Anna, politicians, doctors, clergy, and so many other people from so many countries, I was brought to Butler Aviation Terminal, Logan Airport, Boston, Massachusetts, by Doctor Armand Hammer in his private jet. He had read about our case and now arranged for a great big fruit platter to be on board as we took off. But I could not eat. Only when the pilot announced that we were officially leaving Soviet air space, did Yadviga and I split a kiwi.

ALISON: He looked thinner. Older.

BEN: *(Moving to a make-shift podium)* Senators Kennedy, Kerry, Mrs. Dukakis, friends . . . We thank you. It is privilege to speak with you direct from this tarmac.

ALISON: But he sounded the same.

BEN: *(Again, to crowd)* I am not politician. Today I have no words. So allow me simply to recite . . . the names: Rabbi Mehlman. Rabbi Friedman. Cantor Einhorn . . .

ALISON: One by one, people lined up to shake his hand at the podium.

BEN: *(To audience)* My heart was so full, I was afraid it would explode.

ALISON: Ben?

BEN: Elison.

ALISON: Ben, I . . .

BEN: Elison. *(To audience)* And in her eyes, I could see, they were saying . . . "What now?"

ALISON: *What* now?

BEN: I have hope.

ALISON: You have to get better.

BEN: I do not know when I will work again.

ALISON: First get better.

BEN: I am ready to. And also scared; a little. "But mostly fighter." Right?

ALISON: *(To audience)* And it was like we were picking at a meat pie with our fingers. No forks. No plates. Standing on a tarmac.

BEN: I will speak with you more?

ALISON: Absolutely.

BEN: But first I must do small talk with Mrs. Dukakis.

ALISON: Go.

BEN: Look at all these people! All for who?

ALISON: They love you, Ben.

BEN: How you know this?

ALISON: I just . . .

BEN: Yes?

ALISON: Say hello to Mrs. Dukakis.

(Ben touches her cheek and exits.)

Several surgeries ensued. Tumors removed. A new pacemaker. Kidney stone, blood clot, all treated and eventually, Ben was released. As was I. Or we. All of us. The grip of illness had loosened, and with it, the excuse for calling; for checking in. There were follow-ups, a period of convalescence, but within eight months, Ben was sending out his resumé. Waiting for the phone to ring. For the mail to bring good news. I came back to visit the following spring, upon completion of a dissertation, a job talk, the mail bringing with it some big news of its own. Ben and Yada had moved into the bottom floor of a big house in Brookline with Anna and her family, just like Ben had dreamed, everyone working, everyone busy. Everyone, that is, except for Ben.

(Shift to Ben watching TV)

SCENE 11

BEN: How 'bout some black bean dip?

ALISON: Hi, Ben.

BEN: Baba ganoush? Also called eggplant?

ALISON: How are you feeling?

BEN: I could use some Advil. This television. Is something!

ALISON: We can turn it off.

BEN: Such beautiful pictures. With a capability to express . . . so much. And, of course, freedom to. And to wind up with phenomenon of so-called *Geraldo Show.*

ALISON: I don't watch.

BEN: Oh, you should. Seemingly trained as lawyer, with actual intelligence, and yet, catering to lowest common denominator of such exponential degree as to reduce said denominator to practical negative integer.

ALISON: Like I said, we can just . . .

BEN: Have you seen this episode? Folding chair thrown across studio by neo-Nazi. Thrown back by black man. Hits Old Woman. She bleeds. Geraldo winks. "Back in a flash, after these messages."

ALISON: I told Anna I'd be happy to watch Sima. Or take her for a walk. Is she here? We could *all*—

BEN: Anna is at work. Sima is at new day care, receiving socialization training. So I have no day job as baby-sitter.

ALISON: Oh. So . . .

BEN: Anna is back at seven. She leaves house at eight. Yuri is at minyan three times daily. This black bean dip, I am not allowed.

ALISON: You mean, you're keeping kosher.

BEN: He is. And we are all in compliance, but not happily, least of all, my Anna.

ALISON: I'm sorry to hear that.

BEN: Is funny country. Or maybe Russia is the more. That two people, so different, would find each other in Moscow . . .

ALISON: Yes?

BEN: And have meaning for each other, there, but . . .

ALISON: But?

BEN: Less here. Much less. What will become, do you think?

ALISON: Of?

BEN: Who knows?

(An awkward stillness)

ALISON: So where's Yada?

BEN: Work.

ALISON: Doing?

BEN: She is trained as metalurgical engineer.

ALISON: *(Hopefully)* Yes, I know. And?

BEN: And this is not what she is doing.

ALISON: I see. How 'bout you? Have you . . . ?

BEN: I have turned down several mid-entry-level offers.

ALISON: That's great! That you've *had* . . .

BEN: All arranged by temple.

ALISON: Still—

BEN: A rabbi can arrange for free membership, car loan, also be mortgage cosigner, if one were to accept such. But he cannot create resumé. Nor teach young executive to read one.

ALISON: You'll find something.

BEN: Oh, I am used to not working. I am not working in Soviet Union eight years. But I have always been busy. Apparently no one in America needs secret audiocassette Hebrew lesson made by old Russian.

ALISON: But that's a good thing. Right? That you don't have to make them anymore?

BEN: It is a very good thing.

(Beat. He gets up.)

So you have come to visit.

ALISON: If I can be useful. I mean, if you want to go for a walk—just the two of us—we can do that—

BEN: I am waiting for phone call from potential employer. Also, mail carrier who is half hour late.

ALISON: Right.

BEN: No black bean dip, then?

ALISON: Do you miss it?

BEN: Miss?

ALISON: Just, you know. Nothing. Everything . . .

BEN: I miss nothing from my old life.

ALISON: Not even—? Just knowing your purpose. Because there must be something . . . I mean, it does seem crazy to go halfway around the world just to find . . . Because, I mean, everything here gets so fuzzy, and it doesn't have to be—like you were saying. Just turn on a TV. There is so much Hate in *this* country, and we should be DOING something about it, shouldn't we? Working for the Anti-Defamation—or I dunno—writing letters like we used to in—

BEN: It is not mine to cast blame in America.

ALISON: That's not what I—

BEN: I wait for new job.

ALISON: But—

BEN: You know, Yadviga is working for good samaritan. So-called Salvation Army Thrift Shop in residence at Beth Israel Hospital. She makes six dollars for one hour of back break. Literally. Comes home, lies on floor. She has never been so tired in all her life. *I* make dinner. If this is kind of job you are looking for, I am sure they have Salvation Army in New York City Mount Sinai Medical—

ALISON: I have a job.

BEN: You—?

ALISON: Offer. I have a tenure track *offer* from a political science department in the Midwest. At a good school.

BEN: Wow! This is great!

ALISON: No. It's . . . okay. It's perfectly okay, but it isn't—

BEN: Why didn't you say? Let's have celebration!

ALISON: No.

BEN: We can break open new black bean dip!

ALISON: That isn't why I came up—

BEN: We have Mr. Paul Newman Salsa with blue corn chip!

ALISON: Ben.

BEN: So you like Mild, Medium, or Hot?

ALISON: I don't want a celebration.

BEN: So I am out of Bartyls & James Wine Cooler but can call store delivery from local Stop & Shop.

ALISON: Would you please stop?

BEN: This is most incredible aspect of life here—so-called Home Shopping; QVC. I am so happy to hear your news, Elison, I cannot tell you!

ALISON: Well, I'm not sure I'm going to take it.

BEN: What?

ALISON: The job.

BEN: But why? Why not?

ALISON: Because I don't think that's what I should be doing. I don't want what we did in Russia to be over.

BEN: But you have job in chosen field. You have spent life training for, working for. Not everyone is so lucky.

ALISON: I realize.

BEN: You should go to Midwest, take job, buy house.

ALISON: You sound like my father.

BEN: Only your father . . . is your father.

(A beat)

"So what am I," you are wondering?

ALISON: Sometimes.

BEN: I am a person whose sentence you changed . . . And whose life. Now you must go work . . . change your own.

ALISON: But it has changed. You changed my sentence. We changed each other's.

BEN: Yes?

ALISON: And we have to keep changing.

BEN: You are very right.

ALISON: So how do we change together?

(Pregnant pause. The phone rings.)

BEN: This may be job.

(Ben excuses himself.)

ALISON: *(To audience)* It wasn't. But I took mine. And moved away. And soon Ben did much the same. He got a position as senior programmer for a startup off route 128. Bought a house in the suburbs. Yada, Anna, and Sima moved with. Yuri stayed behind with his minyan. We exchanged New Year's cards, articles. Ben was doing important work with lasers; navigational models onboard airplanes; preventing tragedies. Then one year, a card came back, forwarding address expired. The startup had gone belly-up, and Ben and Yadviga had moved again. But where? Too busy to pursue. I leave the Big Ten a few years after arriving. The tenure clock still ticking but the faith in it flagging. And it showed. In the work. Writing about Remnants after being "strongly advised" not to. Talking about health care when no one seemed to; care, that is. Not in my field. "I am in the wrong field;" it occurs to me. So I call my father.

(Picks up)

"Is he there? Oh, right. Forgot. Say hi, then. Bye, then."

(Hangs up)

Week later.

(A light up Alison's Father)

ALISON'S FATHER: Hey, kiddo!

ALISON: Hi, Daddy!

ALISON'S FATHER: Come to Washington!

ALISON: He said. "Okay, Daddy."

ALISON'S FATHER: Helluva town these days!

(Fade on Father)

ALISON: . . . And when I get there, he's gone. Covering something. But he leaves a list. Of names. So I call. And eventually, wind up here. At the Bank. A place for states in need. And so, sensing potential, they send me on mission. And I'm scheduled to go again. The week of Anna's wedding. And so this . . . invitation.

(Anna steps forward, with Fiancé by her side.)

ANNA: *(Reads)* "Mrs. Benjamin Charny and Dr. Rosalie & Bernard Goodman request the honor of your presence at the wedding of their children, Anna and Adam . . ."

ALISON: I R.S.V.P. "Sorry. Can't. Miss you." And depart.

(Lights shift.)

I arrive in Ukraine on delegation, but no one wants to show us any clinics. The mayor's more interested in Theme Parks than T.B. centers. He's pushing tourist traps; we're pushing toilets.

(A man with a megaphone appears.)

CHERNOBYL MAYOR: ATTENTION! ATTENTION, CHERNOBYL SHOPPERS! BIG SALE ON BOTTLED NORWEGIAN WATER— AISLE FIVE!

ALISON: I stick around anyhow. Looking for something. Someone. I see very few men over fifty. More old women. Who still sell meat pies. And it dawns on me; what I've always known. That my grandmother fled the Cossacks. And I keep coming back in her place. To the home that she left. But Kiev never was. And Minsk is out of the way. So I fly to Moscow to see who's left. I call our old family friends, the Klimovs; Victor's widow, Olya.

OLYA: Come to *dacha,* for weekend. But no sauna. Is broken.

ALISON: Sorry to hear that.

OLYA: Also there is unveiling.

ALISON: Really?

OLYA: For Vitya. We are meeting at grave. You may come, if you like.

ALISON: I would.

(Victor's sons and associates gather in front of a grave.)

I arrive at the cemetery by cab and behold an enormous mausoleum. It's about the size of a two-car garage. And oddly, looks like one. And in the middle, is parked a black Mercedes 600 S.E.L. Much like the one stolen from the garage in front of which Victor was murdered. On the tombstone itself, pictures of Victor in a leather bomber jacket; bunjie jumping with his sons; Olya in a bikini. And next to her, a photograph of a stripper. In a mink coat.

MOURNER A: Best unveiling this month.

MOURNER B: Good deli meat.

MOURNER C: I like the mink, personally.

MOURNER D: Versace.

ALISON: I'd never seen a tombstone with photographs before.

MOURNER A: Cost eight million rubles.

ALISON: Wow.

OLYA: You know, one fantasy my Victor deserved that might actually come true.

MOURNER B: You coming to banquet?

ALISON: Where is it?

MOURNER A: Ramada Inn.

MOURNER C: With the new casino?

MOURNER D: You play?

MOURNER A: Or are you simply additional mistress?

ALISON: No. No, I'm . . . I'm just here to mourn. I missed the funeral.

MOURNERS: Ah.

(The Mourners recede, Olya lingers.)

ALISON: *(To audience)* I missed the funeral. So I stay and try to pray. Not necessarily for Victor.

OLYA: You loved him, yes?

ALISON: Who? Oh. I don't know. Maybe.

OLYA: But still, he was part of your life?

ALISON: Yes. He was.

OLYA: And that part is now gone forever. Except what you *choose* to remember.

ALISON: I suppose.

OLYA: I will remember my Victor on water ski. With big smile. And me in bikini. Gone forever. Except for photograph.

(Olya exits.)

ALISON: *(To audience)* I try to pray . . . for Ben . . . but don't know how; or what. What prayer to say for a dead Jew, in front of an obscene mausoleum, in a land that almost destroyed him, that no longer exists? Ben? . . . Where *was* your funeral? How did you die? What happened . . . to us? What prayer . . . ? A blessing. Any blessing. But not here.

(Flute and guitar music; a traditional Hebrew wedding song)

Cab back to Sheremetevo. Call to Anna, fly on to Dulles. Then into Logan. And straight to a temple off the Fenway.

(A congregation has formed in two rows with an aisle in between. Alison stands at back, in the middle. She is spotted by Eugene Fox, a former Refusenik.)

FOX: Psst. Elison? Yoo-hoo! Sit! Come! Is beginning!

(Alison sits next to Eugene and his wife, Tanya.)

You look great!

ALISON: So do you. You both—

FOX: You remember us? From press conference?

ALISON: Sure . . .

FOX: So this is my wife, Tanya, who was mentioned but not present.

TANYA: Nice to meet you.

ALISON: You had a back problem—

FOX: Is better.

ALISON: And a son. In the film business.

TANYA: Telecommunications. Is safer.

ALISON: It's so wonderful you're here.

FOX: Oh, yes. We love America.

TANYA: But don't see enough of the grandchildren.

FOX: Everyone is so busy here.

TANYA: Shh. There she is.

FOX: You remember Sima?

(All heads crane back to see the start of the procession. Then, in a whisper . . .)

ALISON: She's gotten so big.

TANYA: And smart. Like her grandpa.

(Music plays. They watch.)

ALISON: And there's Anna.

(More music. They watch.)

She looks happy.

FOX: That she is.

TANYA: At long last.

(The music ends, the ring ceremony begins. All watch.)

FOX: So we didn't see you at Benya's funeral.

ALISON: I didn't know about it until it was too late. Where did he die?

FOX: So it was La Jolla.

TANYA: California. New job.

ALISON: And how?

FOX: Cancer.

TANYA: Same cancer.

FOX: But he went in good shape. Next to kidney-shaped pool. Nice town-house. Racked up high long-distance bill.

ALISON: Good for him.

FOX: Oh, yes.

ALISON: And did he ever . . . ?

FOX: Shh! Here comes. The Big Moment. The "Stomp."

(A big moment of quiet. And then the muffled sound of a lightbulb in a cloth napkin being stomped on. The congregation yells . . .)

CONGREGATION: MAZEL TOV!

(As the violin turns to jazzy klezmer, the Foxes dance with each other, as do other couples in the crowd. Lights segue into later in the evening at the reception, the couples switching partners, all the while Alison watching, alone.)

MICHAEL: Hey, stranger! Recognize? Few extra pounds. Touch of gray. You look absolutely the same, Al!

ALISON: Thanks. I'm not. But it's really great to see you, Michael.

MICHAEL: You mean that?

ALISON: I mean that.

MICHAEL: Shhhhoot! I'm married! I can't do anything about it—I mean, she's the rabbi. She was great though, huh?

ALISON: Yeah.

MICHAEL: Two kids.

ALISON: Wow!

MICHAEL: Sam and Gitta.

ALISON: Great names.

MICHAEL: I wanted an Alison . . .

ALISON: That's sweet of you.

MICHAEL: I can't divorce her. I mean, I *would,* but she *is* the rabbi. It'd be a scandal.

ALISON: I understand. I'm glad you're happy, Michael.

MICHAEL: How 'bout you?

ALISON: Oh . . .

MICHAEL: You *look* rich! Bye-bye Graduate School!

ALISON: Yup.

MICHAEL: Those days are gone!

ALISON: Gone for good!

MICHAEL: For better or worse!

ALISON: Better or worse!

MICHAEL: You know who's hurting? I mean, today, *especially?* His wife.

ALISON: Ben's?

MICHAEL: What was her name again?

ALISON: Yadviga.

MICHAEL: Absolutely devastated. He was all she had. And still can't speak the language! Now what? All she had was her family.

ALISON: That's something.

MICHAEL: Yeah, it's *some*thing.

ALISON: It's a lot.

MICHAEL: But they're movin' on! That's what today is all about: New Life! In America! For Better or Worse!

ALISON: For better.

MICHAEL: You think I should go over and talk to her?

ALISON: Let me first. I'd like to. Take care, Michael.

(She crosses. Approaches Yadviga.)

Congratulations.

YADVIGA: *Eli. Ya tak rada tibya vee-deetz.*

ALISON: *Da-da.*

YADVIGA: Is lovely day.

ALISON: And night too!

YADVIGA: Yes.

ALISON: I'm so sorry I've been far away.

YADVIGA: Yes. Me too.

ALISON: And out of touch.

YADVIGA: Also.

ALISON: It's too bad Ben couldn't be here. To see this.

YADVIGA: God takes people when they are ready. Benya was.

ALISON: He was?

YADVIGA: I am not.

ALISON: That's good to hear.

YADVIGA: Nor you. Wedding is happy time. Is not *tragedia*. Is time for us. To be happy! Come! You know this?

(As a new melody begins)

ALISON: No.

YADVIGA: So we fake! Big deal!

(They dance. Ben appears. Asks for Yadviga's hand. Alison makes room for the couple. All watch them dance. Then Yadviga lets go, as Ben turns to Alison.)

BEN: Now is my turn.

ALISON: Ben.

BEN: How 'bout one little tango?

ALISON: I don't know how.

BEN: Me also. But I like the saying, "One little tango." How about we sing? You have beautiful voice. This I know.

ALISON: You do?

BEN: Eyes.

ALISON: But I don't know any songs appropriate for . . .

BEN: Is not true.

ALISON: Not the words. I mean, sometimes I sing to myself, melodies, but not—

BEN: How 'bout something from Minsk? From your grandmother?

ALISON: But the band is still . . .

BEN: They shtink! I get them to stop. HEY! "BAND!" SHA!

(Music stops.)

So, something in Jewish? Or Russian? You have very good Russian, for some reason. Follow me. I have lousy voice, but am good teacher. So. Repeat.

ALISON: Ben.

BEN: *(He sings.) Tum-ba-la, tum-ba-la, tum-ba-la-laika.* Now you.

ALISON: I think . . . what my problem . . . has been . . .

BEN: Shhh . . . I sing. You repeat. Again.

ALISON: Is that we never had enough . . .

BEN: *Tum-ba-la, tum-ba-la, tum-ba-la . . .*

ALISON: Time. I always wanted . . .

BEN: It was enough.

ALISON: But too fraught; *I* was . . . too fraught. And you were always—

BEN: It was blessing. Our time, Elison. And what does a Jew do with his life, but make blessing and deed? Blessing and deed. And when he dies? More blessing; more deed! How? He sings! So we sing . . .

(He sings.)

Tum-ba-la, tum-ba-la, tum-ba-la-laika.

(She continues.)

ALISON: *Tum-ba-la, tum-ba-la, tum-ba-la-laika.*

BEN: You know this!

ALISON: *Tum-ba-la laika/Shpil ba-la-laika . . .*
ALISON AND BEN: *Tum-ba-la laika, freylach zol zayn.*
BEN: Now dance to it!

(Sings)

Shteyt a bocher, shteyt un . . .
ALISON: *Tracht.*
BEN: *Tracht un tracht . . .*
ALISON: *A gan-tse nacht.*
ALISON AND BEN: *Ve men tsu-ne-men, un-nit far-she-men; ve men tsu-ne-men,*
un-nit far-she-men.
BEN: Keep going.
ALISON: *Tum-ba-la, tum-ba-la, tum-ba-la-laika.*
BEN: See, I told you.
ALISON: *Tum-ba-la, tum-ba-la, tum-ba-la-laika.*
BEN: It was in you from before.
ALISON: *Tum-ba-la laika, shpil ba-la-laika . . .*
BEN: Good-bye, my dear.

(As Ben recedes from view)

ALISON: *Tum-ba-la laika*
Freylach zol . . .

(She looks around.)

Ben?

(Sees no one)

Anna?

(Lights isolate her.)

Yada?

(She kneels, as though before a grave.)

A blessing . . .

(She sings alone in the pool of light . . .)

Tum-ba-la laika, shpil ba-la-laika . . .

(Lights begin to fade.)

Tum-ba-la laika
Freylach zol zeyn.

(Hold. Then blackout.)

SEE UNDER: LOVE

by Corey Fischer

See Under: Love. Travelling Jewish Theater production. Pictured (left to right) are Robert Sicular, Joan Mankin, and Julian Lopez-Morillas. Photograph by Ken Friedman.

In 1989, my longtime colleague, collaborator, and cofounder of A Traveling Jewish Theater Naomi Newman gave me an Israeli novel in translation, *See Under: Love,* saying, "You must read this." She also mentioned that she thought it would make an interesting work of theatre. I read David Grossman's novel and was so moved by its shattering and fresh way of looking at the Holocaust and its aftermath that I started a correspondence with his agent regarding the possibility of TJT getting the theatrical rights to the book. After a year of letters and faxes, we had gotten nowhere and I lost my original enthusiasm for the project.

Five years later, I toured a one-man show in Australia for a month and happened to see one of today's most accomplished theatre companies: Théâtre de Complicité. They were performing a brilliant adaptation of a story by John Berger, *The Three Lives of Lucie Cabrol.* I was amazed to see what a vigorously physical ensemble theatre could do with a highly literary text. Walking through the warm Sydney night I could not stop thinking about *See Under: Love.* A few weeks later I resumed the conversation with Grossman's agent and after two more years, we reached an agreement. I spent nearly a year—with several interruptions to create and perform in other projects—reading, rereading, and analyzing the book. I generated a couple hundred pages of notes. I had never encountered a book like this, funny, terrifying, moving, and constantly surprising. At its core, Grossman offers a moral vision of a fierce and necessary compassion that I've found in no other Shoah-related work. *See Under: Love* asks the reader to consider, at the deepest possible levels, the human capacities for evil, for love, and for forgiveness. It's a vision that refuses to name anyone simply "the other" or "the enemy." Grossman insists that we not be ruled by fear, no matter how justified that fear may seem. The power of this worldview would be remarkable in any time and place. That David, an Israeli, has been able to maintain it, to keep his heart open through the chaos and terror of life in the Middle East, fills me with awe and wonder. To make Grossman's vision live on the stage was the greatest artistic challenge I had ever faced. Not to mention the fact that I was proposing to make a two- or three-hour play out of a highly sophisticated work that took advantage of several ingenious literary devices—lexigraphic forms, faux memoir, historical chronicle, surrealistic fantasy, parable, and fairy tale—to create a prismatic experience of the effects of the Shoah on the children of its survivors.

Naomi Newman, who had agreed to direct the play, and I met with David Grossman when he came to San Francisco to give a lecture in 1998, nearly ten years after I'd first read the book. In one sentence, he both liberated and condemned me when he said, "Please, betray my text." He insisted that I not attempt to be too faithful to the book. As I discovered a few years later in Jerusalem, when I saw his play *Riki's Playgroup,* David is also a brilliant playwright, well aware of the demands of theatre, so different from those of literature.

After two more years of work, nine complete revisions, and three readings, the TJT production premiered at the company's theatre in San Francisco. For me, the most intense period of writing came during the rehearsals, as the real nature of the play revealed itself through the work of Naomi, the actors, and the designers. I continued to rewrite the piece up to opening night and, after many conversations with David, who came to San Francisco for the opening, completed some further revisions after the play closed.

The chance to adapt *See Under: Love,* the friendship with David that grew out of the process, the collaboration with Naomi and the talented actors (Norbert Weisser, Mark Samuels, Joan Mankin, Helen Stoltzfus, Robert Sicular, Aaron Davidman, and Julian López-Morillas) and designers (Richard Olmstead, Albert Greenberg, and Todd Roehrman) who created the original performance were among the greatest gifts I've been given in twenty-five years of making theatre.

Notes

I could not have completed the work without the support of my colleagues in TJT and the generous insights of Luan Schooler, Dramaturg at Berkeley Rep at that time. I also owe a considerable debt to Betsy Rosenberg for her masterful translation of the novel.

Financial support for the development and production of *See Under: Love* came from The Kennedy Center's Fund for New American Plays, Koret Foundation, National Foundation for Jewish Culture New Play Commission, National Endowment for the Arts, Flintridge Foundation, California Arts Council, Moses and Susan Libitzky, and the Jewish Community Endowment Fund, Newfeld-Levin Chair in Holocaust Studies, San Francisco Arts Commission, David B. Gold Foundation, The Robert Sillens Family Foundation.

The fragment of the song in Yiddish in Act 1, Scene 1 (*"Es shlogt di sho, mir zaynen do . . .")* is from "Es Shlogt di Sho," words by Kasriel Broydo, composer unknown. It was part of a musical revue performed in the Vilna Ghetto called *Moishe Halt Zikh!* (Hang on, Moishe!). The full song appears in the anthology *We Are Here,* ed. Eleanor Mlotek and Malke Gottlieb (New York: Workmens Circle, 1983).

Characters

MOMIK NEUMAN: A writer in his early forties. He is the grandnephew of Anshel Wasserman.

ANSHEL WASSERMAN: A Hebrew writer of children's stories. Member of the late nineteenth-, early twentieth-century literary-philosophical movement known as Haskalah, or Enlightenment, embraced by many Eastern European Jewish intellectuals as they left the purely religious life of the shtetl behind. Lived all his life in Warsaw until his deportation to the camp. His wife Sarah and daughter Tirzaleh were killed shortly after their arrival in the camp.

KURT NEIGEL: An SS officer *(obersturmbannfuhrer),* commander of the camp.

THE ENSEMBLE—four actors play the following roles:

OTTO BRIG: The heroic leader of the Children of the Heart. He is a non-Jewish Pole who has a reserve of inner strength that never runs out.

ALBERT FRIED: One of the original members of the Children of the Heart; a highly assimilated Jew who has sought refuge from the many losses in his life by devoting himself to science.

PAULA: Otto's sister, and, in a sense, his feminine counterpart. She is generous, vivacious, and wise. She is Fried's lover.

PRINCESS MAGDA: A Gypsy sorceress and member of the Children of the Heart.

YEDIDYA MUNIN: Survivor of the Warsaw Ghetto who joins the Children of the Heart, and believes that his suppressed ejaculations will eventually power his flight to God. He has much kabalistic evidence to support his theory.

HANNAH ZEITRIN: Another recent member of the Children of the Heart. She is a survivor of several *aktions* and deportations who has lost two husbands and several children. She has devised a plan to avenge herself on God.

KAZIK: A mysterious child. (Note: Kazik is "played" by a *bunraku*-style puppet. Alterations to the puppet are introduced as Kazik ages. The puppet is manipulated by various ensemble members. The actor playing Princess Magda supplies Kazik's voice throughout.)

TINA NEIGEL: The wife of Kurt Neigel.

RUTH NEUMAN: The wife of Momik Neuman.

Roles are doubled accordingly:

Otto and Munin and Zalmanson; Ruth and Princess Magda and the voice of Kazik; Paula and Tina and Hannah Zeitrin.

The world premiere of *See Under: Love* was presented by A Traveling Jewish Theatre, February–March 2001 in San Francisco. It was directed by Naomi Newman with original music and sound design by Albert Greenberg, scenic and lighting design by Richard Olmsted, costume design by Todd Roehrman, puppet design and construction by Dennis Ludlow, dramaturgy by Luan Schooler and Naomi Newman, stage management by Joan Sommerfield, directorial assistance by Eric Rhys Miller.

The cast was as follows:

Momik Neuman: Aaron Davidman
Anshel Wasserman: Mark Samuels
Kurt Neigel: Norbert Weisser
Ruth Neuman and Princess Magda and the voice of Kazik: Joan Mankin
Otto and Munin and Zalmanson: Robert Sicular
Paula and Tina and Hannah Zeitrin: Helen Stoltzfus
Albert Fried: Julian López-Morillas

ACT 1

SCENE I

(A large central area is surrounded by unfinished wooden scaffolding which suggests a menacing landscape of guard towers as well as the rough framing of a concentration camp barracks. Raised cubicles in various corners suggest sleeping shelves. As far down stage as possible is a narrow raised flower bed full of soil, with several petunia plants in temporary pots ready to be planted. On a raised platform upstage center is Neigel's office, connected by a ramp to the central, rubble-filled area.

Downstage left is a desk and a worktable piled with books about the Holocaust, identifiable by the presence of swastikas and a wall covered with photographs and maps relating to the Holocaust: Neuman's study. On a platform above the study is a bed in which Neuman and his wife Ruth are sleeping.

The entire stage is dark. Broken moonlight on Neuman's bed. Neuman's sleep is agitated, but not enough to wake Ruth. Gradually, his muttering becomes intelligible.)

NEUMAN: *(In his sleep)* Shut up . . . sick of your story . . . no more story. No more . . . it won't kill the Nazi . . . nazi . . . *nazi kaput* . . . You have to . . . you have to . . .

(His voice becomes thin and reedy.)

But I can't! Too small just just just me don't know *nazi kaput nazi kaput—*

(Ruth stirs, then wakes.)

Herrneigel Herrneigel Herrneigel Doesn't. Like. The. Story.
RUTH: Momik?
NEUMAN: Buthehastolisten.
RUTH: Momik, wake up!
NEUMAN: WHAT KIND OF ANIMAL IS THE NAZI BEAST!?
RUTH: *(She holds him.)* Shh. You're dreaming.
NEUMAN: *(He realizes where he is. Beat.)* I was shouting again?
RUTH: Yes.
NEUMAN: What?
RUTH: The same.
NEUMAN: But what, exactly?
RUTH: "What kind of an animal is the nazi beast."

NEUMAN: *(Listens)* I didn't wake Yariv?
RUTH: I don't think so. I'll go check.

(Ruth gets out of bed and puts on a robe.)

NEUMAN: What kind of an animal is the nazi beast.
RUTH: Go to sleep, Momik. I'll be right back.
NEUMAN: You remember the answer?
RUTH: "The nazi beast can come out of any animal if it gets the right care and nourishment."

(Neuman gets up and pulls on a pair of sweatpants.)

Momik, it's three in the morning. Go back to sleep, please.
NEUMAN: I hope I didn't wake him.

(He crosses down to his study as the lights fade on Ruth and the bedroom. He reads something he wrote the day before and tosses it onto a large pile of rejected material. A new idea:)

Once upon a time, in a place called *dortn,* Over There, the Nazi Beast—may his name be blotted out—imprisoned every Jew he could find. Among them was Anshel Wasserman, who, in better days, had been a teller of wondrous tales that brought joy to countless children in many lands.

(Pause. He looks at the flower bed.)

One day Anshel Wasserman was tending the Nazi Beast's garden—*(Wasserman suddenly enters from stage right and begins planting the petunias, as Neigel marches up ramp to his office. The ensemble follows as camp inmates, creating the racket of the camp as they fall into a "roll call" tableau.)*
When suddenly, the Beast, whose name was Obersturmbannfuhrer Neigel, called out:
NEIGEL: *(Calling down to Wasserman)* Wasserman!

(Wasserman sighs and, with great effort, rises from his planting. He climbs the ramp up to Neigel's quarters. Neuman watches.)

WASSERMAN: *(Out of breath)* Your honor?
NEIGEL: How does my garden progress?
WASSERMAN: The petunias you ordered are in the ground.

NEIGEL: And the radishes?

WASSERMAN: Yes.

NEIGEL: Yes, what? If you can't show a little more enthusiasm for my garden, perhaps you don't deserve to care for it!

WASSERMAN: As you wish.

(Wasserman turns and starts to leave. Neigel picks up his gun and releases the safety catch. Wasserman freezes when he hears the sound.)

NEUMAN: No!

(Neigel freezes.)

WASSERMAN: *(Turns to see Neuman)* Momik?

NEUMAN: Grandfather.

WASSERMAN: *Nu?*

NEUMAN: You can see me?

WASSERMAN: You're all grown up, but I'd recognize you anywhere.

NEUMAN: Listen, Grandfather, maybe I shouldn't be putting you through this. But I don't know how else to do it. You're the only one who knows the way out of this place.

WASSERMAN: Momik, don't say a word. Time is running out. We have a story to tell.

NEUMAN: I know.

WASSERMAN: And I have no idea how to begin.

NEUMAN: But if you don't—

WASSERMAN: Shah!

NEIGEL: What I wish, Scheherazade, is a story. According to our bargain.

NEUMAN: *(Writing)* A bargain. Yes. The previous day, the Nazi and the Jew had struck an unusual bargain.

WASSERMAN: I'm sorry, Your Honor, but the muse seems unwilling to come to me in this place. You can't blame her, *eppes*. All I have been able to . . .

NEIGEL: Enough whining. You are a professional writer. Now, read!

(Wasserman turns to Neigel, slowly takes a notebook from his robe. Pretends to consult it for a moment.)

WASSERMAN: Very well. I will begin by reminding your honor of the four young heroes who make up the Children of the Heart.

(During the following, as each member of the Children of the Heart is named, one of the "inmates" transforms into him or her, with a minor emblematic costume change and a major physical alteration. Each recognizes the others. They exchange secret gestures.)

Otto Brig, noble son of Poland and leader of these partisans of good—

NEIGEL: Yes, Otto, of course. The boy who was their leader! I named my dog after him. And the blonde, his girlfriend, the one with the braid, what was her name—no, don't tell me—Paula, right?

WASSERMAN: Excellent, Commander, only Paula was not his girlfriend, she was—

NEIGEL: Ah, ah, of course, not his girlfriend, his sister! It comes to me now. The other one was in love with her, no? The one who could talk to animals?

WASSERMAN: Albert Fried, conversant with all creatures from lice eggs to buffaloes. And Princess Magda—

NEIGEL: —the gypsy!

WASSERMAN: The Gypsy sorceress, skilled in every work of wonder in the world.

(Struggling to remember)

The new episode begins at the point where . . . one of the old stories ended. I refer to the scene in which the Children of the Heart rescued . . . the gladiator Spartacus from the lion that would have torn him to bits.

NEIGEL: Yes. Spartacus. I remember that one.

(Chuckles)

My God, I must have been six when my father read that episode to me.

WASSERMAN: The Roman legions pursued the tiny band of heroes.

NEIGEL: Yes. They had to escape from the Roman legions. What was it they had . . . a rocket?—

WASSERMAN: *(Remembering)* A time machine.

(The ensemble uses wooden planks and vocal sounds to create the "time machine.")

NEIGEL: A time machine! You see? I remember everything. Everything! How they battled oppression, disaster, ignorance, and disease. They helped out Robin Hood and Pasteur. They even temporarily cured Beethoven's deafness. That was a good one, Scheherazade.

WASSERMAN: True, Your Honor, but they also helped Negroes and Armenians and . . . my people. I'm surprised that you read my humble attempts at . . .

NEIGEL: Times were different then. The century was just beginning. Do you realize I read those stories every week for five years? Maybe more. So. Continue. The young heroes are escaping ancient Rome—

WASSERMAN: On they ventured—

OTTO: *(Reading imaginary gauges)* Something's wrong! The safety controls are not working!

FRIED: You're right.

(Fried checks other instruments)

We've overshot our own time.

PAULA: *(Reading a dial)* 1915 . . . 1920 . . . It's the future!

PRINCESS MAGDA: I'm remembering things that haven't happened yet!

(Each member of the Children of the Heart begins to visibly age.)

FRIED: I've grown up to be a doctor . . .

OTTO: 1933!

PRINCESS MAGDA: A circus? I'm working in a goddamned circus?

PAULA: I'm past forty now. Why don't I have any children? Otto! Use the vision glass, quickly, what do you see?

(Otto looks through the vision glass.)

OTTO: It looks like Gezibowska Street.

PAULA: Good. It's Warsaw at least.

OTTO: But . . . I don't understand. Workmen are filling doors and windows with bricks and plaster. Screams and gunshots.

NEIGEL: *(Growing suspicious)* Wasserman?

FRIED: On Gezibowska Street?

OTTO: Soldiers are throwing something down a sewer hole. Smoke. Now it's all exploding.

(The other Children of the Heart crowd in, trying to see. Otto is having more and more difficulty speaking.)

A sealed chamber. The ceilings are emitting . . . strange vapors. Fires in the chamber. The people inside are . . . dissolving . . . into liquid and ash.

NEIGEL: Just a minute, Wasserman . . .

PAULA: But who could do such things to human—

OTTO: The—new—enemy—more—powerful—than—all—the—others

NEIGEL: What new enemy?

(Wasserman starts to answer, but Neuman interrupts:)

NEUMAN: Be careful, Grandfather!

WASSERMAN: The time machine finally lost power and crashed.

(Otto, Paula, Fried, and Princess Magda knock over the planks, destroying the "time machine." Neigel is distracted by this and drops his questioning. The Children of the Heart look around in confusion. Princess Magda sniffs the air, then bends down and takes a pinch of dirt between her fingers. She holds the dirt to her ear. Fried takes a map out of his pocket and consults it. He then performs some calculations on a slide rule. They group together in solidarity and mutual protection.)

FRIED: According to my calculations, we have arrived somewhere between the years 1940 and 1943.

(Animal sounds in the distance)

PRINCESS MAGDA: We have caught up with ourselves. This is now our present time. There are large animals nearby.

OTTO: *(Understanding dawns at last!)* Of course there are, it's the Warsaw Zoo. Fried, you used to love this place.

FRIED: No Otto, that was you. I hated to see the animals behind bars.

PRINCESS MAGDA: *(Continues listening to her pinch of dirt)* But the animals are alone. And hungry. All the keepers are gone.

OTTO: So. Fried, you will tend to the animals' medical and spiritual needs, Princess Magda will see to their nourishment. Paula will organize our living quarters.

FRIED: Surely we can do more than replace some missing zookeepers?

PAULA: I have a bad feeling about this place, Otto. Fried, can you rebuild the time machine?

(Fried examines a piece of the broken "machine.")

OTTO: No. It's what I saw in the vision glass. This time we will need to fight in a different way.

(Crosses upstage and stands on a piece of rubble to survey the territory)

We will make our home base among the animals while we recruit new members to help us in our battle with the—with the—

(Otto, once again, is overcome with paralysis. Fried rushes to him, quickly performs a series of standard neurological tests: tracking eyes movement, checks his spine, etc.)

FRIED: Some form of autogenic paralysis. Hopefully transient.

WASSERMAN: This strange immobility would come upon Otto Brig whenever he tried to name the enemy the band must now engage.

NEIGEL: What enemy, exactly?

(The Children of the Heart freeze.)

I don't like the sound of this. Warsaw in 1940? You understand that it is absolutely forbidden to produce any writing against the German Reich of Adolf Hitler.

WASSERMAN: *(Stalling)* Of course, Your Honor. But with all due respect, it would help matters if I could convey to you a certain understanding of the writer's process, if you'll indulge me.

NEIGEL: The point, Wasserman!

WASSERMAN: Exactly. And the point, in this instance, is that the as-yet-unnamed-enemy—unnamed because the mysterious powers that inform the myriad infinitesimal choices a writer must make, moment by moment, have not yet chosen to enlighten this humble scrivener.

NEIGEL: *(Interrupting)* I want a story, damn it, not a lecture. Something entertaining. No screaming. No gunshots. And don't kill anyone.

WASSERMAN: What right have you to ask me that, Herr Neigel?

OTTO: *(Still standing on a pile of rubble. Struggling with his paralysis. The others move to help him but he stiffly waves them away as he struggles to regain mobility. To himself:)* Otto—Brig—you—have—to—get—over—this— fear! In the old days there was no corner of the world you couldn't reach when somebody needed help—Armenia, the Ganges after the floods, America to save the Indians, and now you can't even move. Shame on you, Otto Brig! Shame—on—you! I have to do something! Why—can't—I— move!

(He continues to struggle in silence. Paula, Fried, and Princess Magda exchange worried looks. Fried makes signs to Princess Magda that she should attempt some

magic. She tries some hocus-pocus, to no avail. Then, a new idea comes to her. She makes the secret gesture of the Children of the Heart:)

PRINCESS MAGDA: Is the heart willing?

OTTO: *(After a struggle)* The—heart—is—willing!

PRINCESS MAGDA: Come what may?

OTTO: Come—what—may!

(Otto tries to reach out to Fried, but can only move his arm a few inches.)

PAULA: Is the heart willing?

OTTO: The—heart—is—willing!

PAULA: Come what may?

OTTO: Come—what—may!

WASSERMAN: *(Whispers the words of a Yiddish partisan song to Fried)* Es shlogt di sho, mir zaynen do . . .

FRIED: *(Repeats)* Es shlogt di sho, mir zaynen do . . .

(The Children of the Heart pick up the song.)

CHILDREN OF THE HEART: *Mir kukn in di vaytn. S'vert der himl vider blo, skumen naye tsaytn. Un khotsh der vayl iz finster shtok vartn mir geduldik, es kumt der tog, es shlogt di sho—dan falt der, ver s'iz shuldik.*

WASSERMAN: And so it was that the Children of the Heart took up their new life and began preparations for their greatest battle.

OTTO: This zoo shall become Noah's ark in reverse. The animals will save the humans. We will create an island of sanity that will stand as a constant repudiation of the enemy's war against life. We will search for new members among the outcasts of the ghetto.

NEIGEL: *(Shouting)* There will be absolutely no mention of the ghetto in this story!

(Instantly, Children of the Heart transform into the drab inmates and scatter. Action freezes. Neuman looks around, at a loss.)

NEUMAN: This isn't working!

(Ruth appears with some papers in her hand.)

RUTH: Momik, Yariv's playgroup leader sent a note home. He's been hiding under the table again.

NEUMAN: *(Distracted)* I can't say I blame him.

RUTH: *(Ignores this)* So I thought we'd do something different tonight. I'm going to make my grandmother's *kasha varnishkes* and we're going to eat dinner like a family for a change and see if we can get him to talk about what he's so scared of.

NEUMAN: Maybe he's too young for the playgroup.

RUTH: Maybe it doesn't have anything to do with the playgroup.

(Neuman shrugs.)

RUTH: *(She indicates his study.)* You've been in here for a long time.

NEUMAN: I think the story is . . .

RUTH: Come help me cut vegetables like you used to.

(She places a large cooking pot on Neuman's table and takes smaller pots out of it, transforming his study into a kitchen. She takes carrots out of one of the pots and gives him a knife. They chop the carrots. The light shifts and creates huge shadows on the back wall. The ensemble also creates shadow images that underscore the following.)

NEUMAN: Supper . . .

(Remembering)

. . . is when things start getting dangerous.

(Pause)

Mama and Papa chew with all their might. They sweat and their eyes bulge out of their heads.

(He becomes a child.)

They have to eat a lot every night to make themselves strong. They have to get so huge that Death can't carry them away. He almost got them once when they were skin and bones. But now Mama's all red. She's panting and chewing so hard you can't see her neck. The sweat runs down Papa's forehead. They mop the pots with big chunks of bread and gobble them down. I can't eat a thing. I have to keep my eyes on them, but even so, every night, they start to disappear, they float away on the steam from the soup pot; their shadows dance higher and higher on the wall and I almost shriek out loud, "God help them," but I only say it in my heart, and then I translate it to Yiddish so God will understand, "*Mir zol zayn far dayne beyndelekh*"—do something to me and have mercy on their little bones, which is what Mama always says about me.

Then comes the big moment when Papa lays down his fork and gives a long *krechtz* and looks around as if he only just noticed he's at home and he has a son. The battle is over. They will live another day. And this is when I want to ask them to tell me—everything that happened *Over There* but Papa is making nasty remarks to the radio and Mama is in the kitchen counting the knives and forks and I can't open my mouth.

(The light changes; the shadows fade. Neuman speaks directly to Ruth.)

But then they brought Grandfather to us. My mother almost fainted when she saw him. The neighbors had to bring a piece of lemon to revive her. Everyone thought he had died in the camps *Over There*. He'd been at the insane house at Bat Yam but someone had understood a name or two he mumbled in the midst of all his humming and they found us. He wasn't really my grandfather. He was my Grandma Henny's younger brother. But I wanted a grandfather so much, that's what I always called him. He would never sit still. He twitched and gabbled and flapped his arms about. Sometimes the sounds he made sounded like words. I had a feeling that any minute now he would split down the middle like a yellow string bean and another Grandfather would pop out. A Grandfather who would tell me everything about *Over There* that my parents couldn't speak of. Only, it didn't happen. So I hugged him. He felt warm, like an oven. He stopped talking to himself and stayed quiet for half a minute. Then he pointed back over his left shoulder and whispered, *"Nazi kaput."* He leaned close to me and said "Kazik" and made the shape of a little man with his hands and rocked it to his heart. But then his face closed up again.

(Pause)

Oh, Grandfather.

NEIGEL: Wasserman, continue.

(The frozen action resumes, with the ensemble transforming back into the Children of the Heart.)

WASSERMAN: The beauteous Paula, sister of Otto Brig, at the age of sixty-one years, decided to fight her own battle.

(A strange tango is heard. Paula dances toward Fried and takes him in her arms. Through the following, their dance becomes increasingly passionate and sensual.)

PAULA: Against the tyranny and narrow-mindedness of the enemy.

(Wasserman sneaks a glance at Neigel. He is fascinated by the dance.)

WASSERMAN: She mustered her expansive and generous spirit—

PAULA:—to bear witness to the miracle of a woman's body! These thugs in their leather costumes are too stupid to even guess—

NEIGEL: Where is this shit leading?

NEUMAN: *(Putting two and two together)* She wants to have a baby!

WASSERMAN: Despite the fact that certain doctors warned her against it and laughed at her behind her back.

PAULA: This sick old world needs something unheard of!

WASSERMAN: You will remember that in the old days, young Albert Fried was hopelessly in love with Paula.

NEIGEL: But he was too shy to ever tell her.

WASSERMAN: Exactly. But now Paula knew the time was finally right for the two of them. She lay with Fried at all hours of the night and day, in all manner of places.

PRINCESS MAGDA: On the elephant's haystack!

OTTO: Among the rotten cabbages in the storeroom.

PAULA: And by moonlight—

FRIED:—in the empty crocodile pool!

WASSERMAN: She never lost faith that her tremendous creative force would summon an equal potency from Doctor Fried.

(Neigel makes a note in his black book. In the arena, Paula and Fried stop making love. Fried touches Paula's stomach, following its curve with curiosity. He then puts his head to her stomach and listens. He raises his head, amazed.)

FRIED: Paula, my love, this isn't possible. At your age . . . At *my* age!

PAULA: I will name him Kazik.

OTTO: And his existence will be our first victory.

PAULA: His beauty and goodness will overwhelm those worms who try to divide one people from another.

OTTO AND PRINCESS MAGDA: Bravo!

NEIGEL: Wait a minute, Wasserman. Fried is a Jew, isn't he.

WASSERMAN: Although his parents were Jews born in the darkness of the shtetl, he has always considered himself, above all, a Pole—of the Fried persuasion.

NEIGEL: Stop!

(Action freezes.)

This violates German law, Wasserman. An Aryan woman may under no circumstances—

WASSERMAN: As I have tried to explain to you, the story is leading us whither it will.

NEIGEL: But this is not what you used to write about in the old days! I want entertainment, Scheissemeister. Time machines, historical characters, desert islands! Not more reminders of the war. Why do you think I suggested our . . . arrangement? I need distractions, Wasserman. Do you have even the smallest understanding of what it's like to be the sole authority in a place like this?

WASSERMAN: There you have me.

NEIGEL: If I were to let down my guard for a moment, my subordinates would be upon me like sharks. They want my job, Wasserman. An *obersturmbannfuhrer* can have no friends.

WASSERMAN: Like sharks. Your honor is becoming skilled in the use of analogy, if I may say so.

(Pause)

NEIGEL: Thank you.

(Wasserman nods. Neigel makes a note. Action resumes.)

PAULA: No doctors!

OTTO: We can trust this one, Paula. I met her on my travels in the ghetto. She won't talk too much.

PRINCESS MAGDA: *(As doctor, leads Otto to a window)* Each week they add more soldiers to the patrols. Hard times are coming, Brig; some will be able to hold out, others will not. Surely you know what's happening to poor Paulina.

(Paula is now on the ramp ecstatically noting the signs of pregnancy, weighing her breasts, feeling her belly.)

You're her brother. You must warn her that at the age of sixty-nine the body is no longer fit for pregnancy, even an imaginary pregnancy!

(Otto turns away. Fried goes to Paula.)

PAULA: What is he saying?
OTTO: Nothing. Everything will be fine.

(Fried massages her.)

PAULA: My mouth is so dry! I need something sweet. Sweet and sour and moist. Like a grapefruit. If you could only find a grapefruit . . .
FRIED: Paulinka, the city is under—

(Paula moans with the intensity of her craving.)

NEIGEL: Just a minute, Scheherazade. Please write this down: Officer Neigel brought Paula the grapefruit.
NEUMAN: But no grapefruits could be found in the occupied city.
WASSERMAN: *(Smiles to himself)* From where did he get it, may I ask?
NEUMAN: Paula moaned with the pangs of her unfulfilled craving.
NEIGEL: *(Thinks for a moment)* The quartermaster corps sent me a food package. A big grapefruit, direct from Spain. With greetings from General Franco.

(Wasserman writes.)

NEUMAN: Grandfather, really, it makes no sense for the Nazi to . . .
WASSERMAN: Don't be so stiff-necked, Momik. A grapefruit is a grapefruit.
FRIED: *(Puts his hand on Paula's belly)* Boom! Boom! He kicks like a little Hercules.
NEIGEL: *(Quietly)* You have children too, Wasserman?

(Wasserman can't speak. Finally:)

WASSERMAN: One daughter, your honor.

(Neuman writes frantically.)

NEUMAN: A daughter? No one ever mentioned her, Grandfather. What happened—

WASSERMAN: *(To Neuman)* Don't ask me this now, Momik.

(Indicating Neigel)

Something is moving through this one.

NEIGEL: Only someone who has children knows this sort of thing. Boom, boom. Yes.

WASSERMAN: And you?

NEIGEL: Two. Karl and Liselotte. Karl is three and a half. Lise is two. A couple of war babies. I rarely have a chance to see them.

WASSERMAN: You're not a young father, if I may say so, Herr Neigel.

NEUMAN: Listen, Grandfather. We can't get diverted by the Beast's family history. We're not trying to tell *his* story. If we get too involved with his background—

WASSERMAN: It's not so simple. Pay attention.

NEIGEL: We couldn't have children for a long time. We tried for more than seven years.

WASSERMAN: *(Aside to Neuman)* Eight years, my Sarah and I. Eight years we—

NEUMAN: You were married! You see, that's what I need to know about. My parents never told . . . Did your wife . . . when you got here—

NEIGEL: Maybe Paula could have the baby after all.

WASSERMAN: No. She dies. She dies in Dr. Werzler's ward at the military hospital.

(Otto and Princess Magda become bodies in the stage left bunks, moaning as dying soldiers. They also use wood block sounds to heighten sense of urgency and chaos.)

PAULA: Is that me screaming?

FRIED: No, Paula, there are others here.

PAULA: Mothers . . . giving . . . birth . . .

FRIED: And soldiers. There is fighting in the ghetto. They bring the wounded here. The Germans, the Poles.

PAULA: Their screams are all the same.

(Touches her own face)

Is this my face? So dry and cracked . . .

FRIED: No, Paula, your face is beautiful and soft.

PAULA: Don't lie, Albert.

FRIED: Shhh.

PAULA: My breasts ache so.

FRIED: I know.

PAULA: *(A last contraction)* There—will—be—a—child!

(Paula's agony reaches a peak. Then, nothing. Fried checks her pulse, then shakes his head. Princess Magda covers Paula with the sheet. Fried is alone in a spotlight, frozen in a silent scream. Under the sheet, Paula covers her face with white powder. Princess Magda pulls the sheet back to reveal Paula-as-ghost, who climbs the scaffolding.)

WASSERMAN: In later years, whenever Fried felt the sadness in his heart about to crush and destroy him, he would approach Otto and gaze into his eyes, which were the same as Paula's. The same eyes, clear and blue. They were brother and sister, after all. Then happened a small act of real grace. Otto left his own eyes, nobly absenting himself, and allowed Fried to commune with his Paula.

(While Fried gazes into Otto's eyes, Paula floats down from her perch, nearly touching Fried.)

NEIGEL: That could happen. You know, my little one, Karl, has the same eyes I do. But exactly. And my wife, sometimes when she used to—

(Realizing that his use of the past tense reveals the state of his marriage, he quickly corrects himself:)

—*when* she misses me, she picks him up and looks at him in the light—
Go on, go on.

FRIED: *(Still gazing into Otto's eyes, but addressing the dead Paula)* I think of you

WASSERMAN: when I rub half a lemon

FRIED: on my elbows so they won't be rough like tree bark

WASSERMAN: and when I put a rose in a glass of sugar water

FRIED: to keep it fresh.

WASSERMAN: Sarah could stare at a flower for a whole hour.

NEUMAN: Your wife.

WASSERMAN: Yes. She had the most delicate hands. Sarah was an artist, you know. She did the illustrations for the last edition of the Children of the Heart. That's how I met her. I was forty already. Quite the bachelor. Like bird wings, her hands moving across the page. By then I'd stopped writing stories. That was the worst. She always thought of me as the writer, Scheherazade, beloved author of the Children of the Heart, not as Anshel Wasserman the cranky proofreader. She never said a word about it but in my ears her silence rang, may you never know such evil days.

(Neuman makes notes.)

FRIED: I'm sorry I lost my temper with you over such small things. I think of you when I deliberately leave the faucets dripping and the lights on, to show you—wherever you may be—that I, too, am careless and absentminded. And I think of you when—that is, when I—

(Breaks off in embarrassment. Paula makes her way back to the garden.)

OTTO: When you pass wind, Fried. You even think of her when you pass wind. There's no shame in it.

NEIGEL: I thought you were a cultured man, Wasserman.

FRIED: Whenever I thought I was alone and allowed myself to . . . pass wind, she would appear out of nowhere. I wanted to bury myself alive but she only smiled.

WASSERMAN: This happened many times every day, and even now, three years after Paula's death, he farts and shuts his eyes, waiting for the sound of her approaching footsteps.

PRINCESS MAGDA: On a bad day, he wanders around the zoo, honking like a flock of wild geese.

NEIGEL: *(Laughing)* Not bad, Wasserman. Not what I expected, but not bad. Still, it's hard to think of my childhood heroes as a bunch of old farts.

(Pleased with his little joke)

WASSERMAN: *(Dryly)* I hope you will become accustomed to it.

(Pause)

And now I must remind you of our bargain.

NEIGEL: I don't know, Wasserman. We're off to a rather shaky beginning here.

WASSERMAN: "Not bad," was your comment, Herr Neigel. According to the agreement, for each satisfactory installment of—

NEIGEL: All right, all right.

(Neigel motions Wasserman to stand a few feet away. Neigel picks up his revolver, takes aim and fires at Wasserman. Wasserman's body registers the shock of the gunshot. He feels the back of his head. He is unhurt. Neigel freezes.)

NEUMAN: Grandfather!

WASSERMAN: It's all right, Momik. I'm still alive, heaven forbid.

NEUMAN: But he—

WASSERMAN: Yes. I don't understand either. I should be dead many times over by now. Three times they sent me to the gas. Each time, I went willingly. Why not. Sarah and Tirzaleh had been taken from me. As far as I was concerned my life was over. They dropped the pellets down from the ceiling. After a few moments, the others were—

(He makes a gesture of extinction.)

But I just stood there

NEUMAN: You were in the—

WASSERMAN: I told you. Three times.

(Pause)

The third time, I found myself next to Zalmanson, my former editor, from Warsaw. Oy, Zalmanson.

(Otto becomes Zalmanson.)

ZALMANSON: The trouble with you, my little Wasserman, is that you are a coward in life and a coward on paper. You write like a Galizianer. Too long winded. The devil only knows why I go on publishing you!

WASSERMAN: His lungs were turning to leather. He collapsed on the concrete floor and looked up. I stood like a cedar of Lebanon. He understood my unusual situation. And he laughed. With his last breath, he laughed.

NEUMAN: And you didn't—

WASSERMAN: Not by gas and not by bullets, though on the bullets, I still haven't given up.

(Blackout)

SCENE 2

NEUMAN: One night Herr Neigel received a very important telephone call.

(Neigel is seated in his room, uniform loosened, listening to a Wagner aria on his record player. Telephone rings.)

NEIGEL: *(Speaking on the telephone)* Yes?

(Something he hears makes him snap to attention.)

Yes, Reichsfuhrer Himmler. Thank you, sir, I am deeply honored. And may I be so bold as to bring up the subject of my last report? The need to accelerate, accelerate more and more. If you could see fit to send supplies and materiel for three more gas chambers—

(Pause)

Of course . . . I understand . . . Yes, the situation in the east is . . . Thank you again, Reichsfuhrer Himmler, it is my deepest hope that my work continues to . . .

(Himmler has hung up. Neigel takes a bottle of brandy from a cupboard, pours himself a small glass, starts to make a toast, stops.)

NEIGEL: Wasserman.

(Pause)

Wasserman?

(Wasserman staggers awake, and stumbles into Neigel's room.)

WASSERMAN: In tonight's episode we—
NEIGEL: Wait.

(Neigel pours another glass of brandy for himself and one for Wasserman.)

I have a little something to celebrate. My superiors find me worthy of praise.

(He offers Wasserman the glass.)

The Reichsfuhrer said that my work and creative powers are, in their way, as glorious as the operas of Wagner.

(Wasserman, who has just taken a drink, chokes and coughs.)

I forget how delicate you Jews are.

(Neigel sits down. Wasserman recovers. Neigel takes out a blue envelope.)

NEIGEL: By the way, I mentioned you to my wife, Scheherazade. In my last letter. She remembered your stories too. You know what she wrote back?

(Wasserman preens, expecting to hear something flattering.)

She said you were a lousy writer and that your stories were pretty boring except for the hocus-pocus with the time machine and flying to the moon and so on, but even that seemed a little too familiar. She said you were just a curio. How did she put it?

(He finds the line.)

Ah. "A curio who was fortunate enough to find a publisher." That's what she said. I wrote her back, Scheherazade. I defended you for the sake of my happy memories. How do you like that?

WASSERMAN: *(To Neuman)* My perfect reader. Who says there's no God?

(Spits three times)

I'm afraid this Frau Neigel is correct. You know what Pinsky the critic called me? "The writers' matchmaker." I deserved it. In my stories I introduced Jack London to Jules Verne, Karl May to Daniel Defoe, H. G. Wells to Janusz Korczak. Perhaps in my youth I wrote with penetration—

ZALMANSON: but when I began to publish you, you turned coward.

WASSERMAN: Oy, Zalmanson, you *gonef*, stop haunting me!

ZALMANSON: But Wasserman, now that you've been hustled off beyond your life, your writing is showing some improvement. You're putting your milk and your blood into it now. Like you say, you've found you're perfect reader. Keep going! Write with daring! With madness!

(Wasserman is struck with a new inspiration.)

WASSERMAN: Otto's work in the ghetto had borne fruit. The newest member of the Children of the Heart is the incomparable Yedidya Munin, one in a generation, slave and master of his body, a man of flourishing dreams, winged as angels.

NEIGEL: What the hell is that supposed to mean? I thought they were all supposed to have some special skill or talent.

NEUMAN: *(Reads or writes)* A new imaginative current had begun to flow
through Grandfather. It gave him strength enough to hold his ground like
a tree in a storm.

WASSERMAN: Yedidya Munin is an artist of suppressed ejaculation, an arch-
copulator who never knew the touch of woman. Otto found him newly
released from the Paviak on a morals charge and immediately invited him
to join the others in the zoo.

*(Munin enters, a ragged figure with a broom. He can't help but get erotically in-
volved with it as he sweeps. Princess Magda enters and watches.)*

MUNIN: All my life, Pani, I have dreamed of wiping up the caca of a lion.

FRIED: Stop this at once! If you can't control yourself, you have no place in
my zoo!

MUNIN: Ah, but I am controlling myself, Pani, with great precision, if I may
say so. I know you admire precision.

FRIED: Explain yourself!

MUNIN: It's simple. First you have to understand that sperm shoots out of the
body with a terrible force. And I am not speaking in vague generalities.
No, Pani, I read in the most learned scientific journals that the force of
sperm flying is equal to the piston head on an airplane in the sky! Rela-
tively speaking, of course.

FRIED: That's true. So what?

MUNIN: Listen, I'm a simple man. The least in Israel. Vinegar begot of wine.
Baba Yaga's cat. I have not received much learning in my life. In my father's
house, *nu*, of course, the psalms by heart and later, here and there, the
compilations of the Maharan, and a little of the Zohar. Then in Warsaw,
my eyes were opened to the wonders of creation. And in the libraries I
sat and read the latest scientific studies! Of Tsiolkovsky has Your Honor
heard?

FRIED: Of course. Russian. Formulated theories of flight in space using
rockets.

MUNIN: A genius, no? Rockets! And it came into my mind as clear as a voice
from heaven that if I saved the terrible force of the sperm, numerous as

the stars in the sky, if I stored them inside, and if once, just once, I let myself go, that is, a kind of let my people go, what a great and mighty people it would be! For this powerful thrust alone could send me all the way, you see?

(Neigel laughs uncontrollably.)

FRIED: All the way to where?

MUNIN: All the way up. Above the fences; above the wires and the walls and the towers. Up. To God, of course.

(Munin sweeps his way into the darkness. Fried stalks off, looking for Otto.)

FRIED: Otto! You've gone absolutely too far this time.

(Wasserman turns and points at the back of his head.)

NEIGEL: *(Still laughing)* No, no Scheherazade, I don't give out German bullets for Jewish pornography.

WASSERMAN: *(Furious)* Pornography? Pornography? How dare you . . . No. Enough. How could I have thought for one minute that you could begin to hear—no. May my tongue fall out if I speak another word of this story to you!

(Wasserman storms out of Neigel's office downstage to the flower bed. He kneels, facing downstage, and stares straight ahead, immobile.)

NEIGEL: Bravo, Scheissemeister, Some honest feeling for once. You hate me, yes? Because I have power and I use it. Because I kill when I need to. So. In your morality, you are a writer and I am a murderer. Isn't it so? You are good and I am evil. Well, let me tell you something. You and I belong to different species. Your kind will cease to exist in two or three years, when our plan is complete. We will be around for at least a thousand years. And if someone comes along with different ideas they'll have to fight us. And if we are defeated, it will mean they were right.

WASSERMAN: You are being defeated here in this very place with every passing minute.

NEIGEL: Ah, the Jewish mind! Amazing how it never stops turning things inside out. Very well, Scheissemeister, How am I being defeated?

WASSERMAN: By your own cruelty, Neigel. You've learned it well. Can you un-learn it? Evil is not an object you carry with you to take out and use as you please, or leave in your pocket when you prefer.

NEIGEL: You'd be surprised, Wasserman. Most of the ss are model family men. We love our wives and children. We pledge our love to the Fuhrer, the Reich, and the family, in that order. These three loves sustain us when we carry out our orders.

WASSERMAN: Love? In your mouth the word is obscene. What will you do when the order comes to kill your own wife and children for the glory of the Reich?

NEUMAN: *(Writing)* For once the Nazi had no immediate answer. Grandfather had given voice to the Beast's greatest fear.

NEIGEL: There have been cases of nervous collapse among us, I won't deny it. I was acquainted with an excellent officer who committed suicide because he began to have nightmares about murdering his wife and children. But this is rare. Himmler understands these things. I wish I could remember his exact words.

(Neuman finds a note on a file card, reads it to himself.)

Oh yes, "When one hundred or five hundred or a thousand corpses are lying side by side, to continue to be decent human beings anyhow, is what makes us strong." You see, he understands that when we kill mothers and children—I'm not speaking of our *own* mothers and children—we have to be strong. To make decisions that no one else can know about. It's a silent war. In our souls that is. And I will tell you something no one else knows. It's all right to tell you, because with you it's different. In the past few months, due to an . . . *incident* of a private nature, I have been fight-ing a particular secret war of my own. And winning. You can be certain of that. Winning it every day. In order to be a good officer, you have to make decisions, like sending a part of this . . . machine . . .

(Points to his heart)

on leave, till the war is over and then you put it back and enjoy the new Reich.

WASSERMAN: When you finally succeed in turning your heart into a machine, Herr Neigel, on that day you will be completely defeated.

(This time Neigel shoots without being asked, directly in the back of Wasserman's head. As before, Wasserman is unharmed. Lights shift. Neigel and Wasserman return to their respective spaces.)

(Ruth enters.)

NEUMAN: Did you turn off the gas? I don't remember seeing you turn off the gas.

RUTH: I turned it off. And I locked—

NEUMAN: Both locks?

RUTH: —the front door. I need to talk to you about Yariv.

NEUMAN: I took him to the park yesterday . . .

RUTH: And he was a complete mess by the time you got home. You scared him to death.

NEUMAN: He's always scared. Just like I was.

RUTH: Because you keep frightening him!

NEUMAN: I took him to play on the slides. I had to climb up with him because he was afraid to move without me. But then, for some reason that escapes me, I climbed down again. I left him up there, crying. A young mother came up and said, "He's *scared!*" I told her that out in the forests, among the partisans, children his age had to sit in the treetops for hours, keeping guard in absolute silence. Her face went white and she got as far away from me as she could. Then Yariv started screaming. And I thought: if we're caught in a bunker some day with soldiers and dogs searching for us, how will I ever be able to shut him up? Finally I climbed up to get him. His mouth stuck to my neck. He trembled and sobbed. I was shaking too. I almost fell from the ladder. I wanted to say, forgive me, please, Yariv, be wiser and more patient than I am. They didn't teach me how to love.

RUTH: Did you say it?

(Pause)

Did you say it?

NEUMAN: Wait. Do you remember, at our wedding—my Aunt Idka? The one who always wore purple?

RUTH: Can we please talk about Yariv for once!

NEUMAN: I never told you this. I have to tell you this, Ruth.

RUTH: What!

NEUMAN: She had a Band-Aid on her arm. She put it on to cover her concentration camp number. I couldn't tear my eyes away from it, even when I stepped on the glass. Could you feel it? There was an abyss under that little Band-Aid. It was sucking us all in: you, me, all the guests, any hope for a joyful life.

RUTH: What did you tell Yariv?

NEUMAN: I told him to stop crying like a girl.

(Lights change. Wasserman is discovered telling the story to Neigel.)

WASSERMAN: Otto Brig slipped away from the zoo, as he did every evening, just after nightfall to continue his work of rescue in the Warsaw Ghetto. When he closed the gates of the zoo behind him, however, he was struck by a new smell in the air, dark and smoky.

OTTO: It's what I saw in the vision glass. The ghetto is burning.

(Fried and Princess Magda rush to Otto's side.)

WASSERMAN: He gathered the Children of the Heart together and made a mad dash toward the flames, to save anyone they could—

WASSERMAN: *(Finds a bundle of rags and carries it to the three Children of the Heart)* But before they could take one step, something very near their feet gave out with a cry, a wail of enormous distress.

(He places the bundle behind them. Their gazes are fixed on the distance. They don't notice Wasserman, who immediately goes back to his spot upstage. Princess Magda supplies the "wail." Otto bends down and picks up the bundle. It's a small puppet, the size of a newborn baby, wrapped in rags. He carries the baby to Fried.)

FRIED: What is this? What is this? Is it alive?

OTTO: *(They both gaze for a moment, dumbstruck. A dawning realization:)* Look at his eyes, Fried. He recognizes us.

(They stare at each other for a minute. Then Fried takes the baby/puppet and places it on a wooden crate. He washes his hands in a basin of water and gently touches the baby, here and there, examining it. Fried notices that his fingers are covered with something soft and white. He shows this to Otto. Otto sniffs his fingers, then tastes them.)

OTTO: Like the dust from a butterfly's wing.

NEIGEL: No, Wasserman, not butterfly dust. I can tell you this from personal experience, if you don't mind. Not dust. More like a kind of fatty coating. Babies are sometimes born with it. It helps them in some way. I forget just how.

WASSERMAN: You will excuse me, Herr Neigel, but if I say it is like butterfly dust, then butterfly dust it is.

FRIED: *(To Otto, while continuing his examination of the baby)* Not butterfly dust, my friend. It is a fatty coating meant to protect the fetus from the strong waters of the womb.

OTTO: Whatever you say.

(Otto picks up the baby and speaks nonsense to it.)

FRIED: The important thing is—milk! How are we going to feed the child?

NEIGEL: Write that Obersturmbannfuhrer Neigel brings milk to—

WASSERMAN: No, no, no. We've used that already.

NEIGEL: But—

WASSERMAN: *(Motioning for silence)* Besides, it is newly born. It can only take mother's milk.

(Pause)

Ah. Of course. Princess Magda.

NEIGEL: Good. Some magic finally!

PRINCESS MAGDA: Yes. If the child needs milk, I will find it . . . inside . . .

(Princess Magda and Otto begin a flamenco-like dance. The others clap.)

the molecular structure . . . of my earliest memories. I take the voices burning with desire . . . and the dancing mountains of Andalusia and the textures of weathered hands and I . . . squeeeeeeze.

(Milk appears! Fried feeds the baby with a spoon.)

NEIGEL: *(Recollecting)* A warm white liquid. Sweet, too.

WASSERMAN: Very sweet. It melts in your mouth.

NEIGEL: Yes. So creamy.

(They are both suddenly embarrassed and fall silent.)
(Pause)

WASSERMAN: At that moment, the infant, having eaten its fill, opened its mouth in a wide smile revealing the presence of two perfectly formed—

OTTO: Teeth. It already has two teeth, Fried!

FRIED: Such things are possible. Some are born covered with downy hair which soon falls off . . .

(He examines the baby further.)

WASSERMAN: The doctor noticed that the baby was breathing faster and wriggling restlessly. A fearful premonition made him peek at the baby's tummy.

FRIED: *(Clinically, as if dictating to a nurse)* No signs of clotted blood on the navel.

(Pause)

No signs of tearing or cutting on the navel.

(Pause. He looks up, confused.)

No navel.

NEIGEL: No navel?

(Wasserman shakes his head.)

You artists always have to complicate the simplest things! A baby without a navel! This is how you ruin art. Art should entertain people. It should make them feel good.

(Neigel pours himself another drink.)

Tina and I would argue this before the war, you know. She would drag me into dark cellars to watch theatrical presentations that did nothing but encourage doubt. I would leave feeling awkward and confused. Why can't the baby be normal, Wasserman?

WASSERMAN: Because there is no longer such a thing as normal, Herr Neigel.

NEIGEL: *(Momentarily at a loss. Takes another drink.)* You have a point. All right. The baby has no navel. I would not have thought myself capable of listening to such a story. It grows more peculiar each day.

(Makes a note in his black book)

Well, go on. Why stop now?

WASSERMAN: As the night wore on, the baby would not stop hollering. His bitter screams drowned out the clatter and roar of tanks rolling by on the nearby streets and the frightening explosions from the surrounding houses where heavy combat was in progress.

NEIGEL: Now what? Explain!

WASSERMAN: The ghetto, begging your pardon, is being destroyed.

NEIGEL: You're trying to make a war on me with this story of yours. I told you I want entertainment!

WASSERMAN: But the rebellion—

NEIGEL: Don't interrupt. I'm talking now. The Warsaw rebellion? Where will you take me next? To Birkenau? To the Fuhrer's bunker in Berlin? You want to infect me with your famous Jewish suffering? You think you can fight me with your shit words? You are ridiculous. I pity you. I really do. If you had a gun in your hand it would be a lot more convincing than the millions of words you chatter at me.

(Neigel has an idea. He takes his gun from his holster and places it on the table next to Wasserman.)

And now you have one. What are you going to do with it?

(He turns away from Wasserman and raises his hands.)

What are you going to do with it?

(Wasserman picks up the gun. His hand is shaking.)

NEUMAN: *(Crosses to Wasserman)* Do it, Grandfather. Oh my God, yes! Shoot him dead. And then run outside and shoot some guards and start a rebellion. No, wait—hold him hostage and force Himmler himself to come into the camp and then kill *him.*

WASSERMAN: I can't.

NEUMAN: *(Reaches down toward Wasserman)* Then give me the gun!

WASSERMAN: No. We have an obligation to the story. The story is a living, breathing creature, a mysterious, lovely, and delicate creature we must not twist or break to suit our own impetuous whims. And besides, there is now a child living his life in this story. Do you understand? A child.

(He puts the gun back on the table.)

NEUMAN: I've had enough of the story, Grandfather. You can't kill Nazis with a story. You have to beat them to death.

WASSERMAN: No.

NEUMAN: No, of course not.

WASSERMAN: If I can tell the story to him—all of it—it might still be possible to infect him with humanity.

NEUMAN: One infected Nazi? No. I want more. I want to liberate the six million with an undercover mission bigger than you've ever imagined! Tunnels. Parachutes. Submarines. Jet fighters. Can't the Children of the Heart do that? They used to be able to do anything. Have them form a commando unit to kill Hitler and then bomb Germany, wipe out every trace of *Over There*, every good trace and every evil trace and turn back the clock, with the time machine. Let's tell that story. We can do it! Right now!

WASSERMAN: And then what? What happens to the child?

NEUMAN: What happens to him if Neigel and his kind live?

WASSERMAN: We'll see.

NEUMAN: You ask him to shoot you every night but you won't—

(He breaks off.)

B'seder. So be it. I give up. I'm resigning from the project. I'm done with this story.

(Neuman returns to his study. Neigel turns. He and Wasserman both look at the gun on the table. Lights come up on Fried, Otto, Princess Magda, and the baby puppet.)

WASSERMAN: Fried did not know what to do with the screaming baby.

FRIED: *(Looking in the baby's mouth)* We miscounted the number of teeth, Otto. There are four.

OTTO: *(Looks)* I'm counting six.

(In its struggles, the baby strikes Fried in the face.)

FRIED: *Du yassni choleria!* Right in my nose!

(Fried's outburst frightens the baby even more; it starts wailing again. Otto and Fried and Princess Magda distract and comfort the baby, all three of them goo-gooing and cooing, singing fragments of lullabies. Gradually, the baby's wailing changes to laughter.)

NEIGEL: Isn't this baby too young for laughing?

FRIED: Otto, this baby is too young to be laughing. Directed, voluntary laughter begins only at the age of—

NEIGEL: two or three months. Karl started a little later. He is quite serious. With Lischen we saw a smile at two months. She's always first at everything.

FRIED: *(Princess Magda holds the baby puppet while Fried measures it and makes notes.)* Anonymous baby brought to me by Otto Brig at 2005 hours on 5/4/43. Sex: male. Length of body: 51 centimeters. Head measurement: 34 centimeters. Weight, an estimated 3 kilograms. At 2020 Otto Brig saw two teeth in the lower jaw. At 2110 I saw another two teeth in the upper jaw. Approximately one minute later, another two appeared in the lower jaw. All in all, six teeth. At 2120, the baby is alert, even smiling.

WASSERMAN: And as he smiled, in his mouth gleamed—

NEIGEL: Wait, what are you going to tell me now, more teeth?

FRIED: Eight teeth!

WASSERMAN: Exactly so.

(Neigel writes something in his notebook.)
(Fried writes in his notebook.)

It became clear to Fried that every four or five minutes, the child developed at the rate of three months in the life of a normal child.

FRIED: In half an hour he will be eighteen months old. In one hour, he will be three years of age. It can't be. Wersus? Werblov? What was that name?

(Fried finds a small medical dictionary in his pocket.)

"Werner. Werner's syndrome. A process of rapid aging, beginning at thirty years. The deterioration of all systems. See under Progeria."

OTTO: See under what?

NEIGEL: What are you doing to this infant, Wasserman?

FRIED: *(Reading)* "Progeria. The childhood version of Werner's Syndrome (q.v.), . . . only a few cases recorded in medical history. Beginning in infancy, acute symptoms of deterioration, retardation and depression appear. Premature calcification . . . rapid, agonizing death."

NEIGEL: Wasserman, listen to me for just one moment . . .

FRIED: Dear God.

(The baby Kazik crawls out of Princess Magda's lap onto the floor and gradually discovers how to crawl on its hands and knees.)

NEIGEL: *(Pounds the desk)* Enough of this warped story!
WASSERMAN: Enough of your interruptions!
NEIGEL: Don't you dare touch that child!

(Everyone freezes.)

WASSERMAN: *(Slowly and fearlessly)* There are things you must not say to me, Herr Neigel. My life is bitter enough without you. The child will live and die, heaven forbid, according to the story's requirements. It shall be so.
OTTO: Ah, Fried. You might have guessed this is how life would answer the challenge of your grief.
FRIED: Don't worry about me. I'm not ready to give up.
NEIGEL: Good, Fried. Have courage!

(Fried, in a frenzy, works his slide rule and makes calculations in his notebook. By now, The puppet is beginning to get to its feet and take its first few steps.)

FRIED: There—must—be—a—mistake—perhaps—not—Progeria—in—its —acute—form.

(Finally he exhausts himself and becomes still.)

It's like this. If the baby continues to develop at this rate, he'll complete the life cycle of an average human being in exactly twenty-four hours. Yes.

(The puppet falls on its behind.)

NEIGEL: I tell you, Wasserman, you're ruining a good story with these strange ideas. Twenty-four hours. My God.
WASSERMAN: A magnificent twenty-four hours, I assure you.

(The baby gets up again and walks toward Fried. Music.)

PAULA: Kazik. Name him Kazik.
NEUMAN: Kazik? This is Kazik, Grandfather? You spoke that name in our kitchen when I was . . .
FRIED: *(To the baby)* You are Kazik.
KAZIK: *(Reaches out both arms to Fried)* Papa!

(Blackout)

ACT 2

SCENE I

(Lights come up on Neuman's room. His notes and books and his person are in complete disarray. Wasserman approaches the edge of his space and starts to speak.)

NEUMAN: Go away. I've quit the story, remember?

WASSERMAN: Yes, and herrings walk on dry land.

NEUMAN: You can't bring a child into this story. There's no point bringing new life into a dying world.

WASSERMAN: Bite your tongue!

NEUMAN: Ruth and I tried. It's no good. We only hand the fear down, generation to generation. He wakes up screaming every night.

WASSERMAN: A sign of life. Treasure it. This child, this Kazik will surprise us, I promise you.

NEUMAN: He doesn't have a chance!

WASSERMAN: Of course he does! As long as we keep telling the story, the possibilities are infinite.

(Neuman starts to protest.)

Don't say another word! Listen.

(Lights come up on the central area. Fried holds Kazik by the hand and leads him around a small area in the central, rubble-filled arena that now stands for Fried's apartment in the zoo. Princess Magda and Otto manipulate the puppet. Neigel and Wasserman watch from Neigel's room.)

FRIED: *(Pointing to floor)* Ground.

KAZIK: Ground.

FRIED: *(Pointing to and/or touching various objects)* Lamp.

KAZIK: Lamp.

FRIED: Table.

KAZIK: Table.

FRIED: Chair.

KAZIK: Chair.

FRIED: Another chair.

KAZIK: Anotherchair.

(Points to first "chair")

Anotherchair?
FRIED: Yes. No.

(Tries it again)

First chair.
KAZIK: Chairanotherchairfirstchair?
FRIED: *(Points to first chair)* Chair.

(Points to second chair)

Chair.
KAZIK: *(Points to the floor)* Ground.

(Points to another part of the floor)

Ground.
FRIED: Yes. Good.
KAZIK: Yesgood?
FRIED: *(Puts on an exaggerated smile, points to his own face)* Good.
KAZIK: *(Tries to mimic Fried's smile. It looks like a grimace of pain or terror.)*
    Good?
FRIED: Ah, Paula. Why aren't you here to help me? He has so little time. How
    can I teach him everything he needs to know?

*(Growing desperate. He points in various directions, tries to indicate the meaning
of each of the following words with gestures. Kazik tries to imitate the gestures. Indicating the zoo:)*

Poland.

(Clandestinely pointing up toward Neigel, making war noises)

Germans.

(Pointing to himself and to Kazik)

Jew. Jew.

(Again toward Neigel)

Nazi. Bad.

(Pointing far in the distance)

Soviets. Not so bad.

KAZIK: Bad? Badnazi? Notsobadnazibad?

(Kazik makes war noises.)

FRIED: Kazik good.

(Points to himself)

Fried—

(Overcome by the absurdity of his situation)

I can't do this alone, Paula!

(Paula is perched on an upper portion of the stage left scaffolding.)

PAULA: Only tell him what is essential, my darling.

FRIED: *(The sound of her voice is too much for him. He rants:)* Beware of strangers, and doubt your friends, and never tell anyone what you really think, never tell the truth unless there's no choice, someone is bound to use it against you, and don't love anyone too much, not even yourself.

PAULA: Ah, Albert, you sound just like your father. This is not what you believe. Tell him the truth.

FRIED: *(Partly to Paula, partly to Kazik)* I used to sit down with my mother at the piano and the melody flowed out of her fingers like a kind of mist. I dreamed of becoming a pianist, you know. When she died. My father said—

OTTO: *(On an stage left bunk. Becoming Fried's father.)* My boy, your mother has gone away on a long journey. You must forget all about her and attend to your studies.

FRIED: I avoided the other children and spent time alone in the fields. I discovered that animals were not afraid of me.

(Kazik slowly approaches Fried.)

Even the wild rabbits waited patiently for me to touch them. And then I met Otto and Paula and began the happiest days of my life with the Children of the Heart. But even those days passed. And then there was the war—the first one—and I was drafted as a physician and I saw things I would not have believed men capable of.

(Kazik becomes agitated and moves away from Fried.)

PAULA: And what you saw confirmed everything your father had taught you, silently, with his frown of disgust, until you could hardly remember the gentle beauty of your mother's fragrant hand.

FRIED: And then the time machine stranded us here and this time Paula came to me, finally. Even though I never allowed myself to say a single word of longing to her.

PAULA: It didn't matter. I knew everything.

FRIED: Do you know what I really miss? Do you?

(Kazik shakes his head "no.")

I miss the smell of her underarms. And the wrinkles around her eyes. And the way she sat on a chair or bandaged a sore. When I was with her, I knew that there was perhaps something in me deserving of the good life.

(Kazik reaches his hand to Fried, who takes it.)

KAZIK: Good?

(Fried and Kazik look at each other for a long time.)

FRIED: Good.

(Fried holds Kazik in his arms.)

WASSERMAN: And the doctor knew that at last, he was doing something truly important for his son.

NEUMAN: He was doing something truly important for his son.

(Fried sings a lullaby to Kazik.)
(Neuman calls out.)

Ruth? Yariv?

(Lullaby ends.)

WASSERMAN: Fried spent interminable nights —

(Kazik wakes up, looks around.)

which lasted no longer than the twinkling of an eye —

(Kazik goes to sleep.)

at Kazik's bedside.

NEUMAN: Ruth?

(Lullaby resumes. Kazik wakes again.)

FRIED: I will give you the best of lives. I will be the best of fathers and we will
be the best of friends.

*(Kazik wakes. Stands up, steadier on his feet now. Walks downstage to flower bed.
Picks a flower. Smells it. Gives it to Fried.)*

KAZIK: Good?

*(Fried smiles and nods. Kazik notices a tool in flower bed. Picks it up. Hurts hand
on it. Cries out. He hobbles back to Fried, who examines the wound. Otto and
Paula's ghosts come over, concerned.)*

FRIED: No blood. No blood at all. Fine particles of sheer dust. They pulse from
the wound and dissolve in the air.

NEIGEL: No navel and now no blood? And what is this dust he's talking about?

(Fried fingers the invisible dust as it dissolves in the air.)

FRIED: Time. Time itself.

KAZIK: Time. Good.

*(Kazik fingers the invisible dust. He makes idle foot-tapping movements, which
leads him to discover tapping. The tapping turns into a full-blown though awkward dance. The Children of the Heart sing a wordless tune. Suddenly, he stops in
his tracks, breathing audibly, eyes fixed in a trance. Fried consults his watch.)*

FRIED: According to my calculations he is entering the phase of adolescent
dormancy.

*(The Children of the Heart gather around him. As they wait, their breathing
becomes audible, creating contrapuntal rhythms that surround the child. Kazik
awakens and tears at the invisible fibers of breath. The sounds stop. Kazik is now
visibly older [a wig has been placed on the puppet]. He looks around, confused and
angry.)*

KAZIK: Am I—who am I—who—am—I?

FRIED: Whoever you choose to be. This is very important, Kazik. You can choose. Do you understand? You can choose to be a human being.

NEIGEL: *(Calling down from his room)* Tell me, Doctor, how is that done? I always thought one was born so, no?

FRIED: I used to think so. But experience has taught me otherwise. One becomes human by choosing to uphold certain values and precepts.

NEIGEL: *(To Wasserman)* And I have done exactly that. I choose to uphold the values of the party.

WASSERMAN: I mean the higher human values. Re-creating and redeeming one's self.

NEIGEL: You think I haven't done that? It was not easy to choose the extreme actions required by the cause.

WASSERMAN: Killing, you mean.

NEIGEL: Yes. I chose to start killing. That is choice.

WASSERMAN: But you can't simply choose to *start* killing, Herr Neigel, you have to choose to continue killing, each time you do it. No decision is permanently valid, and if you are a man of honor, you must reaffirm your decision each time you kill another prisoner.

NEIGEL: Is that supposed to frighten me? I rather like it. Reaffirming my decision.

WASSERMAN: Every day, Herr Neigel. Every time you shoot your gun and destroy another human being. And twenty-five times when you kill twenty-five prisoners here. Decision after decision. Can you stand it?

NEIGEL: In the words of our Fuhrer—*mit Einsatzfreudigheit*—with pleasure.

(Stamping a series of official documents)

Back in '38 when we were burning your synagogues and stores. Everything went up in flames. We went wild. We killed people in the streets without a trial or anything, without even bothering to cover our tracks. For weeks after that, I remember expecting something to happen, I don't know what. Maybe for a hand to reach out of the sky and smack us in the face. But you know what? Nothing happened. Only the Communists and a few Jew lovers made any fuss at all. But the Church? Neither the Catholic nor the Protestant Church made a sound. Not one bishop in all of Germany wore the yellow star in protest. We're simple folk, Wasserman, what were we supposed to think? That's why I tell you: it's the will of God and nature. The world is getting ready for the new age.

(Blackout)

(Neuman is back in his room.)

NEUMAN: One rainy morning a young Jew not yet beaten down arrives in Neigel's camp. He's forced to run naked with the other new arrivals through a gauntlet of Ukrainian guards who beat him with rifle butts and whips while dogs tear at his feet and legs. But this young naked Jew does something unheard of. He attacks one of the Ukrainian guards and takes his gun. He screams and shoots, running blindly. The Ukrainians begin shooting. Jews run helter-skelter into the line of fire. Neigel runs out of the barracks, strikes the young man, and knocks the rifle out of his hands. The young Jew falls to his knees. He drops his head to the ground, panting like an animal. His skinny rib cage is heaving violently. He's so terrified he lets go a jet of excrement.

WASSERMAN: But Momik, you're leaving out the most important thing. Neigel saw me!

NEUMAN: *(Shocked out of his reverie)* So what? He's still going to—

WASSERMAN: Yes, but he hesitated. And he remembered his choice.

(Pause)

Then he emptied his gun out on the innocent boy. He went on shooting after there was no longer any point. He was furious with himself for keeping his agreement to *choose* his every act of murder. He ran back to his barracks and slammed the door behind him.

NEUMAN: But what does it matter if he chooses, the boy is still dead!

RUTH: Momik, stop it.

NEUMAN: As long as Neigel has his guns and his dogs—

RUTH: Momik!

NEUMAN: As long as *anyone* has whips and dogs and long lines of guards with machine guns what can we possibly tell the children that will—

RUTH: Momik!

(He snaps out of it, agitated.)

NEUMAN: Ruth?

RUTH: It's all right.

NEUMAN: Sometimes I feel I'm so close to understanding what Grandfather is really doing with this story, but then . . .

RUTH: Listen, Momik, It's getting a little too . . . crowded around here, you know? Yariv and I are going to my Uncle Shmuel in Haifa for a while. So you can—

NEUMAN: Shmuel? It's that bad, eh?

RUTH: Just for a while. It will be better like this.

NEUMAN: Don't let him try to teach Yariv any advanced calculus, all right? Shmuel. And you think I scare him.

(They embrace.)

RUTH: Don't forget to eat something once in a while.

(Ruth exits. Beat. Neuman looks at his notes. Thinks.)

NEUMAN: Later that night, Obersturmbannfuhrer Neigel—What? Ah. Yes. Neigel wrote a letter home to his wife.

SCENE 3

(Neigel is alone in his office writing. He periodically consults his small black notebook as he writes. The ensemble watches him from below, occasionally nudging each other and muttering.)

NEIGEL: My darling Christina. As you will recall, in the last episode, Doctor Fried taught Kazik how to speak. And not only that, but he . . .

(Crosses out a line)

. . . In the last episode, Doctor Fried not only taught Kazik how to speak, but he also resolved to become the best of fathers to his son. Two hours later, which, as you know, meant

(Consults notebook)

. . . six years in Kazik's life, the boy entered adolescence.

(Thinks for a moment. Writes again without consulting notebook.)

His voice turned husky, his face coarsened and hair sprouted on his body. Kazik was filled with doubt. He asked the doctor, "Who am I . . ."

(Neigel hunts through the notebook, realizes there's nothing more in it.)

Wasserman!

(Wasserman crosses to Neigel.)

WASSERMAN: Good evening, Your Honor. Have you recovered sufficiently to continue?

NEIGEL: What are you talking about?

WASSERMAN: Only that you seemed troubled by recent events. I thought perhaps you had lost interest in my humble efforts in fabricating the—

NEIGEL: Enough. Get on with it, Wasserman.

WASSERMAN: Very well, Herr Neigel.

(Kazik appears, riding on Otto's shoulders, with Fried and Princess Magda.)

In his twenty-seventh year, which occurred nine hours after his discovery by the Children of the Heart, Kazik's restless mind soon began to hunger for knowledge of the world outside the zoo. He asked the doctor about its inhabitants.

KAZIK: What kind of life do they live?

FRIED: Just life.

KAZIK: Do the people love their lives?

WASSERMAN: The good doctor could not lie to Kazik.

(Fried slowly and regretfully shakes his head.)

KAZIK: *(Indicates the wide world)* How many live there?

FRIED: Oh, millions. Millions.

KAZIK: *(Tries to understand this number. Gives up.)* Never mind how many. One of them loves life. Me—Kazik—am—that—one.

FRIED: What does that mean to you, child?

KAZIK: Something good. Something I want. Something that's there. Let's go get it.

(Kazik and Fried begin a slow motion journey.)

WASSERMAN: And so, forgoing needless preliminaries, the two set off on their way. Fried had no idea which way they should proceed, but that did not matter to Kazik. He felt the doctor's large hand holding his. He saw the fresh grass sparkling with dew and heard the vast night sky breathing above. An uncontainable joy surged through his little body.

KAZIK: I—Love—This—Life!

WASSERMAN: And now, Your Honor, we must settle our accounts.

NEIGEL: But we've hardly begun—

WASSERMAN: I believe our discussion last night may have distracted you. According to my figures, you owe me a bullet. Before I continue I would like to settle our accounts.

NEIGEL: Absolutely not!

WASSERMAN: We have an agreement.

NEIGEL: You can forget about it.

WASSERMAN: What about the word of a German *offizier?*

NEIGEL: Listen, Wasserman, you yourself said I have to make a decision each time I shoot. You're the one who put that into my head. And I have made a decision: I will not shoot you! Not now and not ever. So. Is that clear?

WASSERMAN: You promised, Neigel, Damn you!

NEIGEL: Ach, for you it's nothing, you feel nothing when I shoot you. No pain at all! But for me it's different. I know you now. You're not just another Jew for me like the others out there. No, Wasserman, forget it. I can't do it anymore.

WASSERMAN: You are a German *offizier,* Herr Neigel, paragon of the Third Reich, and I am the lowest of the low, an *untermensch.* And I'll tell you something: if you don't shoot me, I'm going to stop telling you my story.

NEIGEL: You can't stop now! You must continue to tell it!

WASSERMAN: Why do you think I torment myself before you every night? Because I like the color of your eyes?

NEIGEL: Because you enjoy telling the story! You love it!

WASSERMAN: No. Because I wish to die. Shylock the Jew demands his pound of flesh! Shoot, Herr Neigel!

(Neigel gives in and points his gun at Wasserman's temple, his hand shaking.)

WASSERMAN: Stop with the trembling, Neigel. I want a clean shot. Nothing messy, please.

NEIGEL: I'm trying, damn you. This has never happened to me before. What if I lose you this time?

WASSERMAN: *(Smiles)* Release a bullet, Neigel. I am only a Jew, a Jew like all the others! Now, shoot!

(Neigel shoots.)

Momik! I've got it! Now I know what Neigel has been writing down while I tell the story. I know why he insists on hearing more and more. I know!

(Wasserman is unhurt.)
(Blackout.)

SCENE 4

NEUMAN: One night, four prisoners risked their lives to bless the Sabbath in a latrine.

(The ensemble performs a clandestine Sabbath blessing in a corner of the central area. They are on the lookout for guards, as they light a small misshapen candle. Meanwhile, Neigel, in a state of nervous excitement, is packing a small valise while Wasserman watches. He places the last item and snaps it shut. He takes out his small black notebook.)

NEIGEL: My driver will be here in two hours. So, please, tell me what happens on this journey of Kazik and Fried. Where do they go?

WASSERMAN: Where can they go? Fried is one of us, don't forget. And we have established that Kazik is now twenty-seven. He would not survive a journey of any great length. Their travels are confined to the zoo. The crossing of which will take up six years of Kazik's life.

NEIGEL: Very well. Quickly now.

WASSERMAN: May I ask to where the commandant is departing.

NEIGEL: Home, Wasserman. Berlin. I've got forty-eight hours leave. So let's get on with it.

WASSERMAN: *(Pretends to read from his notebook. As the ensemble transforms into the Children of the Heart, Munin is present instead of Otto.)* It was a warm night in early April 1943. The horizon blazed red, and the smell of scorched flesh assailed them from afar. After traveling for three weeks of Kazik's life, which is to say one minute and ten seconds, a lively dispute broke out among the Children of the Heart as to the best way to teach Kazik the principles of life.

FRIED: *(Without much conviction)* We could read to him from the old and new testaments.

PRINCESS MAGDA: No. Words lie. Play him music, the most sublime music.

NEUMAN: Just tell him the truth. Facts. No surprises.

FRIED: We could discourse upon the great philosophies.

NEIGEL: Take him to the mountains! Everything important I learned in the mountains when my grandfather—

MUNIN: He needs a woman.

FRIED: Will you please stay back there where you belong!

MUNIN: I beg your forgiveness, Pani, but since the lions have died I have nothing to do . . .

KAZIK: Woman?

PAULA: Think about it, darling, how much time does he have?

FRIED: My God, you're right. In three hours he'll be well past his prime. This is the only . . .

(Looks around)

But who?

MUNIN: If a worthless *schlimazel* might make a suggestion . . .

WASSERMAN: And it came to pass that Kazik was taken to Hannah Zeitrin, the most beautiful woman in the world.

(Paula transforms into Hannah by removing her shoes and stockings. She puts on a wig of the opposite color of the actor playing the role.)

NEIGEL: A new character? You've never mentioned this one. Who—

MUNIN: Otto found her in a women's shelter. She had been—if you'll pardon me—raped by Poles and Jews and everybody, but she laughed as if she didn't feel it. You see she had lost two entire families. First—

HANNAH ZEITRIN: Dolek was killed in the bombings, then the Germans took Rochka, just like that in April '41. Yehuda Efraim they took in the *gros aktion* in '42.

MUNIN: She remarried—a baker named Barkov who had lost his family.

HANNAH ZEITRIN: But he loved God in spite of everything. He said God commanded us to love life. He convinced me. He had a little girl left and together we made a son. One fine summer night a Polish sentry killed them all. I knew what I had to do. I painted and adorned myself. All over. I decided to be beautiful. So beautiful I would catch His eye, the hungry eye of God Almighty.

MUNIN: Isn't she exquisite? Here, in the zoo, she wanders naked all night long, in the heat and cold, up and down the paths near the carnivore cages, trying to seduce God, fighting her war with him.

(Hannah stops dancing abruptly.)

He has come, Mrs. Zeitrin, He has come for us all.

(Munin takes Kazik to Hannah Zeitrin.)
(Hannah sniffs the air around Kazik.)

HANNAH ZEITRIN: Is it He?

MUNIN: I don't know how Mrs. Zeitrin imagines God will look when He finally comes to her, but I am certain Kazik has the right smell.

(Fried moves Munin and Princess Magda stage right, away from the couple. Hannah caresses Kazik. She turns her back to the audience and holds him between her legs. They begin to make love. Hannah takes a small knife out of her pocket and stabs Kazik repeatedly.)

HANNAH ZEITRIN: Take this, O Lord of Hosts! This is for love and this is for hope. And this is for the joy of life. And this is for renewal. And this is for creation. And this is for the power to forget. And this is for faith. And this is for illusion. And this is for the fucking optimism you implanted in us. And this is for—

(Fried and the others reach Hannah and restrain her.)

FRIED: Stop!

(Fried picks Kazik up and holds him. Munin leads Hannah Zeitrin away. Kazik struggles in Fried's arms.)

Kazik, my Kazik?

WASSERMAN: Thus, Hannah's daring plot against God aborted Kazik's initiation into the fullness of manhood.

NEIGEL: But is Kazik . . . ?

WASSERMAN: His wounds sealed themselves up before any more of his time leaked away.

FRIED: Paula?

(Paula doesn't answer. Kazik reaches out in longing.)

Ah, Kazik. Perhaps it's better this way . . . You know, what happens between a man and a woman, it's not always . . .

(Kazik stops reaching out and abruptly turns to Fried.)

KAZIK: Keep going! Something good! Somewhere. Go find!

WASSERMAN: All he knew was that his great journey was not over and joy was still a possibility. To Fried's great embarrassment, and Munin's delight, he gripped his tiny penis and began to masturbate.

(Neigel, who has been keeping notes, as usual, has been growing increasingly agitated during the preceding.)

NEIGEL: *(Crosses into the central area to Wasserman)* No, no, no! Unacceptable, Wasserman. It's all wrong. I am ashamed of you. This might do here in a barracks, but you have to think of your readers, you know.

(The Children of the Heart transform back into inmates and gather on the upper stage right platform.)

WASSERMAN: *(Laying a trap)* I hadn't thought I had any readers outside this barracks.

NEIGEL: Of course not, only in a manner of speaking, that is. But damn it, Wasserman, we're losing time. My driver—

(Wasserman says nothing.)

You must tell me the rest of Kazik's story. At least the bare outline. You don't know how important this is.

WASSERMAN: No.

NEIGEL: Is the heart willing?

(Wasserman says nothing.)

Is the heart willing?

(Still nothing)

Betrayal!

WASSERMAN: If it is so important, tell the rest of the story yourself.

(Neigel backs Wasserman against the central platform and beats him; the ensemble echoes the sounds of the blows. Wasserman speaks through the blows.)

Good! Like this—you have not yet—tried to kill me. Maybe—with the hands —it will work!

(Neigel collapses on the ramp beside Wasserman, panting and groaning.)

NEIGEL: I beg you, Herr Wasserman, in the name of the story, stop torment-ing me.

WASSERMAN: No, Herr Neigel, you will just have to make up another story for your wife, I'm sorry to say.

NEIGEL: *(Pause)* How did you find out?

WASSERMAN: I thought a little.

NEIGEL: So. You know.

WASSERMAN: You wrote her the whole story, didn't you? In the letters you sent her, you copied out my story. Is that right?

NEIGEL: The whole story, yes.

WASSERMAN: *Nu,* does she still think I'm a curio?

NEIGEL: No, no. She says this is the best story you ever wrote. But she doesn't—

WASSERMAN: Doesn't what? The truth, Neigel!

NEIGEL: Christina doesn't actually know about you. About the two of us, that is.

WASSERMAN: Herr Neigel, please, did I not hear from your own very lips that you told her about me in your letters home?

NEIGEL: I told her, yes of course I told her. I told her you were here. Unfortu-nately, she knows exactly what that means.

WASSERMAN: She thinks that I am dead.

NEIGEL: Yes. She does. And she was upset about it. In her last letter she said you were the only Jew who died here whose name she knows.

WASSERMAN: Please send her my condolences.

NEIGEL: Everything became so complicated. It started out as a joke. Well, not a joke exactly, more like a game. It's too hard to explain. And suddenly I couldn't tell her the truth anymore, you see.

WASSERMAN: This is plagiarism, Neigel!

NEIGEL: I'm sorry.

WASSERMAN: The worst crime you could ever commit against me here!

NEIGEL: I'm sorry.

WASSERMAN: Worse than death! You stole my story, Neigel, you stole my life!

NEIGEL: But I told you I was sorry! How many times do you want to hear it? I'm sorry! I'm sorry! Listen, you can be proud of yourself, Scheherazade, because thanks to your story Tina wrote me to come to her, that things have changed.

WASSERMAN: *(To Neuman)* You hear that, Momik? Gottenyu! Anshel Wasserman, reconciler of Nazi families.

NEIGEL: Before the war, when all this began, it was enough for her to know I was happy in the ss, that after so many years of odd jobs I finally had steady work with a good salary. She never joined the party. She doesn't understand politics. But after her visit here—yes, she was here. The ss has since discontinued such visits—for good reason. After her visit everything changed. She took the children and moved out of our flat to a tiny apartment she rented for herself and she refuses to talk to me.

(Pause)

But then, after you were brought to me, I came up with this strange idea: I thought that if I wrote her a story, maybe she would begin to understand—you see?

WASSERMAN: Understand what? For God's sake, Neigel, stop beating around the bush!

NEIGEL: She would understand that I can be a loyal, obedient member of the ss and still be a human being. That's what I have to tell her. Listen, Herr Wasserman, you don't know the hell I live in. She won't let me touch her. She says I scare her. That there's death on my hands and other female nonsense. She says she'll consider taking me back only if I leave everything here behind. She doesn't even know what she's saying. How can I leave everything behind in the middle of a war? What will I have left? But she says "Remember how much we had to suffer before we could bring Karl into the world? So much pain and suffering for the life of one child, one child, while in your camp, dozens of people every single day, you . . ." She has no idea how many people I really . . . every day . . . Don't judge me,

Herr Wasserman. Don't despise me. She and the children are more precious to me than anything in the world. I have no friends, I have no kin—

WASSERMAN: *(To Neuman)* And now he's going to sing, "*Hob rakhmones, yidn*"
— have mercy on me, Jews, I have no father and no mother.

NEIGEL: I wrote to Tina asking her permission to send her the final unwritten
story of Anshel Wasserman-Scheherazade, a debt of honor to a dead writer.

WASSERMAN: But then you worried that a story full of old farts in a ruined zoo
wasn't suitable?

NEIGEL: I did. But Tina wrote back that she liked the story, that she keeps
my letters by her bed. She wrote something about my imagination, that it
might be a source of hope for us both. After that, I wrote many more letters. Night after night, after you went to sleep, I sat here and grappled with
the story. And what made it even harder is your disorderly mind. Sometimes I couldn't fall asleep trying to imagine how you were going to continue the story. I think that's when I began to feel, well, sort of like a writer.

WASSERMAN: I believe you did.

NEIGEL: *(Looks at his watch)* Only five minutes left, Wasserman. Please, a hint.
At the very least, a hint.

WASSERMAN: You have everything you need to make her come back to you.

NEIGEL: *(Sound of knocking)* My driver! Help me, Herr Wasserman. My life
is in your hands now. You, too, have a wife and a child somewhere. You
must understand me.

WASSERMAN: Listen please, Herr Neigel. Two and one-half months ago, seven
and sixty days, to be exact, I arrived here unwillingly on the morning train
with my wife and daughter. We stepped off the station platform, and my
little girl flew like an arrow to the wonderful buffet you display to calm the
new arrivals. Chocolate was her heart's delight, even though Dr. Blum-
berg had ordained that it was bad for her teeth and that she must abstain.

NEIGEL: Get to the point, Wasserman, my driver's waiting.

WASSERMAN: That is the point, Herr Neigel. The only one. You were standing there with your gun in your hand. My daughter ran to the buffet and
reached for the chocolate. And then, you shot her. That is all, Herr Neigel.

NEIGEL: And you never said a word?

WASSERMAN: A word?

NEIGEL: *(Gets up from ramp, crosses up to his office, puts on coat, takes overnight
bag and newspaper. Starts to leave. Stops.)*

Believe me, Wasserman, I love children.

WASSERMAN: Love?

NEUMAN: *(Crosses to Wasserman, helps him up)* Oh, Grandfather.

WASSERMAN: Write, Momik!

NEUMAN: Now?

WASSERMAN: Now!

NEUMAN: But—

WASSERMAN: Write! It's the only way through this. Write.

NEUMAN: Obersturmbannfuhrer Neigel opened the door of his BMW.

(Suddenly, the ensemble takes on the roles of Neigel's driver, and the parts of his car. Sounds of German words— "Raus," "Achtung," etc.—become the sound of the engine. The car transforms into a crowded train station; German phrases relating to arrivals and departures are heard. Finally, the ensemble creates a train using a plank and a chair. Meanwhile, Neigel's office has been transformed into his wife Tina's apartment, a tablecloth spread over the desk, wine glasses, etc. The actor who plays Paula now takes on the role of Tina, Neigel's wife. She embraces Neigel. They are in the middle of a conversation.)

TINA: And your letters! When I lay in bed after I put the children to sleep, I would laugh, Kurt. When I read them, I would laugh under the sheets. You never made me laugh like this before, Kurt. You're better than Chaplin! But not only laughing. No, I read and I was moved and I cried just as much as I laughed, and I knew you weren't a murderer.

NEIGEL: No, Tina, I—

TINA: I know you're fighting a war inside. You were always so gentle. Now I can see: you entered hell and came out victorious . . .

NEUMAN: He wanted to tell her that he was still in it pretty deep, with the stench of smoke and gas—

NEIGEL:—and those idiot Ukrainians, and the trains coming and going all the time, at night, too, and you can't shut your eyes with all the noise here, and I can't tell anymore whether I'm running this camp or whether I'm a prisoner here. But I want to forget everything—the work and the Reich. I want to be calm and quiet inside, to finish my war and erase everything—

NEUMAN: So he answered her with the only story he could tell. He told her about Fried and Paula.

NEIGEL: When Fried could no longer bear her absence, he would look into Otto's eyes—

TINA: Yes, yes. I loved that part. His eyes would become Paula's eyes.

NEUMAN: And about Kazik.

NEIGEL: He never gave up the possibility of joy!

NEUMAN: And he told her how—

NEIGEL: Fried became the kind of father to Kazik he himself had always wished for.

NEUMAN: Tina listened with the well-known look of a woman who is ready.

NEIGEL: *(He is overcome with desire. He can't hold back any more, takes her in his arms.)* Tina!

TINA: Wait, Kurt.

(She pulls away.)

Let me look at you and remember you like this, yes. This is how you used to be. I think you've come back, Kurt. Welcome home.

(She moves into his arms. They slowly sink onto their "bed." With her mouth close to Neigel's ear, Tina begins to sing a Brecht/Eisler song.)

Und weil der Mensch ein Mensch ist,
drum braucht er was zu essen bittesehr!

NEUMAN: But this wasn't a love song at all. She was singing a satirical anti-Nazi song from the early years . . .

(Tina stops singing mid-phrase.)

TINA: You really do intend to stop it, Kurt, don't you? That's all over with, isn't it? You've come back, Kurt, haven't you come back?

(Neigel doesn't speak. Tina stands up and starts to back away from him. Neigel goes berserk, grabs her, tears her garment, throws her against a post, then forces her face down on the desk and rapes her from behind.)

NEIGEL: *(Screaming as he thrusts)* Spy! Judas Iscariot! Bolshevik! Knife in the back of the Reich!

(He stops suddenly, horrified by what he's doing. He stumbles away as Tina slips to the floor. He grabs his coat and bag and stands silhouetted for a moment before crossing down to the central area.)

NEIGEL: *(To Wasserman)* I hadn't wanted it to be like this. All I wanted was her forgiveness. Damn this war to hell. How did it get into our lives and our beds? I left without a word. I didn't even say good-bye to the children. I had the feeling I might spoil something just by looking at them. I walked through the Hauptbahnhof, and waited all night on a bench for the first train, and when a soldier walked past and saluted and said Heil Hitler, I almost vomited . . . Tell me more, Wasserman.

WASSERMAN: What?

NEIGEL: Tell me more, Wasserman. More about Kazik and the good life in store, only don't stop talking, Wasserman, because there's a terrible noise here and a terrible stench, and when I breathe, my breath smells of smoke, and when the train whistle blows in the station, I want to get up and run away, and I want the sentinels at the gate to shoot me. All day, I scream at the prisoners till I stop hearing the whistle, but now I'm alone. Don't leave me alone tonight. Tell me the story. You and the story are all I have. What a catastrophe.

(Neigel finds a bottle in his desk and drinks from it. Wasserman slowly goes through the motions of opening his notebook but speaks without looking at it.)

WASSERMAN: Kazik was old but he had never found his true métier in life. But none of the Children of the Heart could help him decide this crucial matter.

(Kazik has aged a good deal [the wig has been removed, glasses added]. The Children of the Heart are pacing and musing. Whenever one of them has an idea and is about to speak, he is preempted by Neigel, who is also pacing.)

NEIGEL: Yes. He must have an occupation, mustn't he? A carpenter, maybe? No. He's too small to lift a hammer, isn't he? Let's see. He could be a painter. Yes. Let him be a painter! A silhouette painter? No, no. A painter of deserts? Wait, wait. Oceans? No. Wait.

(Unbuttons shirt. Has a brainstorm.)

Ah. He was, Herr Wasserman, a painter of the imagination!

NEUMAN: *(Stops writing)* Horrible. German schmaltz.

(Mocking)

"A painter of the imagination . . ."

WASSERMAN: In what sense?

NEIGEL: *(With mounting enthusiasm)* I'm surprised you don't get it, Wasserman. He'll paint without a brush. No canvas either. The secret dreams and hopes of each person. And he always found the good in everyone. This way, his life, though brief, had meaning, yes? And he was happy.

WASSERMAN: I don't want to hurt you, Neigel, but the truth is Kazik was miserable. None of his "paintings" brought him relief. Ugliness filled his eyes. He no longer knew how to forgive. He was miserable.

KAZIK: *(He is now an elderly child, still small and unformed, but also old and decrepit, moving, seeing, hearing with difficulty.)* What is it for—all this—living? Someone! Tell me why I'm here!

(Neigel starts to answer. Wasserman raises his arm sternly.)

My life is nothing but preparation. For what?

FRIED: That's the thing, dear one, in return for a lifetime of experience, you have to pay with your life.

(Kazik suddenly crosses another threshold in his rapid decline. He begins shaking.)

KAZIK: Papa!

(He hobbles to Fried, seeking shelter in his arms. When Fried starts to pick him up though, Kazik is overtaken by anger and strikes Fried feebly. Fried lets him.)

No. No. No. No.

WASSERMAN: The little body emitted the stench of rotting. Crooked yellow teeth dropped out of his mouth with every movement.

KAZIK: *(His anger changes to grief and the grief to terror.)* Why? Please! Papa! No! Want-you-gone. You. There. Don't. Be. There.

(With his last, desperate strength, Kazik attacks Fried, pummeling him with his fists.)

NEIGEL: Where did we fail?

WASSERMAN: It's the failure of miracles.

NEIGEL: What do miracles have to do with it?

WASSERMAN: Both you and my own Children of the Heart have tried to work a kind of miracle. An exaggeration of human nature. You in your way and

my Children of the Heart in theirs. We were both trying to create a different kind of human being . . . and we failed. Everything is lost. You by
your actions have caused . . . *nu,* you already know what you have caused,
and I—for once I hoped to tell a beautiful story.

(Pause)

Your wife was right, Herr Neigel: I am a curio.

(Neigel takes Wasserman's hand.)
(To Neuman)

I could not feel the death that was in his hand though I knew it was there.
It was a human hand. Five warm fingers, moist with fear. Fingers which
have touched tears, the tears of the child he was, and the mouth of a baby,
and the thighs of a woman.

NEIGEL: *Bitte,* Herr Wasserman . . .

WASSERMAN: *(To Neigel)* It is not a miracle we need but the touch of a living
person.

OTTO: What do you want to happen to us, child?

KAZIK: Don't-know. I-feel-bad-make-you-feel-bad-too

WASSERMAN: Now, in his last moments, Kazik hungered for the untasted life
beyond the zoo.

KAZIK: *(He gestures to the outside world.)* What? Never saw.

WASSERMAN: They took him to a high place on top of the lions' cage where
he could see very far.

(Fried lifts Kazik as high as he can, supported by Magda and Otto.)

He saw us, Herr Neigel. He saw the mountainous watchtowers and the elec-
trified barbed-wire fences, and the train station which leads nowhere but
to death. Heard the screaming and the snorting of a prisoner hanged all
night long by his feet, and the tortured groans of one Obersturmbannfuhrer Neigel, who was imprisoned with him. And he smelled the smell
of human flesh burned by human beings. A tear burst through the little
one's eye so fiercely that it drew blood.

KAZIK: *(Screams)* Papa!

*(He launches himself into the air, hanging suspended in a beam of light and dis-
appearing. Pause.)*

FRIED: I've betrayed him. I don't know how it happened.

PRINCESS MAGDA: It was all of us. We were not enough.

PAULA: How could you be? Look at what you're up against.

(She indicates the camp surrounding them. They all move toward Neigel.)

OTTO: It was you and your kind, Herr Neigel, who made it impossible for Kazik to live.

(By now, the ensemble and Neuman are all gathered in Neigel's room, staring at him. Unnerved by their stares, he picks up his gun and aims it at them as he backs away.)

NEIGEL: *(Completely broken)* No. I'm not—I'm—I—

(Pause)

Who am I?

(Neigel walks into his shower. He closes the door. Sound of running water. Sound of a gunshot. Long pause as event reverberates. Neuman slowly returns to his desk and closes his notebook. Wasserman, for the first time, crosses down to Neuman's room and reopens his book. They exchange a look. Wasserman crosses upstage.)

NEUMAN: *(Considers the blank page. After a time he begins to write/speak.)*
For Yariv. A New Adventure of the Children of the Heart, by Momik Neuman.
Once upon a time there was a band of worn-out heroes who had seen so many terrible things you wouldn't think they could ever lift a finger or shake a leg again. That's what you'd think. But don't be fooled, for these are the Children of the Heart. One day, their leader, Otto Brig, recovered his strength—which was something he was very good at—and he called them all together to rebuild the time machine which had crashed in a previous episode. Soon the job was done and their voices rose with the familiar heat of passionate debate as they tried to decide where in this still-spinning world their powers were most needed. But even as they went on arguing, Otto led them to their places inside the newly repaired time machine and they took off into the vast confusion of a new life.

(The lights slowly fade.)

THE ACTION AGAINST SOL SCHUMANN

by Jeffrey Sweet

For Dennis, Marcie, and Sandy, with thanks for a home at the Victory Gardens Theater of Chicago.

With thanks to the National Foundation for Jewish Culture, the Center Theatre of Chicago, and David Picker for their parts in the development of this play. Thanks also to Kristine Niven, Ellen Schiff, Tandy Cronyn, Mike Nussbaum, David Pasquesi, Marc Vann, and others who have offered valuable support.

Special thanks to David van Biema, whose article for the Washington Post *was a particularly valuable resource.*

The Action against Sol Schumann. Victory Gardens Theater, Chicago, 2001. *Top:* Bernie Landis (left) and Eli Goodman. *Bottom:* The ensemble cast (Bernie Landis center). Photographs by Liz Lauren.

Sometimes the seed of a play is not an idea but the collision of two ideas. In the mid-1980s, I saw a *Washington Post* article by David van Biema about the Office of Special Investigations case against Jacob Tannenbaum. Soon after I saw a documentary film by Steve Brand called *Kaddish*.

Tannenbaum was a Jew who had been a kapo in a labor camp and who, the OSI alleged, had been particularly brutal to fellow Jews under his charge. After the war, Tannenbaum came to New York, married, had children, and became a pillar of the community. He also wrote regular checks to the Simon Wiesenthal Center. The OSI was preparing its case when he took ill. With Tannenbaum judged incapable of participating in his own defense, the government settled the case by stripping him of his citizenship in return for not deporting him. He ended his days in a nursing home.

Brand's documentary concerns a young American Jew named Yossi Klein whose identity is entirely defined by being the son of a man who survived the Holocaust. The bulk of Klein's energies are focused on political action on behalf of Jewish causes, working to prevent the reoccurrence of conditions that led to the nightmare his father endured. Midway through the film, Klein's father Zoltan dies, and the viewer can't help but be concerned that the son will have a nervous breakdown. The film ends on that note, offering some evidence that Yossi will find his equilibrium.

The play began with my speculating what would happen if this sort of son had been born to that sort of father. Yet, I must emphasize that this is *not* the story of Jacob Tannenbaum and Yossi Klein. The juxtaposition of two real people suggested a situation, and exploring the hypothetical situation mandated the creation of two fictional characters. What my characters do should not be confused with the actions of any real people.

I have, however, tried to ground the play in the world of the real. The procedures and legal language I quote were researched and are as accurate as I can make them. Incidentally, the interrogation scene in the play takes place in the World Trade Center not to harvest associations with 9/11 (the play was written several years before 9/11 and premiered several months before), but because that's where the OSI actually conducted some interviews in New York.

Though I am gratified when my plays are published, I think plays don't easily give up their meaning when read. If they did, why would actors be necessary? Plays (at least *my* plays) aren't so much about what the characters say as about how they behave. As it happens, the part that you can put onto paper

is the words the characters speak, but I think the most fulfilling reading of a
script requires the reader to visualize the constantly shifting spatial relationships between the figures onstage and to imagine that the lines they utter are
not straight declarations but float like icebergs on a sea of submerged objectives that not even the characters themselves fully comprehend.

Much of the meaning and the feeling in this play purposely goes unex-
plained and unarticulated. I think the audience's job is to take in the behavior
they see onstage and to form theories and patterns of meaning out of their ob-
servations. Why does Aaron do this? Why does Diane say that? What does Sol
actually know or remember about his own past? People don't easily volunteer
their truths in real life, so why should they suddenly lose their mystery in the
theatre?

Notes

PRODUCTION

The Action against Sol Schumann was developed and premiered at the Victory
Gardens Theater of Chicago on March 26, 2001, with the support of the NFJC
New Play Commission, under the direction of Dennis Zacek, with the follow-
ing cast: Roslyn Alexander (doubling actress), Kati Brazda (Diane), Melissa
Carlson (Kate), Anthony Fleming III (Paul), Eli Goodman (Michael), Richard
Henzel (doubling actor), Robert K. Johansen (Aaron), Bernie Landis (Sol),
and Amy Ludwig (Leah). The play was nominated for the American Theatre
Critics Association's playwriting prize and was one of the three winners for
2001. Subsequently, it was produced at the Phoenix Theatre (2002) and the
Jewish Theatre of the South (2004).

The New York premiere was given by the Hypothetical Theatre and
opened on June 18, 2004, under the direction of Amy Feinberg. The play was
slightly revised to accommodate a larger cast: Tandy Cronyn (Rivka Glauer),
Douglas Dickerman (Aaron), Kim Donovan (Kate), Catherine Lynn Dowl-
ing (Diane), Margaret A. Flanagan (doubling actress), Bruce Mohat (doubling
actor), Susan O'Connor (Leah), Postell Pringle (Paul Fontana), Jerry Rock-
wood (Israel Frieder), Herbert Rubens (Sol), and Nathan M. White (Michael).

STYLE

Having watched a lot of work in the "Harold" form in recent years at Chicago's ImprovOlympic and Second City, I've become fascinated by the speed

with which group-narrated work can fly. Magpie that I am, I've decided to appropriate some of these devices from improv and incorporate them into a written piece.

In this script, any line that isn't given to a specific character is assigned to a member of the Ensemble. Every time in a passage assigned to the Ensemble the voice is supposed to change, an "em" dash (—) appears before the line. The Ensemble members feel free to roam in and out, chipping in comments, info, questions, and so on. If they sense they are not needed in a particular scene, they may move offstage or sit down on chairs upstage or to the side.

The sense is supposed to be that the group is playing and narrating the story cooperatively. (Yeah, I know, Brecht did this, too.) When scene-setting, members of the Ensemble are involved with moving into place whatever set pieces are necessary.

Incidentally, the role of Paul Fontana may also be played as Paula Fontana; the character's gender is not essential to the story.

Cast of Characters

AARON

MICHAEL

SOL

KATE

DIANE

PAUL

LEAH

Doubling actor plays Holgate, Frieder, Lipsky, Reiner, and Felix

Doubling actress plays Mrs. Shapiro, Rivka, and Nurse

SCENE 1

(Two members of the Ensemble enter, address the audience.)

ENSEMBLE: The smell of cherry blossoms in the air.
—Washington, D.C.
—Paul Fontana.
—Mrs. Shapiro.
—Mrs. Shapiro has been lying in wait for Paul Fontana.

(Paul enters from one side of the stage. Mrs. Shapiro approaches her from the other.)

MRS. SHAPIRO: Mr. Fontana?

PAUL: Mrs.—?

MRS. SHAPIRO: Mrs. Shapiro.

PAUL: Ah, yes.

MRS. SHAPIRO: I thought it was you.

PAUL: I have that feeling myself sometimes.

MRS. SHAPIRO: Excuse me?

PAUL: Nothing. You wanted—

MRS. SHAPIRO: Your secretary—Jennifer I think is her name?—I think maybe
    she hasn't given you all of your messages. I've left messages.

PAUL: Yes, I know.

MRS. SHAPIRO: Oh, you *did* get them?

PAUL: I—yes.

MRS. SHAPIRO: Because, sometimes, you know, secretaries, they decide what
    gets to the desk. Their own judgment of what's important. I think maybe
    your secretary thinks I'm not so important.

PAUL: No, I got your messages.

MRS. SHAPIRO: You never called me back. This is what's got me confused. This
    is why I wait for you here.

PAUL: Oh.

MRS. SHAPIRO: I didn't hear. I thought, like I said, maybe your secretary. And
    you didn't get back to me.

PAUL: I didn't get back because I didn't have anything more to get back to you
    with.

MRS. SHAPIRO: But you're working on it?

PAUL: As I asked Jennifer to tell you, our investigation didn't come up with
    anything we felt we could—

MRS. SHAPIRO: But he's a Nazi. Everybody in the building knows he's a Nazi. Your job—you're *supposed* to be getting rid of these people.

PAUL: Yes, but we have to make our case in court—

MRS. SHAPIRO: Fine, then put me on the stand, I'll tell them. The things he says, the kind of person he is, his accent, his dogs—

PAUL: Mrs. Shapiro, from what you've said, I'm willing to believe he's not a very nice person. But we cannot throw him out of the country just because he's not nice. The law requires more than that.

MRS. SHAPIRO: For instance?

PAUL: Proof.

(She turns to Ensemble members for support.)

ENSEMBLE: Evidence that he obtained his citizenship under false pretenses— —or that he was a member of the Nazi party— —or was involved in war crimes.

MRS. SHAPIRO: But you know that already. He's from Germany, isn't he?

PAUL: The fact that he was born there isn't—*lots* of people have been born in Germany—

MRS. SHAPIRO:—and lots of them are Nazis.

PAUL: Mrs. Shapiro, I don't have an answer that's going to satisfy you. I'm sorry.

(A beat. Mrs. Shapiro nods. Paul starts to walk away. Then—)

MRS. SHAPIRO: What did he do? Pay you off?

(A beat. Paul sighs and continues. Mrs. Shapiro hollers after him.)

You, the Nazis! One government and another. No difference.

(Mrs. Shapiro exits. Paul turns to the audience.)

PAUL: I meet a lot of people like Mrs. Shapiro. Some of them louder. And some—they talk about what they've seen—what happened to parents, or maybe a child. They look at me, and I know they're thinking how can it be fair that they have to put their hopes in—deal with somebody who, from their point of view—they have *children* older than me, some of them. Most of what they tell me about happened in the 1940s. I was being diapered when many of them first arrived in this country, trying to figure out how to make a life after so much death. Being my age, and living now—

ENSEMBLE: —in 1985. This takes place in 1985.

PAUL: I don't pretend, I *can't* claim to understand. But there's work to do, and I'm one of the ones doing it. I asked to be one of the ones doing it.

SCENE 2

ENSEMBLE: Two brothers—

AARON: Aaron—

MICHAEL: —and Michael.

KATE: Michael's wife, Kate.

(Aaron, Michael, and Kate enter. Ensemble members hand Aaron and Michael yarmulkes and offer them chairs to sit at a table. Sol enters carrying a box. He puts it on the table, opens it and pulls out a paroches—*a kind of curtain on which is embroidered a design. At the bottom, there is an inscription.)*

ENSEMBLE: There is an inscription. It reads:

MICHAEL: "Donated by Solomon Schumann, in memory of his family."

ENSEMBLE: This is Sol Schumann's home in Brooklyn.

—An apartment building in Park Slope.

—He and his wife Esther raised the boys here. The boys left to attempt adulthood. His wife died some years before.

AARON: *(To audience)* We come over regularly for dinner.

KATE: What—?

(She hesitates.)

SOL: Yes?

AARON: She wants to know what it is. Isn't that right, Kate?

KATE: Something religious?

SOL: A *paroches.*

ENSEMBLE: *(Spelling)* P-a-r-o-c-h-e-s.

KATE: Oh.

SOL: All right: in a synagogue, you know there is the Ark, and inside the Ark—

KATE: The Torah.

SOL: The Torah, good. So, in front of the Ark sometimes there is a kind of curtain. That's what this is—that curtain.

KATE: Yes, I see. Sorry if I'm asking a stupid question—

SOL: How else would you find out? You weren't brought up with this. No, ask—

KATE: So you give this as a gift to the synagogue.

SOL: Yes.

KATE: And it's okay to put messages like this on it.

SOL: A personal thing, "in the memory of." But you wouldn't see on one, for instance, "Coca-Cola."

(Kate smiles.)

I thought—there are no graves. My mother, my father, my sister. The others. No graves. No place to visit. To leave stones. So this—so they should be remembered. I told the rabbi what I wanted, he recommended someone. On the Lower East Side, a little old man. So old he called me "son." Can you believe such a thing is possible? I told him what I wanted—

AARON: He did a beautiful job, Pop.

KATE: And this is called again—?

SOL: A *paroches.*

KATE: *(Not getting the "ch" sound right)* Paroches.

AARON: No, Kate—"ch."

KATE: "Ch."

AARON: Like there's something in your throat you're trying to get out. "Ch."

KATE: Oh, like in "challah."

AARON: Yes.

KATE: *(Correctly)* Paroches.

AARON: Are you *sure* you aren't Jewish?

MICHAEL: Aaron—

AARON: It's a joke. Michael, I am making a joke.

KATE: *(To Michael)* Honey, you don't have to protect me.

SOL: Sometime this week, Aaron, maybe you can come to services with me? It would be good to help. Some days we have trouble making a minyan.

(To Kate)

A minyan is—

KATE: The ten men you need to hold services.

SOL: Very good.

MICHAEL: You still recruiting people on the street?

(To Kate)

If they don't have ten men, sometimes they go out on the street and ask people
   if they're Jewish.

KATE: They don't have to be Orthodox?

MICHAEL: No, just Jewish.

SOL: People are kind. If they can, they do.

KATE: It's got to be men, though. Not women.

AARON: Tell you what, Pop, I'll see what I can do.

SOL: Besides, my friends ask about my boys. Lipsky thinks I've made you up,
   that you don't exist.

AARON: Sometime this week, I promise.

SOL: And maybe you'll have some good news for me?

AARON: Such as—?

SOL: You've met somebody.

AARON: Oh, Pop, not that again.

SOL: Michael is younger than you, and he's already married.

AARON: Michael has slightly different priorities, all right?

SOL: Having a family, children, this is not important to you?

AARON: Hey, you know what I am? I am hungry. What do you say?

SCENE 3

*(Holgate enters. A member of the Ensemble wheels on a podium as Holgate begins
to speak to the audience. Diane, a reporter, is one of those observing.)*

HOLGATE: *(To the audience)* Germany has worked very hard to reenter the
   community of civilized nations. The Bitburg ceremony is designed to recognize that fact, that achievement.

ENSEMBLE: A Jewish community center in Queens.

—German Chancellor Helmut Kohl has invited President Ronald Reagan to
   visit a German cemetery in Bitburg to honor those who died in World
   War II. Reagan has accepted.

DIANE: Some people have opinions.

LEAH: *(In the audience)* I'm sorry, Mr. Holgate, but it seems to me there had
   to be a way to recognize this without honoring members of the SS.

HOLGATE: There is no question of honoring the SS—

LEAH: There are ss members buried in that cemetery. Laying a wreath there
   will honor their memory.

AARON: *(Rising, in the audience)* I have a question. My name's Aaron Schumann. My question, Mr. Holgate, is, aren't you angry?

HOLGATE: About what?

AARON: *(Approaching the stage)* Probably tonight you would have liked to spend at home with your family, have some pot roast, watch a good cop show on TV. Instead, you're stuck standing up in front of us to defend the indefensible. I think you should ask yourself about the guy who sent you up here — out of the whole office, why did he choose *you* to do this? Because I'm telling you, whoever he is, this man is not your friend.

(Others at the meeting are vocal in support of Aaron.)

HOLGATE: Mr. Schumann, I don't expect to satisfy you. If I were in your position I doubt if *I'd* be satisfied. There are, however, aspects of this situation I think you haven't given full consideration.

AARON: Such as what?

HOLGATE: For one thing, people keep talking about Bitburg as if it were an SS cemetery. In fact, the vast majority of the people buried at Bitburg were ordinary soldiers, a lot of them teenagers drafted into the war against their will. Of the more than two thousand buried there, only forty-eight were members of the SS.

AARON: So only about two percent are SS, which makes this graveyard nearly ninety-eight percent pure.

(Others in the room react. Aaron turns to talk to them.)

No, maybe he's got a point. Maybe we can do a deal.

(Turns back to Holgate)

Tell you what: You tell President Reagan that as far as I'm concerned, he can go to Bitburg, he can stand there and bow his head for ninety-eight seconds provided, after that, he spits for two.

(Lights shift. Holgate exits. The Ensemble members remove the podium. Aaron and Leah end up onstage, looking off after Holgate.)

LEAH: He heard what we had to say.

AARON: Oh, come on, Leah, don't be naive. He didn't hear anything he didn't expect to hear.

LEAH: So why would he—

AARON: Well, what do you think?

LEAH: What is this—a pop quiz?

AARON: Think about it. Why would the administration send this guy to talk to us?

DIANE: *(Appearing off to the side)* So that you *could* yell at him.

AARON: *(Nodding)* Give us a chance to blow off some steam.

DIANE: Maybe you get it out of your system. Yes or no, it gives the appearance they're a little bit responsive to the concerns of the—

AARON: *(Continuing to Leah)* Appearance, yeah. I mean, you don't seriously think that Holgate's gonna fly back to Washington, tell Reagan, "Look, you're gonna have to cancel this Bitburg thing cuz there's a whole lot of angry Jews in Queens." Like Reagan's really going to go, "Angry Jews? Gee! Get Germany on the phone. Tell them if it's okay by the chancellor we'll meet in Disneyworld instead. We'll lay a wreath on the tomb of the unknown Goofy."

(Diane laughs. Aaron looks at her.)

I don't know you.

DIANE: No.

AARON: Do I want to?

DIANE: Diane Abbott.

AARON: You're a writer.

DIANE: Yes.

AARON: *Mother Jones? The Village Voice?*

DIANE: Among others I'd tell you about except I'm too modest.

AARON: What's the story here? For you, I mean. You're doing a story, right?

DIANE: Children of survivors and Bitburg. Your dad's a survivor, right?

AARON: Yes.

DIANE: *(To Leah)* And your parents.

LEAH: You've done your research.

AARON: So you're interested in what?

DIANE: Your reaction to Bitburg, given what your parents went through.

AARON: Are you having any trouble figuring that out?

DIANE: I think I'm beginning to glean it.

AARON: "Glean?"

DIANE: Yes. It's like "infer" only—

AARON: No, I've heard the word. I know the word. Just it's one of those—do you do crossword puzzles?

DIANE: If I did, would you consider me a less credible person?

(Aaron smiles.)

LEAH: *(Persisting)* All right, so if tonight, like you say, meant nothing—

AARON: Worse than nothing.

LEAH: So, according to you, what *would* mean something? What could someone do?

SCENE 4

(Crossfade to Michael, addressing the audience as Aaron, Diane and Leah exit)

MICHAEL: I've heard that there are theories about who you're likely to be, what kind of life you're likely to have, based on when you were born. I don't mean astrology. I mean the order of birth. The first-born boy supposedly has a tendency to do this, the second-born has a tendency to do that. If you're a girl and you're the middle child—and so forth. Well, Aaron's my older brother. So maybe that explains something.

SCENE 5

(Ensemble member appears with airport ground crew signs. Facing us in the audience, he goes through the signals guiding a jet into a terminal as we get corresponding sounds of a jet engine. The engine turns off. Michael is joined by Leah as the Ensemble member signals to Aaron that it's okay for him to enter. Aaron is pleased to see the welcoming committee.)

AARON: Leah!

LEAH: How was the flight?

AARON: More fun than a prostate exam. So, what was the coverage like?

LEAH: Some on the networks, but local carried more.

AARON: Sure, big New York angle.

MICHAEL: That's how I found out you went over.

AARON: TV?

MICHAEL: Kate saw you. On the evening news. "Isn't that Aaron?" I said it couldn't be. "What would he be doing in Germany?"

AARON: But you put that one together, right?

MICHAEL: You didn't tell me you were going.

AARON: It was kind of a quick decision.

MICHAEL: You tell Pop?

AARON: I called from the airport. That's how quick it was.

MICHAEL: It's just—to find out something about a member of your own family from the TV—

AARON: I didn't know that you'd be that interested.

(This is not said with any bitterness, but it registers on Michael nonetheless. Diane enters.)

Look who's here.

DIANE: The gleaning lady.

AARON: What? Oh yeah, I get it. "Gleaning." Cute, yeah.

DIANE: You free to talk?

AARON: You hungry?

DIANE: Is that your way of saying you're hungry?

AARON: Glad you asked.

SCENE 6

(The Ensemble member with the airline signals returns and holds a signal up to have Aaron, Michael, Diane, and Leah wait while other Ensemble members bring on a restaurant table, some chairs, and glasses of beer and wine. The Ensemble member now signals them to their seats.)

AARON: Oh, sure, there were cops there.

DIANE: To protect you?

AARON: German cops protecting people a lot of who—their parents were once dragged away by *other* German cops. Part of me wanted to ask them, "So what did your folks do in the war?"

LEAH: You mean you didn't? There was a possibility for a confrontation and you actually restrained yourself?

AARON: Oh yeah, I recognize this—this is irony, right?

LEAH: No, this is wonderment.

AARON: Me, confrontational?

LEAH: Incredible concept, hunh?

AARON: Michael, am I confrontational?

MICHAEL: Let me think about that for a second.

AARON: *(A joke)* I asked a question: Michael, you asshole, am I confrontational?

DIANE: You were able to just take off like that? From work?

AARON: One of the benefits of being a substitute.

DIANE: Teacher?

LEAH: You got an assignment on Monday?

AARON: In Bed-Stuy.

LEAH: You going to tell the kids you went to Germany?

AARON: I'd be surprised if most of them knew where Germany is.

LEAH: Oh, come on—

AARON: You should come sit in on one of my classes sometime. You think *I'm* confrontational, you should see some of the kids—I feel safer in Germany—

LEAH: Hyperbole alert.

AARON: Yeah? One of the classes I had a couple weeks back, this kid—a friend of his comes in. Fact I have some vague approximation of a lesson going, this doesn't matter. He's got something to talk about with this guy. Something to settle, something to discuss. I tell him this isn't the place or time. He puts his hand in his pocket, says, "Hey, motherfucker, know what I got here? A time machine."

DIANE: What *did* he have?

AARON: I didn't ask. I strolled down the corridor and got one of the security guards. Kid was gone by the time we got back. But you learn quick—you don't get in their face, unless you want an unauthorized nose job. Or worse. You're more likely to be assaulted as a teacher than as a cop.

LEAH: This is an actual statistic?

AARON: An actual statistic. What's more, it's even true.

DIANE: So, aside from the protest itself, did you look much around the country? See anything besides Bitburg?

AARON: Visit a beer hall, tour the Shlossendorfenhoff castle? I wasn't exactly there for cultural enrichment.

DIANE: Granted. But as long as you were there—man does not live by dread alone.

AARON: So to speak.

DIANE: Sorry.

AARON: I almost wanted to visit Bayreuth. You know Bayreuth?

LEAH: The Bayreuth Festival, right? Where they do the Ring Cycle.

AARON: Otherwise known as Wagner Central. Did you know that when he was a conductor—Wagner, I'm talking about—when he was assigned to conduct a score by a Jewish composer, he wore gloves? Yes. And after the piece was done, was finished, he'd throw the gloves away? But he manages to get this place built—Bayreuth—this huge opera house so they can stage his endless nutcase operas. So, years later: Hitler—big Wagner fan. During the war, Hitler keeps the place going full tilt—even when there are shortages cuz of the war—he thinks it's the beating heart of the German soul or something. Including in the orchestra, during the war, Jewish musicians. Yes, playing in the pit. Wrap your mind around that one. You're a Jewish oboe player, at the same time your relatives are being carted away, you're playing *Twilight of the Gods* for Der Fuhrer. How honored they must have been by his applause. So—this is the part I love—when American troops liberate the town, some of the GIs look at this big opera palace and say, "Hey, cool—a vaudeville house!" And they take it over and put up a show. Every comic routine and number they can remember— the Marx Brothers, the Ritz Brothers, Fanny Brice, Jack Benny, Danny Kaye. Wagner's daughter-in-law hears about it, she nearly has a heart attack. This vast, somber temple of high art being desecrated with a bunch of jokes from kike comics. No, if there were any place in Germany I'd actually want to visit, that would be it.

DIANE: In honor of that one performance.

MICHAEL: You know, apart from being an anti-Semitic nutcase, Wagner did write some good stuff.

AARON: And Hitler could sketch. So, okay, what's your point?

MICHAEL: That sometimes you have to separate a person from what they do.

AARON: Why? Why do I have to do that?

MICHAEL: I mean, what they accomplish.

AARON: And again I say why?

MICHAEL: I'm not saying that it makes him less of a nutcase that he wrote some good stuff. But I'm saying that it's not right not to acknowledge that he did write some good stuff.

AARON: You're accusing me of being unfair to Wagner?

MICHAEL: People are more complex than that. You can't just put them in easy categories—good, bad. Besides, some people are good because it's been easy for them to be good. They've never faced a hard choice. And maybe, if they did face one, maybe they wouldn't have measured up.

AARON: So you want more categories? Subcategories? "Good, but untested?" "Bad, but with an excuse?" Should we get a huge rubber stamp, stamp that on Germany? "Bad, but with an excuse?"

MICHAEL: I never said that.

AARON: Oh, so for Germany you'll let me use the "Bad" stamp?

MICHAEL: Maybe I'm suggesting you shouldn't use stamps at all.

AARON: You said we should separate people from what they do.

MICHAEL: *(Attempting to amend) Some* of what they—

AARON: And I say people *are* what they do. What you do, that's who you are. You are the person who does that thing. And, you know, I'm not really concerned about the reasons. The reasons are private. That's for shrinks to worry about. The actions—the actions—if a drunk runs down a five-year-old kid with his car, I don't give a shit if the reason he was drinking was his pet turtle died.

DIANE: So, as far as you're concerned, everybody in the Bitburg cemetery, not just the guys who were in the SS—

AARON: Pretty much, yes. My opinion. You don't have to share it. But if you don't, you're wrong.

DIANE: Tell me something—

AARON: *(Interrupting)* Maybe—

(Diane looks at him, as if to say, "Are you finished?")

I'm sorry, yes, okay. Something you want me to tell you?

DIANE: Have you ever forgiven anyone? For anything?

AARON: You aren't seriously asking me to—

DIANE: No, I'm not talking about Germany now. I'm just talking about you, personally. You. Aaron. Forgive. Somebody who did something, something you thought was wrong, something *to* you maybe—not as a political act particularly—but to you.

AARON: Like what?

DIANE: Hurt you, broke your heart maybe—maybe a girlfriend who cheated on you. I don't know—everybody gets disappointed, feels betrayed by someone sometime. I know I have.

AARON: *(Mock intense interest)* Oh yeah? Tell me about it.

DIANE: We're not talking about me.

AARON: What, aren't you interesting enough to talk about?

DIANE: I'm very interesting. And when you're writing a story about me, I'll be glad to share.

AARON: This story isn't about me. You aren't writing about me.

DIANE: You're going to be in it.

AARON: The story you told me about, that you're writing, is about Bitburg.

DIANE: And about the people who went there. Of which you are one.

AARON: So for this you need to know—

DIANE: Did I say "need"? Just interested.

AARON: You're interested in me?

DIANE: I'm interested in this *aspect* of you. Come on, quit horsing around.

AARON: Okay. Let me think.

(A beat)

Yes.

DIANE: Yes?

AARON: Yes, I have. In twelfth grade, I lent eight bucks to my friend Harvey. He never paid it back. And you know? It's okay. But you know, forgiveness—

DIANE: One of those New Testament things. Kind of revisionist, hunh?

AARON: Fine as a kind of abstract principle, I guess. But in moderation. You don't want to let it get out of hand. I mean, for instance, Nixon.

DIANE: Oh well, Nixon—

AARON: Yeah, well, you see—

DIANE: You've got to draw the line *some*where.

(They share a laugh. A beat. Leah rises.)

LEAH: Well, I've got a meeting with a client tomorrow morning. I should look over his brief.

AARON: Anything interesting?

LEAH: Landlord-tenant thing. Landlord A wants to convert apartment to condos. Tenant B doesn't want to move—

AARON: Fill in the blanks.

LEAH: It's a living.

AARON: Whose side are you on?

LEAH: The side of righteousness and justice.

AARON: Just checking.

LEAH: *(Putting money on the table)* This should cover it.

AARON: What are you doing?

LEAH: You flew to Germany, least I can do is buy a few drinks.

AARON: Okay.

DIANE: Where do you live?

LEAH: Chelsea.

DIANE: I'm heading to the Village. Want to split a cab?

AARON: What, you've got everything you need for your story so it's okay to take off?

DIANE: Absolutely. I never talk to people just to talk to people.

LEAH: Maybe she wants to talk to me, Aaron. Get my perspective.

AARON: Why would she want to do that?

LEAH: *(Giving Aaron a kiss)* Get some sleep, hunh?

AARON: Will do.

(To Diane)

Write a good article.

DIANE: Gee, if just so as not to disappoint you.

LEAH: Night, Michael.

MICHAEL: Night, Leah.

(Leah and Diane exit.)

She's looking good.

AARON: Leah?

MICHAEL: Is she with someone these days?

AARON: Don't know.

MICHAEL: Might be worth finding out.

AARON: You're married.

MICHAEL: I'm talking about you.

AARON: What are you doing? Are you trying to matchmake?

MICHAEL: You like her, she likes you—

AARON: We're friends, yes.

MICHAEL: Okay, I'll shut up.

AARON: In my own good time, okay? When I'm ready.

MICHAEL: At that rate, you'll pay for the honeymoon with your Social Security.

AARON: Who's this talking? Pop? Pop, is that you under a mask?

MICHAEL: All right.

(A beat)

What did he say?

AARON: Pop? When?

MICHAEL: When you told him you were going to Germany. You said you phoned from the airport—

AARON: I phoned, yes.

MICHAEL: And he said?

AARON: "Don't."

MICHAEL: He was afraid that black shirts would jump out and drag you away?

AARON: Not funny.

MICHAEL: I'm not laughing. But, you know, to worry about something like that—

AARON: —given what he went through, I think it's natural—

MICHAEL: You don't have to remind me what he went—

AARON: Sometimes I wonder.

MICHAEL: You wonder?

AARON: Forget it.

MICHAEL: No. You made that crack before, you didn't think I'd be interested about your going to Germany, and now, as if I don't care about what Pop went—

AARON: I didn't say that.

MICHAEL: I'm not reverent enough or something? *Mindful?*

AARON: You've got to admit you're pretty assimilated.

MICHAEL: Why would that qualify as an admission? You think I should feel guilty I'm assimilated?

AARON: It's a reason why some of this other stuff might not be as important to you.

MICHAEL: Other stuff like the camps and Bitburg—

AARON: Or do I have it wrong?

MICHAEL: You have it wrong.

AARON: Yeah? What if I'd called and said, "Hey, come with me."

MICHAEL: What? To Germany?

AARON: Would you have? Okay: It's three days ago. "Michael, I'm going to Germany. I'm going to show Ronny Reagan how I feel about this. Come with."

MICHAEL: It would have been hard to take these particular three days off.

AARON: Oh?

MICHAEL: In case you forget, this is April, and April is a pretty important month in an accountant's life.

AARON: Famous for it.

MICHAEL: All right.

AARON: You wouldn't have gone.

MICHAEL: I *couldn't* have.

AARON: Fine. Wouldn't because you couldn't still comes down to the same—

MICHAEL: Which makes me what?

AARON: Makes us different, that's all. That's what I'm saying. But since when is this news? You haven't set foot inside a synagogue since you were bar mitzvahed. You married a—

MICHAEL: A shiksa?

AARON: Not my word.

MICHAEL: Of course not.

AARON: But when you have kids, you won't raise them Jewish. Probably Unitarian, right? Or Ethical Culture, if anything. When you come to Pop's for Sabbath dinner, you think I don't see that look Kate shoots you when you put on the yarmulke? "Isn't that adorable? Michael's wearing a beanie."

MICHAEL: I think we've just reached the end of the conversation.

(Michael rises.)

AARON: Hey. Michael—

(Michael wheels on him.)

MICHAEL: I don't know where you get off sitting in judgment on me, my wife. We don't even *have* kids yet, already you're making cracks about them.

AARON: Sorry.

MICHAEL: At least *I've* got a life. It ever occur to you, Aaron, this obsession you've got with the past and camps and memorials maybe is a way of avoiding—

AARON: Not just an accountant, a shrink, too.

MICHAEL: Think about it. What does it tell you about someone your age, your education, after twelve, thirteen years is still running around the city as a substitute teacher?

AARON: Well, you may have a case. Of course, I'm teaching kids to read and you're helping rich people dodge taxes. We might draw some conclusions from that, too.

MICHAEL: Okay, fine: you're the righteous Jew and I'm the assimilated sell-out. So I'll do you a favor: I'll keep out of the way so I don't embarrass you anymore.

SCENE 7
(Kate enters, joining Michael as Aaron exits.)

MICHAEL: As if he were handing out licenses to be Jewish.

KATE: Do you feel Jewish?

MICHAEL: I feel Jewish-*ish*.

KATE: What relationship does that have to being Jewish? Like Cheez Whiz is to cheddar?

(A beat)

MICHAEL: Some people—I don't know how they can. Pop—everything he went through—still, every morning he can, he goes to that synagogue.

KATE: Maybe that's what helped him get through it.

MICHAEL: I just can't imagine praying to a God that could let such things happen.

KATE: Did you pick up the dry-cleaning?

MICHAEL: Was I supposed to?

KATE: Never mind.

MICHAEL: Sorry.

KATE: We'll cope. It doesn't ever bother you, does it?

MICHAEL: What?

KATE: That I'm not Jewish?

MICHAEL: What kind of question—

KATE: So the answer's "no"?

MICHAEL: Kate—

KATE: It's such a large part of Aaron's life, and you're brothers—

MICHAEL: I am not my brother.

KATE: I know.

MICHAEL: I am *not* my brother.

(Crossfade to—)

SCENE 8

(Aaron appears onstage. Diane approaches him, hands him a copy of a magazine à la Mother Jones.)

DIANE: Thought you might like to see it.

AARON: Oh?

DIANE: My article. You're in there. It'll be on the stands tomorrow.

AARON: You're welcome.

DIANE: Excuse me?

AARON: No, really, it was my pleasure.

DIANE: Okay, don't tell me. I'll figure it out. You have me thanking you because—

AARON: Well, they paid you for the article, didn't they?

DIANE: I see: I was able to make money because you were worth writing about.
Well, you know, you're welcome, too.

AARON: Right.

DIANE: Hope it helps.

AARON: Diane, because of your article, genocide will be a thing of the past.

DIANE: I'm happy if you think so.

AARON: Now, if you could do something about male pattern baldness—

(She smiles and begins to exit.)

DIANE: See you next time.

AARON: Next time?

DIANE: Or is this it? Are you retiring from the field?

AARON: You've selected yourself to be my chronicler. Ah. And I have nothing
to say about this?

DIANE: Well, you could stop being an interesting person.

AARON: Then you'd drop me.

DIANE: I'm a fairly heartless broad.

AARON: Well, that's obvious.

DIANE: Take care.

(She exits. He opens the magazine, begins to read. He smiles, looks in the direction in which she exited, then exits.)

SCENE 9
(Paul enters, and Ensemble members assemble the suggestion of an office.)

ENSEMBLE: The World Trade Center.
—Photo of Ronald Reagan on the wall.
—Israel Frieder stands at a window. *(Pointing)* Brooklyn.

(Israel Frieder, a very intense elderly man, stands looking out of where the window was placed.)

FRIEDER: I was at a bar mitzvah. A grandson. Donald. Not at the synagogue I usually go to. But there is sometimes in front of the Ark a kind of curtain. And I'm standing there and I'm looking at the curtain in this synagogue, and I see a name stitched into it—as part of the dedication in memory of his family. And I ask the rabbi about the man who donated this curtain. And the rabbi tells me that there is an Orthodox congregation that meets in a room downstairs, and that this man is a member of that congregation. So the next morning, I go. I want to see if it's him. I go. The other members of the congregation, they're glad to see me. They sometimes have trouble making a minyan. You need ten men to have services, you know.
PAUL: Yes.
FRIEDER: And I'm there and I'm waiting. I think maybe I'll try to ask them about him. And then I think maybe I should say nothing, just wait. A couple minutes later, he comes in. Next thing I know, I'm looking at the ceiling. They tell me I've fainted. He doesn't recognize me. I tell them I'll be all right, and I leave.

(A beat)

The bridge, the promenade, Prospect Park. This is some view you've got.
PAUL: It's not really my office. They lend it to me—as a courtesy. When I come up from Washington.

(A beat)

Mr. Frieder, you're sure?
FRIEDER: I'm sure.

PAUL: You understand I have to ask.

FRIEDER: Yes.

PAUL: If I'm going to take this into a courtroom, we have to be certain. After all, to identify someone after so many years. It's been so long since you've seen him.

FRIEDER: Not so long. At least once a week, at night when I close my eyes. He hasn't changed so much. The hair is grayer, but the hands are the same. I remember the hands very well.

(Frieder looks out the window, points.)

I've been living over there since '48. And all this time, he's been living over there, too. Just a few miles away. Raising a family, praying, pretending.

PAUL: If we do this, it could take a long time.

FRIEDER: Mr. Fontana, I've waited forty years.

(Crossfade to—)

SCENE 10

(Schubert chamber music plays. Aaron is waiting. Michael arrives.)

MICHAEL: She come down yet?

AARON: Do you see her?

MICHAEL: Fancy building she works in.

AARON: Oh yes, let's talk about that. Good idea.

(A beat)

She's late. Maybe we should go upstairs.

MICHAEL: She asked us to meet her in the atrium. So why don't we just stay here? What's that?

AARON: Juilliard students play here sometimes.

MICHAEL: No, I mean the piece. The composer.

AARON: Schubert something, I guess.

MICHAEL: It's nice.

AARON: *(With irony)* Yes, it's very soothing.

MICHAEL: You know, you're not going to do Pop or yourself, *any* of us any good if you don't calm down a little.

AARON: Calm down?

MICHAEL: Relent. You know what I mean.

AARON: Take it easy? Be cool? Go with the flow?

(Michael shakes his head, raises his hand as if to say he won't pursue this anymore, and moves away. Leah enters wearing a neatly tailored suit and carrying a briefcase. Aaron sees her.)

Okay, Leah, what's going on? What's the story?

(Leah knows something's just happened between the two of them, but, rather than get into it, she makes the decision to dive into business.)

LEAH: Okay: I've made a few phone calls, and, from what I understand, they haven't formally accused him of anything. It's a request for an interview.

AARON: A request. That means he could say no.

LEAH: Technically, but I wouldn't advise it. With a little luck, we meet with them, we could put an end to the whole thing.

AARON: A little luck being—

LEAH: They see there isn't sufficient basis to continue the—

AARON: Of course there won't be sufficient basis. This is a joke. A sick joke.

MICHAEL: Pardon me for being dumb, but—who are these people?

AARON: You mean the OSI?

MICHAEL: Yes.

AARON: You really don't know who they are?

MICHAEL: I have a general idea. I'm asking for more specific—

LEAH: *(Jumping in before Aaron can reply)* Aaron—

(Aaron covers his mouth with one hand and raises the other to signal he won't say anything more. Leah turns to Michael.)

Okay: it's 1947, '48. The war is over but Europe is still a big mess. You've got a lot of people who, for various reasons, want to come to the United States. Maybe where they used to live is now behind the Iron Curtain and they aren't real eager to go back, or maybe they're Jews and there's nothing much to go back to—

AARON: —except the good neighbors who said nothing when the Nazis dragged you off to the camps.

LEAH: For reasons you can guess, some of the bad guys would also like to get out of Europe—Nazi collaborators and other unpopular types.

MICHAEL: Right.

LEAH: So you have all these people who want to come to America. Which they do. And they apply for citizenship. And when they apply for citizenship, they have to swear that they have not been concentration camp guards and didn't push people into gas chambers. Of course, if you *did* push people into gas chambers, you're not likely to have serious qualms about telling the Immigration Office lies.

AARON: Which they did.

LEAH: And not just two or three either.

AARON: More like hundreds, maybe thousands.

MICHAEL: So the OSI—the OSI?

AARON: *(Impatiently)* The Office of Special Investigations.

MICHAEL: They're supposed to go after them.

LEAH: *(Nodding)* Take away their citizenship, deport them.

MICHAEL: So, what are they going after Dad for? He was a *victim*. It doesn't make sense.

AARON: Obviously they've screwed up. They've confused him with someone else. Sol Schumann—it's a common name. Right?

LEAH: It's possible.

AARON: It's a mistake. We'll go to his place, see him, get this straight. It's a mistake.

SCENE 11

(Sol enters. Aaron, Michael, and Leah turn to face him.)

AARON: Pop?

(A beat)

Pop?

(A beat)

SOL: No.

AARON: What?

SOL: It's not. Not a mistake.

(A beat)

AARON: Are you saying it's true?

SOL: It's more complicated.

(A beat)

AARON: What are you *saying?*

LEAH: Aaron—

(A beat)

SOL: I thought it was behind me. Forty years.

(A beat)

AARON: You were a kapo.

SOL: Yes.

AARON: And you never said. You never told us.

SOL: You didn't need to know. No point to your knowing.

AARON: Of course not.

SOL: Do you think it was a job I asked for? Something I wanted? They came to me. They said, "Schumann, *you. You* will do this." You didn't refuse them. Not if you wanted to live.

(A beat)

I *had* to live. My sister, mother, my father, *their* mothers and fathers—all gone. Only me. The whole family. All gone. Only me.

(A beat)

My *duty* to live.

(A beat. Then, agitated, Aaron rises, leaves the room. Michael looks at Leah and Sol, then follows Aaron.)

SCENE 12

MICHAEL: I follow him up to the roof.

(Michael stands next to Aaron.)

AARON: You know about kapos, don't you? You know who they were? What they did?

MICHAEL: Some of them.

AARON: *Any* of them.

MICHAEL: What they were forced to—

AARON: Where have we heard this before?

MICHAEL: Come on, there's a big difference—

AARON: Right.

MICHAEL: You know there is.

AARON: What a laugh, hunh?

MICHAEL: Laugh?

AARON: The *paroches* he had made in the memory of the family he lost—except it turns out when it comes to memory, his is pretty selective, wouldn't you say?

MICHAEL: It's not something he wanted to remember. Can you blame him?

AARON: That's the question, isn't it?

MICHAEL: Aaron, he needs our help. Come back.

(A beat. Kate, enters, Michael turns to her.)

And I go to the stairs, and he follows me down. When I get to the floor where Pop lives, I open the door from the stairwell to the hallway—

(Aaron hesitates, looks at Michael and exits.)

And he keeps going down the stairs. I hear the door to the lobby slam.

KATE: What did he think, your father's perfect?

MICHAEL: —Aaron grew up with this idea about Pop—this image—

KATE: He didn't grow up with any idea that you didn't grow up with, but are *you* pissing and moaning?

MICHAEL: Well, we're different people.

KATE: Thank God. And what does Aaron think *he'd* do if someone put a gun to *his* head?

MICHAEL: What are you arguing with me for?

KATE: I'm not arguing with you. But if you're going to defend Aaron's behavior—

MICHAEL: I'm not defending. I'm just telling you what it *is* about him.

KATE: *(With a dismissive wave of her hand)* What it is: He's disillusioned, he's hurt. His father isn't pure and perfect. But what gives Aaron the right to expect that? Your dad suffered through something—we can't *begin* to con-

ceive of. But since when does suffering make you a better, more wonderful human being? Except in the case of a few saints, which is why they're
so unusual, which is why they're called saints. I mean, child abusers were
usually themselves abused as children, right?

MICHAEL: Right: Pop's no worse than a child abuser. That'll really give Aaron
comfort.

KATE: Like right now I'm concerned about Aaron's comfort.

MICHAEL: With luck it will all be over after this interview.

SCENE 13

(Sol, Michael, and Leah enter where Paul waits.)

PAUL: Mr. Schumann?

SOL: Yes. This is my son, Michael.

LEAH: I'm Leah Abelson.

PAUL: Yes, we talked on the phone.

LEAH: I'm here as Mr. Schumann's counsel.

PAUL: You understand I'm recording this.

SOL: Yes.

PAUL: All right, then, why don't we—

(Aaron enters.)

Yes?

AARON: I'm Aaron Schumann. I'm his son.

*(He looks at his father. Sol nods. Lights shift. Sol sits. Paul turns on the tape re-
corder. We are in the middle of the questioning.)*

SOL: There were eight of us in Ordenhaupt.

PAUL: Eight kapos?

SOL: Yes.

PAUL: Ordenhaupt was a camp?

SOL: Yes.

PAUL: What sort of labor was done there?

SOL: Pardon?

PAUL: What was done there? What did the prisoners do?

SOL: Different things. Some—what they did before: carpenters, tinsmiths.
Also sorting.

PAUL: Sorting what?

SOL: Eyeglasses, shoes. What had belonged to those who had died.

PAUL: And as a kapo, you supervised this work.

SOL: This is what we were told to do.

PAUL: And you did it.

SOL: What I was told to do. Yes.

PAUL: And what did this consist of? What did you do? As a supervisor.

SOL: To see to it that it is done—the work. To solve problems.

PAUL: And if somebody wasn't doing his job, doing his share of the work—

SOL: You try to get him to.

PAUL: How?

SOL: How?

PAUL: How would you get him to?

SOL: You tell him that he must do it. Everybody must do it. We must all work. We have no choice. He doesn't. I don't. We are not there by choice. We are not there *for* choice. But this we all knew. This we lived with knowing.

PAUL: But, still, if he doesn't do it—

SOL: Maybe he's sick, so you try to protect him.

PAUL: Protect?

SOL: Yes. You try. You put him where you think he might not be noticed.

PAUL: By?

SOL: By the Germans. The guards. You tried to hide him.

PAUL: And you did this?

SOL: Yes.

PAUL: Often?

SOL: When I could. It was dangerous to do. If they thought you were trying to—

PAUL: The Germans?

SOL: If they thought you were trying to help, to protect, they would—

(Sudden agitation)

You know this. I don't have to tell you what they were, what they did. Why do you ask me to tell you what you already know?

PAUL: I'm sorry, Mr. Schumann, it's necessary to our investigation—we need your words. In your own words. How you saw it.

SOL: Yes, I'm sorry. Yes, of course. You ask.

PAUL: If someone still wouldn't work, and he wasn't sick, and you couldn't hide him—how would you deal with that?

SOL: You would try to get him to see. It wasn't just him. It was all of us. If the Germans got angry, it might not be just this one person they might hurt, but maybe four or five others. Just because they were sitting near, or because of the way they were looking. So it wasn't just for yourself. You had to think of the others.

PAUL: And if, after you've explained that, someone still doesn't respond, what might you do?

(A beat)

SOL: You're trying to get me to say I hit them.

PAUL: Did you?

SOL: Only when it was required. For the safety of others. But not to *hurt*.

PAUL: To what, then?

SOL: Sometimes they were—what is the word?—dazed. To wake them.

PAUL: You would hit them to wake them.

SOL: You tried to avoid this. You're a Jew. They are Jews, many of them. You don't want to.

(New beat)

But you're talking about only a part of what happened. You're not talking at all about the people I helped. It was possible to help, which I did as often as I could.

PAUL: How did you help? We would like to know this.

SOL: Food. Sometimes I was able to get extra. I would share. When I had it, when I could do it. There are people alive today—if it weren't for me— they will tell you—people whose lives—you must ask them.

PAUL: We will. We would like to. Any names you can remember, you give to us.

SOL: You'll find them.

PAUL: We'll try.

SOL: You must be fair.

PAUL: We'll look. We'll ask who we can find.

SOL: People think—"a kapo." They think only about the things you were made to do. And this was the worst. That sometimes they made you do things that they would do. The Germans.

PAUL: Such as hit people?

SOL: Yes.

PAUL: With what?

SOL: Well, your hands.

PAUL: Anything else?

SOL: Excuse me?

PAUL: You had a whip.

SOL: Yes. They gave me one. I carried it.

PAUL: You used it.

SOL: Rarely.

PAUL: But you did, sometimes.

SOL: You would try to hold back, but they might say, no, harder. Harder or it will be *your* back. They thought this was—amusing. To make you do what they do. To try to turn you into—

(With force)

Yes, you might be forced to do these things, but inside you hold on to who you are. You know you must not become one of them. You must not lose yourself.

(Lights shift. Paul turns off the machine. Sol looks at Paul wordlessly. Aaron touches his arm. Sol nods. Aaron, Sol, Michael, and Leah leave the room. In a space separately defined by lighting, Aaron turns to Sol.)

AARON: *(Reassuringly)* It's over, Pop.

(Michael, Aaron, Sol, and Leah leave the stage. Paul turns to the audience.)

PAUL: *(To the audience)* I don't want you to think that's all there is to it. We interview other people, we examine documents, records, cross-check. We don't make a decision casually.

ENSEMBLE: *(Reading from a paper)* "This is an action brought pursuant to section 340 (a) of the Immigration and Nationality Act of 1952 to revoke the United States citizenship of Solomon Schumann. It is charged that defendant was at the Ordenhaupt concentration camp, located in what was then southern Germany, which was controlled by the forces of Nazi Germany—that Ordenhaupt concentration camp was operated by the Nazi

ss and relied on prisoner assistants known as 'kapos' in the daily operations of the camp and in disciplining other prisoners—that during the
time he served as a supervisory kapo at Ordenhaupt, defendant partici-
pated in persecution by brutalizing and physically abusing prisoners—"

SCENE 14

(Sol is sitting in a chair, still. Michael enters.)

MICHAEL: Pop? Pop, it's me, Michael. I've been trying to call you, but the
phone's been—

SOL: I took it off the hook. Since they released it to the news, the phone calls
I've been getting.

MICHAEL: Oh.

SOL: I haven't heard from your brother.

MICHAEL: He's gone climbing.

SOL: That was this week he was doing that?

MICHAEL: Yes.

SOL: I forgot.

MICHAEL: Have you had anything to eat? Do you want me to make you something to eat?

SOL: I'm fine.

(A beat)

I don't understand. I answered their questions. What do they want? Why are
they doing this?

*(Lights shift. Sol leaves the stage. Michael stands on one side of the stage, Kate on
the other. They are on the phone with each other.)*

KATE: It was on the TV.

MICHAEL: A camera crew rang the bell, but we didn't open the door.

KATE: They interviewed some of your father's neighbors.

MICHAEL: "We've known him for years. Who would have guessed?"

KATE: Basically. How's it going over there?

MICHAEL: I got him to bed. He's asleep now. It's so—

KATE: What?

MICHAEL: I was just thinking, all the years of him looking in on me when I was a kid. You know, to check on how I was sleeping, make sure I hadn't kicked the covers off in the night—

KATE: And now you're looking in on him.

MICHAEL: I mean, as long as I can remember, he's been the one Aaron and I could always turn to. Chase away bullies, come to bat for us when we needed a hand. Tonight, he looks so—

(A beat)

KATE: You get some sleep yourself, okay?

MICHAEL: Will do.

(Lights shift. Sol appears, wearing a yarmulke, dressed to go out.)

MICHAEL: Pop, what are you doing?

SOL: What I do every morning.

MICHAEL: Pop, I don't know—

SOL: It is what I do every morning.

(Sol hands Michael a yarmulke.)

ENSEMBLE: *(To the audience)* They walk to the shul.

(Lipsky approaches.)

SOL: Do we have a minyan yet?

LIPSKY: Not yet.

SOL: I brought my son. Michael, you remember my friend, Mr. Lipsky.

LIPSKY: I think you should go home.

SOL: Home? But you need us. You don't have enough without us.

LIPSKY: The others won't stay if you stay.

SOL: Are they telling me I can't doven here?

LIPSKY: Not with us.

SOL: "Us?"

LIPSKY: I'm sorry.

(Lipsky walks away. Sol looks at Michael. Michael removes his yarmulke and they exit.)

SCENE 15

(Ensemble brings in a park bench. Reiner appears, wearing a scarf.)

ENSEMBLE: Bernard Reiner.

REINER: *(Taking off scarf)* It's warmer out than I thought.

ENSEMBLE: Washington again. The mall.

REINER: National Art Gallery over there. Over there, the building with the rockets and such.

(Paul enters.)

PAUL: We could have met in my office.

REINER: That would have made it formal.

PAUL: Or in a restaurant.

REINER: Then I'd have to make a fuss with the waiter about not putting salt into the food. No, actually I enjoy sitting here, watching the tourists run in and out of the Smithsonian. Dragging their kids. Of course, the kids are mostly T'd off. What does all this junky old stuff have to do with them?

PAUL: So.

REINER: The Schumann case.

PAUL: Yes?

REINER: This Schumann—you seek to take away his citizenship and deport him for being a kapo.

PAUL: Not for that, exactly. As I'm sure you know, the United States can't prosecute crimes committed on foreign soil.

REINER: *(Nodding)* Not within your jurisdiction.

PAUL: But if he lied about his activities during the war on his application for citizenship, his naturalization can be invalidated, and then, yes, we can move to have him deported.

REINER: But surely many people lied on these applications. About their ages, their health, past political affiliations—any number of things.

PAUL: Yes.

REINER: But you don't pursue them. You don't prosecute them.

PAUL: The question is whether the lies were of sufficient gravity.

REINER: So this is what might be called a selective prosecution.

PAUL: You think that we shouldn't be pursuing this?

REINER: I and some of the people I'm associated with, we question whether you've considered all the implications.

PAUL: Implications?

REINER: I'm sure I don't need to tell you that it is very difficult to be a Jew in the Soviet Union.

PAUL: I don't see how this has anything to do with the Schumann case.

REINER: Then you're lucky to be talking to me. Part of our effort to pressure the Soviets to allow Jews to emigrate involves marshalling public opinion.

PAUL: All right.

REINER: The United States did disgracefully little to help Jews get away from Hitler. We didn't allow many into the country. Most of those we didn't let in ended up dying in the camps.

PAUL: Yes, I know this, but I really don't see what this has to do with Schumann or getting Jews out of the Soviet Union.

REINER: The barriers to Jews coming into this country were the product of anti-Semitism. And now, here you have this man Schumann. A Jew.

PAUL: Yes.

REINER: A Jew who did terrible things to other Jews.

PAUL: So we believe, yes.

REINER: There are some who feel that this can only encourage anti-Semites. "Look, you see, those Jews, give them the opportunity, they even turn on each other. Some of them—no better than Nazis."

PAUL: That's ridiculous.

REINER: Yes, but believe me, that's what some will think. And it will only make our job, our work on behalf of other Jews that much harder. Nobody will *say* anything about this to us, of course, but it will influence the climate. And we're not talking only about the issue of Soviet Jews. Also the Middle East. The political rationale behind Israel is partially based on the idea of reparation. A homeland for people historically persecuted and brutalized. But if you announce to the world—see, some of them *helped* the Nazis do it to their own kind—

PAUL: Schumann is just one man. To generalize from that—

REINER: —is exactly what people do. After all, it isn't the story of the many which captures people's imagination. Four hundred die in an earthquake in Chile. Very sad. By next week, you've forgotten. After all, you can't focus on four hundred people. They're just a mass. Four hundred. Six million. Both big numbers. But *one* person can cast a long shadow in the public's imagination. Schumann has the capacity of casting such a shadow. As far as I'm concerned, what he did puts him beyond the pale. I will not argue that he is anything other than a monster. I talk to you not for his sake, but for the sake of others whose causes may be damaged because of the unhappy fact this man was born a Jew.

PAUL: I'm not prosecuting a Jew, I'm prosecuting a man whose actions demand a response, and that man happens to be a Jew.

REINER: Paul, anti-Semitism isn't something I made up. It's a fact. I am old enough to know firsthand what it can lead to.

PAUL: I'm sorry, I don't think the answer is to back off on this. I understand your concerns. I do. But to not prosecute him *because* he's Jewish, because he violates the accepted image of the concentration camp prisoner as pure victim—don't you see the implications of that?

REINER: Tell me.

PAUL: It would be as if you were trying to—

REINER: Yes? Trying to?

PAUL: To promote the idea that if you're Jewish—if you're born Jewish, you couldn't be capable of such things. That to be born a Jew carries with it a presumption of moral superiority. To be separate from, *better than* others by virtue of ethnicity or nationality.

REINER: And you see a danger in this?

PAUL: Seems to me that's not too far from what the Germans believed.

REINER: (*A small smile*) I think we both have reason to be glad this is not a formal meeting. How are your parents?

PAUL: Fine.

REINER: You remember me to them please.

(*And, after shaking his hand, Reiner makes his way offstage. Paul looks after him, still upset. A beat. He exits in the other direction.*)

SCENE 16

(*Kate opens a door. Leah is standing there.*)

KATE: Michael?

MICHAEL: (*Offstage*) I'm still on the phone.

KATE: Come in.

(*Leah enters.*)

LEAH: I was in the building.

KATE: You have friends in the building?

LEAH: The Laschers. You know them?

KATE: No.

LEAH: Eighth floor.

KATE: No.

LEAH: It's a big building.

KATE: Yes.

LEAH: I should have gone downstairs and rung you up from the door-man's intercom, made sure I wasn't interrupting, instead of just coming straight—

KATE: No, it's okay. People do that, in small towns, you know. They see a light on, they know someone's home, they knock, drop in, say hi. Or if you're on the front porch.

LEAH: You're from a small town?

KATE: I used to visit my grandparents in Ohio.

LEAH: I don't think I've ever been in Ohio.

KATE: Then you probably never met my grandparents. Would you like something to drink—

(Michael enters.)

MICHAEL: Leah.

LEAH: Michael.

MICHAEL: Did we have—was I expecting you?

LEAH: No, this is spontaneous.

MICHAEL: Something the matter?

LEAH: Something we should talk over.

MICHAEL: Without Aaron?

LEAH: Yes.

KATE: Without me?

LEAH: It's about Sol.

MICHAEL: *(To Kate)* Stay. If you want to.

KATE: Is it my business?

MICHAEL: It's family. It's your business.

(To Leah)

Some kind of problem?

LEAH: *(A beat, then—)* You and Aaron called me, asked me to help your father on this.

MICHAEL: We needed a lawyer. You're a lawyer. You're a friend.

LEAH: And also possibly, because my mom's a survivor? Maybe you figured that might help me have a better—appreciation of the situation?

MICHAEL: I don't remember either of us saying anything like that, but maybe.

(A beat)

LEAH: I had dinner at my folks' the other night.

MICHAEL: Oh?

LEAH: My mom and I had a long talk. About my sister, who has three kids. My brother, who has one and a second on the way. About me—

KATE: Your lack of kids?

LEAH: Yeah. And my work.

MICHAEL: And my father?

LEAH: The subject came up.

MICHAEL: She isn't happy about you handling his case.

LEAH: Not excessively.

(A beat)

KATE: She wants you to drop it?

LEAH: That isn't exactly what she said.

MICHAEL: What did she say?

LEAH: "Do what you think is best."

KATE: Your choice.

LEAH: Completely.

(A beat)

You've never come to one of our meetings, have you?

MICHAEL: Meetings?

LEAH: Of our group.

MICHAEL: Kids of survivors?

LEAH: Hasn't Aaron ever invited you?

MICHAEL: Oh, he's asked, but it's not really my kind of thing.

LEAH: Why not?

MICHAEL: I guess I'm arrogant enough to want to believe whatever mess I may or may not make of my life, it's my own mess. And it's got nothing to do with what happened to my father before I was born.

LEAH: So you think that? You think being the son of a survivor has had no—

MICHAEL: Oh, I'm sure it's had some effect—

LEAH: But it's not something you want to look into too closely. Is that it?

MICHAEL: I know it must have had some kind of effect. All I have to do is look at Aaron, see how much a part of him it is. Maybe he gets something out of your group. But I—

LEAH: If it were right for you, you'd do it.

MICHAEL: I couldn't have said it better.

(A beat)

LEAH: I'm worried about him.

MICHAEL: Aaron?

(She doesn't reply.)

KATE: Can I ask something?

LEAH: What? About me and Aaron?

KATE: The two of you like each other, you share the political stuff—I mean, it's your own private concern and so forth and so on—

LEAH: But why didn't anything ever happen between us?

KATE: Yes.

LEAH: It did. Sort of. If a couple of nights counts.

KATE: Why only a couple of nights?

LEAH: I know you may find this hard to believe, but there are times when I want to kick back and forget the weight of history and the rest of what you call the political stuff. Times when I want to put Carly Simon on the stereo, wear slippers with bunny ears and unclench.

MICHAEL: You have slippers with bunny ears?

LEAH: Doesn't everyone?

KATE: I bet Aaron doesn't.

LEAH: Aaron also does not know how to unclench. And therein lies the problem. There's a part of me that for years has been hoping that he would—

KATE: Mellow?

LEAH: Something like that. Not just in the hope that someday we could give it a fair shot, but for his own sake.

(A beat)

MICHAEL: So your mother said you should do what you think is best.

LEAH: Yes.

MICHAEL: Leaving little doubt as to what she thinks that would be.

LEAH: Now I do *lots* of things my mom doesn't agree with.

MICHAEL: But this time it's different?

LEAH: The case is getting a lot of attention. And it's going to keep getting attention. I don't mind that for myself. But my mom—to have me plastered on front pages defending your father on these charges, it'll bring her too close to things I'd just as soon—you see what I'm saying?

(A beat)

KATE: Can you do that? What are the rules? Can you bail out now? Ethically?

LEAH: *(To Michael)* It would be a lot easier if you could tell Aaron and your father you think you need someone else.

MICHAEL: Another lawyer?

LEAH: Yes.

MICHAEL: And what reason would I give?

LEAH: It's an immigration case. You could use someone who's more familiar with immigration law than I am. There's some truth in that.

KATE: So that's why you wanted to bring this up without Aaron around. You want Michael to get you off the hook with him.

LEAH: Pretty chickenshit, hunh? What do you say?

MICHAEL: And what would we do for a lawyer?

LEAH: I've got someone to recommend.

MICHAEL: That would be good.

LEAH: I wouldn't recommend him if I didn't think he was—

MICHAEL: No, I'm sure.

LEAH: I don't look forward to calling your father.

KATE: You wouldn't have to call very far. He's here.

LEAH: Here?

KATE: Asleep in the second bedroom.

LEAH: Oh.

MICHAEL: We had kind of a problem on Sunday. Aaron was off on a camping trip this last weekend.

LEAH: Yeah.

MICHAEL: On Sunday night, he stops by Pop's place on his way back from—

LEAH: From camping.

MICHAEL: Right. He and I have been taking turns staying with him. Anyway, Aaron comes upstairs and finds this idiot with a can of paint painting a red swastika on the door.

LEAH: Of your father's apartment?

MICHAEL: Yes.

LEAH: I hope this idiot has insurance.

MICHAEL: Yeah, well, I'm inside with Pop, right? And I hear this commotion in the hallway. I open the door, and there's Aaron beating the shit out of this guy. And the paint can's been kicked over and there's paint all over the hallway. Red paint. And Aaron's given this guy a bloody nose.

LEAH: Great.

MICHAEL: So he grabs the guy by the back of his shirt and drags him over to the door. And he tells him that he's going to clean it off, if necessary with his tongue.

LEAH: That's Aaron.

MICHAEL: Meanwhile, Pop has come out of the apartment. He looks at this guy. He tells Aaron to let him go. And Aaron does.

LEAH: And that's why he's staying with you. Your father.

MICHAEL: Well, he couldn't stay where he was. And Aaron doesn't have enough room in his place.

LEAH: Oh hell. Never mind.

MICHAEL: What?

LEAH: This conversation didn't happen, okay?

MICHAEL: I'm sorry?

LEAH: Forget what I said about getting someone else. You're stuck with me. If you still want me.

MICHAEL: Hey, that isn't why I told you about this.

LEAH: I know that.

MICHAEL: I wasn't trying to—

LEAH: Michael, it doesn't need to be said. Just do me a favor and don't tell your brother I ever raised the subject.

MICHAEL: Okay. But what about you and your mom?

LEAH: I'll figure out some way to make it up to her.

KATE: You could always get pregnant.

SCENE 17

(Kate exits as Aaron enters. Lights shift. Leah is in conversation with Aaron and Michael.)

LEAH: There's another possibility to consider.

MICHAEL: What is that?

LEAH: Your father might simply take a plane to another country.

AARON: Excuse me?

LEAH: If he were to go to England, for instance—

AARON: And what would that accomplish?

LEAH: If you're stripped of your citizenship and deported, you've got to find some place that's willing to take you. Not real easy to do. But if you go *before* the government can take you through the proceedings, then you have some choice about where you end up.

MICHAEL: And the OSI doesn't pursue any further action?

LEAH: All they're interested in is getting him out of the country. If he's someplace else, he's not within their jurisdiction and the case is over for them.

AARON: But you're talking about giving up.

LEAH: Aaron, it's my responsibility as your father's lawyer to make him aware of the alternatives. That's what I'm doing.

AARON: You seriously advise doing this?

LEAH: The government's going to put a series of witnesses on the stand who will say they saw your father do various things. Your father's case is that these were done under duress. Further, he claims that when the Germans' backs were turned, he used his position to help people when he could.

AARON: So what's wrong with that? Isn't that a viable defense?

LEAH: Yes, if you could find somebody to testify to that. But so far, all these months, we haven't found anybody who will.

AARON: The list of names he gave you, the people he remembers helping—

LEAH: We've advertised, we've gone through the various agencies. Most of them never came to this country. Of those who did, most are dead. Some, frankly, are not in any shape to take the stand. We're talking about some pretty old people. And some we simply haven't found yet, though we're still looking.

AARON: Are you telling me we're going to lose?

LEAH: I'm saying we've got a tough fight ahead, and it would be helpful if we could find someone to back his version of things.

SCENE 18

(The sound of a school bell, the noise of high school kids. Ensemble sets up scene as they move furniture into place.)

ENSEMBLE: Dewey High School.
—The teacher's lounge.

(Aaron is correcting papers. Diane enters.)

DIANE: Aaron?

AARON: Diane.

DIANE: Grading papers?

AARON: Threw a surprise English quiz. Did you know that "tadpole" is the opposite of "fish"?

DIANE: Really?

AARON: *(Holding up paper)* That's what young Mr. Kevin Barkham thinks. I asked him to list three antonyms. You know: good-bad, hot-cold—

DIANE: Tadpole-fish.

AARON: When I sub for history, it's even more illuminating. A lot of them think we fought the Soviet Union in World War II. And a lot of the black kids think that slavery ended sometime in the 1950s.

DIANE: Is that so?

AARON: Jesus, how are people supposed to know who they are if they don't know what's happened before? Whether we like it or not, we live in times that came out of other times, we're part of something. Isn't it better to have some inkling of what?

DIANE: You say that, don't you? To your classes?

AARON: And I inspire them. Yes, I do. Nothing like a white Jewish guy getting up and telling them about A. Philip Randolph to make them want to hit those books.

DIANE: And if they knew about A. Philip Randolph, if they carried this knowledge of him in their hearts—

AARON: Political enlightenment followed by profound social change.

DIANE: Well, that would make it all worth it.

AARON: The thing about history—

(He stops.)

This is just us talking.

DIANE: Hunh? Oh yes, of course.

AARON: No, I mean, that's all this is.

DIANE: Till you say otherwise. All right. "The thing about history?"

AARON: You tell me.

DIANE: Well, what's the old line about being condemned to repeat it? That if you don't know it, if you don't learn from it, you're in danger of—

AARON: And do you believe that?

DIANE: Well, I must, or why am I doing what I do? I have chosen to do this. I have chosen to write about this stuff.

AARON: And do *I* believe it?

DIANE: You went to Bitburg.

AARON: I went to Bitburg.

DIANE: And it's like you said that night—

AARON: Which night?

DIANE: When you came back from Germany. We were in that restaurant— you and your brother and your girlfriend—

AARON: She's not my girlfriend.

DIANE: My mistake.

AARON: Some reporter you are—

DIANE: Hey, I wasn't doing a story about your private life.

AARON: Well, if you did, it wouldn't be much of a story.

DIANE: Sorry to hear that. But that night, you said that thing about people being what they do. What you do is who you are.

AARON: And so, because I went to Bitburg, that makes me who I am.

DIANE: Some people talked, but you—you got on the plane. You flew across the Atlantic Ocean.

AARON: A Jewish Lindbergh.

DIANE: Absolutely.

AARON: What if I went to Bitburg for crummy reasons?

DIANE: How could you do that? How would it be possible to do that?

AARON: Let's say I didn't really deep down give a shit about Reagan or Kohl or the ss or ethical anything. Let's say I went cuz I like showing off or because a girl I was interested in was going and I thought by tagging along I could get into her pants?

DIANE: It still wouldn't take away from the fact that you were there. I mean, yes, take Lindbergh—what if really the only reason *he* flew was to get into someone's pants? The fact is he still flew solo across the Atlantic. He still was the one who did that. Anyway, the meaning of what he did wasn't up to him to decide. He did what he did and people decided what it meant. But the reasons why? Nobody can really know the reasons you do something. Sometimes even you don't know the reasons you do something. I mean, isn't that what people pay money to shrinks to find out?

AARON: Tell me.

DIANE: A shrink says—or may say, "Okay, you say you did this, you did that, you did something else. There's a pattern there. And if you saw somebody else do these things, what would you think that person was about?" And so you say what you'd think, and then you see what you said about a person who did that is what *you* are cuz *you're* the person who did that.

(A beat)

AARON: I assume you're writing an article.

DIANE: Planning to. Yes, I will.

AARON: I won't be part of it. I decline.

DIANE: You didn't like what I wrote about Bitburg?

AARON: I liked it fine.

DIANE: So my writing you like okay.

AARON: Your writing—

DIANE: Content, style, execution—

AARON: You know how to push a pen.

DIANE: I try.

AARON: Don't take it personally. It's not just you I won't do this with.

DIANE: I understand your feelings—

AARON: I'm sure you do. Completely.

DIANE: Well, I don't pretend that.

AARON: No, I'm sure you can read my heart of hearts like the back of a cereal box. Kind of makes talking to me irrelevant, don't you think?

DIANE: I thought you might like the opportunity to present your side.

AARON: And I'm very grateful for the opportunity, but no thank you.

DIANE: I'm going to write this article. If you talk to me or not. I will write it.

AARON: I'm sure you'll find no shortage of people who will say things to you. People you can quote.

DIANE: It must be hard. Given who you are, how active you've been—

AARON: We're back to you reading my soul.

DIANE: People are out there, making assumptions—

AARON: I'm really not all that concerned about what people are assuming—

DIANE: Don't you think it might be worth—

AARON: Excuse me, but I think I gave you a pretty good no. I wasn't hostile—not in an overt way anyhow. You made your case, I considered it, I declined. You're not supposed to be in here, you know. This is a school. Do you want me to call the security guard?

(A beat)

DIANE: I've come across something I thought you should—I saw the list of people you're trying to locate. People your father says he helped. I know where to reach one of them.

AARON: Who?

DIANE: Rivka Glauer.

AARON: Where is she?

DIANE: Canada.

AARON: Could you be more specific?

DIANE: Here's the deal: if I tell you—

AARON:—then I have to talk to you?

DIANE: That's it.

AARON: You're sure it's the right Rivka Glauer?

DIANE: I'm sure.

AARON: But if I don't promise to talk to you, you won't tell me where she is?

DIANE: You've heard my offer.

AARON: This woman could help my father. Are you saying if I don't promise this, you'll stand in the way of that happening?

DIANE: Aaron—let's say you do this, you get your father out of his trouble—

AARON: Yes?

DIANE:—and the Soviet Union lets their Jews go wherever the hell they want, and Israel gets complete security, the Arabs disarm and promise to live in peace, and the surviving concentration camp inmates get reparations and apologies and the whole wish list—

AARON: All right.

DIANE: So what would you see as your life then? What would be Aaron Schumann's path to happiness?

AARON: Well, that's easy. I would take up golf.

(A beat. Diane pulls out a notebook, a pen, and a file card. She writes on the file card and hands it to him.)

DIANE: Rivka Glauer.

(A beat)

AARON: You're paying your own way. You know that.

DIANE: Okay.

AARON: And you don't say anything. I ask the questions.

DIANE: Agreed.

AARON: Okay, let's go.

DIANE: Now?

AARON: Why not?

DIANE: All right.

AARON: You want to make a phone call or something?

DIANE: Phone call?

AARON: If there's someone you want to let know you're taking this trip. Maybe a date to cancel.

DIANE: No, it's okay. I'm cool.

AARON: You've got nobody to call?

DIANE: Nobody I have to.

(A beat. Aaron looks at her for a second with a small smile.)

Don't we want to go somewhere?

AARON: Yes.

SCENE 19

ENSEMBLE: Another plane, this time to Toronto.

—A senior residence home on Kendal Avenue in the northern part of the city.

(Aaron and Diane wait as Felix Glauer helps his wife Rivka into a chair, then stands behind her. They are an aging couple. Aaron pulls out a cassette recorder.)

FELIX: I'm Rivka's husband, Felix. She doesn't see so good.

RIVKA: He's my seeing eye person. I hope you don't mind we meet out here on the patio. You can imagine how noisy it gets when you're in a room with a bunch of people who can't hear.

FELIX: *(To Rivka)* He's got a tape recorder.

(To Aaron)

You're going to tape this?

AARON: If you don't mind.

FELIX: He's going to tape this.

AARON: It could be helpful for our lawyer.

FELIX: You didn't bring him with you, your lawyer.

AARON: *(Correcting)* "Her."

RIVKA: A lady?

AARON: Yes. I wanted to talk to you first.

FELIX: Maybe we should have our lawyer here.

RIVKA: Felix.

FELIX: Or call him, get his advice.

RIVKA: Felix, we don't need a lawyer.

(To Aaron)

Does she know you're here? Your lawyer?

AARON: No.

RIVKA: Shouldn't she?

AARON: When it's time, she will.

RIVKA: *(Referring to Diane)* And this is?

AARON: She came with me.

RIVKA: Yes?

AARON: Diane Abbott.

RIVKA: A friend?

(Diane looks at Aaron.)

AARON: Kind of an interested party.

RIVKA: What do you do, darling?

DIANE: I write.

AARON: She helped me find you.

RIVKA: I didn't know I was lost. Well, all right.

AARON: I'll just turn this on—

(Turns on the tape recorder. A beat.)

RIVKA: We came from the same town, your father and I. I had an older brother, Theo. They were best friends. My brother, he asked your father, if something were to happen to him—

AARON: Yes.

RIVKA: —that your father should promise to keep an eye on me. We were sent to Ordenhaupt, in Germany. A camp. My brother died. An infection. Then the Germans made your father a kapo. He kept his promise to Theo. He looked out for me.

AARON: If you could give me some specifics—? An example. A time when he did something to help—

RIVKA: I see. Yes. One day, I managed to steal some potatoes. The Germans found out they were gone. They started a search while we were at our jobs. I was afraid they would find them, but I couldn't leave to hide them better. I told your father. He managed to get there first and move them. It was a risk. They would have shot him. They didn't hesitate to make an example of kapos.

AARON: If they *had* found out you stole the potatoes—

RIVKA: I would not be here talking to you now.

AARON: He saved your life.

RIVKA: Yes, that's fair to say. And other times when there were selections, people who were going to be sent elsewhere, he protected me. Wouldn't let them take me. "I need her," he'd say. "She's one of my best workers."

AARON: You'll say these things at the trial.

(Rivka looks at Felix.)

FELIX: *(A beat, then—)* Well, that may not be possible.

AARON: Mrs. Glauer, it's very important—

RIVKA: Yes, I know, but there are difficulties—going down there—

AARON: We'll cover your expenses, of course.

RIVKA: No, it's not that.

AARON: Mrs. Glauer, we need you. You tell me he saved your life. Now he needs your help.

FELIX: No, you don't understand.

RIVKA: If I testify for you, then the other side—the prosecution—they can ask me questions?

AARON: Well, yes.

RIVKA: What they ask me, I have to answer. I am under oath. They want to know about what happened in Ordenhaupt. I have to tell.

AARON: Yes.

RIVKA: You don't want me to have to answer those questions. You don't want me to tell what I saw, what I know.

(Gently)

This is why, when I heard about his trouble, I didn't contact you myself.

AARON: But you're talking to me now—

RIVKA: *You* called *me*. I felt I didn't have the right to refuse. And then I thought maybe there was something I could do to help.

AARON: But you just said you can't help him—

RIVKA: Not him. You.

(Aaron doesn't know how to respond. With pain, trying to phrase it correctly, Rivka continues.)

You're going to hear terrible things at the trial. But what I feel you must know is that it wasn't your father who did these things. Not the same person who brought you up. Not the same boy I knew in the village.

AARON: What are you saying?

(A beat)

RIVKA: Do you remember—was it ten years ago?—the girl with the rich father in California, kidnapped—

FELIX: Patty Hearst?

RIVKA: They put her into a closet, yes? Abused her, kept her blindfolded, cut off from the world. At the end of this, she was somebody else. They put a gun into her hands, she helped them rob a bank. She was in that closet four weeks, five? Your father, for him it wasn't weeks—it was *months, years.* The things he was forced to see. A mother, murdered in front of his eyes.

A father shot. Something broke. That's what I believe. That's what you must believe. Or how could he have done such things?

AARON: But they *made* him—the Germans.

RIVKA: No, he did these things even when the Germans were not there. When there was no reason. But that's what I mean: there was no reason. Where there's no reason, all that's left is madness.

(Numbly, Aaron switches off the recorder. He just sits there.)

I'm sorry.

(Rivka looks to Felix. He helps her leave. Aaron is alone with Diane.)

AARON: So, what do you say we head into town, hit some night spots?

DIANE: I would like—

(She stops.)

AARON: What? What would you like?

(A beat)

DIANE: I'm going to write what I think is fair.

AARON: I know that. I don't doubt that.

DIANE: Okay.

AARON: But you know I'm going to hate it anyway.

DIANE: Sure.

(A beat. A laugh.)

You remind me of the boyfriend in college I didn't have.

AARON: You didn't have a boyfriend in college?

DIANE: A few, actually. But none of them were—

AARON: —what—my type?

DIANE: No.

AARON: So I remind you of someone who didn't exist.

DIANE: I'm not saying what I want to say.

AARON: No, my hunch is what you want to say is something sympathetic. Something that would signal to me the fact that, even though you're going to write this, how deeply you—that underneath there's this human being.

But, you know, Diane, even if you could come up with some really good words, they still wouldn't—

DIANE: —mean shit.

(A beat. She looks at him for a moment, nods, then exits.)

SCENE 20

(Ensemble brings on a bench. Aaron heads for it, sits. Michael enters.)

AARON: Must be nice to wake up, look out your window, see the Hudson. Jersey. The sunsets.

MICHAEL: Why don't you come up and look at it from the inside? You haven't seen Pop in days.

AARON: What would I say to him?

MICHAEL: I've never known you to be short of things to say.

(A beat)

Go to the top of the building, you can see jets making approaches to all three airports. When it's nice out, we sometimes go up there with a thermos of coffee, watch the show.

AARON: Were you up watching tonight?

MICHAEL: It was kind of chilly out.

AARON: You might have seen me making an approach to Kennedy.

MICHAEL: You flew somewhere?

AARON: And back. It's been a busy day. Toronto.

MICHAEL: What's in Toronto?

AARON: Rivka Glauer.

MICHAEL: You found her? Why didn't you—

AARON: I didn't want to have to wait to talk to her.

MICHAEL: You should have told Leah. What good is it having a lawyer if—

AARON: I'm not going to argue about this. It's done. I went there, I came back.

MICHAEL: And?

(Aaron hands him the cassette.)

What's on this?

AARON: It ain't good.

(A beat as Michael absorbs this)

He did help her, but mostly—

MICHAEL: Oh, God.

AARON: She thinks he went off his rocker and that's why.

MICHAEL: Off his rocker?

AARON: The shock of some of what he saw, went through. You know the routine.

MICHAEL: But that counts.

AARON: It does?

MICHAEL: It has to.

AARON: Where?

MICHAEL: I mean it's a basic—if you're not in your right mind, you can't be held accountable–

AARON: According to whom?

MICHAEL: It's a legal principle. Diminished capacity I think they call it.

AARON: Well then, we don't have a problem, do we? We're off the hook. Wow, I'm relieved.

MICHAEL: Aaron—

AARON: Except, actually, we're not. It isn't.

MICHAEL: Not?

AARON: Relevant. Legally the issue is did he lie to Immigration when he came into this country. What his frame of mind was before that—beside the point. And, even if it weren't, what could we do? Put him on the stand? To say what? "I was nuts at the time? I didn't know what I was doing? Have a heart, cut me a break?"

MICHAEL: It doesn't match.

AARON: Match?

MICHAEL: With the man we know. The guy we grew up with. He doesn't act like somebody who could have—

AARON: What? Been the ogre of Ordenhaupt?

MICHAEL: I mean, even assuming he did this stuff, does he even know he did?

AARON: So?

MICHAEL: So how can it be right to go after someone, punish someone for something he doesn't even know he did? Doesn't that render the whole idea of punishment meaningless?

AARON: No, I think you're making excellent points. Why don't you ask Leah if they'll allow you to say this at the hearing?

MICHAEL: You don't think it's worth bringing up, getting them to consider?

AARON: You're talking like something can be said or done to change the way it's going to go. Michael, the tracks have been laid and we're on them. The witnesses will climb into the witness box and say their pieces. Leah will do her best to raise doubts about their memories. The judge will look sober and make notes. And you and me—we'll get dressed up in suits and play the loyal sons, walking in and out of the courtroom with Pop.

(A beat)

Oh swell.

MICHAEL: What?

AARON: I don't *have* a suit. I'm going to have to buy a goddamn suit for this!

MICHAEL: The last straw, hunh?

(A beat)

AARON: You remember when Mengele's son was on the TV? Josef Mengele? Talked about visiting his father in South America. Knowing who his father was and what he did. Not excusing, not explaining. But this was his father, and what was he supposed to do? Expose him? Christ, at the very least, if I were him, I would have changed my last name. Even if I *weren't* related and was born with the name Mengele, I would have changed it. I mean, when you look in the phone book, how many Hitlers do you see? But I remember this Mengele kid was on TV—not a kid—a lot older than a kid. But I remember looking at him and thinking, "You poor schmuck." Talk about being stuck with baggage. For all we know, he might have had the talent to be a singer—the German Frank Sinatra. But who would buy a record, "Freddy Mengele—In a Quiet Mood"?

MICHAEL: You aren't comparing, are you?

AARON: Yes, I know: differences, distinctions.

MICHAEL: There are big ones. Mengele and Pop—they're hardly in the same—

AARON: No, you're right. There's consolation—compared to some, Pop wouldn't rate a footnote.

MICHAEL: That's not fair.

AARON: I'm sorry, I don't know what the fairness standard on this is. Where would you even begin to look for such a thing?

(He stops. Then—)

You know, flying back down, all I could think—he did these things and he survived. He survived because—crazy or not—he did these things. And here we are. You and I—the two of us—we are alive because he did these things. I owe my existence to the fact that he—

MICHAEL: You can't look at it that way.

AARON: No?

MICHAEL: You can't.

AARON: If you say so.

(Aaron rises.)

I've got to prepare for a class in the morning. Subbing for geometry. I hate to tell you how little I remember of geometry.

MICHAEL: Aaron—

(Aaron stops, looks at him.)

Give me a call tomorrow. If you have time between classes.

AARON: *(With an ironic smile)* Sure. It'll all look different in the morning.

MICHAEL: *(Overlapping the above; seeing Sol offstage)* It's Pop.

AARON: *(Turning to look as Sol enters)* What?

SOL: *(To Aaron)* I saw you down here with Michael. From the window. Why don't you come up?

AARON: We had a—a few things to talk about.

SOL: Private?

AARON: Stuff there wasn't any point in bothering you with.

SOL: Are you sure you're warm enough?

AARON: I'm fine, Pop.

SOL: It's just, I can see your breath.

AARON: I'm okay.

SOL: Or a hat. You know what you need?

AARON: A wife.

SOL: You laugh. But look at your brother. He doesn't get colds. Look at me. All the time your mother was alive—

AARON: I'll give it real serious thought.

SOL: Come up.

AARON: Can't tonight.

MICHAEL: Aaron's subbing for a class tomorrow. He's got to prepare tonight.

SOL: Of course. But soon?

AARON: Just let me get a little ahead.

(Aaron hugs Sol.)

Night, Pop.

(He exchanges a look with Michael and exits. Sol looks at Michael. They exit.)

SCENE 21

DIANE: *(To the audience)* This is the story I got: Aaron Schumann is in the high school cafeteria. Cesar Segura, age seventeen, comes into the cafeteria and begins yelling at a student named Rosie Alvaro, starts to hit her. Aaron runs over. Segura reaches inside his jacket and pulls out a knife. "Okay, man, come on," he says to Aaron. "Okay, man, try it." And Aaron does.

(A beat)

"I don't understand it," one of the teachers tells me later. "Aaron knew not to do that. He knew better than to challenge that kid. How dangerous it could be. Why did he do it?"

(A beat)

I wanted to go to the service. The funeral. But I figured—well, of course, his father would probably be there. His brother. Friends. Some of them, they know who I am. And if I were to show up—last thing they need. Maybe if I were a better reporter I would have gone, but—

(She exits.)

SCENE 22

(Leah enters from one side, Michael and Kate from the other.)

LEAH: All right, this is the deal: we don't contest the citizenship issue, and they agree not to deport him.

MICHAEL: Don't contest? What does that mean exactly?

LEAH: Your father admits the allegations against him and relinquishes his citizenship. For their part, the government doesn't challenge the assertion that, given your father's recent stroke, deportation would endanger his life. So, they won't take any further action against him.

KATE: So, that's it?

LEAH: That's it.

SCENE 23

(We pick up in the middle of a conversation between Frieder and Paul.)

PAUL: It was the best we could do under the circumstances.

FRIEDER: I don't accept that.

PAUL: Mr. Frieder, what would you have us do?

FRIEDER: What you said you were going to: put him on trial, deport him.

PAUL: He wasn't well enough to stand trial.

FRIEDER: Lies.

PAUL: His son was killed. He had a stroke during the funeral. We had a doctor examine him. He had a stroke, Mr. Frieder. He wouldn't have been able to participate in his own defense. He can barely speak.

FRIEDER: And what about the people he killed? Where are *their* voices? What defense were *they* allowed against him in the camp? I'm telling you, Mr. Fontana—maybe you and your office have closed this case, *I* haven't.

PAUL: Mr. Frieder—

FRIEDER: You think I'm not serious?

PAUL: Don't do anything that would get you into trouble.

FRIEDER: Trouble? Schumann murders dozens, and how do you punish him? Tell him he can't vote any more. For whatever I may do, I'll make you a bargain—you punish me the same.

(And he exits.)

SCENE 24

MICHAEL: *(To the audience)* The rabbi calls and says that, for reasons we may appreciate, he has had to take down the *paroches* my father donated. I decide not to tell Pop when we visit him.

(Nurse wheels Sol in.)

KATE: *(To the audience)* There really was no way to keep Sol at our place and give him proper attention. The doctors believe, given time and therapy, he may regain more of his speech.

MICHAEL: *(To Sol)* I thought maybe I could make a list of your records. Then, if we could figure out which are your favorites, I could make cassettes so that you can listen to them here. Next week.

SOL: *(With difficulty; in a whisper)* Yes.

KATE: Honey, not next week.

MICHAEL: Oh, that's right. I'll be in Seattle on business all next week. But as soon as I get back. And we'll visit regularly. You can count on it.

(Michael and Kate kiss Sol.)

Get some rest, Pop.

(Michael and Kate exit, leaving him alone with the Nurse.)

NURSE: Well, that was a nice visit, wasn't it? You have a very nice son. Why don't we put on the TV now? Would you like that? I think there's a concert on Channel 13.

(She raises a remote control and the sound of symphonic music is heard.)

Too loud.

(She adjusts.)

That's better. I'll look in on you again in a little while, all right, Mr. Schumann?

(She exits. Sol closes his eyes. Frieder enters behind Sol. He takes hold of the chair. Sol opens his eyes.)

FRIEDER: Nice of your son to lead me to you. I feel like some air, don't you?

(He pulls the chair back and offstage. Michael appears.)

MICHAEL: *(To the audience)* When I get to the car, I realize I've left my umbrella. I go back to the room, but Pop isn't there. I ask an attendant. He tells me that he just saw Pop with a friend who said he was taking him for a walk.

SCENE 25

(Frieder has his hands on the wheelchair in which Sol sits, close to the edge of the stage. The sound of traffic roaring by below. During the following, the Ensemble forms a semi-circle around Sol and Frieder.)

ENSEMBLE: The Long Island Expressway.
—In front of them, an exit off the Expressway.
—Cars leaving the expressway curve right and up a hill.
—They are at the top of the hill—
—at the top of the exit.
—Frieder turns Sol's chair.
—It faces down the ramp.
—The wheels are at the edge of the curb.

FRIEDER: I've never trusted people who drive red cars. I think there's a statistic about that. Insurance companies. Something about people who choose to drive red cars, they get into more accidents. Tend to speed more. Risk their necks to maybe save ten seconds. A lot of flash, a lot of hurry. Speed. Still, some people, they love it. Speed. The blood pumping, the heart pounding faster. I could make you that gift. One push. You'd roll slowly for the first few seconds, but then gravity would take effect and you would accelerate. Until something stopped you.

SOL: *(With difficulty; whispering)* Who?

FRIEDER: What?

SOL: Who are—

FRIEDER: You don't remember me, do you? You don't remember which one I am. I understand. There are so many of us. So many with reason. Maybe I won't tell you. Maybe it's better if I let you guess. Something to occupy you on your way—

(Michael breaks through the semi-circle of the Ensemble, grabs Frieder from behind and pulls him away from Sol and the chair. Frieder falls to the ground. Michael pulls Sol back from the edge of the stage.)

MICHAEL: Pop?

(Satisfied that his father is indeed all right, Michael turns to look at Frieder, who is lying on the ground.)

Are you all right?

(Frieder doesn't answer.)

Mr. Frieder, are you all right?

(A beat)

FRIEDER: You know who I am.
MICHAEL: I know who you are.

(A beat)

Can you stand?

(He offers his hand.)

Here.
FRIEDER: I don't want your help.

(Frieder begins to get up, but loses his balance. Michael catches him in his arms, holds him. Frieder holds onto Michael and begins to weep. The sound comes pouring out of him. Sol sits mute in his chair. The lights intensify on the three of them. The rest of the Ensemble stands, witnesses in silhouette. The lights fade.)

EXILE IN JERUSALEM

A Play in Two Acts

by Motti Lerner

Exile in Jerusalem. Jewish Ensemble Theatre production, 1993. Pictured are Evelyn Orbach and Randall Forte. Photograph by Tom Kramer.

xile in Jerusalem was written for Habima National Theatre in Israel in 1989, as a result of a dialogue I had with Omri Nitzan, Artistic Director of Habima during the eighties. We discussed the book *Prophets without Honor,* by Frederick Grunfeld (New York, 1979), eight short biographies of German-Jewish writers, artists, scientists, and philosophers which convey the richness of German-Jewish culture in the early years of the twentieth century, richness which was annihilated by the Nazis in 1933–1945. I felt that each of the many cultural heroes appearing in this book—Freud, Kafka, Einstein, Benjamin, and others—deserved his own play, but I somehow felt closest to Else Lasker Schuller, the greatest German poet of the twentieth century. Perhaps I was intrigued because Else escaped to Palestine in 1939 and died there in 1945. Or because I had heard rumors about this crazy old genius poet who wandered the streets of Jerusalem in rags, feeding the pigeons, scribbling poems in her notebook with a broken pencil. The main reason for my fascination was the realization that Else felt she was an exile in Jerusalem, her beloved city, just as I sometimes feel in Israel, my beloved country.

I was born in Israel in 1949. I've lived here all my life. I married and had my children here. My parents and even my grandparents were born here. But since 1967, I feel that in many respects I do not always belong here. I cannot be part of the political and ideological process, which has not only created the occupation of Palestinian territories and the Palestinian people, but has also severely distorted the moral fabric of Israeli society. I painfully admit that this is the main reason for the bond I felt between me and Else Lasker Schuller.

Since its opening (under the title *Else*) at Habima National Theatre in 1990, the play has had many productions all over the world: in the United States, Europe, and even Australia. The first American production, supported by the NFJC New Play Commission, was done at the Jewish Theatre Ensemble in Detroit in 1993 with Evelyn Orbach as Else. The second American production was mounted by the Williamstown Theatre Festival in 1993, directed by Charles Nelson Reilly, with Julie Harris in the title role. These productions have opened a new era for me—an era of dialogue with American audiences mainly, but not only, in Jewish theatres.

This fascinating dialogue, which I hope will continue, is essential for me, not only as a writer, but as an Israeli who struggles to keep Israel a place for creating Israeli Jewish culture. This Israeli Jewish culture must be part of the world Jewish culture, which is being created in all continents: free, modern, progressive, radical, and rich. It is a culture which stems from our traditional sources, but which must define new boundaries for the human experience in our time, boundaries which will contain the vast changes we are experiencing. Else Lasker Schuller struggled to expand these boundaries, and perhaps this is yet another reason for writing this play about her.

This play would not have reached the American audience without the contribution of Hillel Halkin, one of the finest translators of Hebrew literature into English.

Notes

This play was edited by Stanley Price. Poems by Else Lasker Schuller were translated by Audrei Durchslag and Jeanette Litman-Demeestere, reprinted from *The Hebrew Ballads and Other Poems,* © 1980, with the permission of the publisher, The Jewish Publication Society. Sigrid Bauschinger's translation of "I'm So Sad beyond Measure" is used with permission of the translator.

ACT 1

CHAPTER I

SCENE I

(A winter evening in 1939. A small park in Jerusalem. Werner, a thirty-eight-year-old refugee from Germany who has reached Jerusalem in roundabout ways, sits on a bench and eats his supper. He opens a tin of sardines, cuts slices of bread, and dips the bread in the oil with a flourish of table manners. Else enters, carrying a suitcase. She is a woman of seventy and wears a coat with a colorful kerchief around the collar and a hat. Upon closer inspection she turns out to have a small hump on her back that she tries to hide by means of the coat.)

ELSE: *(Testing to see if he speaks German) Guten Abend? . . .*

WERNER: *(Happily) Ja, ja . . . guten Abend . . .*

ELSE: *(Relieved) Gott sei Dank . . .* I hope you are not the only creature in Jerusalem, *mein guten Herr,* who can be spoken to in an intelligible language . . .

WERNER: Of course not, *meine Dame.* For the past hour I've been speaking German to these unfortunately mute sardines . . . In Hebrew, by the way, you say *sardeen* too. *(He points to the tin.)*

ELSE: That must be because they're Hebrew sardines . . . *(Chuckles)*

WERNER: You should know, *meine Dame,* that the public here thinks very highly of the Hebrew sardine. There are patriots who even claim it has the bouquet of smoked salmon . . . But the trees, unfortunately, they speak Hebrew here . . . *(He laughs in a shrill voice and opens his suitcase.)* Would *meine Dame* care to buy some perfume or lipstick?

ELSE: *(Peering for a moment into the suitcase) Nein, danke.* You haven't by any chance seen the mayor of Jerusalem and his entourage, have you, *mein Herr?*

WERNER: No . . .

ELSE: I must be a bit early. *(Pause)* Or a bit late. *(Sits down)*

WERNER: These Levantines, *meine Dame,* are far from punctual . . . Even if they promise to come, there's not much chance they ever will. Are you planning to wait for the mayor here?

ELSE: He wrote that all of Jerusalem was looking forward to my arrival. I wouldn't want him to comb the streets for me. *(Takes a letter out of her pocket)*

WERNER: *(With a hint of sarcasm)* On a winter day like this . . .

ELSE: He also asked me to dine with him in the town hall.

WERNER: I'm sure his servants will be glad to reheat the goose for you . . . *(He laughs his strange laugh.)*

ELSE: *(With enthusiasm)* He even wrote to me about a cave in which King David's harp is kept. Tomorrow I'll play a song of praise to Jerusalem on it.

WERNER: *(Casts a suspicious glance at her and looks away)* All that's left in the caves of Jerusalem, *meine Dame,* is crumbling bones. This city is the biggest graveyard in the world. For the time being, of course. Our Fuhrer is planning even bigger ones . . . *(He gestures toward a bottle.)* Tea?

ELSE: And a bit of smoked salmon, *bitte* . . .

WERNER: *(Handing her a sardine and a lemon)* With lemon? A squashed survivor from a Hebrew lemon boat sunk by a submarine of the Reich and washed up in Jaffa. I rescued it as it lay dying in a pile of rubbish in the marketplace. Perhaps *meine Dame* would like to buy something after all? Some soap?

ELSE: *Danke* . . . *(Points to the bottle)* and is there sugar for the tea?

WERNER: *(Pouring her some)* The sugar sank and melted in the sea. The water, on the other hand, is from the spring King David drank from. For a minute, *meine Dame,* you looked familiar to me. To tell the truth, I haven't spoken German for quite awhile . . . *(Laughs)*

ELSE: *(While eating and drinking)* The poor mayor must be so hungry by now that he's chewing his coattails. If you promise not to tell him I've eaten already, I'll have him invite you to my heavenly banquet of saints. Do you think he'll like my dress? *(She opens her coat enough for him to see a bright red dress.)* I also have a flaming green silk scarf with real peacock feathers that I was given by a young Tibetan prince. Perhaps I should change hats, though. Mayors have a weakness for hats. I once met one who went down on his knees every time he saw a feather hat. Do you think the mayor of Jerusalem will be as passionate? Anyone sitting on King David's throne must surely have a little bit of the poet in him.

WERNER: *(Tentatively)* Frau Schuller?

ELSE: You look so like my little son Paul, whose curls had garlands of red and white roses . . .

WERNER: *(Interrupting her, astonished)* Frau Lasker-Schuller! It is you! . . . Good God . . . what are you doing in Jerusalem? I was told you had left for Switzerland back in '33! It's unbelievable . . . why, just a week ago I read two of your poems in an old issue of the *Zurich Literatur* . . . wonderful poems, Frau Schuller . . . "And I drink quiet wine from the moon . . ." *(He is speechless.)* Here, have some more tea. I can't tell you how surprised I was, Frau Schuller, to find Baroque imagery in those poems . . .

ELSE: And you, *mein Herr,* must be . . . *(She tries to remember.)*

WERNER: Doktor Werner Hermann. I left Germany for Paris a week before you did. The day before that I ate cream cakes at the table next to you in the Grossenwahn Café . . . *(Laughs)*

ELSE: *(She seems to remember.)* Ah . . . Werner Doktor Hermann from Heidelberg!

WERNER: No, no. From the Grossenwahn Café, near the Kaiser Wilhelm Church. My wife is Gertrud Wendel of the opera . . .

ELSE: Gertrud? . . .

WERNER: She stayed behind with the girls . . . She's of pure Aryan aristocratic stock . . . don't you remember me, Frau Schuller? Back in '29 I wrote an article about you in the Frankfurter *Zeitung* called "Passion and Death in Expressionist Poetry."

ELSE: *(Pretending to know him)* Werner Doktor Hermann! How are you, my dear man? For a moment I thought you were Stefan Zweig or Arthur Kostler. I dreamt about them last night . . . *(Laughs)* Could I have a little more of the smoked salmon, *bitte?*

WERNER: *Ja, ja* . . . Here's some more tea too . . . I have got half a cup of sugar in my room, but I'm keeping it to sweeten harder times. Perhaps you haven't heard, my dear Frau Schuller, but Stefan Zweig managed to get to Brazil with his wife, and I ran into Arthur Kostler six months ago in Marseilles. A broken man, shaking with fear that the French might hand him over to the SS . . . I gave him half of my morphine, enough to kill a horse . . . *(Laughs)* . . . apropos of horses, it's just possible that the mayor doesn't know you've arrived. Perhaps we should go to the town hall . . .

ELSE: I'll certainly tell him about your generosity, dear Doktor Hermann. I'm sure he'll reward you handsomely. You wouldn't happen to have any chocolate, would you? I'm very fond of chocolate with almonds and walnuts . . .

WERNER: So am I. Don't you remember how it stuck to my beard once?

ELSE: To your beard?

WERNER: And then I had to shave it . . .

ELSE: *(Remembering)* Werner Hermann! My "Prince of Cairo"! Isn't that what I called you?

WERNER: Yes, it is . . .

ELSE: You sat every night in the Grossenwahn Café playing songs from Brecht operas on the piano with your nose . . .

WERNER: That's right . . .

ELSE: You used to organize a choir from the beggars in the street . . . I paid them with cigarette butts from the ashtrays . . . and your Gertrud used to sing. I heard her "Die Tote Stadt." Oh, my Prince of Cairo. So you're still alive?

WERNER: Apparently it's not so easy to kill me . . . *(Laughs)*

ELSE: And does your nose still play the piano?

WERNER: It does . . . *(They both laugh.)*

(Else mimics him, swaying back and forth as he plays and starts to sing a Brecht song about Hitler. Werner joins in laughingly.)

TOGETHER: Mister Hitlerhousepainter said,
"You want a painter, sir?
Step aside, that's me!"
He took a can of paint
And in colors far from faint
He painted Germany He painted Germany
Mister Hitlerhousepainter
Said, "You want a painter, sir?
I'm the man for it!"
In no time flat the job was done,
And before the paint could run
He whitewashed all the shit,
He whitewashed all the shit.

(They laugh. In the background British policemen can be heard announcing a curfew.)

SCENE 2

(Werner and Else are in Werner's room, in an old building near downtown Jerusalem. The room is rundown and almost empty. It has a table with a typewriter and another piece of furniture that serves as a bed. The sole window faces the street.)

WERNER: I lit the paraffin burner. The smoke will go away soon. I'm truly sorry, Frau Schuller, to have had to drag you here so unexpectedly. The British can be very unpleasant in a curfew . . . *(He doesn't notice that she has fallen asleep.)* Over here they call this lamp a "Lux," although it gives off more soot than light. They haven't invented Hebrew words for everything yet . . . The water must have boiled by now. I'll bring you your tea . . . *(Exits. Comes back after a short moment with a cup of tea.)* I almost forgot how to make tea for more than one . . . *(Notices that she is asleep)*

SCENE 3

(Morning. Else rises from the bed. Birds chirp outside. She notices Werner's suitcase of perfumes and sniffs at it. Unable to resist temptation, she opens the suitcase and takes out a bottle of perfume. She smells it and sprays some of it on her throat. Werner speaks from outside the room.)

WERNER: Frau Schuller?

ELSE: *Ja, ja . . . bitte . . . (She quickly returns the perfume to the suitcase.)*

WERNER: *Guten Morgen . . . (He smells the perfume but is not sure where the odor comes from.)* I've brought you a cup of fresh tea. And this is the same bread that King David ate. It's called "pita."

ELSE: Pita? *(The word amuses her.)* Pita . . . pita? pita! That's a word the birds must understand. Pit . . . pit . . . pit . . . pit . . . pita! Pita, *bitte*, pita . . . *(She breaks off some crumbs for the birds.)*

WERNER: *(Stopping her)* Frau Schuller . . .

ELSE: They're also looking for a safe haven until the storm blows over . . . I met them in Trieste. They hovered over the ship all the way to Haifa and escorted me from there by train to Jerusalem. Now and then they knocked on the windowpane and I gave them crumbs . . . *(She throws them more crumbs.)*

WERNER: *(Quickly taking the bread away from her)* Frau Schuller, I bought this pita for you . . . *(He realizes where the smell of perfume is coming from.)* That scent . . . it's very familiar . . .

ELSE: I always had good taste in perfume . . .

WERNER: *(Catching on)* Frau Schuller! I barely make a living from those perfumes. My university job doesn't start until the spring.

ELSE: *(Consolingly)* Is it so hard to sell perfume in such a sweaty country?

WERNER: My Gertrud always said I couldn't sell water to a thirsty man in the Sahara . . .

ELSE: She was right. Give me that suitcase and I'll sell all its contents in a day . . .

WERNER: That's very kind of you . . .

ELSE: Picture me wrapped in a gold silk robe, smelling of myrrh and cinnamon as I ride about Jerusalem on a camel with your suitcase.

WERNER: *(Succumbing to her charm)* Even the Chasidim will line up to buy. *(They laugh.)*

ELSE: *(She finishes laughing, takes off her coat, and hangs it up. She opens her suitcase.)* The Prince of Cairo mustn't be upset if I hang up a few of my things . . . just in the corner. They'll blossom there like white, red, and blue lilies growing out of the rocks. The angels will come and peek at us through the cracks in the walls . . .

WERNER: Ahem . . . yes, indeed . . .

ELSE: *(Taking her clothes out of the suitcase and hanging them in the room)* You mustn't dream of sleeping in the hallway again, Werner. You can bring your blanket in here and stand it by the door. I'll go and sell your perfume today.

WERNER: By all means . . . But look, Frau Schuller, I've no objections to being your host, but perhaps we had better ask the landlord . . .

ELSE: No, no. You mustn't interrupt me when I'm working on a new idea, Werner. Didn't you say you had found Baroque imagery in my poems? Baroque! What a wonderful title that would make! I'll compose a few poems, you'll write an article about them, and my friend Professor Buber will publish it in the newspapers. You'll be the leading literary critic of the Levant! Every landlord in Jerusalem will be happy to have you for a tenant . . .

WERNER: That's a wonderful idea, Frau Schuller, but too much intimacy between a poet and her critic might be detrimental both to the poetry and the criticism.

ELSE: There's nothing intimate about living together! What's intimate is that I'm willing to publish a whole book for you. A big book, bound in fragrant leather . . . My little son Paul will illustrate it with lovely spring flowers . . .

WERNER: *(Startled)* Paul? But he's . . . *(mumbles)* . . . over ten years ago . . .

ELSE: Such gentle young boys never die, Werner . . . *(In a torrent of words)* He'll illustrate it and you'll add your notes in the corners . . .

WERNER: Frau Schuller, you don't know the landlord. He's a fascist . . .

ELSE: You're the man for it. What would poets be without their critics? It's only through your insight that our poems gain their rightful place.

WERNER: *(Firmly)* Frau Schuller. I assume you have no other place to live, and I'm happy to be able to share this room with you, but . . .

ELSE: *(Interrupting him)* You don't understand, Werner Doktor Hermann. You yourself will choose the poems and edit them . . .

WERNER: *(Weakening)* We're in Jerusalem, not Berlin. In Jerusalem you can only publish books in Hebrew . . .

ELSE: In Hebrew?

WERNER: I stopped writing in German the day I left Germany.

ELSE: Werner . . .

WERNER: I refuse to be at the mercy of their language any more, Frau Schuller . . .

ELSE: *(Taking a looseleaf notebook with a few pages from her suitcase)* And what am I supposed to do with these poems? Tear them up? I don't have any other language. *(She kisses the pages and holds them out to him.)* God has sent me to you with a treasure that only comes the way of a chosen few.

WERNER: *(He hesitates at first to look at the poems but then cannot restrain himself. His face lights up as he reads them.)* New poems! If you have no objection, I'll try to translate them. I write Hebrew better than I speak it . . .

ELSE: God kisses you with my lips, Werner, you dear, dear man . . . *(She kisses him on the forehead, then skips away with surprisingly childlike gaiety.)*

WERNER: About the room, Frau Schuller—

ELSE: *(Interrupting him)* I won't bother you. I promise to be a very considerate tenant . . . You can sit quietly in a corner and write . . . You won't even notice I'm here . . . I'll spend the days riding our camel, selling perfume, and at night I'll go to the cinema . . .

WERNER: I still think I should talk to the landlord and—

ELSE: *(Interrupting)* And now I'm off to see the poor mayor, who went hungry all night while he waited for me. *Auf Wiedersehen.* *(She kisses him again and leaves. He reads from her papers.)*

WERNER: O, God. Wrap up your robe around me fast

I know I'm just the drop left in the glass

And as the last man stands pouring out the world,

Out of your power you'll never let me pass,

And a new globe around me will be furled.

SCENE 4

(Werner turns to the audience as if it were gathered in the German synagogue in Jerusalem for a poetry recital by Else Lasker-Schuller. Else is late. Werner stalls for a time while he waits for her.)

WERNER: *Guten Abend, meine Damen und Herren.* Good evening, Mister Mayor. Good evening, Professor Buber . . . It is a great honor and pleasure to present you with our renowned poet who will read us a selection of her latest poetry, written in defiance of the Fuhrer and his murderous henchmen. These poems are dedicated by her to her unforgettable friends who have been driven into exile all over the world. *Meine Damen und Herren,* Frau Else Lasker-Schuller! . . . *(Apologetically)* She'll be with us in a minute . . . Meanwhile, let me thank the rabbi of this synagogue and his assistants for making this distinguished evening possible. All of us, I am sure, share the hope that we will soon be holding evenings of poetry in Hebrew . . . *(Seeing Else)* Please accept my apologies for the delay. Frau Else Lasker-Schuller—*bitte!* . . .

(Else comes on stage. Werner vacates his place for her. She is wearing a colorful robe and a hat with a huge feather in it. Her throat, arms, and hands are adorned with heavy jewelry. In one hand she holds a candle, and in the other a little bell. She puts down the candle and begins reading her poetry, accompanying herself now and then with the bell.)

ELSE: "My Mother"
The candle burns on my table
All night long for my mother
For my mother . . .
My heart burns beneath my shoulder blade
All night long. For my mother.

"The End of the World"
There is a weeping in the world
As if the good Lord now lay dead.
And heavy as the grave, the weight
of the shadow falls like lead.
Come, Let's go sneaking
In everybody's heart life lies

As in a coffin.
Ah! Let's kiss deeply, you and I
A longing's knocking at the world
From which we'll surely die.

"My Blue Piano"
At home I have a blue piano
But have no note to play.
It stands in the shadow of the cellar door,
There since the world's decay.
Four star-hands played harmony
—The Moon-maiden sang in her boat—
Now the rats dance janglingly,
Broken is the keyboard . . .
I weep for the blue dead.
Ah, dear angel, open to me
—What bitter bread I ate—Even against the law's decree,
In life, heaven's gate.

(There is scattered applause. Else bows to the audience.)

Good evening, Mister Mayor. How is Your Grace? I have something wonderful and precious to tell you. Your Grace will never believe it. On our way here we stopped to rest at the number fifteen bus stop, Werner and I— and who do you think was sitting on the other side of me? Who? *(There is silence. Else shifts her glance elsewhere.)* You can't guess either, Herr Professor Buber? *(No one answers.)* King David! None other than King David in person, isn't that so, Werner? And I, who all my life have wanted to know what King David wore—I reached out quite shamelessly to touch him. And what do you think he was wearing? Well? . . . *(No one guesses.)* A tweed jacket. I swear by my little son Paul! English tweed. *(Laughing)* You tell them, Werner . . . Tell them . . .

(Werner steps up hastily to put an end to the embarrassing moment.)

WERNER: Many thanks to our renowned poet—and thank you all for coming!
ELSE: I have something else quite wonderful to tell you too . . .
WERNER: Permit me to apologize for the slight misunderstanding . . . Inciden-

tally, next Saturday night our poet will give another recital in the synagogue. The cost of a ticket will be three *piastres,* even for poetry lovers. No substitutes, such as eggs or tomatoes, can be accepted. Thank you very much, *und auf Wiedersehen.*

CHAPTER 2

SCENE I

(Werner's room. Night. Werner sits at his typewriter, lights a cigarette, and tries to translate "The Blue Piano" into Hebrew.)

WERNER: At home I have a blue piano . . . At home I have a blue piano . . . *(He types.)* No, no . . . *(He crosses out and types again.)* . . . But have no note to play . . . But have no note to play . . . *(He opens a dictionary.)* But have no note to play . . . Yes, yes . . . that's it . . . *(He types.)*

(Else enters.)

ELSE: Are you planning to work all night, Werner?

WERNER: If your poems are published in Hebrew, the mayor may forgive you that scene at the synagogue . . .

ELSE: I didn't make any scene. He laughed along with everyone . . .

WERNER: He certainly did.

ELSE: They all laughed . . .

WERNER: Certainly . . . *(He continues translating.)* It stands in the shadow of the cellar door . . .

ELSE: I don't understand how such a poem can be translated.

WERNER: Professor Buber was quite enthusiastic about my translations. "Your command of Hebrew is impressive," he said to me . . . *(He goes on typing.)*

ELSE: Even your typewriter is groaning.

WERNER: If you give me some of your books, Frau Schuller, I can do some more tonight.

ELSE: What books?

WERNER: Buber suggested including some of your early poetry too.

ELSE: But I don't have a single one of my books . . .

WERNER: You don't?

ELSE: I fled Berlin with the dress on my back . . . I found this suitcase thrown away in Zurich. At the bus station.

WERNER: *(Surprised)* You don't even have one book?

ELSE: No. Don't you?

WERNER: I left everything behind in Paris.

ELSE: *(Alarmed)* There must be someone in this country who has a book of mine.

WERNER: Maybe in a second-hand bookshop . . .

ELSE: Someone has to have my books!

WERNER: *(Hesitantly)* Of course. I'll go and look tomorrow—

ELSE: *(Interrupting him)* You'll go and look this minute and you'll keep on looking until you find them! They're being burned right now in Germany, huge piles of them, hundreds of poems going up in flames! The mayor must make an announcement on the radio. *(She starts to leave and returns.)* I want to know the truth, Werner. I have written poems in my life, haven't I? Nineteen books . . . I haven't suddenly woken up from a dream, have I? Did I or did I not stay up every night in the Grossenwahn Café, reading them aloud? My Paul sat next to me listening . . . didn't he?

WERNER: He did.

ELSE: And then one day men in brown and black shirts appeared in the streets. They broke the windows of the café and beat me with their clubs . . .

WERNER: They did.

ELSE: I even have a big scar on my scalp, don't I? *(She bends her head.)*

WERNER: Frau Schuller, your books are safe in the libraries of Zurich. You needn't worry about the immortality of your poems. We can put out a new book without them.

ELSE: *(Making him look at her scalp)* Do I or do I not have a scar?

WERNER: Today, you're writing different poems . . . about the hell our lives have become . . .

ELSE: *(Interrupting him)* I have a scar and I wrote books! *The Hebrew Ballads, The Prince of Thebes, The Miracle Rabbi of Barcelona.* Now they're hiding in the suitcases and coat pockets of refugees. I hear them calling me, banished books in battered bindings, trembling with shame in the darkness, waiting for me, Else Lasker Schuller, to come and save them . . . *(She storms out.)*

(Werner starts to follow her but stops after a single step and remains standing where he is.)

SCENE 2

(Werner is waiting for Else by the front gate of Professor Buber's house in Jerusalem. Street sounds can be heard. A wagon driver cries, "Ice! Ice!" Dogs bark with pent-up fury and children cry. Werner's patience is running thin. Suddenly he notices a cigarette butt on the pavement. He picks it up and lights it. A minute later Else enters, dressed in colorful clothes. Werner hurries over to her.)

ELSE: *(A slim book in her hand)* The Hebrew Ballads . . .

WERNER: That's all?

ELSE: I sent it to him myself in 1910. *(Hands him the book)*

WERNER: *(Reading aloud)* "To Martin Buber, the Holy Prophet of the Jews, With a primal Kiss" . . .

ELSE: You should have seen how he adored my scarves. He even said I looked like Greta Garbo in this hat!

WERNER: Even a blind man could tell you that. *(They both laugh. Werner stops laughing and says reluctantly:)* And now . . . to the great writer Agnon?

ELSE: You know, when Agnon lived in Berlin he used to wait in the doorway of the Grossenwahn Café every morning just to hear me laugh. His lovely wife Esther turned green with envy. Even then I was prettier than she was. *(She takes a partly chewed loaf of bread from her pocket.)* This is for you . . .

(Werner does not know whether to laugh or be angry. She holds out the loaf of bread to him.)

WERNER: You stole that from Martin Buber?

ELSE: Stole? He served me a whole meal. I kept the bread, that's all—for you.

WERNER: Thank you. I've already eaten. I'm full.

ELSE: *(She takes an ashtray from her pocket.)* And this is for your room . . .

WERNER: You walked off with that too!

ELSE: You really do need an ashtray, and you haven't eaten, Werner. You're hungry . . .

WERNER: I said I'm full. And I must ask you to return this ashtray.

ELSE: If you were a poet, you would know how to accept humiliation.

WERNER: It's not a question of humiliation. *(Silence)* Sometimes, when I walk down this street with my suitcase of perfumes, I see Herr Professor Buber sitting on his terrace and writing . . . A philosopher for salons and newspapers! If I could have stayed one more year in Germany, I'd have man-

aged to publish my studies on Goethe. All the universities in the world
would be after me today . . .

ELSE: I'll wait here while you're seeing Agnon . . .

WERNER: While I'm seeing him?

ELSE: He lives just around the corner.

WERNER: Absolutely not . . .

ELSE: He must have a few of my books.

WERNER: No, no . . . You may not know this, Frau Schuller, but I once wrote
a piece for *Literarische Welt* in which I said that Agnon's books about the
black-garbed Jews of the shtetl are millstones about the neck of the modern Jew . . .

ELSE: But I told you his Esther can't stand me. She'll never let me in to see
him . . .

WERNER: Nor me. She thinks I ruined his career in Berlin.

ELSE: Go and see him, Werner. I beg you, go . . .

WERNER: Agnon can't abide people like us. I once heard him say that we turned
a blind eye to Nazism and sold our souls to the devil just to go on sitting
in the cafés of Berlin . . . To him I'm an assimilated Jew who married a
goy, and I can go on pounding these pavements, selling perfume for the
rest of my life . . .

ELSE: *(Angrily)* For days on end you've been poking through my poems, Werner, pawing at them as if you owned them . . .

WERNER: Frau Schuller . . .

ELSE: And now, when finally I beg you for some help, all you do is give me excuses. You're nothing but a wretched critic . . . a nobody who follows me
around and lives off the crumbs of my genius . . .

WERNER: *(Controlling himself)* Frau Schuller, our friendship is the most precious thing to have happened to me since I came to Jerusalem!

ELSE: You want to be friends with the Poet, but you'll do nothing for the person inside . . .

WERNER: *(Truthfully)* Agnon will slam the door in my face. I've already seen
him several times about a position at the university, and he turned me out
of his house like a pariah.

ELSE: You're still young, Werner . . . you'll make him pay for it one day . . .
I'm ten thousand years old . . .

WERNER: Go and see him yourself. Maybe you'll get some pudding. *(He looks at the loaf of bread she's still holding.)* You had your main course at Buber's, haven't you?

ELSE: Of course I did! He poured me a glass of port, and his wife served me petits fours and . . . *(She trails off.)*

WERNER: *(Angrily realizing the truth)* Fine, fine. So the holy prophet of the Jews didn't even offer you a bite. If you hear Agnon screaming through the window you'd better come to his rescue . . . *(Exits)*

SCENE 3

(Else is left alone on the bench. She huddles there, sunken into herself like a sudden victim of old age. After a minute she reaches into her pocket, takes out the bread, and munches on it slowly. Soon Werner returns with a broad smile.)

WERNER: He had a postcard. One poem. Untitled. *(Shows her)* They did everything they could to throw me out. His Esther was pale with fright. *(He mimics her.)* "You're not to write a word about him, do you hear? Not a word! . . ." *(He laughs.)*

ELSE: He didn't ask about me?

WERNER: Of course he did. He even invited you to visit him . . . When I wanted to sit on a chair, she said it was broken . . . *(Laughs)*

ELSE: *(Interrupting)* When did he invite me?

WERNER: Anytime you like . . . *(Else understands. He continues.)* So I went to sit on the couch—and she told me my trousers were dusty . . .

ELSE: *(Interrupting)* And my books?

WERNER: He'll ask his friends . . . When I began to brush them off, she pushed me off the rug . . .

ELSE: *(Interrupting him again)* What friends?

WERNER: I went back to the chair, sat down . . . and went sprawling. It was broken. *(He laughs.)*

ELSE: *(Angrily)* He did not invite me to visit him . . .

WERNER: Of course, he did . . . He wants to help. He's even ready to recommend a native Hebrew speaker to translate your poems. *(Ironically)* Not that he doesn't think my Hebrew is good . . . *(Laughs)* I went sprawling on the floor . . .

ELSE: *(Angrily)* I'm not letting anyone touch my poems . . .

WERNER: *(Incredulously)* And just how do you expect anyone to read them?

ELSE: I've been a Hebrew poet all my life. My poems are already in Hebrew.

WERNER: Agnon knows they're full of Hebraic symbols. But he was referring
to the actual language in which they are written . . .

ELSE: My poems are Hebrew poems. I will not start patching and cobbling
them now . . .

WERNER: Frau Schuller, He's right. Nobody in this country is going to read
poetry in the language abused by the housepainter . . .

ELSE: But that's how I wrote them . . . I can't write any other way . . . If you
whitewash a violet, is it still a violet?

WERNER: We're trying to make a life for ourselves here. Living means writing
. . . and your violets that wilted there can only bloom here in the language
people live in. If Agnon thinks I'm not the person to translate your poetry,
I'm willing to abide by his judgment . . .

ELSE: *(Interrupting him)* My violets never wilted, Werner. They never did and
never will . . . *(She waves the copy of* Hebrew Ballads.*)* With these letters
I drew them . . . With these commas and colons I decorated them . . .
that's how they fell into my lap, like ripe pears . . . like pomegranates . . .
and I will not allow them to be skinned alive . . .

WERNER: Goethe and Heine have been translated.

ELSE: My poems are the word of the living God. Yes, the word of God. This
is the way He wanted them written. In these very words. In these very
lines. He chose me and sent me. His angels from the clouds, bearing gifts
wrapped in softest silk. He watched me through the window as I sat at my
typewriter . . . Whenever I wrote anything He disliked, He tapped on the
pane with His ring . . . *(Agitatedly)* I won't change the tail of one comma
for these Philistines. A Jewish poet knocks on their door—and they shut
the bolts and sit inside jabbering away in their own oriental patois—so
pleased with themselves . . . The swine aren't worthy of my poetry . . .
they aren't worthy of anything . . . anything . . . they aren't worthy of God
. . . *(She suddenly faints. Werner rushes over and catches her.)*

WERNER: Frau Schuller . . . Frau Schuller? *(He carries her off to her bed.)*

CHAPTER 3

SCENE I

*(Else and Werner are in their room. Else is lying in bed. Werner lights a cigarette
and listens to the voices of the children outside.)*

CHILDREN: Crazy Else
Ate a mouse.
She hides Nazis
In her house!

(The chanting and laughter fade away. Werner puts out his cigarette and picks up a newspaper from the table.)

WERNER: The Wehrmacht entered Paris yesterday. No doubt the Gestapo are there today. Would you like me to read you what it says about them in the "Hebrew Made Easy for Immigrants" column? *(Else doesn't answer.)* If my books have been gathering dust in Montmartre, now they'll be gathering crowds to watch them burn on the Champs Elysée . . . I left a pair of woolen slippers there too . . . *(He puts the paper down angrily.)* Hell! My little girls are in Berlin and all I can think of is my slippers. *(He reaches for the paper again but throws it back down at once.)* I'm embarrassed to read this. It's like it's written for children . . . *(He puts the paper away in a drawer.)* Would you like a glass of tea, Frau Schuller? *(Else doesn't answer.)* Grass will grow on my palms before I master this language! I understand every rule and every exception to every rule, and I still can't compose a single elegant phrase. *(Pause)* You're looking much better today. As an amateur doctor and a professional patient, I give you my permission to go out for a walk . . . and to go back to work, if you'd like to. *(She doesn't answer.)* Perhaps, Frau Schuller, you could write another letter to Thomas Mann about your books . . . *(He takes a letter from his pocket.)* He left Switzerland two months ago. The last one you sent came back . . . He managed to get his wife and children to New York. *(Angrily)* Aryan exiles are even able to save their books . . . *(Pause)* Does your arm still hurt? I can give you a bit of morphine. If Arthur Kostler had taken all the morphine I offered him in Marseilles, I wouldn't be walking around with enough in my pocket to kill a horse . . .

ELSE: Hold me, Werner. Embrace me. Not a soul in Jerusalem has held me yet. *(She clings to him.)*

WERNER: Frau Schuller . . .

ELSE: Call me Else, Werner . . .

WERNER: Frau Schuller . . .

ELSE: Caress me, Werner. Please, caress me . . .

WERNER: *(Embarrassed)* Frau Schuller . . . I just told you that Paris has fallen to the Wehrmacht and that Thomas Mann has fled to New York. I should also have confessed that the mayor has refused to see me about your books . . .

ELSE: Forget about the mayor . . . the two of us are alone on this earth . . . if only a tiger would bridge the distance between us with his body . . .

WERNER: The distance is even greater between me and my . . . *(Trails off)*

ELSE: Look at me, Werner. I was also created in God's image.

WERNER: Frau Schuller, I know you're beautiful. But I've always kept away from beautiful women on account of my long nose . . .

ELSE: Don't be evasive. I know the chariots must be thundering in your heart too . . .

WERNER: *(Breaking away from her)* Please, Frau Schuller . . .

ELSE: I've been talking nonsense again, haven't I? Well, I've been a foolish woman all my life, and yet they say the sky is never so deep as when seen through my babbling . . .

WERNER: You're not foolish, Frau Schuller. You're probably the world's greatest poetess. You're a unique personality. I'm a great admirer. But this kind of intimacy is in . . .

ELSE: *(Impatiently)* Don't humiliate me, Werner . . . *(She grabs him.)* Kiss me . . . kiss me . . . Please. The stars destined me to love, and I love . . . Yes, I love . . .

WERNER: Frau Schuller, I'm a critic . . . a critic and scholar, not a lover. I'm perfectly happy . . . I'm delighted to share my room with you, but you must respect the privacy of my feelings . . .

ELSE: *(Unyieldingly)* I have no one else here but you. In this whole horrible desert, no one . . .

WERNER: *(Angrily)* Frau Schuller, I'm a married man. I have a wife and children in Berlin, although it's been two years since I've heard from them . . . *(He starts to leave.)*

ELSE: *(Hurrying after him)* Werner! Werner! Forgive me . . . *(She grabs hold of him.)* I just suddenly felt so sad. If only you could understand how it hurt . . .

WERNER: I have my own reasons to feel sad.

ELSE: I know . . . Don't go . . .

WERNER: *(Relenting and lighting a cigarette)* These past few days my nightmares have become unbearable. If I were to shed a single tear, it would be followed by a flood . . . They'd have been worse off if I'd stayed, wouldn't they?

ELSE: Of course . . .

WERNER: I wanted to smuggle them out with me, but Gertrud wouldn't hear of it. Until the war I wrote to them every day . . . I begged them to join me . . .

ELSE: They're perfectly well, Werner . . . I know they are . . .

WERNER: *(Adamantly)* Of course they are! *(Pause. Werner puts out his cigarette and sticks the stub in a box.)* I never meant to leave you either, Frau Schuller. You're very dear to me.

ELSE: *(Reading what she wants to in his words and kissing his hands)* There, you see? Your heart is full of love for me! Kiss me . . . kiss me, please . . .

WERNER: Can't you see I'm falling apart right in front of you?

(Else embraces him. He tears himself away.)

WERNER: Can't you realize that all I can think about is the morphine in my pocket?

(Werner leaves. Else hesitates for a moment, then hurries after him.)

ELSE: Werner! Your coat!

(But Werner is already gone. She returns to the room and sits down. She is cold. She gets up and puts the coat on.)

SCENE 2

(Morning. Else is sleeping in Werner's chair with his coat on. Werner enters. His clothes are wet and he is shaking from the cold. He sees her in his coat and is furious. Quietly, he goes to look for dry clothes and finds some near her chair. He takes off his trousers. She wakes up.)

ELSE: Werner?

WERNER: *(Quickly putting on the dry trousers before she can see him in his underwear)* Guten Morgen, Frau Schuller. You must be very warm in my coat . . .

ELSE: I looked everywhere for you last night. I went to the Café Europa and the Café Zichel and the Café Atara—from there I ran to the railway station . . .

WERNER: *(Angrily)* I was out walking on the Friedrichstrasse . . .

ELSE: *(Almost believing him)* You were walking on the Friedrichstrasse?

WERNER: And I'm going to have a glass of tea before I have to go back there . . .

ELSE: *(Handing him a sheaf of papers)* Look, Werner: ancient pearls and crystal, diamonds hidden in dust. I was sitting here in the dark when I suddenly saw them glitter. *(She reads aloud.)*

ELSE: I have chosen you
Under all the stars.
And lie awake—an eavesdropping flower
In the buzzing leaves
Our lips would make honey.
Our shimmering nights have broken into bloom.
My heart lights its sky
From your body's blissful gleam.
My dreams hang on your gold.
I have chosen you under all the stars.

WERNER: "Secretly by Night." You wrote it in 1910!

ELSE: For the King of Bavaria. How I loved him! *(She shows him some more sheets.)* And here are poems I wrote for Georg Grosz and Franz Werfel. I loved them too . . .

WERNER: You did all this tonight??!

ELSE: *Ja, Ja* . . .

WERNER: Even poets cried when you read this in the Grossenwahn Café . . .

ELSE: And the more they cried, the more coins they threw in my hat. *(They laugh.)* I was the richest beggar in Berlin . . . Do you remember how I used to stand like a scarecrow in the fountain in the Alexanderplatz and let the birds land on my wet felt hat? *(They laugh.)*

WERNER: We've got *The Hebrew Ballads* you found at Buber's, the postcard from Agnon, the blue piano poems you've written here . . . and now these too . . . it's a book! A thin book, but a book . . . I can write an afterword, and perhaps you'll add a few sketches—it's practically ready for the printer . . . we'll give another poetry recital too . . .

ELSE: *(Taking his hands in hers)* Are you happy, Werner? Do you really like my poems? I traveled a long way back in time to dig up these treasures for you . . .

WERNER: Frau Schuller . . .

ELSE: No, no, Werner . . . I'm sorry if my poems are an illustrated map of my soul . . . that my inmost caves are open to you . . .

WERNER: *(Interrupting her)* Frau Schuller . . . I don't want to have to sleep out-of-doors again . . .

ELSE: I won't say another word. I'll sit here quietly. *(She sits.)* You won't hear one more bit of nonsense from me. Even the angels will be amazed by my silence . . . Aren't you proud of me for being so quiet?

WERNER: Marvelous. *(He tries removing his coat from her. She doesn't let him get near her hump and slips out of it by herself.)* And now I'm off to Dvir Publishers. *Auf wiedersehen! (He leaves. Else kisses him on the mouth and bursts out laughing at her triumph.)*

ELSE: *(After him)* My dreams hang on your gold!

SCENE 3

(Werner's room. Werner enters, hiding an ice cream cone behind his back.)

ELSE: I'm keeping quiet, Werner. I haven't said a word since you left. I've been waiting for hours in absolute silence . . .

WERNER: *(Grinning)* I could hear you keeping quiet from the bottom of the stairs. It had me worried. *(He shows her the ice cream and announces)* Ice cream! Vanilla fudge with cherry and chocolate!

ELSE: Cherry and chocolate? . . . *(She reaches out for the cone.)*

WERNER: *(Holding it at arm's length and declaiming)* Vanilla . . . like in Berlin . . . *(Else tries again.)* No, no. I want a poem first.

ELSE: Werner . . .

WERNER: At least a stanza.

ELSE: *(Unable to contain herself)* Werner!

WERNER: Not bad . . . let's have another line . . .

ELSE: Werner . . .

WERNER: *(As if quoting her)* "Werner, Werner, Werner . . ." Would you call that expressionistic? Surrealistic? Dada?

ELSE: *(Suddenly suspicious)* They don't want to publish my book, do they?

WERNER: Of course they do . . . We even set a date . . .

ELSE: When?

WERNER: *(After a slight hesitation)* In a few months . . . Frau Schuller, your ice cream . . . "Werner, Werner, Werner" . . .

ELSE: *(Anxiously)* They said they're not interested in my poems . . .

WERNER: Not at all.

ELSE: That they're muddled expressions of a feeble mind. That for the healthy Hebrew people they're just morbid flights of fancy . . .

WERNER: Nothing of the sort.

ELSE: Just like the Nazis wrote about me in *Der Stürmer!*

WERNER: *(Offering her the ice cream)* How could you even think such a thing? Yours are among the most lyrical poems being written anywhere today . . . They suggested translating them into Hebrew. They just need time to look for a translator . . .

ELSE: Translating them?

WERNER: I told them I would have to discuss it with the poet.

ELSE: But didn't you promise that you would never let anyone peck out the eyes of my poems? . . . *(She drops the ice cream.)*

WERNER: Frau Schuller, that ice cream cost me my whole fortune.

ELSE: I'm not the gullible old fool you take me for, Werner.

WERNER: Frau Schuller . . .

ELSE: I still have eyes and ears. And I understand everything. Did you think I could be seduced with an ice cream? You were the only friend I had here. *(She goes to pack her suitcase.)*

WERNER: *(Now desperate)* We have to translate these poems into Hebrew. No one is going to publish them in German . . .

ELSE: No, Werner . . .

WERNER: We have no choice. If you're my friend, you have to compromise. For your own sake—and for mine.

ELSE: Absolutely not!

WERNER: Frau Schuller, for three years I've been running around the streets of this city selling perfume. Is that what I came here for? Your book is my one chance to stake an intellectual claim here . . .

ELSE: I'll publish it in Switzerland . . .

WERNER: It has to be published here, and in Hebrew, so that I can write something for it. Anything—an introduction, an afterword, notes, anything at all . . . if not with one publisher, then with another . . .

ELSE: Poets are truth-tellers, Werner. I would have gone to any lengths for you, had you only told me the truth. But you've deceived me . . . you've betrayed me like all the other Jews in Jerusalem. The day will yet come when you'll tear out my soul to get some appointment at the university . . . *(She finishes packing her suitcase.)*

WERNER: Where will you go? Please, Frau Schuller, be reasonable. Put down that suitcase. You were expelled from Switzerland—you'll never be allowed back . . .

ELSE: Jerusalem should have been entrusted to poets, not to ordinary Jews. That's why it's such a mean place. I will not be stoned by the city for whose sake I have written all my life . . .

WERNER: I shouldn't have gone to Dvir. It was a mistake. They were the wrong publisher. I admit it. I'm sorry. They think you have to come from Russia to be a poet. We should go to Schocken. Herr Schocken is a good German Jew. He knows your reputation.

ELSE: There is no place for a poet in Jerusalem. If King David came and offered his psalms to Dvir, or Solomon his songs, they'd be thrown out on their ear . . .

WERNER: Frau Schuller . . . Please. A little patience. The audience for your poetry is right here in Jerusalem . . . Or else in Dachau . . .

ELSE: I'm an old woman, Werner. I can't wait any longer . . . I want to go home . . .

WERNER: *(Holding her hands)* You have no home. The home you had is destroyed . . .

ELSE: It's hard for me here, Werner.

WERNER: It will be far harder without you . . .

ELSE: *(Cradling her cheeks in his palms)* I walked up King George Street today in the rain that God cried, and I didn't see any angels. The sky was empty . . .

WERNER: *(Moving away from her)* Even when this war is over, there'll be nowhere else to go. If there are still angels in the world, this is the place to look for them . . .

ELSE: *(Taking hold of him again)* Werner . . .

WERNER: *(Moving away once more)* You need to rest a little and calm down . . .

ELSE: *(Fiercely)* I don't want to calm down, Werner! I want you to love me . . . I want someone on this earth to love me. Hold me! *(She embraces him.)*

WERNER: Frau Schuller, I beg you . . . You can't flirt with everyone in Jerusalem . . . The mayor himself has declared you unwelcome in his office because of the eyes you make at him . . .

ELSE: I do not!

WERNER: Everyone at the town hall saw you pinch his cheek . . .

ELSE: That's a lie! You're the only one I love . . . *(She kisses him on the face and mouth.)* Here, take my poems . . . do what you want with them . . .

WERNER: *(Struggling to break free and losing his temper)* You can't seduce me with your poems. What do you take me for? Don't you ever touch me again! Don't ever come near me . . . *(Hastily gathering a few of his things)* Your writing gives you no rights over me . . . I warned you . . .

ELSE: *(Adamantly)* Don't do it for the poems, Werner. Do it for me.

WERNER: *(Pushing her away)* Leave me alone! I still love women. Yes. I still want women. But I'm not so desperate that I have to accept your advances . . . Good-bye, Frau Schuller. *(He turns and goes.)*

ELSE: I'll help the sun paint your face on all the houses . . . I'll hang your smile from the branches of every tree . . . I want someone on this earth to love me! Werner!! *(Blackout)*

ACT 2
CHAPTER 4
SCENE I

(Werner's new room, which looks even poorer and more threadbare than his old one. Werner sits in his underwear by the table, soaking his feet in a bucket of water. Else suddenly enters.)

ELSE: *Guten Tag,* Herr Werner Doktor Hermann!

WERNER: *(Surprised)* Guten Tag, Frau Schuller . . . *(He rises politely.)*

ELSE: So, here you are at last!

WERNER: I've always been here . . .

ELSE: I waited a whole year for you to visit me, but you never came . . .

WERNER: I meant to visit you. I really did . . .

ELSE: You meant to? *(Surveying the room)* What a sad room this is, Werner! How empty and gray . . .

WERNER: This past year has been a self-portrait in black and white, Frau Schuller . . . *(Else laughs. He shows her a bundle of manuscripts.)* I managed to translate my never-to-be-published book on Goethe into Hebrew and I've begun to talk like him . . .

ELSE: You look at the world through merely human eyes, while I see its reflection in the running water . . . I think you urgently need some of your old chief's magic prairie tea . . . What a tiny window . . .

WERNER: Did you find my new address reflected in the running water too?

ELSE: What an idea! . . . The other day I was taking the river route through the jungle on my way to darkest Chicago when a sudden flash of lightning revealed your smiling ox-face . . .

WERNER: *(Bellowing)* Moo . . . moo . . . *(They both laugh.)* Will plain local tea be good enough for *meine Dame?*

ELSE: *Nein, danke! (She peers behind the bed.)* I see, Herr Doktor, that you still haven't found any plain local woman . . .

WERNER: The local women seem to prefer local men . . .

ELSE: *(Taking heart)* You'll never guess what made the angels bring me to your abode, Werner . . .

WERNER: *(Ironically)* Perhaps they discovered how much I missed you.

ELSE: Doctor Spitzer at Tarshish Books is putting out a volume of my new poems. Your introduction will be the golden bridge which the pilgrims cross to the true Promised Land. *(She hands him the manuscript.)*

WERNER: *(Looking at it with emotion) My Blue Piano* . . . And Spitzer is going to publish it like this . . . in German?

ELSE: *(Excitedly) Ja, ja* . . . In German . . . *(He kisses her. She kisses him back. He pulls away.)*

WERNER: In happier times we'd have lit up the Friedrichstrasse with fireworks and rung all the bells of the Kaiser Wilhelm Church. I will be delighted to write an introduction, *meine Dame*. And if you care to leave the manuscript with me for a day or two, I'll write an afterword . . . a bridge for the pilgrims to return by . . .

ELSE: Can I also leave you a few other belongings for safekeeping?

WERNER: Yes, yes of course, Frau Schuller . . . *(She exits. He reads one of the poems out loud.)*

If only I could go home.

The lights go out,

Out goes their last farewell.

Where now?

Oh, mother, do you know?

Our garden too is dead.

I have no sisters, no, nor brothers, anymore.

Winter played with Death in all the nests,

And frost killed off the many songs of love.

(As Werner absorbs the pain expressed by the poem, he grows sad. A minute later Else reappears, dragging her suitcase behind.)

ELSE: It's just for a few days, Werner, until I find a new room . . .

WERNER: *(Flabbergasted)* What was the matter with the room I left you?

ELSE: The landlord came with his Gestapo gang. They grunted and groaned and chased away the birds who lived on the window sill . . .

WERNER: Frau Schuller, it was a comfortable, quiet, inexpensive room right in the middle of town . . .

ELSE: It was a dark, dank room, Werner, and I loathed it . . .

WERNER: If *meine Dame* can afford more luxurious quarters, who am I to object? I'll be glad to look after your things in the meantime. *(Else turns to go. He stops her.)* And if you have nowhere else to go, you can always stay here. Until you find another room.

ELSE: You're very generous, Herr Werner Doktor Hermann, but I already have many kind offers of accommodation. Buber and Agnon have both asked me to stay with them . . .

WERNER: I'm rarely here at night. I'm working night shifts in a bakery. It's only temporary. I start teaching at the university in the spring . . .

ELSE: *(Ironically)* Why, how marvelous, Werner . . .

WERNER: And as for my afterword, I can already see the opening. "These poems express the destruction of an entire spiritual world. 'Our garden too is dead . . . Winter has played with Death in every nest'—here you have the clean, simple essence of Horror, a drop of pure blood on a white cloth."

ELSE: You keep talking and talking, and you haven't even asked me to stay yet . . .

WERNER: *(Realizing she is right and clearing his throat)* I would like you, Frau Schuller, to stay here. *(She puts down her suitcase.)* As a matter of fact, it was rather sad without you. I really did miss you . . . truly . . . if you've paid the landlord for this month's rent, you can ask for it back . . .

ELSE: I haven't paid him for a year, the swine. This morning I sneaked into his kitchen and took a fork, a spoon, and a cup . . . *(She takes them from her dress pocket.)*

WERNER: What, no tablecloth?

(She shows him tablecloth too. Werner breaks into a shrill laugh.)

SCENE 2

(The scene changes suddenly to the Atara Café on Ben-Yehuda Street. Noises from the street mingle with the conversations of the customers and the music of a saxophone. Werner serves Else a cup of tea.)

WERNER: A lonely ship sails down the Rhein
Sails straining toward the sea.
Seventy sailors pull its oars,
Bringing you your tea.

ELSE: You sing like Kurt Weill, Werner . . . he's just a little hoarser. *(She sings in a grotesquely hoarse voice.)* "Surabaya Johnny . . . how you hurt me so? Surabaya Johnny . . . God, I love you so . . ."

WERNER: Weill once told me that song was a variation of "Kol Nidrei." His father, you know, was the cantor of a synagogue in Dessau . . .

ELSE: *(To the tune of "Surabaya Johnny")* "*Kol Nidre-e-e-i ve'esorei . . .*" Take that damn pipe out of your mouth! *(They both laugh.)* If only we were in Berlin now, I'd put a chair on my table at the Grossenwahn, sit, open my new book, and read. And Herr Albert Professor Einstein would stand behind me and accompany me on his violin. He's always very excited, Herr Albert, when I give birth to a new book . . . Do you know what Herr Sigmund Professor Freud will say when he reads it?

WERNER: *(Mimicking Freud)* "Frau Lasker-Schüller's Oriental delusions stand in total contradiction to the psychoanalytic concept of the subconscious, which is why I consider them mere hallucinations . . ." *(He laughs shrilly.)*

ELSE: No, no, no, Werner. He'll cough a bit because of his throat cancer, and sigh: "You are a transparent woman, Frau Schüller. The curtains of your soul fly in the breeze like swallows. Would you do me the great kindness of stretching out on my couch?" *(She laughs.)* Did you hear that, Werner? Dirty old man! That's what he said each time I sent him a new book . . . "Would you stretch out on my couch?" *(They both laugh.)*

WERNER: Did you know that he died in London three years ago?

ELSE: Sigmund died? It's not possible. Stubborn old men like him never die. But if they buried him alive, we'll send a copy to the cemetery . . . We'll send another to Pope Pius, and a third to Mussolini. Did you know how wild the Duce is about me? He invited me to eat *gelato* with him in Rome. *Una grande cassata.* Just last week I wrote to him about my wonderful plan to end the war . . .

WERNER: You wrote to Mussolini?

ELSE: Yes. I sent him a recipe for strudel. Peace strudel. If he and Churchill sat down together over some strudel . . .

WERNER: And is the Fuhrer wild about you too? *(They laugh.)*

ELSE: *(She wedges a strip of paper between her nose and upper lip and sings, mimicking Hitler.)*

Ja. Jawohl. Let them eat strudel.

Und give each Frau a poodle,

And swastikas we'll doodle

From Moscow to the Rhein.

And you, Herr Doktor Noodle,

Please take a piece of kugel . . . *(They laugh.)*

ELSE: And I hereby appoint you, Herr Doktor, National Critic of German Poetry—in perpetuity.

WERNER: Shhh . . . *(He tries to check his laughter.)* I still haven't got my university appointment . . . *(She goes on laughing.)* And if some professor should see me now, I won't get it either . . .

ELSE: *Heil!* . . . *(They both laugh.)*

(Else puts the chair on the table, climbs up and sits on it. She pulls out her book from her dress.)

WERNER: *(Introducing her)* Ladies and Gentlemen, I give you Frau Else Lasker-Schuller at the Café Atara! . . .

(Else's laughter vanishes as she opens the book. As soon as she reads the first line, Werner is struck dumb too.)

ELSE: "I Know"

I know that soon I must die,

Yet all the trees are radiant

After the longed-for kiss of July—

My dreams have grown pale with time—

Never have I drawn so dark an end

In my books of rhyme.

You break off a flower to greet me—

I loved it already in the bud.

Yet I know that soon I must die.

My breath hovers over God's river—
Softly I set my foot
On the path to my eternal home.

(Werner helps her down into a second chair standing on the floor.)

SCENE 3

(Else sits silently by the table in Werner's room. Werner is setting the table. He spreads a newspaper for a tablecloth and puts two plates, one spoon, and one fork on it.)

WERNER: Doesn't that smell good? I've fried the croutons, and in a minute we'll have a good German soup made from good Jewish onions. This is a celebration. It's not every day a new book gets published here. *(He puts the spoon down next to her.)* The spoon is for you. You're about to see someone eat soup with a fork for the first time in your life. The next time you have dinner with one of your admirers, steal a soup spoon for me . . . *(He laughs shrilly and goes to fetch the soup pot. In a minute he returns while glancing out the window.)* It's unbelievable! A herd of cows is marching up King George Street. Do you hear that? *(He moos at them and laughs.)* Moo . . . moo . . . just look how proud they are! *(He sets the pot on the table.)* Ah, to be a bull in Jerusalem! *(He laughs.)* Did you know that the Dutch cow has adjusted to Palestine with no problems at all? Who would have thought a cow could be so cosmopolitan? And now why don't you take off your coat and tuck yourself into this napkin. *(Else doesn't respond. Werner takes off her coat. For the first time she makes no attempt to hide her hump. He ties a kind of napkin to her neck and pours the soup. He notices that she is not eating.)* Aren't you hungry? The soup is really good . . .

ELSE: I would like to die, Werner . . .

WERNER: To die, Frau Schuller? Whatever gave you such an idea? Now, of all times, when we've shown them that we can survive . . . that we can go on writing our books no matter where they stick us? At least taste it, please. I made it for you. *(He tries feeding her with the spoon.)* You were so beautiful reading your poem at the café. Your face beamed . . . your eyes shone . . . your voice was as clear and full as a choir of angels. *(He strokes her hands and face.)* Frau Schuller, you're such a precious woman . . . such a dear . . . *(He falls silent for a moment.)* Before, when Jews went into exile, they had to leave their houses and belongings behind, but they could still take their spiritual property. Who else wanted it? This war has robbed us of everything, even of the Spirit . . . *(He is silent.)* The soup is cold already. I forgot all about the flower I picked for you! *(Quotes)* "You break off a flower to greet me. I loved it already in the bud." That's the saddest poem I've ever heard . . . *(He takes a flower from his jacket pocket and gives it to her.)* If only I could express my suffering . . . but I can't. I can't forgive myself . . . how could I have let Gertrud keep the girls? She swore they would be safe with her. She swore! I tried to be logical . . . her parents promised to obtain new birth certificates for them . . . last night I saw them . . . they were running hand in hand chasing pigeons in Goethe Park, in white dresses with ribbons in their hair. *(He sobs.)* I want to live, Frau Schuller. I want to live . . . only to live . . .

(Werner seizes Else and embraces her. She yields. The physical contact between them becomes openly sexual. Werner starts sobbing.)

CHAPTER 5

SCENE 1

(Morning. Else rises, combs her hair, sticks Werner's flower into it, puts on some jewelry, dons her coat, and heads for the door while humming a German children's song. Werner enters, returning from the night shift in the bakery. His hair is unkempt and his face and his hands are sooty. He is tired and in a bad mood.)

ELSE: *(Noticing his blackened face)* Your beautiful lashes are charred—and your eyebrows too . . . your eyes are weeping pearls . . . *(She strokes his face. He pushes her gently away.)* Doesn't my Prince want his face cooled by my kisses?

WERNER: Your prince is in a hurry to get to the University. *(She persists.)* Frau Schuller, I've asked you more than once . . .

ELSE: I've tried keeping all my promises. It's you who . . . *(She stops herself.)* You look so gray I only want to color you red a little.

WERNER: *(Noticing some postcards on the table)* What are those?

ELSE: I'm going to fly some little messages up over the rooftops to tell the pedestrians below about my recital. *(She points to one of them.)* On this one I drew the dream I had the other night about you and me—David and Abigail . . . *(She sticks the cards in her coat pocket.)*

WERNER: I hate to spoil your dreams, but I very much doubt that anyone will be at your recital. *(He takes a newspaper out of his pocket.)* As I was leaving the bakery this morning I looked at last week's *Davar* and thought I would faint. *(He reads quickly.)* "The German Invasion of Palestine. Last week I came across a book of German poems by a new immigrant called Else Lasker-Muller, published by Tarshish Books." Muller! *(He throws the newspaper on the table and lights a cigarette.)* We ran away from one nationalism to fall into the clutches of another!

ELSE: *(Picking up the paper and looking at it while turning it this way and that)* I don't think God reads this newspaper, Werner . . .

WERNER: I'm not God, Frau Schuller. And I do read it. *(He reads)* "Are we so lacking treasures of our own that we must rummage in the garbage thrown out by the anti-Semites?" We laughed at Goebbels and Streicher for asking such questions too, and look where we are now . . .

ELSE: *(Grinning)* If it were me instead of that Muller woman, I'd be tearing my hair out . . .

WERNER: But it *is* you this Polish Yid is writing about! It's your book that he's calling rubbish . . .

ELSE: My name is Schuller . . . Lasker-Schuller, not Lasker-Muller . . .

WERNER: There aren't any poets called Lasker-Muller in Jerusalem . . .

ELSE: *(Still turning the newspaper and examining it)* Is this where he writes about my poems?

WERNER: He doesn't write anything about your poems. They're in German, and this fool refuses to look at a Gothic letter . . . We were driven out of Germany because we're Jews, and here the door is slammed in our face because we're Germans. *(Bitterly)* Only that God of yours still loves us. The doors of His heaven are the only ones still open to us . . . Stefan Zweig killed himself in Brazil. Kurt Tucholski in Sweden. Ernst Toller hanged himself in New York. Walter Benjamin swallowed morphine in Spain. And the list keeps growing . . . *(He grunts with pain as he tries taking off his shoes.)* Everyone in the bakery works barefoot, but I'm the only one who gets blisters. *(He massages the bottoms of his feet.)* Once I stank of soap and perfume, now it's of smoke . . . I can't understand such chauvinism. We were exiled here against our will, and we're not wanted here either. Who knows why I've been summoned to the dean's office today. A few more articles like this and he'll cancel all the German literature courses . . .

ELSE: How can you say I'm not wanted, Werner? Yesterday at the Rex Cinema the man at the kiosk gave me a free chocolate bar. And when I went in everyone applauded and asked me to read my poems . . .

WERNER: *(Belligerently)* I find it hard to believe after what I had to go through to arrange this Saturday's recital.

ELSE: You needn't have bothered. The angels would have done it for me. Just yesterday, as I was walking down Jaffa Street, one of them landed on my shoulder and said: "Dear poet, here are a thousand more years of life for you." And my Paul, he was so annoyed that he said: "Just a thousand? Why, a thousand years are hardly a single day . . ."

WERNER: *(Mockingly)* Your Paul? Your Paul—

ELSE: *(Interrupting him fiercely)* Yes . . . my Paul . . .

WERNER: *(In despair)* Frau Schuller, there are no angels on Jaffa Street. There are nothing but petty, narrow-minded Jews who care only for patriotic marches . . . It's time you faced up to it. No one out there cares about you or your poems . . .

ELSE: You're wrong . . .

WERNER: To date your book has sold a grand total of eleven copies. Four were bought by libraries, five by collectors, and only two by the public. That article has ruined any chance you had of selling more . . .

ELSE: Don't try to be so logical, Werner. We've already seen that nothing is less logical than logic . . .

WERNER: *(Angrily)* I wish I had some other straw to clutch at . . .

ELSE: If you would just look up, you would see the angels sitting in the branches of the cypress trees and playing Kurt Weill's melodies on their flutes . . .

WERNER: Perhaps Chagall can afford to see it that way. Not us.

(Else hums some popular tune and leaves. Werner puts his shoes back on, dons his jacket; he clears his throat and turns to the audience.)

SCENE 2

(A side room in the German synagogue on Shmuel Hanagid Street. Werner addresses the audience in the theatre as if it were the handful of people who have come to hear Else read her poems.)

WERNER: *Guten Abend, meine Damen und Herren,* and my special thanks to our sexton, Herr Kurt Stark, for making this evening possible. Tonight the renowned poet Else Lasker-Schuller will read to us from her new book, *My Blue Piano,* which was published with the generous help of the distinguished Dr. Spitzer. *(He bows to Spitzer.)* I am sure that if only the British had ended the curfew earlier, there would be more of us here to make the acquaintance of this great poet and her poems. Frau Lasker-Schuller, *bitte* . . .

(Else enters, wearing a lace robe and a feather hat. She holds her book and her little silver bell. She bows to the audience, desperately trying to hide her disappointment at its small size. Werner continues.)

If only the British had ended their curfew earlier, there would have been more of us here . . .

ELSE: *(Ignoring him and turning to the audience)* Thank you very much for taking the trouble to come to the heart of Jerusalem to hear my poems. Of course, God would have been happier had a few more of his chosen people troubled themselves, but God's sorrow does not seem to move many people these days. *(She smiles.)* And apropos of God, there's something very, very funny that I must tell you about Him. Naturally, you'll have to keep it a secret. *(In a whisper)* God wears a big ring on His right hand. It's a plain bronze ring, but it's so rough and thick that you can't hold His hand because of it. Do you get me? When he grips the hands of the angels, His ring hurts their fingers so that they scream with pain . . . *(She laughs.)* What a pity there aren't more people here! I'm sure they would have laughed too . . . *(She counts the audience.) Eins, zwei, drei, vier, funf, sechs, sieben* . . . the seven righteous men of Sodom . . . Good evening, Herr Doktor Spitzer . . . *(She laughs again, but at once grows serious.)* I also have something very serious to tell you about Him. *(She points overhead.)* Well, it's not so serious, because God himself isn't as serious as He looks in our paintings of Him. That at least is the opinion of the birds, who are no doubt the closest to Him. Yesterday, by the way, I saw a bird . . . No, that isn't what I wanted to tell you. Yesterday I was looking at the sky and sketching some small children as they rode their sheep through the clouds. They were shouting "Giddyap" when who should look down and fear they might fall but little God Himself . . . And so He ran after them, whistling through a hole in an apricot stone . . . *(She whistles.)* Isn't that something? *(She bursts into loud laughter. Werner steps up to her. She apologizes.)* Yes, yes, just one more little thing and then I'll read. When I gave recitals in the Grossenwahn Café in Berlin, all the other cafés were deserted. Even the whores came to peek through the windows . . . *(She laughs.)* Oof, I shouldn't utter such a word in a synagogue. The rabbi will be angry with me. But I am a poet after all. Or, to be more precise, I am a woman in whom poems happen. That is, the words run around inside me, and I play with them like children with colored buttons. *(Happily)* And when I'm stuck in the middle of a poem, I throw the buttons on the floor and choose my words by how the colors go together . . . *(She laughs.)*

WERNER: Frau Schuller . . . I think you had better start reading . . .

ELSE: Yes, yes. I'll start in a minute, Herr Doktor Spitzer. There's just one more thing I want to say. When I think of Jerusalem and all the people in it, I say to myself: how happy I am to be with you all! How good and cozy you make me feel! How much love you shower on me! If only two or three more of you could have come tonight . . . And now I'll begin. *(She opens her book and reaches for her bell. She looks at the audience, still unable to accept how small it is.)* Herr Albert Professor Einstein once told me that he never played his violin unless he was sure the walls were listening . . . Herr Albert is such a funny man. If I were a bird, I'd sit on his bald patch and weave a nest from his curls . . .

WERNER: Please, can you start reading?

ELSE: *(Laughing)* But I'm starting, can't you see. *(Reads from the book)*
"A Prayer"
My God, my heart is filled with pain
So take and cup it in your hands
Till the evening sun has set again
In time and Nature's ordered plan.

(She can't go on and is silent for a moment.)

One more little thing . . . if anyone here has any golden sweet wrappers . . . anything bright or shiny . . . please let me have them. I can make wonderful flowers out of them. My Paul colors them and we sell them for ten *pfennings* apiece . . . *(She begins to weep.)* and for five *pfennings* more, I'll autograph the petals . . .

(Werner sees she has lost control of herself and hurries to her side.)

WERNER: Frau Schuller . . . perhaps you need to rest a bit . . . *(He takes her hands.)*

ELSE: *(Angrily)* I'm reading my poems . . .

WERNER: Frau Schuller . . . Perhaps you'd like to sit down for a minute . . .

ELSE: *(Venting all her frustration on him)* Let go of me, you pig . . . I haven't finished . . . you're driving away my audience . . . it's your fault no one came . . .

WERNER: Frau Schuller . . .

ELSE: Mind your own business, you pest of a critic . . . you literary parasite, you!

WERNER: The recital is over, ladies and gentlemen . . .

ELSE: *(To the audience)* This heartless man abandoned his daughters back there.

WERNER: Stop it!

ELSE: He cared only for saving his own neck, the worm . . .

WERNER: Stop it!!

ELSE: Imagine . . . two little girls . . . abandoned . . . alone with the pigeons in Berlin . . .

WERNER: Stop it!!!

(He seizes her and claps his hand over her mouth. She goes limp and loses consciousness. He carries her to bed. He stands looking at her for a moment, checks her breathing, and leaves.)

SCENE 3

(Else is lying in bed in Werner's room. Out in the street the children are singing a jeering song about her. Werner enters.)

CHILDREN: Else the whore
Is Hitler's wife!
If you see her,
Run for your life . . .

(The children's voices fade away.)

ELSE: I don't know how to apologize, Werner. You're as dear to me as my own Paul . . .

WERNER: I have to go to the bakery . . . *(He changes into his work clothes without out caring whether she looks at him.)*

ELSE: I'm sorry for saying what I did, Werner. You've been a wonderful father to your girls. I know how you worry about them.

WERNER: *(Ironically)* You were a wonderful mother to Paul, too. It's not your fault he caught tuberculosis . . .

ELSE: Don't hurt me so . . .

WERNER: You don't hurt me? *(There is a brief pause.)*

ELSE: You're not going to forgive me, are you?

WERNER: No.

ELSE: *(Mollifyingly)* You know, Werner, I thought that if the book doesn't do well, we can always open a little fun-fair in Talbiya, across from the leper hospital . . . A fun-fair would be something holy and precious. We could rent donkeys for tourists to ride to the Old City on. For five *pfennings* a ride . . . what do you think?

WERNER: *(Sarcastic)* That's a wonderful idea, Frau Schuller . . . I can't begin to tell you how excited I am.

ELSE: I knew you'd love it . . .

WERNER: I sincerely hope you manage to earn a living from it, because I can barely earn one for myself.

ELSE: There'll be a huge carousel. The Grand Mufti of Jerusalem can ride with the Princes of the Jewish Agency, and there will be peace.

WERNER: *(Unable to keep his anger from showing)* That's a wonderful dream too . . .

ELSE: I love you so, Werner. I'll carry you in my teeth like a jaguar through the jungle . . .

WERNER: Frau Schuller . . .

ELSE: Forgive me for talking to you in poetry, but it's the tenderest way to show you my soul . . .

WERNER: *(Impatiently)* Frau Schuller, I'm begging you. You're a very profound woman. You live every minute of your life with a poetic intensity that is too much for me. Werner Hermann is a simple, shallow, superficial creature. My soul lacks the depths of yours. I really am the literary parasite you said I was . . .

ELSE: You are an Indian Prince and I'm your . . .

WERNER: *(Desperate)* Please . . . you promised . . .

ELSE: I'm a nymph floating down the river on water lilies . . .

WERNER: You're not a nymph . . . and I'm begging you to leave me alone. I have nowhere left to escape from you . . .

ELSE: If we embrace each other, we won't die . . . *(She seizes him.)*

WERNER: *(Exploding furiously)* I can't embrace. You . . . Anybody. I have no love left. If I ever had any, you killed it with your own hands . . . with your insanity . . . it's time you took a good look at what you've done to me . . . *(Quoting)* "At home I have a blue piano, But have no note to play." I have no culture left. I have no love left. You've drained me dry. I've become an abyss of hatred and despair. I've become a reflection of the world we live in, every bit as crude, as cruel, and as vile as it is . . . but no, that's not true . . . I was always like this. They made a terrible mistake about me back there. I'm a German, just like everyone says I am. I was born in Germany. May 10th 1902. I lived there all my life. I'm as German as the German butcher in the German butcher's shop and the German grocer in the German grocery and the German barman in the German beer cellar. I never had any other home or language. If they'd have accepted me in their party, I'd have marched in the streets with them, and sieg-heiled with them, and burned synagogues and stoned Jews with them . . . I would have clubbed you just like they did . . .

ELSE: *(Holding him and trying to calm him)* Werner . . . my little Paulchen . . .

WERNER: I'm not your Paulchen! Paul was a miserable, sickly Jew and I'm a German . . . I hate Jews and poets . . . I can't stand their vileness and their poetry . . . and I can't stand you . . . no, I can't stand you either. *(He pounces on her suitcase.)* Out!! I want you out of here right now! Out before I throw you out with my own hands! I'll show no mercy . . . you're nothing but an ugly old hunchbacked Jewess! Your Paul would still be alive if you had taken care of him. Out!!!

(There is a long pause. Else picks up her suitcase and starts to leave. Werner takes out a pack of cigarettes, discovers that it is empty, and flings it irately on the floor. Suddenly, struck by how terribly pathetic Else is, he caves in and changes his mind.)

WERNER: Come back! Come back! I'll go. The children will chase you and throw stones. *(He takes her suitcase.)* No, no. I'm just a weak, spoiled Jew myself who was kicked out of his own home. It's time I faced it. I didn't mean to hurt you. You're very dear to me. I have no one else but you, either. *(He chokes on his tears, which he tries to hide from her.)* I'd better go out for a walk. I should have been at the bakery by now anyway. *(He hurries out.)*

(The steps leading up to Werner's room. A winter afternoon. From afar the muezzin's call to prayer rises above the sounds of the street. Else stands on the steps talking to a droopy-winged lark. She has clearly aged and looks shockingly weak.)

ELSE: I'll wear the blue straw bonnet with a green feather . . . I'll hold my arms out . . . and stand on one leg, looking up at the sky . . . and you, my love, will flutter over me, and chase away the flies. *(She laughs.)* Peck away, you clever little lark, peck away . . . And I'll stick a flower in my hump. Just imagine, a hunchbacked Jewish scarecrow with a lily blooming out of it. *(She laughs.)* And if the British come, I'll scare them away, pssst, pssst, pssst. And if Hitler comes, I'll hiss right in his face, hsss, hsss, hsss . . . Schicklegruber . . . *(She laughs.)*

(Werner enters.)

WERNER: Frau Schuller, you're making a laughingstock of yourself in front of all the neighbors. And you're making one of me, too. You promised to stop talking to birds in the street.

ELSE: I didn't start it. The bird did.

WERNER: It's four o'clock . . .

ELSE: It's a pity you didn't hear the legend of the scarecrow he just told me. The scarecrows are a very odd people, Werner . . . and the birds are actually fond of them. Perhaps because of their sadness at having their legs stuck in the ground . . .

WERNER: *(Interrupting her)* I can't stand how pathetic you've become . . .

ELSE: I just wanted to make you laugh . . .

WERNER: I beg you try to keep your sanity, that's all . . . because if you lose it, I'll lose mine too . . .

ELSE: *(Insulted)* Why should you lose your sanity? *(He sneezes.)* Gesundheit!

WERNER: Don't you know I'm allergic to birds? And what are you doing here anyway? Professor Buber is waiting for us . . .

ELSE: If you hadn't started arguing with me, we'd be chatting in his living room right now . . .

WERNER: Please, forget the bird . . . *(He frightens it away.)*

ELSE: Not this one. He's the reincarnation of my Paul . . .

WERNER: He's not your Paul. Your merciful God was kind enough to kill Paul with tuberculosis fifteen years ago . . .

ELSE: That's not true. We listen to the "Barcarelle" every night . . .

WERNER: I wish He were as kind to us . . . And leave your scarves and chains behind too. You'll have to try to look civilized . . . *(He helps take off her scarves.)*

ELSE: What's wrong with this one?

WERNER: Please don't argue. *(He helps her out of it.)* When we get to Professor Buber's, you're to sit opposite him in a chair, cross your arms, and let me do the talking. All you have to say is that Doktor Hermann is one of Europe's leading literary scholars and an expert on the libraries of Frankfurt and Berlin . . .

ELSE: Doktor Hermann is one of Europe's leading literary scholars and an expert on the libraries of Frankfurt and Berlin . . .

WERNER: Good!

(She takes a scarf that Werner has removed from her neck and tries putting it on again.)

WERNER: *(Removing the scarf)* Frau Schuller, I asked you . . .

ELSE: What's wrong with this scarf?

WERNER: You must also say that Doktor Hermann is the most suitable candidate for the available position of assistant librarian at the university . . .

ELSE: Doktor Hermann is the most suitable candidate for . . .

WERNER: . . . the available position of assistant librarian at the university . . .

ELSE: . . . the available position of assistant librarian at the university . . .

WERNER: And that's all

ELSE: And that's all

WERNER: I don't want you saying anything else . . .

ELSE: Nothing else . . .

WERNER: And keep your hands away from his cheeks . . .

ELSE: His cheeks? I never laid a hand on his cheeks!

WERNER: I know. I'm just taking precautionary measures. And don't try to walk off with his ashtray . . .

ELSE: Since when do I walk off with people's ashtrays?

WERNER: *(Impatiently)* I have the distinct impression that you took an ashtray of Buber's once before . . .

ELSE: I did not!

WERNER: . . . that I then had to return. *(He gathers up the scarves and chains and goes to put them away.)*

ELSE: *(Angrily)* It was you who took that ashtray! You've been taking things from me too . . . you go through my pockets and steal my jewelry . . .

WERNER: Frau Schuller . . .

ELSE: Oh, no, you don't . . . don't touch me! Don't touch me! Just who do you think you are, ordering me to sit there with my arms crossed? *(She takes a chain back.)*

WERNER: I didn't order you. I asked you . . . *(He seizes her hand.)* And now I'm asking you to put down that chain.

ELSE: I will not!

WERNER: *(Angrily)* Do you want me to go on working in the damn bakery until hell freezes over?

(Werner grabs the chain and throws it on the floor. Else backs away in fright.)

ELSE: Don't touch me . . . you want to choke me . . . I know you do . . .

WERNER: Frau Schuller . . . you'd better go home. To hell with Buber. It's going to rain soon . . .

ELSE: No, no . . . I'll never find the way without you . . .

WERNER: Frau Schuller . . .

ELSE: The landlady will hit me with her broom . . . she's crazy . . . this whole city is full of crazy people speaking a foreign language I can't understand . . .

WERNER: It's called Hebrew . . .

ELSE: You're not leaving me all alone in the dark . . .

WERNER: There's nothing to be afraid of. I'll take you home and light the oil lamp for you . . .

ELSE: You're lying, Werner! You'll dump me on the way . . . I know you will . . .

WERNER: Frau Schuller . . .

ELSE: You'll let the children throw stones at me . . .

WERNER: I don't understand what I'm doing here with you . . . I simply don't understand . . . *(He tries to go.)*

ELSE: Just write a few more lines, Werner . . . *(She holds out a tattered paper and gestures to him to write on it.)* My fingers hurt so much . . .

WERNER: I'm asking you to leave me alone!

ELSE: *(Stubbornly)* I can't hold the pencil. I'll tell you what to write . . .

WERNER: Well, I've had enough of your writing.

ELSE: Don't you believe that the riddle of life can be solved by poetry?

WERNER: *(Angrily)* No!! *(He throws the paper on the ground.)*

(Else is thunderstruck. She can't pick up the paper. She is trembling. Werner takes off his coat and drapes it over her shoulders.)

ELSE: I've been running after you through the streets for the last two days, bleeding poetry for you . . .

WERNER: Leave me alone, Frau Schuller . . . leave me alone . . .

ELSE: There's a rose blooming between my thighs, Werner . . . a soft, tender rose . . .

WERNER: *(Trying to maintain control)* You're making my life hell . . . can't you understand that? Do I have to put you in an asylum? Do you want me to stick my head in the oven at the bakery? To swallow morphine? Is that what you want?!

(He tears himself away and walks off. Else picks up the paper. She tries to follow him but cannot make her legs obey her. She is panic-stricken.)

ELSE: Goddie? Where are you? Come out. Coo-coo . . . Goddie? Where are you? Come out . . . *(She runs into some children who taunt her.)* No, no. Let me be, children. Let me be . . . Goddie? Coo-coo . . . Where are you? I said let me be, you little bastards . . . *(Stones begin to fly at her. She tries to protect herself. Her forehead is bleeding.)* Not with the stones of Jerusalem, you bastards, not with the stones of Jerusalem! *(She tries to flee but cannot walk. She collapses and starts to crawl.)* Goddie? Goddie? . . . Coo-coo . . . Where are you? Come out . . . where are you? *(No one answers. Gripped by terror, she continues crawling.)* Oh, God, open the door . . .

(She crawls this way and that until, sobbing hysterically, she reaches her bed in Werner's room, which she is too weak to get onto.)

SCENE 2

(The noise of the street fades away. Else is alone in the room, sprawled at the foot of the bed and panting heavily. Werner enters, holding his suitcase. He sees her and rushes over.)

WERNER: Frau Schuller . . . *(He puts her in bed and spreads his coat over her. She shows no resistance.)* I'm sorry I left you, but you make it impossible for me to stay. I've slept the last three nights on a park bench, but I'm not giving anyone the pleasure of watching me die of pneumonia. *(He opens his suitcase and takes out a cake.)* A sponge cake. I stole it from the bakery. Like the rest of them . . .

(Werner offers her some cake. She does not respond and her breathing grows heavier. He bends down to look at her.)

You should eat something . . . you should take better care of yourself . . . do you hear me? Paris has been liberated . . . the trains are running from Marseilles . . . we'll start out for Haifa today! We'll be on the deck of the first ship to sail. You have to be strong for the trip . . . we don't want any complications . . . is that clear? No complications! You can stay with me in Paris until you get back on your feet. We'll get in touch with Gertrud when we get there. They're alive, Gertrud and the girls. They're still alive, aren't they? *(He takes the bag of morphine from his pocket.)* If we spend one more night here, I'm going to swallow this damned poison . . . *(He goes over to the window.)* In Paris I can jump into the Seine . . .

(Werner lifts his hand as if to pour out the morphine. Suddenly he stops and looks at Else, whose loud breathing has stopped. He puts the bag down on the table and hurries over to her.)

Frau Schuller? . . . Frau Schuller? . . . What's the matter? Answer me! Frau Schuller? *(He hugs her.)* Else . . . Else . . . Else? *(He notices the tattered page in her hand, takes it, looks at it, and reads it.)*
I'm so sad beyond all measure
I who once sat on the branches
Full of joyous song.
O God, how should my lament move you
Since so many people on earth Carry their deep burden
And Children are starving at all doors.
The need is great. I know.
Therefore my lips should be silent.

(It is suddenly dark.)

ASHER'S COMMAND

by Marilyn Clayton Felt

Asher's Command. J. Howard Wood Theatre production, Sanibel, Florida, 2002. Pictured are Robert Schelhammer (left) and Dan Harvey. Photograph by Michael Pistella, *Island Reporter,* Sanibel.

In December of 1987, my first play, *Acts of Faith,* was in rehearsal at New York's 92nd Street Y for a production by the small, new, experimental Mosaic Theater. Since this was a play about an Arab terrorist and his Jewish American captive, there was an underlying anxiety that the theme might alienate the audience, primarily Jewish subscribers with traditional tastes. As opening night neared, we followed the news vigilantly, hoping no clash in the occupied territories would occur to heighten anti-Arab sentiment.

This Israeli news watch became an addiction, so that several months later, when the first intifada broke out, I absorbed every detail. Most intriguing was the emergence of a young general appointed commander of the West Bank occupation, who showed a surprising regard for the human dignity of the "locals" (as they were called then).

The general was treading a narrow path between security and humanity, and in the third month of his command, an incident erupted that forced his hand. A Jewish settlement on the West Bank sent its children on the traditional Passover walk of "the length and breadth of the land" in the midst of the intifada. They obeyed no security precautions, as if tempting an incident to happen. The result was a clash in an Arab village that caused the death of a girl from the settlement, as well as the deaths of village youths; the commanding general had no choice but to punish the villagers, using the method, established in British times, of the demolition of homes.

As news reports brought out the details, a second character emerged, a village man who had protected some Jewish youths from the rage of his village. His explanation was, "They were children." The next day it was reported that his home had been among those demolished, a tragic mistake of the army.

The events unfolded like a Greek tragedy. Weighed down by history, feuds, and prophecies, the nature of the Middle East conflict seemed epitomized in this incident and in the downfall of its central character, the humane young general.

The incident and fates of these two men brought me to Israel and the West Bank for six weeks. I interviewed people at the Jewish settlement and the Arab village; I met the young general, but I never did meet the villager who protected the young settlers. People in the village told me frankly that acknowledging that some villagers "protected the settlers" was tantamount to admitting that the settlers had been in danger at the hands of the villagers.

The two men became the characters Asher and Samir, for whom I created a friendship from youth. In successive drafts the actual incident came to occupy less and less time as the relationship itself came to dominate the play. Both are men of noble intentions, both are "protagonist" and "antagonist." I have been surprised to find little precedent in political theatre in which hero and villain are not clearly marked as such.

To my sorrow, this play makes some Jewish audiences angry. I think it likely that the anger and sense of threat come from seeing Jews on stage who do not fit the image of the underdog. The Jews in this play are in power and face the same moral dilemmas faced by all people in power—how to protect one's own without oppressing others. The protagonists face the timeless dilemma that emerges when care for "the other" conflicts with loyalty to the tribe. Jewish moral sense is at the base of both these loyalties, deeply rooted in the soul of the general. At the end he finds himself torn apart, a commander with no choices.

Not surprisingly, both Jews and Arabs often think the other is portrayed more favorably in the play. A more serious concern is that Jews worry that the play will reinforce anti-Semitism, a possibility that freezes my heart. Personally, I have not found the raising of controversy to be either an artistic triumph or even a public relations boost.

When you are reading *Asher's Command,* it is important to remember that it is written about earlier times, the late eighties, and though less than twenty years ago, those times were very different. Few Israelis used the word "Palestinian"; even saying it was to take a forbidden position. The word does not appear in the play because it did not appear in the daily dialogue. Also different is the fact that the weapons available to the "locals" in the territories were much less lethal than they are today.

I think that what I want the play to say, as Asher does, is that all life needs to find a place between extremes. While adversity may improve the human spirit by bringing out courage, resourcefulness, protectiveness, and so on, continual threat and hatred can destroy even the noblest of human spirits.

Notes

The NFJC Commission was used toward a weekend series concert readings directed by Ugo N. Toppo and presented at the Rainbow Theatre in Stamford, Connecticut in 1995. The play premiered in 2002 at the J. Howard Wood Theatre in Sanibel, Florida.

Although this play was suggested by an actual incident, all names have been changed and fictional characters have been added.

Time and place: The play takes place in 1988 in the Galilee, and, in recall, during the period from 1970 to 1988 in the occupied West Bank.

Sets: No major set is required. Settings change frequently and should be suggested minimally, with pantomime used to suggest all but the most significant props. An important feature of the staging is lighting, to suggest dawn, hot midday, sunsets, starlight. A backdrop might depict at ground level piles of stones so that they are ever-present and reflect the changing light.

Characters: The two main characters are Asher, an Israeli military officer, and Samir, a Palestinian auto mechanic. In the play's "present time," Asher is in his mid-thirties, Samir mid-forties. Flashbacks take Samir and Asher back as far as eighteen years. In addition to the two main characters, the play requires a supporting cast of three men and three women taking multiple roles.

Supporting Cast Roles

Protesters
Four Reporters
Lila, Asher's wife
The Aide
Tarik, an Arab youth
A Soldier
Two Dancers
A Rabbi
The Chief-of-Staff
Two Village Women
Reuben, a young Jewish man
Rivka, Samir's daughter
Sara, a Jewish youth
Hannah, a Jewish youth
Two Voices-in-the-Dark
A Military Police Officer
Three News Hawkers
An Interrogator
A Doctor
A Sergeant

Supporting Cast Role Assignments

MALE ROLE ASSIGNMENTS

Actor 1 (can play over age forty): the Aide, Chief-of-Staff, a Soldier, Voice-in-the-Dark 1, News Hawker 1

Actor 2 (can play late teens to thirties): Tarik, Reuben, Military Police Officer, Interrogator, News Hawker 2, Reporter 3

Actor 3 (can play over forty): the Rabbi, Voice-in-the-Dark 2, News Hawker 3, Sergeant, Reporter 4

FEMALE ROLE ASSIGNMENTS

Actor 4 (can play thirties to forties): Lila, Doctor

Actor 5 (can play teens and twenties): Reporter 1, Dancer 1, Village Woman 1, Sara, Rivka

Actor 6 (can play teens and twenties): Reporter 2, Dancer 2, Village Woman 2, Hannah

Protesters (can be played by all)

ACT 1

(The Galilee, 1988. A deep red sunset reflects on the stonescape. In silhouette, Asher enters wearily.)

ASHER: The dark is kind. Even in the middle of a war, if it's pitch black—you
    stay in a crevice and you're safe.

(He takes out cigarette and lighter, lights the cigarette.)

There has been a war going on here for as long as anyone can remember. This
    land of stones and olive trees has been soaked with the blood of Hit-
    tites, Canaanites, Assyrians, Babylonians, Crusaders, Turks. Right now
    it's Arabs and Jews. I am one of the Jews. We have our own land, and we
    occupy two small territories that fell to us twenty years ago.

(In the background, shouts of Protesters start to rise. Then camera flashes and TV lights.)

PROTESTERS: *(In the background)* Houses to rubble, peace to dust!

(Lila, Asher's wife, peers out her back door into the night.)

LILA: Asher? When did you get here? . . .

(Lila comes out to join him.)

Come inside. Do you see what's happening out front?
ASHER: I needed to come home . . .
LILA: People are gathering. Come inside.
ASHER: *(Softly)* Not yet.

(The protests and the Reporters' "on-camera live" broadcasts that are going on in front of the house can be heard out back.)

PROTESTERS: Shame on you! Come out and face us! Shame on you! Shame!
REPORTER 1: Camera ready? . . . We are outside the home of the young com-
    mander who was the bright hope of the Labor administration. But—his
    career seems to be the casualty of a tragic clash involving Jewish settlers
    in an Arab village. You can hear the peace protesters all around me.
REPORTER 2: Peace groups demonstrated today from here to Jerusalem asking
    for the ouster of the commander of the West Bank occupation. They are

protesting what they see as an overreaction of the army. Troops punished a West Bank village in such haste that they demolished the home of an Arab man who apparently sheltered some of the Jewish settler children.

PROTESTERS: Houses to rubble! Peace to dust! Shame on him! Come out and face us! Shame! *(The protesters' cries rise and fall.)*

ASHER: You know what would have happened with any other commander?

(Pause)

Any other commander would have blown that village to hell!

LILA: You need some sleep.

ASHER: They sell each other for a shekel.

LILA: Who? . . . Who sells each other for a shekel?

(Silence)

What's this? . . . Looks like blossom petals in your hair . . .

(She shows him the petals, but he does not respond.)

In your hair . . . your collar . . . your cuffs . . . on your boots . . . What are you holding? *(Gently opening his fist)* A sprig of blossoms . . .

(A reporter tiptoes into the yard.)

REPORTER 2: Ma'am, does the general want to make a statement?

LILA: Not tonight. No interviews. This is our home—please go and leave us alone here! Tell the others there'll be no interviews tonight.

(The Reporter backs away.)

PROTESTERS: *(Swelling)* Come out and face us! Shame on you! Houses to rubble! Peace to dust! Shame!

(Lila peers around the house.)

LILA: The reporters are trying to retreat, but they can't get through the protesters. Like trying to part the Red Sea! Hmmm. *(Joking)* I don't know, Asher. I'm used to you inviting people home for dinner without telling me, but this is too much! *(Asher smiles.)* Too much. You tell me, who's going to cook for them tonight—you or me? Let's see . . . that's the peace crowd out there, isn't it . . . Between the veggies and the koshers . . . *(Brightly)*

cheeseburgers should do it . . . Rare cheeseburgers! With bacon. Like holding out a cross to a vampire. They'll all vanish.

ASHER: Lila, you could make a dead man laugh.

LILA: *(Gently) Are* you a dead man?

ASHER: Am I a dead man? Look out front.

LILA: *(Gently)* I didn't mean your career.

ASHER: Am I a dead man?

(Pause)

Just a different man.

LILA: Different from what?

(The protests begin to fade, and as they do they are drowned out by a new sound: a muezzin's call to prayer comes up, distant. [This call to prayer will be heard several times in the play.] Samir appears stage right in a dim spotlight. Only Asher sees him. Samir looks up at the sky, sniffs the air.)

SAMIR: When you're a farmer, you walk out everyday and look up at the sky
and sniff the air for rain. You love the earth. You know everything about
her—her smell, her feel . . .

LILA: *(Gently)* Asher? . . .

ASHER: *(Still talking to Lila, but moving into a different time)* Different from
how I thought I'd be when I was seventeen . . .

SAMIR: *(To Asher)* Are you lost? Young man, are you lost?

(Lila freezes. Asher is seventeen. The year is 1970.)

ASHER: *(To Samir)* No. I'm not at all lost. My car broke down, that's all.

(Lights dim on the backyard. Lila recedes. Asher walks over to Samir's garage, where Samir and his young assistant, Tarik, are at work. The call to prayer fades.)

My car won't start up. It's right across the street. I saw your sign . . .

SAMIR: Come in . . . Come, come, I won't bite.

ASHER: It was working this morning. I drove it three hours. Then I stopped
here, went into that bakery, came back to the car, and it wouldn't start up.

SAMIR: You have petrol?

ASHER: Of course.

TARIK: *(Just loud enough to be heard)* Lyahoudi lyome bitsaado, bukra bukhudlak beitak. [The Jew you help today, will take your house tomorrow.]

SAMIR: *(Ironically)* Tarik is my watchdog!

ASHER: *(Turning to go)* Forget it.

SAMIR: No, no, no . . .

ASHER: I caught the message.

SAMIR: There is no other garage you can walk to . . . I apologize for my assistant . . . How old are you?

(Silence)

If you will trust me with your key . . . Your soldiers come to me with their own cars. *(Lightly)* Best stock of reconditioned parts in town, good prices, *(Pointedly)* service you can trust.

ASHER: *(Handing Samir the key)* I'll come with you.

SAMIR: No . . . wait in here, please.

(Samir exits.)

ASHER: *(To Tarik)* What did you say before?

(Silence)

What did you say before? *"Lyahoudi"* . . . what's the rest of it? I want to know what we're accused of.

TARIK: *(Coolly, without looking at Asher)* Lyahoudi lyome bitsaado, bukra bukhudlak beitak.

ASHER: What does it mean?.

TARIK: "The Jew you help today will take your house tomorrow."

(Silence. Asher goes to the doorway to wait. Offstage, the vroom-vroom of an engine. Turning his back to the doorway and Tarik, Asher takes money from his pocket and counts it. Then he reaches into his sock, takes out money and counts it. He puts all the money in his pocket and waits. With nervous energy to spare, Asher paces and begins glancing at the bits of paper posted on the walls. Tarik quickly comes from behind the bench and sweeps his hand over the papers to indicate "not for your eyes." Asher resumes waiting at the doorway. Samir returns, a small object in his hand.)

SAMIR: Tarik, go keep an eye on the car. The blue Renault . . . You can watch it from the doorway . . . Now!

(Tarik moves slowly to the doorway. Samir hands the keys to Asher. Then he opens his other hand and reveals the object.)

Somebody put this in your tailpipe.

ASHER: *(Alarmed)* What is it?

SAMIR: A small potato. A little warning.

ASHER: *(Regaining his cool)* Who from?

SAMIR: Somebody doesn't like that a Jewish boy buys lunch in an Arab bakery. And doesn't wear a kipa. Not kosher.

(Asher is surprised by Samir's sudden use of Yiddish idiom, but he tries not to show it.)

It could be one of ours, it could be one of yours—the black hats with the beards. They're very strict with young Jews who come around here. You know that?

ASHER: Of course.

SAMIR: Potato, can you tell us who did this? . . . You won't talk? *(To Asher)* It is too young to have eyes.

ASHER: *(Firmly, collecting evidence)* Can I have that potato?

SAMIR: Certainly. *(Handing it over)* Maybe when it grows up it will be able to tell you something. Your car's ready to go. I pumped it a few times, aired out the carburetor for you. *(Pause)* You're surprised that this happens to your car?

ASHER: *(Coolly)* No. *(Pocketing the potato, fumbling for change)*

SAMIR: *(Echoing the tone)* "No."

ASHER: Can you come out and start my car?

SAMIR: *(Simmering)* I told you I did that and the car starts.

ASHER: But I want you to start it with me.

SAMIR: Look here—I am telling you that's not necessary. I do safe work.

(Silence)

Do your parents know where you are?

ASHER: *(Alerted, shams)* Of course. The army knows too.

SAMIR: *(Laughing)* No, no, no. I am not going to harm you! That's okay. Nobody trusts anyone . . . If you don't mind advice from me—call your parents. Tell them where you are. It could be dark before you get back. Easy to take the wrong road. Maybe they'll suggest something to you. Here's the phone . . . Please. Dial.

(Asher dials.)

ASHER: *(Coolly)* Hello? I'm calling to say I'm going to get home a little late. I took a drive . . . Into the West Bank . . . Just outside Nablus . . . I'll tell you when I get home . . . I'll tell you when I get home! I had a little trouble with the car. A mechanic here fixed it. Hold on . . .

(He gestures to Samir "do you want to talk?" Samir nods and takes the phone. During the following conversation between Samir and Asher's mother, Asher visibly relaxes.)

SAMIR: *(On phone)* Shalom, I am the mechanic . . . Your son's car had a little problem. I have fixed it so it is safe . . . This is what I do for a living . . . I'm sorry to hear that — I understand — I have just had a son . . . Today . . . Early, early today . . . Thank you. So today I can help someone else's son. His car is safe and I will send him straight home to you . . . I will give you to your son . . . I am Samir . . . Just, Samir.

ASHER: *(Taking the phone from Samir)* Yes . . . I'm okay . . . You don't need to . . . You don't need to . . . *(To Samir)* Where are we?

SAMIR: Jamal Motors, South Nablus Road.

ASHER: Jamal Motors, South Nablus Road. *(He hangs up.)*

SAMIR: Your mother was so thankful, she must have thought we would cook you in a stew. And God forbid not a kosher stew! *(Asher laughs in spite of himself.)*

ASHER: You know our expressions . . .

(Samir nods acknowledgment.)

I'm seventeen — you asked before.

(Samir smiles.)

She . . .

SAMIR: She says your father passed away this winter.

ASHER: Yes, he did.

SAMIR: So. Be on your way home.

ASHER: You know, when I saw that solar collector outside, I said, he'll be able to fix the car. There's a modern mechanic there.

SAMIR: But the problem your car had was not a modern problem.

(Asher laughs.)

ASHER: Did you put that up—the collector and the tank? I didn't know they had them out here yet.

SAMIR: *Popular Mechanics* and my hands. Where is your home?

ASHER: In Herzliya. I'm not a settler. What do I owe you?

SAMIR: Nothing . . . May I ask what part of Herzliya?

ASHER: On a kibbutz. I want to pay you.

SAMIR: No—I don't like what happened to you. Is your kibbutz near the town center?

ASHER: No, it's on the coast.

SAMIR: I see. *(Pause)* So. This teaches you to go sightseeing!

ASHER: I'm not sightseeing. Not like a tourist . . . I came to see things for myself.

SAMIR: The flora and fauna of the West Bank . . . If you came here to see things, why were you so afraid of me?

ASHER: I wasn't afraid.

SAMIR: I'm being harsh on you. You came here like a very moral young man to see the truth with your own eyes. And you got a lesson!

ASHER: I guess I did.

SAMIR: You came to see the occupation . . . And soon you will *be* the occupation.

ASHER: I hope not. I'm hoping to be a pilot.

SAMIR: You don't need my permission.

ASHER: My grandparents were all killed in the Holocaust. My parents got here alone. They were fourteen, fifteen . . .

SAMIR: What is your name?

ASHER: Asher.

SAMIR: Asher, these are subjects for big politicians, not for us.

ASHER: How do you see what's going on here? . . . I mean the occupation . . .

SAMIR: *(Interrupting)* Also for big politicians.

ASHER: I want to know what you think of us. The truth. I know there are problems . . . but I think there are terrific things—like if you're interested

in building things like solar collectors, you could build things for hydro-
ponic farming—there are terrific things we could do together. It depends
how you see us.

SAMIR: Then here's the truth. If we talk about the occupation, the Holocaust,
the big world . . . we'll anger each other. If we talk about cars and potatoes,
parents and sons, we can be friends. Start home now. It's going to rain.

ASHER: It's going to rain?

SAMIR: When you're a farmer you can smell everything on the air.

ASHER: But you're a mechanic.

SAMIR: *(Amused)* We are all farmers here.

(Beep-siren of an army patrol car)

VOICE OF SOLDIER: *(Loud and intrusive)* Asher! Asher!

(Tarik quickly leaves by a back door.)

ASHER: She called a patrol to escort me back to the checkpoint.

*(A Soldier enters, gun at the ready, looking for Asher. [Note: Soldiers should not be
played as heel-clicking sadists. This army is no better or worse than other occupation armies, but their style is informal.] Asher, embarrassed, holds up his hand—
unnecessarily, of course; it's obvious who is the lost kid. The Soldier signals to Asher
"get behind me," and focuses his attention on Samir. Asher obeys awkwardly.)*

SOLDIER: *(To Samir)* Identity card?

*(Samir fumbles for the identity card, hands it over. The Soldier takes a long time
reading the card.)*

ASHER: He fixed my car.

(No response from the Soldier, who continues reading)

He gave me his phone to call home.

SOLDIER: *(To Asher)* Show me your driver's permit?

(Asher hands him the permit.)

(Scanning the permit) Tell me what happened.

ASHER: I parked my car, went into a bakery, and when I came out the car
wouldn't start.

SOLDIER: How long was it out of your sight?

ASHER: Maybe fifteen minutes.

SOLDIER: Then what did you do?

ASHER: I came in here, asked him to have a look at it. He found a potato in the tailpipe.

SOLDIER: Any other evidence of tampering with the car?

ASHER: I don't know, I haven't seen it yet.

SOLDIER: How do you know the problem was caused by the potato?

ASHER: He told me. *(Taking out the potato)* Here it is.

SOLDIER: Did you watch him when he fixed the car?

ASHER: No.

SOLDIER: Why not?

(Pause)

Why didn't you go out with him to see what was wrong?

(Pause)

SAMIR: Because I asked the young man to stay inside.

SOLDIER: Why?

SAMIR: I didn't know what was wrong with the car, I thought it might be sabotaged.

SOLDIER: *(Sarcastically)* You wanted to protect him.

SAMIR: *(Simmering but trying not to show it)* It was obvious that someone outside was angry. The sight of the two of us together could cause trouble.

SOLDIER: *(To Samir)* In your view, who was the perpetrator— *(Giving him no time to answer; rewording, patronizingly and slowly)* who put the potato in the tailpipe?

SAMIR: It could be anyone.

ASHER: I was getting very angry looks from the settlers.

SOLDIER: *(To Asher)* You went through the green line checkpoint today?

ASHER: *(Pause)* Yes.

SOLDIER: And you told them this was your destination?

ASHER: *(Pause)* No. I lied.

SOLDIER: You lied?

(Asher nods.)

What business do you have here?

ASHER: I wanted to see things for myself.

SOLDIER: "Things"? What things?

ASHER: *(Pause)* The occupation.

SOLDIER: You know it is a very serious offense to mislead security forces.

ASHER: I'm aware of that.

SOLDIER: If we book you, if you want to be an officer, this could be the end of it.

(He scans Asher's driver's permit and keeps hold of it.)

(To Samir) Now you—come outside and start the car.

ASHER: He doesn't need to do that. He started it already. Look, all he did was fix my car. You should reward him, not hassle him. Take my license, book me, but stop hassling him.

SOLDIER: *(To Asher)* You see what a lie leads to? You see the consequences? You see how many people are drawn in? You see the security problem you created?

(To Samir) Outside.

(Samir, the Soldier, and Asher go out the front door. We still see them. The soldier turns and looks up at the roof.)

Is that a solar collector behind the water tank?

(Samir nods yes.)

Show me your permit for the construction.

SAMIR: A permit is needed?

SOLDIER: You bet. Where did you get the solar collector?

SAMIR: I built it.

SOLDIER: No ideas as to the perpetrator?

(Samir shakes his head no.)

That's an illegal construction you have up there. *(Aiming his gun at the roof)*

ASHER: Don't do that!

(The Soldier fires a shot. Water spurts out and as the lights dim we hear the sound of rushing water. When the lights come up, Asher, eighteen, is washing up, looking into a mirror, adjusting a military beret.)

(To us) When I entered the army, whenever there was talk about the Arabs, my mind went to Samir. He became a kind of touchstone. Whenever I wanted to talk to that cryptic population beyond the green line, I used Samir's face. In my imaginary debates Samir talked a lot, and he never let me off easily. I wanted to go back just to thank him for being a decent human being. I got the chance when I was sent to Nablus for a training session.

(Samir appears in spotlight. This takes place "in memory"—Asher and Samir are in separate spotlights.)

SAMIR: *(Unsettled)* Is there some problem?

ASHER: *(To us)* He didn't recognize me. I don't think he spent the year having imaginary debates with *me*. I took off my hat, as I should have done immediately on a social visit.

SAMIR: The young man from Herzliya!

ASHER: I'm sorry. The uniform surprised you.

(Silence)

No choice.

(Silence)

No, that's not true. If I can't be straight with you, what's the point.

SAMIR: If you've come all this way you must have some coffee.

ASHER: I was looking for the solar collector and water tank . . .

SAMIR: They're not here anymore.

ASHER: *(To us)* He gave me the coffee in a small cup and it was deep and rich—a different drink than kibbutz Nescafé! I swallowed it in one gulp before he even started his. He teased me about how fast I drank it, and said I had to learn to sip good coffee slowly. He said, *(As Asher)* "Each time you visit you will get a lesson in something." *(As Samir)* *"Each time you visit you will get a lesson in something."* *(As Asher)* "Each time you visit . . ." He made it sound like he wanted me to come back. I didn't get to thank him the way I wanted to. I never got to thank him the way I wanted to—something always got in the way. Maybe that's what kept bringing me back.

(1978, Lights up on Samir's garage. Asher bounds in holding Lila behind him.)

Glad you're still open—

SAMIR: You're in luck—sometimes I stay a little late . . . Is someone with you?

ASHER: Yes. I brought someone to meet you.

(Lila steps out.)

My fiancée, Lila.

LILA: Asher talks so much about you that I said, "It sounds like he's a really good friend—I'd really like to meet him—"

ASHER: So I took her up on that—

LILA: Asher took me up on the idea of meeting you so fast that I think it's what he wanted to do all the time—to introduce me to you.

SAMIR: I'm very honored.

LILA: Actually I think it's my test. Asher places great value in your judgment.

SAMIR: *(Embarrassed)* No, no, no. *(Pause)* Asher, you took me by surprise. I don't have a clean chair to offer . . .

LILA: I've been sitting all the way up here. And there's an inviting stack of tires if I want to sit again.

SAMIR: Please.

(Samir starts the coffee preparations.)

So, have you been suffering from the same cold snap we have here?

ASHER: We had snow!

SAMIR: Is your car behaving well or is it stalling?

ASHER: It's stalling. I'd like you to check the tuning, if that's okay.

SAMIR: No problem. I'm glad you remember where you can find a good garage . . . So. *(To Lila)* Welcome to Jamal Motors. Is your home in Herzliya too?

LILA: No, the Galilee.

SAMIR: And how did fate bring you together?

LILA: The army. That's how most people meet each other.

SAMIR: So you must be a soldier.

LILA: I was. But I've just done my two years.

SAMIR: And you don't want to stay in the army like our Asher here?

LILA: No!

SAMIR: Why do you say no like that? Your fiancé believes the army is a wonderful thing.

LILA: *(To Asher)* You do?

SAMIR: He does. We have many debates about this.

LILA: No. With you he feels he has to defend it—that's the truth. He complains about it plenty. But—he thinks he can change it.

SAMIR: *(Bringing over coffee)* And what do you think?

LILA: *(Lightly)* Mmmm. I think this coffee smells wonderful. I think he probably can.

SAMIR: I see. Asher, you're a lucky young man. So. *(To Lila)* Your parents must be happy that you'll marry a nice Jewish boy.

(Lila laughs.)

Why are you laughing?

LILA: The way you say "nice Jewish—"

SAMIR: *(Interrupting, mock offended)* There's something funny about the way I speak?

LILA: It's like a Jewish comedian. Have you spent time in Israel? Or in the States?

SAMIR: I've spent a bit of time in Israel.

ASHER: You have?

LILA: Asher, a woman can find out in ten minutes what it takes a man ten years.

SAMIR: Never forget that, Asher.

ASHER: What did you do there?

SAMIR: A long story. For another time.

(Lights dim on Samir's garage. Two Reporters appear.)

REPORTER 3: Today on the Nablus Road a car traveling to the nearby settlement was trapped by a road block and stoned.

REPORTER 4: Fortunately an army patrol car arrived on the scene, and the local attackers fled.

REPORTER 3: Settlement leaders have convened to draw up their demands for protection.

REPORTER 4: *(More softly)* And at the settlement, the young pioneers are calming the fears of the younger children with a performance. Here we have the performance live.

(Spotlight on two girls, who enter dancing. They twirl in religious ecstasy.)

DANCER 1: *(Softly, about to tell a miracle)* A miracle happened, in our day, at this spot, just outside Shem. The Arabs call the city Nablus but it is our ancient city of Shem. The Arabs call this land the West Bank, but it is our ancient Samaria.

DANCER 2: Seven is a powerful number.

DANCER 1: Seven days in the Lord's week.

(They do a walk of seven steps, counting out the numbers.)

DANCER 2: Seven times our settlement tried to set down roots in Samaria, and seven times we were uprooted. Our parents would put up a fence and plant saplings, but each time our government would order our own army to evict us. That didn't stop us! We defied the army year after year and returned to this very spot and danced—thousands of us.

DANCER 1: Eight is a miraculous number.

DANCER 2: Eight days the temple oil lasted on Hanukah.

(They do a walk of eight steps, counting out the numbers.)

DANCER 1: Today, on Hanukah, we made our eighth attempt. And our new miracle is this. The government gave the army an order: "You must open your camp to the settlers!" And so the army had to give us housing right here. Today is our beginning!

DANCER 2: Now settlements are taking root throughout the West Bank. In our ancient Sinai Desert, where we are making the desert bloom. We are reclaiming God's land.

(Spotlight off the dancers)

REPORTER 3: A curfew has been announced throughout Nablus and the surrounding region.

(Spotlight off Reporter. A year later, 1979. Lights up on Samir's garage. Samir stares into space. Asher appears at the entrance. An iron grate is pulled down over the door [suggested in pantomime].)

ASHER: Samir? . . . Samir?

SAMIR: Asher—wait, wait—I'll be right there. *(At the door)* How long are you going to be in town?

ASHER: I can wait around a bit. Whose orders are you closed for?

SAMIR: I'm trying to remember. What I remember is when I can be open—one to three. I'm not even supposed to be in here. I come in to protect the place.

ASHER: Okay *(Checking his watch)*, it's almost that now. Five more minutes. If it's an army regulation, I could say I waived the order.

SAMIR: No, no. It is not good for me to look different.

ASHER: Of course. And if it's your guys you certainly don't want to open up on my account.

SAMIR: *(Ironically)* God forbid.

(A whistle blows.)

It was *our* regulation.

(He opens the grate, Asher enters.)

Ours are signaled by whistles, yours by sirens.

ASHER: *(Sympathetically)* You're really getting squeezed.

SAMIR: *(Starting coffee preparation)* Tarik hardly comes in now. But that means we can have our coffee uninterrupted. Sit, sit, sit.

(Asher sits down.)

It was kind of you to bring your fiancée to meet me.

ASHER: It was important to me.

SAMIR: Her name is Lila?

ASHER: Lila. *(Pause, then casually asking the question he's burning to ask)* What do you think of her?

SAMIR: It's not important what I think. What does your mother think? What do your—

ASHER: I'm asking you.

SAMIR: There is no way to know a person the first time you meet.

ASHER: I know our women are different . . .

(Silence)

More forward sometimes . . .

(Samir is distant for a split second.)

Samir?

SAMIR: Asher, it doesn't matter so much who you marry but what you make of it. And if I can give you any good advice about Lila, here it is—I hope she has a strong back.

ASHER: A strong back?

SAMIR: A strong back.

ASHER: *(Pause)* What . . . what for?

SAMIR: *(Wryly)* What for . . .

ASHER: I'm sorry to sound stupid, but there are several things you could mean . . .

SAMIR: What do you think I mean?

ASHER: *(Pause)* Well, you could mean I'll be giving a woman a lot of burdens . . .

SAMIR: *(Amused)* No, no, no . . .

ASHER: I know you're not saying something . . . off color.

SAMIR: "Off color"?

ASHER: About sex.

SAMIR: *(Embarrassed)* No, no, no.

(Asher takes out a cigarette for each of them and a lighter. The lighter doesn't work.)

SAMIR: What's wrong with your lighter? Give it here.

(Asher passes the lighter over. Samir tinkers with it. Lighting both cigarettes with the lighter and handing it back to Asher.) No charge. All right. Suppose you have two bookends.
(He mimes what he's describing.)

If they are solidly built and firmly placed, everything they hold between them is safe. But if just one is weak, not firm—then everything they hold falls over. Even if the other is very strong. The strong one pushes to hold everything together and will push the weak one over. A husband and wife must be like bookends—back-to-back—equally strong, each one supports the other—steadfast. You get the idea?

ASHER: *(Joking)* Back-to-back? Not face-to-face looking into each other's eyes? Not side-by-side walking into the sunset?

SAMIR: We get married forever. We are the most steadfast people on earth.

We're like the trees that bookends are made from. Olive trees. Olive trees are low—which helps them take the storms—sturdy, planted forever.

ASHER: I hear you. I hear about the marriage and I hear about the politics. You can't help slipping that in, can you?

(Samir smiles.)

SAMIR: That is how my father talked with me before my wedding. And you no longer have a father, so.

ASHER: *(Softly, seriously)* Thank you.

SAMIR: Lila will move to Herzliya?

ASHER: As a matter of fact, I'm going to move to her kibbutz. It's up north, cooler, more land, less tourists.

(Pause)

SAMIR: Do you know that I lived for two years in Israel?

ASHER: I wanted to ask you—

SAMIR: Do you know that I was a student at Hebrew University?

ASHER: You know I don't.

SAMIR: There's a story I want to tell you. I was waiting until you were old enough not to act rashly.

ASHER: *(Amused)* And you're realizing I'll never be old enough for that!

SAMIR: But I want to tell you before you leave Herzliya.

ASHER: I'm getting more mature by the minute. Tell me.

SAMIR: When I was nineteen I went to stay with my cousin in Nazareth for the summer. My uncle was building a store and I was sent to help them. My cousin was a pretty smart fellow and he was taking the exams for Hebrew University. At night I'd take a look at what he was studying . . . to make a long story short, I studied hard, I applied from Nazareth, and I got in.

ASHER: And you never told me.

SAMIR: I fell in love with a Jewish girl. She was living near the university and when her roommates were away we'd go to her flat. It was a different world. The freedom was something new. I had no experience and . . . she became pregnant. I wanted to marry her. She wanted to marry me. I brought her to my uncle's home to introduce her to my family. They made a feast to welcome her.

ASHER: They did?

SAMIR: Why are you surprised?

ASHER: Why do you think I'm surprised?

SAMIR: *(Waits a moment, no response)* You won't be surprised by the rest of the story. From the welcome of my family, she took courage to tell her parents. And they pulled her out of the university.

ASHER: Did you see her again?

SAMIR: I disgraced myself some. I went to her home to try to ask for her hand in an honorable way. They turned me away like a stray dog. But I did get a few letters from her. The child was a girl. So, I have an Israeli daughter. "Rivka."

ASHER: I don't know what to say . . . Have you ever seen her?

SAMIR: The family persuaded her mother that it would be better for a child to grow up fatherless than to have an Arab father. Too much shame.

ASHER: I don't know what to say . . .

SAMIR: So when there are bombs, attacks . . . I watch the television.

ASHER: She lives in Herzliya?

SAMIR: The mother's family does. That's all I know.

ASHER: So how did you think I'd act rashly?

(Samir gestures how would I know?)

ASHER: How old is she now?

SAMIR: *(Thinks for a moment)* Almost a young woman.

ASHER: What were you afraid of? That I'd think less of you? . . .

SAMIR: No, no, no.

ASHER: That I'd run to her family and try to bring you together?

SAMIR: Exactly. You think you can stir things up and change the world. You think you can make things happen the way you want to. But I'm afraid of taking away her foundation.

ASHER: *(Goading him)* So you're never going to see her.

SAMIR: I didn't say that. Asher—think about your own nature. Then answer this: Can you get information and leave it at that? Take no action?

ASHER: What do you take me for? You know, they give me a lot of responsibility in the army. I don't talk about it because I know your views.

SAMIR: Good—we don't need to go into that. What I want you to do is move cautiously, slowly . . . first, just see, without anyone knowing, if you can find her. I will write down the family's name . . . Go slow. You know why olive trees are strong? Because they grow slowly.

(Blackout. Three years later, 1982. In a spotlight a Rabbi appears, seated, bereaved. Asher approaches the Rabbi's door. Asher is now in his thirties, and we see a new maturity.)

ASHER: May I come in, Rabbi? I'm armed only with a box of chocolates.

RABBI: Suit yourself.

ASHER: I've been asked to visit you this evening, and to tell—

RABBI: *(Interrupting)* We've told you already what we're going to do . . .

ASHER: I've been asked to tell you that the evacuation will go ahead tomorrow morning as—

RABBI: *(Interrupting)* And we've sent a message regarding our intentions to the prime minister.

ASHER: I'm here to see if I can help you—boxes, packing, anything that—

RABBI: *(Interrupting)* We will wall ourselves up in the bunker; when the evacuation starts one of our number will commit suicide every hour and the last one to remain will open the bunker and fire on whoever enters; he will go down fighting.

ASHER: I'm here to beg you not to create more sorrow but to let the will of the majority be carried out. I want to tell you how sad we all are to have to dismantle this beautiful little village.

(The Rabbi nods cynically.)

We're transplanting the fruit trees, we'll salvage whatever possible.

RABBI: Wait, wait, wait. What are your qualifications for this job?

ASHER: *(Pause)* To be an army officer?

RABBI: To destroy this settlement.

ASHER: May I sit down?

(The Rabbi points him to a seat.)

I love this land and I've fought for it. When I was only eighteen, my commander was wounded and I took command in the middle of an attack. I've commanded a tank battalion, I've been wounded twice . . .

RABBI: Those are your medals. That's not what I'm talking about.

ASHER: *(Pause)* What do you want me to tell you?

RABBI: Tell me if you were ever powerless.

ASHER: *(Thinks a moment)* Once, on a patrol, we were ambushed. And a young

soldier was mortally wounded. And I watched the medic trying to keep
the life going in him—

RABBI: But you all wanted him to live?

ASHER: Of course.

RABBI: Everybody was gathered around helping you?

ASHER: Of course.

RABBI: I want you to tell me about when you were powerless among strangers.

(Silence)

Give me one instance.

(Pause)

Can you imagine that—a Jew who has not been powerless among strangers
    . . . And this is who they send to destroy the defenses.

ASHER: Once, when I was about seventeen . . .

RABBI: Yes . . .

ASHER: *(Long pause)* No, it wasn't a big thing. Nothing really happened.

RABBI: This is who they send to destroy our defenses.

(Pause)

So—you just failed that test.

(Silence)

Is that your first failure?

ASHER: Well, I'd say it's the most serious one.

RABBI: Believe me, this is just the beginning . . .

*(Later the same year, Lights up on Samir's garage. Asher enters holding an envel-
ope. Samir is occupied with his coffee preparation.)*

SAMIR: *(Calling over to Asher, in good humor)* So what did you do to get onto
    my television?

ASHER: I was in the Sinai. Basically, I had to supervise my men evicting settlers
    from their homes. You can't imagine what we had on our hands—they
    were threatening mass suicide, they were cursing and screaming at us:
    "Arab lovers!" "Traitors!"

(Samir comes over with the coffee.)

I had to visit the head rabbi the night before we evicted him — all officers were
assigned to "socialize." Look, there's one thing that happened that I want
you to know about. He kept asking if I'd ever been powerless among
strangers . . . One time was stuck in my mind. The day my car broke
down — among strangers. Angry eyes everywhere and a dead car that was
turning into an oven. But then a very decent stranger helped me.

SAMIR: What did the rabbi say about that?

ASHER: I couldn't tell him about that, of course. And the problem was I
couldn't think of any other example because what you did that day filled
my mind.

SAMIR: *(Bristling)* Why couldn't you tell him?

ASHER: Why? Because he would think my views, my actions even, were biased
. . . not based on . . . what's the right word? Rationality.

SAMIR: *(Ironically)* Of course. Why didn't I see that?

(Asher picks up the envelope.)

ASHER: Herzliya! *(Waving the envelope)* I have something for you from Herzliya. *(Joking)* If I could tell anyone about my detective work, they'd give
me a top position in the mossad! No, actually, it was a piece of cake.

(Samir pours a cup of coffee.)

Your hands are shaking. It turned out okay. Luckily, the name was not a common one — if we'd had a Cohen or a Levy, forget it. There's a deli in town
with a proprietor of the name you gave me. So I decided to try to get to
know the owner. I came in for a few blintzes, a few coffees, and we started
talking about children and grandchildren. It was easy because he has photos up behind the cash register. When he got to his granddaughter Rivka,
who was just the right age, I thought bull's-eye! But then he pointed out
her photo and I thought maybe I was on the wrong track because she's a
redhead — a *gingi,* we call it . . .

SAMIR: From her mother.

ASHER: I'd been imagining a girl with your coloring. But then he started telling me how her father "fell" in some mysterious "action" —

SAMIR: So at least her mother married.

ASHER: Maybe by now, but not then, not to someone who "fell"—that's what I'm telling you. That was my confirming clue to the child. The moment he said that, I smelled something wrong. Because I know just who fell and where and when. Then suddenly he said, "Here she comes now—" And the girl from the wall photo—the same girl a few years older—walked in with a friend to have an after-school blintz at her grandpa's.

SAMIR: So you actually saw her.

ASHER: I had my little standard issue camera with me. I waited until everyone was distracted, looking over some homework paper she brought from school . . .

(Opening the envelope, Asher takes out a photo and hands it to Samir. Samir looks at the photo for a long time.)

She has your eyes . . . So the good news is I found her. The bad news is that her grandfather is a political supporter of the extreme right. Extreme, extreme. Posters all over the deli.

SAMIR: I fell into the right family!

ASHER: You didn't know about them from . . . what was her name? I don't want to say "your girlfriend."

SAMIR: No, no, no . . . her name was Shoshana. She was a great believer in everybody loving everybody else . . .

ASHER: And, you were her rebellion!

SAMIR: *(A pause as Samir stills the reverberations of the past)* Does Rivka need anything? *(Pause)* It's odd to have a daughter in the world and know in your heart there's nothing you can give her.

ASHER: That can change. It can. I'll keep an eye on her. We won't lose her.

(Samir gazes at the photo.)

SAMIR: I feel like she's just been born.

ASHER: Congratulations . . . Congratulations.

(Pause)

I meant to ask—what happened to your studies?—At Hebrew University?

SAMIR: I came home at the end of the year. I came back to my life. I married Mouna, who I always thought I would marry. And we had Jamal—born,

in fact, the day that you drove up here; and then we had three more — all
sons — only sons. They're not giving me an easy time these days.

ASHER: The occupation?

SAMIR: The occupation.

*(Blackout. 1984. Lights up, sounds from a distant rally — cheers, jeers, whistles; the
mood is both jubilant and threatening. Tarik enters.)*

TARIK: *(To us)* Today is the most magnificent day. We have a new martyr, and
he is already within the gates of paradise. Abu Rami. Last night Abu Rami
flew over the occupier's northern border in a hang glider. He rode on the
wings of Mohammad's angels. He saw the stars and the crescent moon,
and the mighty occupier's land lying before him. A hang glider is just like
an innocent sparrow. It cannot be detected by radar. Abu Rami touched
down right outside an army camp, Allah be praised. He got his Kalishnikov ready, and his grenades, and he walked around the barbed wire to find
an opening. He knew, of course, that he would not return. He entered,
and he hurled a grenade. The guard saw him coming, and what did the
guard do? He ran away! He turned his back and fled! So Abu Rami killed
six enemy soldiers! Within their own fort. Still in their pajamas! They got
Abu Rami, but, I tell you, he is the most glorious martyr of the war. You see
from this, we all see from this, that they are vulnerable. They run away and
fall and die like all other men. Now every ten-year-old boy here will take
out his slingshot and practice with renewed strength. Our Davids — our
"cubs of the stones" — can beat the occupier's Goliath. Allah be praised.

*(Crossfade from Tarik to Samir's garage. Asher and Samir are playing back-
gammon.)*

ASHER: Your throw. Today, while we're playing, let's see if we can avoid a single
mention of the occupation.

SAMIR: Have your arguments gone sour?

(Silence)

Okay. Other topics. Mint tea. I'm curious why you don't like mint tea. Here
we always have mint tea before our coffee. But you — in the early days you
accepted it a few times to be diplomatic, but you let it sit in your glass.
Now I know not to offer.

ASHER: I'm sure you ask because you have a theory.

SAMIR: Mint tea is light, soothing, slow. It has a delicate flavor. You have to pay attention to it to enjoy it. But with you everything has to be intense, dark, serious.

ASHER: That's because what I have to do is intense, dark, and serious . . .

SAMIR: Stop. You're going to get to the forbidden topic.

ASHER: Okay. Good save.

(They play for a while silently.)

I have a subject. Love. Love between a man and a woman.

SAMIR: An excellent choice.

ASHER: I have something to thank you for. Remember after I brought Lila to meet you? And you gave me advice about bookends.

SAMIR: I remember well.

ASHER: Well, bookends came in handy last week. My latest controversy with Lila started over this stupid medication she takes when she feels a flu coming on . . . she wants the children to take it, she wants me to take it . . . It's some concoction diluted a million times. Maybe one atom is left. I said, this is irrational, this is dark ages. She said, "You only believe what you can see, you don't listen to underlying meanings, you do things too fast to enjoy them"—a whole catalog of everything wrong with me. So you know what I said to her? "Bookends. We don't have to be the same, sometimes all we have to do is support each other. Bookends." She really liked that. She likes it whenever I use a metaphor. Once in a while I come up with a really good one. Of course that one came from you . . . That evening I took her to the old city and bought her a pair of bookends for her "medical" books. Olive wood.

SAMIR: They'll last you a long time.

ASHER: Marrying Lila was the best thing I ever did.

SAMIR: I can hear that.

ASHER: Even if you wouldn't agree with my judgment at the time.

SAMIR: All I said was that I could not know a person the first time.

ASHER: Yet you knew me the first time, and I knew you the first time. We knew each other at once.

(Samir throws the dice.)

I was at headquarters last week and learned something about the service record of a certain young soldier—a certain Rivka.

SAMIR: Yes . . . *(Samir stops mid-move.)*

ASHER: And I found what she does . . . want to guess?

SAMIR: *(Wryly)* She's a secret service agent turning in Arabs right and left.

ASHER: She's a mechanic.

SAMIR: A mechanic?

ASHER: An ace mechanic. She repairs jeeps and she teaches new soldiers the techniques.

SAMIR: Rivka's a mechanic?

ASHER: Just in case you want proof, there was a little story in an IDF magazine. *(Taking out a small magazine, finding a page in it, and handing it to Samir)* With a photo.

SAMIR: She doesn't look like a mechanic!

(Asher smiles. Samir reads the article and begins to glow.)

(Reading) "The corporal has developed her own twist on dealing with sand . . ."

ASHER: Keep the magazine. It's for you.

(Samir can't take his eyes off the page)

Does Mouna know about Rivka? If I'm overstepping by asking, just tell me.

SAMIR: No, no, no. *(Small pause)* Everyone here knew that I brought Shoshana to my uncle's house. It was before I'd ever declared anything to Mouna. But when it was finished and I came home, Mouna was just very happy to see me return. Over time I told her everything.

(Samir looks over the newspaper once more. Lights fade on Samir's garage. Spotlight on Asher.)

ASHER: *(To us)* Despite quiet moments in Samir's garage, tempers were getting hotter in the West Bank, and attacks were being launched against us from other borders. We overreacted badly and I spoke my mind about that at the time, but several years later things reached a point where I realized that speaking out wasn't enough. I knew I had to resign from the army. I went in to see the chief-of-staff . . . I wasn't prepared for what happened.

(1987. Spotlight on the Chief-of-Staff at his desk. Asher strides in, expected.)

CHIEF-OF-STAFF: Asher, could I get you to apologize for a five-year-old insult to our big general?

ASHER: When you hear why I've come, you won't find it necessary.

CHIEF-OF-STAFF: When you hear what I've got to offer, you'll see it is.

ASHER: The subject of this apology is our very own General Attila-the Hun?

CHIEF-OF-STAFF: *(Amused)* Now, now. Asher, You have a fine career ahead of you . . .

ASHER: I was coming in, as a matter of fact—in view of the latest massacre—to resign. I want to separate myself—

CHIEF-OF-STAFF: Asher. I'm not talking politics, I'm talking tactics.

ASHER: There's very little we do that I'm proud of.

CHIEF-OF-STAFF: That's why we need you to stay. We need men who look at things in new ways . . . I know you've become familiar with the West Bank . . . You and I know one day we'll be saying good-bye to those territories . . . The job now is to create a climate of safety and security, cool things down, keep the settlers in check, keep the locals in check, cut down the provocations. How's that for a mission statement?

ASHER: *(Ironic)* It's a fine statement.

CHIEF-OF-STAFF: But will it be put into action? You're the one who can tell us. *(Pause)* I'm offering you the West Bank command.

(Pause)

Don't you get it? You're an ace at establishing rapport. I watched how you handled the settlers at Sinai—kept things in balance, gave everyone a little, took your time, kept your eye on the objective. You've got a better way to run the occupation? Good. Here's your chance.

(Asher is speechless.)

Apologizing to Attila-the-Hun's a small price, huh?

(Crossfade from the Chief-of-Staff's office to two Village Women outside Samir's garage.)

VILLAGE WOMAN 1: *(Casually)* You know who the new commander is. The one who comes into the bakery . . . and here *(Motioning to the garage)*.

VILLAGE WOMAN 2: Last week he bought a big box of rose-water cakes. So I said to him—he always has a smile in his eyes, you can talk to him—I say,

"You are going to eat all these?" He says, "My wife asks me to bring a box home. She's a fan of yours." He comes in to buy a box to bring home to his wife.

VILLAGE WOMAN 1: He's won you over.

VILLAGE WOMAN 2: He's a nice man, polite.

VILLAGE WOMAN 1: They say he got the job to make the occupation look good for the television. And to put us to sleep.

(The Village Women walk off. Lights up on Samir's garage.)

TARIK: Two alternators to rewind today, and the boss is polishing a coffee pot.

SAMIR: The bottom was so blackened the heat couldn't get through. *(He hums as he works.)*

TARIK: You're not expecting a visitor today, are you?

SAMIR: Any customer who wants to sit and talk gets a good cup of coffee.

TARIK: Especially if that visitor is the new commander of the occupation!

SAMIR: If Asher comes in today, he has the hospitality of this garage.

TARIK: You really think the commander of the occupation is going to walk in that door.

(Silence)

What do you want to bet me . . . a day's wages. I work for you free today if he comes in.

SAMIR: I'd be very surprised if he comes his first day on the job.

TARIK: But you hope. I hear your heart humming.

SAMIR: Enough. Get to work.

(Silence)

TARIK: People are asking me if you're a collaborator.

(Silence)

People are asking me if you're a collaborator.

SAMIR: Only the stupid ones. Only the sheep. If you don't know how to answer them, I'll tell you. You tell them, Samir is a man who is loyal to his friends. And one of his friends happens to be this man, Asher, who came in need as a boy of seventeen and comes back in good will to visit every year of his life. You tell them that Samir thinks it is better to maintain a friendship that can help his friends than to destroy it. And tell them to go talk to the families whose sons I got out of prison . . . I have nothing to hide. Tell them to be here when the general comes. Tell them to have coffee with us.

TARIK: I'll tell Hammad to come and ask why his house got demolished . . . You'll be luckier if the general doesn't show his face.

(Silence)

He's the king of the occupation and what are we—what were we called today? Oh yes, here it is . . . "if the Arabs want to continue to escalate the unrest, we will crush them under our feet like *grasshoppers.*"

SAMIR: Without seeing the paper, I can tell you Asher's not the one who said it. Asher would spit on the one who said it.

TARIK: *(Scanning the paper)* The great prime minister said it. *(Tearing out the article)* Your friend's boss. *(Posting the article)*

SAMIR: We don't need that posted here.

TARIK: I want to post it in front of me so I can learn my correct position, show that we're all working hard at complying with their wishes. Let's see . . . how does a grasshopper walk? . . . Does it walk at all or does it just hop?

SAMIR: Take it down.

TARIK: *(Teasing)* But he's not coming in today, right? No way he'd come the first day on the job.

SAMIR: Now!

(Tarik practices walking with a hop.)

TARIK: Let's see, how would a grasshopper hop in an "unrest," whatever that is . . .

(Tarik puts a twitch into his hop.)

SAMIR: Why do you want to put me in this position? Why confrontation? Why fights? Go home. I can't trust you. Go home.

TARIK: As you say, boss. *(Getting up and bowing to Samir)* I obey you—and your friend will obey his boss.

(On his way out Tarik takes a can of petrol.)

SAMIR: Why are you taking petrol?

TARIK: In honor of the new commander, the leadership has designated tomorrow as "Petrol Bomb Day."

SAMIR: What a glorious name for a day!

TARIK: They want to know which side you're on.

(Silence)

If you don't *give* the petrol, a unit will break in at night and take it. They plan to ignite the shops that refuse. By taking the petrol myself I am doing you a favor.

(Tarik leaves. Samir tears down the posted article. Checks his watch. Gets the coffee pot ready. Checks his watch. Takes from his pocket a folded piece of paper, unfolds and scans it, refolds and pockets it. Checks his watch. Asher walks in beaming like a ray of sunshine.)

SAMIR: So . . . *(Starting up the coffee)* So. The commander comes to me.

ASHER: *(Good naturedly)* Cut it out, Samir.

SAMIR: The chosen of the chosen.

ASHER: That's a lot of rubbish. If we were chosen, it was for suffering. And we were lonely so God chose you to be our partner!

SAMIR: You look the same. I thought you would be full of medals, have a big escort . . .

ASHER: Of course I look the same. And my car is outside. A simple staff car. With driver.

SAMIR: Not broken down I hope? *(Bringing over the coffee)*

ASHER: Not broken down. But the driver is on high alert for a potato.

SAMIR: *(Joking)* Let's hope that's all he'll get! Sip it slowly, slowly.

ASHER: *(Not responding in the same spirit)* What's the psychology of it? You tell me. Why can't they get it through their heads here that the stonings, the petrol bomb attacks, don't get them what they want. If we felt secure, public opinion would shift, you'd get the land back. Simple as that. Win in a week by stopping the violence. Why can't they get that through their heads?

SAMIR: *(Smoldering)* I'll tell you that if you'll tell me something else. Explain to me . . . blowing up houses. Are you trying to blow us off the map, house by house? . . . Or is it not polite to ask such a question on your first day?

ASHER: No, I want to defend it. It's stones and concrete. It's not lives.

SAMIR: *You* won't be able to stomach it. Watching the poor elderly parents carrying out whatever they can save . . . You're very quiet. Have you supervised these things already?

ASHER: You know that until today I've had little to do with the occupation.

SAMIR: And now you're high enough to avoid the whole messy business. You can let the troops do the dirty work.

ASHER: No. I experience everything my men have to.

SAMIR: Give this man a medal for suffering!

ASHER: It's not lives. It's stones and concrete.

SAMIR: A man without a home? Can't shelter his family, can't raise his head.

ASHER: All pride.

SAMIR: You see, you don't know. You don't know what it is to have a home in a village that was your parents' and their parents' and their parents' . . .

ASHER: *(Interrupting)* You're right. I don't. My father never knew, my grandfather . . .

SAMIR: *(Interrupting)* You know who placed each stone . . . you know where each child was born, where each person died, you know which generation made each addition . . . you know the place of every tree and every rock. It is in your blood. You don't know what it is . . .

ASHER: You're so right. But we haven't had your luck. My grandfather used to say, "The best rewards are not of this world." That's because he was never able to have the rewards of this world . . . *You* work yourself up over pride —my grandparents would have kissed the ground to be allowed to live.

SAMIR: *(Frustrated at being one-upped)* Period. End of conversation.

(A beat)

ASHER: *(Standing)* I'd better go.

SAMIR: *(Sitting him down)* Asher . . . Asher, I won't allow you to leave until you have one of the small rewards of this world—Mouna's baklava.

ASHER: Mouna's baklava can make peace any day!

SAMIR: *(Bringing over baklava)* West Bank mechanic holds commanding general hostage until he eats baklava.

ASHER: Mmmm.

SAMIR: Eat it slowly. Enjoy it. I have something to read to you. *(He takes the folded paper from his wallet.)* Tell me if there's anything that is offending in this. "My Dear Rivka, Some years ago, a very trustworthy and honorable friend in Israel looked you up for me. He has been watching over you as a guardian angel all the years since that time, and he tells me about your progress in life. I look forward to the time when you and I might meet, but I do not want to bring any trouble or shame into your life. As for myself, I have nothing to be ashamed of in my life, except that I have not been able to help or guide you in yours. If you would ever like to visit, my wife and I invite you warmly. We have a modest but good home, and there will always be a room in it for you. I would like to show you my garage. I read that you are quite the mechanic, so we will have many things to talk about. My friend, a man you will realize you can trust when you know who he is, would see that you are escorted here very safely, even secretly if you wish." I'm not sure how to sign it . . .

ASHER: Yes—you haven't introduced yourself as her father . . .

SAMIR: I can't explain who I am in a letter. Someone has to determine first whether she should know. Someone who understands Rivka's life. You see that?

ASHER: Yes. Someone who can talk to Rivka, see how she thinks about things . . .

SAMIR: The person has to first determine that it won't cause her shame. If that person truly believes that it would be good that Rivka knows about me, he . . . or she . . . would tell her.

(Pause)

Could your Lila . . .

ASHER: Of course, of course.

SAMIR: A woman knows a woman's heart.

(Pause)

How should I sign the letter?

ASHER: "Your loving father." Since she's going to know you *are* her father before she reads it.

SAMIR: *(Signing it)* "Your loving father." Asher, I had this letter ready for your visit for a reason. With the mood getting worse here, and your new position . . .

ASHER: Go on.

SAMIR: It's better if you don't visit for a while.

(A beat. Asher is stung.)

Don't tell me you don't know how your secret service sets up an Arab . . . "Secret" agents who everybody knows come to visit him, force him to walk outside, and then embrace him. That's all. The neighbors finish the job.

(Silence)

Why do I have to tell you this? Could you really not know?

ASHER: For one, there's nothing secret about me—it's all in the open. Second, you used to tell me soldiers came here for their cars—

SAMIR: A very long time ago.

ASHER: And mainly, you never said this before. I thought you wanted me to come. To tell the truth, I made a rule for myself as I began to rise in the army—that I would not stop visiting until *you* asked me to.

SAMIR: Don't take offense.

ASHER: They're making it that hard on you.

SAMIR: Asher—on the one hand you and I are old friends—look what I've just trusted you to do. On the other, standing in my garage is the head of this monster that puts my friends' sons in jail, demolishes houses, diverts water . . .

ASHER: Look—we're going to get out of here! That's what I'm working for. But until we do, I'm going to run the most decent occupation on earth. Last week two soldiers asked some local residents to load their military gear into a truck while they stood by and had a cigarette. Their case is coming up before me tomorrow. Do you know where they're going to have their cigarettes for the next month? In jail.

SAMIR: Someday you'll see you can't make the world over.

ASHER: Is that your lesson for the day? I came here to . . . to share my hopes with you . . . Yes, that's what I came here to do.

SAMIR: *(Tone lightens)* You're destined for a big life. How does it feel?

ASHER: *(Lightly)* Just destined for a lot of people angry at me. Are you one of them, or are you going to give me the letter?

(Samir hands over the letter. Asher starts to embrace Samir, but then, thinking of Samir's caution, he pulls back and stiffly offers his hand. Samir looks out to check that no one is watching, then embraces Asher warmly.)

SAMIR: God be with you, Asher.

ACT 2

(Spotlight on Reuben, an intense young man who leaps up into a dance.)

REUBEN:Ya-ta-te-dum-ta-te-dum-ta-te dum, ya-ta-te-dum-ta-te-dum-dum!

(Springing to face us)

I am Reuben, servant of the Lord! This is the tomb of our forefather Joseph. Feel the dampness. Feel the age. Ancient, holy stones. From the time when our Lord walked with us. Moses brought Joseph's body back from Egypt so that Joseph could rest forever in the land of the Jews. What would you think if I told you that the only people not allowed to visit here freely are — us, the Jews? This tomb lies on the outskirts of our ancient city Shem, where Abraham built the first altar to our Lord. During our exile the Arabs swarmed in, changed holy names, defiled holy places. But, in 1967 we re-captured our land. And what did we do about it? Remove the traces of Arab defilement? Send the defilers packing? Isn't that what you'd expect? But no — our army has its face toward the international press and does not want to upset the Arabs, so they try to keep us out of our city and our holy places. In direct contradiction to the word of the Lord who has com-manded us to settle every corner of the land of Israel. When I visited the holy sites and saw Joseph's tomb in alien hands I vowed to redeem it. So, young as I am, I established here a yeshiva — a place of study — because, until nightfall, the army is not allowed to keep Jews out of yeshivas. I run roadblocks, I trick soldiers, I stop Arab traffic by leading comrades into the center of town to dance and sing to the Lord so the Arabs know whose city this is. I test every crevice of the law to redeem the Lord's land. I find the Lord's spirit in these stones. And where do I live? I live in my car be-cause until the Lord's people are established in Shem I have no home.

(A soldier handcuffs Reuben, pulls him off.)

(To us) Today we have a new commander here. He wants to give away this land. Never fear — we'll open his eyes.

(Lights up on Asher's office, stage right.)

ASHER: *(To us)* We are occupiers for the first time in 2000 years. In control of the lives of others — in a position to regulate every detail of their daily comings and goings. We can order the stores closed and a mother can't buy milk, a farmer watches his produce rot. We can impose a curfew and a family can't water their crops or feed their animals. We can close roads, schools, borders which twenty thousand people cross to work everyday. We have a lot of power and we have to use it well. I mean to set a precedent for how a just occupier behaves.

(A Soldier enters with Reuben, who is cradling a Bible in his handcuffed hands.)

SOLDIER: *(To Asher)* He was brought in last night for a vigilante shooting at Nablus. Other recent charges: physical and verbal clashes with soldiers, a shooting at the refugee camp, squatting attempts, breakings and enterings, running military roadblocks, and this morning—the disturbance at Joseph's tomb. And minor incidents . . . taking food from Nablus merchants and refusing to pay . . .

ASHER: Explain that one to me.

REUBEN: I dance in the streets of Shem to show them whose city it is. I use every breath the Lord has given me to make them want to get out as fast as their legs will carry them.

ASHER: I see. *(Quietly)* Reuben, I have taken a special interest in your case. I am giving you a sentence never before given a Jewish settler. I am banning you for three months from the city of Nablus.

REUBEN: Banning?

ASHER: You set foot in Nablus and you go to jail.

REUBEN: Every filthy Arab can spit in the streets of Shem, and you're "banning" me? You're going against the Lord. Use me. I put the fear of God into the Arabs. I do things you'd be afraid to.

ASHER: We reward those on the side of peace. We punish those on the side of war.

REUBEN: What about the side of God?

(The Soldier pulls Reuben out.)

(Offstage) What about the side of God? . . . What about the side of God? . . .

(Crossfade to stage left, Samir's garage. Samir is at work. A female soldier enters; fatigues, a cap, long curly red hair in a braid. She stands quietly at the entrance and gazes at Samir. Samir turns from his work, sees her, grasps instantly who she is, and is stunned.)

RIVKA: Good morning. I notice that you have a Citroen outside. I have an old Citroen and I'm having trouble finding parts for it. Do you happen to keep any?

SAMIR: *(Trembling, yet trying not to show it)* Yes, yes, I keep a stock of old parts for everything. Can you tell me what you need?

RIVKA: It's not for right now, just in general . . . Like, once I needed a timer . . .

SAMIR: Would you like me to look at your car? See what vintage it is?

RIVKA: No, my car isn't here. My unit dropped me off. I only have a few minutes before they pick me up.

SAMIR: Well, I can show you my stock so you know what you can find here.

RIVKA: *(Softly)* Is it all right for you if I'm in your garage?

SAMIR: It is kind of you to ask. I was just thinking if it was safe for you. But if your unit is watching out for you—

RIVKA: *(Interrupting and finishing his thought)*—yes, there's no problem. *(Pause)* It's very important that I be here.

SAMIR: *(Pause)* May I ask why?

RIVKA: Did you ever live in Israel? Please—I'm not with security. I'm not on duty, I'm asking for a personal reason.

SAMIR: Yes. I did live in Israel for a few years. And I went to Hebrew University.

(Rivka is silent; having gotten so far so fast, she does not know how to go on.)

(Softly) Rivka?

(Rivka is silent, now she is crying.)

You came to the right place.

(He wants to comfort Rivka, but is afraid to touch her.)

Welcome, Rivka. Welcome to my garage.

(Rivka nods in acceptance.)

How did you find me? *(Hastily)* I'm very happy you found me . . . I don't know how to say it.

RIVKA: My mother told me a long time ago.

SAMIR: I have tried to learn if it was right to make myself known to you. I gave a letter to a friend—

RIVKA: Yes, yes, I got the letter. I have so many questions, and no time . . .

SAMIR: Why didn't you come with him, safely?

RIVKA: There was no need.

(Pause)

Does it offend you that I'm a soldier?

SAMIR: I know many soldiers.

RIVKA: So many questions *(She makes a gesture of frustration.)* — I came today —

SAMIR: *(Interrupts)* We will go slowly. You'll come back many times. Now that you know where I am, you'll come many times.

RIVKA: Yes, of course. But I came today because I'm going to be married . . .

SAMIR: Congratulations, Rivka!

RIVKA: And I want you to be at my wedding.

(Silence)

I want you to be at my wedding.

SAMIR: Rivka . . . We must go slowly.

RIVKA: I talked this over with my mother, and she understands.

SAMIR: I cannot.

RIVKA: My fiancé, Rafi, wanted me to find you. He wants my life to be whole. It's how he feels about that, that told me he's right for me.

SAMIR: Rivka, I cannot.

(Silence)

It's your family's celebration . . . They won't want me there, and . . . I cannot, Rivka.

(Silence)

Your grandfather will walk with you, won't he, Rivka? It's his responsibility to do that.

(Silence, as she absorbs his refusal)

Rivka, I will have a wedding feast for you. In my home. That's the way it will be.

(Pause)

My wife — Mouna — will welcome you. We will prepare a feast for you and your fiancé. You will have two wedding feasts. That's the way it will be.

(Pause)

Mouna will make *mahmool* [mah-MOOL], you've had *mahmool?*

RIVKA: Little cakes made from rosewater . . . Anytime my mother would see
them in a bakery, she would buy one for me.

SAMIR: So. We will have *mahmool* and we will give everyone gifts of almonds,
just the way it would be at a wedding. Do you know, Rivka, you are my
only daughter?

(Rivka shakes her head no.)

Will you accept my hospitality?

(Rivka nods yes.)

I will decorate my home with olive branches and almond blossoms.

(Crossfade to stage right, Asher's Office. The Aide brings in Tarik.)

AIDE: The perpetrator of the petrol bomb attempt on the Bet Shayan road.

ASHER: Tarik, I'm sorry to see you here. Do you dispute the charge?

TARIK: *Allahu akbar!*

ASHER: Tarik, you've become a potential murderer. But you have the luck that
your attempt failed. Under military law, the penalty is demolition of your
home—the walls that sheltered the bomb making. But because I'm dedi-
cating my command to peace, and because of my esteem for your employer, I am ordering sealing rather than demolition. I'm going to tell you
something to pass on to your friends. You are giving powerful ammuni-
tion into the hands of the settlers. Every time there is a stoning or a petrol
bomb attack, the settlers win sympathy. They win support, votes, power.
Think carefully—is this what you want?

TARIK: *(Raising handcuffed wrists in a power gesture) Allahu Akbar!*

AIDE: He was carrying a bulletin about "Petrol Bomb Day" that had an added
little sermon. The translation is roughly, "The vices and corrupt ways of
Jews have been noted as far back as the Koran. Any tie between Arab and
Jew is forbidden. No Arab may rest or sleep until revenge has been taken
and the Jewish defiler has been expelled from every corner of our sacred
land." Not the format of the communiqués we've been seeing. Some fringe
group.

(The Aide begins to pull Tarik out, but as Tarik passes in front of Asher, he comes in close.)

TARIK: *(To Asher)* I did not tell your police . . . *(He is pulled away by the Aide.)*
ASHER: Let him speak to me.
TARIK: I did not tell them who supplied the petrol.

(A beat)

ASHER: Out!

(The Aide pulls Tarik out. Asher sits down at his desk. The Rabbi strides in. Asher recognizes him reluctantly and rises.)

Good morning, Sir.
RABBI: The hero of the Sinai campaign against the Jews!
ASHER: That was a difficult time for all of us. I hope we can put it behind us and work together.
RABBI: So I do not need to introduce myself.
ASHER: I remember you well.
RABBI: Last time we met you addressed me as "Rabbi."
ASHER: You wear many hats these days—
RABBI: When you were softening me up you addressed me as "Rabbi".
ASHER: I know that now you head the delegation of West Bank Settlements. I did not know which hat you wished me to address.
RABBI: Rabbi.
ASHER: Rabbi.
RABBI: A soldier-philosopher. You walk in the footsteps of Joshua, in the footsteps of David.
ASHER: I'm just a soldier who carries out policy.
RABBI: I'm here to offer our help. We know that the army cannot be at every roadblock the Arabs devise to trap and slaughter Jews. Our Committee for Safety has voted a militia to patrol the roads. We need the proper arms.
ASHER: It's the army's job to protect the roads, . . . Rabbi. I intend to create a climate of safety, not of fear.
RABBI: So it's the Jews who should live in fear? We're the only people who pave the road for our enemies.

(Pause)

We gave up land—and what did we get?

(Pause)

You don't want to answer that out of shame.

(Pause)

Do you know what it's like to be driving alone at night, be stopped by some
   wreck, and know that behind the rocks Arabs are waiting for you with
   knives and crowbars?

ASHER: That's exactly the kind of situation we're aiming to avoid. I plan to . . .

RABBI: *(Interrupting)* You plan! God has a plan before which all human plans
   are dust. Have you read His plan?

ASHER: I am a soldier, Rabbi, not a biblical scholar.

RABBI: Then even if you are ignorant about the power of the Lord, you must be
   acquainted with the power of men. You must know that every time we let
   down our guard, every time we trusted in the good will of others, we were
   slaughtered. General, will you go down in history as the man who handed
   our haven to the enemy? What is different about today? Enlighten me.
   Are people kinder? Do we have fewer enemies? Are their weapons weaker?
   Enlighten me, General. If there is nothing different about today, perhaps
   you think *you* are what is different—you have everything under control.

(Pause)

Let me ask you this question, then. What are you going to do if I tell you
   that tonight we will take revenge for the Jew whose throat was slit in Gaza
   today? How will you control us?

ASHER: I am trying to avoid a confrontation with you, Rabbi.

RABBI: Enlighten me. Do you plan to put me in jail? Pass a law against me?
   (Pause) The fact is you cannot control me because you lack the power.
   Power is what counts here.

ASHER: If you know history, . . .

RABBI: *(Interrupting)* That was only hypothetical. No Jew's throat was slit in
   Gaza today, yet. But I see you accept that it happens often enough not
   even to raise an eyebrow.

ASHER: You caught me off guard.

RABBI: Or shed a tear.

ASHER: You caught me again. Rabbi, if you know history, you know that what weakened us every time was internal war. As you just pointed out, I must rely on your good will.

RABBI: So easily he backs down! Do not be afraid to be proud, General—God has made you in his image! We are both of the house of David. I will go only so far in opposing you.

ASHER: *(Trying to end the visit)* Thank you, Rabbi. I've got to . . .

RABBI: *(Interrupting)* That's more than you'll be able to say for your Arab friends. *(Pause)* I have been remiss. I've allowed our talk to stay on strategy and tactics rather than on the important thing you and I share—our covenant with God.

ASHER: That talk has to wait for another day, Rabbi. I've got to get on with my job.

RABBI: I don't think you know your job. God has written your job description. I hope you will allow me to read it—it's no more than a paragraph. *(Opening to a ribboned page in a Bible.)* "When the Lord your God brings you to the land to take possession of it, and clears away many nations before you, then you must utterly destroy them; you shall make no covenant with them, and show no mercy to them . . . you shall break down their altars, and dash in pieces their pillars, and burn their graven images with fire." Deuteronomy, Chapter 7, Verses 1 and 5. That is your job.

ASHER: Rabbi, you and I do have a common interest. This land. I'm going to ask you for a gift.

RABBI: A gift . . .

ASHER: A period of peace. No provocations.

RABBI: No provocations? . . . Earlier today, I passed one of my students being led out in handcuffs.

ASHER: Reuben.

RABBI: Reuben . . . Do you know what a provocation it is to punish a young man for his loyalty? You are in no position to talk about provocations!

(The Rabbi leaves. Spotlight on Asher.)

ASHER: *(To us)* My father always remembered my grandmother growing plants from orange seeds on her windowsill in Germany. He remembered her saying, "Look at the miracle—this tiny seed holds the complete plan for an orange tree." When he decided to make his life on a kibbutz, he took

great pleasure in the orange trees. Watching him at work I learned that all
things need order to flourish, and protection from extremes. Life is fragile, and all life exists only by finding a narrow crevice between extremes.
But here, everyone here is a messenger of God, whipping up the winds
with words, fanning sparks into firestorms.

(Pause)

Tending the occupation, I kept the damage of the storms in check. Until the
season of the Passover arrived, and with it developed a tragedy that aimed
itself like a tornado and set down in a small village that happened to be
Samir's. It started with Reuben and his settlement during the Passover
celebration. Or maybe earlier with Reuben and me when I took that unusual action of banning him. Or maybe earlier with Reuben and the locals
he offended. Or maybe at the beginning of time.

*(Morning light comes up across the stage. Two girls—Sara and Hannah, walk in
with picnic baskets; the effect should be that there is a whole group of youngsters
following along behind them. They read from their Bibles.)*

To celebrate the Passover, the youth groups—the "Young Pioneers"—take
hikes throughout the land here.

*(Asher recedes. Reuben, the group's guard, follows the girls holding a gun, constantly
on high alert, surveying the surroundings. Thus protected, the girls sometimes interrupt their reading to bend down and pick flowers.)*

HANNAH: "Go out in joy and be led forth in peace. The mountains and the
hills shall break forth into singing."

REUBEN:"When the house of Jacob came forth out of Egypt, The sea saw it
and fled; The Jordan turned backward. The mountains skipped like rams,
The hills like young sheep. Tremble, thou earth, at the presence of the
Lord, At the presence of the God of Jacob!" *(Reuben walks on in the lead.
Walking quickly, he will soon be out of sight.)*

HANNAH: "Lo, the winter is past . . ."

SARA: "The rain is over and gone . . ."

HANNAH: "The flowers appear on the earth . . ."

SARA: "The time of the singing of birds is come . . ."

HANNAH: "And the voice of the turtle is heard in our land."

SARA: But—if you make your home in Judea or Samaria, do not walk un-
   guarded.

HANNAH: Reuben and Misha are with us; their guns protect us.

SARA: *(Glancing back)* Hey guys, c'mon, keep up with us.

HANNAH: *(Looking back, amused)* Avi's hat got blown into the stream.

SARA: Debra's collecting flowers.

(A muezzin's call to prayer starts up. For a moment it casts a chill over Sara and Hannah and they are silent.)

(Calling ahead) Hannah, wait! We should stay together.

HANNAH: We have to keep up with Reuben!

SARA: Reuben! Why doesn't he wait? *(Calling ahead)* Reuben, wait for the
   others!

(Hannah has now reached the stage, stage right, and the morning light closes in, capturing her in a small spotlight.)

Wait! Hannah!

HANNAH: *(To us)* Finally, Reuben stops, the others reach us, and we spread
   a cloth and set out our breakfast. *(Sara recedes.)* Suddenly we realize that
   Arabs are on the hillside watching us, stones in their hands. A stone cuts
   through the air. Reuben raises his gun. Misha grabs his arm, but Reuben
   pushes him away and fires into the air. We want to get back to the main
   road, but we're not sure of the way. We don't want to go into the riverbed
   because they could trap us there. We keep our heads high to not show fear.
   Stones are falling closer. Reuben fires more warning shots. Misha grabs his
   arm, and this time they start to fight. We read our psalms. In grave danger we read our psalms.

(Tarik enters.)

TARIK: *(To us)* Soon, I will tell you what really happened. *(He watches Hannah
   intently.)*

HANNAH: *(To us)* They come down holding stones. Reuben shouts, "They
   want the gun. Make a circle around me so they can't reach the gun! Protect
   the gun!" We circle around Reuben just in time. The Arabs swarm down
   from the hills, surrounding us with their heat, their breath, their smells,
   their pushing. Some are shouting, "Give them safe passage and get rid of

them." Others say, "Let them walk into the hills and get lost." Others say, "Take them to the village center." They say the *mukhtar* [MOOKH-tar] will decide how many deaths and who will die.

TARIK: This village is my village. We had scores to settle, but we weren't lying in wait for armed settlers. Everybody knows their guard—he's a lunatic. His "warning" bullet killed Rasheed. "Who is Rasheed," you are saying. "Why do we need to hear those names?" The newspapers don't give our names. Nobody asks our names. So I will say our names. I will say Rasheed, I will say Reema, I will say Ahmed, and I will say "the *shabeeb*"—the name for all our heroic youth! Rasheed is a boy who was out with his plow until the settler's bullet found his heart. After the first shots, men ran to the mosque to sound an alarm. The *shabeeb* wanted blood for blood right there. But the older ones said take the settlers to the *mukhtar*. The older ones won this time, but be warned—their time is running out.

HANNAH: They force us into the center. The streets get narrower, the mob presses in. "Kill the Jews," "Death to the Jews!" *"Allahu Akbar!"* Women and girls doing that weird screaming. Everywhere—hands raised with stones. A man came up behind us silently. He took my elbow and led me and Debra into his house. He shut the door against the mob. *(Pause)* When I came out of the Arab's house, everything was quiet. I was in an Arab street, kneeling over Sara, giving her mouth-to-mouth resuscitation.

TARIK: *(Subdued)* Ahmed, a teacher, pushed on the settler girl's chest to revive her heart.

HANNAH: Blood was flowing from her head.

TARIK: People ran to call for ambulances.

HANNAH: They had stoned Sara to death.

TARIK: That is not what happened. I saw with my own eyes what happened.

HANNAH: We don't leave blood on a street. Our teachings tell us that when someone dies and the blood is spilled, you must bring back the blood and bury it with the body. Daniel and Avi took off their shirts to soak it up. While they collected Sara's blood, Arab boys stood on a roof and made victory signs.

(The sun is now an enormous blood-red disk. It becomes molten and then chars, blackening into sunset. In a moment the darkness of the night is shattered by sirens, flashbulbs, TV lights, reporters.)

REPORTER 1: Today in the West Bank the escalating uprising erupted into a fight between civilians; this time it was a fight to the death. In a moment we will bring you the commander.

(Asher enters with an Aide, who starts to block the cameras.)

ASHER: No, let them film—we want everyone to know what's happening and how we're responding. *(To the cameras)* The children were forced to go into the village . . . When they arrived there the crowd grew larger and violence broke out. Some of the locals tried to rescue the children. We have begun an investigation and the village is closed.

REPORTER 2: At dusk hundreds of soldiers in full combat gear poured into the area, fanning out to hunt for any lost children. Helicopters hung overhead. The army put the village under curfew.

REPORTER 1: From the very start of the uprising there have been dire predictions that it had to come down to war between the people who live in the West Bank—the Arabs and the Jews.

(Blackout. Two village men meet in the glare of searchlights. They speak in whispers.)

VOICE-IN-THE-DARK 1: *(Hurriedly)* They're past the Baradis.

VOICE-IN-THE-DARK 2: Every truck in the occupation is driving into this village.

MILITARY POLICE OFFICER: Every male resident over the age of fourteen is required to go to the square in front of the schoolhouse! You must have an identity card.

VOICE-IN-THE-DARK 1: The Khalifa boys ran up into the hills.

VOICE-IN-THE-DARK 2: Don't try it. They've got patrols out there by now.

VOICE-IN-THE-DARK 1: Yusef got caught.

MILITARY POLICE OFFICER: Every male resident over the age of fourteen is required to go to the schoolhouse square! You must have your identity card.

VOICE-IN-THE-DARK 2: Now let me warn you about how they question you.

VOICE-IN-THE-DARK 1: I'll show you my arms and my legs.

VOICE-IN-THE-DARK 2: Listen! They ask something they know about your family to make you think they're on to everything. And you know where they get the information?

VOICE-IN-THE-DARK 1: Collaborators!

VOICE-IN-THE-DARK 2: No! That's what they want you to think. They get
   it from you, me, anyone—who tells them something, just to get off the
   hook. Whatever you say gets used against somebody. So—you plant something false.

VOICE-IN-THE-DARK 1: About some*one* false.

VOICE-IN-THE-DARK 2: They listen for a name that gets given a few times.
   Then they zero in on it.

MILITARY POLICE OFFICER: Every male resident over the age of fourteen to
   the square in front of the schoolhouse!

*(The Village square at night. Searchlights rove. The Military Police Officer checks
through identity cards as he surveys a sea of detainees.)*

(Over a bullhorn) Samir the mechanic! . . . Who is Samir the mechanic? *(Pause)*
   Identify yourself by rising! Samir the mechanic!

VOICE-IN-THE-DARK 2: *(Whispered)* Back row.

VOICE-IN-THE-DARK 1: *(Whispered)* Next to the well.

(The spotlight searches the area.)

MILITARY POLICE OFFICER: Samir the mechanic?!

*(The spotlight zeros in as Samir, handcuffed and blindfolded, rises. Blackout.
Across the stage, out of the dark come murmurs of the Kaddish.)*

ALL: *(In a round) Yisgadal v'yiskadash sh'me rabbo . . .*

(Newspaper headlines are shouted, drowning out the Kaddish.)

VOICE OF NEWS HAWKER 1: "Girl Mobbed and Stoned to Death in West Bank
   Village!"

VOICE OF NEWS HAWKER 2: "Day of Blood!"

VOICE OF NEWS HAWKER 3: "Fourteen-Year-Old Settler Girl Stoned to Death
   by Arabs!"

*(Night light up on an entrance to the village. In the background—glare of torch-
lights, protesting settlers.)*

AIDE: We've set up the roadblocks, the backup troops are in position. And all
   the remaining children are safely accounted for.

ASHER: Excellent . . . How can I get to speak with a particular man in the village . . .

AIDE: They're all under guard outside the schoolhouse, sir. I could get a car to drive you over there . . .

ASHER: No, I'm needed here now . . .

AIDE: Or I could ask MPs to bring him to you . . .

ASHER: He'd have to come under guard?

AIDE: If he walks here on his own, he'd be stopped at every point.

ASHER: I see.

AIDE: Should I call for an MP, sir?

ASHER: *(Pause)* No, no—not now, not priority . . .

PROTESTERS: *(Over a bullhorn, from a distance, with swelling repetitions from a crowd)* A new settlement where her blood was spilled!

AIDE: We've ordered the settlers to keep the demonstration *across* the road from the village, sir.

PROTESTERS: *(Over a bullhorn, from a distance, with swelling repetitions from a crowd)* A collective crime gets collective punishment!

AIDE: We told them the bonfires had to stay contained, and out in the open field.

PROTESTERS: *(Over a bullhorn, from a distance, with swelling repetitions from a crowd)* Raze the village to the ground!

ASHER: *(To the Aide)* All right. We've got two objectives. Keep the settlers out; keep the locals in. I want a trench dug out at every road to the village. I want the troops to form a human chain around the entire perimeter of the village. Keep the locals in, keep the settlers out. A tight chain, linking hands, around the entire perimeter. The operative word is *safe*. We are going to ensure everyone's safety.

(Spotlight on a sheet-covered body on a gurney table. A Doctor stands by.)

AIDE: Sir, the autopsy of the girl has been completed. The doctor asks you to come for the report.

(The Aide and Asher approach the gurney. The Doctor raises the sheet. Asher looks at the girl's face for a long moment.)

DOCTOR: General, we have a very surprising finding.

(The Doctor holds out a bullet.)

This bullet was in the girl's brain. This —

ASHER: *(Interrupting)* The locals didn't have firearms. We did a search last week.

AIDE: It's the same caliber as the guard's gun, sir.

ASHER: What are you saying?

DOCTOR: That this bullet, and not a stone, was the cause of death.

(Asher takes the bullet and examines it.)

AIDE: We've been putting together the scenario, and, from the angle of entry, it seems that as the guard fell, his trajectory must have altered. *(He illustrates the arc.)* And that produced the bullet that killed the girl.

ASHER: You're certain of this? There's no doubt?

AIDE: Yes, sir. The girl was standing close to him. He'd told the children to encircle him to protect the gun. The bullet entered through the base of her brain.

ASHER: And the stone?

DOCTOR: Sir, there is no wound here that is not the result of the bullet.

ASHER: No more tests needed? This is certain?

DOCTOR: Yes, General.

(Asher walks away from the autopsy.)

AIDE: *(Coming after him)* Sir, are you going to release the information?

ASHER: There's no way we could keep it from the press if we wanted to. And we don't want to.

AIDE: There are people you'll want to inform first, sir?

ASHER: *(Reminded)* Of course. But carefully, carefully.

(The Aide exits.)

Carefully, carefully. We're a frightened people. And with good reason. And we don't like to be told that the world might be a little less malevolent than we thought. We're afraid we'll be gulled into carelessness. We're an angry people. And with good reason. And we don't like to have the fuel stolen away. We're a moral people. Which is why we have to close our eyes. We don't like to see that the people we step on everyday for the sake of the haven might be decent people. When this bullet is made public . . .

(Crossfade to a detention room, where an Interrogator faces Samir, who sits with hands bound, blindfolded.)

INTERROGATOR: So, Samir, tell us what you were doing when the clash started.

SAMIR: I came home for lunch.

INTERROGATOR: Was anyone else with you?

SAMIR: Yes.

INTERROGATOR: Who?!

SAMIR: *(Softly)* My wife.

INTERROGATOR: *(Loudly)* Your wife *(Writing it down)*. What was your first contact with the children?

SAMIR: *(Trying to be cordial, expecting all will turn out well)* I heard shouting, I looked outside. There was a big crowd. The young people were at the center. People were shouting at them, pushing them. They looked very frightened, some were crying. To me, youngsters are youngsters. I see they're children. They're born into this. They cannot help it. I know how I'd want mine to be protected. *(Assuming everyone knows the rest of the story and not wanting to brag)* So . . . May I have a cigarette? Look *(Raising his hands to the blindfold)*, is this necessary?

(The Interrogator knocks Samir's hands away, startling him.)

INTERROGATOR: Go on.

(Silence)

INTERROGATOR: Go on!

SAMIR: *(Pause)* About what?

INTERROGATOR: Who was doing the stone throwing and the shouting?

SAMIR: I couldn't see, I was in the house.

INTERROGATOR: But people *were* throwing stones and shouting.

SAMIR: Yes.

INTERROGATOR: You said before you were at the window. Who did you see? . . . Who?!

SAMIR: *(Pause)* There's been a lot of trouble here, and people are very anxious.

INTERROGATOR: A beautiful soul! Who?!

SAMIR: What do you want from me?

INTERROGATOR: You've been identified as a ringleader. You were seen hurling stones at the children.

SAMIR: *(Slowly, realization is hitting hard)* What is this?

INTERROGATOR: And inciting others with shouts of *"Allahu akbar"* and "Death to the Jews".

SAMIR: Is this the way you do things?

INTERROGATOR: Who was shouting? You said you saw them. Give me names.

SAMIR: You want me to accuse my neighbors.

INTERROGATOR: Five separate witnesses identified you. Five witnesses from this village identified you. Because your house is used as a base for stonings, it has been declared a critical hazard. Under emergency regulations it will be demolished at dawn.

SAMIR: I don't do these things.

INTERROGATOR: Five witnesses from this village. You think they have something against you? Tell us who would have something against you. Names.

SAMIR: You have all been in my shop. I don't do these things. *(Samir's mouth is turning to cotton.)* Please . . . some water.

INTERROGATOR: There's water right here. Who went to the mosque and used the loudspeaker to call out the crowd? Names.

(Samir can't get words out.)

(Interrogator puts a cup into Samir's hand.) Here's water. Six hours 'til dawn.

(Samir takes a sip. The Interrogator pulls away the cup.)

SAMIR: *(Disoriented)* When I heard the shouting, I looked out. I saw that I could reach two of the girls, so I went out and brought them into my house. I shut the door to keep out the crowd.

INTERROGATOR: A lily white dove! Is that what you are—a lily white dove? Let's see you flap your wings.

(Samir does nothing.)

Are your wings clipped? . . . Well how are you going to prove you're a lily white dove? Let's hear you coo.

SAMIR: *(Strong again with anger)* You know me. I fix your cars for you.

INTERROGATOR: *You* fix *our* cars? What do you do, install bombs? Of course not, everybody loves us. No one ever throws a stone. You love us, right?

(Silence)

You whipped up the mob! You hurled stones! A girl is dead.

SAMIR: You decided I am guilty; why are you asking me?

INTERROGATOR: So that you can help us and we can help you.

(Silence)

Look, Samir, if you cooperate, maybe we could see about sealing rather than
demolition . . .

(Silence)

Give me names. Who was shouting?

(Silence)

Who put up the flags?

(Silence)

Want a cigarette? Here's a cigarette.

SAMIR: No.

INTERROGATOR: Maybe we need to bring in your wife for questioning.

SAMIR: No!

INTERROGATOR: No? Then coo to prove you're a dove. Flap your wings.

*(Samir, hands cuffed together, moves his elbows up and down, and makes a cooing
sound.)*

All right then. We're making progress. Who put up the flags?

(Crossfade from the detention room to Asher and the Aide)

AIDE: *(Gently waking Asher)* Sir . . . sir, the Rabbi is here on behalf of the settlements . . .

ASHER: He hasn't been told yet, has he?

AIDE: Yes, sir, I think he has . . . by the chief-of-staff, sir.

(The Aide exits as the Rabbi enters.)

RABBI: *(Approaching from a distance)* What's this about a bullet? I cannot
fathom what difference a bullet makes.

(Asher rises.)

A beautiful soul! Everyday you look in the mirror and see reflected your beautiful soul. When the Arabs look at you do you know what they see? Weakness. The Arabs see weakness in your face. They have a name for you—
you know what it is? "General Zigzag." That is what the Arabs call you.
If, and I'm only saying if, that bullet came from Reuben's gun, it was directly propelled by a stone thrown at him with deadly intent. What court
in the world would not convict the stone thrower? No witness denies that
Reuben was hit in the head by a stone. He's unconscious.

ASHER: The stone thrower will be charged. No disagreement. Beyond that,
what's your point, Rabbi?

RABBI: What do you plan to do about the mob?

ASHER: I intend to find out what precipitated it.

RABBI: Does anything make it right to mob and stone innocent children? The
whole world finally sees the fear we have to live with. Concretely. Dra-
matically. And you are going to declare to the press, "Forget it. It was a
mistake."

ASHER: Are you advising me to cover up the truth?

RABBI: Truth?! How do you know an Arab did not grab the gun and shoot it?

ASHER: None of the children suggested anything like that.

RABBI: The children are saying that there was an Arab on the roof of a house
with a Kalishnikov aiming at them.

ASHER: There were no firearms in that village. Rabbi, if we're not an honest
society, we're not worth preserving.

RABBI: (Stunned, softly) Would you repeat that?

(Asher is silent.)

RABBI: Repeat it, please. I want to know who we are dealing with.

ASHER: (Trying to minimize it) If we're not an honest society, we're not worth
preserving.

RABBI: Perhaps you would allow God to make that judgment! . . . Or do you
think you are God?

(A moment of silence)

Asher, I have been thinking about how to appeal to you, how to make you
understand . . . Answer just one question for me. Why? Even animals don't

go against their own. Why do the Arabs need to hear this? Why does the world need to hear this?

ASHER: Not the Arabs, or the world. Us. In this bullet exists a moral.

RABBI: A general teaching morals.

ASHER: No . . .

RABBI: I'd be ashamed of you if you did not teach morals. I'm talking only about the strategy. Asher, here is my lesson for today: a people who are terrified for their lives can't hear morals. First you punish our enemies—you show we are a mighty people who cannot be intimidated. Then our people will see that here is a general who cares about our safety, and they will listen. Let pictures of houses blasting to the sky introduce the sop about the bullet!

(The Interrogator bustles in.)

INTERROGATOR: We've got substantial agreement on six points, General.

ASHER: Can you leave us, Rabbi . . .

RABBI: Asher, we don't always understand God's ways, but remember this: we are doing God's work here.

(The Rabbi leaves.)

INTERROGATOR: Substantial agreement on six points, General. One—about 10:15, the group entered the fields, the guard started off with a quick finger on the trigger—when he saw locals were gathering he fired "in the air" to scatter them, but it seems that he killed one. Two—around 10:45, the locals mobbed the kids, threatened with stones, made them go into the village, whooped up the atmosphere with *"Allahu Akbars"* and "Kill the Jews." Three—during that time, some locals did protect the kids. Four—at about 11:00 the final clash was triggered when the sister of the man who was killed hurled a stone at the guard. The guard fired, bullets and stones were flying, and the girl fell at that time. Five—around 11:15, village families ran to call ambulances and get help. Six—we have identified four ringleaders who generally incited the mob.

ASHER: Strong testimony? We're not going to be stampeded.

INTERROGATOR: At least five witnesses have identified each of the four. And five is all that's required.

ASHER: There's no need to carry out demolitions *today* if there's any question about the guilt of any of them.

INTERROGATOR: No question. Plenty of corroboration.

ASHER: I'll go with you. I want to see each man who's accused.

(They start off, but the Chief-of-Staff strides in from the direction the Rabbi exited, puts a friendly but controlling arm around Asher, turns him around and brings him back.)

ASHER: *(To the Interrogator)* I'll follow shortly.

(The Interrogator exits.)

CHIEF-OF-STAFF: *(Indicating the direction from which the Rabbi exited)* Asher, you owe me one!

ASHER: Steamrollered by "Old Thunderbolt!" What did I lose?

CHIEF-OF-STAFF: Nothing, really.

ASHER: C'mon.

CHIEF-OF-STAFF: *(Tentatively)* We're going to announce the bullet.

ASHER: On the condition that . . .

CHIEF-OF-STAFF: The Rabbi wants us to hold the announcement until after the funeral.

ASHER: *(Sarcastically)* Good thinking. Keep the anger boiling.

CHIEF-OF-STAFF: He sees the announcement of the bullet as disrespectful to the family, to their grief.

ASHER: Disrespectful . . . How do you see it?

CHIEF-OF-STAFF: Just difficult. Another condition—he wants demolitions before the announcement, before the funeral, the first item on the morning news.

ASHER: You agreed already?

CHIEF-OF-STAFF: Provisionally. I said we'd talk about it. Ultimately it's your call.

ASHER: I wanted the freedom . . .

CHIEF-OF-STAFF: *(Interrupting)* They're doing a war dance in the settlement. If we don't move fast, they'll move first.

ASHER: I know the script.

CHIEF-OF-STAFF: You can preempt a lot of ugliness.

ASHER: I didn't want my hand forced . . .

CHIEF-OF-STAFF: Is there a problem?

ASHER: There are people in this village who didn't want that tragedy to happen. I want to strengthen their position. I wanted time to consider. An hour.

CHIEF-OF-STAFF: Take your time. But it won't get easier.

ASHER: For strategy—how to use that bullet to turn things around.

CHIEF-OF-STAFF: Just how are you thinking of doing that, Asher?

ASHER: I want to make it crystal clear here that our own fears are contributing to our tragedies. It was an unstable situation with the locals. It could've gone either way. The guard's own bullet, fired in panic, killed the girl he was protecting . . . it's a symbol of what's happening to us.

CHIEF-OF-STAFF: Symbol?! The settlers don't listen to philosophy. They're very practical. The conclusion they'll draw is that we aren't providing enough protection.

ASHER: Not enough protection?!!! They didn't inform us of the hike, they didn't have working communication devices . . . there's not one single regulation they paid attention to!

CHIEF-OF-STAFF: Then you have to tell them that. I'll back you up. *After* this blows over. Otherwise you're pouring fuel on the fire. Once they feel protected, then maybe you'll have your audience. It's a question of timing. Come, Asher, we need you to brief the settlement leaders, calm them down.

(Asher hesitates.)

You'll be back by dawn.

(The Chief-of-Staff sweeps Asher off. Blackout. Sounds of roosters crowing. The sun rises on a street in Samir's village. Muezzin's call to prayer comes up. Asher enters, walking quickly. Sounds of army trucks rumbling in drown out the call to prayer. Across the stage, a Sergeant is measuring a house.)

ASHER: Is this one of the houses?

SERGEANT: Yes, sir, it is.

ASHER: I haven't signed any orders yet.

SERGEANT: We've been told to have everything ready, sir.

ASHER: Make sure that's understood.

SERGEANT: Yes, sir.

ASHER: Where are the accused being held?

SERGEANT: Still at the schoolhouse, sir . . .

(Asher starts to walk off.)

Sir, may I show you something?

(Asher turns back.)

Just a side thing, sir, but the last house we wired up—we found a photo. Can I show it to you sir? *(Showing it to Asher)* Now it looks like it's just a photo of a girl. But—look carefully at the poster in the background. See what I mean there? This is in some kind of café, and there's a poster of a political candidate in the background. Writing's in Hebrew. Now, that café's not on the West Bank, that's for dead sure. I know that candidate and you probably do too, sir, and he's just the political stripe for you know what . . . For his supporters to be a target, if you know what I mean . . . Should I hand this over to an MP, sir?

ASHER: *(Coolly)* No, I'll take care of it. Who owns the house?

SERGEANT: It's owned by . . . *(Reading)* "Samir the mechanic" . . . Charged with "inciting the mob" . . . Maybe we nipped something in the bud . . .

(Blackout. Lights up on the detention room. Samir sits blindfolded and bound. Asher enters.)

ASHER: Samir! *(Taking off Samir's blindfold)* Samir . . .

(Samir is impassive.)

Please forgive us. *(Untying the ropes on Samir's wrists)* I found out less than ten minutes ago. When a soldier showed me this photo they found in the house.

(Silence)

Why didn't you ask to speak to me?

(Samir is now untied but he does not move out of the position in which he was bound. Samir counters Asher with a cool, absent-from-body withdrawal.)

(Trying for lightness) In any case, as you would say, "The commander comes to you."

(Silence)

Why the hell didn't you ask for me?

SAMIR: I did not want to embarrass you.

ASHER: Wonderful!

SAMIR: I thought maybe this is a game your boys play to get names.

ASHER: No . . . you were identified as a ringleader.

SAMIR: I see.

ASHER: People from this village. Five witnesses.

SAMIR: I see.

ASHER: Of course your home's safe, there's no doubt of that.

SAMIR: *(After a moment)* If others will be punished I must be punished too.

ASHER: Samir—look at me . . . Get up, cut this out.

SAMIR: You must blow up my home.

ASHER: I'm going to destroy the home of an innocent man?

SAMIR: *(Taunting)* How could five witnesses be wrong?

ASHER: *(Pause)* Are they punishing you because of me?

SAMIR: I'm wondering why you're doubting my neighbors.

ASHER: Okay. You were hurling stones and shouting, "Death to the Jews."

SAMIR: Maybe the witnesses' words mean nothing to you because we are Arabs.

ASHER: You're playing with me.

SAMIR: You know how treacherous Arabs are.

ASHER: God damn you. This is turning nasty and twisted.

SAMIR: We *are* nasty and twisted. Like the olive trees. Do you know that you can't uproot an olive tree? You think you've torn it out, but its roots twist so far underground that new sprouts appear where you never expect them.

ASHER: What do you want me to do?

SAMIR: As a man interested in our land, you should know about the olive trees . . .

ASHER: Okay. I know you're angry beyond words, and I do know about olive trees. You've told me. *(Pause)* Your house will be as steadfast as the olive trees and that's that.

SAMIR: You're not listening.

ASHER: If you're afraid that the village will take revenge on you, I can protect you . . . Is that or isn't that what's behind this? *(Pause)* You're your own worst enemy with your secrecy.

(Silence)

You want me to say I was wrong? Say we make mistakes? I'm saying I was wrong! I'm saying mistakes got made! I said something must have gone wrong!

(The Sergeant approaches the door, knocks, peers in.)

SERGEANT: Sir, they're waiting for you to sign the command.

(Asher motions he should go away.)

Crowds are beginning to gather, sir.
ASHER: Thank you.

(The Sergeant leaves.)

(To Samir) What about the house that will always have a room for Rivka?
SAMIR: *(Pause)* That was a house in a village where people respected me.
ASHER: You offered her a wedding feast!
SAMIR: Do you understand? That house is already destroyed. That's all there is to it.
ASHER: She doesn't care about the hotheads in the village!

(Pause)

If I don't get out there soon we're going to have a riot on our hands.

(He holds the photo out to Samir.)

This girl is now a young woman who has, for the first time in her life, met her father, been invited to his home . . .
SAMIR: I don't want to hear another word about her!
ASHER: You're going to ruin your life for pride. And you want me to be the instrument of it.
SAMIR: I'm really a father to be proud of now!

(Taking the photo, he tosses it to the floor.)

You have demolitions waiting. You want to participate with your men. You better be on your way.
ASHER: God damn you, Samir. We've trusted each other all these years.

SAMIR: You cannot put yourself in my shoes. You have no understanding. We are fundamentally different. You cannot put yourself in my shoes, and you show repulsive arrogance in thinking that you can.

(Asher strides to the door.)

(Slowly, coolly) Now listen to me. Listen carefully. Don't make a special case of me. You'll do me no favor. If you want to show consideration for me, you will not spare my house. If you spare my house you are doing it for yourself.

(Blackout. The call to prayer starts up. Explosion. A cloud of smoke and dust. Ululating cries from the women. Seen through the cloud, dimly lit, Asher at first stands at attention, then bows his head.)

MALE VOICES: *(In a low rumble) Allahu akbar! Allahu akbar!*
ECHOES: *Allahu akbar! Allahu akbar!*

(From the opposite corner of the stage, still shrouded in smoke, comes Hannah's girlish voice, which finally drowns out the call to prayer.)

HANNAH: No . . . , no . . . , no, that's not him . . . *(Suddenly, warmly)* That's him!
INTERROGATOR: Are you sure?
HANNAH: Certain.

(As the smoke clears and the dust settles, we see Hannah going through a stack of identity cards with the Interrogator.)

INTERROGATOR: That's the man who took you in?
HANNAH: Definitely.
INTERROGATOR: Okay, now that I know the general configuration, let me show you some others.

(He selects some cards from the pack and shows them, one by one, to Hannah.)

HANNAH: No . . . no . . . no . . . The one you showed me before . . . That's him.
INTERROGATOR: Tell me once again what happened.
HANNAH: We were surrounded by Arabs. Then a man came up behind me and touched my elbow, and whispered, "Come with me." He said that to me and Debra.

(The Interrogator shuffles the cards.)

INTERROGATOR: You know that you are never supposed to leave your group, don't you?

HANNAH: The group was all separated. We were separated from the others already.

INTERROGATOR: *(Handing her the cards)* Again. Show me the one.

(Asher approaches the Interrogator's doorway.)

HANNAH: This one.

INTERROGATOR: General, I'm afraid there's been an unfortunate mistake.

(Crossfade from the Interrogator to the detention room. Asher storms in.)

ASHER: You set me up . . .

(Samir smiles to himself.)

That's funny?! It's funny that you've made me look like a tyrant and a fool?

SAMIR: No, Asher. We were friends a long time.

ASHER: I told you I'd protect you!

SAMIR: But some things even you can't do.

ASHER: You showed me that! When I told you I could protect you, I could protect you. You and your family. And with respect. You had skills . . .

SAMIR: Empty words, Asher, empty words. Who would you protect me from? This whole village is my family. What's your idea? That you'd punish my enemies here? Or that I'd take Mouna and all the children and pack up our belongings and my garage, and go where? Some destination where nobody knows us? You take me away from here and you take my life. Our lives are in this village. They fed me from the time I was born, and they'll bury me here when I die.

ASHER: *We* moved from town to town—from country to country—children had to be sent off without parents, parents without children—and don't you dare, don't you dare say, "period, end of conversation"! *(Pause)* Acknowledge that I offered what any of *us* would have accepted with joy! You acknowledge that I've offered something acceptable and decent, and something I could deliver! You acknowledge to me that they are not empty words!

(Silence)

We developed independence, and courage, and wits, because we had to. Everywhere we were turned out. Put down roots, tear them up! Put down roots, tear them up! But no. You'd rather live in rubble among people who betrayed you. Because *that's* what happened! That's the only way this could have happened! Your neighbors betrayed you!

SAMIR: I will have to accept their judgment of me. I understand them better now.

ASHER: What does that mean? I'm fed up with you talking in circles! Can you say anything directly? Just one thing. Give it a try.

SAMIR: Did you ever think that Jews might be responsible for what happens to them?

(Silence)

You put yourselves above everyone else—Jewish blood must not be spilled! Land for Jewish graves instead of people's farms. But when you're a farmer you love the earth. You know her feel, her smell—you know everything about her.

ASHER: And we don't. Let me get just what the hell you're saying—all that "when you're a farmer" mumbo-jumbo—

SAMIR: We accept what the land gives us. You grow things in the air, in the water . . .

ASHER: Where the hell is that coming from?!

SAMIR: You can't come in and buy the earth with money or with experiments. You cannot make the earth love you.

ASHER: No? We're doing better than you did with years of stupidity and neglect.

SAMIR: You wanted my love to be your passport here, but it can't be.

(Silence)

It is there now for everyone to see that "the land of the Jews" is not a just land. Not a wise land. Even under the most just commander they could find. Even God will see. God will see what His chosen really are.

ASHER: This has been inside you all the time? Under everything? Under everything between us?

SAMIR: Just take your precious souls and your graves and get out and leave us alone.

ASHER: You want to know about Jews? I'll tell you something about Jews —
we don't turn our own people over to the enemy!

(Silence)

And I'll tell you something else. That story you're feeling so self-righteous over.
So *(With mock sympathy)*, the parents turned you out. If that woman were
an Arab her parents would have killed her. You live in the middle ages.
Worse than animals. We don't kill our own.

(Silence)

That secrecy of yours was like a knife, wasn't it? You crafted it, you sharpened
it, you waited in the dark, and when the chance came you stabbed me in
the back. They stab you. You stab me.

*(Crossfade to a village road. The call to prayer starts up. Asher appears. A Sergeant
awaits him.)*

SERGEANT: A Molotov cocktail was thrown at a settler's car, sir. Right up the
road. The perpetrators fled.

ASHER: How do we usually respond in such a case? *(He knows the answer.)*

SERGEANT: Uproot the trees that give cover to the perpetrators, sir.

ASHER: Then why are we waiting? Order it done.

SERGEANT: Yes, sir. *(Pause)* How extensive, sir?

ASHER: How extensive?

SERGEANT: It's an almond orchard. I thought you'd want to say whether or
not the whole orchard.

ASHER: If it creates a screen from the road, tear it up. Back to a hundred meters
from the road. That's the regulation.

SERGEANT: Yes, sir. *(Pause)* It's in full bloom. I thought you'd want to be consulted. *(Pause)* The bulldozers are ready.

ASHER: Then get 'em started. We can't spend our lives in this village.

SERGEANT: Sir?

ASHER: It's time to close ranks, Sergeant!

SERGEANT: Thank you, sir. *(A moment, then, seeing Asher hasn't budged)* It's a
full day for you, sir. The men can take it from here.

ASHER: I'll be right here with them.

(The Sergeant motions in an invisible bulldozer, whose approaching rumble drowns out the call to prayer. He positions it with hand signals, talks to the driver over a walkie-talkie.)

SERGEANT: Start with those babies there! Molotov haven.

(Crunch of a bulldozer crashing into wood, breaking, uprooting a multitude of trees)

(After inspecting the uprooting) Continue down the line!

(Asher kneels to inspect the uprooting. Petals start to fall. A wind blows and petals waft in from every direction.)

ASHER: Hold it, Sergeant!
SERGEANT: Hold it!
ASHER: Sergeant, over here.

(The Sergeant kneels next to Asher.)

There are still roots.
SERGEANT: Just pieces. They're not gonna go anywhere, sir.
ASHER: Get the bulldozer back. They have to get to the roots.

(Asher is tearing out roots with his hands.)

SERGEANT: Sir . . .
ASHER: All the roots. Every single goddamned root.

(The Sergeant tries gently, in vain, to pull Asher up.)

SERGEANT: Sir, we'd have to bring in a backhoe.
ASHER: I don't think they know about olive trees . . .
SERGEANT: *(Interrupting)* Sir, these are almond trees . . .

(Blitz-out by wind-borne almond petals. Blackout. Night light up on the yard behind Lila and Asher's house. This is the scene of the start of the play.)

ASHER: And then they brought me home.
LILA: Listen how quiet it is *(Lila peers out the window.)* The protesters have
    gone . . . They must be flocking somewhere else.

(Silence)

So you had to give the command to blow up Samir's house . . . I don't think
  you had a choice.

(Silence)

(Compassionately) Asher, tomorrow there'll be some new disaster and this will
  be forgotten.

(Silence)

ASHER: It's what I felt when I did it. I felt a revenge so primitive . . .
LILA: Against the village?
ASHER: No, let it be.
LILA: Against Samir?
ASHER: Against Samir.
LILA: For protecting his future?
ASHER: No, I understand that.
LILA: For what, then? . . . For not loving you? For not giving you his blessing
  to live on this land?
ASHER: Something like that . . . It was a fear. A fear so deep, so sickeningly
  deep . . . "we're all farmers here, you're aliens, we know the earth, we love
  the earth, you can't come in and buy it . . ."
LILA: Asher, that's just the old cant.
ASHER: Not when it comes from Samir . . . Because if it's inside Samir, it's in-
  side everyone.
LILA: Come inside, Asher.
ASHER: In a moment. You go in.

*(Lila goes into the house. He takes out cigarette and lighter. He lights the cigarette.
After a moment a young woman appears. In the dark it is difficult to see that she's
in uniform. Asher looks up wearily.)*

I'm not giving any interviews tonight.
RIVKA: I'm not a reporter . . .

(Pause)

I'm Rivka . . . Your wife gave me the letter—
ASHER: Rivka, of course . . .
RIVKA: The news—that was *his* house, wasn't it?

ASHER: Yes, it was his. It was a very sad mistake.

RIVKA: Can you help me go to see him? They're not allowing anyone in.

ASHER: No, it's too dangerous. *(Pause)* Rivka, he doesn't want to see you right now . . .

RIVKA: He doesn't want to see me now?

ASHER: He believes he has nothing to offer you . . .

RIVKA: Nothing to offer?

ASHER: No house to receive you, no home for a wedding—

RIVKA: Open the door, close the door—

ASHER: *(Interrupting)* That's not fair. He never closed the door until this moment. Until he was caught in this . . . *(A beat)* He thinks differently from you and me. You have to go beyond yourself to understand. Do you see what I'm saying, Rivka? You have to go beyond yourself to understand him.

(A long silence)

What are you thinking, Rivka?

RIVKA: That I never had a father, and I never will.

(Pause)

ASHER: Rivka, Samir told me what he would want to say to you before your wedding. It's about marriage.

RIVKA: He told you something to say to me?

ASHER: Yes. Yes, he did. Are you listening?

RIVKA: *(Softening)* Of course I'm listening.

ASHER: All right. Imagine you have two bookends . . .

(Asher begins to demonstrate the bookends as Samir did.)

You know—the type you see in the old city, made out of olive wood . . . Close your eyes now, and imagine I'm Samir.

(Rivka closes her eyes.)

If your bookends are solidly built and firmly placed, everything they hold between them is safe. But if even one is weak, everything they hold falls. People must be like bookends—back to back—each one supports the other—steadfast.

(The stage becomes black and we no longer see Rivka. Spotlight on Asher.)

The dark is kinder. Even in the middle of a war, if it's pitch black you can stay in a crevice and you're safe there. Eventually the stars will come out . . .

(The stars do come out, slowly.)

And living things will send out green shoots again. Modest shoots, modest efforts.

Curtain

THE LAST SEDER

by Jennifer Maisel

The Last Seder. Theater J production, 2000. Pictured (left to right) are Carla Briscoe, Bernard Engel, Bill Hamlin, Halo Wines, Susan Rome, Kerri Rambow. Photograph copyright © by Stan Barouh.

The first draft of *The Last Seder* was the last piece of mine my mother read before her sudden death and for that it will always hold a special place in my heart. For years I had wanted to write a play about a family at Passover—it's always been my favorite holiday and the ritual of a seder, much like the ritual of a mass, reflects dramatic structure so perfectly. I just didn't know how it was going to work, how I was going to enter the world, whose world it actually was. And then one day it hit me, a monologue I had written years before about a woman standing in Penn Station trying get someone to come home with her for the holiday. That holiday had to be Passover, those words had to be the daughter's first entrance into the world of the play. And then the play came streaming out—

The first draft was one of those writing experiences that writers wish for with each first draft—fast, deep, and furious—possibly because the steps of the seder let me plow through whatever walls sprouted in my path and possibly because it was just one of those times that the magic took hold.

I'm always asked if the play is autobiographical and as much as some audience members have fought me on it, the answer still remains no. People always want to know which of the four daughters I am, and once someone ambushed my sister relentlessly with the same question (I don't think anyone has approached my brother about it). I'll cop to the fact that for fun the house is inspired by the house I grew up in, and the chomping of the horseradish root is evidently something my mom's father did at every seder. But that's where it ends. Really.

What I have come to realize, however, is that at each subsequent reading or performance of the play I relate more to a different daughter. I wrote the first draft as the youngest—and very single—daughter living far from my long-married long-in-love parents. By the first staged reading—when I had lost my mother and was on the verge of being engaged—I realized that the year before I had written a moment that at the time I hadn't known I was going to soon long to experience: the wish of getting to say good-bye to a love who was already gone. I got married while developing the play with Playwrights Theatre of New Jersey, and was just pregnant (and didn't know it) when I flew to Washington, D.C., to receive the Kennedy Center's Fund For New American Plays award only a few weeks after 9/11. The Organic Theatre's production closed the day before I gave birth to my daughter Julia, and I had her in tow when we started to rehearse at Theater J. In a sense the play has become more reflective of my life over time, as if I've grown into it, and I hope for the day when I go to a performance and recognize some of Lily in myself.

The Last Seder is dedicated to the memory of my mother, Joan Maisel. It may not be about you, Mom, but in so many ways, without you, it never would have been written.

In 2000, Playwrights Theatre of New Jersey (John Pietrowski, Artistic Director) was awarded a commission grant from the National Foundation for Jewish Culture, sponsored by the Winnick Family Foundation, to workshop *The Last Seder*. The play was presented publicly in two concert readings on October 28 and 29, 2000, directed by Joseph Megel. It has also been read at The Streisand Festival of New Jewish Plays at the La Jolla Playhouse (dir. Dan Oliverio), The Upper West Side JCC's premiere Springboard reading series (dir. Joseph Megel), and Ensemble Studio Theatre—The LA Project—First Look series (dir. Tamara McDonough).

The Last Seder was given the 2002 Fund for New American Plays Award from the Kennedy Center, a project of the John F. Kennedy Center for the Performing Arts with the support of Countrywide Home Loans, Inc., and the Horace W. Goldsmith Foundation in cooperation with the President's Committee on the Arts and the Humanities. The Fund for New American plays also honored the playwright with the Charlotte Woolard award for most promising new writer. *The Last Seder* was produced at the Organic Theatre in Chicago as part of the Fund for New American Plays grant in May 2002, and was subsequently staged at Theater J in Washington, D.C., in January 2003, both productions directed by Joseph Megel.

The Stage

The set needs to imbue the audience members with a sense of how in this house stories are woven and lives move forward simultaneously. Minimal prop pieces can indicate a room—things pulled out of moving boxes that litter the house. The set and the lights need to facilitate the action moving forward without blackout, conveying that some characters are continuing their lives and action onstage when they are not the ones currently in focus.

In any home a family lives, at once, the same life and different lives. It is my intention that the play and its production reflect that.

Characters

LILY PRICE: sixties, family matriarch

MARVIN PRICE: seventies, her husband, suffering from Alzheimer's

JULIA PRICE: oldest daughter, mid-thirties, very pregnant

CLAIRE PRICE: second daughter, early thirties

MICHELLE PRICE: third daughter, late twenties

ANGEL PRICE: the youngest, early twenties

HAROLD FREEDMAN: seventies, next-door neighbor

JANE: Julia's lover

JON: Claire's fiancé

KENT: late twenties, early thirties

LUKE: Angel's ex-boyfriend, of color, early twenties

There is no intermission.

Man plans and God laughs.

—YIDDISH SAYING

Black

(Marvin stands in his own light.)

MARVIN: Why am I in some place with angels?

(The rhythmic lulling sounds of a train on the tracks—lights crossfade to Michelle.)
Penn Station

MICHELLE: Ummm, excuse me—hi?—look, I know you don't know me, but you look like someone who might . . . might be open to a complete stranger asking you . . . I'm not some psycho-chick, in case you're thinking I am which I'm sure you are—here's my license, so you know I'm me . . .

(There's a shadow of a man at the edge of her light. She hands him card after card from her wallet.)

. . . here . . . library card, museum membership, prescription card—so at least you know I'm a semi-cultured literate insured psycho, I guess—Thank you for not running away. It's just that for months I've known this was coming, there's been this impending dread which was only exacerbated by

(Michelle continues speaking as we see the various members of her family. Lights rise on Angel Price, outside, backpack, rolling up her sleeping bag.)

the Hallmark store across from me—its windows a mad succession of hoblins goblins witches and candy accented by Happy Jewish New Year and Day of Atonement cards and Halloween wasn't even over before they added Indians and Pilgrims decorating *(Lights up on Claire Price and Jon Prescott, driving a U-HAUL truck. She drives and he shifts gears, his hand snaking in to her lap. She laughingly slaps it away.)* Christmas trees sprouting out of Plymouth Rock, of which I doubt the historical accuracy and then

(192 Waverly Ave, the Price family home. Lights up on Lily Price, sixties, small with great strength, stands before her husband, Marvin Price, seventies, unbuttoning his shirt.)

Valentine's day, hearts everywhere since New Year's and now they have Easter Barbie, Easter Barbie for Christ's sake which really gets me up in arms even though I'm not religious—

(Lily pulls Marv's head down to kiss her.)

really, it's more of a cultural thing I have to admit, but all they'd have to do is stick a jar of gefilte fish and a Haggadah in the leftover Easter Barbie's hands and we'd make all the little girls with mezuzzahs on their Malibu dream houses very *(She catches herself in the rant.)* happy . . .

(Lights up on Julia and Jane. Julia Price, mid-thirties, very pregnant, packing a suitcase as Jane, her girlfriend, strokes Julia's stomach.)

Right. Well—every day . . . every day some relative calls me to confirm whether I'm bringing flourless chocolate cake this year to seder—with my family Passover is a

(Angel stands outside #55—Luke's House—transfixed—a huge baby wreath that says "IT'S A GRANDSON!" circles the house number. She backs away from the door as if hoping no one sees her.)

big hulabaloo—not so much in a do-everything-according-to-the rules sense but more in a digging-horribly-and-obsessively-into-every-detail-of-your-life-between-appetizers-and-desserts sense—and since it's the last time . . . well . . . it's all much more . . . that.

(192 Waverly—Lily and Marv recline against each other in a huge bathtub.)

But they're really not calling to find out what I'm bringing, but who I'm bringing and I couldn't put up with hearing Aunt Mabel say, "So Michelle, why don't you have a man yet?" in her frog voice. Again. I'm tired of making excuses and I'm tired of sympathetic "I've-got-a-friend"s. And this, this is the last year so it becomes important in a way I can't explain. So I'm walking up to you, and you must think I'm crazy and I know you don't know me but you're wearing a nice suit and you looked somehow . . . right . . . and that's a step in the right direction anyhow. Do you like matzah?

(The four daughters: Julia, Claire, Michelle, and Angel, speak to the audience.)

DAUGHTERS: The last seder.

(Shift to)
Train Trestle
(Michelle and Kent, suitcases)

MICHELLE: You know what? . . . This is a mistake. We can check the schedule downstairs and I can pay your ticket to wherever you were going to before I—well, before—

KENT: It's an adventure—look, you've enticed me this far, don't get cold feet now.

MICHELLE: I was so worried that you might think I was psycho, that I completely forgot to consider the possibility that you might be.

KENT: I'll show you my library card later—

(He picks up their bags and goes. She follows.)
192 Waverly
(Angel rings the bell.)

LILY: Shit.

(Ring)

Go away!

(Insistent doorbell ringing. Lily appears, wet, wrapped in a towel.)

Fucking Jehovah's witnesses. Fucking door-to-door Fuller Brush guy, frigging campaign to elect some right-wing fat ass. This better be good! This better be very very good.

(Lily throws open the front door. Angel stands there. Silence.)

ANGEL: Hi . . .
LILY: Keys?
ANGEL: I lost them.
LILY: No keys and a day early.
ANGEL: I'm not early.
LILY: You're early.
ANGEL: You're dripping.
LILY: You're early. You've been skulking around town for days already, you don't call and now you're early.
ANGEL: How did you—
LILY: I'm your mother, I know things. You love the great outdoors so much? You've got a sleeping bag. Come back tomorrow.

(Michelle rushes up the walk, Kent stands back. Chaos ensues.)

MICHELLE: Mom! Angel!

LILY: Early.

ANGEL: All of us?

(Julia and Jane, lugging suitcases. Angel runs over and drops down on her knees, putting her head to Julia's belly.)

Oh, hi hi hi hi hi hi.

LILY: You're early.

JULIA: What?

JANE: I've given up Easter for Lent. Besides, I'm told this family gives good sater.

JULIA/ANGEL/MICHELLE/LILY: Seder.

JANE: Whatever.

ANGEL: *(To Julia's belly)* Hi hi hi hi hi hi.

JULIA: *(To Angel)* Hello? Up here—

LILY: You're all early.

MICHELLE: We're not early.

(Harold Freedman—next-door neighbor, seventies—comes outside. They wave—)

HAROLD: Hi girls.

MICHELLE: Hi Mr. Freedman.

JULIA: Hi Mr. Freedman. You look fabulous!

HAROLD: Golf. No cart. Four times a week.

JANE: *(To Julia)* Golf?

JULIA: *(To Harold)* You're coming to seder, aren't you?

HAROLD: Wouldn't miss it.

(He goes inside.)

MICHELLE: How's he doing?

LILY: As well as can be expected—whatever the hell that means. *(To the kids)* You're early. You're early. You're all early. Etiquette. I forgot to teach you etiquette.

(From offstage the U-HAUL honks.)

Who the hell is that?

(To Kent)

And who the hell are you?

CLAIRE: *(From off)* Hey everyone!!!!

LILY: Claire and Jon—Oh God.

MICHELLE: Yup.

LILY: They're never early.

MICHELLE: Nope.

LILY: Damn it.

MICHELLE: Yup.

(Claire and Jon rush on. Julia and Claire hug over Angel, head still pressed against fetus.)

JULIA: A U-HAUL.

ANGEL: Never one for subtlety.

CLAIRE: Why—what did you guys bring?

JULIA: The car.

MICHELLE: A suitcase.

ANGEL: A backpack.

CLAIRE: Yeah, well, I thought we might need something a little bigger.

JULIA: Hide the silver. And the piano.

(Claire flips Julia off.)

MICHELLE: My evil big sisters.

JULIA: Hey, watch who you call big!

LILY: Move out of the way. Out of the way.

(To Julia's stomach)

I'm warning you, stay in there as long as possible. It's a dangerous world.

JANE: Where's Marv?

LILY: Oh shit. I left him in the bathtub.

JULIA: Mom?

LILY: It *is* contagious. Your father is contagious. I probably know you—

(She points to Kent.)

Do I know you? Shit.

MICHELLE: The bathtub? Jesus, Mom, what were you doing?

LILY: Reliving the magic. Marvin! You haven't wandered off somewhere, have you? I found him strolling down the middle of East Rockaway Road last week. No traffic at 3 a.m.—beauty of the suburbs.

MICHELLE: Mom!

LILY: I'm thinking that one of those electronic leashes they have for dogs, that would be good for your father.

(The inside of the house is revealed. They follow Lily.)

MICHELLE: I thought you were putting the alarm on at night—

LILY: What do you think woke me up to find out he was gone in the first place?

Bathroom

(Marvin sits in the now-empty bathtub, shivering.)

ANGEL: Oh, Daddy.

(Lily grabs a towel and gets into the bathtub to get Marvin to stand. She wraps him in the towel, drying him off tenderly.)

LILY: Come on in, the water's fine. Come on in, the water's fine. That's what you always said. The water could be turning you every shade of blue and you'd just say, come on in, the water's fine.

(Jane hands over a quilt.)

JANE: Hello, Marvin.

MARVIN: Hello.

JULIA: Hey Dad.

MARVIN: Who are you?

(He turns to Lily. Sometimes Marvin loses words, but he covers valiantly.)

Who are these people? I'm not . . . I'm naked for God's sake. You like this? You like what you see? Who—

JANE: That's your daughter, Julia, Mr. Price. I'm Janie. And your daughter, Claire, and Jon. And Michelle—

MICHELLE: Hi Daddy.

(She kisses him. He flinches.)

JANE: And Angel. Your youngest.

MARVIN: Angel—Angel. Have I died? Am I dead?

ANGEL: No, Daddy.

MARVIN: Why am I someplace with angels then?

(He appeals to Lily.)

Why am I someplace with angels?

LILY/ANGEL: *(Lily)* It's a nickname. *(Angel)* You named me that.

(Marvin approaches Kent.)

MARVIN: It's been a long time. Too long.

(He throws his arms around Kent. The quilt falls off. Kent bravely rolls with it, as if being embraced by a strange naked man is an everyday occurrence.)

You look . . . well, you look well.

KENT: And you, sir.

MARVIN: Scotch, scotch! That's what we need.

(Still naked, he ushers Kent out of the bathroom. The rest stand silent.)

LILY: Who the fuck is he?

(They all look at Michelle.)

MICHELLE: My . . . my—Kent.

DAUGHTERS: Step one. THE SEARCH FOR CHAMETZ. Clean the house of the impure and evil or get the yeast out.

Front Yard

(Jon and Jane gather the bags that were left outside.)

JON: Passover with the Price family. You could publish a dysfunctional best seller on this one, Doctor.

JANE: Hey, considering my folks won't even let me and Julia in the door, this is a dream holiday. Could I divorce my parents, Jon? You and Claire could handle it. Make litigation history?

(Angel comes outside.)

ANGEL: I'm leaving.

JON: Don't even start.

ANGEL: No one will notice if I'm gone. He certainly won't.

JANE: Angel.

ANGEL: He won't.

JON: Did you think your blowing town for years was going to make him better?

ANGEL: No. I don't know. No. *(Yes)* He's just . . . he's not him. I'll write. *(She shoulders her bag, waiting to be stopped.)*

JANE: Angel baby, you're going nowhere.

JON: Suck it up, kiddo.

ANGEL: I can't.

JANE: Look, there'll never be another seder at this house again and on top of that, if I know your sisters, they've already staked out their claim on all the good stuff and if you don't stick around your childhood is going to be picked over by families in old station wagons wanting to pay a quarter for your most precious possessions and don't give me that crap about not needing anything material in your life because I definitely remember that before you took off on whatever finding yourself journey the last few years have been, mall was your middle name.

ANGEL: It's just . . . it's not the same. It's better from far away. It's never going to be the same.

(They look at the For Sale sign.)

JANE: I know . . .

(Lily joins them.)

LILY: I'm making hot chocolate!

JON: Make mine a double.

LILY: I will. As soon as you come back with the milk.

JON: My pleasure.

LILY: What a son-in-law.

JON: Not yet.

LILY: That's something else we have to discuss.

JON: Discuss it with Claire. The caterer has fired *us*.

LILY: Hang in there.

JON: The band sent us a tape of their new song "why did she say yes . . . when who knows what she really meant at all . . ."

LILY: Hang in there.

JANE: I'm voting for an ultimatum.

ANGEL: Ooh. Bad idea.

LILY: No, not with Claire—now with Julia, I agree that made perfect sense, but Claire—

JANE: Second child syndrome.

LILY: Julia strategies would not work at all—I'm thinking that if he would just—

JANE/LILY/ANGEL: —hang in there—

JON: Okay, okay, okay . . . Milk . . . and anything else?

(She hands him a list.)

I knew we brought the U-HAUL for a reason.

LILY: Yeah, well there's a seder tomorrow, in case it hadn't totally slipped *my* fragile aging mind. Angel will go with you.

ANGEL: I will?

LILY: Go on. Jane—I need your height.

Den
(Marvin serves Kent a drink.)

MARVIN: Scotch, straight up.

(Claire stands at the bookshelves, setting aside some hardcovers, putting others back.)

DAUGHTERS: More step 1: THE SEARCH FOR CHAMETZ. Clean the house of the impure and evil—

MICHELLE: —and don't forget the profit margin.

MARVIN: Cheers. *(The men sit down. To Kent:)* You still haven't introduced me to your lovely wife. I'm Marvin—

(This is a blow to Michelle—Marvin extends a hand to her. She just looks at it.)

KENT: Marvin, this is Michelle. Michelle, Marvin.

MARVIN: Lovely.

MICHELLE: I have to—I can't—

(Michelle stands abruptly to leave. She snaps at Claire on her way out of the room.)

Should I get you a box, Claire? Or maybe another truck.

CLAIRE: I'm looking for first editions. You want to go through the garage sale
pile over there, feel free.

MICHELLE: Oh . . . how very generous of you.

(She grabs the book out of Claire's hand.)

CLAIRE: Hey.

MICHELLE: I gave this to Daddy—

CLAIRE: It's not as if he's going to be rereading it anytime soon.

(Michelle grabs another book from the first edition pile and walks away.)

Michelle!

MICHELLE: Put it on my tab.

U-Haul

(Angel and Jon outside #55 with bags of groceries.)

JON: The ice cream's melting.

ANGEL: Okay. Wait!

*(Jon digs in one of the bags for a pint of ice cream and pries off the lid of the melted
stuff. He drinks some and hands the pint to her. She drinks without taking her eyes
from the house.)*

JON: Ahh . . . young love.

ANGEL: It's not love.

JON: Curiosity.

ANGEL: Obsession.

Kitchen

*(Jane, on a stepstool, reaches dishes on high shelves, passes them to Lily, who hands
them to Julia to wrap and place in one of the several boxes on the kitchen table.)*

LILY: My box. Angel's box. Michelle's.

(Jane hands a glass pitcher to Julia.)

JANE: This is pretty.

LILY: Never been used.

JULIA: Which box?

LILY: You get all these wedding presents. A lot of them are things maybe you're not old enough to want yet or they're just not your taste yet or you've got so much other stuff. I swear there's an Osterizer up there that's still in its original box.

JULIA: We'll never know.

LILY: There's always Vermont.

JULIA: It's not quite the same thing.

LILY: Well you're not missing anything except thank you notes. And decades after the wedding it's still all new and untouched. Unlike me . . .

(Jane hands her another dish. Julia holds up the pitcher.)

JULIA: Which box, Ma?

(Lily takes the dish from Jane's hand and throws it against the wall. CRASH.)

DAUGHTERS: THE SEARCH FOR CHAMETZ. Clean the house of the impure and evil—

MICHELLE: —or just break everything.

LILY: That felt good.

(She grabs the next dish from Jane's hand and does it again. CRASH. Claire rushes in.)

CLAIRE: I heard—oh, man, was that real Fiestaware?

LILY: A cheap imitation.

CLAIRE: Mom!

LILY: It slipped.

CLAIRE: It slipped all the way over there?

LILY: Go away.

CLAIRE: Be careful.

LILY: Go away.

CLAIRE: Just don't—

LILY: Now!

(Claire leaves. Lily surveys the mess.)

The only problem with catharsis is you have to clean up afterward.

(Lily puts her hand out for the next dish. Jane holds it slightly above her reach.)

I'll be good. I promise.

JULIA: Mom?

(The pitcher)

LILY: Make Jane a box.

JULIA: She can share my box.

LILY: Well that Osterizer is going to take up most of it.

Den
(Marvin and Kent)

MARVIN: Tell me about business.

KENT: Well, y'know—

MARVIN: You don't have to tell me. Rough times out there. Rough rough rough. Can't find a job, eh? Don't look so surprised. You might as well have interview suit monogrammed on the pocket.

KENT: That bad, huh?

MARVIN: There are men who wear suits like they're cut just for them. Some have that from the moment they put the first one on, some get it from years of wearing them five days a week.

KENT: I'm making another career change. Again.

MARVIN: Mmmmhmmm. You've got what it takes. I've always thought that about you. You have got what it takes.

Angel's Room
(Claire, Angel, cordless phone)

CLAIRE: I thought you had given that up.

ANGEL: I haven't given anything up. I am holding on to everything as tightly as I can so don't plan on sticking any tangibles or intangibles of mine into that truck.

(Claire peers into Angel's boxes.)

Claire!

CLAIRE: God! Everybody's gotten so touchy.

ANGEL: Well you've gotten so predatory. What's that about?. . . Claire.

CLAIRE: It's not about anything.

ANGEL: Claire—

CLAIRE: Maybe if you just stopped thinking about him.

ANGEL: Maybe if you stopped changing the subject — *(Claire can beat her at this game.)* I did stop thinking about him. I stopped for a long time.

CLAIRE: Which brings you to sitting in front of his house long enough for milk to sour?

ANGEL: I started again.

CLAIRE: Doesn't all this just sap your energy completely? Aren't you completely . . . sapped?

ANGEL: Sapped?

CLAIRE: Sapped . . .

ANGEL: I might be a sap, but am I sapped?????? I am a sap. A complete and total sapped out sap. There was a baby wreath on his parents' door. It's a grandson. Spelled it out for me right there. He's had a kid. Luke has a son so therefore, it is completely and totally over and any obsessing on my part would be beyond pathetic, beyond sappish so — so I called him.

CLAIRE: You called him! Jesus, Angel.

ANGEL: I hung up.

CLAIRE: Angel—

ANGEL: I hung up. You don't know what self-control that took.

CLAIRE: So what if he star-69ed you?

ANGEL: Oh God.

CLAIRE: What if they have caller ID?

ANGEL: Oh God. Ohgodohgodohgod.

CLAIRE: I can't believe you don't think of those things.

ANGEL: Oh God. Technology — I hate technology. I don't believe in technology.

(Jane enters.)

JANE: Well, it exists.

ANGEL: Just be eternally grateful, you two. Eternally — that you fell in love in a much easier, less technologically advanced time. Oh God.

Marv and Lily's Bedroom
(Lily lies with her head on Julia's belly.)

JULIA: So this morning on the news they were talking about this woman who was so devoted to her mother that she gave up everything in her own life—

everything, the possibility of anything but taking care of her mother—so somehow they found her mother, lying in her bed, very well cared for, perfectly preserved, mummified, dead for six years from natural causes. Because even after her mother died, she just didn't know what else she could do.

(A beat. Then Lily starts to laugh. So does Julia.)

LILY: Not my kids. Not my grandson either!

JULIA: Mom, there was no penis on the ultrasound.

LILY: He still has time. You got two months, kid, start growing one! It's not good that we should be a family of just women and with the way things are going . . .

(She gets up and walks to the door.)

JULIA: Mom? Aren't there things to discuss—conversations we're supposed to have, family decisions . . .

LILY: Absolutely.

JULIA: So, we're not talking about them because . . .

LILY: You promised me an analyzation-free weekend, Julia, so don't go all fucking therapist on me.

JULIA: This cursing thing—

LILY: You like it? It's the new me.

JULIA: It's just—

LILY: Hey, you're the one who told me to stop swallowing my anger. And you know what, it feels really fucking good.

JULIA: *(Julia puts out a hand.)* Mom—

LILY: Session over.

JULIA: But I—

LILY: I'm fabulous as long as no one asks me or lets me think. Don't go there, Julia.

(Julia puts out a hand.)

JULIA: I need help getting up.

Angel's Room

ANGEL: You cannot plan love.

CLAIRE: Poor Jon, he never knew what hit him.

JANE: You should be a general. You should run wars. You should be president.

ANGEL: You can't strategize love. It's against the rules.

CLAIRE: If there are rules there are ways around them. Basic business strategy—Dad always said—

ANGEL: With business maybe, but not with love. You can't, you can't do that—

JANE: Please—Julia has no idea what I manipulated to get to her.

CLAIRE: I thought it was who you manipulated.

JANE: What?

CLAIRE: The way Norman tells it you went to enormous lengths to see if he and Julia were more than just roommates.

JANE: Oh shit. Julia knows?

ANGEL: Since that very manipulative night.

CLAIRE: Norman likes to get into it in gory detail—how he knew exactly what you were trying to find out but was having too much fun to let on.

JANE: I'll kill him.

CLAIRE: She was flattered.

JANE: I'll still kill him.

ANGEL: She was very flattered.

JANE: Well . . . for the record . . . by no means did I go to "enormous lengths."

(Lights up to include Michelle in her room, filled with boxes, listening to the laughter leaking from Angel's room. Their scene continues as Michelle unwraps the plastic from several of her father's suits in dry cleaning bags. She holds her father's suit in her hands, stroking the fabric. She has surrounded herself with other objects of his—the books, some shirts.)

CLAIRE: You know, Mom once said that the reason why Dad never had a problem with you and Julia was because you looked exactly like his first love, so he totally understood everything.

JANE: She told me that it was because I reminded him of his mother.

ANGEL: He never had a problem because there was nothing to have a problem with.

(Julia enters.)

JULIA: You're still overromanticizing us.

JANE: You were eavesdropping.

JULIA: You were loud.

CLAIRE: Watch out, the two therapists fight. You guys do fight, don't you?

JANE: A Freudian free-for-all.

ANGEL: I want to talk to my nephew.

(Julia lies down with them. Angel sticks her face against Julia's belly and whispers.)

JULIA: Everybody only wants to talk to my stomach these days. My patients want to touch my stomach which I'm not sure is not a breach of some ethical standard—and they really really want to know without "prying" in which unnatural way this all came about which makes me wonder, do I owe them a framed photo of sperm donor 83971 for the waiting room since I know every morbid little detail of their lives? And to top it all off, I wind up feeling guilty about charging them when they spend their entire hour talking about how my stomach makes their biological clocks tick.

(Angel puts her ear against Julia's belly.)

ANGEL: Shhhhh. I'm waiting for an answer.

Den
(The men. TV light.)

MARVIN: Place is kind of dead tonight. I've never seen a sports bar where they had *It's a Wonderful Life* on the TV.

KENT: Think of it as an intellectual sports bar.

MARVIN: *(To Jon)* Well it's not working for you, Stuart, you're going to have to take your business in another direction.

JON: You know I have no business sense.

MARVIN: It shows. It shows. You know what you need in here?

JON: What?

MARVIN: Women.

Angel's Room

CLAIRE: So the question is—who is this Ken guy?

JULIA: Kent.

CLAIRE: Kent?

JULIA: I think so.

JANE: Kent. Man of mystery.

ANGEL: Man of steel, perhaps?

CLAIRE: Oh, wouldn't that be nice. She's never been this closemouthed about a boyfriend before.

JULIA: Maybe she was and we just assumed that no details meant no guy.

(They look at Angel.)

ANGEL: I know nothing.

CLAIRE: Michelle! Michelle!

JULIA/JANE/ANGEL/CLAIRE: Michelle! Michelle!

(In her room, Michelle has pulled a bunch of wire coat hangers out of the suits and is twisting them into a larger sculptural shape. She can't stop to join the others.)

Den

(Lily enters.)

MARVIN: An answer to my prayers. Now I saw her first, guys, she's mine.

LILY: Howdy, stranger. Care to buy a lady a drink?

MARVIN: I most certainly would. You guys take a hint.

(Jon and Kent leave.)

LILY: Let's go.

MARVIN: You just got here.

LILY: It's late, Marvin.

MARVIN: Where'd the bartender go? The service here is terrible.

LILY: Don't make me play this all the way through.

MARVIN: What's your name?

LILY: Shit. C'mon, cowboy. We're going back to my place.

MARVIN: That was fast.

LILY: I don't consider conversation foreplay. Let's blow this joint.

(Marv searches his pockets.)

MARV: I lost . . . I lost my, my car keys —

(He begins to get agitated.)

I lost my — where do — would you help me look? Where are my car keys — where are my car keys. *(Lily takes his hands.)*

LILY: We don't need the car. It's a very short walk.

Michelle's Room

(Kent enters. Michelle's work is beginning to resemble a wire figure.)

KENT: You're not going to answer the call of the wild siblings?—what are you doing?—

MICHELLE: I don't know. Something . . . nothing.

I really shouldn't have dragged you into this. It wasn't right. I can tell everyone that we had a fight and I drove you to the train station and you went back to the city and that's it, we're over, they'll believe that, and I won't be subjecting you to this anymore.

KENT: Why?

MICHELLE: Why? Because this whole thing is a shambles. The place is half-packed up, my mother is half off her rocker, my sister is practically putting price tags on our childhood, not to mention my father—I come out here to see him all the time, to talk to him, give my mom a break, whatever, and every time I think maybe he's getting better, I'm wrong. Have you noticed that no one will mention my father?—they're just kind of existing around him as if he hadn't disintegrated to the point where this is what we're left with, a house that's being sold and a last seder that he can't even lead so I guess technically last year was the last seder only we didn't know that then and we weren't all here, God knows the last time we were all here and now he's not all here and I don't even know you—

(She stops—she really doesn't know him.)

What kind of freak are you that you actually came home with me?

(He looks at her, amused.)

What? What?

KENT: What kind of freak are you that you actually asked?

I don't want to go.

MICHELLE: You have no other place to be?

KENT: Nope.

MICHELLE: Shouldn't you have some other place to be?

KENT: If I did, I wouldn't be here and you wanted me here, didn't you? So be glad my social calendar had a vacancy.

Okay—I was escaping. Y'know, train to Montauk, some cheesy motel in the off season, walk on the beach, watch cable, figure out my life. My family is everywhere but here—so, gefilte fish out of jar under the stars seemed like a good idea after the day I had had. New York's like that for me sometimes, I just have to get out and then I get out and all I want to do is go back.

MICHELLE: I'm offering you going back.

KENT: But now I'd rather have my gefilte fish off of a plate.

I'll mention your father if you want me to—or you mention him and I'll nod and smile.

(The stage transitions to night . . .)

Lily and Marvin's Bedroom

(Lily holds an adult diaper. Marvin stays away from her.)

LILY: Don't be like this.

MARVIN: No.

LILY: It's just for sleeping. It's just for the night.

MARVIN: No.

LILY: Marvin—please.

MARVIN: Stay away from me! Stay away from me! Stay away from me!

LILY: Keep your voice down. For once, Marvin, for once will you just—

MARVIN: *(Screaming)* Noooooooooo!

(His cry echoes through the house—and, simultaneously, in their rooms—
Angel crams her hands over her ears to drown out the sound of her father.
Claire and Jon are in the middle of making love. They stop, not knowing what to do.
Michelle bolts out her door. Kent follows.
Jane and Julia: Jane is shaving Julia's legs for her. The sound makes her miss.)

JULIA: Ow!

JANE: Maybe we should be the kind of dykes who don't shave their legs. At least 'til the baby's born.

JULIA: Maybe we should be the kind of dykes who wax . . . Poor Daddy. God— poor Mom.

(Marvin is trying to open the bedroom door, but it's locked, which he doesn't realize.)

MARVIN: Help me . . . help me . . . Stay away . . . somebody—

(Michelle reaches the other side of the door.)

MICHELLE: Mom—open the door.

LILY: Go away!

MARVIN: Help me!

MICHELLE: Mom—

LILY: Go away, Michelle.

(Marvin cringes against the door.)

MARVIN: I don't want to I don't want to I don't want to—would you help me? Would somebody help me?

MICHELLE: What are you doing to him?

LILY: It's a sex game, Michelle. It's our little nightly ritual. Now just let me deal with it.

MARVIN: Please, please, please please . . .

(A stain appears at the front of his pants.)

LILY: Fuckfuckfuckfuck.

MICHELLE: Mom!

LILY: I am diapering your father. When you were two you protested in much the same way. If you want to help me, help me by going away.

(Kent, who has been hanging back, comes over to lead Michelle away. She jerks away at his touch. Julia and Jane show up.)

MICHELLE: Go to bed.

JULIA: It'll be easier once he's in Serenity Willows.

MICHELLE: Easier for who?

JULIA: Clients of mine—

MICHELLE: We're not clients, Julia.

JULIA: You know I don't think that.

MICHELLE: You know what? I'm not so sure.

MARVIN: Lily! Lily!

MICHELLE: God, Daddy. God.

JULIA: I know it's difficult to—

MICHELLE: Don't, okay, Julia? I know you mean well. Just please don't.

(She leaves.)

JULIA: You're probably not used to that yet.

KENT: Definitely not yet.

JANE: Well, acclimate fast.

JULIA: Y'know, Angel was always his baby, but Michelle was Daddy's girl. There's a really comfortable couch in the den if you'd rather—

KENT: I'm gonna . . .

(He gestures after Michelle and follows her.)

JULIA: Oh, a keeper.

Michelle's Bedroom
(Kent enters; Michelle holds up a bunch of brochures.)

MICHELLE: Dear Mr. Price. We are pleased to welcome you to Serenity Willows with our serene grounds and our big willow trees and your own personal restraints attached to your bed. Here you can stop reading the paper, running on the beach and taking your old business partner to lunch so he can beg you to come back to work again. Here you can serenely contemplate the bars on your window and serenely perform all sorts of juvenile therapeutic activities to make you forget you're not at home—oh, that's right, forgetting won't be a problem at all.

(She tears up the brochures and starts inserting the strips through the wires, holding back tears. Kent watches her for a moment. She sniffs and wipes her eyes.)

KENT: I'm sorry.

MICHELLE: He was always the one I could talk to—he listened. And every time I come home I keep hoping for that, that he'll . . .

KENT: Don't you think somewhere inside there he's listening—

MICHELLE: Don't. Don't do that. Please. It's disgusting and demeaning and patronizing to me, rather than some kind of spiritual Band-Aid.

(Beat)

I don't know, maybe he is listening. But that's the problem—I. Don't. Know. He's disappearing. I'm watching him disappear.

(Beat)

I would think the intrigue is over by now. There's an 11:21 back into the city. We'd be cutting it close but you'll make it.

(Silence)

KENT: So—I actually don't have my library card on me, but I'll give you my resumé which I do happen to have in my briefcase in that convenient whip-it-out-during-the-interview pocket. You can call any of the references on it. Ask them anything about me.

I'm not getting on a train for anywhere, Michelle.

(This overlaps with)
Lily and Marvin's Bedroom

LILY: C'mon . . . c'mon sweetheart . . . let's get you cleaned up. C'mon.

(She offers her hand. He takes it.)

Good boy . . . good boy.

(This occurs simultaneously with)
Roof
(Angel crawls out her window onto the roof, pulling a quilt after her. She hunts under the eaves for something and then pulls out a weathered child's safe. She opens it and takes out a very old pack of cigarettes and matches and lights up.)
Michelle's Room
(Michelle and Kent continue. She works on the sculpture.)

MICHELLE: Whoo whoo, chugachuga, chuga chuga. All aboard. Long Island eat my dust. City lights up ahead . . .

KENT: C'mon, sometimes it's easier to talk to strangers.

MICHELLE: Oh please.

KENT: Beside, I'm a master of distraction. Comes from my days working as a magician at kids' parties.

MICHELLE: Really.

KENT: No. But I distracted you. Briefly.

MICHELLE: Go away.

KENT: You invited me.

MICHELLE: It was a moment of desperation.

KENT: Y'know, inviting a stranger to seder is a mitzvah.

MICHELLE: I know.

KENT: And taking it back would be—

MICHELLE: Bad . . . very very bad . . . I should sleep. I'll never sleep.

(He dangles the resumé at her.)
Julia's Room

JANE: Justin. Jacob. Jeeves.

JULIA: Jeeves?

JANE: Maybe he'll grow up orderly with an English accent. Malcolm?

JULIA: Not an M.

JANE: I like Malcolm.

JULIA: I don't even want it to cross anybody's mind that we're naming the baby for him. I don't want it to be a thought in anyone's head . . . I wanted him to know his grandchild.

JANE: He'll experience him. Or her. We really should be doing her names—

JULIA: But he won't know the baby. The weird thing is is that the baby won't miss Dad either. I mean, how can you miss someone you didn't ever get to know?

JANE: We'll just have to miss Marvin for him.

(This overlaps with)
Lily and Marvin's Room
(Lily watches Marvin sleep, then leaves to go to the backyard.)
(This overlaps with)
Angel's Roof
(Angel smokes. The rooftop is on the side of the house, facing the neighbors, over-looking a path. She looks down at the path. Luke is standing there.)

LUKE: My wandering angel. Hi.

ANGEL: Hi.

(A moment. He climbs up the side of the house as if he's done it a million times before. Sees her with the cigarette.)

DAUGHTERS (except Angel): Clean the house of the impure and evil and you never know who will show up.

LUKE: Some things never change.

ANGEL: Stale. But still here.

(He bends and kisses her. The chemistry hasn't changed either. She pushes him away.)

LUKE: Stale but still here?

ANGEL: You've got a kid.

LUKE: We've got a kid?

ANGEL: No, you, you have a kid. I saw the baby wreath on your parents' door. It's a boy. Congratulations. Have a stale cigarette. Keep your distance.

(He grins. Leans in for a kiss. She backs off.)

I don't do that. I don't poach.

LUKE: And I don't have a kid. It's Lynn's.

ANGEL: Lynn? Lynn is twelve.

LUKE: Lynn is seventeen.

ANGEL: Lynn is not seventeen.

LUKE: Seventeen and we're making the best of it.

(They kiss again.)

Backyard

(Lily sits in the backyard on a yard chaise, smoking. Harold enters.)

HAROLD: I thought they were coming tomorrow.

LILY: I thought they were coming tomorrow.

(He sits down opposite her and puts her feet in his lap.)

I lost a fucking day.

HAROLD: So . . . what's a day? You've had plenty.

(He takes off her shoes.)

Everything's going to get easier.

LILY: Everything's going to change. I never thought I could be so tired. I never thought I could resent him. I don't want to resent him. *(He starts rubbing her feet.)* Some young couple is going to buy this house. Some young fresh-from-the-altar honeymooners and they won't know why they have to have it because of the magnolia tree or why one of their girls grows up to love women or why another one will be a wanderer or why minds tend to falter before the body gives out. They won't have any idea that the fights they have will be déjà vu to the house. That it's all coming out of the walls, trapped between the layers of wallpaper and insulation. They won't have any idea.

(Silence.)

HAROLD: And you'll be watching it all from next door.
LILY: I'll be watching it all from next door.

(Pause)

I still haven't figured out how I'm going to tell them that.
HAROLD: They haven't asked?
LILY: They wouldn't dare.

Roof
(Angel lies back as Luke slips her clothes off of her. She unbuckles his pants and pulls them off a little too forcefully. They roll off the side of the roof, spilling change and keys.)

ANGEL: Oooops.
LUKE: Shit.
ANGEL: Shhhh . . . *(Luke throws Angel's bra over the side.)* Hey.
LUKE: Ooops.
ANGEL: Let's hope Mr. Freedman doesn't get up early to trim the hedges.
LUKE: Maybe he's staying up late to peer out his attic window and get a few
    thrills.

Backyard
(Mr. Freedman's a little busy with Lily's feet.)

LILY: Tell me you still miss her.
HAROLD: I miss her most moments of every day.
LILY: And she wouldn't mind.
HAROLD: She would mind. But she would understand, and in her own way,
    she'd be happy.
LILY: You were Marvin's favorite golf partner.
HAROLD: He never won.
LILY: But it was always close. It was always so close he'd be looking forward
    to next time. Because next time—

(Lily closes her eyes and leans back against him.)
Michelle's Room
(She reads Kent's resumé.)

MICHELLE: Systems analyst. Systems analyst?

KENT: I'm horribly, exceedingly, good at it. I have the knack. It's the bane of my existence. Worst Job Ever. Spill.

MICHELLE: Telephone solicitations. For one of those meet-on-the-phone party lines.

KENT: Ouch—

MICHELLE: A great way to make bucks while doing my art, I thought. The problem with those scam "big money" jobs, the scam's on you, there's no money. Three weeks. And I didn't even get a date out of it. Of course my dad never let me forget that.

(Beat—then she goes back to the resumé.)

MBA? You don't seem MBA-ish.

KENT: MBA-ish?

MICHELLE: Y'know, Claire and Jon give off lawyer scents, Julia reeks of thera-pist/oldest sister—you can practically smell her coming. My dad's an in-ventive yet business savvy fatherly advice combo platter. And I give off the fruity bouquet of overworked but loving it elementary school art teacher waiting for her big gallery show to materialize with a few notes of impa-tience and the slight waft of turpentine.

KENT: So that's that sexy smell—

(Pause)

MICHELLE: Yeah. Um . . . Investment banker.

KENT: And I'm even better at that. A wizard.

MICHELLE: You're everything I've never dated.

KENT: Dream job?

MICHELLE: Parks department muralist.

KENT: That sounds good.

MICHELLE: I'm keeping my fingers crossed.

(She sticks her hand into one of the boxes and comes up with a batch of photos, shuffles through them.)

That's the side of my school.

KENT: I know this. On Third Street—that's yours?

MICHELLE: That's mine.

KENT: I am truly truly impressed.

(Silence)

MICHELLE: Okay, something that's not on the resumé.

Claire's Room
(Afterglow. Jon is sleeping.)

CLAIRE: You're hoping you did it, aren't you? *(She pokes him.)* Jon . . . Jon?

JON: *(He's talking in his sleep)* No.

CLAIRE: Yes you are.

(Jon snuggles into her. Snores.)

JON: Hit the sleep switch.

CLAIRE: You're hoping you fertilized me.

(Jon sits up, awake now.)

JON: Jesus, Claire.

CLAIRE: What?

JON: You make this shit up.

CLAIRE: What? What am I making up? You must be dreaming.

JON: What would be wrong with that? What would be wrong with actually going through with something we've planned? What would be wrong with hoping for something we've agreed to hope for?

CLAIRE: You don't wake up well.

JON: God only knows what's going on in your head—that is, if you let Him in on it. You make all this meaning around stuff and then don't have the decency to tell me so I can at least defend myself against your delusions.

CLAIRE: You don't—I don't, I'm not—I am not delusional.

JON: You think I'm trying to stealth-fertilize you. Is that what you're really thinking?

CLAIRE: No. Yes. Not really. No.

JON: The whole having a baby thing was your idea. Having sex tonight was your idea.

CLAIRE: You just looked so cute.

JON: God!

CLAIRE: You're not cute?

JON: Claire! Please! I'm not the one who stealths anything. We made love. It was pretty good—not our best, but being in your parents' house is always titillating and inhibiting at the same time. Marry me or don't marry me, I won't stop loving you, but I want an answer, Claire.

(She doesn't answer.)

You exhaust me.

(He pulls the covers over his head.)

Michelle's Room

KENT: Oh . . . I can't tell you this—

MICHELLE: One incredibly embarrassing sexual thing.

KENT: But I can't—

MICHELLE: It was your idea.

KENT: I can't—

MICHELLE: It was your idea.

KENT: I was just trying to take your mind off things.

MICHELLE: And you will—as soon as you tell me.

KENT: You weren't actually supposed to take me up on it.

MICHELLE: Coward.

KENT: Okay okay okay—I had to be recircumsized when I was fifteen.

MICHELLE: What?

KENT: The moyle did kind of a half-assed job the first time.

MICHELLE: Ooooh.

KENT: And my parents were so traumatized, so traumatized they couldn't go through it again—

MICHELLE: Did they sue?

KENT: Did they sue?

MICHELLE: Nowadays people would sue. Claire would sue.

KENT: No—they didn't sue. The moyle was my grampa—suing her own father —my mom couldn't do it. But she wouldn't even let him carve a pot roast after that.

MICHELLE: Oh God . . .

KENT: But when he died, his tendency toward unevenness worked in my financial favor—he paid for the MBA—though I don't think my cousins ever wanted to trade places. Okay.

MICHELLE: What?

KENT: Your turn.

MICHELLE: I can't.

Backyard

HAROLD: Stay at my house tonight.

LILY: I can't.

HAROLD: You'll sneak back in the morning.

LILY: Not until everything is taken care of.

HAROLD: I'm an old man, you know. Take advantage of me while you can.

LILY: You'd have thought I'd have had enough of old men by now.

Claire's Room

(Jon sleeps. Claire disentangles herself from him and goes to her handbag. She takes out a packet of birth control pills and pops one and then, as she's putting it away, drops it. Jon wakes.)

JON: . . . Now what?

CLAIRE: Nothing . . . just go back to sleep . . .

Michelle's Room

MICHELLE: Okay. Okay. But don't look at me.

KENT: I won't.

MICHELLE: I'm not kidding—one look in my direction and that's it.

KENT: See no evil. Hear evil okay, but no see evil.

MICHELLE: I can't.

KENT: Be bold.

MICHELLE: I can't.

KENT: Pretend it's confession. All Jews secretly want a chance to go to confession.

MICHELLE: We do?

KENT: We do.

MICHELLE: Okay—don't look.

KENT: I'm going to look if you don't start soon.

MICHELLE: Okay—I don't even fantasize about men anymore. I fantasize about my vibrator. And the funny thing is that I don't even like my vibrator. It disappoints me. It doesn't do for me what I've been promised it will do, what all the women's magazines say. It lets me down. I don't even know why I keep it, but how do you throw out a vibrator? You'd have to wrap it in something and be really surreptitious about it and make sure nobody saw you because it would be really obtrusive and embarrassing to be caught.

KENT: Just how big is this vibrator?

MICHELLE: Big. Big big.

(She kicks him to stop him from laughing; he lowers his hands.)

You looked.

KENT: How'd you get it home from the store?

MICHELLE: It came Fed Ex. I had to sign for it. It was a gift.

KENT: A gift. A gift from whom?

MICHELLE: Well, put it this way—my sisters and I got the exact same thing for Hanukah last year.

KENT: You're kidding.

MICHELLE: My mom has a very strange sense of what it means to be a mother.

(The following overlaps with this scene.)
Lily and Marvin's Room
(Marvin bolts upright from sleep).

MARVIN: Lily?

(He smiles as if she's right there next to him and sinks back into sleep.)
Michelle's Room
(They continue.)

KENT:—Look, Michelle, I want to tell you—

MICHELLE: Thank you.

KENT: What?

MICHELLE: For tonight. Thank you.

Angel's Bedroom
(Angel and Luke, half clothed, work their way in the window.)

ANGEL: Careful, careful, careful—

Backyard
(Sleepy silence)

HAROLD: When that young honeymoon couple sleeps at night you and I will sneak back here and cut blooms from the magnolia tree.
LILY: Mmmmm.

The House Quiets
(Simultaneously in:)
Julia's Room
(They sleep.)
Claire's Room
(They sleep.)
Backyard
(Lily and Harold each doze on an outdoor chaise.)
Angel's Bedroom
(Angel kisses Luke and then pulls out a box of doll clothes.)

ANGEL: Right where we left them—

(She pulls out a couple of condoms from the box.)

Do these things have an expiration date?

(She looks up at him. Luke is stopped with a strange expression on his face.)

What? What?
LUKE: I need to go. My goddamn pants. My goddamn pants.
ANGEL: What just happened?

(He leans out the window to pull in a sock.)

Luke—

(She reaches across the floor and grabs his underwear.)

LUKE: Give me that.
ANGEL: Hostage. You never wear boxers.
LUKE: I never wore boxers. Now I do.

(She pulls them on.)

Give them back, Angel.

ANGEL: Take them back.

LUKE: I'm leaving.

ANGEL: Make love to me first.

(She looks up at him sweetly; it's an old game. But he's not playing.)

Come on.

(He pulls away at her touch.)

You came back here for me, Luke—come on—

(The following action overlaps with Angel and Luke's scene.)

Michelle's Room

(Kent sleeps, fully clothed, having dozed off on the floor. Michelle reaches out a hand to caress his face and, asleep, he closes his own over hers and brings it to his chest. She finally pulls her hand away and leaves the room. Michelle walks the house, checking in on her sisters' rooms, while they sleep. She skips Angel's room when she hears voices coming from it. She heads toward Lily and Marvin's room.)

Angel's Room

(Angel and Luke continue.)

LUKE: I came here to see.

(She poses alluringly.)

ANGEL: Take a good look.

LUKE: When my mom told me you were here—

ANGEL: Your mom told you?

LUKE: She ran into your mother, who claimed you were lurking around town. I
    wanted to stop thinking about whether I'd run into you, or whether you'd
    just show up on my doorstep . . . so I showed up on yours.

ANGEL: Your mom told you?

LUKE: How else did you think I knew you were here? I'm not psychic.

(The look on Angel's face shows she was hoping he was.)

Oh Christ.

ANGEL: What?

LUKE: That thing—you think I feel you close by. You think I know when you think about me.

ANGEL: Not—exactly.

LUKE: Christ.

(The following action overlaps with this scene.)

Lily and Marvin's Room

(Michelle stands over Marv sleeping. She moves into the bathroom, looking for Lily, whispering—)

MICHELLE: Mom?

(Through the window—Michelle sees where Lily and Harold sleep in their separate chaises.)

Angel's Room

(Angel and Luke continue.)

ANGEL: It's not so flaky. You make it sound so flaky, as if love—

LUKE: I came here to see you, to prove to myself I've moved on and you just suck me right in as if no time—as if love means don't write, don't call because who needs to breach thousands of miles because he can just feel my thoughts—

ANGEL: I wrote—

LUKE: Postcards. You wrote postcards, Angel. You quoted Emily Dickinson and Rilke and didn't say one word of your own. As if I have some secret decoder ring that can decipher whatever the hell you meant. You just thought you could go and come back and I'd still be here when you deigned to return.

ANGEL: But . . . but you are still here.

LUKE: It's too much. Too many breakups, too much drama. It's never really you, it's never really me—it's us. I don't want to love you anymore, Angel.

ANGEL: There is something. You feel it. You know you feel it. There is something.

LUKE: You're right, Angel. There is something. The past.

(He storms out, as dignified as he can be with just a shirt—and no pants on.)

ANGEL: Luke! Luke!

(Pulling her shirt closed, she follows him.)

Front Door
(Luke pulls open the front door. The ALARM goes off.)

ANGEL: Shit.

(She punches futilely at the panel—trying to remember the sequence of numbers.)
Backyard
(The alarm keeps going as Harold and Lily wake.)

LILY: Son of a bitch. Not again.

Front Door
(Michelle arrives—Angel and Luke are crowded at the panel. Fast and furious.)

ANGEL: I can't remember.
LUKE: Well, give me my damn boxers before everyone wakes up.
MICHELLE: Too late.

(Michelle starts punching at the panel.)

What did you do to this thing? Hi, Luke.
LUKE: Hi.

(Julia, Jane, Claire, Jon arrive.)

JULIA: Luke, hi!

(Julia throws her arms around him. Claire glares at Angel.)

CLAIRE: Hi Luke. You remember Jon?

(Marvin arrives holding a bat.)

MARVIN: Get out!
ANGEL: Daddy!
MARVIN: Get out!
CLAIRE: Daddy, watch out!
MARVIN: Breaking into my house. Get out—

(He's swinging the bat wildly.)

Get out. Get out.
MICHELLE: Daddy, stop it. Stop it!
MARVIN: You think you're going to hurt my family?

(Approaches Angel, menacing and dangerous, waving the bat)

You're not hurting my family.

(Lily arrives.)

LILY: Marvin!
MARVIN: Stay back!

(He swings the bat.)

LILY: God! What are you doing? Put it down.
MARVIN: Stay away.

(He's focused on Angel.)

ANGEL: Daddy?

(Julia steps in his path.)

JANE: Julia, don't!
MARVIN: Get out!
JANE: Get away from him. Don't—you'll hurt her!
JULIA: We're all family here, Daddy. Look, this is your grandkid. Look—

(She's got him distracted enough for Luke to grab the bat and Michelle to grab his flailing hands. Lily gets to the panel and turns off the alarm.)

MICHELLE: Here . . . you want to feel him, Daddy? You want to feel your
  grandson?
JULIA: It's okay.

(Michelle puts his hands on Julia's stomach.)

MARVIN: What's in there?
JULIA: He's yours, Daddy, he's a part of you . . .

(Angel has tears running down her face. Lily pulls it together.)

LILY: All my children gathered together and no one remembers our anniver-
  sary. 10-0-5. Luke.
LUKE: Lily.
LILY: Call me Mrs. Price.

(A moment of really really really awkward silence. Jane goes to Julia, furious.)

JANE: You don't do that!

JULIA: Everything's okay.

JANE: You don't put our child—put you—in danger like that—you don't do that!

JULIA: Shhh.

JANE: Don't shhhh me! God, Julia!

JULIA: I'm sorry. I'm sorry I'm sorry I'm sorry—

(Julia pulls her into an embrace and calms her. The others have tried to stay out of the interchange.)

LUKE: Good night.

(He turns to walk out the front door, only to be confronted by Harold.)

MICHELLE: Right on cue.

HAROLD: Everything all right?

LILY: It's wonderful.

(He holds out Luke's pants.)

HAROLD: And these would belong to . . . ?

(Luke snatches them. Harold holds out Angel's bra.)

This yours too?

(Except for Angel and Luke, the others are struggling to keep straight faces—and then the laughter breaks through, from Lily's guffaw on. Luke hands the bra to Angel.)

LILY: C'mon, Luke and Angel are cooking breakfast. Penance for waking us up.

CLAIRE: Luke makes the best pancakes.

JULIA: Just put your pants on first, huh? . . . mmmm. Coffee. C'mon, Daddy, you and I will make the coffee.

(The group begins to move toward the kitchen.)

JANE: You don't get coffee.

JULIA: Isn't this a special circumstance?

JANE: Don't push it.

LILY: October 5th. Is that so hard to remember? October 5th. Ten, o, five.

JON: Where's Kent?

MICHELLE: Sleeping?

CLAIRE: Does this mean he can sleep through your snoring?

(They leave Luke and Angel to sort out clothes. He pulls on his pants. She indicates the boxers.)

ANGEL: You want these?

LUKE: No . . . it's okay.

ANGEL: You staying?

LUKE: You heard the lady. I'm making pancakes.

(She follows him into the—)

Kitchen

CLAIRE: Dibs on the first one.

LUKE: The first one gets sacrificed to the pancake gods.

JON: You should know well enough that this family does not sacrifice food.

LILY: Seder stuff. Seder stuff. Where's the f—

(She sees a box on the floor.)

I packed it.

(Lily pulls out Haggadahs and a seder plate and other assorted seder paraphernalia.)

Okay—so this will not be the most brilliant seder of them all. This has got to be a group thing. Everybody's roasting eggs and making kugel and setting tables.

CLAIRE: Tables?

LILY: Floors, whatever. And no extended family.

MICHELLE: I thought you invited everyone.

LILY: And then I uninvited everyone.

MICHELLE: But I told Kent that the whole family—oh, God, I dragged him all the way here to—to . . .

JULIA: To meet us, right?

JANE: Trial by fire.

CLAIRE: Just us?

LILY: Just us.

CLAIRE: Wow.

LILY: And Harold—of course.

(At this Michelle leaves the room.)

Where are you going? Michelle??

(She's gone.)

JON: I'm going to miss Aunt Mabel.

JULIA: Oh, the horror.

Michelle's Room

MICHELLE: Kent, wake up. Kent—come on.

(He rolls over, lying on his resumé.)

Watch out.

(She picks up his resumé and unsnaps his briefcase to put it away. She takes a CD out of his briefcase. She picks up press releases and lyrics and music—under the name Josh Kent. Kent wakes and sees her with his stuff—)

KENT: Michelle—

MICHELLE: What is this? This is you? Josh Kent—

KENT: Michelle.

MICHELLE: You've got a CD?

KENT: A demo.

MICHELLE: All last night . . . everything you said . . . you lied to me.

KENT: I didn't totally lie to you.

(She snaps the briefcase shut.)

MICHELLE: You didn't even tell me your name. Your resumé doesn't say any of this. This says your name is Josh. This is you?!

KENT: Sometimes—

MICHELLE: Oh . . . God—I am a total idiot.

KENT: Michelle.

MICHELLE: What the fuck was I thinking? I told you . . . I told you everything. I am so stupid! A stupid gullible idiot.

(Michelle rips up Kent's resumé.)

KENT: It's simple—
MICHELLE: It is not simple—
KENT: Please—
MICHELLE: We're having breakfast. I came up to get you.

(He reaches out to grab her, she pulls away.)

Don't. You came here to do me a favor. The fact that you've lied your way
    through the entire thing—
KENT: You asked me to lie.
MICHELLE: Not to me! I suppose the circumcision story isn't true either.
KENT: It is.
MICHELLE: Right.
KENT: You want me to show you?
MICHELLE: Just stay away from me.

(She storms out of the room. He follows. Their action overlaps with the action in the—)

Kitchen
(Lily and Harold flank Marvin. Cross dialogue.)

HAROLD: They have got the most beautiful course, Marv—

Hallway
(Kent pursues Michelle.)

MICHELLE: I want you to leave.
KENT: I didn't totally lie to you.

(She keeps moving.)

MICHELLE: You partially lied to me—much better—

Kitchen
(Lily and Harold flank Marvin. Cross dialogue.)

HAROLD: . . . It's like—screw getting the little ball into the little hole, I want
    to stay here as long as humanly possible.

(Lily cuts up Marv's pancakes for him and guides his fork to his mouth when he seems to forget what to do. Michelle enters, Kent at her heels. Marv sees Kent.)

KENT: I just didn't get a chance—

MARVIN: There's my guy. Sit down, grab a cup of coffee.

LILY: I never understood the thrill of that game anyway.

HAROLD: When you turn sixty-five it will come to you magically.

KENT: *(Quietly)* I tried—

MICHELLE: Leave me alone, Kent. Or is it Josh? Or is it something else?

HAROLD: Marv and I used to say the same thing—then it changed when the Social Security checks started coming in—remember that?

MICHELLE: No—he doesn't. He doesn't remember a fucking thing. He doesn't recognize anyone, do you, Daddy? except him.

(She points to Kent.)

KENT: Don't—

LILY: Stop it.

MICHELLE: You know who the hell he is, Daddy? Because I don't.

KENT: Michelle.

JULIA: Michelle—

MICHELLE: That's your guy, Daddy? That's your guy? Who is he—

ANGEL: What are you doing?

LILY: Stop it.

ANGEL: Leave him alone.

MICHELLE: Who is he—? Tell me. C'mon . . .

LILY: Cut it out.

MARVIN: We're . . . we're old friends.

LILY: Don't you dare behave like a child in this house. I won't have it.

MICHELLE: They're just about to put you out to pasture, Daddy. They're farming you out to Serenity Willows as if it's for your own good—what a fucking joke. Yet another lie.

MARVIN: A lie?

LILY: Grow up.

HAROLD: Michelle, I think you should—

MICHELLE: You know, I saw you two.

JULIA: *(Quietly)* Oh shit.

HAROLD: What?

MICHELLE: Let's just all of us come clean, why don't we. Kent and I—we're not even Kent and I, we're nothing. Actually, I'm just a complete fool and he's not even Kent. And I saw you.

HAROLD: You don't know—

MICHELLE: Do tell us, then, Harold, in the spirit of my confessional of one girl who practically begged for a guy to treat her dishonestly—

KENT: Come on!

MICHELLE: Exactly what you *(To Harold)* and you *(To Lily)* are getting so cozy about.

ANGEL: That isn't true, is it?

MICHELLE: I saw—couldn't you at least wait until you stuck him in that place? You couldn't even wait until then, could you? I'm not even saying wait for him to be dead. Oh, that would be rich—put him right next to your dead wife, Harold, and then you and Mom can keep doing it in eternal rest.

MARVIN/ANGEL/JON: *(Marvin)* Young lady—*(Angel)* Stop it all of you stop! *(Jon)* Michelle—

MARVIN: —you ought to learn to be—more quiet—

ANGEL: Why can't you just leave things alone?

JULIA: This is not the way for something that's a private matter—

MICHELLE: Shove it, Dr. Freud.

(She turns to Lily.)

You're saying it's over and it's not over . . . it's not over!

(Lily doesn't dignify this with a response. She starts dumping any leavened items into Michelle's hands.)

MICHELLE: Mom?

(Lily keeps pushing things into Michelle's arms until she's practically throwing them at her.)

LILY: Can't have any of this in the house. Look at this—a loaf of bread, and brownies—rice cakes? Can I keep rice cakes in the house during Passover?

MICHELLE: Mom—

LILY: Let's get rid them, too.

JULIA: Michelle.

MICHELLE: Don't you try to intervene. I don't need you to intervene, because you knew, didn't you? You knew! And there you are, "facilitating" putting Daddy away.

(One last bag of bagels thrown at Michelle)

LILY: Go. Go to the beach. Take this stuff to the pigeons.

DAUGHTERS (except Michelle): THE SEARCH FOR CHAMETZ. Finally, actually, getting the yeast out.

MICHELLE: Mom—

LILY: Get this shit out of my house!

(She points to Kent and to Marvin.)

Take him and take him. Or don't come back. The car keys are in my bag. *(She walks out of the kitchen. Silence.)*

KENT: Let's go.

(He offers her a hand which she bats away. He reaches to Marvin who goes with him easily.)

We'll wait outside.

(Harold leaves—and Jon and Luke, with a glance shared between them, follow. The sisters and Jane watch as the packages of bread, crackers, and cookies fall one by one out of Michelle's hands as she keeps trying to keep the pile in her arms. She finally gives up and they go tumbling to the floor.)

MICHELLE: He recognizes Kent who isn't even Kent. Is it so bad to want him to know who I am? Is it so bad . . .

(Angel runs out of the room.)

JULIA: Michelle—

MICHELLE: Maybe you shouldn't say anything, okay Julia—because in all likelihood it'll be something brilliant and insightful and I can't listen to that right now. It'll be like you're bossing me around again—

JULIA: I don't boss—

MICHELLE: Hah—

JULIA: —and I don't facilitate. I didn't know, I guessed. And as much as it may suck for us, it's good for her and doesn't hurt him a damn bit, so get over it. I'm worried about you. Mom says you come out here all the time—

MICHELLE: I'm trying to help.

JULIA: Are you? I see your face when Daddy doesn't recognize you. As if it's only you he doesn't know and not the world. And don't think I haven't figured out you only call me back when you know I'm in session. And this guy you haven't told any of us about—

MICHELLE: You don't get it—you've got Jane and the baby and this perfect life and you're Mom's favorite which means you're just not losing the same thing.

CLAIRE: Michelle!

MICHELLE: Don't even go there, tag sale lady. You'll be too busy tallying up the profits—

CLAIRE: Fuck you, Michelle—

(Claire leaves. Julia pulls out a grocery bag and packs the bread, etc., into it. She hands it to Michelle.)

JULIA: They're waiting.

(Jane and Julia leave Michelle standing there, arms full, alone.
The sound of the OCEAN swells.
Marvin stands in his light. Michelle "sees" him.)

MARVIN: Come on in, the water's fine.

(Lights fade on Michelle.)

Come on in, the water's fine.

(The ocean sound takes over momentarily—Marvin's light goes out as we cross-fade to—)

Living/Dining Room

(Claire and Jon are moving boxes into a makeshift dining room table.)

CLAIRE: And in the dream we're making out against my old bean bag chair in my room but not my room and you're naked—

(Jane comes in with plates which she sets down—then she goes back.)

—you're naked, and I'm about suck on your penis—and by the way, your penis is acting really strange.

JON: Strange.

CLAIRE: It was so weird—and then—

JON: Strange how?

CLAIRE: It's not really part of the dream.

(Julia brings in a pile of Haggadahs and leaves.)

JON: Strange how?

CLAIRE: Jon—

JON: It's my penis we're talking about here.

CLAIRE: In my dream. A dream penis. A strange dream penis. A very very long and very very thin and kind of forked and squiggly like a puppy or a forked tongue so totally unfamiliar but still your penis.

(Jane comes in with more dishes; Jon stares at Claire, Jane leaves.)

It turned back, y'know, after I sucked it it turned back into the one we both know and we both love but the point is is that there I am sucking away and your body is responding the way it responds and I look up and see that it's just your torso there. Your head is missing. Your head is on the phone on the other side of the room. That's where your head is.

(Jon's looking at her oddly, and then says what he may have been waiting to say.)

JON: Do you think these dreams have anything to do with your hormone fluctuations since you went back on the pill?

CLAIRE: Oh shit.

JON: Give me a little credit.

CLAIRE: There are just things I want in my life first . . . before that.

JON: Y'know—so do I.

CLAIRE: You do?

JON: Yeah.

CLAIRE: Oh. I didn't know.

JON: See what it feels like when someone has a plan concerning you and doesn't let you in on it?

CLAIRE: I know.

JON: No—you don't know, Claire. You just blithely go ahead with life and assume I'll catch up. We had it all figured out, the wedding, you're off the pill for six months—we have those stupid matching filofax calendars with all these dates figured out because you bought them. You did. The last time you postponed the wedding I found out from the fucking florist.

CLAIRE: I . . .

JON: Maybe I'm the one reevaluating now. Maybe I'm canceling the next wedding date. Maybe I don't want to have a kid with you.

(She can't say anything.)

What's going to happen the day I decide I don't want to catch up anymore?

CLAIRE: I don't know.

JON: I kept waiting for you to tell me, Claire. All you had to do was tell me.
 (Julia walks in.)

JULIA: Claire, I — oh, I'm sorry.

JON: She's all yours.

(He walks away.)

CLAIRE: We're not laughing. We did all the way here. But now —

JULIA: What made you think you get to keep laughing?

CLAIRE: You two. Mom and Dad. The beginning.

JULIA: Get over it. It's a relationship. Sometimes you have to talk.

Den

(Angel, Lily, Jane)

LILY: I'm not talking about it.

ANGEL: Good.

LILY: I'm an adult — and your mother — and I don't have to talk about it with you.

ANGEL: Good.

LILY: Good?

ANGEL: Because I don't want to hear about it.

LILY: You don't.

ANGEL: No — I don't. I can't.

LILY: You think I'm not in need of whatever you had last night.

ANGEL: Mom.

LILY: You think I don't need to be touched sometimes.

ANGEL: Mom —

LILY: That I don't need someone to take care of me — to rub my feet —

ANGEL: Oh.

LILY: To need to feel a man's hands —

ANGEL: Please—

LILY: You think I'm impervious to that, because I'm not—

ANGEL: Mommy! . . . I just can't.

(She runs out of the room.)

JANE: Hi.

LILY: You've been around us too long to be a fucking buffer system anymore—

(She leaves.)

JANE: Welcome to the family.

Kitchen

(Lily enters. Luke holds a cookbook.)

LUKE: I'm trying to figure out what's okay to go in and what's not—I've got
   the chicken broth going and sweet potatoes and the pot roast is started.

LILY: We'll make a Jew out of you yet.

LUKE: I think the matzah ball thing is beyond me.

*(He's got a lump of mush in a pot. Lily starts to lose it—just barely—tears run
down her face but she keeps moving around, taking the kitchen by storm.)*

LILY: Look at this mess. I should have moved out last week and not told any
   of them. Just gone, no forwarding address, show up on their doorsteps for
   major holidays and no reason at all. Big fucking surprise.

LUKE: I don't remember you ever cursing before.

LILY: It feels good. Whatever feels good these days goes.

LUKE: Mrs. Price—

LILY: Don't be ridiculous, Luke, call me Lily.

(She starts patting the mush into matzah balls.)

LUKE: Would it be better if I go?

LILY: Who the hell else will cook dinner? What about the restaurant?

LUKE: They can live without me for the day. Here.

(He hands her a towel to dry her eyes. She bats it away.)

LILY: It's the niceness. I wouldn't cry if you weren't so fucking nice.

(Silence)

Y'know I always wanted you two to wait so you could grow into each other but you wouldn't. You just wouldn't. You may just have ruined it.

Julia's Room
(Julia and Claire going at it over Julia's boxes, which Claire has opened)

JULIA: It's MY Barbie collection. It's MY Nancy Drews. Hands off.
CLAIRE: I'm just looking.
JULIA: These boxes were packed. What have you got in your hand?
CLAIRE: Nothing.
JULIA: Give it up.
CLAIRE: Nothing.
JULIA: Jesus, Claire, what has gotten into you? Give it back.

(She grabs at Claire's hand—Claire waves an unwrapped Barbie thing from the seventies.)

CLAIRE: *(Teasing)* Barbies—isn't there some law against dykes' children having Barbies?
JULIA: Give it back.
CLAIRE: Y'know, pregnancy has really made you lose your sense of humor. God, all of you, packing away stuff in boxes you're never going to open as if the memories are something you can actually—when was the last time you even looked at these things, anyway?
JULIA: Give it back. I have now got forty pounds on you and my hormones are not my responsibility AND if you fight with a pregnant woman you are going to look really really bad.

Hallway
(Jon carries a box labeled "possible first editions." Harold watches.)

HAROLD: Need a hand?
JON: I'm fine.
HAROLD: Loose reins. Love and a really good sense of humor.

The Beach
(Michelle, Kent, Marvin, the bag of Chametz)

KENT: Coming?
MICHELLE: No.

KENT: It's not as if there's anything between us. It's not as if anything happened. It's—not as if you were planning on seeing me again. Were you?

MICHELLE: I guess not.

KENT: You pick me out of a crowd, you use me to distract your family—to distract your self and I come along and I play your game which is my own fault, I admit, my desire for intrigue gets the best of me and I blew it, I admit I blew it but you are, you are . . . that moment and you are the kind of opportunity I could have spent my whole life regretting not seizing. You could at least let me explain. You could at least listen to me.

(Marvin starts wandering down the beach—and offstage.)

MICHELLE: No. I can't.

KENT: What did I betray, Michelle?

(She finally turns around.)

MICHELLE: Potential—there was potential. I know that me walking up to you in the train station was ridiculous and risky and beyond insane. I know that. God, I would scream at any of my friends who did something so stupid. Taking you home. You coming with me. And maybe I mistook you seizing the moment for potential and I mistook that potential for something—I don't know—something strong, something that could withstand the familial disintegration. Maybe it wasn't particularly fair to you, but that's what I did. In this house full of craziness you were the one stable thing. And you were my stable thing . . . and then you weren't. But there was something almost there. And that's what there was to betray.

(She looks around.)

Daddy!!!! Daddy, wait up.

(She runs after Marvin; he is holding the bread. Kent stays there.)
Julia's Bedroom
(They're actually tussling now.)

CLAIRE: Stop it.

JULIA: I—can't—believe—you—

(Julia finally pins Claire and sits on her.)

CLAIRE: Ow.

JULIA: I told you!

CLAIRE: Get off!

(Jane and Jon enter just as Claire manages to flip Julia over.)

JULIA: Shit.

JON: Claire!

(He and Jane yank her off of Julia).

JANE: What is your problem, Claire?

CLAIRE: She started it.

JULIA: You greedy little Barbie-monger—I did not. Keep your grubby hands off my memories—and stay the hell away from me.

(Jane pulls her to her feet. Julia storms off. Jon picks up the Barbie toy from where Julia has been lying on it. It is crushed.)

JON: So—who does this belong to?

DAUGHTERS: CHAMETZ inferno. Burn baby burn.

Kitchen

LILY: I've never done this.

LUKE: You haven't—

LILY: Don't look at me like that.

LUKE: I don't know—I just thought—it's in the book—you do it. Like it's not a seder if you don't follow it exactly.

LILY: We're reform Jews, Luke. Very very reform.

LUKE: Which means?

LILY: Flexibility.

Where's the damn book?

(He hands it to her and points out a page.)

All leaven in my possession—

LUKE: You're not going to do it in Hebrew?

LILY: Don't push me. *(Reads)* All leaven in my possession which I have seen or not seen, which I have removed or not removed, is hereby nullified and ownerless as the dust of the earth.

(He strikes a match and hands it to her.)
The Beach
(Michelle is trying to catch up with Marvin, who—offstage—is wading knee deep into the ocean, flinging the bread to the seagulls. She stands at the edge of the waves.)

MICHELLE: Daddy!

(He keeps going.)

Daddy come back!

(Her words echo over her family as, at the same time—)
Kitchen
(Lily sends the crumbs into flames while—)
Julia's Bedroom
(Jane and Julia play with a Barbie on Julia's belly while—)
Claire's Room
(Claire enters the room. Jon leaves while—)
Dining Room
(Angel lights candles.)
The Beach
(Kent is suddenly there. Way ahead of her.)

KENT: Marvin!
MARVIN: *(From off)* Come on in—the water's fine! Come on in—the water's fine.

(Offstage, Marvin slips and goes under. He disappears.)

MICHELLE: Daddy!

(She and Kent go after him—offstage—and gently, slowly they bring him back, all soaking wet. They collapse, Michelle has her arms around her father, but their positions switch subtly so it's apparent that he is holding her, rather than vice versa. Marvin strokes her hair. Kent looks out over the ocean.)

MARVIN: What a nice girl. You're the nice girl. You've always been the nice girl.

(They stay that way.)
192 Waverly Ave
(The family rushes to meet the returning, soaking wet, three. Marvin is wrapped in a blanket.)

LILY: There you are—
ANGEL: Which beach did you go to—
CLAIRE: Michelle what did you do?—
MICHELLE: Don't ask.

(She hands Lily the car keys.)

I'm sorry. I am so so sorry.

(They grip hands tightly.)

LILY: Twenty minutes 'til dinner. Take a hot shower.
DAUGHTERS (except Michelle): URCHATZ. Always wash your hands before
   you eat.

(Lily towels Marvin's face.)

LILY: Are you cold?
MARVIN: Fine.

(Lily looks at Harold—and in that look is all the love she has for her husband.)

HAROLD: I wouldn't have it any other way.

Michelle's Room
*(She is standing, shivering, slipping the shreds from Kent's resumé into her wire
sculpture, when Kent comes in. He goes to her, putting his hand on her shoulders
from behind. He moves her hair off her neck and bends to kiss it. He lifts his face
with a wry grin.)*

KENT: Karpas—
MICHELLE: Parsley? I taste like parsley?
KENT: The sea . . . you taste like the sea.

(And then they really kiss.)

DAUGHTERS (except Michelle): KARPAS. Dip parsley in saltwater and eat it
   leaning to the left.
MICHELLE: Kent is so not a Jewish name.
KENT: Joshua Kent Green. Kent was my mother's maiden name—the Ellis
   Island mangling. And as for what I do—that's been the problem. What I
   love is music but the other stuff, it just comes much easier for me. So I go

back and forth. I leave the interview and they've offered me all this money and I'm really good at this stuff but I hate it. I really really hate it . . . so I'm going off to think things through and you walk up to me in the middle of Penn Station. You walk up to the guy in the suit . . . so how can I say, I'm not . . . that—and then this whole time, with everything, your father . . .

MICHELLE: You're a musician.

KENT: Sometimes.

MICHELLE: A musician in a suit.

KENT: Sometimes.

DAUGHTERS: Light two candles.

Dining Room

(The daughters, Jane, Jon, and Luke gather. Angel dims the overhead lights and then lights the dozens of candles around the room. Everyone starts taking their places around the room—sitting on the floor—with the seder plate in the middle. They pass out Haggadahs. Lily, Marvin, and Harold arrive. Everyone's attention focuses on the leader's chair—a special cushion at the head of the "table." Silence. Who should lead?
Lily leads Marvin to the leader's cushion. She puts a yarmulke on his head. He pulls it off. She puts it back on and goes to walk to her place at the other end of the table. Marvin grabs at her—suddenly frightened at being left alone.)

MARVIN: No!

LILY: I'll be sitting right there.

MARVIN: No!

LILY: You'll be able to see me. I'll just be—

(He holds onto her arm tightly. She turns to Angel, sitting beside Marvin with a horrified look on her face.)

Scoot.

Fuck tradition. Fuck the way it's always been. We're starting a new way it's always been.

(She starts rearranging people.)

You—over there. Move together, come on. And you two—

(She's got Claire and Julia sitting together)

CLAIRE/JULIA: *(Claire)* But Mom—*(Julia)* I don't want to sit next to her—
LILY: Tough shit.

(She puts Harold on Michelle's other side and Kent several seats from Michelle.)

There. Let discord and harmony have a field day duking it out.

(She pulls the "leader's pillow" from behind Marvin.)

We'll each take a turn leading. Pour the first cup of wine.

(She reads from the Hagaddah.)

Blessed art thou, O Lord, our God, king of the universe, who has kept us alive, sustained us and enabled us to reach this day.
DAUGHTERS: KIDDESH, Blessed art thou, king—or queen—of the universe who has given us four glasses of the one thing that will get us through this night.
LILY: Drink the first cup of wine.

(They do. She tosses the leader's cushion to Jon.)

Let the games begin.
DAUGHTERS: YACHATZ. If you don't find your *afikomen* you don't get any dessert.

(Jon grabs three matzahs that are covered with a cloth and breaks the middle one—he covers it in another napkin and holds it up.)

JON: I've always wanted to do this.
JANE: Do what?
JULIA: Daddy had the best hiding places.
MICHELLE: Yeah—they were like, in plain sight—
JANE: Hello? Token shiksa goddess buffer system here. Help!
LUKE: It's the *afikomen*—technically it's the dessert but it's a piece of matzah wrapped in a cloth. So the seder leader hides the *afikomen* when no one's looking and the seder can't be finished until one of the children finds it and returns it to him.

(They all look at him.)

I spent all afternoon reading the damn book.

(Lily laughs. Angel beams at him.)

JANE: That cracker is dessert? I'm going for ice cream.

CLAIRE: Don't forget the ransom. Whoever finds the *afikomen* ransoms it.

JULIA: You would never forget the ransom.

CLAIRE: Shut up! Who held the *afikomen* until Dad agreed to help you through grad school?

MICHELLE: As if you didn't buy it from me for fifty bucks so you could hit Mom and Dad up for law school.

LILY: You sold the *afikomen?*

MICHELLE: Yeah, well, I was young.

JON: And obviously working in nonprofit from the beginning.

MICHELLE: Unlike some people.

CLAIRE: So that's at me too, huh?

JULIA: Recognizing yourself?

HAROLD: Girls—

ANGEL: You have to admit, Claire—

JANE: Buffer zone here.

JULIA: Greedy. That's what you've been all weekend, greedy!

CLAIRE: I have not!

JULIA: You pawed through the stuff I had set aside for the baby.

ANGEL: You've been picking through everyone's things.

MICHELLE: You're searching for first editions—

JULIA: Gram's china—suddenly it's not in the cabinet, gee, where could it have gone?

ANGEL: Don't even ask if anybody else wants any of this stuff.

JANE: Wow, this is just like Easter at home.

LUKE: Yeah, next thing you know, they'll break out the ham.

MICHELLE: Maybe some of it has sentimental value. Have you heard of that? It's different than monetary value—let's look it up—oh, you took the dictionary too.

CLAIRE: You don't understand.

JULIA: You brought a fucking U-HAUL!

(Jane stands up waving the leader cushion.)

JANE: Hello! Hello!

ANGEL: Stay out of it.

JANE: No—I've got the leader cushion. So I am the leader. Is that right? So as the leader I say go to your damn respective corners—

LILY: You go, girl.

(A moment of respite. Then Jane points to Claire.)

JANE: If they don't understand, make them understand.

(Claire pulls out a small notebook.)

CLAIRE: It's for Daddy.

JULIA: Give me a break.

MICHELLE: Right—

JANE: Quiet from the peanut gallery.

CLAIRE: I did my research . . . the books—there are first editions I know no one here has read, and your coin collection, Angel, and Michelle, the stamp collection you started in third grade and forgot about after three months. I mean, I know we were planning on a garage sale but then I did my research and so far not very much junk which we were tossing and some of slight sentimental value like the Barbie stuff—so far that's thirty-eight thousand dollars, which is eleven months in Serenity Willows. So far. So maybe you wouldn't have to sell the house, Mom, if you don't want to. Or whatever. I just didn't want you to have to worry about the money.

(She looks at Jon.)

I probably should have said something.

(Lily walks over to Claire and kisses her.)

DAUGHTERS (except Claire): Shefokh Hamatekha. Pour out thy wrath—we keep doors open.

LILY: You have a lovely heart.

(She turns to Jane—)

Give me that—

DAUGHTERS: Go directly from step eight through fifteen. We really need that second cup of wine as fast as possible.

(Jane tosses Lily the leader cushion. They all drink.)

LILY: *(She leafs through the Haggadah.)*
The plagues—we have to do the plagues—

(Michelle—still standing, shellshocked—starts to leave—she needs air.)

Where are you going?
MICHELLE: To open the door for Elijah.
DAUGHTERS: Elijah, lucky invisible prophet, goes from house to house to drink the cup of wine waiting for him at each one.
LILY: You're out of order.
MICHELLE: Fuck order.
LILY: That's my girl.

(Michelle goes outside—we see her under the magnolia tree as inside they name each plague—everyone takes a drop of wine from their glass with their finger and touches it to their plates.)

GROUP (except Marvin and Michelle): *Dahm*—Blood. *Tzfardayah*—Frogs. *Kinim*—Lice. *Ahrove*—Flies. *Dehvehr*—Blight.

(Wind begins to blow through the trees on the lawn. Wind chimes go crazy.)

GROUP (except Marvin and Michelle): *Shechine*—Boils. *Bahrahd*—Hail.

(Michelle closes her eyes—and silently moves her mouth—"please, oh please . . .")

Arbeh—Locust. *Choshech*—Darkness. *Makkot Be-Chorot*—Striking of the Firstborn.
ANGEL: Watch out, Julia.
JULIA: I hate that. You know I hate that.

(Wind sweeps through the house.)

MARVIN: *(Singing)* Had Gad-yaaaaa, Had Gad Ya.

(His voice is weak, his awareness still dim. They look at him, stunned, as he continues . . .)

My father bought for *bizret zuzim* . . .

(Harold prompts Marvin to continue.)

MARVIN/HAROLD: Had Gad-yaaaa. Had Gad Ya . . .

HAROLD: The only kid, the only kid. My father bought for two *zuzim*.

(Jane, Julia, and Jon leaf furiously through their Haggadahs to join in.)

MARVIN/HAROLD/JON/JULIA/JANE: Had Gad-yaaaa. Had Gad Ya . . .
JULIA: Then came the cat and ate the kid my father bought for two *zuzim*—

(Marvin slowly gains strength and vigor with each refrain.)

MARVIN/HAROLD/JON/JULIA/JANE/CLAIRE: Had Gad-yaaaa. Had Gad Ya . . .
CLAIRE: Then came the dog and bit the cat that ate the kid my father bought
for two *zuzim*.
ALL: Had Gad-yaaaa. Had Gad Ya . . .

(They look to Angel to do the next verse but she can't. Luke grabs the Haggadah.)

LUKE: Then came the stick and beat the dog that bit the cat that ate the kid
my father bought for two *zuzim*.
ALL: Had Gad-yaaaa. Had Gad Ya . . .

(Luke shoves the Haggadah at Angel . . .)

LUKE: Do it—
ANGEL: Then came the fire and burnt the stick that beat the dog that bit the
cat that ate the kid my father bought for two *zuzim*.
ALL: Had Gad-yaaaa. Had Gad Ya . . .
JANE: Then came the water that quenched the fire that burnt the stick that beat
the dog that bit the cat that ate the kid my father bought for two *zuzim*.
ALL: Had Gad-yaaaa. Had Gad Ya . . .

(Marvin bangs the beat on the table. Nobody takes a breath; they speak the sequence as fast as they can.)

KENT: Then came the ox and drank the water that quenched the fire that burnt
the stick that beat the dog that bit the cat that ate the kid my father bought
for two *zuzim*.
ALL: Had Gad-yaaaa. Had Gad Ya . . .
JON: Then came the butcher and slaughtered the ox that drank the water that
quenched the fire that burnt the stick that beat the dog that bit the cat
that ate the kid my father bought for two *zuzim*.
ALL: Had Gad-yaaaa. Had Gad Ya . . .

(Marvin shouts above them.)

MARVIN: Lily, you're up!

LILY: Then came the Angel of Death who killed the butcher who slaughtered the ox that drank the water that quenched the fire that burnt the stick that beat the dog that bit the cat that ate the kid my father bought for two *zuzim*.

ALL: Had Gad-yaaaa. Had Gad Ya . . .

(Michelle reenters the house to see her father picking up his Haggadah, taking a deep breath and saying fast—)

MARVIN: Then came the Holy One, blessed be he, and slew the Angel of Death who killed the butcher who slaughtered the ox that drank the water that quenched the fire that burnt the stick that beat the dog that bit the cat that ate the kid my father bought for two *zuzim*.

(He's back. Marvin's back. And the rest are too stunned to sing.)

Had Gad-yaaaa. Had Gad Ya . . .

(Marvin settles back down, not noticing the others' looks.)

Okay—we return from the brief commercial interruption to join our regularly scheduled seder. Michelle—come sit down.

(She does, warily. Marvin holds up a huge horseradish root. He continues.)

This—as my family who has heard this story before—is my favorite part of the seder. This is horseradish root. Now there's the chopped white version of this with some sugar or whatever somewhere on the table. And for those of you wimps who just can't handle even that I'm sure Lily has slipped the red pansy-assed stuff onto the spread somewhere. You eat the horseradish to experience just a little bit of the suffering that our people have had to go through during the ages. Now my father and my grandfather started this a long time ago and I hereby continue the tradition—who's joining me? Julia?

(He passes out horseradish root.)

JULIA: I'm suffering for two, daddy, I'll stick with the red.

MARVIN: Claire.

CLAIRE: I'm in.

MARVIN: Thatagirl. Jon—you're in by default. Michelle—

MICHELLE: Sure, Daddy—

MARVIN: Okay, Kent—time to be a man and join in. *(To Jane)* You too. Snow-Angel?

(She can't say anything.)

LUKE: She's in.

MARVIN: Okay—follow me—one, two, three—

(Marvin takes a big bite of the horseradish root—and puts it in his mouth—tears run down his face. The others follow suit . . . tears running down their faces as well, though not necessarily for the same reasons.)

Okay—for all of you who have never been to a seder before, hold on to your hats, fasten your seatbelts, and don't believe everything you read because I do it my way.

(He leafs through the Haggadah—)

I like to personalize things and I knew my daughters followed suit the year I took out the Haggadahs and opened to the part about the four sons—the wise son, the wicked son, the simple son, and the son who does not know how to ask—had all been changed to daughters. And then the next year—possibly because the four daughters weren't so infatuated with their titles—that part was crossed out altogether in black crayon.

KENT: *(To Michelle)* Which one were you?

MICHELLE: Suffice it to say, I wasn't happy with the birth order assignment. And I wield a mean black crayon.

MARVIN: And I have never been one to stand on ceremony—have I, Lily?

(She manages to eke out the words—)

LILY: No fucking way!

MARVIN: Now that is my woman! So we're going to do a little original Dayenu—which means, for the first timers—"it would have been enough."

(He starts them off—and they join in—)

ALL: Day, dayenu, day dayenu, day dayenu dayenu dayenu—

MARVIN: Had He given me the love of my life, but not anything else. Dayenu.

Had He given me my daughters but not blessed my life with such comfort and joy.

ALL: Dayenu.

(Marvin points to each and they speak.)

HAROLD: Had He given me just Elizabeth but no golden wedding anniversary to remember. Dayenu.

JANE: Had He given me Julia but not her family who I love and the family I'm about to have. Dayenu.

JULIA: Had He given me all the love I've gotten and not this baby to share it with. Dayenu.

CLAIRE: Had He given me Jon, but nothing else. Dayenu.

(That doesn't seem to make Jon happy.)

JON: Had He given me the career I love but nothing else. Dayenu.

KENT: Had He given me this day and nothing else. Dayenu.

LILY: *(To Marvin)* Had He given me you and nothing else. Dayenu.

LUKE: Had He given me my family, but not cooking or the restaurant . . .

ALL: Dayenu.

(They're all looking at Angel. She looks at Luke.)

ANGEL: Oh . . . Had He given me only love but not the adventures. Dayenu.

(And then it's Michelle's turn.)

MICHELLE: . . . had He given me this meal and . . . and . . .

DAUGHTERS (except Michelle): It's never enough.

(Kent picks up the chorus to save Michelle.)

KENT: Day dayenu . . .

(But his song trails off when he sees they're too upset to join in—Marvin surveys his daughters.)

MARVIN: Okay—The Four Questions—Angel, until my grandchild pops out you're still the youngest. You read.

JULIA: But don't sing.

MARVIN: Please don't sing.

(Angel tries to read—)

ANGEL: Why is this night different from all other nights?

(And then she starts to sob. Lily leaves the room, followed by Harold.)

MARVIN: This is not supposed to be happening like this—

Front Door
(Lily runs to make sure the front door is locked.)

HAROLD: What are you doing?
LILY: If it's Elijah who came in tonight I'm not letting him out.

(She punches in the alarm code.)

HAROLD: Lily—
LILY: Don't take it personally.

(The alarm is activated.)

There.

(Big band music spills out of the den—)

Marvin?!

Den
(Marvin has the stereo blasting—and the rest of the gang surrounding him.)

MARVIN: It's a musical interlude. I can't stand these sad faces and I have taught
   my daughters well—

(He bows to Julia—)

May I have this dance?

*(And they're dancing. He is a smooth and incredibly good dancer. Everybody
watches.)*

DAUGHTERS: The real four questions.
MARVIN: *(To Julia)* That's it—rock step. There you go. Let me lead—
JULIA: I'm used to leading . . . we took a class . . .

(He draws her close.)

MARVIN: Don't name the baby for me, Julia. I never liked the name Marvin.

JULIA: Daddy—

MARVIN: They really should have named me Brick.

JULIA: Daddy!

MARVIN: Bring her to see me.

JULIA: Her?

MARVIN: I'll know her. Because she's yours and you're mine. I'll know her.

(He spins her out. He turns to Jane.)

Time for you to cut in.

(She takes Julia's hand and he turns to Claire. Julia and Jane dance while Claire and Marvin dance. Michelle turns to Angel and Jon.)

MICHELLE: The *afikomen*.

ANGEL: Oh, God.

JON: What?

ANGEL: If Daddy gets the *afikomen* back, the seder's over.

MICHELLE: Where did you hide it, Jon?

(They leave the den.)

MARVIN: *(To Claire)* Michelle and Angel, you should be warming up! Rock step—good. You teach this to Jon yet?

CLAIRE: We're kind of hopeless at it. I guess after today . . .

Dining Room
(Michelle and Angel are frantically searching. Kent comes in.)

JON: It's not here.

ANGEL: It can't be gone, it can't be gone.

KENT: Your father's waiting for you two.

MICHELLE: But—

JON: It's gone, Michelle. Maybe it's gone for good.

(Jon leads Angel into the den. Kent grabs Michelle's hand and they follow.)
Den

MARVIN: Will you take some advice from an old man?

CLAIRE: I'll take some advice from you.

MARVIN: Honey . . . it won't matter if you and I don't dance at your wedding.

CLAIRE: But Daddy—

MARVIN: It's not the important part.

CLAIRE: I just . . . I could always see it, y'know?

MARVIN: *(In Yiddish) Man Tracht und Gott Lacht.*

CLAIRE: I object to the use of an unfamiliar language, Daddy. No Yiddish.

MARVIN: Man plans and God laughs . . .

CLAIRE: Daddy, I can't . . .

MARVIN: *(He stops and looks at her.)* Let people know, Claire.

CLAIRE: What?

MARVIN: Let people know you. That's your answer.

(He spins her—and stops her. She looks for Jon to take her over but he's not there. Marvin puts a hand out to Angel.)

MARVIN: My snow-angel.

ANGEL: Tell me the story again.

(And meanwhile, they're dancing—but it's Angel's particular brand of freestyle.)

MARVIN: You were two, maybe three. And I was supposed to be watching you. Your mother was out buying school clothes with your sisters and you were down for your nap. Or I thought you were down for your nap—your mother hadn't warned me of your wandering nap nature. So I go in to check on my baby and she's not there. She's actually managed to open her door and toddle down the hallway and open the front door and fling herself into the snow. And there, while I've been looking all over the house for her—she's been making snow angels, a dozen probably—all over the yard. And since I never really liked the name Amy anyhow . . . thus Angel was born.

ANGEL: I love that story.

Oh Daddy, why does it all have to change?

MARVIN: You don't always have to live so much in the moment, Angel baby.

ANGEL: It's just—it's that—Daddy—

MARVIN: I know, baby . . . I know. Timing, it's all about timing. Knowing when to grab tight—knowing when to let go—

(He spins Angel out and looks to Michelle. Kent hands Michelle over to her dad.)

KENT: Save the next dance for me.

MARVIN: The one with two left feet.

MICHELLE: There's got to be one, doesn't there?

MARVIN: You've got many other talents. Many other talents.

MICHELLE: I love you, Daddy.

MARVIN: I know, sweetheart. Don't ever think I don't know that.

*(He spins her out to Kent and moves on to Lily. The music changes to their song—
they don't need to speak. They just need to dance, close.
Harold exits.
The daughters watch as their parents dance their dance. Lily and Marvin finish
in a dip with a flourish. And as he brings her up close to him and kisses her, he
says—)*

Dayenu.

(And he lets her go. They see that he is pulling the afikomen *out of his breast pocket.)*

LILY: Marvin—

*(He waves the end-of-seder token. The look on each of the sisters' faces as they see
their father about to be taken from them again.)*

MARVIN: I always have the best hiding places.

ANGEL: Don't, Daddy!

CLAIRE: Daddy—

MARVIN: No lawyers allowed in the *afikomen*-bartering process. I guess I don't
have to pay the ransom this year.

JULIA: Daddy please—

MICHELLE: Just not yet—don't do it yet.

MARVIN: I think we're just about done with this seder.

(He gives his family a wry grin—)

Next year in Serenity Willows.

(He unwraps the afikomen *and bites it—and in that moment, the seder and magic
are over.
Marvin straightens—his face has lost itself again. His gaze on the crowd recognizes
no one except Lily. He extends a shaky hand to her. Lily takes it and pulls him in*

close to her again. They dance with her leading, barely moving their feet. Fade to the flickering candles—and then)

Kitchen

(Later. Angel searches for food. Julia enters.)

JULIA: We're starving.

(Claire enters from the other side.)

CLAIRE: Yeah, well, we never ate.

(They start spreading food out on the table.)

JULIA: It's strange to think I'll drive my kid by this place someday and point it out and say, look, that's where Mommy grew up.

(Michelle enters.)

MICHELLE: So hungry . . .

(They sit down and eat—picking things off each other's plates, offering to one another—but not saying anything. They've done this midnight meal a hundred times before but never will again in this kitchen. Lily stands in the doorway, unseen, watching the girls eating. She turns and goes back to her room.)

Lily and Marvin's Bedroom

(Marvin stares out the window, which is covered by the boughs of a huge spruce pine. Lily joins him.)

LILY: That was Julia's tree. Girl Scouts. It was about this high—

(She measures out the height with her hand against his calf.)

And I forgot all about it, really, until one day I was up in her room and I realized that it was scraping against the window up there too and I told you and you said the branches against the window was what let you go to sleep at night. Safe.

MARVIN: I know.

LILY: They're good girls. We'll be okay.

MARVIN: I know.

LILY: Come to bed.

MARVIN: In a minute.

(They stand there, together.)

Backyard

(Michelle's got a big pair of pruning shears. She, Julia, Claire, and Angel contemplate the magnolia tree.)

MICHELLE: Just stick the branch in water and voilà, new tree?

CLAIRE: Why not?

MICHELLE: I kill plants, y'know. It's a well documented fact.

CLAIRE: Well, if you kill this one then you'll just have to come over to mine and Jon's house and we'll clip you a new one.

JULIA: You're getting a house?

CLAIRE: He doesn't know yet.

ANGEL/MICHELLE/JULIA: Claire!

CLAIRE: okay, okay, I'll tell him, I'll tell him . . . Just as soon as I propose.

ANGEL/MICHELLE/JULIA: Claire!

CLAIRE: Do you think diamonds look tacky on a man?

Den

(Luke is crashed on the couch. The sisters stare at him.)

ANGEL: *(whispering)* I can't.

JULIA: Do it.

ANGEL: I can't . . .

CLAIRE/MICHELLE: Do it!

ANGEL: Shhhh.

JULIA: Now.

(Angel crawls onto the couch with Luke.)

LUKE: . . . Huh?

ANGEL: I'm growing this tree and it means it's going to take a while to take root and I thought—I wanted to—just let me know if I should leave you alone, because I don't want to leave you alone, Luke. I don't want to leave you alone again.

(Luke is still sleeping.)

Luke? Luke?

(Angel looks at her sisters—what's she going to do with no real answer?)

JULIA: Sleep tight.

(As they move to their rooms)

Ooh.

MICHELLE: Are you all right?

JULIA: She kicked.

(Claire and Michelle feel Julia's belly before heading off to their rooms . . .)

Michelle's Room

(Kent sleeps on the mattress on the floor. Michelle's sculpture stands semi-finished—a wire figure of her father, dressed in his suit, combined with all sorts of found objects of his from the house, and the Serenity Willows brochure. Michelle enters with her branch and a bottle of water. She sticks the branch in the water and places it beside the bed. Kent wakes as she gets into bed beside him.)

KENT: What's that?

MICHELLE: That is what's next.

(They settle into each other as the lights fade on
Julia and Jane
Claire and Jon
Angel and Luke
Lily and Marvin
Michelle and Kent.)

About the Playwrights

Two previous plays by **MARILYN CLAYTON FELT** have been produced. Her first, the two-act *Acts of Faith,* premiered at the Mosaic Theater of the 92nd Street Y in 1987 and entered the 2005 repertory of the Augsburg State Theater in Germany. *Asher's Command* typifies her work, which follows encounters that cross political lines. She is intrigued by the way characters develop when they are trapped between humanitarian and tribal loyalties.

COREY FISCHER has been creating and performing theatre for over thirty years. In 1978 he cofounded A Traveling Jewish Theatre and still serves the company as writer, actor, and director. He has received numerous awards and fellowships, including a Kennedy Center Fund for New American Plays award for *See Under: Love.* Fischer's fiction and nonfiction have appeared in *Because God Loves Stories* (Simon and Schuster, 1997), *The Sun, American Theatre, Callboard, Ocean Realm, The San Francisco Examiner, Skin Diver,* and *Belief.com.* Before the founding of ATJT, he worked in film, television, and theatre with, among others, Robert Altman, Joseph Chaikin, and The Committee.

NORA GLICKMAN was born in Argentina. She coedited *Argentine Jewish Theatre: Tradition and Innovation* and *Crossing Continental Bridges: Cinematic and Literary Representations in Latin American Themes.* Her plays are anthologized in *Teatro de Nora Glickman* and in *Dramaturgas en la escena del mundo.* Her fiction is collected in *Uno de sus Juanes, Mujeres memorias malogros* and *Puerta entreabierta.* Her critical writings include *Leib Malach y la trata de blancas* and *The Jewish White Slave Trade.* Glickman is a professor at Queens College, City University of New York.

MOTTI LERNER was born in Israel in 1949. He writes mostly on political issues. His plays have been produced in Israel, England, the United States, Austria, and Australia. They include *Kastner, Pangs of the Messiah, Pollard, Exile in Jerusalem, Passing the Love of Women, Autumn, Hard Love,* and *The Murder of Isaac.* Among his films are *The Kastner Trial, Bus 300, Egoz, The Institute, A Battle in Jerusalem,* and *The Silence of the Sirens.* He teaches political playwriting at Tel Aviv University.

JENNIFER MAISEL has been awarded with several honors by the Kennedy Center's Fund for New American Plays. She won the California Playwrights competition and was a PEN West Literary Award Finalist. Her plays, including *Mallbaby, Mad Love, Dark Hours, Eden, impenetrable,* and *. . . and the Two Romeos,* have been mounted across the country. Her *Goody Fucking Two Shoes* is a Heideman Award finalist and was produced at the 2005 Humana Festival at the Actors Theatre in Louisville.

DONALD MARGULIES' plays include *Brooklyn Boy, Collected Stories, God of Vengeance, The Model Apartment, Sight Unseen, The Loman Family Picnic, What's Wrong with This Picture?, Found a Peanut,* and *Luna Park.* He has won the Sidney Kingsley Award for Outstanding Achievement in the Theatre, two Obie Awards, two Drama-Logue Awards, five Drama Desk Award nominations, the Lucille Lortel Award, the Outer Critics' Circle Award, the Los Angeles Drama Critics' Circle Award, and the American Theatre Critics Association New Play Award. Short-listed twice for the Pulitzer Prize, he won in 2000 for *Dinner with Friends.* He teaches playwriting at Yale University.

ARI ROTH is the author of *Born Guilty,* based on Peter Sichrovksy's book, commissioned and produced by Washington's Arena Stage; and its sequel, *Peter and the Wolf.* Roth has been the recipient of the National Foundation for Jewish Culture's New Play Commissions for *Peter and the Wolf, Goodnight Irene, Ali Salem Drives to Israel,* and *Life in Refusal.* He is as well the author of *Love and Yearning in the Not-for-Profits and Other Marital Distractions* and *Oh, the Innocents.* Since 1997, he has served as the Artistic Director of Theater J in Washington, D.C.

JEFFREY SWEET is a resident playwright of the Tony-winning Victory Gardens Theater, which has produced world or Chicago premiers of eleven of his plays. His work includes *Porch, The Value of Names, Flyovers, The Action against Sol*

Schumann, Bluff, and *Berlin '45.* Sweet has won prizes from the American Theatre Critics Association and Chicago's Joseph Jefferson Award. His plays are produced in New York, regionally, and internationally. He serves on the council of the Dramatists Guild. Sweet is the author of two books on playwriting and a book on Second City, *Something Wonderful Right Away.*

ELISE THORON'S other works include *Charlotte: Life? or Theater?,* with music by Gary Fagin. It premiered at Philadelphia's Prince Music Theater in 2001 and was mounted at the United States Holocaust Museum (Washington), The Hermitage Museum (St. Petersburg), Soho Studio Theatre (London), and the Joods Historische Museum (Amsterdam). Her *Prozak and the Platypus,* a rock play with music by Jill Sobule, was done at the Summer Play Festival in New York in 2004. *The Great Gatsby,* adapted and directed in Russian, entered the 1995–2003 repertory at the Pushkin Theatre in Moscow.